Principles of auditing

The Willard J. Graham Series in Accounting
Consulting Editor   **Robert N. Anthony**   Harvard University

Seventh Edition

PRINCIPLES OF
Auditing

Walter B. Meigs
University of Southern California

O. Ray Whittington
School of Accountancy
San Diego State University

Robert F. Meigs
School of Accountancy
San Diego State University

1982
RICHARD D. IRWIN, INC.   Homewood, Illinois   60430
Irwin-Dorsey Limited   Georgetown, Ontario   L7G 4B3

ISBN 0-256-02568-1

Library of Congress Catalog Card No. 81– 84904

Printed in the United States of America

1 2 3 4 5 6 7 8 9 0 D 9 8 7 6 5 4 3 2

Preface

This Seventh Edition of *Principles of Auditing* includes significant additions and revisions. These changes reflect the rapid change occurring within the profession of public accounting and the expanding role of the attest function in our society.

Our goal in this book is to emphasize concepts which enable the student to understand the philosophy and environment of auditing. Thus, the first 10 chapters provide a sweeping overview of the public accounting profession with special attention to auditing standards, professional ethics, the legal liability inherent in the attest function, the study and evaluation of internal control, the nature of evidence, the growing use of audit sampling, the impact of electronic data processing, and the basic approach to planning an audit.

In addition to this conceptual approach to the work of the auditor, this edition, like the preceding ones, presents auditing techniques in an organized and understandable manner.

New features of this edition

Among the many new features of this edition are the following:

Increased emphasis is placed on *planning the audit,* including the screening of prospective clients, obtaining a knowledge of the client's business, working with audit committees of the board of directors, and developing appropriate audit strategies.

More attention is given to *transaction cycles* in the study and evaluation of internal control. However, the traditional emphasis upon substantive testing of financial statements items is retained.

The use of flowcharts and graphic illustrations has been increased throughout the text.

A carefully revised and easy-to-understand chapter on *audit sampling,* includes the important concept of beta risk and a clear explanation of modern sampling techniques such as dollar-unit sampling. Emphasis is placed on basic concepts of importance to every auditor rather than on statistical formulas of interest primarily to sampling specialists.

A sustained effort has been made to consolidate material and create a textbook truly suited to a one-semester course in auditing. For example, the chapters on cash and marketable securities have been combined into a single chapter, as have the chapters covering long-term debt and owners' equity. Despite the inclusion of much new material, this Seventh Edition is shorter both in number of chapters and in total pages than the preceding edition.

Expanded coverage of reports by auditors and accountants is now presented in two chapters. The second of these is an all new chapter (Chapter 19), "Other Reports by CPAs." It includes compilations reviews, limited reviews on quarterly data, and opinions upon the adequacy of internal control.

Both text discussion and problem material have been updated to include the latest pronouncements of the Auditing Standards Board, the SEC, and the FASB. This material is integrated into text and problems to assure coverage of all topical areas included in recent CPA examinations.

The selection of questions and problems at the end of each chapter has been substantially increased.

An increased number of concise *Illustrative Cases* are used to demonstrate important audit concepts in "real-world" situations.

Achievement tests and comprehensive examination

Three Achievement Tests and a Comprehensive Examination (all in objective form) are available with the Seventh Edition. Each Achievement Test covers about six chapters, and the Comprehensive Examination covers the entire book. The Achievement Tests are of a length that may conveniently be fitted into the normal class meeting time, and the Comprehensive Examination may be used as a final exam. The CPA Examination in Auditing has used objective questions extensively in recent years. Many of the questions in the Achievement Tests and Comprehensive Examination have been drawn from this source. Thus, they may serve the dual purpose of providing a rapid and efficient means of testing student understanding of course content and also giving the student some first-hand experience with the kinds of questions now playing such an important role in the CPA Examination in Auditing.

Questions, problems, and case studies

The questions, problems, and case materials at the end of each chapter are divided as follows: Group I—Review Questions; Group II—Questions Requiring Analysis; Group III—Problems; and Group IV—Case Studies in Auditing.

The review questions are closely related to the material in the chapter and provide a convenient means of determining whether the student has grasped the major ideas and implications contained in that chapter.

The questions requiring analysis call for thoughtful appraisal of realistic auditing situations and the application of generally accepted auditing standards. Many of these Group II questions are taken from CPA examinations, others from actual audit engagements. These thought-provoking questions requiring analysis differ from the Group III Problems in that they are generally shorter and tend to stress value judgments and conflicting opinions.

Many of the Group III Problems have been drawn from CPA examinations; in the selection of these problems consideration was given to all auditing problems which have appeared in CPA examinations in recent years. Other problems reflect actual audit situations from the experience of practicing accountants. Many of the problems are new, but problems appearing in the previous editions have been retained (usually with some modification) if they were superior to other available problems. In response to the recent shift in content of the auditing section of the CPA examination, problems requiring extensive working papers and quantitative applications have been minimized, and short case-type questions have been emphasized.

Case studies in auditing

The six case studies in auditing appear at the ends of the chapters on "Audit Working Papers: Quality Control for Audits"; "Cash and Marketable Securities"; "Accounts and Notes Receivable and Sales Transactions"; "Inventories and Cost of Goods Sold"; "Debt and Equity Capital: Loss Contingencies"; and "Further Verification of Revenue and Expenses." The cases present specific issues covered in these chapters, but they also place these issues in proper perspective in relation to the entire examination and to the issuance of an audit report.

The authors' experience in teaching the auditing course has been that the use of case studies at strategic intervals is one of the highlights of the course. Case studies in auditing are a means of viewing audit engagements through the eyes of a partner in a CPA firm and also from the viewpoint of the client. Students enjoy the cases thoroughly because of the lively class discussions they produce and the arguments of opposing views. In preparing and discussing these cases the student must identify the important issues, weigh the opposing arguments, and then reach a conclusion. Class discussions in which each student evaluates the arguments of others and participates in reaching common grounds of agreement can bring the auditing course close to the realities of the professional practice of the certified public accountant.

References to authoritative sources

Numerous references are made to the pronouncements of the Financial Accounting Standards Board, the Securities and Exchange Commission, the Auditing Standards Board, and the American Institute of

Certified Public Accountants. Special attention is given to the Code of Professional Ethics, and to Statements on Auditing Standards. The cooperation of the AICPA in permitting the use of its published materials and of questions from the Uniform CPA Examination brings to an auditing text an element of authority not otherwise available.

Contributions by others

We gratefully acknowledge the able and thorough reviews of Dorothy Brandon of East Carolina University, Wai P. Lam of the University of Windsor, and John A. Tracy of the University of Colorado. Their many suggestions for this Seventh Edition were most valuable.

Finally, to the many faculty members at various schools who used the preceding editions and offered constructive suggestions, and to the students in the auditing courses taught by the authors—our sincere thanks.

Walter B. Meigs
O. Ray Whittington
Robert F. Meigs

Contents

ix

Relationship of revenue to balance sheet accounts. Miscellaneous revenue.
EXPENSES. Audit objectives. Relationship of expenses to balance sheet ac-
counts. The budget—a vital element in controlling costs and expenses. Payrolls.
Internal control. Methods of achieving internal control. The employment function. Timekeeping. Payroll records and payroll preparation. Distributing
paychecks or cash to employees. Description of internal control for payroll.
AUDIT PROGRAM FOR PAYROLLS. AUDIT PROGRAM FOR SELLING,
GENERAL, AND ADMINISTRATIVE EXPENSES. INCOME STATEMENT
PRESENTATION. How much detail in the income statement? Reporting earnings per share. Reporting by diversified companies. Examination of the statement of changes in financial position.

Financial statements. Financial statement disclosures. The auditors' standard
report. Restatement of basic points concerning the standard report. EXPRES-
SION OF AN OPINION BY THE AUDITORS. Unqualified opinions. Qualified
opinions. Adverse opinions. Disclaimer of opinion. Negative assurance clause
in audit report. Comparative financial statements in audit reports. Dating the
audit report; dual dating. Reports to the SEC. The auditors' responsibility for
information accompanying audited financial statements. Reporting on audits of
personal financial statements. Special reports. Basis other than generally accepted accounting principles (GAAP). Specified elements, accounts, or items.
Compliance reports.

Unaudited financial statements. Disclaimers on unaudited financial statements
of public companies. Reports on unaudited interim financial data. Compilation
and review for nonpublic companies. Letters for underwriters. Reviews of financial forecasts. Reports on internal accounting control. Operational audits.

1

The role of the auditor in the American economy

Financial reporting—an essential in achieving social and economic goals

In our complex, industrialized society the communication of financial and other economic data is vitally important. Our economy is characterized by large corporate organizations that have gathered capital from millions of investors and that control economic resources spread throughout the country, or even throughout the world. Top management in the corporate headquarters is remote from the operations of company plants and branches and must rely on financial reports and other communications of economic data to control the company's far-flung resources. In brief, the decision makers in a large organization cannot get much information on a firsthand basis. They must rely on information provided by others.

The millions of individuals who have entrusted their savings to corporations by investing in securities rely upon annual and quarterly financial statements for assurance that their invested funds are being used honestly and efficiently. Even greater numbers of people entrust their savings to banks, insurance companies, and pension funds. However, these financial institutions, in turn, invest the money in corporate securities. Thus, directly or indirectly, almost everyone has a financial stake in corporate enterprise, and the public interest demands prompt, *dependable* financial reporting on the operations and the financial health of publicly owned corporations.

1

The need for honest, candid public disclosure exists for federal, state, and city governments as well as for business entities. The federal government expends a major share of the gross national product and, in so doing, relies upon the communication of financial data to assure that the costs it incurs are reasonable, regardless of whether the project be a trip to the moon, a mass transit system, or a foreign aid program. The financial crises in large city governments in recent years are further reminders that all large organizations must be held accountable for proper management of resources entrusted to them if they are to carry out the responsibilities with which they are charged.

The importance of dependable financial reporting applies to the revenue of federal, state, and local governments as well as to their expenditures. The revenue of the federal and state governments is derived in large part from income taxes based on the reported incomes of individuals and corporations. Thus the financial support of the government rests on the measurement and communication of information concerning taxable income.

Good accounting and financial reporting aid society in allocating its resources in the most efficient manner. The goal is to allocate our limited capital resources to the production of those goods and services for which demand is greatest. Economic resources tend to be attracted to the industries, the areas, and the organizational entities that are shown by accounting measurements to be capable of using more resources to the best advantage. Inadequate accounting and inaccurate reporting, on the other hand, conceal waste and inefficiency and thereby prevent our economic resources from being allocated in a rational manner.

Finally, most of our national policies, such as developing energy sources, controlling inflation, combatting pollution, and increasing employment rely directly on quantitative measurement of economic activity and the communication of these data. Appropriate accounting standards and reliable financial reporting are key factors in the pursuit of our economic and social goals.

What we have said thus far clearly indicates the importance of good financial reporting to the very existence of our society. Implicit in this line of reasoning is recognition of the social need for independent auditors—individuals of professional competence and integrity who can tell us whether the financial reports being provided to the public by corporations and by governmental units constitute a fair and complete picture of what is really going on.

The attest function

The principal reason for the existence of a public accounting profession is to perform the attest function. To *attest* to financial statements means to provide assurance as to their fairness and dependability. The attest function includes two distinct steps or stages. First, the independent public accountants must carry out an examination (or audit); this examination provides the objective evidence that enables the auditors to express an informed opinion on the financial statements. The second stage of the attest function is the issuance of the auditors' report, which conveys to users of the financial statements the auditors' opinion as to the fairness and dependability of the financial statements.

It may be helpful to pose the question: Who is qualified to perform the attest function? As a brief answer, we can say that the persons who attest to financial statements must be both *technically competent* to conduct an audit and *independent* of the company being audited, so that the public will have confidence in their objectivity and impartiality. One reason for retaining a firm of independent public accountants to attest to financial statements is the conflict of interest which may exist between the company preparing the financial statements and those persons who use the financial statements. For example, a business that prepares financial statements to support its application for a bank loan has an incentive to emphasize the strong aspects of its financial position and downplay the weak points. In other words, there is an incentive to prepare distorted financial statements in order to secure the loan.

Regular audits by independent public accountants offer the most important kind of protection to the public. Although every investment involves some degree of risk, investors will incur unnecessary risks if they invest in companies that do not have regular audits of their financial statements by independent public accountants.

Recognition of the responsibility of independent accountants to third parties led to the organization in Scotland and England more than a century ago of Institutes of Chartered Accountants. The technical competence of persons desiring to become chartered accountants was tested by examinations. Independence, integrity, and professional responsibility were recognized as qualities quite as important in chartered accountants as technical skill. Through the Institutes of Chartered Accountants, ethical principles were evolved to encourage auditors to follow professional standards in performing the attest function of auditing. In the United States, the American Institute of Certified Public Accountants (AICPA) has played a similar role in establishing professional standards for its members.

Credibility—the contribution of the independent auditor to financial reporting

The contribution of the independent auditor is to give credibility to financial statements. *Credibility*, in this usage, means that the financial statements can be *believed*; that is, they can be relied upon by outsiders, such as stockholders, creditors, government, and other interested third parties.

Audited financial statements are now the accepted means by which business corporations report their operating results and financial position. The word *audited* when applied to financial statements means that the balance sheet, statements of income and retained earnings, and statement of changes in financial position are accompanied by an audit report prepared by independent public accountants, expressing their professional opinion as to the fairness of the company's financial statements.

What is an audit?

An audit is an examination of a company's financial statements by a firm of independent public accountants. The audit consists of a searching investigation of the accounting records and other evidence supporting those financial statements. Through the study and evaluation of the company's system of internal control, and by inspection of documents, observation of assets, making of inquiries within and outside the company, and by other auditing procedures, the auditors will gather the evidence necessary to determine whether the financial statements provide a fair and reasonably complete picture of the company's financial position and its activities during the period being audited.

The following authoritative definition of an audit appears in *Statement on Auditing Standards (SAS) No. 1*, "Codification of Auditing Standards and Procedures":

> The objective of the ordinary examination of financial statements by the independent auditor is the expression of an opinion on the fairness with which they present financial position, results of operations, and changes in financial position in conformity with generally accepted accounting principles. The auditor's report is the medium through which he expresses his opinion or, if the circumstances require, disclaims an opinion.[1]

The examination conducted by the independent auditors provides the basis for the audit report. *Never do auditors express an opinion on the fairness of financial statements without first performing an audit.* Personal experience with the business, audits made in prior years, belief in the integrity of the owners and managers—none of these factors is sufficient to warrant an expression of opinion on the financial statements by the independent public accountants. Either they make an audit of the current year's financial statements or they do not. If they do not perform an audit, they do not express an opinion on the fairness of the financial statements.

The evidence gathered by the auditors during an examination will prove that the assets listed in the balance sheet really exist, that the company has title to these assets, and that the valuations assigned to these assets have been established in conformity with generally accepted

---

[1] American Institute of Certified Public Accountants, *Statement on Auditing Standards No. 1*, AICPA (New York, 1973), par. 110.01.

accounting principles. Evidence will be gathered to show that the balance sheet contains *all the liabilities* of the company; otherwise the balance sheet might be grossly misleading because certain important liabilities had been deliberately or accidentally omitted. Similarly, the auditors will gather evidence about the income statement. They will demand proof that the reported sales really occurred, proof that the goods were actually shipped to customers, and proof that the recorded costs and expenses are applicable to the current period and that all expenses have been recognized.

The audit procedures comprising an examination will vary considerably from one engagement to the next. Many of the procedures appropriate to the audit of a small retail store would not be appropriate for the audit of a giant manufacturing corporation such as General Motors. Auditors make examinations of all types of business enterprise, and of not-for-profit organizations as well. Banks and breweries, factories and stores, colleges and churches, airlines and labor unions—all of these are regularly visited by auditors. The selection of the audit procedures best suited to each engagement requires the exercise of professional skill and judgment.

Other types of audits and auditors

The type of audit we are primarily concerned with throughout this book is an independent, financial audit performed by a firm of certified public accountants. Such an audit is sometimes referred to as a *financial compliance audit*, because it emphasizes compliance of the financial statements with generally accepted accounting principles.

The Internal Revenue Service also conducts a type of financial compliance audit when its revenue agents audit the income tax return of an individual or a business to determine that the tax return is in compliance with tax laws and regulations. Bank examiners are another group of government auditors who conduct financial compliance audits.

The performance of any type of compliance audit is based on the existence of recognized criteria or standards, established by an authoritative body. The existence of such authoritative standards makes it possible to determine whether the entity being audited is or is not in compliance with the standards.

Operational audits.   An operational audit (in contrast to a compliance audit) is designed to measure the *efficiency* of a business or governmental organization. Often the operational audit focuses on a single department or other unit of an organization. The operations under study may be accounting, manufacturing, marketing, personnel, or any other elements of the organization's operations. Because the criteria for efficiency are not as clearly established as are generally accepted accounting standards, an operational audit tends to require more subjective judgments than do financial compliance audits. The end product is usually a report to management containing recommendations for improvements in operations.

Internal auditing.   Nearly every large corporation maintains an internal auditing staff. The internal auditors conduct many operational audits designed to determine whether a given branch or department of the company understands its role, is properly staffed, maintains adequate records, protects its resources, and generally is effective in carrying out its assigned function. Internal auditing is discussed further in Chapter 5.

General Accounting Office.   Congress has long had its own auditing staff, headed by the controller general and known as the General Accounting Office, or GAO. The work of GAO auditors includes both compliance audits and operational audits. These assignments include audits of government agencies to determine that spending programs follow the intent of Congress and operational audits to evaluate the efficiency of selected government programs. GAO auditors also conduct examinations of corporations holding government contracts to verify that contract payments by government have been proper.

Unaudited financial statements—the credibility gap

Financial statements prepared by management and transmitted to outsiders without first being audited by independent accountants leave a credibility gap. In reporting on its own administration of the business, management can hardly be expected to be entirely impartial and unbiased, any more than a football coach could be expected to serve as both coach and official referee in the same game.

Unaudited financial statements are not acceptable to absentee owners or other outsiders for several reasons. The financial statements may have been honestly but carelessly prepared. Liabilities may have been overlooked and omitted from the balance sheet. Assets may have been overstated as a result of arithmetical errors or through violation of generally accepted accounting principles. Net income may have been exaggerated because revenue expenditures were capitalized or because sales transactions were recorded in advance of delivery dates.

Finally, there is the possibility that unaudited financial statements have been deliberately falsified in order to conceal theft and fraud, or as a means of inducing the reader to invest in the business or to extend credit. Although deliberate falsification in financial statements is not common, it has occurred and has caused disastrous losses to persons who relied upon such misleading statements.

For all these reasons (accidental errors, deviation from accounting principles, unintentional bias, and deliberate falsification) unaudited annual financial statements are not acceptable in the business community.

Illustrative case.   Some years ago, the bankruptcy of Allied Crude Vegetable Oil Corporation, a major exporter of vegetable oils, stunned the world of finance. Fifty-one companies and banks that were creditors of Allied held warehouse receipts for nearly two billion pounds of salad oil purportedly owned by Allied. Investigation disclosed that the bulk of the warehouse receipts, ostensibly issued by a warehousing subsidiary of American Express Company, had been forged and that an inventory of salad oil with a reported value of $175 million did not exist.

Bankruptcy hearings disclosed that none of the creditors received current audited financial statements of Allied before making loans to the company. Had the creditors insisted upon receiving audited statements before granting or renewing loans to Allied, the shortages would have been discovered by the auditors before reaching large amounts.

Auditing—then and now

Although the objectives and concepts that guide present-day audits were almost unknown in the early years of the 20th century, audits of one type or another have been made throughout the recorded history of commerce and of government finance. The original meaning of the word *auditor* was "one who hears" and was appropriate to the era during which governmental accounting records were approved only after a public hearing in which the accounts were read aloud. From medieval times on through the Industrial Revolution, audits were made to determine whether persons in positions of fiscal responsibility in government and commerce were acting and reporting in an honest manner. During the Industrial Revolution, as manufacturing concerns grew in size, their owners began to use the services of hired managers. With this separation of the ownership and management groups, the absentee owners turned increasingly to auditors to protect themselves against the danger of fraud by both managers and employees. Before 1900 auditing was concerned principally with the detection of fraud. In the first half of the 20th century the direction of audit work tended to move away from fraud detection toward the new goal of determining whether financial statements gave a fair picture of financial position, operating results, and changes in financial position. This shift in emphasis was a response to the needs of the millions of new investors in corporate securities.

In the last 10 years or so, however, the detection of large-scale management fraud has assumed a larger role in audit philosophy. This latest shift of emphasis is a result of the dramatic increase in the number of lawsuits charging that management fraud has gone undetected by independent auditors. This issue is considered more fully in Chapter 2.

Determining fairness of financial statements—a major auditing objective

Shortly before 1900 many Scottish and English chartered accountants came to the United States to represent British investors in this era of rapid industrialization in America. These chartered accountants were influential in the formation of an American accounting profession. In 1896 legislation was enacted by New York providing for the first licensing of certified public accountants in the United States.

In 1900 auditing work was concentrated on the balance sheet; in fact most companies at that time regarded the income statement as confidential information not to be made available to outsiders. The principal distribution of audited financial data outside the company was to bankers from whom loans were being requested. These bankers were interested in the balance sheet rather than the income statement, and they were strongly in favor of a conservative valuation of assets. In brief, they wanted assurance of debt-paying ability before they granted a loan. The independent public accountants of this era were much influenced by the attitudes of bankers who were the major users of audited financial statements. Today, corporate income statements audited by independent public accountants are eagerly awaited by the public and by government as a most significant measure of business trends.

After World War I, as American securities markets expanded rapidly, the public accounting profession in the United States focused on an important new objective—determining the *fairness* of financial statements. The emphasis of auditing changed from fraud detection and measurement of solvency to determining the fairness with which corporate financial statements reported operating results, earnings per share, and income trends. The advent of federal income taxes added another dimension to the auditors' work; the expanding role of income taxes involved not only the actual preparation of tax returns, but also a new acquisitive interest by the government in the fairness of reported income. This interest was augmented by the enactment of the Securities Act of 1933 and the Securities Exchange Act of 1934—the "truth-in-securities" laws.

The demand for more disclosure

Corporations that offer their securities for sale to the public must disclose all material information about their financial affairs. The disclosure system that has evolved in the United States is intended to develop an efficient market by making available promptly to all investors all material information concerning companies whose shares are publicly bought and sold.

Prompt disclosure is necessary for both favorable and unfavorable developments. Any failure to make disclosure in a timely, complete, and accurate manner makes possible the abuse of information by insiders and lessens the efficiency of the market place. Occasionally, a corporation may be placed at a business disadvantage by making disclosure. However, it may be argued that such disadvantage is a necessary consequence of the decision to become a publicly owned company.

The question of whether or not disclosure should be made of confidential information that could be quite harmful to a company, its employees, and stockholders is presently receiving a great deal of study. Current demands for more and more disclosure of corporate actions appear to call upon independent auditors to disclose any business actions that may violate moral standards. If such trends prevail, the public accounting profession will face a difficult new challenge in defining its responsibilities. The disclosure issue has been particularly critical when auditors have discovered that some multinational companies have made political contributions or paid bribes in other countries in which such payments were considered to be customary practice.

Illustrative case. The chairman of the board of Exxon Corporation, in a letter sent to all its stockholders, disclosed that political contributions had been made in Italy by an Italian subsidiary of Exxon. Although contributions by corporations to political parties were legal in Italy, Exxon ordered the practice stopped. The chairman's public letter recognized that local customs differed from one country to another, but emphasized that honesty is not subject to criticism in any culture, and that "a well-founded reputation for scrupulous dealing is itself a priceless company asset."

Disclosure of unfavorable news may in some cases force a company into insolvency. Banks, for example, have always been reluctant to disclose adverse news, such as large-scale losses, for fear that depositors might become alarmed and withdraw their deposits to an extent that would cause a run on the bank and inevitably force its closure. Thus, the disclosure of unfavorable developments by a bank may be a self-fulfilling prophecy of financial disaster.

Materiality. In the financial statements of very large corporations, such as American Telephone or General Motors, dollar amounts are shown in millions—an amount of $100,000 may not be regarded as material. An item that is not material to one company may be quite material to another. For example, the uninsured destruction of $15,000 worth of inventory in a small store would be a relatively important transaction. This $15,000 loss might represent one fourth of a year's net income and 10 percent of the total assets of a small store. On the other hand, destruction of inventory costing $15,000 would definitely not be a material item in the financial statements of Sears, Roebuck, which recently reported net income of more than half a billion dollars and total assets in excess of $28 billion.

A general definition of the adjective *material* is "of substantial importance, of great consequence, pertinent or essential to, likely to influence." In *Statement No. 4*, the APB commented on materiality in these words: "Financial reporting is only concerned with information that is significant enough to affect evaluations or decisions."[2] Thus, the concept of materiality as used in accounting may be defined as a state of relative

---

[2] *APB Statement No. 4*, "Basic Concepts and Accounting Principles Underlying Financial Statements of Business Enterprises," AICPA (New York, 1970), par. 128.

importance. Unfortunately, there is no handy rule of thumb to tell us whether a given item is material. Some accountants have tended to dismiss the concept of materiality as meaning nothing more than "if it isn't important, don't bother with it." In actual auditing practice, however, one of the most significant elements of professional judgment is the ability to draw the line between material and immaterial errors or departures from good accounting practice. The auditor who raises objections and creates crises over immaterial items will soon lose the respect of both clients and associates. On the other hand, the auditor who fails to identify and disclose material information may be liable for the losses of those who rely upon audited financial statements. In brief, applying the concept of materiality to corporate financial statements is one of the most complex problems faced by accountants.

The relative dollar amount involved is an important consideration in judging materiality, but not necessarily the controlling factor. If a corporation sells assets to a member of its top-management group and that individual in turn sells the same assets back to the corporation at a profit, this *related party transaction* warrants disclosure, even though the dollar amounts are not large in relation to the financial statements as a whole. Such a transaction suggests the possibility of a conflict of interest and warrants disclosure. Both quantitative and qualitative elements should be considered in the determination of materiality.

Perhaps the most useful working rule in applying the test of materiality is to ask the question: "Is the item of sufficient importance to influence the conclusions that will be reached by users of the financial statements?" This view of materiality has been well expressed by the American Accounting Association in *Accounting and Reporting Standards for Corporate Financial Statements:*

> The materiality of an item may depend on its size, its nature, or a combination of both. An item should be regarded as material if there is reason to believe that knowledge of it would influence the decisions of an informed investor.

As a rough rule of thumb, some accountants tend to regard items that are less than 4 or 5 percent of net income as not material. Such an approach is oversimplified, in the opinion of the authors. For example, the percentage relationship of an item to total net income or to earnings per share will vary widely when computed for companies that are profitable as compared with companies that are barely breaking even or operating at a loss. For a company that is breaking even, the percentage relationship of an item to net income has no significance; the more important criteria may then become the nature of the item in question, its absolute amount, and its relationship to such factors as total assets, current assets, and stockholders' equity. Materiality should not be measured by any single quantitative device.

Current status of the materiality issue. In summary, materiality requires informed judgment based on the particular facts in each set of circumstances. Both quantitative and nonquantitative guidelines are needed, at least to identify items clearly not material, but the auditors' judgment cannot be replaced by an arbitrary percentage relationship. Specific rules cannot be formulated that would be valid for determining materiality for all situations. Materiality decisions will probably continue to constitute an area requiring broad experience and informed judgment. The AICPA Task Force on Materiality and Audit Risk is working to develop rules for the guidance of auditors in assessing materiality.

Development of sampling techniques

In the early days of the auditing profession, a normal audit was one that included a *complete review of all transactions.* However, about 1900, as large-scale business enterprise developed rapidly in both Great Britain and the United States, auditors adopted a *sampling technique.* This new auditing technique transformed the audit process into the making of tests of selected transactions rather than the verification of all transactions. Auditors and business managers gradually came to accept the proposition that careful examination of relatively few transactions selected at random would give a reliable indication of the accuracy of other similar transactions.

Internal control as a basis for testing and sampling

As auditors gained experience with the technique of sampling, they became aware of the importance of the system of internal control. The meaning of internal control and the methods by which auditors evaluate the system of internal control are thoroughly explored in Chapter 5 and illustrated throughout this book. At this point a concise definition will serve to explain why good internal control makes it possible for auditors to rely greatly upon sampling techniques. A system of internal control consists of all measures used by a business for the purposes of (1) safeguarding its resources against waste, fraud, and inefficiency; (2) promoting accuracy and reliability in accounting and operating data; (3) encouraging and measuring compliance with company policy; and (4) judging the efficiency of operations in all divisions of the business.

One example of internal control is an organization plan that separates the custody of assets from the function of record-keeping. Thus, a person handling cash should not also maintain accounting records. Another example is the subdivision of duties so that no one person handles a transaction in its entirety, and the work of one employee serves to prove the accuracy of the work of another.

Evaluation of internal control became recognized as a prerequisite to successful use of sampling techniques. Auditors found that by studying the client's accounting system, and by considering the flow of accounting work and the methods provided for automatic proof of recorded data, they could determine the extent and direction of the tests needed for a satisfactory audit of the financial statements. *The stronger the system of internal control, the less testing required by the auditors.* For any section of the accounts or any phase of financial operations in which controls were weak, the auditors learned that they must expand the scope and intensity of their tests.

The impact of EDP on the audit process

Auditing standards and objectives are the same for companies with EDP systems as for those with manual systems. However, EDP affects specific auditing *procedures,* because it causes changes in the client's organization and in the information available for audit. One of the challenging tasks confronting auditors is to modify auditing procedures to fit the computer age. The accounting data that auditors wish to verify may, for example, be stored on magnetic tape rather than in loose-leaf ledgers. The auditors must, therefore, be familiar with electronic data processing systems and their impact upon internal controls and the information system; they must also be competent to use the computer as a tool for performing audit functions.

Major auditing developments of the 20th century

Many of the ideas mentioned in this brief historical sketch of the development of auditing will be analyzed in detail in later sections of this book. Our purpose at this point is merely to orient ourselves with a quick overall look at some of the major auditing developments of the 20th century:

1. A shift in emphasis to the determination of fairness in financial statements.
2. Increased responsibility of the auditor to third parties, such as governmental agencies, stock exchanges, and an investing public numbered in the millions.
3. The change of auditing method from detailed examination of individual transactions to use of sampling techniques, including statistical sampling.
4. Recognition of the need to evaluate the system of internal control as a guide to the direction and amount of testing and sampling to be performed.
5. Development of new auditing procedures applicable to electronic data processing systems, and use of the computer as an auditing tool.

6. Recognition of the need for auditors to find means of protecting themselves from the current wave of litigation.
7. An increased demand for prompt disclosure of both favorable and unfavorable information concerning any publicly owned company.

The certified public accountant

In recognition of the public trust imposed upon independent public accountants, each state recognizes public accountancy as a profession and issues the certificate of Certified Public Accountant. The CPA certificate is not only a license to practice, but also a symbol of technical competence. This official recognition by the state is comparable to that accorded to the legal, medical, and other professions. A CPA certificate is issued by state and territorial governments to those individuals who have demonstrated, through written examinations and the satisfaction of educational and experience requirements, their qualifications for entry to the public accounting profession.

Why should the states license independent accountants by granting CPA certificates? Such action by the various state governments is based on the assumption that the public interest will be protected by an official identification of competent professional accountants who offer their services to the public. The opinion of an independent public accountant concerning the fairness of a set of financial statements is the factor that causes these statements to be generally accepted by bankers, investors, and government agencies. To sustain such confidence, the independent public accountant must be a professional person of the highest integrity and competence.

In addition to passing an examination and meeting certain educational requirements, the candidate for a CPA certificate in many states must also complete from one to five years of public accounting experience. The requirements as to amount of education and public accounting experience differ considerably among the various states.

The CPA examination

Although certified public accountants are licensed by State Boards of Accountancy, a uniform examination is given twice a year on a national basis. Preparation and grading of the uniform examination are performed for the state boards by the AICPA.

The CPA examination is essentially an academic one; in most states candidates are not required to have any work experience to sit for the examination. In the opinion of the authors, the ideal time to take the examination is immediately after the completion of a comprehensive program of accounting courses in a college or university. The examination extends over two and a half days and covers four fields: auditing, accounting theory, accounting practice, and business law. Although the subject of federal income taxes is not presented as a separate field, this topic is usually emphasized in several parts of the examination. The Uniform CPA examination is given twice a year, in May and November. In addition to the Uniform CPA Examination, some states require a separate examination on professional ethics or other topics.

The compilation of the questions and problems included in this textbook involved a review of all CPA examinations of the past 10 years and the selection of representative questions and problems. Use of this material is with the consent of the American Institute of Certified Public Accountants. Many other problems and questions (not from CPA examinations) are included with each chapter.

CPA firms: size and services

In addition to the making of audits, nearly all CPA firms do a substantial amount of professional work in the fields of taxation and management advisory services. Tax work includes advising clients on business policies that will hold the burden of taxation to a minimum as well as the actual preparation of income and other tax returns. Management advisory services include a wide range of activities, such as the design and installation of accounting systems, budgeting, and financial forecasting. Another type of work, particularly important to smaller CPA firms, is *accounting services.* This service features preparation of financial statements for companies with limited accounting personnel. Write-up work, including the posting of transactions to ledgers, may also be performed. The end product of these engagements for many small business concerns is unaudited financial statements. The CPA's contribution in these circumstances is not verification of data, but preparation of financial statements with proper classification and disclosures.

A certified public accountant may practice as a sole proprietor, form a partnership with other CPAs, or become a member of a professional corporation. In numbers of professional staff, a firm may range from one person to several thousands. In terms of size, CPA firms are often grouped in the following categories.

Local firms. Local firms typically have one or two offices, include only one or a few CPAs as partners, and serve clients in a single city or area. The services provided emphasize income tax returns, management advisory services, and accounting services. Auditing is usually only a small part of the practice. Audit clients tend to be small business concerns that find need for audited financial statements to support applications for bank loans.

Regional firms. Many local firms have become regional firms by opening additional offices in neighboring cities or states and increasing the number of professional staff. Merger with other local firms is often a route to regional status. This growth is often accompanied by an increase in the amount of auditing as compared to other services.

National firms. CPA firms with offices in most major cities in the United States are called national firms. Some of these firms operate in other countries as well.

Big Eight firms. Often in the news are the eight largest CPA firms in the United States, known as the Big Eight. All of these firms maintain offices in major cities throughout the world. Since only a very large CPA firm has sufficient staff and resources to audit a giant corporation, these Big Eight firms audit nearly all of the largest American corporations. Although these firms offer a wide range of services, auditing represents the largest share of their work. Annual revenue of a Big Eight firm is in the hundreds of millions of dollars. In alphabetical order, these eight firms are Arthur Andersen & Co.; Arthur Young & Co.; Coopers & Lybrand; Deloitte Haskins & Sells; Ernst & Whinney; Peat, Marwick, Mitchell & Co.; Price Waterhouse & Co.; and Touche Ross & Co.

American Institute of Certified Public Accountants

The AICPA is the national organization of certified public accountants engaged in research and in promoting high professional standards of practice. Throughout its existence, the AICPA has contributed enormously to the evolution of generally accepted accounting principles as well as to development of auditing standards. The many technical divisions and committees of the institute (such as the Auditing Standards Board) provide a means of focusing the collective experience and ability of the profession on current problems. Such governmental agencies as the Securities and Exchange Commission and the Internal Revenue Service continually seek the advice and cooperation of the institute in improving laws and regulations relating to accounting matters.

Division for CPA firms. The AICPA recently organized a division in which the members are CPA firms, rather than individual CPAs. The Division for Firms was created for the purpose of improving the quality of practice in CPA firms of all sizes. The Division for Firms has two sections: the Private Companies Practice Section and the SEC Practice Section. Membership is voluntary; a CPA firm may belong to either section or both. Each section has its own membership requirements, which include mandatory peer review. The formation of two sections for CPA firms reflects the belief that the performance of audits for large corporations subject to SEC regulations involves significantly different problems from the audit of small private companies. The SEC Practice Section has more rigorous membership requirements than does the Private Companies Practice Section. This new division of the AICPA represents a significant step in the accounting profession's efforts at self-regulation.

**Research and publications of the AICPA—auditing litera-
ture.** Among the most important AICPA publications bearing directly
on the work of the CPA are *Statements on Auditing Standards*. These
authoritative pronouncements on auditing matters are issued by the
Auditing Standards Board and are referred to as *SAS*s. The first of the
series, *Statement on Auditing Standards No. 1*, issued in 1973, is a compilation of 54 previous statements on auditing procedure issued by the
AICPA over a span of 30-odd years. Since 1973 more than 30 new *SAS*s
have been issued dealing with current problems.

Another important set of pronouncements serving as guides to the
independent auditor are the *Statements on Standards for Accounting and
Review Services (SSARS)*. These pronouncements deal with the responsibility of CPAs when they are associated with unaudited financial
statements. An example is the case of a small company retaining a CPA
to prepare its financial statements, but not to perform an audit.

A third important publication of the AICPA of great importance to
auditors is the *Code of Professional Ethics*. It is discussed thoroughly in
Chapter 2.

Peer review. A peer review occurs when one CPA firm arranges for
a critical review of its practices by another CPA firm. Such an external
review clearly offers a more objective evaluation of the quality of performance than could be made by self-review. The purpose of this new
concept is to encourage rigorous adherence to the best professional
standards. It signifies the interest of the profession in effective self-
regulation. Peer review is required for CPA firms belonging to the SEC
Practice Section of the AICPA.

Financial Accounting Standards Board. Auditors must determine whether financial statements are prepared in compliance with
generally accepted accounting principles. The AICPA has designated
the Financial Accounting Standards Board as the body with power to set
forth these principles. Thus *FASB Statements*, exposure drafts, public
hearings, and research projects are all of major concern to the public
accounting profession.

The structure, history, and pronouncements of the FASB (and its
predecessor, the Accounting Principles Board) are appropriately covered in introductory and intermediate accounting courses.

Securities and Exchange Commission

The SEC is an agency of the U.S. government. It administers the
Securities Act of 1933, the Securities Exchange Act of 1934, and other
legislation concerning securities and financial matters. The function of
the SEC is to protect investors and the public by requiring full disclosure of financial information by companies offering securities for sale to
the public. A second objective is to prevent misrepresentation, deceit,
or other fraud in the sale of securities.

The term *registration statement* is an important one in any discussion of the impact of the SEC on accounting practice. To *register* securities means to qualify them for sale to the public by filing with the SEC financial statements and other data in a form acceptable to the Commission. A registration statement contains *audited financial statements,* including a balance sheet and income statements for a three-year period.

The legislation creating the SEC made the Commission responsible for determining whether the financial statements presented to it reflected proper application of accounting principles. To aid the Commission in discharging this responsibility, the Securities Acts provided for an examination and report by an *independent* public accountant. Thus, from its beginning, the Securities and Exchange Commission has been a major user of audited financial statements and has exercised great influence upon the development of accounting principles, the strengthening of auditing standards, and especially upon the concept of independence.

Protection of investors, of course, requires that the public have available the information contained in a registration statement concerning a proposed issue of securities. The issuing company is therefore required to deliver to prospective buyers of securities a *prospectus,* or selling circular, based on the registration statement. The registration of securities does not insure investors against loss; the SEC definitely does not pass on the merit of securities. There is in fact only one purpose of registration: that purpose is to provide disclosure of the important facts so that the investor has available all pertinent information on which to base an intelligent decision on whether to buy a given security. If the SEC believes that a given registration statement does not meet its standards of disclosure, it may require amendment of the statement or may issue a stop order preventing sale of the securities.

To improve the quality of the financial statements filed with it and the professional standards of the independent accountants who report on these statements, the SEC has adopted a basic accounting regulation known as *Regulation S-X* and entitled *Form and Content of Financial Statements.* The Commission has also published, in *Accounting Series Releases,* its decisions on accounting issues presented in important cases, and opinions of the Commission's Chief Accountant on many complex accounting problems. Both of these publications have been most influential in the improvement of accounting practices and auditing standards.

The audit report

The end product of an audit of a business enterprise is a report expressing the auditor's opinion on the client's financial statements. The auditor's standard report usually consists of only two short paragraphs. The first, or scope, paragraph is a concise statement of the scope of the examination; the second paragraph is an equally concise statement of the auditors' opinion based on this examination. The wording of the auditor's standard report usually follows quite closely the pattern recommended by the AICPA.

To the Board of Directors and Stockholders
XYZ Company:

We have examined the balance sheet of XYZ Company as of December 31, 19— and the related statements of income, retained earnings and changes in financial position for the year then ended. Our examination was made in accordance with generally accepted auditing standards and, accordingly, included such tests of the accounting records and such other auditing procedures as we considered necessary in the circumstances.

In our opinion, the financial statements referred to above present fairly the financial position of XYZ Company as of December 31, 19— and the results of its operations and the changes in its financial position for the year then ended, in conformity with generally accepted accounting principles applied on a basis consistent with that of the preceding year.

Blue, Gray & Company

Los Angeles, Calif.

Certified Public Accountants
February 26, 19xx

The audit report is addressed to the person or persons who retained the auditors; in the case of corporations, the selection of an auditing firm is usually made by the board of directors and ratified by the stockholders.

Importance of the auditors' report

The writing of the auditors' report is the *final* step in completing an examination. Why, then, should we study the auditors' report at the *beginning* of a course in auditing? The answer is that if we appreciate the significance of the auditors' report, understand why it is prepared and how it is used as a basis for financial decisions, we are then in an excellent position to understand the purpose of the various audit procedures that comprise an examination. Every step in the auditing process is taken to enable the auditors to express an informed opinion on the fairness of the client's financial statements. Later chapters of this book present the auditors' work in verification of cash, inventories, and other financial statement topics. In these chapters students may appropriately ask themselves at each step: How does this verification work relate to the preparation of the auditors' report?

Since the auditors' report is so very briefly and concisely worded, a full understanding of its meaning requires that we consider the signifi-

cance of each of the phrases included. Phrases such as "generally accepted auditing standards" and "generally accepted accounting principles" mean very different things, and a clear understanding of each is
essential to an appreciation of the purpose and nature of auditing. In
the following sections of this chapter we shall, therefore, give careful
consideration to each of the main ideas in the auditors' short-form
report.

Auditors' reports and clients' financial statements

In the scope paragraph of the auditors' report, the first sentence
reads: "We have examined the balance sheet of XYZ Company as of
December 31, 19— and the related statements of income, retained earnings and changes in financial position for the year then ended." To gain
a full understanding of this sentence we need to emphasize the following two points:

1.   **The client company is primarily responsible for the financial statements.**

The management of a company has the responsibility of maintaining
adequate accounting records and of preparing proper financial statements for the use of stockholders and creditors. Even though the financial statements are sometimes constructed and typed in the auditors'
office, primary responsibility for the statements remains with management.

The auditors' product is their report. It is a separate document from
the client's financial statements, although the two are closely related
and often transmitted together to stockholders and to creditors.

Once we recognize that the financial statements are the statements of
the company and not of the auditors, we realize that the auditors have
no right to make changes in the financial statements. What action then
should the auditors take if they do not agree with the presentation of a
material item in the balance sheet or income statement? Assume, for
example, that the allowance for doubtful accounts is not sufficient (in
the auditors' opinion) to cover the probable collection losses in the
accounts receivable.

The auditors will first discuss the problem with management and
point out why they believe the valuation allowance to be inadequate. If
management agrees to increase the allowance for doubtful accounts, an
adjusting entry will be made for that purpose, and the problem is
solved. If management is not convinced by the auditors' arguments and
declines to increase the doubtful accounts allowance, the auditors will
probably *qualify* their opinion by stating in the report that the financial statements reflect fairly the company's financial position and
operating results, *except that the provision for doubtful account
losses appears to be insufficient.* Usually such issues are satisfactorily disposed of in discussions between the auditors and the client, and a

qualification of the auditors' opinions is avoided. A full consideration of the use of qualifications in the auditors' report is presented in Chapter 18.

2. The auditors render a report on the financial statements, not on the accounting records.

The auditors' examination and opinion cover not only the balance sheet but the statements of income, retained earnings, and changes in financial position as well. The auditors investigate every item on the financial statements; this investigation includes reference to the client's accounting records, but is not limited to these records. The auditors' examination includes observation of tangible assets, inspection of such documents as purchase orders and contracts, and the gathering of evidence from outsiders (such as banks, customers, and suppliers), as well as analysis of the client's accounting records.

It is true that a principal means of establishing the validity of a balance sheet and income statement is to trace the statement figures to the accounting records and back through the records to original evidence of transactions. However, the auditors' use of the accounting records is merely a part of the examination. It is, therefore, appropriate for the auditors to state in their report that they have made an examination of the *financial statements* rather than to say that they have made an examination of the accounting records.

Auditing standards

The second sentence in the scope paragraph of the auditors' report reads as follows: "Our examination was made in accordance with generally accepted auditing standards and, accordingly, included such tests of the accounting records and such other auditing procedures as we considered necessary in the circumstances."

Standards are authoritative rules for measuring the *quality* of performance. The existence of generally accepted auditing standards is evidence that auditors are much concerned with the maintenance of a uniformly high quality of audit work by all independent public accountants. If every certified public accountant has adequate technical training and performs audits with skill, care, and professional judgment, the prestige of the profession will rise, and the public will attribute more and more significance to the auditor's opinion attached to financial statements.

What are the standards developed by the public accounting profession? The AICPA has set forth the following basic framework:

General standards
1. The examination is to be performed by a person or persons having adequate technical training and proficiency as an auditor.

2. In all matters relating to the assignment, an independence in mental attitude is to be maintained by the auditor or auditors.

3. Due professional care is to be exercised in the performance of the examination and the preparation of the report.

Standards of field work

1. The work is to be adequately planned and assistants, if any, are to be properly supervised.

2. There is to be a proper study and evaluation of the existing internal control as a basis for reliance thereon and for the determination of the resultant extent of the tests to which auditing procedures are to be restricted.

3. Sufficient competent evidential matter is to be obtained through inspection, observation, inquiries, and confirmations to afford a reasonable basis for an opinion regarding the financial statements under examination.

Standards of reporting

1. The report shall state whether the financial statements are presented in accordance with generally accepted accounting principles.

2. The report shall state whether such principles have been consistently observed in the current period in relation to the preceding period.

3. Informative disclosures in the financial statements are to be regarded as reasonably adequate unless otherwise stated in the report.

4. The report shall either contain an expression of opinion regarding the financial statements, taken as a whole, or an assertion to the effect that an opinion cannot be expressed. When an overall opinion cannot be expressed, the reasons therefore should be stated. In all cases where an auditor's name is associated with financial statements, the report should contain a clear-cut indication of the character of the auditor's examination, if any, and the degree of responsibility he is taking.

This statement of auditing standards has been officially adopted by the membership of the AICPA. The expression "generally accepted auditing standards" as used in the short-form audit report refers to the 10 standards listed above.

Application of auditing standards

The 10 standards set forth by the American Institute of Certified Public Accountants include such intangible and subjective terms of measurement as "**adequate** planning," "**proper** evaluation of internal control," "*sufficient competent* evidential matter," and "*adequate* disclosure." To decide under the circumstances of each audit engagement what is adequate, proper, sufficient, and competent requires the exercise of professional judgment. Auditing cannot be reduced to rote;

the exercise of judgment by the auditor is vital at numerous points in every examination. However, the formulation and publication of carefully worded auditing standards are of immense aid in raising the quality of audit work, even though these standards require professional judgment in their application.

Training and proficiency

How does the independent auditor achieve the "adequate technical training and proficiency" required by the first general standard? The AICPA considers *continuing professional education* to be essential. In addition to on-the-job training during audit assignments, the practicing CPA must participate in formal training programs of the CPA firm and the AICPA and must read and study current literature in accounting and related fields. This dedication to continuing professional education is essential to meet the requirements of the first general standard.

Independence—the most important auditing standard

An opinion by an independent public accountant as to the fairness of a company's financial statement is of no value unless the accountant is truly independent. Consequently, the auditing standard that "in all matters relating to the assignment an independence in mental attitude is to be maintained by the auditor" is perhaps the most essential factor in the existence of a public accounting profession.

If auditors owned shares of stock in a company which they audited, or if they served as members of the board of directors, they might subconsciously be biased in the performance of auditing duties. A CPA should therefore avoid any relationship with a client that would cause an outsider who had knowledge of all the facts to doubt the CPA's independence. It is not enough that CPAs be independent; they must conduct themselves in such a manner that informed members of the public will have no reason to doubt their independence. Independence is more readily maintained when a CPA firm is large enough that no one client represents a significant portion of a partner's income.

A possible difficulty in the maintenance by auditors of an attitude of independence lies in the fact that they are selected and paid by the management of the company they audit. Moreover, they often serve as financial advisers and consultants to management. These circumstances naturally create in auditors a tendency to react sympathetically toward the attitudes and objectives of management and to identify themselves with the management group.

The long-run welfare of the public accounting profession—in fact, its very existence and recognition as a profession—is dependent upon the independence and integrity of the auditor. If auditors assume the role of partisan spokesmen for management, they thereby sacrifice their professional status as independent public accountants.

Accumulating evidence

The three standards of field work relate to accumulating and evaluating evidence sufficient for the auditors to express an opinion on the financial statements. One major type of evidence is the client's system of internal control. By studying and evaluating the system of internal control, the auditors can judge whether the system offers assurance that the financial statements will be free from material errors and irregularities. A second major type of evidence consists of information that substantiates the amounts on the financial statements being audited. Examples of such evidence include written confirmations from outsiders and first-hand observation of assets by the auditors. The gathering and evaluating of evidence lies at the very heart of the audit process and is a continuing theme throughout this book.

Auditing standards contrasted with auditing procedures

Auditing *standards* must not be confused with auditing *procedures.* Auditing standards are basic principles governing the nature and extent of the investigation necessary on each examination; auditing procedures, on the other hand, are the detailed acts or steps comprising the auditors' investigation. A familiar example of an audit procedure is the inspection and counting of a client's assets, such as cash, marketable securities, and notes receivable.

To illustrate the distinction between auditing standards and procedures, let us consider the auditors' work on inventories. One of the standards of field work is the obtaining of *sufficient competent evidential matter* to provide a basis for an opinion. As related to inventory, this standard requires evidence as to quantities and prices of merchandise owned by the client. One phase of the standard requires that the auditors satisfy themselves that the inventory is fairly priced. To meet this standard, the auditors might utilize such auditing *procedures* as (1) observe the taking of physical inventory, (2) compare prices applied to the inventory with prices on purchase invoices, and (3) determine that the carrying value of items in inventory does not exceed net realizable value. These three investigative steps are auditing procedures.

A decision as to how many purchase invoices should be examined and how extensive the comparison with current market prices should be requires the exercise of judgment by the auditors and invokes an auditing standard—the judging of how much evidence is sufficient under the circumstances. This decision should ideally be the same if made by different auditors facing the same set of circumstances.

No single set of procedures will fit all examinations. The selection of audit procedures is made by the CPA without any restriction by the client. The auditors' report states that the auditors used all procedures that *they* considered necessary in the circumstances. In each engagement, the nature of the accounting records, the quality of the internal control, and other circumstances peculiar to the company will dictate the audit procedures to be used. Auditing standards, however, do not and should not vary from one examination to the next. Standards should be uniform; procedures should vary to fit the circumstances of each engagement.

The opinion paragraph of the auditors' report

The opinion paragraph consists of only one sentence, which is restated here with certain significant phrases shown in italics:

> *In our opinion*, the financial statements referred to above *present fairly* the financial position of XYZ Company as of December 31, 19—, and the results of its operations and the changes in its financial position for the year then ended, in conformity with *generally accepted accounting principles* applied on a basis consistent with that of the preceding year.

Each of the italicized phrases has a special significance. The first phrase, "in our opinion," makes clear that the auditors are expressing nothing more than an informed opinion; they are not guaranteeing or certifying that the statements are accurate, correct, or true. In an earlier period of public accounting, the wording of the audit report contained the phrase "We certify that . . . ," but this expression was discontinued on the grounds that it was misleading. To "certify" implies a positive assurance of accuracy, which an audit simply does not provide.

The auditors cannot guarantee the correctness of the financial statements because the statements themselves are largely matters of opinion rather than of absolute fact. Furthermore, the auditors do not make a complete and detailed examination of all transactions. Their examination is limited to a program of tests that leaves the possibility of some errors going undetected. Because of limitations inherent in the accounting process and because of practical limitations of time and cost in the making of an audit, the auditors' work culminates in the expression of an opinion and not in the issuance of a guarantee of accuracy. The growth of public accounting and the increased confidence placed in audited statements by all sectors of the economy indicate that the auditors' opinion is usually sufficient assurance that the statements may be relied upon.

In the opinion paragraph of the report, the auditors are really making four assertions about the financial statements: (1) the statements present fairly the financial position and results of economic activity; (2) the presentation is in conformity with generally accepted accounting principles; (3) generally acceptable accounting principles have been consistently applied; and (4) by implication (third standard of reporting), disclosure is adequate.

The financial statements "present fairly . . ."

The next phrase of the opinion paragraph that requires special consideration is the expression "present fairly." Since many of the items in financial statements cannot be measured exactly, the auditors cannot say that the statements present exactly or correctly the financial position or operating results.

The meaning of "present fairly" as used in the context of the auditors' report has been much discussed in court cases and in auditing literature. Some accountants believed that financial statements were fair if they conformed to GAAP; others insisted that fairness was a distinct concept, broader than mere compliance with GAAP. This discussion led to the issuance by the AICPA of *SAS No. 5*, "The Meaning of 'Present Fairly in Conformity with Generally Accepted Accounting Principles' in the Independent Auditor's Report." This statement emphasized that an auditor's judgment as to the fairness of financial statements should be applied within the framework of generally accepted principles."[3] In the opinion of the authors, the essence of *SAS No. 5* is to equate the quality of *presenting fairly* with that of *not being misleading.* Financial statements must not be so presented as to lead users to forecasts or conclusions that a company and its independent auditors know are unsound or unlikely.

Adequate informative disclosure. If financial statements are to present fairly the financial position and operating results of a company, there must be adequate disclosure of all essential information. A financial statement may be misleading if it does not give a complete picture. For example, if an extraordinary item arising from an uninsured flood loss of plant and equipment were combined with operating income and not clearly identified, the reader might be misled as to the earning power of the company.

Generally accepted accounting principles

In our study of the main ideas contained in the auditors' report, the next key phrase to be considered is "generally accepted accounting principles." The wording of the audit report implies that generally accepted accounting principles represent a concept well known to CPAs. Examples of such principles have long been agreed upon; the cost principle, the realization principle, the matching concept, the going-

---

[3] American Institute of Certified Public Accountants, *Statement on Auditing Standards No. 5*, "The Meaning of 'Present Fairly in Conformity with Generally Accepted Accounting Principles' in the Independent Auditor's Report." AICPA (New York, 1975), par. 3.

concern assumption, and others are familiar to every accounting student. However, no official list of accounting principles exists, and a satisfactory concise definition is yet to be developed.

To qualify as *generally accepted*, an accounting principle must have substantial authoritative support. At present, the body designated by the AICPA Council to establish accounting principles is the Financial Accounting Standards Board. The *Statements of Financial Accounting Standards* thus represent generally accepted accounting principles. In addition, the older *Accounting Research Bulletins* and *APB Opinions* have also been designated as statements of accounting principles, except when superseded by FASB statements.

Another source of detailed accounting principles is the series of accounting releases by the SEC, which is stated to be a "program for the publication, from time to time, of opinions on accounting principles for the purpose of contributing to the development of uniform standards and practices on major accounting questions." The American Accounting Association has contributed significantly to the development of a unified body of accounting standards by such publications as its *Accounting and Reporting Standards for Corporate Financial Statements*.

The conceptual framework project currently being carried on by the FASB may eventually provide a more sharply defined meaning for generally accepted accounting principles.

Consistency in the application of accounting principles means that the same accounting principles should be followed from year to year by an individual business so that the successive financial statements issued by the business entity will be comparable. The concept of consistency as used in the audit report does not mean that the accounting principles used by a business are identical with the principles used by other companies in the same industry.

Other types of auditors' reports

The form of auditors' report discussed in this chapter is called an *unqualified opinion.* Such a report may be regarded as a "clean bill of health" issued by the auditors. An unqualified opinion denotes that the examination was adequate in scope and that the financial statements present fairly financial position and results of operations in conformity with generally accepted accounting principles applied on a basis consistent with that of the preceding year. Under these circumstances the auditors are taking no exceptions and inserting no qualifications in the report. An unqualified opinion is the type of report the client wants and also the type auditors prefer to issue. In some audits, however, the circumstances will not permit the auditors to give their unqualified approval to the financial statements. The other possible alternatives are a *qualified opinion,* an *adverse opinion,* and a *disclaimer of opinion.*

In some audit engagements, the auditors may find that one or more items in the financial statements are not presented in accordance with generally accepted accounting principles. Perhaps the auditors do not regard as reasonable the valuation assigned to certain assets by management. If the auditors cannot persuade the client company to change the unsatisfactory items in the financial statements, they will issue a qualified opinion or an adverse opinion. The choice between these two options depends upon the materiality of the shortcomings in the financial statements. A decision to issue a qualified opinion would indicate that the auditors believed that the deficiencies, although significant, were not so material as to invalidate the financial statements viewed as a whole.

An *adverse opinion* states that the financial statements *are not fairly presented.* In practice an adverse opinion is rare, because it would be useless to the client. If the financial statements are so deficient as to warrant an adverse opinion by the auditors, this situation will be discussed between the auditors and the client early in the engagement. At this point, the management of the client company probably will agree to make the changes necessary to avoid an adverse opinion or will decide to terminate the audit engagement and thus avoid paying additional audit fees.

The auditors will issue a *disclaimer of opinion* if they are unable to determine the overall fairness of the financial statements. This type of result might occur if the audit revealed the system of internal control to be grossly inadequate or if the auditors for any reason did not perform sufficient work to have a basis for an opinion. Sometimes, the client may want only a limited investigation and therefore understands that a disclaimer of opinion will be the only type of audit report possible. However, if the auditors *know* that the financial statements do not constitute a fair presentation, they must not disclaim an opinion, but must issue an adverse opinion. In other words, the fact that the audit was not complete would not justify the auditors in disclaiming an opinion on financial statements that they knew to be misleading.

Extensions of the auditors' attest function

In recent years many suggestions have been made for the extension of the auditors' attest function beyond reporting on annual financial statements. Among the various reports currently issued by auditors are reports on a client's internal control, reports to various regulatory agencies, letters to the underwriters of an issue of securities, and other special reports. It has been suggested that CPA firms attest to quarterly financial statements, to financial forecasts, and to the quality of management performance. The reputation of CPA firms for integrity and skilled professional investigation has led to requests that they participate in a variety of other special assignments.

In making decisions on the possible extension of the attest function to these many new proposed areas, we should keep in mind certain basic conditions necessary for successful performance of the attest function. These conditions include independence and technical competence of the attestor, the existence of evidential matter and of accepted standards for presentation, adequate disclosure, and a clear indication of the responsibility assumed by the attestor.

A vigorous profession in a rapidly changing society should expect that its role will change to meet changing needs. The CPA may appropriately ask: "How can I expand or modify my services to make them of greater value to my clients and to the entire community?"

KEY TERMS INTRODUCED OR EMPHASIZED IN CHAPTER 1

Adverse opinion   An opinion issued by the auditors that the financial statements they have examined *do not present fairly* the financial position, results of operation, or changes in financial position in conformity with generally accepted accounting principles.

American Institute of Certified Public Accountants (AICPA)   The national professional organization of CPAs engaged in promoting high professional standards and improving the quality of financial reporting.

Attest function   The primary function of the independent public accountant—to attest to financial statements; that is, to bear witness as to their reliability and fairness—the independent opinion of the CPA lends credibility to audited financial statements.

Audit   An examination or investigation by independent public accountants of a set of financial statements, and the accounting records and other supporting evidence both within and outside the client's business.

Auditing procedures   Detailed steps comprising an audit; for example, counting cash on hand, confirming accounts receivable, and observing the physical inventory.

Auditor's standard report   A very precise document designed to communicate exactly the character and limitations of the responsibility being assumed by the auditor; in standard form, the report consists of a scope paragraph and an opinion paragraph, which cover the basic financial statements.

Certified Public Accountant   A person licensed by the state to practice public accounting as a profession, based on having passed the Uniform CPA Examination and having met certain education and experience requirements.

Consistency   The concept of using the same accounting principles from year to year so that the successive financial statements issued by a business entity will be comparable.

CPA examination   A uniform examination administered twice a year by the American Institute of Certified Public Accountants for state boards of accountancy to enable them to issue CPA licenses. Covers fields of auditing, accounting theory, accounting practice, and business law.

Disclaimer of opinion   Form of report in which the auditors state that they do not express an opinion on the financial statements; should include a separate paragraph stating the auditor's reasons for disclaiming an opinion and also disclosing any reservations they may have concerning the consistent application of generally accepted accounting principles—should not be used in lieu of an adverse opinion (that is, in cases in which the auditors know that material departures from generally accepted accounting principles exist).

Disclosure Making public all material information about financial affairs.

Financial compliance audit An audit to determine whether financial statements, income tax returns, or other financial reports are in compliance with established criteria.

Fraud Misrepresentation by a person of a material fact, known by that person to be untrue or made with reckless indifference as to whether the fact is true, with intent to deceive and with result that another party is injured.

Generally accepted accounting principles (GAAP) Concepts or standards established by such authoritative bodies as the APB, FASB, and AICPA and accepted by the accounting profession as essential to proper financial reporting.

Generally accepted auditing standards (GAAS) A set of 10 standards adopted by the AICPA and binding on its members—designed to ensure the quality of the auditor's work.

Independence A most important auditing standard, which prohibits CPAs from expressing an opinion on financial statements of an enterprise unless they are independent with respect to such enterprise; independence is impaired by a material financial interest, service as an officer or trustee, loans to or from the enterprise, and various other relationships.

Internal control All the measures used by a business for the purposes of (1) safeguarding its resources from waste, fraud, and inefficiency; (2) promoting accuracy and reliability in accounting and operating data; (3) encouraging compliance with company policy; and (4) judging the efficiency of operations in all divisions of the business.

Material Being of substantial importance. Significant enough to affect evaluations or decisions by users of financial statements. Information which should be disclosed in order that financial statements constitute a fair presentation. Involves both quantitative and qualitative criteria.

Operational audit A review of a department or other unit of a business or governmental organization to measure the efficiency of operations.

Qualified opinion The appropriate form of audit report when some factor is sufficiently significant to require mention in the auditors' report but not so material as to necessitate the expression of an adverse opinion or the disclaiming of an opinion. May be viewed as falling into two groups: "except for" and "subject to" opinions. The "except for" clause indicates such limitations as a lack of sufficient evidence, a departure from generally accepted accounting principles, or a change between periods in the application of accounting principles. The "subject to" clause is used when an uncertainty is not subject to reasonable estimation.

Securities and Exchange Commission (SEC) A government agency authorized to review financial statements of companies seeking approval to issue securities for sale to the public.

Statements on Auditing Standards (SAS) A series of statements issued by the Auditing Standards Board of the AICPA. Considered to be interpretations of generally accepted auditing standards.

Unqualified opinion The form of audit report issued when the examination was adequate in scope and the auditors believe that the financial statements present fairly financial position and operating results in conformity with generally accepted accounting principles applied on a basis consistent with that of the preceding year.

GROUP I: REVIEW QUESTIONS

1–1.   The attest function is said to be the principal reason for the existence of a public accounting profession. What is meant by attesting to a client's financial statements, and what two steps are required?

1–2.   Identify the two principal qualifications that should be possessed by a person who is to perform the attest function for a company's financial statements.

1–3.   You are to evaluate the following quotation.

"If a CPA firm completes an examination of Adam Company's financial statements following generally accepted auditing standards and is satisfied with the results of the audit, an *unqualified* audit report may be issued. On the other hand, if no audit is performed of the current year's financial statements, but the CPA firm has performed satisfactory audits in prior years, has confidence in the management of the company, and makes a quick review of the current year's financial statements, a qualified report may be issued."

Do you agree? Give reasons to support your answer.

1–4.   Distinguish between a financial compliance audit and an operational audit.

1–5.   Identify some of the social and economic factors that have encouraged the development of the attest function to its present importance.

1–6.   CPA firms are sometimes grouped into the categories of local firms, regional firms, and national firms. Explain briefly the characteristics of each. Include in your answer the types of services stressed in each group.

1–7.   Contrast the objectives of auditing at the beginning of this century with the objectives of auditing today.

1–8.   Why should the state license certified public accountants?

1–9.   How does the role of the Securities and Exchange Commission differ from that of the AICPA?

1–10.   Describe briefly the function of the General Accounting Office.

1–11.   Which of the following statements is preferable?
   a.   The X Company retains a CPA firm to conduct an annual audit of its accounting records.
   b.   The X Company retains a CPA firm to conduct an annual audit of its financial statements.
   Give reasons for your answer.

1–12.   Pike Company has had an annual audit performed by the same firm of certified public accountants for many years. The financial statements and copies of the audit report are distributed to stockholders each year shortly after completion of the audit. Who is primarily responsible for the fairness of these financial statements? Explain.

1–13. An attitude of independence is a most essential element of an audit by a firm of certified public accountants. Describe several situations in which the CPA firm might find it somewhat difficult to maintain this independent point of view.

1–14. List two of the more important contributions to auditing literature by the American Institute of Certified Public Accountants.

1–15. Draft the standard form of audit report commonly issued after a satisfactory examination of a client's financial statements.

1–16. Jane Lee, a director of the Ralston Corporation, suggested that the corporation appoint as controller, John Madison, a certified public accountant on the staff of the auditing firm that had made annual audits of Ralston Corporation for many years. Lee expressed the opinion that this move would effect a considerable saving in professional fees because annual audits would no longer be needed. She proposed to give the controller, if appointed, sufficient staff to carry on such continuing investigations of accounting data as appeared necessary. Evaluate this proposal.

1–17. Apart from auditing, what other professional services are offered by CPA firms?

1–18. Davis & Co., Certified Public Accountants, after completing an audit of Samson Company decided that it would be unable to issue an unqualified opinion. What circumstances might explain this decision?

1–19. "I have never issued a qualified audit report," said Auditor Smith. "Such reports satisfy no one. I find it much more satisfactory to change the financial statements if the client is using unacceptable accounting methods."

You are to criticize this quotation.

1–20. State four principal assertions made by the auditor in the opinion paragraph of the auditor's standard report.

1–21. Alan Weston, CPA, completed an examination of Kirsten Manufacturing Company and issued an unqualified audit report. What does this tell us about the extent of the auditing procedures included in the examination?

1–22. A CPA firm does not guarantee the financial soundness of a client when it renders an opinion on financial statements, nor does the CPA firm guarantee the absolute accuracy of the statements. Yet the CPA firm's opinion is respected and accepted. What is expected of the CPA firm in order to merit such confidence? (AICPA, adapted)

1–23. What is the principal use and significance of an audit report to a large corporation with securities listed on a stock exchange? To a small family-owned enterprise?

1–24. What were some of the factors that caused auditors to adopt a sampling technique rather than make a complete review of all transactions?

1–25. Describe several business situations that would create a need for a report by an independent public accountant concerning the fairness of a company's financial statements.

1–26. A student of auditing, when asked to distinguish between auditing standards and auditing procedures, stated that auditing standards relate to the preparation of the audit report, whereas auditing procedures are concerned with the examination of the financial statements before writing the report. Do you agree? Explain.

1–27. If a CPA firm has made a thorough professional examination of a client's financial statements, should it not be able to issue a report dealing with facts rather than the mere expression of an opinion? Explain.

1–28. Why did the auditors of a generation or more ago usually limit their examinations principally to balance sheet accounts?

1–29. The auditor's standard report usually contains a sentence such as the following: "Our examination was made in accordance with generally accepted auditing standards and, accordingly, included such tests of the accounting records and such other auditing procedures as we considered necessary in the circumstances."

a. Distinguish between auditing standards and auditing procedures.

b. Quote or state in your own words four generally accepted auditing standards. (AICPA)

1–30. "The auditors' work is essentially complete when they have determined that the dollar amounts in the financial statements are in agreement with the amounts in the client company's ledger accounts." Do you agree with this quotation? Explain.

1–31. Spacecraft, Inc., is a large corporation audited regularly by a CPA firm and also maintaining an internal auditing staff. Explain briefly how the relationship of the CPA firm to Spacecraft differs from the relationship of the internal auditing staff to Spacecraft.

GROUP II: QUESTIONS REQUIRING ANALYSIS

1–32. In a political speech, a candidate for public office stated: "If a large corporation takes any action that violates moral standards, it is the responsibility of that corporation's independent auditors to make full and prompt disclosure of such action." Evaluate this quotation.

1–33. James Chan, while working as a member of the audit staff of Wilkins and Lee, CPAs, was assigned to the audit of Bayside Corporation. During the next several years, Chan regularly participated in the audit of this client and eventually was placed in charge of the Bayside engagement. During this period he received his CPA certificate. Finally, Chan, who had made a very favorable impression upon the officers of Bayside Corporation, was offered a position as controller of the company. He accepted the position. Immediately after this appointment, a member of the board of directors introduced a motion for discontinuance of the annual audit on the grounds that the corporation now had the services of Chan on a full-time basis.

While considering this motion, the board invited Chan to express his views. Put yourself in the role of the new controller and explain fully your views on the proposed discontinuance of the annual audit.

1–34. Jensen and Landry, CPAs, in its first audit of Milltown Corporation, found that certain assets of material amount had been valued by the client by use of methods that Jensen and Landry did not approve. Should the auditors change the financial statements to reflect proper valuation of the items in question, should they qualify the audit report by indicating that generally accepted accounting principles had not been followed in certain respects, or should they take some other action? Explain.

1–35. The role of the auditor in the American economy has changed over the years in response to changes in our economic and political institutions. Consequently, the nature of an audit today is quite different from that of an audit performed in the year 1900. Classify the following phrases into two groups: (1) phrases more applicable to an audit performed in 1900, and (2) phrases more applicable to an audit performed today.

   a. Complete review of all transactions.

   b. Evaluation of the system of internal control.

   c. Auditors' attention concentrated on balance sheet.

   d. Emphasis upon use of sampling techniques.

   e. Determination of fairness of financial statements.

   f. Audit procedures to prevent or detect fraud on the part of all employees and managers.

   g. Registration statement.

   h. Fairness of reported earnings per share.

   i. Influence of stock exchanges and the investing public upon use of independent auditors.

   j. Generally accepted auditing standards.

   k. Bankers and short-term creditors as principal users of audit reports.

   l. Pressure for more disclosure

   m. *Certification* by the auditors.

1–36. Select the best answer for each of the following items and give reasons for your choice.

   a. The auditor's report makes reference to the basic financial statements, which are customarily considered to be the balance sheet and the statements of—

   (1) Income and changes in financial position.

   (2) Income, changes in retained earnings, and changes in financial position.

   (3) Income, retained earnings, and changes in financial position.

   (4) Income and retained earnings.

   b. The general group of the generally accepted auditing standards includes a requirement that—

   (1) The auditor maintain an independent mental attitude.

   (2) The audit be conducted in conformity with generally accepted accounting principles.

   (3) Assistants, if any, be properly supervised.

   (4) There be a proper study and evaluation of internal control.

   c. The general group of the generally accepted auditing standards is primarily concerned with—

   (1) The personal qualifications of CPAs.

   (2) Negotiation with the client about the audit engagement and arrangements for the audit.

   (3) Conformity to generally accepted accounting principles.

   (4) The overall audit program including provision for a review of internal control.

   d. An unqualified standard audit report by a CPA normally does not
       explicitly state—
       (1) The CPA's opinion that the financial statements comply with
            generally accepted accounting principles.
       (2) That generally accepted auditing standards were followed in
            the conduct of the audit.
       (3) That the internal control system of the client was found to be
            satisfactory.
       (4) The subjects of the audit examination. (AICPA, adapted)

GROUP III: PROBLEMS

1–37. John Clinton, owner of Clinton Company, applied for a bank loan and
       was informed by the banker that audited financial statements of the
       business must be submitted before the bank could consider the loan
       application. Clinton then retained Arthur Jones, CPA, to perform an
       audit. Clinton informed Jones that audited financial statements were
       required by the bank and that the audit must be completed within
       three weeks. Clinton also promised to pay Jones a fixed fee plus a bonus
       if the bank approved the loan. Jones agreed and accepted the engage-
       ment.

       The first step taken by Jones was to hire two accounting students to
       conduct the audit. He spent several hours telling them exactly what to
       do. Jones told the students not to spend time reviewing internal controls
       but instead to concentrate on proving the mathematical accuracy of the
       ledger accounts and summarizing the data in the accounting records
       that support Clinton Company's financial statements. The students fol-
       lowed Jones' instructions and after two weeks gave Jones the financial
       statements which did not include any footnotes. Jones reviewed the
       statements and prepared an unqualified audit report. The report, how-
       ever, did not refer to generally accepted accounting principles nor to
       the year-to-year application of such principles.

       Required:
       List on the left side of the sheet of paper the 10 generally accepted
       auditing standards and indicate how the actions of Jones resulted in a
       failure to comply with each standard. Organize your answer as follows:

Generally Accepted Auditing Standard	*Actions by Jones resulting in failure to comply with generally accepted auditing standards*
General standards (1) The examination is to be performed by a person or persons having adequate technical training and proficiency as an auditor.	(1)

1–38. The business activities of Far Horizons, Inc., consist of the administra-
       tion and maintenance of approximately 400 condominiums and com-
       mon property owned by individuals in a suburban residential de-
       velopment. Revenue consists of monthly fees collected from each
       condominium owner, plus some miscellaneous revenue. The principal

expenses are property taxes and maintenance of all the buildings, shrubbery, swimming pools, lakes, parking lots, and other facilities. The furniture, fixtures, and equipment owned by the corporation and used to perform its maintenance functions represent about 25 percent of its total assets of $400,000.

The corporation retained James Brown, CPA, to perform an audit of its financial statements for the current year and received from him the following audit report.

Board of Directors
Far Horizons, Inc.

I have examined the balance sheet of Far Horizons, Inc., at December 31, 19— and the related statements of income and retained earnings and changes in financial position for the year then ended. My examination was made in accordance with generally accepted auditing standards and, accordingly, included such tests of the accounting records and such other auditing procedures as I considered necessary in the circumstances.

As further amplified in Note 3 to the financial statements, my engagement did not include an examination of records relating to furniture, fixtures, equipment, or other plant assets indicated on the balance sheet.

In my opinion, except for the effects, if any, on the financial statements that an examination of plant assets might have produced, the financial statements referred to above present fairly the financial position of Far Horizons, Inc., at December 31, 19—, and the results of its operations and the changes in its financial position for the year then ended, in conformity with generally accepted accounting principles applied on a basis consistent with that of the preceding year.

James Brown, CPA

The note to the financial statements referred to in the audit report read as follows: "The equipment necessary for administration and maintenance was acquired in various years going back as far as the origin of the corporation 10 years ago. Therefore, the records do not lend themselves readily to application of standard auditing procedures and are not included in our engagement of independent auditors. The equipment is being depreciated using the straight-line method over various estimated useful lives."

Required:

a. What type of audit report did the CPA issue? Was this the appropriate type of report under the circumstances? Explain.
b. What contradiction, if any, exists between the scope paragraph of the audit report and the note to the financial statements? Do you consider the note to be a reasonable statement? Why or why not?
c. Did the omission of the examination of plant assets from the audit engagement have any bearing on the evidence needed by the auditor

in order to express an opinion on the income statement? Explain fully.

1–39. Helen Farr, president of Farr Corporation, has become convinced that the quality of work being performed in the company's accounting operations has not shown the progress achieved in some other sections of the company. To remedy this situation, Farr decides to retain the services of a firm of certified public accountants. The company has never been audited. On October 1, Farr invites you, as a CPA, to conduct an audit covering the current calendar year. The request includes mention of the fact that subsidiary ledgers are not in balance with control accounts, the posting of transactions is approximately two months in arrears, and bank statements have not been reconciled for several months.

Required:

You are to evaluate each of the following courses of action and state which, if any, you would follow. Give reasons for your choice. If none of the suggested courses of action is satisfactory, in your opinion, describe what you consider to be the appropriate action by the auditor. In drafting your answer to this problem, prepare a separate section for each of the six alternative courses of action.

   a. Urge the management to take whatever steps are necessary to have the accounting records in balance and all transactions recorded on a current basis before the end of the year, so that the audit work can begin as scheduled and be completed in a reasonable time.

   b. Advise the management of the serious deficiencies in operation of the accounting department, and explain that one of the benefits of your audit will be the balancing of subsidiary ledgers with control accounts and the bringing of the posting work up to date.

   c. Offer to make an immediate analysis of the condition of the records and then to undertake the necessary corrective work as a separate engagement before the year-end audit already agreed upon.

   d. Offer to make an immediate analysis of the records and a review of accounting personnel with the objective of making recommendations that will aid the client's own staff in getting the records into acceptable condition.

   e. Advise the client that no corrective action is feasible until after the year-end audit. Explain that the performance of that audit will provide information on the nature and source of accounting shortcomings, which should permit more efficient operation in the future.

   f. Advise the client that you cannot accept the engagement, as you would not be able to express an opinion on the financial statements of a business having such poorly kept records.

1–40. Joe Rezzo, a college student majoring in accounting, helped finance his education with a part-time job maintaining all accounting records for a small business, White Company, located near the campus. Upon graduation, Rezzo passed the CPA examination and joined the audit staff of a national CPA firm. However, he continued to perform all accounting work for White Company during his "leisure time." Two years later Rezzo received his CPA certificate and decided to give up his part-time work with White Company. He notified White that he would no longer be available after preparing the year-end financial statements.

On January 7, Rezzo delivered the annual financial statements as his final act for White Company. The owner then made the following request: "Joe, I am applying for a substantial bank loan, and the bank loan officer insists upon getting audited financial statements to support my loan application. You are now a CPA and you know everything that's happened in this company and everything that's included in these financial statements, and you know they give a fair picture. I would appreciate it if you would write out the standard audit report and attach it to the financial statements. Then I'll be able to get some fast action on my loan application."

Required:
a. Would Rezzo be justified in complying with White's request for an auditor's opinion? Explain.
b. If you think Rezzo should issue the audit report, do you think he should first perform an audit of the company despite his detailed knowledge of the company's affairs? Explain.
c. If White had requested an audit by the national CPA firm for which Rezzo worked, would it have been reasonable for that firm to accept and to assign Rezzo to perform the audit? Explain.

1–41. The following audit report is deficient in several respects.

To Whom It May Concern:

We have examined the accounting records of Garland Corporation for the year ended June 30, 19—. We counted the cash and marketable securities, studied the accounting methods in use (which were consistently followed throughout the year), and made tests of the ledger accounts for assets and liabilities. The system of internal control contained no weaknesses.

In our opinion the accompanying balance sheet and related income statement present correctly the financial condition of the corporation at June 30, 19—.

The accounting records of Garland Corporation are maintained in accordance with accounting principles generally observed throughout the industry. Our examination was made in accordance with generally accepted auditing standards, and we certify the records and financial statements without qualification.

Required:
You are to criticize the report systematically from beginning to end, considering each sentence in turn. Use a separate paragraph with identifying heading for each point, as for example, Paragraph 1, Sentence 1. You may also wish to make comments on the overall contents of each paragraph and upon any omissions. Give reasons to support your views. After completing this critical review of the report, draft a revised report, on the assumption that your examination was adequate in all respects and disclosed no significant deficiencies.

1– 42. After completing the audit field work on September 17, 19—, Roger Triola prepared and delivered the following audit report to Wheat Corporation.

To the Board of Directors and Stockholders of Wheat Corporation:

We have examined the balance sheet and the related statement of income and retained earnings of Wheat Corporation at July 31, 19—. In accordance with your instructions, a complete audit was conducted.

In our opinion, with the exception of some minor errors that are considered immaterial, the aforementioned financial statements present fairly the financial position of Wheat Corporation at July 31, 19—, and the results of its operations for the year then ended, in conformity with pronouncements of the Accounting Principles Board and the Financial Accounting Standards Board applied consistently throughout the period.

Roger Triola, CPA
September 17, 19—

Required:
List and explain deficiencies and omission in the auditors' report. The type of opinion (unqualified, qualified, adverse, or disclaimer) is not the issue and need not be discussed.

Organize your answer by paragraph (scope and opinion) of the auditor's report. (AICPA, adapted)

1– 43. Bart James, a partner in the CPA firm of James and Day, received the following memorandum from John Gray, president of Gray Manufacturing Corporation, an audit client of many years.

Dear Bart:

I have a new type of engagement for you. You are familiar with how much time and money we have been spending in installing equipment to eliminate the air and water pollution caused by our manufacturing plant. We have changed our production processes to reduce discharge of gases; we have changed to more expensive fuel sources with less pollution potential; and we have discontinued some products because we couldn't produce them without causing considerable pollution.

I don't think the stockholders and the public are aware of the efforts we have made, and I want to inform them of our accomplishments in avoiding damage to the environment. We will devote a major part of our annual report to this topic, stressing that our company is the leader of the entire industry in combating pollution. To make this publicity more convincing, I would like to retain your firm to study what we have done and to attest as independent accountants that our operations are the best in the industry as far as preventing pollution is concerned.

To justify your statement, you are welcome to investigate every aspect of our operations as fully as you wish. We will pay for your services at your regular audit rates and will publish your "pollution opinion" in our annual report to stockholders immediately following some pictures and discussion of our special equipment and processes for preventing industrial pollution. We may put this section of the annual report in a separate cover and distribute it free to the public. Please let me know at once if this engagement is acceptable to you.

Required:

Put yourself in Bart James's position and write a reply to this client's request. Indicate clearly whether you are willing to accept the engagement and explain your attitude toward this proposed extension of the auditor's attest function. (In drafting your letter, keep in mind that Gray is a valued audit client whose goodwill you want to maintain.)

Professional ethics

The need for professional ethics

All recognized professions have developed codes of professional ethics. The fundamental purpose of such codes is to provide members with guidelines for maintaining a professional attitude and conducting themselves in a manner that will enhance the professional stature of their discipline.

To understand the importance of a code of ethics to public accountants and other professionals, one must understand the nature of a profession as opposed to other vocations. Unfortunately, there is no universally accepted definition of what constitutes a profession; yet, for generations, certain types of activities have been recognized as professions, while others have not. Medicine, law, engineering, architecture, and theology are examples of disciplines long accorded professional status. Public accounting is a relative newcomer to the ranks of the professions, but has achieved widespread recognition in recent decades.

All of the recognized professions have several common characteristics. The most important of these characteristics are (*a*) responsibility to serve the public, (*b*) a complex body of knowledge, and (*c*) a need for public confidence. Let us briefly discuss these characteristics as they apply to public accounting.

Responsibility to serve the public. The certified public accountant is the representative of the public—creditors, stockholders, consumers, employees, and others—in the financial reporting process. The role of the independent auditor is to assure that financial statements are *fair to all parties* and not biased to benefit one group at the expense of another. This responsibility to serve the public interest must be a basic motivation for the professional. If a CPA firm's only concern were maximizing its income, the firm would presumably work for the benefit of creditors, investors, management, or whichever group offered the highest fee.

There is a saying in public accounting that "The public is our only client." This expression is an oversimplification, since the entity being audited pays the auditor's fee and is, in fact, the client. Yet the saying conveys an ideal that is essential to the long-run professional status of public accounting. Public accountants must maintain a high degree of independence from their client (the company) if they are to be of service to the larger community. Independence is perhaps the most important concept embodied in public accounting's code of professional ethics.

Complex body of knowledge. Any practitioner or student of accounting has only to look at the abundance of authoritative pronouncements governing financial reports to realize that accounting is a complex body of knowledge. One reason why such pronouncements continue to proliferate is that accounting must reflect what is taking place in an increasingly complex environment. As the environment changes—such as the trend toward business combinations in the 1960s and the increase in litigation and government intervention in more recent years—accounting principles and auditing practices must adapt. The continual growth in the "common body of knowledge" for practicing accountants has led many states to enact continuing education requirements for CPAs. The need for technical competence and familiarity with current standards of practice is embodied in the code of professional ethics.

Need for public confidence. Physicians, lawyers, certified public accountants, and all other professionals must have the confidence of the public to be successful. To the CPA, however, public confidence is of special significance. The CPA's product is creditability. Without public confidence in the attestor, the attest function serves no useful purpose.

Professional ethics in public accounting as in other professions have developed gradually and are still in a process of change as the practice of accounting itself changes. Often new concepts are added as a result of unfortunate incidents that reflect unfavorably upon the profession, although not specifically in violation of existing standards.

Professional ethics in public accounting

A principal factor in maintaining high professional standards of practice has been the development of a code of professional ethics under the leadership of the American Institute of Certified Public Accountants. Careless work or lack of integrity on the part of any CPA is a reflection upon the entire profession. Consequently, the members of the profession have acted in unison through their national organization to devise a code of ethics. This code provides practical guidance to the individual member in maintaining a professional attitude. In addition, this code gives assurance to clients and to the public that the profession intends to maintain high standards and to enforce compliance by individual members.

Evidence that public accounting has achieved the status of a profession is found in the willingness of its members to accept voluntarily standards of conduct more rigorous than those imposed by law. These standards of conduct cover the relationships of the CPA with clients, with fellow practitioners, and with the public. To be effective, a body of professional ethics must be attainable and enforceable; it must consist not merely of abstract ideals, but of attainable goals and practical working rules that can be enforced.

In the short run the restraints imposed on the individual CPA by a body of professional ethics may sometimes appear to constitute a hardship. From a long-run point of view, however, it is clear that the individual practitioner, the profession as a whole, and the public all benefit from the existence of a well-defined body of professional ethics.

THE AICPA CODE OF PROFESSIONAL ETHICS

The AICPA *Code of Professional Ethics* consists of four parts. The first part, Concepts of Professional Ethics, is a philosophical discussion that is not intended to establish enforceable standards of ethics. The second part, Rules of Conduct, is a group of enforceable ethical standards approved by the membership of the AICPA. Interpretations of Rules of Conduct issued by the AICPA's Professional Ethics Division Executive Committee constitute the third part of the Code. The Interpretations provide guidelines for the scope and applications of the Rules of Conduct. The fourth part of the Code consists of Ethics Rulings, which are also issued by the Professional Ethics Division Executive Committee. The Rulings explain the application of the Rules of Conduct and Interpretations to *specific* factual circumstances involving professional ethics.

A portion of the Concepts of Professional Ethics section is quoted below, followed by that portion of the Code that sets forth specific Rules of Conduct.[1]

A distinguishing mark of a professional is his acceptance of responsibility to the public. All true professions have therefore deemed it essen-

---

[1] The words *he* and *his* in the following material refer to both male and female CPAs.

tial to promulgate codes of ethics and to establish means for ensuring their observance.

The reliance of the public, the government, and the business community on sound financial reporting and advice on business affairs, and the importance of these matters to the economic and social aspects of life impose particular obligations on certified public accountants.

Ordinarily those who depend upon a certified public accountant find it difficult to assess the quality of his services; they have a right to expect, however, that he is a person of competence and integrity. A man or woman who enters the profession of accountancy is assumed to accept an obligation to uphold its principles, to work for the increase of knowledge in the art and for the improvement of methods, and to abide by the profession's ethical and technical standards.

The ethical Code of the American Institute emphasizes the profession's responsibility to the public, a responsibility that has grown as the number of investors has grown, as the relationship between corporate managers and stockholders has become more impersonal, and as government increasingly relies on accounting information.

The Code also stresses the CPA's responsibility to clients and colleagues, since his behavior in these relationships cannot fail to affect the responsibilities of the profession as a whole to the public.

The Institute's Rules of Conduct set forth minimum levels of acceptable conduct and are mandatory and enforceable. However, it is in the best interests of the profession that CPAs strive for conduct beyond that indicated merely by prohibitions. Ethical conduct, in the true sense, is more than merely abiding by the letter of explicit prohibitions. *Rather it requires unswerving commitment to honorable behavior, even at the sacrifice of personal advantage.* [Emphasis supplied.]

The conduct toward which CPAs should strive is embodied in five broad concepts stated as affirmative Ethical Principles:

Independence, integrity, and objectivity. A certified public accountant should maintain his integrity and objectivity and, when engaged in the practice of public accounting, be independent of those he serves.

General and technical standards. A certified public accountant should observe the profession's general and technical standards and strive continually to improve his competence and the quality of his services.

Responsibilities to clients. A certified public accountant should be fair and candid with his clients and serve them to the best of his ability, with professional concern for their best interests, consistent with his responsibilities to the public.

Responsibilities to colleagues. A certified public accountant should conduct himself in a manner which will promote cooperation and good relations among members of the profession.

Other responsibilities and practices. A certified public accountant should conduct himself in a manner which will enhance the stature of the profession and its ability to serve the public.

The foregoing Ethical Principles are intended as broad guidelines as distinguished from enforceable Rules of Conduct. Even though they do not provide a basis for disciplinary action, they constitute the philosophical foundation upon which the Rules of Conduct are based.

RULES OF CONDUCT

Applicability of rules

The Institute's Code of Professional Ethics derives its authority from the bylaws of the Institute, which provide that the Trial Board may, after a hearing, admonish, suspend, or expel a member who is found guilty of infringing any of the bylaws or any provisions of the Rules of Conduct.

The Rules of Conduct, which follow, apply to all services performed in the practice of public accounting including tax and management advisory services except (a) where the wording of the rule indicates otherwise and (b) that a member who is practicing outside the United States will not be subject to discipline for departing from any of the rules stated herein so long as his conduct is in accord with the rules of the organized accounting profession in the country in which he is practicing. However, where a member's name is associated with financial statements in such a manner as to imply that he is acting as an independent public accountant and under circumstances that would entitle the reader to assume that United States practices were followed, he must comply with the requirements of Rules 202 and 203.

A member may be held responsible for compliance with the Rules of Conduct by all persons associated with him in the practice of public accounting who are either under his supervision or are his partners or shareholders in the practice.

A member engaged in the practice of public accounting must observe all the Rules of Conduct. A member not engaged in the practice of public accounting must observe only Rules 102 and 501, since all other Rules of Conduct relate solely to the practice of public accounting.

A member shall not permit others to carry out on his behalf, either with or without compensation, acts which, if carried out by the member, would place him in violation of the Rules of Conduct.

Independence, integrity, and objectivity

Rule 101—Independence. A member or a firm of which he is a partner or shareholder shall not express an opinion on financial statements of an enterprise unless he and his firm are independent with respect to such enterprise. Independence will be considered to be impaired if, for example:

A. During the period of his professional engagement, or at the time of expressing his opinion, he or his firm
    1. (a) Had or was committed to acquire any direct or material indirect financial interest in the enterprise; or
         (b) Was a trustee of any trust or executor or administrator of any estate if such trust or estate had or was committed to acquire any direct or material indirect financial interest in the enterprise; or

2. Had any joint, closely held business investment with the enterprise or any officer, director, or principal stockholder thereof which was material in relation to his or his firm's net worth; or

3. Had any loan to or from the enterprise or any officer, director, or principal stockholder thereof. This latter proscription does not apply to the following loans from a financial institution when made under normal lending procedures, terms, and requirements:

   (*a*) Loans obtained by a member or his firm which are not material in relation to the net worth of such borrower.

   (*b*) Home mortgages.

   (*c*) Other secured loans, except loans guaranteed by a member's firm which are otherwise unsecured.

B. During the period covered by the financial statements, during the period of the professional engagement, or at the time of expressing an opinion, he or his firm

   1. Was connected with the enterprise as a promoter, underwriter, or voting trustee, a director or officer or in any capacity equivalent to that of a member of management or of an employee; or

   2. Was a trustee for any pension or profit-sharing trust of the enterprise.

The above examples are not intended to be all-inclusive.

Rule 102—Integrity and objectivity. A member shall not knowingly misrepresent facts, and when engaged in the practice of public accounting, including the rendering of tax and management advisory services, shall not subordinate his judgment to others. In tax practice, a member may resolve doubt in favor of his client as long as there is reasonable support for his position.

General and technical standards

Rule 201—General standards. A member shall comply with the following general standards as interpreted by bodies designated by Council, and must justify any departures therefrom.

A. Professional competence. A member shall undertake only those engagements which he or his firm can reasonably expect to complete with professional competence.

B. Due professional care. A member shall exercise due professional care in the performance of an engagement.

C. Planning and supervision. A member shall adequately plan and supervise an engagement.

D. Sufficient relevant data. A member shall obtain sufficient relevant data to afford a reasonable basis for conclusions or recommendations in relation to an engagement.

E. Forecasts. A member shall not permit his name to be used in conjunction with any forecast of future transactions in a manner which may lead to the belief that the member vouches for the achievability of the forecast.

Rule 202—Auditing standards. A member shall not permit his name to be associated with financial statements in such a manner as to imply that he is acting as an independent public accountant unless he has complied with the applicable generally accepted auditing standards promulgated by the Institute. Statements on Auditing Standards issued by the Institute's Auditing Standards Board are, for purposes of this rule, considered to be interpretations of the generally accepted auditing standards, and departures from such statements must be justified by those who do not follow them.

Rule 203—Accounting principles. A member shall not express an opinion that financial statements are presented in conformity with generally accepted accounting principles if such statements contain any departure from an accounting principle promulgated by the body designated by Council to establish such principles which has a material effect on the statements taken as a whole, unless the member can demonstrate that due to unusual circumstances the financial statements would otherwise have been misleading. In such cases his report must describe the departure, the approximate effects thereof, if practicable, and the reasons why compliance with the principle would result in a misleading statement.

Rule 204—Other technical standards. A member shall comply with other technical standards promulgated by bodies designated by Council to establish such standards, and departures therefrom must be justified by those who do not follow them.

Responsibilities to clients

Rule 301—Confidential client information. A member shall not disclose any confidential information obtained in the course of a professional engagement except with the consent of the client.

This rule shall not be construed (a) to relieve a member of his obligation under Rules 202 and 203, (b) to affect in any way his compliance with a validly issued subpoena or summons enforceable by order of a court, (c) to prohibit review of a member's professional practices as a part of a voluntary quality review under Institute authorization or (d) to preclude a member from responding to any inquiry made by the ethics division or Trial Board of the Institute, by a duly constituted investigative or disciplinary body of a state CPA society, or under state statutes.

Members of the ethics division and Trial Board of the Institute and professional practice reviewers under Institute authorization shall not disclose any confidential client information which comes to their attention from members in disciplinary proceedings or otherwise in carrying out their official responsibilities. However, this prohibition shall not restrict the exchange of information with an aforementioned duly constituted investigative or disciplinary body.

Rule 302—Contingent fees. Professional services shall not be offered or rendered under an arrangement whereby no fee will be charged unless a specified finding or result is attained, or where the fee is otherwise contingent upon the findings or results of such services. However, a member's fees may vary depending, for example, on the complexity of the service rendered.

Fees are not regarded as being contingent if fixed by courts or other public authorities or, in tax matters, if determined based on the results of judicial proceedings or the findings of governmental agencies.

Responsibilities to colleagues (reserved)

Other responsibilities and practices

Rule 501—Acts discreditable. A member shall not commit an act discreditable to the profession.

Rule 502—Advertising and other forms of solicitation. A member shall not seek to obtain clients by advertising or other forms of solicitation in a manner that is false, misleading, or deceptive.

Rule 503—Commission. A member shall not pay a commission to obtain a client, nor shall he accept a commission for a referral to a client of products or services of others. This rule shall not prohibit payments for the purchase of an accounting practice or retirement payments to individuals formerly engaged in the practice of public accounting or payments to their heirs or estates.

Rule 504—Incompatible occupations. A member who is engaged in the practice of public accounting shall not concurrently engage in any business or occupation which would create a conflict of interest in rendering professional services.

Rule 505—Form of practice and name. A member may practice public accounting, whether as an owner or employee, only in the form of a proprietorship, a partnership, or a professional corporation whose characteristics conform to resolutions of Council.

A member shall not practice under a firm name which includes any fictitious name, . . . or is misleading as to the type of organization (proprietorship, partnership or corporation). However, names of one or more past partners or shareholders may be included in the firm name of a successor partnership or corporation. Also, a partner surviving the death or withdrawal of all other partners may continue to practice under the partnership name for up to two years after becoming a sole practitioner.

A firm may not designate itself as "Members of the American Institute of Certified Public Accountants" unless all of its partners or shareholders are members of the Institute.

ANALYSIS OF AICPA CODE

Some of the rules stated in the *Code of Professional Ethics* are self-explanatory, but discussion and illustration may be necessary to a full understanding of several other sections of the Code.

Independence

The first AICPA Rule of Conduct is concerned with the problem of independence. Two distinct ideas are involved: first, accountants must *in fact* be independent of any enterprise they audit; and, second, the relationships of CPAs with clients must be such that they will *appear* independent to third parties.

The point concerning *appearance of independence* to an informed third part was only recently added to the code. Previously accountants had been prone to say that independence was a state of mind, a mental attitude, which was not subject to objective measurement and therefore could be judged only by CPAs themselves. For example, CPAs who own stock in a corporation or serve as directors might argue that their interest in the company does not modify by one hair their objective approach to an audit. Despite such arguments it seems reasonable that an investor or banker using audited financial statements would prefer that the audits be performed by CPAs who have no financial or management interest in their clients and therefore have no conflict of interest. CPAs must not only *be* independent of the company on whose statements they report; they must also *appear* independent to outsiders who are given all pertinent information about the relationships between the auditors and the company being audited.

Independence of partners and staff. Does Rule 101 apply to a CPA's employees? The term *he and his firm* in the first sentence of Rule 101 applies to (1) partners of the firm, and (2) all professional staff assigned to an office involved in the audit. These individuals are prohibited from having certain financial interests and business relationships, as described in Rule 101.

Independence of partners and staff implies impartiality with respect to a client. Naturally, outsiders will question the auditors' impartiality if the auditors have a financial interest in the client's business. However, Rule 101 goes further and prohibits CPAs from participating with clients in joint, closely-held ventures. Examples include closely-held corporations, partnerships, and joint ventures. In such projects, each investor must be concerned with the financial well-being of the others. Interests in the investment project may have to be liquidated, for example, to satisfy an investor's other obligations. The auditors' appearance of independence is impaired if the financial well-being of a client (or its key personnel) may affect the auditors' own investments. Therefore, Rule 101 prohibits a CPA from having joint financial investments with a client that are material in amount as compared with the auditor's net worth.

Financial interests in audit clients. When a CPA firm acquires a new audit client, the firm will notify its partners and staff that they must dispose of any stockholdings in the company before the audit engagement begins. By disposing of any such investments, the auditors avoid a challenge to their independence in dealing with the new client company.

Direct and indirect interests. The *Code of Professional Ethics* makes a distinction between direct and indirect financial interests. A CPA may have an *indirect* interest in an audit client that is not material to the auditor's net worth; any *direct* financial interest impairs the auditor's independence. This distinction between direct and indirect interests enables auditors to invest in companies that have minor interests in audit clients.

Illustrative case.   John Jones, a partner in the CPA firm, Reynolds and Co., owns shares in a regulated mutual investment fund, which in turn holds shares of stock in audit clients of Reynolds and Co. The CPA firm inquired of the AICPA Professional Ethics division whether this financial interest by Jones affected the firm's independence.

The response was that this indirect interest would not normally impair the independence of the CPA firm, because investment decisions are made only by the mutual fund's management. However, if the portfolio of the mutual fund were heavily invested in securities of a client of Reynolds and Co., the indirect interest could become material and thereby impair the independence of the CPA firm.

Business relationships with client companies.   Assume that a CPA firm were to accept as a new audit client the Zone Corporation. Assume also that Jones, one of the CPA firm's partners (or staff), had been serving Zone Corporation as controller on a part-time basis. Even though Jones were to resign his post with Zone Corporation as soon as it became an audit client, the CPA firm could not audit Zone Corporation for any accounting period in which Jones had served the company in a management capacity. To do so would violate the basic concept that one cannot act independently in evaluating one's own work.

Interests of a CPA's relatives.   Another question that often arises in discussions of independence may be stated as follows: How is independence affected by a financial interest or business position held by a relative of a CPA? The answer depends on the closeness of the family relationship and on whether the CPA works in a firm office that participates in the audit. The financial interests and business positions of a CPA's spouse, dependent children, or relatives supported by the CPA are attributed directly to the CPA. Accordingly, if the CPA's spouse owns even one share of a client's stock, the situation is evaluated as if the CPA owned the stock. Independence is impaired.

A problem of independence also may result from financial interests or business activities of other close relatives, such as parents, brothers, sisters, and nondependent children. However, the financial interests of these relatives are not attributed directly to the auditor, and independence is impaired only by investments that are material to the relative's net worth. Independence problems concerning closer relatives may be mitigated if the CPA is geographically separated from the relatives and the CPA is not assigned to an office that participates in the audit. To avoid an impairment of independence, it sometimes is necessary for a CPA firm to transfer a partner or staff member to an office that does not participate in a particular audit.

Impairment of independence does not result from an investment or business relationship by distant relatives of a CPA, unless there are close financial ties between the CPA and the relative.

Other problems of independence.   It is impossible to describe all the situations that impair the appearance of independence. Interpretations and Ethics Rulings are issued regularly describing the application of Rule 101 to new situations. Three particularly significant situations involve the activities of retired partners, client gifts, and litigation.

A retired partner's activities may affect the independence of the CPA firm. Typically, these partners are paid retirement benefits and may continue to function as a part of management of the CPA firm. If the retired partner wishes to be employed by an audit client of the firm, the partner must no longer be associated in any way with the CPA firm. For example, the partner cannot use office space in the CPA's firm's offices or be named on the firm's stationery. Retired partners who continue to be associated with a CPA firm are prohibited from serving audit clients in a management capacity or having financial interests as described in Rule 101.

An outsider may question the independence of a CPA firm in situations in which a partner or employee accepts an expensive gift from a client. It would appear that special considerations might be tied to the acceptance of the gift, and the auditor might not act with complete impartiality. To avoid this implication of lack of independence, auditors should decline all but token gifts from audit clients.

Litigation may also affect the independence of auditors, if the litigation involves the client and the auditors. The relationship between the auditors and client management must be characterized by complete candor and full disclosure. A relationship with these characteristics may not exist when litigation places the auditors and client management in an adversary position. Auditors in litigation with a client must evaluate the situation to determine whether the significance of the litigation affects the client's confidence in the auditors or the auditors' objectivity.

Independence as defined by the SEC. A discussion of professional ethics would be incomplete without considering the important role played by the Securities and Exchange Commission. A principal aim of the Commission throughout its existence has been the improvement of auditing standards and the establishment of high levels of professional conduct by the independent public accountants practicing before the Commission.

The laws administered by the SEC require that financial statements be examined by "independent public or certified public accountants." The Commission therefore faces the task of deciding upon the meaning of *independence* on the part of accountants. The following was adopted as part of Rule 2–01 of *Regulation S-X:*

> The Commission will not recognize any certified public accountant . . . as independent who is not in fact independent. For example, an accountant will be considered not independent with respect to any person . . . (1) in which, during the period of his professional engagement to examine the financial statements being reported on or at the date of his report, he or his firm or a member thereof had, or was committed to acquire, any direct financial interest or any material indirect financial interest; or (2) with which, during the period of his professional engage-

ment to examine the financial statements being reported on, at the date of his report or during the period covered by the financial statements, he or his firm or a member thereof was connected as a promoter, underwriter, voting trustee, director, officer, or employee, ... For the purposes of Rule 2–01 the term "member" means all partners in the firm and all professional employees participating in the audit or located in an office of the firm participating in a significant portion of the audit.

In applying this rule to specific cases, the SEC has held that the public accountant was not independent in the following situations, among others:

1. A partner in an accounting firm also acted as legal counsel for the audit client.
2. An accounting firm performed the month-end accounting work of the audit client, including the making of adjusting and closing entries for the general ledger.
3. A partner of an accounting firm that audited a wholly-owned subsidiary company invested in a nominal amount of stock of the subsidiary's nonclient parent company.

Independence when the auditors perform accounting services. One difference between the concept of independence required by the SEC and that set forth in the AICPA *Code of Professional Ethics* relates to auditors who perform accounting services for a client. Can the auditors who post the general ledger, make closing entries, and maintain subsidiary records also serve as independent auditors for the company? The SEC answer is no; the CPA is not independent under these circumstances. The auditor should be an outsider who reviews the work performed by the client's accounting employees. If independent auditors perform the original accounting work, they cannot maintain the posture of an outside critic. In *Accounting Series Release No. 126*, the SEC stated: "The Commission is of the opinion that an accountant cannot objectively audit books and records which he has maintained for a client."

Illustrative case.   The SEC found in one famous case (In the Matter of Interstate Hosiery Mills, Inc., 4 SEC 706, 717 [1939]) that a staff member of the CPA firm had been maintaining the accounting records of a client; the financial statements had been falsified, and the audit staff member was responsible for the falsification. Clearly the dual role of internal accountant and independent auditor played by this individual had resulted in defeating the purpose of the audit.

The AICPA, on the other hand, has often considered the propriety of combining the performance of manual or automated accounting services with the conduct of an independent audit for a client, but has not opposed the practice as damaging to the auditor's independence. As long as the client takes responsibility for the financial statements and the auditors perform their engagement in accordance with generally accepted auditing standards, the AICPA indicates that independence is not impaired. Of course, the accounting services cannot include consumating transactions or performance of any other management function. If the AICPA ruled that independence is impaired whenever the auditors perform accounting services, such a ruling would no doubt be a blow to many small public accounting firms with practices including considerable write-up work and occasional audits for write-up clients. Despite this attitude of the AICPA, the SEC position denying the independence of a CPA who maintains a client's accounting records appears much sounder in terms of basic auditing philosophy.

Does rendering of management advisory services threaten the auditors' independence? A problem to be considered in rendering management advisory services is the possible threat to the auditors' independence when auditing as well as a variety of consulting services are performed for the same client. Can a public accounting firm that renders extensive management advisory services for a client still maintain the independent status so essential in an audit and in the expression of an opinion on the client's financial statements.

A CPA who becomes a part-time controller for a client and assumes a *decision-making* role in the client's affairs is not in a position to make an independent audit of the financial statements. On the other hand, public accounting firms have long been rendering certain purely *advisory* services to management while continuing to perform audits in an independent manner that serves the public interest. Advisory services can generally be distinguished from management proper; the work of the consultant or adviser consists of such functions as conducting special studies and investigations, making suggestions to management, pointing out the existence of weaknesses, outlining various alternative corrective measures, and making recommendations.

Independence—a matter of degree. The concept of independence is not absolute; no auditors could claim complete independence of a client. Rather, independence is relative—a matter of degree. As long as the auditors work closely with client management and are paid fees by their clients, complete independence can be considered merely an ideal. Auditors must strive for the greatest degree of independence consistent with their environment.

Recent developments have served to increase the auditor's independence in dealings with management. One of these developments is the widespread adoption of audit committees by corporation. Members of these audit committees are selected from the company's board of directors. Ideally, audit committee members are outside directors, that is, board members who are not also officers of the company. The functions of the audit committee include appointing and discharging the independent auditors, determining the scope of the auditors' services, reviewing audit findings, and resolving conflicts between the auditors and management.

A second development that has strengthened the CPA's independence is a recent SEC requirement applying to public companies that change auditors. These companies must file an informative disclosure (Form 8-K) describing the reason for the change in auditors. The discharged auditors may also respond if they disagree with management's analysis. This requirement and the widespread establishment of audit committees restrict management from *shopping for accounting principles.* Shopping for accounting principles occurs when a company changes auditors to a CPA firm that is more likely to sanction a disputed accounting principle. A company's management might search for auditors, for example, who would accept a questionable inventory valuation method as being in accordance with generally accepted accounting principles. Consequently, auditors who are consulted on a question of accounting or auditing by a company other than a client should be sure they are aware of all the facts and circumstances before responding. This would include obtaining permission from the company's management to make inquiries of the current auditors. Although cases in which management has actually shopped for accounting principles are rare, it is clear that if management can change auditors casually and without explanation, undue pressure is placed on auditors' independence.

General and technical standards

In addition to performing audits, CPAs also provide accounting, review, tax, and management advisory services. Clients and the general public expect these services to be performed with competence and professional care. Therefore, ethical standards have been established under the category of general and technical standards that apply to all CPA services.

Forecasts of future transactions. Owners of a business who wish to sell all or part of the enterprise sometimes prepare optimistic forecasts of expected future earnings. Similar projections may be prepared to support an application for a bank loan. To make these forecasts more convincing, the business executive may seek to have a CPA attest to the achievability of the projections. Such endorsements are not permitted under the *Code of Professional Ethics*.

One reason CPAs are ethically prohibited from attesting to the achievability of forecasts is the lack of evidential matter supporting the outcome of future events. Without the existence of evidential matter, the attest function cannot be performed in a credible manner. Accountants can make an objective verification of *past* earnings and vouch for their fairness; they cannot read the future, and therefore they must not vouch for the achievability of a forecast of *future* earnings.

Rule 204, in prohibiting AICPA members from vouching for the achievability of forecasts, does not prevent CPAs from aiding management in preparing budgets, pro forma financial statements, cash forecasts, and the like. These studies are essential tools of management and aid in the formulation of sound decisions. CPAs may prepare or assist their clients in preparing forecasts; they may even review these forecasts. However, if the CPA firm's name is associated with this work, the firm must make sure that the major assumptions underlying the forecast are disclosed and the source of data is indicated in the document. The auditors should provide a report indicating the nature of their work, such as a compilation or review of the information and a statement that the firm does not vouch for the achievability of the forecast.

Auditing standards and accounting principles. Rule 202 obligates a CPA performing an audit to comply with the 10 generally accepted auditing standards discussed in Chapter 1, and clarifies the enforceability of *Statements on Auditing Standards*. Rule 203 requires the CPA to recognize the pronouncements of the Financial Accounting Standards Board and its predecessor, the Accounting Principles Board, as primary sources of generally accepted accounting principles.

The consequence of these two rules is a strengthening of the authority of the AICPA and the FASB, and a lessening of the opportunities for wide variations in the quality of auditing services or the options available for accounting procedures. In addition, Rule 202 essentially precludes a CPA who performs the *accounting* service of preparing *unaudited* financial statements for a client from implying that *auditing* services were applied to the financial statements.

Other technical standards. Rule 204 requires CPAs to adhere to professional standards issued by other bodies. To date the Council of the AICPA has recognized three such bodies: (1) the Management Advisory Services Executive Committee to prescribe standards for management advisory services, (2) the Accounting and Review Services Committee to prescribe standards for unaudited financial information services for nonpublic clients, and (3) the FASB to prescribe disclosure standards for supplemental information outside financial statements. CPAs must become familiar with such standards and apply them to their engagements. To violate standards prescribed by these bodies is to violate the Rules of Professional Conduct.

Responsibilities to clients

The conduct of an audit requires that the client entrust the CPA with complete information about the business being audited. To safeguard this sensitive relationship between the CPA and the client, the AICPA has established several ethical rules.

Confidential client information. Rule 301 stresses the confidential nature of information obtained by CPAs from their clients. The nature of the accountants' work makes it necessary for them to have access to their clients' most confidential financial affairs. Independent accountants may thus gain knowledge of impending business combinations, proposed financing, prospective stock splits or dividend changes, contracts being negotiated, and other confidential information that, if disclosed or otherwise improperly used, could bring the accountants quick monetary profits. Of course, the client would be financially injured, as well as embarrassed, if the CPAs were to "leak" such information. Accountants must not only keep quiet as to their clients' business plans, but they rarely even mention in public the names of their clients. Any loose talk by independent public accountants concerning the affairs of their clients would immediately brand them as lacking in professional ethics. On the other hand, the confidential relationship between the CPA and the client is *never* a justification for the CPA to cooperate in any deceitful act. The personal integrity of the CPA is essential to the performance of the attest function.

Illegal acts by clients.   We have previously emphasized that unswerving commitment to honorable behavior is the essence of ethical conduct. If CPAs permit doubts to arise about their personal integrity, they have destroyed their usefulness as independent auditors. This concept should govern the CPAs' reaction when they encounter dishonest, illegal, or possibly illegal acts by a client. In recent years investors have been deceived by a few gigantic frauds including falsified financial statements, as in the widely publicized *Equity Funding* case. In considering the responsibility of auditors for detection of fraud, it is helpful to distinguish *nonmanagement fraud* from *management fraud*. Nonmanagement fraud consists of dishonest actions that occur within a company despite management's efforts to prevent such actions. Protection against nonmanagement fraud is provided by a strong system of internal control, as discussed in Chapter 5. The independent auditors' contribution in preventing nonmanagement fraud is to study and evaluate the system of internal control and to make recommendations for improvement in internal controls. The normal audit is not designed to detect small scattered instances of theft, embezzlement, or other dishonest acts. Such small localized cases of fraud will not have a material effect on the overall fairness of the financial statements.

Management fraud occurs only when the top executives of a company deliberately deceive stockholders, creditors, and independent auditors. The purpose of management fraud is generally to issue misleading financial statements that exaggerate corporate earnings and financial strength. Such overstatements of operating results and financial position may enable the management of the company to obtain increased salaries and bonuses, or to benefit from stock options and from higher market prices for their holdings of the company's securities. The theft of assets may also be involved.

If management fraud is so material as to make the financial statements misleading, the independent auditors cannot avoid responsibility. Although the normal audit is not designed to detect fraud, the auditors do accept responsibility for the fairness of audited financial statements. Before issuing an audit report the auditors should do everything necessary to be reasonably satisfied that the financial statements are not materially in error for *any reason,* including possible management fraud.

As explained in *SAS No. 17,* an auditor's examination carried out in accordance with generally accepted auditing standards is not designed to detect illegal client acts.[1] Unfortunately, the media and the public sometimes tend to blame auditors because illegal acts by a client company are not brought to light during an audit. Only those persons who understand the scope and limitations of an audit realize that audits by their very nature cannot be relied on to detect illegal acts by the client. Of course, audit procedures such as inquiries of management and of the client's legal counsel sometimes will result in the discovery of certain illegal acts. Under no circumstances should the CPAs condone or ignore actions they *know* to be dishonest or illegal. This does not mean that the CPAs should report such acts to governmental authorities; it does mean that they should not permit their firm's name to be associated with financial statements that are misleading, or that conceal morally indefensible actions by a client.

If the CPAs have knowledge of dishonest or clearly illegal actions by a client, they should discuss the situation with the client so that action can be taken to remedy the situation and make disclosures or adjustments to the financial statements. In some cases this may mean discussing the situation with the audit committee of the board of directors. If the client fails to take corrective action, the CPAs should withdraw from the engagement. This action on the part of the CPAs makes clear that they will not be associated in any way with dishonorable or illegal activities. The performance of the attest function by independent public accountants is a valuable and important service to society if two conditions are met: personal integrity and professional competence on the part of the CPAs.

Client confidences and privileged communications. The communications of a client to a certified public accountant are not privileged under common law, as are communications to a lawyer, clergyman, or physician. However, some states have adopted statutes indicating that public accountants should not be required in court to give evidence gained by them in confidence from clients.

Contingent fees. An accountant is prohibited (Rule 302) from making an audit on a contingent fee basis. For example, a company in need of an auditor's report to support its application for a bank loan might offer to make the auditor's fee contingent upon approval of the loan by the bank. Such an arrangement would create an undesirable temptation for the auditor to abandon an independent viewpoint and to

---

[1] *Statement on Auditing Standards No. 17,* "Illegal Acts by Clients," AICPA (New York, 1977), pp. 1–2.

lend support to the statements prepared by management. In the handling of tax work, on the other hand, the accountant does not assume an independent status, and contingent fees are permissible if they are determined as a result of judicial proceedings or of government agency findings.

Responsibilities to colleagues

Society's impression of a profession is affected by the way members conduct their business affairs. Cutthroat competition or general lack of cooperation among its members casts a poor image on any profession. Currently there are no Rules of Conduct governing responsibilities to colleagues. Still, CPAs should strive for goodwill and mutual cooperation with other members of their profession.

In the past, Rules of Conduct existed to restrict competitive bidding for engagements, offers of employment to employes of other CPA firms, and endeavors to take clients from other CPAs (encroachment). However, the Department of Justice and the federal courts have taken the position that such rules violate the antitrust laws. This development resulted in revisions of the ethical rules of all the major professions. Accordingly, the membership of the AICPA voted to rescind these rules.

Other responsibilities and practices

Acts discreditable. Rule 501, prohibiting acts discreditable to the profession, applies to all members of the AICPA, whether they work in public practice, industry, or government. The rule permits the disciplining of those members who act in a manner damaging to the reputation of the profession. The rule is not specific as to what constitutes a discreditable act; it is subject to interpretation. In the past, such acts as signing a false or misleading opinion or statement, committing a felony, and engaging in discriminatory employment practices have been interpreted to be violations of Rule 501.

One interesting practice that has been interpreted to be discreditable is failure to return client records. These situations generally arise when the CPAs have been discharged and not paid for their services. To refuse to return a client's ledger is clearly wrong, but what if the CPA retains working papers needed by the client? To enforce collection of a fee, some CPAs have refused to allow the client or the successor CPAs access to their working papers. Since the working papers are the CPAs' property, this is a legitimate business practice, not a violation of Rule 501. However, a problem sometimes arises in the definition of working papers. Documents that provide the only support or analysis for entries in client records are considered part of the client's records, even if the papers were prepared by the CPAs. Failure to provide the client with access to such documents constitutes a violation of Rule 501.

Advertising. Until 1978, advertising by CPAs was strictly forbidden by the Rules of Professional Ethics. Most certified public accountants considered advertising in any form to be unprofessional. However, this prohibition was dropped because it was deemed a possible violation of the federal antitrust laws. Members of the public accounting profession may now advertise their services so long as the advertising is not false, misleading, or deceptive. Unethical advertising includes advertising that creates unjustified expectations of favorable results, makes incomplete comparisons with other CPAs, or indicates an ability to influence a court or other official body.

Acceptable advertising is that which is informative and based upon verifiable fact. Indications of the types of services offered, certificates and degrees of members of the firm and fees for services are all acceptable forms of advertising. However, endorsements or testimonials by clients or others should be avoided.

Incompatible occupations. Rule 504 prohibits the AICPA member from engaging in any business or occupation that "would create conflict of interest in rendering professional services." For example, an accountant should not act as an insurance broker because CPAs often perform management advisory services involving a review of the adequacy of the client's insurance coverage. An objective appraisal of insurance coverage would be difficult if the accountant were in a position to benefit personally by the sale of insurance. For similar reasons, CPAs in public practice should not act concurrently as investment advisors. To do so might put the CPAs in a position of making recommendations regarding investment in their audit clients.

Form of practice. Corporations have certain tax advantages not available to partnerships, such as tax deductibility of pension and profit sharing plans. Therefore, many state laws as well as the AICPA Rules of Professional Ethics allow CPAs to form professional corporations. However, the AICPA did not wish to allow the corporate form to be used to limit CPA's liability or to allow them to undertake unethical activities. For this reason the requirements for professional incorporation are very specific. In addition to providing for unlimited liability, all corporate stock must be owned and the corporate control must rest with individuals authorized to practice public accounting. The name of the corporation cannot be impersonal or fictitious; it must contain only the names of one or more present or former owners of the firm.

The CPA as tax adviser—ethical problems

What is the responsibility of the CPA in serving as tax adviser? The CPA has a primary responsibility to the client: that is, to see that the client pays the proper amount of tax and no more. Rule of Conduct No. 102 provides that in the role of tax adviser, the certified public accountant may properly resolve questionable issues in favor of the client; the

CPA is not obliged to maintain the posture of independence required in audit work. When CPAs express an opinion on financial statements, they must be unbiased; freedom from bias is not required in serving as a tax adviser. On the other hand, CPAs must adhere to the same standards of truth and personal integrity in tax work as in all other professional activities. Any departure from these standards on a tax engagement would surely destroy the reputation of certified public accountants in performing their work as independent auditors.

A second responsibility of CPAs on tax engagements is to the public, whose interests are represented by the government—more specifically by the Internal Revenue Service. To meet this responsibility, CPAs must observe the preparer's declaration on the tax returns they prepare. The declaration requires the preparer to state that the return is "true, correct, and complete . . . based on all information of which the preparer has any knowledge." To comply with this declaration, what steps must the CPA firm take to acquire knowledge relating to the tax return? The firm is not required to make an audit; knowledge of the return may be limited to information supplied to the firm by the client. However, if this information appears unreasonable or contradictory, the CPAs are obligated to make sufficient investigation to resolve these issues. Information that appears plausible to a layman might appear unreasonable to CPAs, since they are experts in evaluating financial data. CPAs are not obligated to investigate any and all information provided by the taxpayer, but they cannot ignore clues that cast doubt on the accuracy of these data.

In addition to being guided by the declaration on the tax return, CPAs engaged in tax practice are also bound by the AICPA *Code of Professional Ethics*. This code is in general applicable to every type of work CPAs undertake, although those portions of the Rules of Conduct relating to the examination of financial statements *are clearly not applicable to tax engagements*. However, in tax work as in auditing or any other area of their practice, CPAs pledged to high standards of morality and integrity. Only by unswerving conformance with these standards can CPAs uphold the dignity and honor of the public accounting profession.

To further identify appropriate standards of tax practice for CPAs, the AICPA has issued a series of *Statements on Responsibilities in Tax Practice*. The nine statements issued to date have focused on CPAs' responsibilities, in varying circumstances, for signing the preparer's declaration on tax returns which they have prepared or reviewed, for use of estimates in preparing returns, for errors in previously filed returns or client failure to file returns, for advice to clients on tax matters, and for certain procedural aspects of preparing tax returns.

Unless certified public accountants approach tax engagements with full recognition of the responsibilities imposed on them by the AICPA code, by the preparer's declaration on the return, and by the *Statements on Responsibilities in Tax Practice*, they may quickly destroy public confidence in the profession. The interests of the taxpayer and of the government are directly opposed, and this conflict requires a most careful delineation of the responsibility of CPAs. Because of public confidence in the CPA certificate and the reputation of the profession for integrity, any financial data to which CPAs lend their names gain in credibility, even though no examination is made and no opinion is expressed. This level of public confidence and respect is an invaluable asset of the profession that deserves to be guarded with the greatest care.

Enforcement of professional ethics

The AICPA *Code of Professional Ethics* is binding only upon accountants who are members of the AICPA. Violation of the Code may result in admonition, suspension, or expulsion of the offending member by the AICPA's Trial Board. Although expulsion from the AICPA would not in itself cause the loss of a CPA license and would not prevent the expelled member from continuing the practice of public accounting, the damage to the CPA's professional reputation would probably be so great as to make this penalty disastrous to the individual or the firm.

Many provisions of the AICPA Rules of Conduct have been adopted by numerous states as part of state accountancy acts; in these states the revocation of license to practice is a possible consequence of the violation of the standards previously discussed. The several state societies of certified public accountants also follow the leadership of the AICPA to a great extent in urging compliance by their members with the policies set forth in the Code. In summary, a problem of enforcing professional ethics exists and will no doubt continue to exist, but with a few exceptions most public accounting firms recognize the value of professional ethics and attempt to conform fully with the standards enunciated by the AICPA.

KEY TERMS INTRODUCED OR EMPHASIZED IN CHAPTER 2

Audit committee   A committee of a corporation's board of directors that engages independent auditors, reviews audit findings, monitors activities of the internal auditing staff, and intervenes in any disputes between management and the independent auditors. Preferably, members of the audit committee are outside directors, that is, members of the board of directors who do not also serve as corporate officers.

Ethics Rulings   Pronouncements of the AICPA Professional Ethics Executive Committee that explain the application of Rules of Conduct and Interpretations of the *Code of Professional Ethics* to specific factual circumstances involving professional ethics.

Independence   A most important Rule of Conduct that prohibits CPAs from expressing an opinion on financial statements of an enterprise unless they are independent with respect to such enterprise; independence is impaired by a material financial interest, service as an officer or trustee, loans to or from the enterprise, and various other relationships.

Interpretations of Rules of Conduct Guidelines issued by the AICPA Professional Ethics Executive Committee for the scope and applications of the Rules of Conduct.

Management fraud Exists when the client management makes a deliberate effort to present misleading financial statements, supported by falsified accounting records.

Nonmanagement fraud Dishonest actions (usually involving the theft of assets) that occur within a company despite management's efforts to prevent such actions.

Profession An activity that involves a responsibility to serve the public, has a complex body of knowledge, and has a need for public confidence.

Rules of Conduct A group of enforceable ethical standards approved by the membership of the AICPA, included in the *Code of Professional Ethics.*

Shopping for principles Undesirable conduct by some enterprises that discharge one independent auditing firm after seeking out another firm that will sanction a disputed financial statement presentation or disclosure.

GROUP I: REVIEW QUESTIONS

2–1. In Chapter 1 the 10 generally accepted auditing standards were discussed. How does the AICPA *Code of Professional Ethics* relate, if at all, to these 10 generally accepted auditing standards?

2–2. Wallace Company is indebted to John Greer, a CPA, for unpaid fees and has offered to issue to him unsecured interest-bearing notes. Would the CPA's acceptance of these notes have any bearing upon his independence in his relations with Wallace Company? Discuss. (AICPA, adapted)

2–3. Arthur Brown is a CPA who often serves as an expert witness in court cases. Is it proper for Brown to receive compensation in a damage suit based on the amount awarded to the plaintiff? Discuss. (AICPA, adapted)

2–4. Sara Kole, CPA, has been requested by the president of Noyes Company, a closely held corporation and audit client, to cosign Noyes Company checks with the Noyes treasurer when the president is away on business trips. Would Kole violate the AICPA *Code of Professional Ethics* if she accepted this request? Explain.

2–5. Is it ethical for a CPA firm to determine its fee for audit services in connection with a bond issuance as a percentage of the proceeds of the bond issue? Explain.

2–6. Laura Clark, wife of Jon Clark, CPA, is a life insurance agent. May Jon Clark refer audit clients needing officer life insurance to Laura Clark or to another life insurance agent who will share a commission with Laura Clark? Explain.

2–7. Bill Terry, a CPA who had reached retirement age, arranged for the sale of his practice to another certified public accountant. Their agreement called for the transfer of all working papers and business correspondence to the accountant purchasing the practice. Comment on the propriety of this plan.

2–8. Sally Jones is a partner in a large CPA firm. Her husband, Zane Jones, is employed as bookkeeper by Coast Company, an audit client of Sally's firm. Under these circumstances is the independence of the CPA firm impaired? Explain. (AICPA, adapted)

2–9. Cary Beal, a CPA in public practice, has proposed to enter into an arrangement with Susan Dunlap, a management specialist. Dunlap would seek engagements to study companies' operations, and suggest where improvement might be made. If the study indicates deficiencies in the accounting system, Dunlap would recommend Beal to perform the proposed services. Beal would pay Dunlap compensation for the referral. Would such an arrangement violate the AICPA *Code of Professional Ethics?* Explain. (AICPA, adapted)

GROUP II: QUESTIONS REQUIRING ANALYSIS

2–10. Willis Martin, a CPA in public practice, owns a limited partnership interest in an oil drilling business in which an audit client also owns a limited partnership interest. The interest is material to Martin's net worth. Is Martin in violation of the AICPA *Code of Professional Ethics?* Explain fully. (AICPA, adapted)

2–11. Mary Carr, a staff accountant of the CPA firm, Bell & Co., is participating in the audit of Fashions, Inc., a manufacturer of women's apparel. During a conversation with the vice president of sales, Carr is offered any items of apparel she might want for her wardrobe, at no cost to her. Should Carr accept the gifts? Explain.

2–12. A CPA is approached by a prospective tax client who promises to pay the CPA a fee of "5 percent of whatever amount you save me in taxes." Can the CPA accept the tax engagement under this fee arrangement? Explain. (AICPA, adapted)

2–13. A CPA is considering establishing a small-loan company, while continuing in the practice of public accounting. Is this permissible under the AICPA *Code of Professional Ethics?* Why?

2–14. With the approval of its board of directors, Thames Corporation made a sizable payment for advertising during the year being audited by Leslie Wade, CPA. The corporation deducted the full amount in its federal and state income tax returns. The controller, John Warren, acknowledges that this deduction probably will be disallowed because it related to political matters. He has not provided for this disallowance in his income taxes provision and refuses to do so because he fears that this will cause the federal and state revenue agents to believe that the deduction is not valid. What is the CPA's responsibility in this situation? Explain. (AICPA, adapted)

2–15. Ward Nolan retired from the large CPA firm of Oates, Pyle and Company after an association of 20 years. Nolan then accepted directorships in several corporate clients of Oates, Pyle and Company. Nolan has re quested permission from the managing partners of Oates, Pyle and Company to maintain a small office in the firm's suite, to receive mail and telephone calls through the firm, and to perform occasional consulting services for the firm on a fee basis. May the managing partner of Oates, Pyle and Company ethically grant Nolan's request? Explain.

2–16. Harvey Jackson publishes a well-known book entitled *The Best of Everything*. In his book Jackson lists retailers of products and services who have demonstrated excellence in service to their customers. Carl Swift, a CPA in public practice, has been nominated for listing in Jackson's book. Should Swift allow his name to be associated with such a publication? Explain.

2–17. Harris Fell, CPA and member of the AICPA, was engaged to audit the financial statements of Wilson Corporation. Fell had half-completed the audit when he had a dispute with the management of Wilson Corporation and was discharged. Hal Compton, CPA, was promptly engaged to replace Fell. Wilson Corporation did not compensate Fell for his work to date, therefore, Fell refused to allow Wilson Corporation's management to examine his working papers. Certain of the working papers consisted of adjusting journal entries and supporting analysis. Wilson Corporation's management had no other source of this information. Did Fell violate the AICPA *Code of Professional Ethics?* Explain fully.

2–18. A CPA owns a one-tenth interest in an investment club composed of six members. The investment club periodically meets to invest pooled resources in listed securities, or to sell portions of the securities portfolio and invest in other securities. At the current meeting of the investment club, the president, who owns a one-fifth interest, proposes that the club make a substantial investment in shares of common stock of a major corporation that is the audit client of the CPA's employer firm. What should the CPA do? Explain.

2–19. John Mason, a resident of California and a partner in a national CPA firm, has participated for several years in the audit of X Company, which is listed on the New York Stock Exchange. Richard Mason, a brother of John Mason, resides in France and is a successful real estate developer. The two brothers have seen each other briefly on two occasions in the last 10 years.

X Company is now in financial difficulties, and some of its creditors have challenged the fairness of its audited financial statements. During the current audit of the company, John Mason happened to notice his brother's name and address in a list of X Company's stockholders. Richard Mason was listed as the owner of 500 shares. John Mason had had no knowledge of his brother's investments. After coming across this information, John telephoned his brother and learned that Richard owned securities in 25 listed American corporations. The value of the investment in X Company was about 4 percent of the total market value of Richard's investment in securities.

Do these facts warrant a presumption of impairment of independence on the part of John Mason, CPA, with respect to the audit of X Company? Discuss.

2–20. What effect, if any, does each of the following have upon the auditor's independence? Explain.

    a. The auditor's acceptance of a fee from the client.

    b. The client's preparation of working papers for the auditor's files.

    c. The auditor's inquiries of client employees, in the course of gathering evidence.

2–21. Auditors must not only appear to be independent; they must also be independent in fact.

    Required:

    a. Explain the concept of an "auditor's independence" as it applies to third-party reliance upon financial statements.

    b. (1) What determines whether or not an auditor is independent in fact?

        (2) What determines whether or not an auditor appears to be independent?

    c. Explain how an auditor may be independent in fact but not appear to be independent.

    d. Would Joe Marks, a CPA, be considered independent for an examination of the financial statements of a—

        (1) Church for which he is serving as treasurer without compensation? Explain.

        (2) Women's club for which his wife is serving as treasurer-accountant if he is not to receive a fee for the examination? Explain. (AICPA, adapted)

2–22. Select the best answer for each of the following. Explain the reasons for your selection.

    a. Which of the following best describes why publicly traded corporations follow the practice of having the outside auditor appointed by the audit committee of the board of directors?

        (1) To comply with the regulations of the Financial Accounting Standards Board.

        (2) To emphasize auditor independence from the management of the corporation.

        (3) To encourage a policy of rotation of the independent auditors.

        (4) To provide the corporate owners with an opportunity to voice their opinion concerning the quality of the auditing firm selected by the directors.

    b. Gray and Moore, CPAs, is the firm that audits the financial statements of Mock Company. Mock's board of directors has requested Gray and Moore to perform management advisory services in the area of inventory management, which the board believes to be inefficient. Which of the following services by Gray and Moore could impair the CPA firm's audit independence?

        (1) Identify the inventory-management problem as caused by the procedures presently operative in the purchasing, receiving, storage, and issuance operations.

        (2) Study and evaluate the inventory-management problem and suggest several alternative solutions.

        (3) Develop a time schedule for implementation of the solution

adopted by Mock Company's board, to be carried out and supervised by Mock personnel.

  (4) Supervise the purchasing, receiving, storage, and issuance operations.

 c. A CPA firm's report accompanying a financial forecast of a client should—

  (1) Not be issued in any form, because it would be in violation of the AICPA *Code of Professional Ethics*.

  (2) Disclaim any opinion as to the achievability of the forecast.

  (3) Be prepared only if the client is a not-for-profit organization.

  (4) Be a qualified short-form audit report if the client is a commercial enterprise.

 d. *Statements on Auditing Standards* issued by the AICPA's Auditing Standards Board are—

  (1) Part of the generally accepted auditing standards under the AICPA *Code of Professional Ethics*.

  (2) Interpretations of generally accepted auditing standards under the AICPA *Code of Professional Ethics*, and departures from such statements must be justified.

  (3) Interpretations of generally accepted auditing standards under the AICPA *Code of Professional Ethics*, and such statements must be followed in every engagement.

  (4) Generally accepted auditing procedures that are not covered by the AICPA *Code of Professional Ethics*.

 e. Glen Page, CPA, accepted the audit engagement of Todd Company. During the audit, Page became aware of his lack of competence required for the engagement. What should Page do?

  (1) Disclaim an opinion.

  (2) Issue a qualified opinion.

  (3) Suggest that Todd Company engage another CPA to perform the audit.

  (4) Rely on the competence of client personnel. (AICPA, adapted)

GROUP III: PROBLEMS

 2–23. Lauren Brown, CPA, has been requested by the management of Walker Corporation, an audit client, to perform a nonrecurring engagement involving the implementation of an information and control system. Walker's management requests that in setting up the new system and during the period before conversion to the new system that Brown:

  (1) Counsel on potential expansion of business activity plans.

  (2) Search for and interview new personnel.

  (3) Hire new personnel.

  (4) Train personnel.

In addition Walker's management requests that during the three months subsequent to the conversion, that Brown:

  (1) Supervise the operation of the new system.

  (2) Monitor client-prepared source documents and make changes in basic data generated by the system as Brown may deem necessary without concurrence of the client.

Required:

a. If Brown completes the engagement for implementation of the system as outlined before she begins the audit of Walker Corporation, is her independence impaired? Explain.

b. Which of the services may Brown perform and remain independent with respect to Walker Corporation?

c. If Walker Corporation was Brown's tax client and not her audit client, could Brown implement the system as outlined and continue to perform tax services for the client? Discuss. (AICPA, adapted)

2–24. Thomas Gilbert and Susan Bradley formed a professional corporation called "Financial Services Inc.—A Professional Corporation," each taking 50 percent of the authorized common stock. Gilbert is a CPA and a member of the AICPA. Bradley is a CPCU (Chartered Property Casualty Underwriter). The corporation performs auditing and tax services under Gilbert's direction and insurance services under Bradley's supervision.

One of the corporation's first audit clients was Grandtime Company. Grandtime had total assets of $600,000 and total liabilities of $270,000. In the course of his examination, Gilbert found that Grandtime's building with a carrying value of $240,000 was pledged as collateral for a 10-year-term note in the amount of $200,000. The client's financial statements did not mention that the building was pledged as collateral for the 10-year-term note. However, as the failure to disclose the lien did not affect either the value of the assets or the amount of the liabilities, and his examination was satisfactory in all other respects, Gilbert rendered an unqualified opinion on Grandtime's financial statements. About two months after the date of his opinion, Gilbert learned that an insurance company was planning to loan Grandtime $150,000 in the form of a first-mortgage note on the building. Realizing that the insurance company was unaware of the existing lien on the building, Gilbert had Bradley notify the insurance company of the fact that Grandtime's building was pledged as collateral for the term note.

Shortly after the events described above, Gilbert was charged with a violation of professional ethics.

Required:

Identify and discuss at least five ethical implications of those acts by Gilbert that were in violation of the AICPA *Code of Professional Ethics.* (AICPA, adapted)

2–25. Hillcrest Corporation was formed on October 1, year 5, and its fiscal year will end on September 30, year 6. You audited the corporation's opening balance sheet and rendered an unqualified opinion on it.

A month after issuing your report you are offered the position of secretary of the company because of the need for a complete set of officers and for convenience in signing various documents. You will have no financial interest in the company through stock ownership or otherwise, will receive no salary, will not maintain any corporate records, and will not have any influence on Hillcrest's financial matters

other than occasional advice on income tax matters and similar advice
normally given a client by a CPA.

Required:

a. Assume that you accept the offer, but plan to resign the position
before conducting your annual audit with the intention of again
assuming the office after rendering an opinion on the statements.
Can you render an independent opinion on the financial statements? Discuss.

b. Assume that you accept the offer on a temporary basis until the
corporation has gotten under way and can elect a secretary. In any
event you would permanently resign the position before conducting
your annual audit. Can you render an independent opinion on the
financial statements? Discuss. (AICPA, adapted)

2–26. Roland Company, a retail store, has utilized your services as independent auditor for several years. During the current year the company
opened a new store; in the course of your annual audit, you verify the
cost of the fixtures installed in the new store by examining purchase
orders, invoices, and other documents. This review brings to light an
understated invoice nearly a year old in which a clerical error by the
supplier, Western Showcase, Inc., caused the total of the invoice to
read $28,893.62 when it should have been $82,893.62. The invoice was
paid immediately upon receipt without any notice of the error, and subsequent statements and correspondence from Western Showcase, Inc.,
showed that the account with Roland Company had been paid in full.
Assume that the amount in question is material in relation to the financial position of both companies.

Required:

a. What action should you take in this situation?

b. If the client should decline to take any action in the matter, would
you insist that the unpaid amount of $54,000 be included in the
liabilities shown on the balance sheet as a condition necessary to
your issuance of an unqualified audit report?

c. Assuming that you were later retained to make an audit of Western
Showcase, Inc., would you utilize the information gained in your
examination of Roland Company to initiate a reopening of the
account with that company?

2–27. Bell & Davis, CPAs, has been requested by the board of directors of
Worthmore, Inc., to audit the company's financial statements for the
year ended November 30, year 5. Worthmore, Inc., has never before
had an audit. For each of the following cases, indicate whether Bell &
Davis would be independent with respect to Worthmore, Inc., and explain why.

a. Two directors of Worthmore, Inc., became partners in Bell &
Davis, CPAs, on July 1, year 5, resigning their directorships on that
date.

b. During year 5 Lee Bell, the former controller of Worthmore, Inc.,
now a partner of Bell & Davis, was frequently called upon for

assistance by Worthmore. He made decisions for Worthmore's management regarding plant and equipment acquisitions and the company's marketing mix. In addition, he conducted a computer feasibility study for Worthmore. (AICPA, adapted)

2–28.   An audit client, March Corporation, requested that you conduct a feasibility study to advise management of the best way the corporation can use electronic data processing equipment and which computer, if any, best meets the corporation's requirements. You are technically competent in this area and accept the engagement. Upon completion of your study the corporation accepts your suggestions and installs the computer and related equipment that you recommended.

Required:
a.   Discuss the effect acceptance of this management advisory services engagement would have upon your independence in expressing an opinion on the financial statements of March Corporation.
b.   A local company printing data processing forms customarily offers a commission for recommending it as supplier. The client is aware of the commission offer and suggests that you accept it. Would it be proper for you to accept the commission with the client's approval? Discuss. (AICPA, adapted)

3

Legal liability of auditors

Legal environment of the times

We live in an age of litigation. Persons having real or fancied grievances against business and professional persons are likely to take their grievances to court. Consumer organizations and various special interest groups often request courts to assess damages against professionals and business executives for alleged wrongs to society. The Securities and Exchange Commission, in its administration of federal laws, has frequently asked courts to enjoin CPAs and other professional persons from committing acts forbidden by those laws. The result has been clogged court calendars at every judicial level, and such crises as the medical malpractice insurance problem.

The rapid growth of the public accounting profession during the past several years has been accompanied by a sharp increase in the number of court cases involving independent public accountants. These court cases have included criminal charges as well as lawsuits involving civil matters. A man or woman entering the public accounting profession today should be aware of the legal liability inherent in the practice of public accounting. Awareness of the causes of past litigation can improve performance by all certified public accountants. This chapter will describe briefly some aspects of common law and of statutory law having a bearing on the work of the CPA, and some related court cases. It should be emphasized, however, that the court cases discussed in this chapter are isolated occurrences; the tens of thousands of satisfactory audits performed each year by certified public accountants do not result in court cases or newspaper headlines.

By way of comparison, let us assume that 1 million commercial airline flights are safely completed during a year, but that two crashes occur. It would seem unreasonable to assert on the basis of these assumed facts that commercial aviation is unsafe and should be prohibited by law. On the other hand, there is every reason to investigate every detail relating to the two crashes with the goal of improving the safety record of commercial aviation.

Definition of terms

Discussion of auditors' liability is best prefaced by a definition of some of the common terms of business law. Among these are the following:

Breach of contract is failure of one or both parties to a contract to perform in accordance with the contract's provisions. A CPA firm might be sued for breach of contract, for example, if the firm failed to deliver its audit report to the client by the date specified in the *engagement letter* representing the contractual arrangement between the CPA firm and the client.

Fraud is defined as misrepresentation by a person of a material fact, known by that person to be untrue or made with reckless indifference as to whether the fact is true, with the intention of deceiving the other party and with the result that the other party is injured. Rule of Conduct 102 of the AICPA's *Code of Professional Ethics* (discussed in Chapter 2) states that a member of the AICPA shall not knowingly misrepresent facts. A CPA found to have violated this provision of Rule 102 might be sued for fraud by the client or another injured party.

Constructive fraud differs from fraud as defined above in that constructive fraud does not involve a misrepresentation with intent to deceive. Reckless performance of a legal obligation is considered constructive fraud. A very substantial failure to observe generally accepted auditing standards during an audit engagement is considered to be constructive fraud by the CPAs.

An *independent contractor* is a party to a contract who performs contractual obligations essentially without control or supervision by the other contracting party. The generally accepted auditing standard dealing with independence makes it essential that a CPA firm's role in the examination of a client's financial statements be that of an independent contractor rather than an employee, despite the firm's receipt of a fee from the client.

Negligence is violation of a legal duty to exercise a degree of care that an ordinarily prudent person would exercise under similar circumstances with resultant damages to another party. For the CPA, negligence is failure to perform a duty in accordance with applicable professional standards. The two subdivisions of negligence are *ordinary negligence,* defined as lack of reasonable care; and *gross negligence,* which is lack of even *slight* care, indicative of reckless disregard for duty. A CPA firm that failed to gather sufficient competent evidence to support the figure for cash in the client's balance sheet might be accused of *ordinary negligence* by an injured party if all other phases of the audit conformed to generally accepted auditing standards. In contrast, if the CPA firm failed substantially to comply with generally accepted auditing standards, it might be charged with *gross negligence* by an aggrieved party. Gross negligence by auditors is considered constructive fraud.

Proximate cause exists when damage to another is directly attributable to a wrongdoer's act.

Contributory negligence is negligence on the part of a party damaged by another party's negligence. For example, a CPA charged by a client with *ordinary negligence* for failure to discover a cash shortage during the course of the audit might countercharge the client with *contributory negligence* for failing to establish an adequate system of internal control for cash.

Privity is the relationship between parties to a contract. A CPA firm is in privity with the client it is serving, as well as with any *third party beneficiary,* such as a creditor bank, named in the engagement letter representing the contract between the CPA firm and its client.

A *third-party beneficiary* is a person—not the promisor or promisee—who is named in a contract or intended by the contracting parties to have definite rights and benefits under the contract. For example, if Warren & Co., CPAs, is engaged to examine the financial statements of Arthur Company and to send a copy of its audit report to Third National Bank, the bank is a third-party beneficiary under the contract between Warren & Co. and Arthur Company.

Common law is unwritten law that has developed through court decisions; it represents judicial interpretation of a society's concept of fairness. For example, the right to sue a person for fraud is a common law right.

Statutory law is law that has been adopted by a governmental unit, such as the federal government. CPAs must concern themselves particularly with the federal securities acts and state blue-sky laws. These laws regulate the issuance and trading of securities.

Auditors' liability to clients

We have pointed out that CPA firms are independent contractors in their performance of audit engagements. In undertaking the customary audit engagement—the examination of and the expression of an opinion on the client's financial statements—auditors are responsible for carrying out their assignment in accordance with generally accepted auditing standards and for complying with the *Code of Professional Ethics*. Under the common law, if the auditors do not comply with their obligations to the client and there is consequent harm to the client, the latter may sue the auditors for breach of contract or for torts, such as fraud or negligence. To recover its losses, an injured client need prove only that the auditors were guilty of *ordinary negligence* and that the auditors' negligence was the proximate cause of the client's losses.

CPAs can be held liable to clients for the negligent performance of any type of services: auditing, accounting, review, tax, or management-advisory services. However, cases involving the performance of audits or the preparation of unaudited financial statements are most common. Many court actions by clients have arisen from employee defalcations that were not detected by the auditors' examinations. In defense, auditors attempt to prove that they were not negligent in the performance of their examination or that there was contributory negligence on the part of the client.

Illustrative case. Calvert Roth, CPA, has audited the financial statements of Metro Bank for the last five years. At the conclusion of each audit, Roth has suggested improvements in Metro Bank's internal controls over consumer loans. However, Metro's management failed to make the recommended improvements in internal controls. Recently, it was discovered that Harold Kay, a loan officer, had embezzled funds through the creation of fictitious consumer loans. Metro Bank filed suit against Roth for negligence in the performance of his audits. By means of expert testimony by other CPAs, it was established that Roth had been negligent in the performance of the last two audits. The court concluded that if Roth had performed his audit work adequately there was a reasonable chance that the defalcations would have been detected. However the court also concluded that Metro Bank's management was negligent in not carrying out the suggested improvements in internal control. Because of this **contributory negligence** on the part of the client, the court barred the bank from recovering its losses from Roth.

Auditors' liability to third parties

Lawyers, physicians, and most other professionals render services to people who contract directly with them. The work performed by independent auditors, however, is regularly used by persons who have not entered into contracts with the auditors. Auditors' reports are used by many third parties, including stockholders, potential stockholders, and creditors. Legal liability to these third parties has developed under common law and also has been codified in the federal securities acts. We shall consider each of these two types of liability in the following sections.

Liability to third parties under common law

Auditors' liability under common law varies somewhat from one jurisdiction to another. For example, liability in the state of New York is not identical to liability in the state of California. However, in all jurisdictions, certain third parties have the same rights as a client in litigation against the auditors. A third-party beneficiary is *in privity* with the CPA firm and with the client being audited, and therefore has the same rights as the client under common law. Thus, an aggrieved third-party beneficiary need prove only that: (1) the auditors were guilty of ordinary negligence and (2) losses were sustained as a result of reliance on the auditors' opinion. Proving these two points will entitle the third-party beneficiary to recover damages from the CPA firm.

Courts of certain jurisdictions have been willing to make more liberal interpretations of common law liability to third parties. These courts have increased the classes of third parties who have the same rights as clients in litigation against the auditors. In *Rusch Factors, Inc.* v. *Levin*, 284 F. Supp. 85 (1968), the court extended these rights to any limited class of persons who could be foreseen to rely on the auditors' report, despite the auditors' lack of knowledge of the specific third parties. This principle of auditor liability for ordinary negligence to a limited class of foreseen third parties was also supported by the American Law Institute's *Second Restatement of the Law of Torts*, which guides many courts in common law rulings.

Illustrative case.   Dianne Holiday, CPA, performed the audit of Lyman Corporation for the year ended December 31. Holiday was aware that Lyman intended to use the audit report to obtain bank loans. However, no specific banks were identified to Holiday. After the report was issued, Lyman obtained loans from First National Bank and Dime Box State Bank. Also, Wallace Manufacturing Co. relied on Holiday's opinion in providing trade credit to Lyman. If the court applied the principles contained in the *Second Restatement of the Law of Torts,* Holiday could be held liable to First National and Dime Box if she were found guilty of ordinary negligence in the performance of her examination. The banks form a limited class of third parties who could be foreseen to rely on the audit report. On the other hand, a strict application of the primary beneficiary principle by the court would not give First National and Dime Box the same rights as the client under common law because the parties were not specifically identified at the time the examination was performed. Under either set of principles, Holiday would not be held liable for ordinary negligence to Wallace Manufacturing Co. The audit was not performed for the use of trade creditors; therefore, Wallace would not be considered a part of a limited class of foreseen parties.

But what of liability to third parties who are not given the same rights as clients under common law? Can the auditors be held liable to these other third parties? This question was answered in a landmark court case, *Ultramares* v. *Touche & Co.*, 255 N.Y. 170 (1931). In the *Ultramares* case, the defendant CPAs issued an unqualified opinion on the balance sheet of a company engaged in the importation and sale of rubber. On the strength of the CPAs' opinion, the plaintiff, a factor, made a number of loans to the company. Shortly thereafter, the company was declared bankrupt, and the factor sued the CPAs for negligence. Even though the case was ultimately settled out of court, Justice Cardoza established the principle that auditors could be held liable to any third party for *gross negligence* (constructive fraud).

Thus, under common law, bankers and other creditors or investors who use financial statements covered by an audit report can recover from the auditors if it can be shown that the auditors were guilty of *fraud* or *gross negligence* in the performance of their professional duties. Fraud is obviously present if the auditors surrender their independence and cooperate with the client to give outsiders a false impression of the financial position or operating results of the business. Gross negligence exists if the auditors have not conducted an examination of any real substance and consequently have no real basis for an opinion. To express an opinion in their role of independent experts when in fact they have no basis for an opinion is considered as gross negligence and provides a basis for legal action by injured third parties.

The burden of proof. Legal actions under the common law require the plaintiffs to bear most of the burden of affirmative proof. Thus, the plaintiffs seeking damages from a CPA firm must prove that they sustained losses, that they relied upon audited financial statements that were misleading, that this reliance was the proximate cause of their losses, and that the auditors were guilty of a certain degree of negligence. The auditors named as defendants in a common law action are in the position of having to refute the charges brought by the plaintiffs.

As indicated in the following section, legal actions brought against auditors under the Securities Act of 1933 tend to shift much of the burden of proof to the auditors. The plaintiffs must prove only that they sustained losses and that the financial statements were misleading. The auditors must then bear the burden of proof to show that they were not negligent or that the misleading financial statements were not the proximate cause of the plaintiffs' losses. For these and other reasons, it is important in considering specific cases involving auditors' liability to third parties to determine whether the legal action is being brought under the statutes administered by the SEC.

Auditors' liability under the securities acts

Statutory liability for auditors is codified in the federal securities acts, primarily the Securites Act of 1933 (1933 act) and the Securities Exchange Act of 1934 (1934 act). The 1933 act regulates the initial sale of securities in interstate commerce, and the 1934 act regulates the trading of securities after initial distribution.

Securities Act of 1933. The 1933 act states that accountants who express an opinion in a *registration statement* concerning a proposed offering of corporate securities may be held liable to third parties for their losses if the statements are later shown to include untrue statements of material fact or to omit material facts necessary to prevent the statements from being misleading. The wording of Section 11(a) of the Act on this point is as follows:

In case any part of the registration statement, when such part became effective, contained an untrue statement of a material fact or omitted to state a material fact required to be stated therein or necessary to make the statements therein not misleading, any person acquiring such security (unless it is proved that at the time of such acquisition he knew of such untruth or omission) may . . . sue. . . .

The third parties who have sustained losses may sue for recovery from the accountants and *need not prove that they relied upon the statements or that the accountants were negligent.* The burden of proof is placed upon the accountants to show that their audit work was adequate to support their opinion (the "due diligence" defense) or that the losses of third parties were not the result of errors or omissions in the financial statements.

In summary, the 1933 act establishes the highest level of auditor liability. Third parties who purchase securities registered under this Act have rights greater than the rights of a client under common law. In audits for registration statements, the auditors are liable not only for fraud and gross negligence, but also for losses to third parties resulting from ordinary negligence. In addition, the burden of proof is shifted to the auditors to prove that they were not negligent in the performance of their examination.

A significant case involving auditors' liability under the Securities Act of 1933 was the *BarChris* case. *Escott* v. *BarChris Construction Corporation*, 283 F. Supp. 643 (1968), was an action under Section 11 of the Securities Act of 1933 undertaken by purchasers of BarChris's registered debentures against the directors, underwriters, and independent auditors of BarChris. Subsequent to issuance of the debentures, Bar-Chris, a builder of bowling alleys, became bankrupt. The plaintiffs claimed that the registration statement for the debentures contained material false statements and material omissions; the defendants all countered with due diligence defenses. The court found that the registration statement was false and misleading and that with a few exceptions none of the defendants had established their due diligence defenses. The court also found that the CPA firm had failed to comply with generally accepted auditing standards. The court was especially critical of the CPA firm's conduct of the S-1 review, so-called because it is a special investigation carried out by a CPA firm some time after completion of the audit but just prior to the effective date of the S-1 or similar registration statement filed with the SEC. In an S-1 review, the CPAs look for any evidence that events since their audit have made the registration statement misleading as filed. The court cited the CPA firm's excessive reliance on questioning of client management during the S-1 review, with no substantiation of management's answers.

Subsequent to the decision of the court in *BarChris*, the AICPA's Auditing Standards Executive Committee issued a statement entitled

"Subsequent Events," now a section of *SAS No. 1*. This statement, which clarified the auditing procedures required in an S-1 review, is discussed in Chapter 7.

Securities Exchange Act of 1934. In addition to the registration statements required in connection with new issues of securities, companies listed on the stock exchanges and certain companies whose stock is traded over the counter *must file audited financial statements each year* with the SEC, in accordance with provisions of the 1934 act. Section 18(a) of that act provides the following liability for misleading statements:

> Any person who shall make or cause to be made any statement in any application, report, or document filed pursuant to this . . . (Act) or any rule or regulation thereunder . . . , which statement was at the time and in the light of the circumstances under which it was made false or misleading with respect to any material fact, shall be liable to any person (not knowing that such statement was false or misleading) who, in reliance upon such statement, shall have purchased or sold a security at a price which was affected by such statement, for damages caused by such reliance, unless the person sued shall prove that he acted in good faith and had no knowledge that such statement was false or misleading.

In addition, Rule 10b–5 promulgated by the SEC under the 1934 Act reads as follows:

> It shall be unlawful for any person, directly or indirectly, . . .
> (1) to employ any device, scheme, or artifice to defraud,
> (2) to make any untrue statement of a material fact or to omit to state a material fact necessary in order to make the statements made . . . not misleading, or
> (3) to engage in any act, practice, or course of business which operates or would operate as a fraud or deceit upon any person, in connection with the purchase or sale of any security.

Most lawsuits against certified public accountants have been filed under Section 18(a) and Rule 10b–5 of the 1934 act. The wording of this act implies that the act was written to create liability for fraudulent misrepresentations. In some court decisions, however, the act has been interpreted more broadly and auditors have been held liable for losses proximately caused by their negligence even though fraudulent intent was not established. However, the recently decided *Hochfelder* case appears to have redefined auditor liability under the 1934 act.

The Hochfelder case and its impact on accountants' liability. The expansion of auditors' liability to third parties may have been slowed by the decision of the U.S. Supreme Court in *Ernst* v. *Hochfelder* (44 LW 4451 [1976]). This decision was in a suit instituted against a national public accounting firm that for 21 years had audited the financial statements of First Securities Company of Chicago, a small brokerage firm. The president of First Securities, who was also its majority stockholder, committed suicide, leaving a note stating that the firm was insolvent and disclosing a fraud that he had perpetrated upon several investors. The president had persuaded the investors to mail him their personal checks, the funds from which he was to invest in escrow accounts yielding high returns to the investors. There were no such escrow accounts in the accounting records of First Securities Company; instead, the president converted the investors' checks to his own use immediately upon receipt.

The investors filed suit under SEC Rule 10b–5 (and the related Securities Exchange Act of 1934 Section 10[b]) against the CPA firm, charging it with negligence, and thus with responsibility for the investors' losses in the fraud. During court hearings, the plaintiffs acknowledged that they had not relied upon the audited financial statements of First Securities Company or upon the auditors' reports; further, they did not accuse the CPA firm of fraud or intentional misconduct. The basis for the plaintiffs' charge of negligence was that the CPA firm failed during its audits to discover a weakness in First Securities Company's internal control that enabled the president of First Securities to carry on the fraud. The internal control weakness was manifested in the president's rule that *only he* could open mail addressed to him at First Securities, or addressed to First Securities to his attention.

The U.S. district court which heard the case dismissed it, holding that there was no issue of material fact as to whether the CPA firm had conducted its audits of First Securities in accordance with generally accepted auditing standards. The U.S. Court of Appeals, in reversing the district court's dismissal of the case, stated that the CPA firm was liable for damages for aiding and abetting the First Securities president's fraud because the CPA firm had breached its duty of inquiry and disclosure regarding the First Securities internal control weakness.

The U.S. Supreme Court reversed the court of appeals, deciding that an action for damages under Section 10(b) of the 1934 Act and the related SEC Rule 10b–5 was not warranted in the absence of *intent* to deceive, manipulate, or defraud on the CPA firm's part. In the Court's opinion, Mr. Justice Powell wrote:

> The words "manipulative or deceptive" used in conjunction with "device or contrivance" strongly suggest that (Section) 10(b) was intended to proscribe knowing or intentional misconduct.

*　*　*　*　*

> When a statute speaks so specifically in terms of manipulation and deception, and of implementing devices and contrivances—the commonly understood terminology of intentional wrongdoing—and when its history reflects no more expansive intent, we are quite unwilling to extend the scope of the statute to negligent conduct.

Many accountants believe that the *Hochfelder* case, despite its narrow application to a CPA firm's responsibility for discovering a weakness in internal control, should help limit auditors' responsibility to third parties who are not third-party beneficiaries, and restrain the SEC's efforts to widen that responsibility. In *Hochfelder* the Supreme Court rejected the SEC's *amicus curiae* brief supporting the plaintiffs, pointing to the Commission's acknowledgement that the CPA firm was unaware of the existence of the plaintiffs, and thus could not foresee that its audit reports could influence the plaintiffs' investments—as indeed they did not.

Based on the *Hochfelder* case, it now appears that auditors' liability under the 1934 act is the same as the auditors' liability to third parties under common law. Third parties will be able to recover their losses from reliance upon an auditor's report only if the auditor has performed in a grossly negligent manner.

Auditors' civil liability: a summary

The auditors' civil liability under common law and under the federal Securities Acts is summarized graphicly in Figure 3–1. The wavy lines

Figure 3–1
Summary of auditors' civil liability

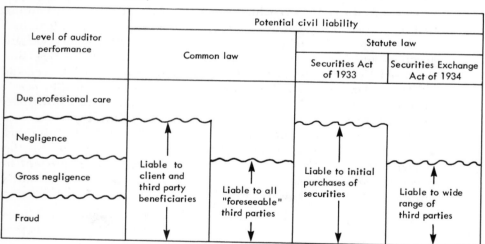

Level of auditor performance	Potential civil liability		
	Common law	Statute law	
		Securities Act of 1933	Securities Exchange Act of 1934
Due professional care			
Negligence	Liable to client and third party beneficiaries	Liable to initial purchases of securities	
Gross negligence			Liable to wide range of third parties
Fraud	Liable to all "foreseeable" third parties		

between the various levels of auditor responsibility are intended to emphasize that clear-cut boundaries defining these levels do not exist. The level of an auditor's performance is established by the courts on a case-by-case basis; what constitutes negligence in the view of one court may not be considered negligence in a similar case tried in another court. Therefore, the safest policy for a CPA firm is to perform every engagement with a level of care that no court could interpret as negligent.

Auditors' criminal liability under the securities acts

Both the Securities Act of 1933 and the Securities Exchange Act of 1934 include provisions for criminal charges against persons violating provisions of the act. These provisions are found in Section 17(a) of the Securities Act of 1933 and Section 32(a) of the Securities Exchange Act of 1934.

The *Continental Vending Machine Corporation* civil case was accompanied by a celebrated criminal case involving three members of the CPA firm that audited Continental's financial statements. The criminal charges rocked the profession, because there was no intent to defraud on the part of the CPAs; they were convicted of criminal fraud on the basis of gross negligence. The verdict of guilty was affirmed by a U.S. court of appeals, and the U.S. Supreme Court refused to review the case. The three CPAs were later pardoned by the President of the United States. The president of Continental, who had originally been indicted with the three CPAs and who pleaded guilty, received a six-month jail sentence.

The principal facts of the *Continental Vending* case (*United States* v. *Simon*, 425 F. 2d 796 [1969]) are as follows. The U.S. government's case of fraud against the three CPAs hinged upon a footnote to Continental's audited financial statements, which read:

> The amount receivable from Valley Commercial Corp. (an affiliated company of which . . . [Continental's president] is an officer, director, and stockholder) bears interest at 12 percent a year. Such amount, less the balance of the notes payable to that company, is secured by the assignment to the Company of Valley's equity in certain marketable securities. As of . . . [the date of the auditors' report] . . . the amount of such equity at current market quotations exceeded the net amount receivable.

The U.S. government charged the CPAs should have insisted that the note be worded as follows:

> The amount receivable from Valley Commercial Corp. (an affiliated company of which . . . [Continental's president] is an officer, director and stockholder), which bears interest at 12 percent a year, was uncollectible at . . . [the balance sheet date], since Valley had loaned approximately the same amount to . . . [Continental's president] who was unable to pay. Since that date . . . [Continental's president] and others have pledged as security for the repayment of his obligation to Valley and its obligation to Continental (now $3,900,000, against which Continental's liability to Valley cannot be offset) securites which, as of . . . (the date of the auditors' report) . . . , had a market value of $2,978,000. Approximately 80 percent of such securities are stock and convertible debentures of the Company.

The receivable from Valley amounted to $3.5 million, of which more than $2.1 million was included in current assets (totaling $20.1 million) with the $1.4 million balance in other assets. The amount payable to

Valley was slightly more than $1 million, of which about one half was included in total current liabilities of $19 million and the remainder in long-term debt.

The CPA firm had been auditors for Continental for several years. The court found that the CPAs had been concerned with the amounts receivable from and payable to Valley for at least five years, especially as they involved loans to Continental's president; yet the CPAs had continued to issue opinions on Continental's financial statements despite the continued growth of the receivable from Valley. The court also found that the CPAs were not furnished audited financial statements for Valley, in spite of their repeated requests and that the CPAs had never themselves been the auditors for Valley. In response to the defendent CPAs' claims that they had no motive for the alleged fraud, the U.S. government demonstrated to the appellate court's satisfaction that the CPAs were motivated to preserve their firm's reputation and to conceal the alleged derelictions of their predecessors and themselves in preceding years.

The *Continental Vending* case has significant implications for the public accounting profession. Not only is civil liability an ever-present hazard for public accountants, but criminal charges may also be involved.

The SEC's regulation of accountants

The SEC has issued rules for the appearance and practice of CPAs, attorneys, and others before the Commission under the statutes it administers. Rule of Practice 2(e), giving the SEC the power of suspension and disbarment, has the following wording:

> The Commission may deny, temporarily or permanently, the privilege of appearing or practicing before it in any way to any person who is found by the Commission . . . (1) not to possess the requisite qualifications to represent others, or (2) to be lacking in character or integrity or to have engaged in unethical or improper professional conduct.

On several occasions the Commission has taken punitive action against public accounting firms when it has found the audit work deficient with regard to financial statements filed with the Commission. These actions against public accounting firms usually arise when a listed corporation encounters financial difficulties and it later appears that misleading financial statements had served to conceal for a time the losses being incurred by the company. In recent years the SEC has taken action against CPA firms by the use of consent decrees in which the CPAs have agreed to certain penalties or restrictions. For example, a CPA firm may agree under pressure from the SEC not to accept new clients during a specified period and to permit a review of its practice.

Accountants' liability for accounting and review services

To this point we have discussed the liability of CPA firms that serve their clients as independent auditors. CPA firms are also associated with unaudited financial statements. For example, CPAs may be engaged to compile or review the financial statements of nonpublic companies. When a CPA firm is engaged to perform financial statement services that are less than an audit, there is always a danger that the client or third parties will misunderstand the extent of the CPAs' involvement with the financial statements.

The risks to CPA firms engaged in the preparation of unaudited financial statements were brought sharply into focus by the *1136 Tenants' Corporation* v. *Rothenberg* case. In this common law case, an incorporated apartment cooperative, which was owned by its shareholder-tenants and managed by a separate realty agent, orally retained a CPA firm for a period of 17 months to perform services leading to the preparation of financial statements for the cooperative, and also including letters containing tax information to the shareholders. The CPA firm's fee was to be only $600 per year.

The CPA firm submitted financial statements of the corporation for one full year and the first six months of the following year. The financial statements bore the notation "subject to comments in letter of transmittal." The referenced letter of transmittal read in part:

> Pursuant to our engagement, we have reviewed and summarized the statements of your managing agent and other data submitted to us by . . . [the agent], pertaining to 1136 Tenants' Corporation. . . .
>
> The following statements were prepared from the books and records of the Corporation. No independent verifications were undertaken thereon. . . .

The client corporation later sued the CPA firm for damages totaling $174,000 for the CPA's alleged failure to discover defalcations of the corporation's funds committed by the managing agent. The client contended that the CPAs had been retained to render all necessary accounting *and auditing* services for it. The CPAs maintained they had been engaged to do write-up work only, although a working paper they had prepared supporting accrued expenses payable in the balance sheet included an entry for "audit expense."

The New York state trial court ruled in favor of the plaintiff client, as did the Appellate Court of New York. The latter found that the CPAs' working papers indicated that the CPAs had examined the client's bank statements, invoices and bills, and had made notations in their working papers concerning "missing invoices." The New York Court of Appeals (the state's highest court) affirmed the decision.

There are many lessons for CPA firms in the *1136 Tenants' Corporation* case.

1. CPAs who prepare unaudited financial statements should adhere closely to Rules of Conduct 102 and 202 of the AICPA's *Code of Professional Ethics*. Rule 102 states that a CPA shall not knowingly misrepresent facts, and Rule 202 prohibits a CPA firm from implying that it acted as an independent auditor unless it complied with the generally accepted auditing standards. The actions of the CPA firm described in the preceding paragraph might be construed as violating both rules.

2. Engagement letters are as essential for accounting and review services as they are for independent audits. Oral arrangements for accounting and review services are of scant assistance when there is a dispute as to the nature of the services to be rendered by the CPA firm to the client.

3. A CPA engaged to perform *accounting or review* services should be alert for, and follow up on, such unusual items as missing invoices. As professional persons, CPAs are bound to exercise due professional care, even though their engagements do not include independent audits of the client's financial statements.

4. CPAs should report on financial statements clearly and concisely, using as far as possible the standardized language set forth in *Statements on Auditing Standards* and *Statements on Standards for Accounting and Review Services*. Reports should indicate the nature of the services rendered and the degree of responsibility being assumed by the CPA firm.

Auditors' responsibility for detection of errors and irregularities

Any discussion of the legal liability of auditors would be incomplete without the inclusion of auditors' obligation to discover errors and irregularities. As pointed out in Chapter 1, the typical audits performed early in this century by CPAs were primarily concerned with the discovery of management and nonmanagement fraud. In later years, however, the public accounting profession directed its auditing emphasis to the compliance of the client's financial statements with generally accepted accounting principles.

In recognition of this change in audit emphasis, the AICPA issued *SAS No. 16*, which describes the auditors' responsibility for the detection of errors and irregularities. *SAS No. 16* defines the term *errors* as unintentional mistakes in financial statements and underlying accounting records. On the other hand, the word *irregularities* refers to intentional distortions of financial statements, including management fraud and misappropriations of assets (defalcations).

The auditors' standard report states that the financial statements are presented in accordance with generally accepted accounting principles. Implicit in this statement is the belief that the financial statements taken as a whole are not materially misstated as a result of errors and irregularities. Therefore, auditors have an obligation, within the limitations of the auditing process, to (1) plan their examination to search for errors or irregularities that would have a material effect on the financial statements and (2) exercise due skill and care in the conduct of their examination. The auditors' search for errors and irregularities is accomplished through the performance of those auditing procedures they consider appropriate in the circumstances. If the auditors' examination indicates that material errors or irregularities may exist, they should discuss the matter and the extent of further investigation with appropriate management that is at least one level above those involved, and with the board of directors or its audit committee. Also, the auditors should extend their audit procedures to determine whether the material errors or irregularities exist and their effect on the financial statements.

Does failure to detect errors or irregularities constitute proof of negligence on the part of the CPA firm? Auditors do not guarantee the accuracy of financial statements; they merely express an opinion as to the fairness of the statements. Furthermore, auditors do not make a complete and detailed examination of all records and all transactions. To do so would entail an almost prohibitive cost, which would certainly not be warranted under ordinary business conditions. The nature and extent of the auditors' examination is determined by the auditors' judgment after a study and evaluation of the client's system of internal control. If the scope and direction of the audit procedures have been well chosen, the conclusions of the auditors should generally be sound. However, there can never be any absolute assurance that errors or irregularities did not exist among the transactions not included in the auditors' tests. There is also the possibility that fraudulent documents have been so skillfully forged or other irregularities so expertly concealed that the application of normal auditing techniques would not reveal the irregularities. When a CPA firm's examination has been made in accordance with generally accepted auditing standards, the firm is not liable for failure to detect the existence of errors or irregularites.

The Equity Funding Corporation of America fraud. The AICPA's posture on auditors' responsibility for discovery of irregularities was challenged by many critics as a result of the celebrated Equity Funding Corporation of America fraud. Nineteen persons—principally employees of Equity Funding—pleaded guilty to criminal fraud associated with Equity Funding's published financial statements covering a period of several years. Three accountants who were tried and found guilty of comparable criminal charges appealed their convictions. These accountants were members of the CPA firm retained to audit Equity Funding's financial statements.

Because of the furor caused by the Equity Funding fraud, the AICPA appointed a five-member Special Committee on Equity Funding to consider whether the fraud suggested a need for changes in generally accepted auditing standards or in the auditing procedures by which auditing standards are implemented. The Committee also sought to determine any need for a change in the scope of, or a clarification of, auditors' responsibilities for the detection of irregularities.

In the *Report of the Special Committee on Equity Funding*, the Committee concluded that, with few exceptions, generally accepted auditing standards are adequate and no changes are required in procedures commonly used by auditors. The exceptions dealt with confirmation of an insurance company's insurance in force and with the audit of related party transactions. The Committee further concluded that *customary auditing procedures properly applied* would have provided reasonable assurance of detection of the fraud at Equity Funding.

The Committee reached the following conclusions with respect to auditors' responsibilities for the detection of fraud:

> In sum, the committee reaffirms the soundness of the accounting profession's understanding with respect to the role of audits in the detection of fraud. A change in this basic understanding to make the auditor's opinion into more of a guarantee of the absence of fraud would represent a major change in the conception and performance of audits and would vastly increase their expense—yet still not furnish a complete guarantee. To ask that a professional opinion be made into an absolute assurance would, moreover, be to seek a degree of certainty which is seldom to be found in any other area of commercial life—or, for that matter, in any area of our lives, private or public. However, even though such absolute assurance is not feasible, the application of generally accepted auditing standards will often result in the discovery of material frauds. Audits also can be expected to deter frauds which might otherwise occur.[1]

The CPAs' posture in the age of litigation

In addition to the preceding court cases, several other actions against CPAs, under both common law and the securities acts, are pending trial. It is apparent that lawsuits will continue to plague the public accounting profession, as they have the legal and medical professions. The question thus is: What should be the CPAs' reaction to this age of litigation?

In the opinion of the authors, positive actions helpful to CPAs in withstanding threats of possible lawsuits include the following:

1.   Greater emphasis upon compliance with the public accounting profession's generally accepted auditing standards and *Code of Professional Ethics*. Close analysis of the court cases and other actions described in this chapter discloses numerous instances in which the auditors appear not to have complied fully with one or more auditing standards and Rules of Conduct.

2.   Emphasis on professionalism rather than growth. Some CPA

---

[1] *Report of the Special Committee on Equity Funding*, AICPA (New York, 1975), pp. 39–40.

firms may have emphasized growth of their practices more than high quality of their work. Very rapid growth may bring excessive overtime work by overextended staff members and responsibilities too heavy for insufficiently experienced accountants.

3. **Thorough investigation of prospective clients.** As indicated in preceding sections of this chapter, many court cases involving CPAs have been accompanied by criminal charges against top management of the CPAs' clients. CPAs should use great care in screening prospective clients to avoid the risks involved in professional relationships with the criminally inclined.

4. **Use of engagement letters for all professional services.** Controversies over what services are to be rendered by a CPA can be minimized by a clearly written contract describing the agreed-upon services and pointing out that the ordinary audit is not designed to uncover irregularities. Engagement letters are discussed in Chapter 4.

5. **Exercising extreme care in audits of clients in financial difficulties.** Creditors and shareholders of companies that are insolvent or in bankruptcy are likely to seek scapegoats to blame for their losses. As the court cases described in this chapter demonstrate, litigation involving CPAs tends to center around auditing of clients who later become bankrupt.

6. **More extensive use of peer reviews.** CPA firms should arrange for independent review of their quality controls and other aspects of their professional practice. The interchange of professional skills among CPAs is a policy worthy of encouragement. Periodic peer review is a membership requirement for CPA firms joining the AICPA's Division for Firms.

7. **Obtaining a thorough knowledge of the client's business.** One of the major causes of audit failures has been a lack of understanding by auditors of the client's business and of industry practices.

8. **Maintenance of adequate liability insurance coverage.** Although liability insurance coverage should not be considered a substitute for the CPA's compliance with the preceding recommendations, public accountants must protect themselves against possible financial losses from lawsuits. Adequate liability insurance is essential.

KEY TERMS INTRODUCED OR EMPHASIZED IN CHAPTER 3

Common law Uncodified principles of law developed through court decisions.

Constructive fraud Violation of a legal duty or a contractual obligation that requires the exercise of exceptional good faith.

Due diligence defense A CPA firm's contention that its audit work was adequate to support its opinion on financial statements included in a registration statement filed with the SEC under the Securities Act of 1933.

Errors Unintentional mistakes in financial statements and accounting records, including mistakes in the application of accounting principles.

Fraud Misrepresentation by a person of a material fact, known by that person to be untrue or made with reckless indifference as to whether the fact is true, with intent to deceive and with result that another party is injured.

Gross negligence Lack of even slight care.

Irregularities Intentional distortions of financial statements, often accompanied by use of false or misleading records.

Management fraud Exists when management of the client company makes a deliberate effort to present misleading financial statements, supported by falsified accounting records.

Negligence Violation of a legal duty to exercise a degree of care that an ordinarily prudent person would exercise under similar circumstances, with resultant damages to another party.

Peer review Review of a CPA firm's public accounting practice—especially quality control—by another CPA firm.

Statutory law Laws adopted by the United States Congress, state legislatures, and legislative bodies of other governmental units in the United States.

Third-party beneficiary A person—not the promisor or promisee—who is named in a contract (or known to the contracting parties) with the intention that such person should have definite rights and benefits under the contract.

GROUP I: REVIEW QUESTIONS

3–1. What is meant by the term *privity?* How does privity affect the auditor's liability under common law?

3–2. State briefly a major distinction between the Securities Act of 1933 and the Securities Exchange Act of 1934 with respect to the type of transactions regulated.

3–3. Should auditors who are engaged in the examination of a client's financial statements thoroughly investigate suspected material irregularities? Explain.

3–4. Is privity a valid defense against third-party charges of negligence against an auditor? Explain.

3–5. How does the SEC regulate CPAs who appear and practice before the commission?

3–6. In the *1136 Tenants* case, what was the essential difference in the way the client and the auditors viewed the work to be done in the engagement?

3–7. Compare auditors' common law liability to clients, third-party beneficiaries, and foreseen third parties with their common law liability to other third parties.

3–8. Define the term *third-party beneficiary.*

3–9. Which of the following court cases tended to slow the expansion of auditors' liability to third parties? *BarChris, Hochfelder, Westec, Rusch Factors, Inc., Equity Funding, Continental Vending.*

3–10. Compare the rights of clients under common law with the rights of persons who purchase securities registered under the Securities Act of 1933 and sustain losses. In your answer emphasize the issue of who must bear the burden of proof.

3–11.   Distinguish between common law and statutory law.

3–12.   Distinguish between ordinary negligence and gross negligence within the context of a CPA's work.

3–13.   How was the *Continental Vending* case unusual with respect to penalties levied against auditors?

3–14.   Are engagement letters needed both for audits and for accounting and review services performed by CPAs? Explain.

3–15.   Were the auditing procedures customary at the time of the *Equity Funding* case sufficient to have disclosed the fraud if the auditors had functioned reasonably, or did the case indicate the need for modification of customary procedures? Explain.

GROUP II: QUESTIONS REQUIRING ANALYSIS

3–16.   Rogers and Green, CPAs, admit they failed substantially to follow generally accepted auditing standards in their audit of Martin Corporation. "We were overworked and understaffed and never should have accepted the engagement," said Rogers. Does this situation constitute fraud on the part of the CPA firm? Explain.

3–17.   Jensen, Inc., filed suit against a CPA firm, alleging that the auditors' negligence was responsible for failure to disclose a large defalcation that had been in process for several years. The CPA firm responded that it may have been negligent, but that Jensen, Inc., was really to blame because it had completely ignored the CPA firm's repeated recommendations for improvements in the system of internal control.

   If the CPA firm was negligent, is it responsible for the loss sustained by the client? Does the failure by Jensen, Inc., to follow the CPAs' recommendation for better internal controls have any bearing on the question of liability? Explain.

3–18.   Dandy Container Corporation engaged the accounting firm of Adams and Adams to examine financial statements to be used in connection with a public offering of securities. The audit was completed, and an unqualified opinion was expressed on the financial statements that were submitted to the Securities and Exchange Commission along with the registration statement. Two hundred thousand shares of Dandy Container common stock were offered to the public at $11 a share. Eight months later the stock fell to $2 a share when it was disclosed that several large loans to two "paper" corporations owned by one of the directors were worthless. The loans were secured by the stock of the borrowing corporations, which was owned by the director. These facts were not disclosed in the financial statements. The director involved and the two corporations are insolvent.

   Required:
   State whether each of the following statements is true or false, and explain why.
   a.   The Securities Act of 1933 applies to the above-described public offering of securities in interstate commerce.

    b. The accounting firm has potential liability to any person who acquired the stock.

    c. An insider who had knowledge of all the facts regarding the loans to the two paper corporations could nevertheless recover from the accounting firm.

    d. An investor who bought shares in Dandy Container could make a prima facie case by alleging that the failure to explain the nature of the loans in question constituted a false statement or misleading omission in the financial statements.

    e. The accountants could avoid liability if they could show they were neither negligent nor fraudulent.

    f. The accountants could avoid or reduce the damages asserted against them if they could establish that the drop in the stock's market price was due in whole or in part to other causes.

    g. It would appear that the accountants were negligent in respect to the handling of the secured loans in question—if they discovered the facts regarding the loans to the paper corporations and failed to require adequate disclosure in the financial statements.

    h. The Securities and Exchange Commission would defend any action brought against the accountants in that the SEC examined and approved the registration statement (AICPA, adapted)

3–19.   Gordon & Groton, CPAs, were the auditors of Bank & Company, a brokerage firm and member of a national stock exchange. Gordon & Groton examined and reported on the financial statements of Bank, which were filed with the Securities and Exchange Commission.

     Several of Bank's customers were swindled by a fraudulent scheme perpetrated by Bank's president who owned 90 percent of the voting stock of the company. The facts establish that Gordon & Groton were negligent, but not reckless or grossly negligent in the conduct of the audit, and neither participated in the fraudulent scheme nor knew of its existence.

     The customers are suing Gordon & Groton under the antifraud provisions of Section 10(b) and Rule 10b–5 of the Securities Exchange Act of 1934 for aiding and abetting the fraudulent scheme of the president. The customers' suit for fraud is predicated exclusively on the negligence of the auditors in failing to conduct a proper audit, thereby failing to discover the fraudulent scheme.

Required:
Answer the following, setting forth reasons for any conclusions stated.

    a. What is the probable outcome of the lawsuit? Explain.

    b. What other theory of liability might the customers have asserted? (AICPA, adapted)

3–20.   A CPA firm's accounting services to a client sometimes involve the compilation of unaudited financial statements. Discuss the need for an engagement letter for compilation of unaudited financial statements. (AICPA, adapted)

3–21.   The partnership, Watkins, Miller & Fogg, CPAs, was engaged for the first time to examine the financial statements of Flinco Corporation. Flinco is the largest manufacturing concern in the locale. It is engaged in a multistate business and its stock is traded on the over-the-counter market. The CPA firm has enjoyed considerable stature in the business community but has traditionally served small to medium-sized businesses. The firm has never audited a publicly held corporation before.

Required:
  a. State the general guidelines a CPA firm may look to in assessing its legal liability when assuming the responsibility for a publicly held client.
  b. Discuss the significant additional potential liabilities imposed by federal statutes and related regulations that the Watkins firm is assuming in accepting the Flinco engagement. (AICPA, adapted)

3–22. Wanda Young, doing business as Wanda Young Fashions, engaged the CPA partnership of Small & Brown to examine her financial statements. During the examination, Small & Brown discovered certain irregularities that would have indicated to a reasonably prudent accountant that James Smith, the chief accountant, might be engaged in a fraud. More specifically, it appeared to Small & Brown that serious defalcations were taking place. However, Small & Brown, not having been engaged to discover defalcations, submitted an unqualified opinion in its report and did not mention the potential defalcation problem.

Required:
What are the legal implications of the above facts as they relate to the relationship between Small & Brown and Wanda Young? Explain. (AICPA, adapted)

3–23. Donald Sharpe recently joined the CPA firm of Spark, Watts, and Wilcox. He quickly established a reputation for thoroughness and a steadfast dedication to following prescribed auditing procedures to the letter. On his third audit for the firm, involving a partnership client, Sharpe examined the underlying documentation of 200 disbursements as a compliance test of purchasing, receiving, vouchers.payable, and cash disbursement procedures. In the process he found 12 disbursements for the purchase of materials with no receiving reports in the documentation. He noted the exceptions in his working papers and called them to the attention of the in-charge accountant. Relying on prior experience with the client, the in-charge accountant disregarded Sharpe's comments, and nothing further was done about the exceptions.

Subsequently, it was learned that one of the client's purchasing agents and a member of its accounting department were engaged in a fraudulent scheme whereby they diverted the receipt of materials to a public warehouse while sending the invoices to the client. When the client discovered the fraud, the conspirators had obtained approximately $700,000, of which $500,000 was after the completion of the audit.

Required:
Discuss the legal implications and liabilities to Spark, Watts, and Wilcox as a result of the above facts. (AICPA, adapted)

3–24. The partnership of Porter, Potts, & Farr, CPAs, was engaged by Revolutionary Products, Inc., a closely held corporation, to examine its financial statements for the year ended June 30, 1983. The engagement letter said nothing about the CPA firm's responsibility for defalcations. Porter, Potts & Farr performed its examination in a careful and competent manner, following generally accepted auditing standards and using appropriate auditing procedures and tests under the circumstances.

Subsequently, it was discovered that the client's chief accountant was engaged in major defalcations. However, only an audit specifically designed to discover possible defalcations would have revealed the fraud. Revolutionary Products asserts that Porter, Potts & Farr is liable for the defalcations.

Required:
Is Porter, Potts & Farr liable? Explain. (AICPA, adapted)

3–25. Barton and Company, CPAs, has been engaged to examine the financial statements of Mirror Manufacturing Corporation for the year ended September 30, 1983. During that year, Mirror needed additional cash to continue its operations. To raise the cash, it sold its common stock investment in a subsidiary. The buyers insisted upon having the proceeds placed in escrow because of the existence of a major loss contingency involving additional income taxes assessed to the subsidiary by the Internal Revenue Service. William Carter, president of Mirror, explained this to Carl Barton, the partner in charge of the Mirror audit. Carter indicated that he wished to show the proceeds from the sale of the subsidiary as an unrestricted current account receivable. He stated that in his opinion the claim of the IRS against the subsidiary was groundless and that he needed an "uncluttered" balance sheet and a "clean" auditor's opinion to obtain additional working capital through loans. Barton acquiesced in this request. The IRS claim proved to be valid, and pursuant to the agreement with the buyers the purchase price of the subsidiary was reduced by $450,000. This coupled with other adverse developments caused Mirror to become insolvent. Barton and Company is being sued by several of Mirror's creditors who loaned money in reliance upon the audited financial statements.

Required:
What is the liability, if any, of Barton and Company to the creditors of Mirror Manufacturing? Explain. (AICPA, adapted)

3–26. In conducting the examination of the financial statements of Farber Corporation for the year ended September 30, 1983, Anne Harper, CPA, discovered that George Nance, the president who was also one of the principal stockholders, had borrowed substantial amounts of money from the corporation. Nance indicated that he owned 51 percent of the corporation, that the money would be promptly repaid, and that the financial statements were being prepared for internal use only and would not be distributed to the other six shareholders. He requested that these loans not be accounted for separately in the financial statements but be included in the other current accounts receivable. Harper acquiesced in this request. Nance was correct as to his stock ownership and the fact that the financial statements were for internal use only. However, he subsequently became insolvent and was unable to repay the loans.

Required:
What is Harper's liability? Explain. (AICPA, adapted)

3–27. The CPA firm of Bigelow, Barton, and Brown was expanding very rapidly. Consequently it hired several staff assistants, including James Small. Subsequently, the partners of the firm became dissatisfied with Small's production and warned him that they would be forced to discharge him unless his output increased significantly.

At that time Small was engaged in audits of several clients. He decided that to avoid being fired, he would reduce or omit entirely some of the required auditing procedures listed in audit programs prepared by the partners. One of the CPA firm's non-SEC clients, Newell Corporation, was in serious financial difficulty and had adjusted several of its accounts being examined by Small to appear financially sound. Small prepared fictitious working papers in his home at night to support purported completion of auditing procedures assigned to him, although he in fact did not examine the Newell adjusting entries. The CPA firm rendered an unqualified opinion on Newell's financial statements, which were grossly misstated. Several creditors subsequently extended large sums of money to Newell Corporation relying upon the audited financial statements.

Required:
Would the CPA firm be liable to the creditors who extended the money in reliance on the erroneous financial statements if Newell Corporation should fail to pay the creditors? Explain. (AICPA, adapted)

3–28. Select the best answer for each of the following questions and explain the reasons for your choice.

a. Which of the following best describes a trend in litigation involving CPAs?
   (1) A CPA cannot render an opinion on a company unless the CPA has audited all affiliates of that company.
   (2) A CPA may not successfully assert as a defense that the CPA had no motive to be part of a fraud.
   (3) A CPA may be exposed to criminal as well as civil liability.
   (4) A CPA is primarily responsible for a client's footnotes in an annual report filed with the SEC.

b. An independent auditor has the responsibility to plan the audit examination to search for errors and irregularities that might have a material effect on the financial statements. Which of the following, if material, would be an *irregularity* as defined in Statements on Auditing Standards?
   (1) Misappropriation of an asset or groups of assets.
   (2) Clerical mistakes in the accounting data underlying the financial statements.
   (3) Mistakes in the application of accounting principles.
   (4) Misinterpretation of facts that existed when the financial statements were prepared.

    c. The *1136 Tenants'* case was chiefly important because of its emphasis upon the legal liability of the CPA when associated with

        (1) A review of interim statements.

        (2) Unaudited financial statements.

        (3) An audit resulting in a disclaimer of opinion.

        (4) Letters for underwriters.

    d. A CPA is subject to *criminal* liability if the CPA

        (1) Refuses to turn over the working papers to the client.

        (2) Performs an audit in a negligent manner.

        (3) Willfully omits a material fact required to be stated in a registration statement.

        (4) Willfully breaches the contract with the client. (AICPA)

GROUP III: PROBLEMS

3–29. Risk Capital Limited, a publicly held Delaware corporation, was considering the purchase of a substantial amount of the treasury stock held by Florida Sunshine Corporation, a closely held corporation. Initial discussions with the Florida Sunshine Corporation began late in 1983.

    Wilson and Wyatt, CPAs, Florida Sunshine's public accountants, regularly prepared quarterly and annual unaudited financial statements. The most recently prepared unaudited financial statements were for the fiscal year ended September 30, 1983.

    On November 15, 1983, after protracted negotiations, Risk Capital agreed to purchase 100,000 shares of no-par, Class A treasury stock of Florida Sunshine at $12.50 per share. However, Risk Capital insisted upon audited statements for the calendar year 1983. The contract specifically provided: "Risk Capital shall have the right to rescind the purchase of said stock if the audited financial statements of Florida Sunshine for calendar year 1983 show a material adverse change in the financial position of the Corporation."

    At the request of Florida Sunshine, Wilson and Wyatt audited the company's financial statements for the year ended December 31, 1983. The December 31, 1983 audited financial statements furnished to Florida Sunshine by Wilson and Wyatt showed no material adverse change from the September 30, 1983, unaudited statements. Risk Capital relied upon the audited statements and purchased the treasury stock of Florida Sunshine. It was subsequently discovered that as of the balance sheet date, the audited statements contained several misstatements and that in fact there had been a material adverse change in the financial position of the corporation. Florida Sunshine has become insolvent, and Risk Capital will lose virtually its entire investment.

    Risk Capital seeks recovery against Wilson and Wyatt.

Required:

    a. Discuss each of the theories of liability that Risk Capital will probably assert as its basis for recovery.

    b. Assuming that only ordinary negligence by Wilson and Wyatt is proven, will Risk Capital prevail? State yes or no and explain. (AICPA, adapted)

3–30. Mark Williams, CPA, was engaged by Jackson Financial Development Company to audit the financial statements of Apex Construction Company, a small closely held corporation. Williams was told when he was engaged that Jackson Financial needed reliable financial statements that would be used to determine whether or not to purchase a substantial amount of Apex Construction's convertible debentures at the price asked by the estate of one of Apex's former directors.

Williams performed his examination in a negligent manner. As a result of his negligence, he failed to discover substantial defalcations by Carl Brown, the Apex controller. Jackson Financial purchased the debentures, but would not have if the defalcations had been discovered. After discovery of the fraud Jackson Financial promptly sold them for the highest price offered in the market at a $70,000 loss.

Required:
a. What liability does Williams have to Jackson Financial? Explain.
b. If Apex Construction also sues Williams for negligence, what are the probable legal defenses Williams's attorney would raise? Explain.
c. Will the negligence of Mark Williams, CPA, as described above prevent him from recovering on a liability insurance policy covering the practice of his profession? Explain. (AICPA, adapted)

3–31. Charles Worthington, the founding and senior partner of a successful and respected CPA firm, was a highly competent practitioner who always emphasized high professional standards. One of the policies of the firm was that all reports by members or staff be submitted to Worthington for review.

Recently, Arthur Craft, a junior partner in the firm, received a phone call from Herbert Flack, a close personal friend. Flack informed Craft that he, his family, and some friends were planning to create a corporation to engage in various land development ventures; that various members of the family are presently in a partnership (Flack Ventures), which holds some land and other assets; and that the partnership would contribute all of its assets to the new corporation and the corporation would assume the liabilities of the partnership.

Flack asked Craft to prepare a balance sheet of the partnership that he could show to members of his family, who were in the partnership, and to friends, to determine whether they might have an interest in joining in the formation and financing of the new corporation. Flack said he had the partnership general ledger in front of him and proceeded to read to Craft the names of the accounts and their balances at the end of the latest month. Craft took the notes he made during the telephone conversation with Flack, classified and organized the data into a conventional balance sheet, and had his secretary type the balance sheet and an accompanying letter on firm stationery. He did not consult Worthington on this matter or submit his work to him for review.

The transmittal letter stated: "We have reviewed the books and records of Flack Ventures, a partnership, and have prepared the attached balance sheet at March 31, 1983. We did not perform an examination in conformity with generally accepted auditing standards, and therefore do not express an opinion on the accompanying balance sheet." The balance sheet was prominently marked "unaudited." Craft signed the letter and instructed his secretary to send it to Flack.

Required:

What legal problems are suggested by these facts? Explain. (AICPA, adapted)

3–32. Chriswell Corporation decided to raise additional long-term capital by issuing $3,000,000 of 15 percent subordinated debentures to the public. May, Clark & Company, CPAs, the company's auditors, were engaged to examine the June 30, 1983 financial statements, which were included in the registration statement for the debentures.

May, Clark & Company completed its examination and submitted an unqualified auditor's report dated July 15, 1983. The registration statement was filed and became effective on September 1, 1983. Two weeks before the effective date, one of the partners of May, Clark & Company called on Chriswell Corporation and had lunch with the financial vice president and the controller. He questioned both officials on the company's operations since June 30 and inquired whether there had been any material changes in the company's financial position since that date. Both officers assured him that everything had proceeded normally and that the financial position of the company had not changed materially.

Unfortunately, the officers' representation was not true. On July 30 a substantial debtor of the company failed to pay the $400,000 due on its account receivable and indicated to Chriswell that it would probably be forced into bankruptcy. This receivable was shown as a collateralized loan on the June 30 financial statements. It was collateralized by stock of the debtor corporation that had a value in excess of the loan at the time the financial statements were prepared but was virtually worthless at the effective date of the registration statement. This $400,000 account receivable was material to the financial position of Chriswell Corporation, and the market price of the subordinated debentures decreased by nearly 50 percent after the foregoing facts were disclosed.

The debenture holders of Chriswell are seeking recovery of their loss against all parties connected with the debenture registration.

Required:

Is May, Clark & Company liable to the Chriswell debenture holders? Explain. (AICPA, adapted)

3–33. Meglow Corporation, a closely held manufacturer of dresses and blouses, sought a loan from Busch Factors. Busch had previously extended $25,000 credit to Meglow but refused to lend any additional money without obtaining copies of Meglow's audited financial statements.

Meglow contacted the CPA firm of Winslow & Watkins to perform the audit. In arranging for the examination, Meglow clearly indicated that its purpose was to satisfy Busch Factors as to the corporation's sound financial condition and to obtain an additional loan of $50,000.

Winslow & Watkins accepted the engagement, performed the examination in a negligent manner, and rendered an unqualified opinion. If an adequate examination had been performed, the financial statements would have been found to be misleading.

Meglow submitted the audited financial statements to Busch Factors and obtained an additional loan of $35,000. Busch refused to lend more than that amount. After several other factors also refused, Meglow finally was able to persuade Maxwell Department Stores, one of its customers, to lend the additional $15,000. Maxwell relied upon the financial statements examined by Winslow & Watkins.

Meglow is now in bankruptcy, and Busch seeks to collect from Winslow & Watkins the $60,000 it loaned Meglow. Maxwell seeks to recover from Winslow & Watkins the $15,000 it loaned Meglow.

Required:

a. Will Busch recover? Explain.

b. Will Maxwell recover? Explain. (AICPA, adapted)

3–34. Cragsmore & Company, a medium-size partnership of CPAs, was engaged by Marlowe Manufacturing, Inc., a closely held corporation, to examine its financial statements for the year ended December 31, 1983.

Before preparing the audit report William Cragsmore, a partner, and Joan Willmore, a staff senior, reviewed the disclosures necessary in the notes to the financial statements. One note involved the terms, costs, and obligations of a lease between Marlowe and Acme Leasing Company.

Willmore suggested that the note disclose the following: "The Acme Leasing Company is owned by persons who have a 35 percent interest in the capital stock and who are officers of Marlowe Manufacturing, Inc."

On Cragsmore's recommendation, this was revised by substituting "minority shareholders" for "persons who have a 35 percent interest in the capital stock and who are officers."

The audit report and financial statements were forwarded to Marlowe Manufacturing for review. The officer-shareholders of Marlowe who also owned Acme Leasing objected to the revised wording and insisted that the note be changed to describe the relationship between Acme and Marlowe as merely one of affiliation. Cragsmore acceded to this request.

The audit report was issued on this basis with an unqualified opinion. But the working papers included the drafts that showed the changes in the wording of the note.

Subsequent to delivery of the audit report, Marlowe suffered a substantial uninsured fire loss and was forced into bankruptcy. The failure of Marlowe to carry any fire insurance coverage was not noted in the financial statements.

Required:

What legal problems for Cragsmore & Company are suggested by these facts? Discuss. (AICPA, adapted)

3–35. Reed & Belt, a regional CPA firm, has been named as a defendant in a class action by purchasers of the shares of stock of the Newly Corporation. The offering was a public offering of securities within the meaning of the Securities Act of 1933. The plaintiffs allege that the CPA firm was either negligent or fraudulent in connection with the preparation of the audited financial statements that accompanied the registration statement filed with the SEC. Specifically, they allege that Reed & Belt either intentionally disregarded, or failed to exercise reasonable care to discover, material facts that occurred subsequent to January 31, 1983, the date of the auditors' report. The securities were sold to the public on March 16, 1983.

The plaintiffs have subpoenaed copies of Reed & Belt's working papers. Reed & Belt is considering refusing to relinquish the papers, asserting that they contain privileged communication between Reed & Belt and Newly Corporation.

Reed & Belt will, of course, defend on the merits irrespective of the questions regarding the working papers.

Required:
a. Can Reed & Belt rightfully refuse to surrender its working papers? Explain.
b. Discuss the liability of Reed & Belt in respect to events that occur in the period between the date of the auditors' report and the effective date of the public offering of the securities. (AICPA, adapted)

3–36. The limitations on professional responsibilities of CPAs when they are associated with unaudited financial statements are often misunderstood. These misunderstandings can be reduced substantially if CPAs carefully follow professional pronouncements in the course of their work and take other appropriate measures.

Required:
The following list describes seven situations CPAs may encounter in their association with and preparation of unaudited financial statements. Briefly discuss the extent of the CPAs' responsibilities and, if appropriate, the actions to be taken to minimize misunderstandings. Identify your answers to correspond with the letters in the following list.
a. A CPA was engaged by telephone to perform accounting work including the compilation of financial statements. His client believes that the CPA has been engaged to audit the financial statements and examine the records accordingly.
b. A group of business executives who own a farm managed by an independent agent engage Linda Lopez, a CPA, to compile quarterly unaudited financial statements for them. The CPA compiles the financial statements from information given to her by the independent agent. Subsequently, the business executives find the statements were inaccurate because their independent agent was embezzling funds. The executives refuse to pay the CPA's fee and blame her for allowing the situation to go undetected, contending that she should not have relied on representations from the independent agent.
c. In comparing the trial balance with the general ledger a CPA finds an account labeled Audit Fees in which the client has accumulated

the CPA's quarterly billings for accounting services including the compilation of quarterly unaudited financial statements.

d. To determine appropriate account classification, John Day, CPA, reviewed a number of the client's invoices. He noted in his working papers that some invoices were missing but did nothing further because he thought they did not affect the unaudited financial statements he was compiling. When the client subsequently discovered that invoices were missing, he contended that the CPA should not have ignored the missing invoices when compiling the financial statements and had a responsibility to at least inform him that they were missing.

e. A CPA had compiled a draft of unaudited financial statements from the client's records. While reviewing this draft with her client, the CPA learns that the land and building were recorded at appraisal value. (AICPA, adapted)

3–37. The CPA firm of Arnold and Bates was engaged by the trustee in bankruptcy for Martin & Co., a stockbrokerage firm that had incurred substantial embezzlement losses, to examine the financial statements of Martin & Co. for the nine years of its existence from July 1, 1974 through June 30, 1983. The U.S. bankruptcy court had authorized the engagement. The former owners of Martin & Co., who had perpetrated the embezzlement, were serving terms in federal prisons.

Roger Bates, a senior partner of Arnold and Bates, assumed charge of the Martin & Co. assignment. As the audit progressed, Mr. Bates became aware of the irrefutable fact that the CPA who had examined the financial statements of Martin & Co. for the eight years ended June 30, 1982, had missed obviously material misstatements and omissions in Martin's financial statements for those years. Martin's trustee in bankruptcy had indicated he planned to seek recovery from the predecessor CPA if he had been guilty of gross negligence. To complicate Mr. Bates's problem, several other stockbrokerage clients of Arnold and Bates had filed with Martin's trustee substantial claims for unpaid amounts due them from transactions with Martin & Co.

Required:

Discuss the action, if any, that Bates should take in this situation with respect to the following:

a. Examination of the predecessor's working papers.

b. Communication with the AICPA and the state society of CPAs, if the predecessor is a member.

c. Communication with the state board of accountancy.

d. Disclosure of the predecessor's negligence in the audit report of Arnold and Bates.

e. Recommending establishing a receivable for damages from the predecessor CPA.

f. Notifying the other stockbrokerage clients of Arnold and Bates regarding their possibility of recovery from the predecessor CPA.

3–38. In a preliminary discussion, before beginning your audit of Mark Company, the chairman of the board of directors audit committee states that he would like to ascertain whether any key employees have

interests that conflict with their duties at Mark Company. He asks that
during your regular audit you be watchful for signs of these conditions
and report them to him.

Required:

Briefly discuss your professional position in this matter. Include the
following aspects in your discussion:

a. The responsibility of the CPA for the discovery of conflicts of interest. Give reasons for your position.

b. The advisability of requesting that the client furnish you with a
   letter of representations that contains a statement that no conflict of
   interests is known to exist among the company's officers and employees. What action, if any, would you take if the client refused to
   provide the letter? How would his refusal affect your opinion?

c. At the same time that you are conducting the audit of Mark Company, you are also conducting the audit of Timzin Company, a
   supplier of Mark Company. During your audit of Timzin Company, you determine that an employee of Mark Company is receiving kickbacks.

   (1) Discuss your responsibility, if any, to reveal this practice to
       the audit committee of Mark Company.

   (2) Discuss your professional relationship with Timzin Company
       after discovering the kickbacks. (AICPA, adapted)

4

The public accounting profession: Planning the audit

Most public accounting practices are organized as partnerships, although a CPA may also practice as a sole practitioner or as a member of a professional corporation. In comparison with a sole proprietorship, the partnership form of organization offers several advantages. When two or more CPAs join forces, the opportunity for specialization is increased, and the scope of services offered to clients may be expanded to include such areas as tax planning and management-advisory services. Also, qualified members of the audit staff may be rewarded by admission to the partnership. Providing an opportunity to become a part owner of the business is an important factor in a CPA firm's ability to attract and retain competent personnel. A partnership also provides opportunities for professional growth through the exchange of ideas and frequent discussions among partners concerning audit problems and the issues confronting the profession.

CPA firms organized as partnerships vary in size from local offices with as few as two partners to international organizations with 300 or more partners. Only a very large public accounting firm can perform an audit of a business such as Sears, Roebuck or IBM, with plants and branches in many different countries. At present, there are eight international public accounting firms, often called the Big Eight.[1] Each of

---

[1] The Big Eight include Arthur Andersen & Co.; Arthur Young & Co.; Coopers & Lybrand; Deloitte Haskins & Sells; Ernst & Whinney; Peat, Marwick, Mitchell & Co.; Price Waterhouse & Co.; and Touche Ross & Co.

these firms has several hundred partners, thousands of employees, and hundreds of offices located in cities all over the world. Most large corporations are audited by these eight firms. In addition to the Big Eight, there are many national firms and more than 10,000 regional and local public accounting firms that offer a wide variety of auditing, tax planning, and management-advisory services.

In past decades, state laws generally prohibited professionals from organizing their practices as corporations. This prohibition was founded on the premise that professionals should not be able to "hide behind the corporate veil" and avoid taking personal responsibility for their professional acts. Now, however, most states recognize the *professional corporation* as a permissible form of organization for professional practices. Professional corporations differ from traditional corporations in a number of respects. For example, all shareholders and directors of a professional corporation must be licensed practitioners of the profession. In addition, the professional corporation must carry adequate liability insurance to cover damages caused by negligent actions.

Professional corporations provide CPAs with significant advantages with respect to personal income taxes. However, a public accounting firm may not organize as a professional corporation unless all states in which the firm will practice permit this form of organization. Thus, the large national public accounting firms will remain as partnerships for the foreseeable future. Many local CPA firms, on the other hand, are organized as professional corporations.

Responsibilities of the professional staff

Human resources—the competence, judgment, and integrity of personnel—represent the greatest asset of any public accounting firm. The professional staff of a typical public accounting firm includes partners, managers, senior accountants, and staff assistants.

Partners.   The principal responsibility of the partner is to maintain contacts with clients. These contacts include discussing with clients the objectives and scope of the audit work, resolving controversies that may arise as to how items are to be presented in the financial statements, and attending the client's stockholders' meetings to answer any questions regarding the financial statements or the auditors' report. Other responsibilities of the partner include recruiting new staff members, general supervision of the professional staff, reviewing the audit working papers, and signing the audit reports.

Specialization by each partner in a different area of the firm's practice is often advantageous. One partner, for example, may become expert in tax matters and head the firm's tax department; another may specialize in SEC registrations; and a third may devote full time to design and installation of data processing systems.

The partnership level in a public accounting firm is comparable to that of top management in an industrial organization. Executives at this level are concerned with the long-run well-being of the organization and of the community it serves. They should and do contribute important amounts of time to civic, professional, and educational activities in the community. Participation in the state society of certified public accountants and in the AICPA is, of course, a requisite if the partners are to do their share in building the profession. Contribution of their specialized skills and professional judgment to leadership of civic organizations is equally necessary in developing the economic and social environment in which business and professional accomplishment is possible.

An important aspect of partners' active participation in various business and civic organizations is the prestige and recognition that may come to their firms. Many clients select a particular public accounting firm because they have come to know and respect one of the firm's partners. Thus, partners who are widely known and highly regarded within the community may be a significant factor in attracting business to the firm.

Managers. In large public accounting firms, managers or supervisors perform many of the duties that would be discharged by partners in smaller firms. A manager may be responsible for supervising two or more concurrent audit engagements. This supervisory work includes reviewing the audit working papers and discussing with the audit staff and with the client any accounting problems that may arise during the engagement. The manager is responsible for determining the audit procedures applicable to specific audits and for maintaining uniform standards of field work. Often, managers have the administrative duties of compiling and collecting the firm's billings to clients.

Familiarity with tax laws and with SEC regulations, as well as a broad and current knowledge of accounting theory and practice, are essential qualifications for a successful manager. Like the partner, the audit manager may specialize in specific industries or other areas of the firm's practice.

Senior auditors. The senior auditor is an individual qualified to assume full responsibility for the planning and conducting of an audit and the writing of the audit report, subject to review and approval by the manager and partner. In conducting the audit, the senior delegates most audit tasks to assistants based on an appraisal of each assistant's ability to perform particular phases of the work. A well-qualified university graduate with a formal education in accounting may progress from staff assistant to senior auditor within two or three years, or even less.

One of the major responsibilities of the senior is on-the-job staff training. When assigning work to staff assistants, the senior should make clear the end objectives of the particular audit operation. By assigning assistants a wide variety of audit tasks and by providing constructive criticism of the assistants' work, the senior should try to make each audit a significant learning experience for the staff assistants.

The review of working papers as rapidly as they are completed is another duty of the senior in charge of an audit. This enables the senior to control the progress of the work and to ascertain that each phase of the engagement is adequately covered. At the conclusion of the field work, the senior will make a final review, tracing all items from individual working papers to the financial statements.

The senior will also maintain a continuous record of the hours devoted by all members of the staff to the various phases of the examination. In addition to maintaining uniform professional standards of field work, the senior is responsible for preventing the accumulation of excessive staff-hours on inconsequential matters and for completing the entire engagement within budgeted time, if possible.

Staff assistants. The first position of a college graduate entering the public accounting profession is that of a staff assistant. Staff assistants usually encounter a variety of assignments that fully utilize their capacity for analysis and growth. Of course some routine work must be done in every audit engagement, but college graduates with thorough training in accounting need have no fear of being assigned for long to extensive routine procedures when they enter the field of public accounting. Most firms are anxious to assign more and more responsibility to younger staff members as rapidly as they are able to assume it. The demand for accounting services is so far beyond the available supply of competent individuals that every incentive exists for rapid development of promising assistants.

The larger public accounting firms maintain well-organized training programs designed to integrate new staff members into the organization with maximum efficiency. One of the most attractive features of the public accounting profession is the richness and variety of experience acquired even by the beginning staff member. Because of the high quality of the experience gained by certified public accountants as they move from one audit engagement to another, many business concerns select individuals from the public accounting field to fill such executive positions as controller or treasurer.

Professional development within the CPA firm

A major problem in public accounting is keeping abreast of current developments within the profession. New business practices; new pronouncements by the Auditing Standards Board, the SEC, and the FASB; and changes in the tax laws are only a few of the factors that require members of the profession continually to update their technical knowledge. To assist in this updating process, most large public accounting firms maintain a separate professional development section.

Professional development sections offer a wide range of seminars and educational programs to personnel of the firm. The curriculum of each program is especially designed to suit the needs and responsibilities of participants. Partners, for example, may attend programs focusing on the firm's policies on audit quality control or means of minimizing exposure to lawsuits; on the other hand, programs designed for staff assistants may cover audit procedures or use of the firm's computer facilities. In addition to offering educational programs, the professional development section usually publishes a weekly newsletter or monthly journal for distribution to personnel of the CPA firm and other interested persons.

The professional development section may also have a technical research staff that studies emerging issues in the profession. This staff assists in developing the "firm's position" on complex accounting issues arising in client's financial statements or FASB Discussion Memoranda. Often, a position paper conveying the firm's viewpoint is prepared by the research staff and sent to the research staff of the FASB. Thus, the professional development section may take an active hand in shaping current developments in the profession as well as in updating and informing personnel of the firm.

Continuing education—the CPAs' response to change

The need for CPAs to expand their knowledge and improve their skills continues throughout their professional careers. Many states have recognized this need by adopting continuing education legislation. Such legislation requires all licensed practitioners within the state to devote at least a specified number of hours each year (or every two years) to acceptable professional development programs. Professional development sections of CPA firms, the AICPA, various state societies of certified public accountants, and many universities provide numerous programs that meet the continuing education criteria. Home study materials providing continuing education credit are also available through the AICPA.

The CPA as an expert witness

As business affairs have grown more complex, the number of court cases involving accounting issues has increased greatly. The testimony of accountants and other experts is needed in order that the judge or jury gain the necessary understanding of the pertinent facts. *Expert witnesses* are persons who have special knowledge, experience, or training in a given field or profession. They are able to analyze and evaluate matters within a specialized body of knowledge, on which the judge or jury lacking such specialized experience could not readily form an opinion.

Among the types of cases in which a CPA may appropriately serve as an expert witness are the following: (*a*) income tax cases, including both criminal fraud cases and civil tax cases; (*b*) partnership dissolutions; (*c*) interpretations of contracts involving valuation of assets, bonuses, or determination of net income; (*d*) regulatory cases involving the rates and earnings of public utilities, and (*e*) other cases involving complex accounting measurements.

Seasonal fluctuations in public accounting work

One of the traditional disadvantages of the public accounting profession has been the concentration of work during the "busy season" from December through April, followed by a period of slack demand during the summer months. This seasonal trend was caused by the fact that most companies kept their records on a calendar-year basis and desired auditing services immediately after the December 31 closing of the accounts. Another important factor has been the spring deadline for filing of federal income tax returns.

Auditors often work a considerable number of hours of overtime during the busy season. Some public accounting firms pay their staff a premium for overtime hours. Other firms allow their staff to accumulate the overtime in an "overtime bank" and to "withdraw" these hours in the form of additional vacation time during the less busy times of the year.

Relationships with clients

The wide-ranging scope of public accountants' activities today demands that CPAs be interested and well informed on economic trends, political developments, sports events, and the many other topics that play a significant part in business and social contacts. Although an in-depth knowledge of accounting is a most important qualification of the CPA, an ability to meet people easily and to gain their confidence and goodwill may be no less important in achieving success in the profession of public accounting. The ability to work effectively with clients will be enhanced by a sincere interest in their problems and by a relaxed and cordial manner.

The question of the auditors' independence inevitably arises in considering the advisability of social activities with clients. The partner in today's public accounting firm may play golf or tennis with the executives of client companies and other business associates. These relationships actually may make it easier to resolve differences of opinions that arise during the audit, if the client has learned to know and respect the CPA partner. This mutual understanding need not prevent the CPA from standing firm on matters of accounting principle. This is perhaps the "moment of truth" for the practitioners of a profession.

However, the CPA must always remember that the concept of independence embodies an *appearance* of independence. This appearance of independence may be impaired if an auditor becomes excessively involved in social activities with clients. For example, if a CPA frequently attends lavish parties held by a client or dates an officer or employee of a client corporation, the question might be raised as to whether the CPA will appear independent to outsiders. This dilemma is but one illustration of the continual need for judgment and perspective on the part of an auditor.

PLANNING THE AUDIT

Auditors do not merely accept a new audit client and then arrive at the client's premises to "start auditing." The first standard of field work states:

> The work is to be *adequately planned* and assistants, if any, are to be *properly supervised.* (Emphasis added.)

In addition, the Auditing Standards Board has issued *SAS No. 22,* "Planning and Supervision," to provide CPAs with guidance in adequately planning each audit engagement.

The concept of adequate planning includes investigating a prospective client before deciding whether to accept the engagement, obtaining an understanding of the client's business operations, and developing an overall strategy to organize, coordinate, and schedule the activities of the audit staff. Although much planning is done before beginning the actual audit field work, the planning process continues throughout the engagement. Whenever a problem is encountered during the audit, the auditors must plan their response to the situation. For example, if weaknesses are discovered in the client's system of internal control, the auditors must plan audit procedures to satisfy themselves that these weaknesses have not resulted in material errors in the financial statements. In short, the planning process begins with the auditor's decision on accepting a prospective audit client and continues until the audit report is signed and delivered.

Accepting new audit clients

Public accounting is a competitive profession, and most CPA firms are anxious to obtain new clients. However, a CPA firm's principal product is its reputation for credibility. No auditor can afford to be associated with clients who are engaging in management fraud or other misleading reporting practices.

The recent wave of litigation involving auditors underscores the need for CPAs to investigate prospective audit clients before undertaking an engagement. The CPAs should investigate the history of the prospective client, including such matters as the identities and reputations of the directors, officers, and major stockholders. The incentive for management to overstate operating results is increased when the client company is in a weak financial position or is greatly in need of capital. Therefore, auditors should consider the financial strength and credit rating of a prospective client as factors in the overall risk of an association with that client. Even if there are no misrepresentations in the financial statements, the auditors usually are named as defendants in lengthy and costly lawsuits whenever an audit client goes bankrupt. Many CPAs choose to avoid engagements entailing a relatively high risk of overstated operating results or of subsequent litigation; others may accept such engagements, recognizing the need to expand audit procedures to compensate for the unusual levels of risk.

Audit committees.   To enhance the auditors' independence from management, many companies organize an audit committee within the board of directors to maintain contact with the independent auditors. The committee may decide which auditing firm to retain, determine the scope of the services to be performed, and review the progress of the audit and the final audit findings.

An audit committee usually is composed of three to five *outside directors*—that is, directors who are neither officers nor employees of the client organization. The exclusion of officer-directors from the audit committee allows the CPAs to discuss more openly such problems as weaknesses in internal control, disagreements with management as to accounting principles, or possible indications of management fraud or other illegal acts by corporate officers. The communications between the audit committee and the CPAs provide the board of directors with up-to-date information about the financial position of the business, as well as with information useful in evaluating the efficiency and integrity of the company's management.

The New York Stock Exchange requires all listed companies to have an audit committee composed exclusively of outside directors. Not all audit clients, however, have audit committees. For example, the concept of an audit committee is not applicable to clients organized as sole proprietorships, partnerships, or small, closely held corporations. Arrangements for an audit of a small or medium-size business often are made with the owner, a partner, or an executive, such as the president, treasurer, or controller.

Obtaining a knowledge of the client's business

When should a racquetball club recognize its revenue from the sale of lifetime memberships? Is a company organized to produce a motion picture a going concern? Is it appropriate for a real estate developer to use the percentage-completion method of revenue recognition? What is a reasonable useful life for today's most advanced computer system? We will not attempt to answer these questions in this textbook; we raise them simply to demonstrate that the auditors must have a good working knowledge of an audit client's business and business environment if they are to express an opinion on the fairness of the client's financial statements.

The auditor's knowledge of the client's business should include an understanding of such factors as the client's organizational structure, accounting policies and procedures, capital structure, product lines, and methods of production and distribution. In addition, the CPA should be familiar with matters affecting the industry within which the client operates, including economic conditions and financial trends, inherent types of business risk, governmental regulations, changes in technology, and widely used accounting methods. Without such a knowledge of the client's business environment, the auditor would not be in a position to evaluate the appropriateness of the accounting principles in use or the reasonableness of the many estimates and assumptions embodied in the client's financial statements.

Numerous sources of information on prospective clients are available to the auditors. AICPA audit and accounting guides, trade publications, and governmental agency publications are useful in obtaining an orientation in the client's industry. Previous audit reports, annual reports to stockholders, SEC filings, and prior years' tax returns are excellent sources of financial background information. Informal discussions between the auditor-in-charge and key officers of the prospective client can provide information about the history, size, operations, accounting records, and internal controls of the enterprise.

Communication with predecessor auditors. An excellent source of information about a prospective client who previously has been audited is the predecessor auditor. The *successor auditors'* examination may be greatly facilitated by consulting with the *predecessor auditors* and reviewing the predecessors' working papers. Communication with the predecessor auditors can provide the successor CPAs with background information about the client, details about the client's system of internal control, and evidence as to the account balances at the beginning of the year under audit.

On occasion, a client may seek to change auditors because of disagreements with the predecessor auditors over accounting principles or audit procedures. For this reason, *SAS No. 7* requires the successor auditors to make certain inquiries of the predecessor auditors *before accepting the engagement.*[2] These inquiries should include questions regarding disagreements with management over accounting principles, the integrity of management, the predecessor's understanding of the reason for the change in auditors, and other matters that will assist the successor auditors in deciding whether to accept the engagement. (Regulations of the SEC require companies subject to its jurisdiction to

---

[2] *Statement on Auditing Standards No. 7,* "Communications between Predecessor and Successor Auditors," AICPA (New York, 1975).

report changes in independent auditors, and the reasons therefor, to the Commission.)

Auditors are ethically prohibited from disclosing confidential information obtained in the course of an audit without the consent of the client. The successor auditors should therefore obtain the prospective client's consent before making inquiries of the predecessor auditors. In addition, they should ask the client to authorize the predecessor auditors to respond fully. If a prospective client is reluctant to authorize communications with the predecessor auditors, the successor CPAs should consider the implications in deciding whether or not to accept the engagement.

The auditors may also make inquiries of other third parties in obtaining background information about a prospective audit client. For example, the client's bankers can provide information regarding the client's financial history and credit rating. The client's legal counsel can provide information about the client's legal environment, including such matters as pending litigation and regulatory requirements.

Tour of plant and offices. Another useful preliminary step for the auditors is to arrange an inspection tour of the plant and offices of a prospective client. This tour will give the auditors some understanding of the plant layout, manufacturing process, principal products, and physical safeguards surrounding inventories. During the tour, the auditors should be alert for signs of potential problems. Rust on equipment may indicate that plant assets have been idle; excessive dust on raw materials or finished goods may indicate a problem of obsolescence. A knowledge of the physical facilities will assist the auditors in planning how many audit staff members will be needed to participate in observing the physical inventory.

The tour affords the auditors an opportunity to observe firsthand what types of internal documentation are used to record such activity as receiving raw materials, transferring materials into production, and shipping finished goods to customers. This documentation is essential to the auditors' study and evaluation of internal control.

In going through the offices, the auditors will learn the location of various accounting records. The auditors can ascertain how much subdivision of duties is practical within the client organization by observing the number of office employees. In addition the tour will afford an opportunity to meet the key personnel whose names appear on the organization chart. The auditors will record the background information about the client in a *permanent file* available for reference in future engagements.

Preliminary arrangements with clients

The auditors' approach to an engagement is not that of detectives looking for evidence of fraud; instead, the approach is the positive, constructive one of gathering evidence to prove the fairness and validity of the client's financial statements.

A conference with the client before beginning the engagement is a useful step in avoiding misunderstandings. The conference should include discussion of the nature, purpose, and scope of the audit and any matters that could conceivably produce friction. Since the fee is usually in the mind of both client and auditors, it should be frankly discussed, but without creating the impression that the auditors' chief interest is in the earning of a fee.

A clear understanding between the client and the auditors concerning the scope of the examination and the condition of the accounting records at the starting date is an essential step in planning an audit. Otherwise, the auditors may arrive to begin an examination only to find that transactions for the period to be examined have not yet been fully recorded. It is not the auditors' job to draft routine adjusting entries or to balance the subsidiary ledgers with the control accounts. By doing this type of work for an audit client, the auditors would violate the SEC's definition of independence.

A new client should be informed as to the extent of investigation of the beginning balances of such accounts as plant and equipment and inventories. To determine the propriety of depreciation expense for the current year and the proper balances in plant and equipment accounts at the balance sheet date, the auditors must investigate the validity of the property accounts at the beginning of the current period. If the auditors are unable to obtain satisfactory evidence as to the balance of *beginning inventory*, it may be necessary to disclaim an opinion on the income statement in the first audit of a new client.

In some cases, satisfactory audits of the business in preceding years by other reputable auditing firms may enable the auditors to accept the opening balances of the current year with a minimum of verification work; in other cases, in which no satisfactory recent audit has been made, an extensive analysis of transactions of prior years will be necessary to establish account balances as of the beginning of the current year. In these latter situations the client should be made to understand that the scope and cost of the initial audit may exceed that of repeat engagements, which will not require analysis of past years' transactions.

Fees.   When a business engages the services of independent public accountants, it will usually ask for an estimate of the cost of the audit. In supplying this estimate after being engaged, the accountants will give first consideration to the time probably required for the audit. Staff time is the basic unit of measurement for audit fees. Each public accounting firm develops a per hour or per diem fee schedule for each category of audit staff, based on direct salaries and such related costs as payroll taxes and insurance. The direct rate is then increased for allocated overhead costs and a profit element.

In addition to basic per diem or per hour fees, clients are charged for direct costs incurred by the public accounting firm for staff travel, report processing, and other out-of-pocket expenditures.

Estimating a fee for an audit thus usually involves the application of the CPA firm's daily or hourly rates to the estimated time required. Since the exact number of days cannot be determined in advance, the auditors may merely give a rough estimate of the fee. Or they may multiply the rates by the estimated time, add an amount for unforeseen problems, and quote a range or bracket of amounts within which the total fee will fall. Once the auditors have given an estimate of the fee to a client, they naturally feel some compulsion to keep the charges within this limit.

Per diem rates for audit work vary considerably in different sections of the country, and even within a given community, in accordance with the reputation and experience of the accounting firm. Of course, the salaries paid to audit staff members are much less than the rates at which audit time is billed to clients. In many firms salaries represent about 40 percent of billing rates; the remainder is required to cover the cost of nonbillable time when auditors are not assigned, overhead expenses of the office, and a profit to the partners.

Use of the client's staff.   Another issue to be discussed in the preliminary conference is what the client's staff can do to prepare for the audit. As previously mentioned, the client's staff should have the accounting records up to date when the auditors arrive. In addition, many audit working papers can be prepared for the auditors by the client's staff, thus reducing the cost of the audit and freeing the auditors from routine work. The auditors may set up the columnar headings for such working papers and give instructions to the client's staff as to the information to be gathered. These working papers should bear the label *Prepared By Client* or *PBC*, and also the initials of the auditor who verifies the work performed by the client's staff. Working papers prepared by the client should never be accepted at face value; such papers must be reviewed and tested by the auditors in order that the CPA firm maintain its independent status.

Among the tasks that may be assigned to the client's employees are the preparation of a trial balance of the general ledger, preparation of an aged trial balance of accounts receivable, analyses of accounts receivable written off, lists of property additions and retirements during the year, and analyses of various revenue and expense accounts. Many of these working papers may be in the form of computer printouts.

Engagement letters

These preliminary understandings with the client should be summarized by the auditors in an *engagement letter*, making clear the nature of the engagement, any limitations on the scope of the audit, work to be performed by the client's staff, scheduled dates for perfor-

═══════ **Figure 4–1**
Engagement letter

Adams, Barnes and Company

CERTIFIED PUBLIC ACCOUNTANTS

July 17, 19X5

Mr. J. B. Wilson
Chairman of the Audit Committee
Board of Directors
Barker Tool Company
1825 LeMay Street
Chicago, Illinios 60642

Dear Mr. Wilson:

This letter is to confirm our arrangements for our examination of the financial statements of Barker Tool Company for the year ended December 31, 19X5.

Our examination will be performed in accordance with generally accepted auditing standards and will include all procedures which we consider necessary to provide a basis for expression of our opinion as to the fairness of the financial statements. Our examination will include a study and evaluation of the Company's system of internal accounting control, and we will prepare a letter with our recommendations for correcting weaknesses brought to light by this study.

An examination performed in accordance with generally accepted auditing standards includes a search for errors and irregularities which would have a material effect upon the financial statements. However, such an examination cannot be relied upon to disclose all cases of fraud and defalcation.

Our examination is scheduled for performance and completion as follows:

Begin field work	September 10, 19X5
Delivery of internal control letter	November 15, 19X5
Completion of field work	February 20, 19X6
Delivery of audit report	March 1, 19X6

Our fees for this examination will be based on the time spent by various members of our staff at our regular rates, plus direct expenses. We will notify you immediately of any circumstances we encounter that could significantly affect our initial fee estimate of $35,000.

In order for us to work as efficiently as possible, it is understood that your accounting staff will provide us with a year-end trial balance by January 15, 19X5, and also with the schedules and account analyses descibed on the separate attachment.

If these arrangements are in accordance with your understanding, please sign this letter in the space provided and return a copy to us at your earliest convenience.

Very truly yours,

Charles Adams

Charles Adams, CPA

Accepted by:_____

Date: _____

mance and completion of the examination, and the basis for computing the auditors' fee. When the engagement letter is accepted by the authorized client official, it represents an *executory contract* between the auditor and the client. Engagement letters do not follow any standard form; an example of such a letter is presented in Figure 4–1.

The use of engagement letters is not limited to audit engagements; documentation of the mutual understanding between the CPAs and the client is desirable before rendering any type of professional service.

Illustrative case. In the *1136 Tenants' Corporation* v. *Rothenberg* case, an incorporated apartment cooperative sued its CPAs for failing to detect embezzlement losses caused by a managing agent. The CPAs maintained they had been engaged only to do write-up work and not to perform any audit procedures. The court found that the CPAs had not made it sufficiently clear to the client that the engagement did not include audit procedures and held the CPAs liable for damages totaling $174,000. (The CPAs' fee for the engagement had been only $600.) Had the CPAs clearly set forth the scope of the engagement in an engagement letter, the case might never have been brought to court.

Developing an overall audit strategy

After obtaining a knowledge of the client's business, the auditor-in-charge should formulate an overall audit strategy for the upcoming engagement. The best audit strategy is the approach that results in the most *efficient* audit—that is, an effective audit performed at the least possible cost to the client. In formulating this audit strategy, the CPA should consider such factors as whether statistical sampling or EDP audit techniques might be used to advantage, the appropriate experience levels of the audit staff to be assigned to the engagement, and whether another CPA firm might be engaged to audit a branch location rather than having audit staff members travel to a distant city.

Developing an efficient audit strategy requires considerable audit experience as well as a familiarity with the client's business operations. For a large audit client, the audit strategy would be developed by a partner or manager; for smaller clients, the strategy might be formulated by a senior, subject to review by the manager.

Audit plans

The planning process is documented in the audit working papers through the preparation of *audit plans, audit programs,* and *time budgets.* These "planning and supervision" working papers serve a dual purpose. First, they provide documentary evidence of the CPA firm's compliance with the "adequate planning" requirement of the first standard of field work. Second, these working papers provide the auditor-in-charge with a means of coordinating, scheduling, and supervising the activities of the audit staff members involved in the engagement.

An audit plan is an overview of the engagement, outlining the nature and characteristics of the client's business operations and the overall audit strategy. Although audit plans differ in form and content among public accounting firms, a typical plan includes details on the following:

1. Description of the client company—its structure, business, and organization.
2. Objectives of the audit (e.g., audit for stockholders, special purpose audit, SEC filings).
3. Nature and extent of other services, such as preparation of tax returns, to be performed for the client.
4. Timing and scheduling of the audit work, including determining which procedures may be performed before the balance sheet date, what must be done on or after the balance sheet date, and setting dates for such critical procedures as cash counts, accounts receivable confirmations, and inventory observation.
5. Work to be done by the client's staff.
6. Staffing requirements during the engagement.
7. Target dates for completing major segments of the engagement, such as the study and evaluation of internal control, tax returns, the audit report, and SEC filings.
8. Any special problems to be resolved in the course of the engagement.

The audit plan is normally drafted before starting work at the client's offices. However, the plan may be modified throughout the engagement as special problems are encountered and as the auditors' study and evaluation of internal control lead to identification of areas requiring more or less audit work.

Audit programs

An audit program is a detailed outline of the auditing work to be performed, specifying the procedures to be followed in verification of each item in the financial statements and giving the estimated time required. As each step in the audit program is completed, the date, the auditor's initials, and the actual time consumed may be entered opposite the item. An audit program thus serves as a useful tool both in scheduling and in controlling audit work. It indicates the number of persons required and the relative proportions of senior and staff assistant hours needed, and it enables supervisors to keep currently informed on the progress being made.

The inclusion of detailed audit instructions in the program gives assurance that essential steps in verification will not be overlooked. These written instructions enable inexperienced auditors to work effectively with less personal supervision than would otherwise be required, and thus permit seniors and managers to concentrate upon those features of the examination that demand a high degree of analytical ability and the discriminating exercise of professional judgment.

Audit programs are considerably more detailed than audit plans. The audit plan outlines the objectives of the engagement; the audit program lists the specific procedures that must be performed to accomplish these objectives.

Illustrative audit program.   A typical example of the detailed audit procedures set forth in an audit program is the following partial list of procedures for the audit of investments in marketable securities:

X COMPANY
Partial Audit Program—Securities
December 31, 19—

Working paper refer- ence	*Date and initials*			*Time*	
				Esti- mated	*Actual*
		1.	Inspection of securities:		
		a.	Obtain or prepare list of securities owned as of balance sheet date.		
		b.	Compare list of securities with corresponding ledger account.		
		c.	Inspect securities on hand at or near date of balance sheet and compare with list of securities at balance sheet date. Reconcile securities to date of balance sheet and vouch transactions for intervening period. Maintain control of securities during this period.		
		d.	Compare serial numbers of securities inspected with serial numbers listed for these securities in prior year's audit.		

Tailor-made audit programs.   The conditions and problems encountered differ with every audit engagement; hence it is necessary for the auditor-in-charge of each examination to determine what procedures are appropriate under the circumstances. In the advance planning of an engagement, only a *tentative* audit program can be prepared. The auditor should expect this first draft of the program to be modified during the audit as strengths and weaknesses in the client's system of internal control and other special considerations are encountered.

Weak internal control, as manifested by poor accounting records, incompetent personnel, or lack of internal auditing, necessitates much more extensive auditing than would be necessary for a well-staffed concern with strong internal controls, good accounting records, and an effective internal auditing department. Internal control is sometimes adequate for certain operations of the company but weak or absent in other areas. The amount of testing by the auditors should be increased in areas of operations for which internal controls are deficient and may properly be minimized in areas subject to strong internal controls. The great variation in quality of internal controls encountered, coupled with the variety of accounting methods and special problems peculiar to individual business concerns, requires that the audit program be modified as the auditors learn more about the circumstances of the individual audit engagement.

The value of the audit program as a means of giving coherence, order, and logical sequence to the investigation is beyond dispute. The audit program must not, however, be considered a substitute for an alert, resourceful attitude on the part of the audit staff. They should be encouraged to explore fully any unusual transactions or questionable practices that come to their attention from any source and cautioned not to restrict themselves to the investigative routines set forth in a prearranged audit program.

Time budgets for audit engagements

Public accounting firms usually charge clients on a time basis, and detailed time records must therefore be maintained on every audit engagement. A time budget for an audit is constructed by estimating the time required for each step in the audit program for each of the various grades of auditors and totaling these estimated amounts. Time budgets serve other functions in addition to providing a basis for estimating fees. The time budget is an important tool of the audit senior—it is used to measure the efficiency of staff assistants and to determine at each stage of the engagement whether the work is progressing at a satisfactory rate.

There is always pressure to complete an audit within the estimated time. The staff assistant who takes more than the normal time for a task is not likely to be popular with supervisors or to win rapid advancement. Ability to do satisfactory work when given abundant time is not a sufficient qualification, *for time is never abundant in public accounting.*

The development of time budgets is facilitated in repeat engagements by reference of the preceding year's detailed time records. Sometimes time budgets prove quite unattainable because the client's records are not in satisfactory condition, or because of other special circumstances that arise. Even when time estimates are exceeded, there can be no compromise with qualitative standards in the performance of the field work. The CPA firm's professional reputation and its legal liability to clients and third parties do not permit any shortcutting or omission of audit procedures to meet a predetermined time estimate.

The audit trail

In developing audit procedures, the auditors are assisted by the organized manner in which accounting systems record, classify, and summarize data. The flow of accounting data begins with the recording of thousands of individual transactions on such documents as invoices and checks. The information recorded on these original documents is summarized in journals; and at the end of each month, the amounts in the journals are posted to ledger accounts. At the end of the year the balances in the ledger accounts are arranged in the form of a balance sheet and income statement.

In thinking of the accounting records as a whole, we may say that a continuous trail of evidence exists—a trail of evidence that links the thousands of individual transactions comprising a year's business activity with the summary figures in the financial statements. In a manual accounting system, this *audit trail* consists of source documents, journal entries, and ledger entries. An audit trail also exists within a computer-based accounting system, although it may have a substantially different form; this will be discussed in Chapter 6.

Just as a hiker may walk in either direction along a mountain path, an auditor may follow the audit trail in either of two directions. For example, the auditor may follow specific transactions from their origin forward to their inclusion in the financial statement summary figures. This approach provides the auditor with assurance that the transactions have been properly interpreted and processed.

On the other hand, the auditors may follow the stream of evidence back to its sources. This type of verification consists of tracing the various items in the statements (such as cash, receivables, sales, and expenses) back to the ledger accounts, and from the ledgers on back through the journals to original documents evidencing transactions. This process of working backward from the financial statement figures to the detailed evidence of individual transactions provides assurance that financial statement figures are based upon actual transactions.

Although the technique of working along the audit trail is a useful one, bear in mind that the auditors must acquire other types of evidence obtained from sources other than the client's accounting records.

Planning a recurring engagement

Planning a repeat engagement is far easier than planning for a first audit of a new client. The auditor-in-charge of a repeat engagement generally was involved in the previous year's audit and has a good working knowledge of the client's business. Also, the previous year's audit working papers contain a wealth of information useful in planning the recurring engagement. For example, the audit plan provides background information about the client and explains the overall strategy employed in the last audit. The prior year's audit program shows in detail the procedures performed and the length of time required to perform them. In addition, last year's working papers substantiate the beginning balances for the current year's audit.

While the prior year's working papers are extremely useful in planning the new engagement, the auditor-in-charge should not merely duplicate last year's audit program. Each audit should be a learning experience for the auditors, enabling them to design a more efficient audit in the following year. Also, the auditors may need to modify their approach to the audit for any changes in the client's operations or business environment.

THE AUDIT PROCESS

Although specific audit procedures vary from one engagement to the next, the fundamental steps underlying the audit process are essentially the same in almost every engagement:

1. Review the client's system of internal control and prepare a description of the system in the audit working papers.
2. Conduct tests to determine the reliability of the key internal control procedures.
3. Evaluate the effectiveness of the system of internal control in preventing material errors in the financial statements.
4. Prepare a report to management containing recommendations for improving the system of internal control.
5. Complete the audit—conduct tests to substantiate specific account balances and perform other auditing procedures.
6. Form an opinion and issue the audit report.

The sequence of these steps provides a logical framework for the audit process. However, the auditors need not complete each of these tasks before moving on to the next; several steps of the process may be undertaken concurrently. Of course the audit report cannot be issued until all other audit work is complete.

1. Review internal control and describe it in the working papers

The nature and extent of the audit work to be performed on a particular engagement depends largely upon the effectiveness of the client's system of internal control in preventing material errors in the financial statements. Before auditors can evaluate the effectiveness of the system, they need a knowledge and understanding of how it works: what procedures are performed and who performs them, what controls are in effect, how various types of transactions are processed and recorded, and what accounting records and supporting documentation exist. Thus, a review of the client's system of internal control is a logical first step in every audit engagement.

Sources of information about the client's system include interviews with client personnel, audit working papers from prior years' engagements, plant tours, and the client's procedures manuals. In gathering information about a system, it is often useful to study the sequence of procedures used in processing major categories of transactions. The sequence of procedures used for processing each major type of transaction is often termed a *transaction cycle.* In a manufacturing business, for example, the major transaction cycles might include: (*a*) *sales cycle,* involving sales, accounts receivable, and cash receipts; (*b*) *purchase cycle,* involving various assets and expenses, accounts payable, and cash disbursements; (*c*) *production cycle,* involving production costs, inventories, and the cost of goods sold; (*d*) *payroll cycle,* involving payroll expense, payroll taxes, and cash disbursements; and (*e*) *financing cycle,* involving long-term debt, capital stock, and cash receipts and disbursements.

To illustrate one of these transaction groups, let us consider sales transactions. The procedures used in processing sales transactions might include receiving a customer's purchase order, credit approval, shipment of merchandise, preparation of sales invoices, recording the sale, recording the account receivable, billing, and handling and recording the cash received from the customer.

A working knowledge of the client's system of internal control is needed throughout the audit; consequently the auditors should prepare a working paper fully describing their understanding of the system. Frequent reference to this working paper will be made to aid in designing audit procedures, ascertaining where documents are filed, familiarizing new audit staff with the system, and as a refresher in beginning next year's engagement.

The description of the system of internal control is usually prepared in the form of systems flowcharts. As an alternative to flowcharts, parts of the system may be described by written narratives or by the completion of specially designed questionnaires. All of these systems description working papers are illustrated and discussed in Chapter 5.

2. Test the system

Many internal control procedures are designed to prevent material errors in the financial statements. For example, the periodic reconciliation of bank statements to the accounting records should prevent material errors in the Cash account. By studying and evaluating the internal control procedures in force, the auditors can judge the risk of material error in various financial statement amounts.

Tests of compliance. Audit tests to determine whether key internal control procedures have been *operating effectively* throughout the period under audit are called *tests of compliance.* To illustrate a compliance test, consider the control procedure in which the accounting department accounts for the serial sequence of all shipping documents before preparing the related journal entries. The purpose of this control is to provide assurance that each shipment of merchandise is recorded in the accounting records. As a compliance test of this control procedure, the auditors might select a sample of shipping documents prepared at various times throughout the year and inspect the related journal entries.

Notice that a compliance test measures the effectiveness of a particular *control procedure*; it *does not* substantiate the dollar amount of an account balance. Actually, a particular control procedure may affect several financial statement amounts. If, for example, the test described above indicates that the accounting department does not account for the serial sequence of shipping documents, the auditors should be alert to the possibility of material errors in sales revenue, accounts receivable, cost of goods sold, and inventories.

The second standard of field work states:

> There is to be a *proper study* and *evaluation* of the existing internal control as a basis for reliance thereon and for the determination of the resultant extent of the tests to which auditing procedures are to be restricted. (Emphasis added.)

The first two steps of the audit process complete the auditors' study of internal control by providing them with an understanding of the system and with reasonable assurance that the procedures are in use and operating effectively. The next logical step in the audit process is for the auditors to evaluate the effectiveness of the system of internal control in preventing material errors in the financial statements.

3.   Evaluate the system

Auditors evaluate the system of internal control in order to determine the *nature, timing,* and *extent* of the audit procedures necessary to complete the audit. A major objective of internal control is to produce accurate and reliable accounting data. Thus, auditors should make an intensive investigation in areas for which internal control is weak; however, they are justified in performing less extensive auditing work in areas for which internal controls are strong. This process of deciding upon the matters to be emphasized during the audit, based upon the evaluation of internal control, means that the auditors will modify their audit program by expanding audit procedures in some areas and reducing them in others.

Not all weaknesses in internal control require action by the auditors. For example, poor internal control over a small petty cash fund is not likely to have a material impact upon the fairness of the financial statements. On the other hand, if one employee is responsible for initiating cash disbursements and also for signing checks, this combination of duties might result in material error in the financial statements and substantial defalcations. In each instance, the auditors must exercise professional judgment in determining whether to modify the nature and extent of their audit procedures and whether to make recommendations to the client for improving the system of internal control.

4.   Report to management

When serious deficiencies in internal control are discovered, the auditors should issue a recommendation letter to the client containing suggestions for overcoming the weaknesses. This *management letter* not only provides the client with valuable suggestions for improving internal control, but also serves to minimize the liability of the auditors in the event that a major defalcation or other serious loss is later discovered. The management letter should be issued as soon as possible after the auditors complete the evaluation of internal control. If the evaluation of internal control is completed before the balance sheet date, the auditors' recommendations may be implemented quickly enough to contribute to the reliability of the financial statements for the year under audit.

5. Complete the audit

Some procedures for verifying account balances may be performed early in the audit. However, only after completing the study and evaluation of internal control are the auditors in a position to determine fully the nature, timing, and extent of the procedures necessary to substantiate account balances.

Tests designed to substantiate the fairness of a specific financial statement item are termed *substantive tests*. Examples of substantive tests include confirmation of accounts receivable, observation of the taking of physical inventory, and determination of an appropriate *cutoff* of transactions to be included in the year under audit. In addition to conducting substantive tests, the auditors will perform other audit procedures in completing the audit, as, for example, investigating related party transactions that may warrant special disclosure.

6. Issue the report

The date upon which the last audit procedures are completed is termed the *last day of field work*. Although the audit report is dated as of the last day of field work, it is not actually issued on that date. Since the audit report represents an acceptance of considerable responsibility by the CPA firm, a partner must first review the working papers from the engagement to ascertain that a thorough examination has been completed. If the auditors are to issue anything other than an unqualified opinion of standard form, considerable care must go into the precise wording of the audit report. Consequently, the audit report is usually issued a week or more after the last day of field work.

Relationship between tests of compliance and substantive tests

Compliance tests provide auditors with evidence as to whether prescribed internal control procedures are in use and operating effectively. The results of these tests assist the auditors in evaluating the *likelihood* of material errors having occurred. Substantive tests, on the other hand, are designed to *detect* material errors if they exist in the financial statements. The amount of substantive testing done by the auditors is greatly influenced by their assessment of the likelihood that material errors exist.

To illustrate, assume that a client's procedures manual indicates that the finished goods warehouse is to be locked at all times and accessible only to authorized personnel. Through a compliance test consisting of inquiry and observation, the auditors learn that the warehouse often is unlocked and that several unauthorized employees regularly eat lunch there. As the client's internal control procedure is not operating properly, the auditors should recognize that the *risk* of inventory shortages is increased. However, the compliance test has *not* determined that an inventory shortage does, in fact, exist.

The principal substantive test to detect shortages of inventories is the auditors' observation of a physical inventory taken by the client. As part of this observation, the auditors make test counts of various items. In our case of the unlocked warehouse, the auditors' compliance test has shown that the system of internal control cannot be relied upon to prevent shortages. Therefore, they should increase the number of test counts in an effort to detect any shortage that might exist.

Timing of audit work

The value of audited financial statements is enhanced if the statements are available on a timely basis after the year-end. To facilitate an early release of the audit report, auditors normally begin the audit well before the balance sheet date. The period before the balance sheet date is termed the *interim period.* Audit work that can be performed during the interim period includes the study and evaluation of internal control, issuance of the management letter, and some of the substantive testing. Other substantive tests, such as confirmation of year-end bank balances, establishing a proper cutoff of transactions to be included in the year, and searching for unrecorded liabilities must necessarily be performed on or after the balance sheet date.

Performing audit work during the interim period has numerous advantages in addition to facilitating the timely release of the audited financial statements. The independent auditors may be able to evaluate internal control more effectively by observing and testing the system at various times throughout the year. Also, they will be on hand to advise the client whether complex transactions, such as business combinations, are being recorded in conformity with generally accepted accounting principles. Another advantage is that interim auditing creates a more uniform workload for CPA firms. With a large client, such as General Motors, the auditors may have office space within the client's buildings and carry on auditing procedures throughout the entire year.

Auditing terminology

The terms used to describe the various phases of audit work need to be precisely defined in order that audit programs, other working papers, and reports may be clearly understood. The following terms are among those most commonly employed; others will be defined as they are introduced in later chapters.

Analyze—the process of identifying and classifying for further study all the debit and credit entries contained in a ledger account. Accounts are analyzed in order to ascertain the nature of all the transactions that gave rise to the balance. An account such as Miscellaneous Expense, for example, requires analysis before any real understanding of its contents is possible.

Compare—the process of observing the similarity or variations of particular items in financial statements from one period to the next. If the comparison of a given type of revenue or expense for two successive years shows substantial change, further investigation to ascertain the cause of the change is necessary. The term may also be used by the auditor to mean ascertaining the agreement or lack of agreement between a journal entry and the corresponding entry in a ledger account, or between such related documents as a purchase order and an invoice.

Confirm—the process of proving the authenticity and accuracy of an account balance or entry by direct written communication with the debtor, creditor, or other party to the transaction. Obtaining proof from a source outside the client's records is thus a basic element of confirmation. It is standard practice to confirm bank balances by direct correspondence with the bank, and to confirm accounts receivable by direct correspondence with customers. The letters or forms sent to outsiders for this purpose are called *confirmation requests*.

Examine—to review critically or to investigate. An "examination of the financial statements" has the same meaning as an "audit of the financial statements."

Extend—to compute by multiplication. To extend the client's physical inventory listing is to multiply the quantity in units by the cost per unit. The resultant product is the extension.

Foot (or down-foot)—the process of proving the totals of vertical columns of figures; *cross-foot* means the proving of totals of figures appearing in horizontal rows. By footing and cross-footing schedules and records, the auditor derives positive assurance of their arithmetical accuracy.

Inspect—a careful reading or point-by-point review of a document or record. Other terms frequently used by the auditor to convey the same or a similar meaning are *scrutinize* and *examine*.

Reconcile—to establish agreement between two sets of independently maintained but related records. Thus, the ledger account for Cash in Bank is reconciled with the bank statement, and the home office record of shipments to a branch office is reconciled with the record of receipts maintained by the branch.

Test—to select and examine a representative sample from a population of similar items. If the sample is properly chosen, the results of this limited test should reveal the same characteristics as would be disclosed by an examination of the entire lot of items.

Trace—the process of following a transaction from one accounting record to another. The purchase of machinery, for example, might be verified by tracing the transaction from the voucher register to the check register.

Verify—to prove the validity and accuracy of records or to establish the existence and ownership of assets. Verification of plant and equipment, for example, might include analysis of ledger accounts, proof of footings, tracing of postings from journals, examination of documents authorizing acquisitions and retirements, and physical observation of the assets.

Voucher—a term used to describe any document supporting a transaction. Examples are petty cash receipts, receiving memoranda, and paid checks.

Vouching—establishing the accuracy and authenticity of entries in ledger accounts or other records by examining such supporting evidence of the transactions as invoices, paid checks, and other original papers.

KEY TERMS INTRODUCED OR EMPHASIZED IN CHAPTER 4

(Note: the preceding section of this chapter contains definitions of specific audit terminology that are not repeated in this glossary.)

Audit committee A committee composed of outside directors (members of the board of directors who are neither officers nor employees) charged with responsibility for maintaining contacts with the company's independent auditors.

Audit plan A broad overview of an audit engagement prepared in the planning stages of the engagement. Audit plans usually include such matters as the objectives of the engagement, nature of the work to be done, a time schedule for major audit work and completion of the engagement, and staffing requirements.

Audit program A detailed listing and explanation of the specific audit procedures to be performed in the course of an audit engagement. Audit programs provide a basis for assigning and scheduling audit work and for determining what work remains to be done. Audit programs are specially tailored to each engagement.

Audit trail A trail of evidence linking individual transactions to the summary totals in the financial statements. In a manual accounting system, this trial consists of source documents, journal entries, and ledger entries.

Compliance tests Audit procedures designed to provide reasonable assurance that prescribed control procedures within the client's system are (1) in use and (2) operating as planned.

Effective audit An audit that provides the auditors with sufficient evidence to express an opinion on the fairness of the financial statements.

Efficient audit An effective audit performed at the lowest possible cost to the client.

Engagement letter A formal letter sent by the auditors to the client at the beginning of an engagement summarizing the nature of the engagement, any limitations on the scope of audit work, work to be done by the client's staff, and the basis for the audit fee. The purpose of engagement letters is to avoid misunderstandings, and they are essential on nonaudit engagements as well as audits.

Interim period   The period under audit prior to the balance sheet date. Many audit procedures can be performed during the interim period to facilitate early issuance of the audit report.

Management letter   A report to managment containing the auditors' recommendations for correcting any deficiencies disclosed by the auditors' study and evaluation of internal control. In addition to providing management with useful information, a management letter may also help limit the auditors' liability in the event a control weakness subsequently results in a loss sustained by the client.

Predecessor auditor   The CPA firm that formerly served as auditor, but has resigned from the engagement or has been notified that its services have been terminated.

Professional corporation   A form of organization for professional practices that is now permitted in some states. Professional corporations enable practitioners to limit their exposure to legal liability and to obtain the tax benefits of incorporation. All shareholders and directors of a professional corporation must be licensed practitioners of the profession, and the corporation must carry adequate amounts of professional liability insurance.

Successor auditor   An auditor who has accepted an engagement or who has been invited to make a proposal for an engagement to replace the CPA firm that formerly served as auditors.

Substantive tests   Tests of account balances and transactions designed to detect any material errors in the financial statements. The nature, timing, and extent of substantive testing is determined by the auditors' study and evaluation of the client's system of internal control.

Time budget   An estimate of the time required to perform each step in the audit program.

GROUP I: REVIEW QUESTIONS

4–1.   Why are the national public accounting firms organized as partnerships?

4–2.   How does a professional corporation differ from the traditional corporation?

4–3.   Describe the various levels or grades of accounting personnel in a large public accounting firm.

4–4.   Distinguish between the responsibilities of a senior auditor and a staff assistant.

4–5.   List three of the more important responsibilities of a partner in a public accounting firm.

4–6.   Describe the activities of a professional development department in a large public accounting firm.

4–7.   List four types of court cases in which the CPA may serve as an expert witness.

4–8.   What information should a CPA firm seek in its investigation of a prospective client?

4–9.   Describe the preferred composition and role of the audit committee of a board of directors.

4–10.   What topics should be discussed in a preliminary meeting with a prospective audit client?

4–11.   Are auditors justified in relying upon the accuracy of working papers prepared for them by employees of the client?

4–12.   State the purpose and nature of an engagement letter.

4–13.   Define and differentiate between an *audit plan* and an *audit program*.

4–14.   Should a separate audit program be prepared for each audit engagement, or can a standard program be used for most engagements?

4–15.   "An audit program is desirable when new staff members are assigned to an engagement, but an experienced auditor should be able to conduct an examination without reference to an audit program." Do you agree? Discuss.

4–16.   Suggest some factors that might cause an audit engagement to exceed the original time estimate. Would the extra time be charged to the client?

4–17.   The following statements illustrate incorrect use of auditing terms. You are to substitute the proper terms for the italicized words.
  a. We *checked* the cash on hand.
  b. We *analyzed* the bank statement with the ledger balance for Cash in Bank.
  c. We *confirmed* the ledger account for Miscellaneous Expense by classifying and reviewing the various kinds of debit and credit entries in the account.
  d. We *vouched* the accounts receivable by direct written communication with customers.
  e. We *reconciled* the minutes of directors' meetings for the entire period under audit.

4–18.   Define and differentiate between a compliance test and a substantive test.

GROUP II: QUESTIONS REQUIRING ANALYSIS

4–19.   Morgan, CPA, is approached by a prospective audit client who wants to engage Morgan to perform an audit for the current year. In prior years this prospective client was audited by another CPA. Identify the specific procedures that Morgan should follow in deciding whether or not to accept this client. (AICPA, adapted)

4–20.   How does a knowledge of the client's business help the auditor in planning and performing an examination in accordance with generally accepted auditing standards? (AICPA adapted)

4–21.   Arthur Samuels, CPA, agreed to perform an audit of a new client engaged in the manufacture of power tools. After some preliminary discussion of the purposes of the audit and the basis for determination of the audit fee, Samuels asked to be taken on a comprehensive guided tour of the client's plant facilities. Explain specific ways that the knowledge gained by Samuels during the plant tour may help in planning and conducting the audit.

4– 22. A CPA has been asked to audit the financial statements of a publicly held company for the first time. All preliminary discussions have been completed between the CPA, the company, the predecessor auditor, and all other necessary parties. The CPA is now preparing an engagement letter.

List the items that should be included in the engagement letter, and describe the benefits derived from preparing an engagement letter. (AICPA, adapted)

4– 23. The audit plan, the audit program, and the time budget are three important working papers prepared early in an audit. What functions do these working papers serve in the auditor's compliance with generally accepted auditing standards? Discuss.

4– 24. The first standard of field work requires, in part, that "the work is to be adequately planned." An effective tool that aids the auditor in adequately planning the work is an audit program.

What is an audit program and what purposes does it serve? (AICPA, adapted)

4– 25. How can a CPA make use of the preceding year's audit working papers in a recurring examination? (AICPA, adapted)

4– 26. Should a CPA accept a request to serve as an expert witness for the plaintiff in a case involving another CPA as defendant? Explain.

4– 27. Ann Knox, president of Knox Corporation, is a close friend of a client of yours. In response to a strong recommendation of your audit work by her friend, Ann Knox has retained you to make an audit of Knox Corporation's financial statements. Although you have had extensive auditing experience, you have not previously audited a company in the same line of business as Knox Corporation.

Ann Knox informs you that she would like to have an estimate of the cost of the audit. List all the steps you would take in order to have an adequate basis for providing an estimate of the audit fee for the Knox Corporation engagement. (AICPA, adapted)

4– 28. Select the best answer for each of the following. Explain the reasons for your selection.

  a. To emphasize auditor independence from management, many corporations follow the practice of—

  (1) Appointing a partner of the CPA firm conducting the examination to the corporation's audit committee.

  (2) Establishing a policy prohibiting social contact between employees of the company and the staff of the independent auditor.

  (3) Requesting that a representative of the CPA firm be on hand at the annual stockholders' meeting.

  (4) Having the independent auditor report to an audit committee of outside members of the board of directors.

  b. When a CPA is approached to perform an audit for the first time, the CPA should make inquiries of the predecessor auditor. This is a necessary procedure because the predecessor auditor may be able

to provide information that will assist the successor auditor in determining whether—
- (1) The predecessor's work should be utilized.
- (2) The company follows a policy of rotating its auditors.
- (3) The predecessor is aware of any weaknesses in internal control.
- (4) The engagement should be accepted.

c. One step in the audit process involves preparing a written description of the client's system of internal control. The next step should be—
- (1) Determine the extent of audit work necessary to complete the audit.
- (2) Gather enough evidence to determine if the system of internal control is functioning as described.
- (3) Write a letter to management describing the weaknesses in the system of internal control.
- (4) Form a final judgment on the effectiveness of internal control.

d. Which of the following portions of an audit may *not* be completed before the balance sheet date?
- (1) Compliance testing.
- (2) Issuance of a management letter.
- (3) Substantive testing.
- (4) Evaluation of the system of internal control. (AICPA, adapted)

GROUP III: PROBLEMS

4–29. For many years the financial and accounting community has recognized the importance and use of audit committees and has endorsed their formation.

At this time the use of audit committees has become widespread. Independent auditors have become increasingly involved with audit committees and consequently have become familiar with their nature and function.

Required:
a. Describe what an audit committee is.
b. Identify the reasons audit committees have been formed and are currently in operation.
c. What are the functions of an audit committee? (AICPA, adapted)

4–30. In a discussion between Peters and Ferrel, two auditing students, Peters made the following statement:

"A CPA is a professional person who is licensed by the state for the purpose of providing an independent expert opinion on the fairness of financial statements. To maintain an attitude of mental independence and objectivity in all phases of audit work, it is advisable that the CPA not fraternize with client personnel. The CPA should be courteous but reserved and dignified at all times. Indulging in social contacts with clients outside of business hours will make it more difficult to be firm and objective if the CPA finds evidence of fraud or of unsound accounting practices."

Ferrel replied as follows:

"You are 50 years behind the times, Peters. An auditor and a client are both human beings. The auditor needs the cooperation of the client to do a good job; you're much more likely to get cooperation if you're relaxed and friendly rather than being cold and impersonal. Having a few beers or going to a football game with a client won't keep the CPA from being independent. It will make the working relationship a lot more comfortable, and will probably cause the client to recommend the CPA to other business people who need auditing services. In other words, the approach you're recommending should be called 'How to Avoid Friends and Alienate Clients.' I will admit, though, that with so many women entering public accounting and other women holding executive positions in business, a few complications may arise when auditor-client relations get pretty relaxed."

Evaluate the opposing views expressed by Peters and Ferrel.

4–31. Valley Finance Company opened four personal loan offices in neighboring cities on January 2. Small cash loans are made to borrowers who repay the principal with interest in monthly installments over a period not exceeding two years. Ralph Norris, president of the company, uses one of the offices as a central office and visits the other offices periodically for supervision and internal auditing purposes.

Required:

Assume that you agreed to examine Valley Finance Company's financial statements for the year ended December 31. No scope limitations were imposed.

a. How would you determine the scope necessary to complete your examination satisfactorily? Discuss.

b. Would you be responsible for the discovery of fraud in this examination? Discuss. (AICPA, adapted)

4–32. You are invited by John Bray, the president of Cheviot Corporation, to discuss with him the possibility of your conducting an audit of the company. The corporation is a small, closely held manufacturing organization that appears to be expanding. No previous audit has been made by independent certified public accountants. Your discussions with Bray include a review of the recent monthly financial statements, inspection of the accounting records, and review of policies with the chief accountant. You also are taken on a guided tour of the plant by the president. He then makes the following statement:

"Before making definite arrangements for an audit, I would like to know about how long it will take and about how much it will cost. I want quality work and expect to pay a fair price, but since this is our first experience with independent auditors, I would like a full explanation as to how the cost of the audit is determined. Will you please send me a memorandum covering these points?"

Write the memorandum requested by John Bray.

4–33. McKay Company found its sales rising rapidly after the opening of a large military installation in its territory. To finance the increase in accounts receivable and the larger inventory required by the increased volume of sales, the company decided for the first time in its history to seek a bank loan. The president of the local bank informed McKay Company that an audit by a CPA would be a necessary prerequisite to approval of the loan application. Jill McKay, sole proprietor of the business, engaged the newly formed CPA firm of Marshall and Wills to conduct the audit and provide the report requested by the bank. McKay Company had not previously been audited.

From the beginning of the audit engagement, nothing seemed to go well. Robert Corning, the staff accountant sent out by Marshall and Wills to begin the work, found that the accounting records were not up to date and not in balance. He worked for a week assisting the McKay Company accountant to get the accounting records in shape. The problem was not reported to the partners until the following week because Marshall was out of town and Wills was suddenly taken ill. In the meantime, the McKay accountant complained to Jill McKay that the auditor was impeding his work.

After the audit work was well under way during the second week, McKay refused to permit the auditor to confirm accounts receivable, which were the largest current asset. She also stated that the pressure of current business prevented interrupting operations for the taking of a physical inventory. Corning protested that confirmation of accounts receivable and observation of a physical inventory were mandatory auditing procedures, but Jill McKay rejected this protest.

Upon his return to town Marshall was informed of the difficulties and went immediately to McKay's office. He explained to McKay that the omission of work on receivables and inventories would force the auditors to disclaim an opinion on the financial statements taken as a whole. McKay became quite angry; she asserted that she could borrow the money she needed from her mother-in-law and thereby eliminate any need for bankers or auditors in her business. McKay ordered Marshall and Corning off the premises and asserted that she would pay them nothing. Marshall replied that he had the McKay Company general ledger and other accounting records in his own office, and that he would not return them until he received payment in full for all time expended, at the firm's regular per diem rates for Corning plus a charge for his own time.

Evaluate the actions taken by Marshall and Wills in this case and advise Marshall on the action to be taken at this point.

5

Internal control

Our consideration of internal control has three major objectives: first, to explain the meaning and significance of internal control; second, to outline the steps required to create and maintain strong internal control; and third, to show how auditors go about their study and evaluation of internal control. No attempt is made in this chapter to present in detail the internal control procedures applicable to particular kinds of assets or to particular types of transactions, such as purchases or sales. Detailed information along these lines will be found in succeeding chapters as each phase of the auditors' examination is presented.

The meaning of internal control

Many people interpret the term *internal control* as the steps taken by a business to prevent employee fraud. Actually, such measures are rather a small part of internal control. The basic purpose of internal control is to *promote the efficient operation of an organization.* The system of internal control consists of all measures employed by an organization to (1) safeguard assets from waste, fraud, and inefficient use; (2) promote accuracy and reliability in the accounting records; (3) encourage and measure compliance with company policies; and (4) evaluate the efficiency of operations. In short, internal control consists of all measures taken to provide management with assurance that everything is functioning as it should.

Internal control extends beyond the accounting and financial functions; its scope is company-wide and touches all activities of the organization. It includes the methods by which top management delegates authority and assigns responsibility for such functions as selling, purchasing, accounting, and production. Internal control also includes the program for preparing, verifying, and distributing to various levels of supervision those current reports and analyses that enable executives to maintain control over the variety of activities and functions that constitute a large corporate enterprise. The use of budgetary techniques, production standards, inspection laboratories, time and motion studies, and employee training programs involve engineers and many other technicians far removed from accounting and financial activities; yet all of these devices are part of the mechanism now conceived as a system of internal control.

This broad, sweeping concept of internal control is most significant when viewed against the backdrop of a large nationwide industrial organization, for internal control has developed into a technique of vital importance in enabling management of large complex enterprises to function efficiently. Since internal control has attained greatest significance in large-scale business organizations, the greater part of the discussion in this chapter is presented in terms of the large corporation. A separate section is presented at the end of the chapter, however, dealing with the problem of achieving internal control in a small business.

Internal accounting controls versus internal administrative controls

Auditors are primarily interested in internal controls of an accounting nature—those controls bearing directly upon the dependability of the accounting records and the financial statements. For example, preparation of monthly bank reconciliations by an employee not authorized to issue checks or handle cash is an *internal accounting control* that increases the probability that cash transactions are presented fairly in the accounting records and financial statements.

Some internal controls have no bearing on the financial statements and consequently are not of direct interest to the independent public accountant. Controls of this category are often referred to as *internal administrative controls.* Management is interested in maintaining strong internal control over factory operations and sales activities as well as over accounting and financial functions. Accordingly, management will establish administrative controls to provide operational efficiency and adherence to prescribed policies in all departments of the organization.

An example of an internal control device of an administrative nature is a requirement that all employees entering a certain work area wear protective hardhats. Important though such a control device may be from a safety standpoint, it is not directly related to the dependability of the financial statements. Consequently, the auditors would probably not concern themselves with determining whether employees actually comply with this policy.

In *Statement on Auditing Standards No. 1,* the AICPA provided the following definitions to assist in the distinction between accounting and administrative internal controls:

> *Administrative control* includes, but is not limited to, the plan of organization and the procedures and records that are concerned with the decision processes leading to management's authorization of transactions. Such authorization is a management function directly associated with the responsibility for achieving the objectives of the organization and is the starting point for establishing accounting control of transactions.
>
> *Accounting control* comprises the plan of organization and the procedures and records that are concerned with the safeguarding of assets and the reliability of financial records and consequently are designed to provide reasonable assurance that:
>
> *a*. Transactions are executed in accordance with management's general or specific authorization.
>
> *b*. Transactions are recorded as necessary (1) to permit preparation of financial statements in conformity with generally accepted accounting principles or any other criteria applicable to such statements and (2) to maintain accountability for assets.
>
> *c*. Access to assets is permitted only in accordance with management's authorization.
>
> *d*. The recorded accountability for assets is compared with the existing assets at reasonable intervals and appropriate action is taken with respect to any differences.

The auditors' study and evaluation of internal control will always include review and testing of major accounting controls. The review of internal controls of a purely administrative nature does not ordinarily fall within the responsibility of the independent auditors, whose objective is to express an opinion on the fairness of financial statements.

The need for internal control

The long-run trend for corporations to evolve into organizations of gigantic size and scope, including a great variety of specialized technical operations and numbering employees in tens of thousands, has made it impossible for corporate executives to exercise personal, firsthand supervision of operations. No longer able to rely upon personal observation as a means of appraising operating results and financial position, the corporate executive has, of necessity, come to depend upon a stream of accounting and statistical reports. These reports summarize current happenings and conditions throughout the enterprise; the units of measurement employed are not only dollars but labor-hours, material weights, customer calls, employee terminations, and a host of other denominators.

The information carried by this stream of reports enables management to control and direct the enterprise. It keeps management informed as to whether company policy is being carried out, whether governmental regulations are being observed, and whether financial position is sound, operations profitable, and interdepartmental relations harmonious.

Business decisions of almost every kind are based at least in part on accounting data. These decisions range from such minor matters as authorizing overtime work or purchasing office supplies to such major issues as a shift from one product to another or making a choice between leasing or buying a new plant. The system of internal accounting control provides assurance to management of the dependability of the accounting data used in making these decisions.

Decisions made by management become company policy. To be effective, this policy must be communicated throughout the company and consistently followed. Internal control aids in securing compliance with company policy. Management also has a direct responsibility of maintaining accounting records and producing financial statements that are adequate and reliable. Internal control provides assurance that this responsibility is being met.

To the independent public accountants, internal control is of equal significance. The quality of the internal controls in force, more than any other factor, determines the pattern of their examination. The independent auditors study and evaluate the system of internal control in order to determine the extent and direction of the other auditing work necessary to permit them to express an opinion as to the fairness of the financial statements.

Foreign Corrupt Practices Act

In the mid-1970s, a number of American corporations acknowledged having made payments (which could be interpreted as bribes) to officials in foreign countries. In most cases the payments were legal under the laws of the countries in which they were made, but they were not in accordance with American business ethics. In some instances, these questionable payments were made without the authorization or knowledge of top executives of the corporations involved.

In the Foreign Corrupt Practices Act of 1977, Congress ordered an end to this practice. Payments to foreign officials for the purpose of securing business were specifically prohibited. However, the act goes far beyond the issue of illegal payments and requires *every corporation under the jurisdiction of the SEC to maintain a system of internal accounting control that will provide reasonable assurance that transactions are executed only with the knowledge and authorization of management.* In addition, the act requires the system of internal control to limit the use of corporate assets to those purposes approved by management. Finally, the act calls for accounting records to be reconciled at reasonable intervals with assets actually on hand. These requirements are designed to prevent the creation of secret slush funds or other misuses of corporate resources. Violations of the act can result in fines of up to $1 million and imprisonment of the responsible individuals. Thus, a strong system of internal accounting control, long viewed as essential to the operation of a large organization, is now required by federal law.

MEANS OF ACHIEVING INTERNAL ACCOUNTING CONTROL

Systems of internal control vary significantly from one organization to the next. The specific control features in any system depend upon such factors as the size, organizational structure, nature of operations, and objectives of the organization for which the system was designed. Yet certain factors are essential to satisfactory internal control in almost any large-scale organization. These factors include a logical plan of organization, a well-designed accounting structure, an internal audit function, and the quality and training of personnel.

Plan of organization

An *organization plan* refers to the division of authority, responsibilities, and duties among members of an organization. A well-designed organization plan is a first step to assure that transactions are executed in conformity with company policies, to enhance the efficiency of operations, to safeguard assets, and to promote the reliability of accounting data. These objectives may be achieved in large part through adequate separation of responsibilities for (1) initiation or approval of transactions, (2) custody of assets, and (3) record keeping.

Internal control over transactions. A fundamental concept of accounting control is that *no one person or department should handle all aspects of a transaction from beginning to end.* If management is to direct the activities of a business according to plan, every transaction should involve five steps; it should be *authorized, initiated, approved, executed,* and *recorded.* Accounting control will be enhanced if each of these steps is performed by relatively independent employees or departments. No single department will then be in a position to complete a transaction that has not been reviewed, approved, and recorded by other departments.

A credit sales transaction may be used to illustrate an appropriate division of responsibilities. Top management of a company may authorize the sale of merchandise at specified credit terms to customers who meet certain criteria. Orders from customers are *initiated* in the sales department and sent to the credit department for *approval.* The credit department reviews the transaction to ascertain that the extension of credit and terms of sale are in compliance with company policies. Once the sale is approved, the shipping department *executes* the transaction by obtaining the merchandise from the inventory stores department and shipping it to the customer. The accounting department uses copies of the documentation created by the sales, credit, and shipping departments as a basis for *recording* the transaction and billing the customer.

When responsibilities for authorizing, initiating, approving, executing, and recording transactions are separated in this manner, no one department can initiate and complete an unauthorized transaction. The possibility of unrecorded transactions is greatly reduced because of the documentation that must be prepared as information concerning the transaction moves from one department to another. (Sequential numbering of this documentation will assist the accounting department in determining that all transactions have been accounted for.) Also, division of responsibilities permits specialization of labor, which should contribute to the overall efficiency of operations.

Accountability for assets. A traditional step in achieving internal accounting control is separation of the accounting function from custody of related assets. When the accounting and custodial departments are relatively independent, the work of each department serves to verify the accuracy of the work of the other. Periodic comparisons should be made of accounting records and the physical assets on hand. Investigation as to the cause of any discrepancies will uncover weaknesses either in procedures for safeguarding assets or in maintaining the related accounting records. If the accounting records were not independent of the custodial department, the records could be manipulated to conceal waste, loss, or theft of the related assets.

Illustrative case. A manufacturer of golf clubs operated a large storeroom containing thousands of sets of golf clubs ready for shipment. Detailed perpetual inventory records were maintained by the employee in charge of the storeroom. A shortage of several sets of clubs developed as a result of theft by another employee who had acquired an unauthorized key to the storeroom. The employee responsible for the storeroom discovered the discrepancy between the clubs in stock and the quantities of clubs as shown by the records. Fearing criticism of his record keeping, he changed the inventory records to agree with the quantities on hand. The thefts continued, and large losses were sustained before the shortages were discovered. If the inventory records had been maintained by someone not responsible for physical custody of the merchandise, there would have been no incentive or opportunity to conceal a shortage by falsifying the records.

Figure 5–1 illustrates the use of an independently maintained record to establish accountability for assets. It is not essential that *all three* parties in the diagram (A, B, and C) be employees of the company; one or more may be an outside party or a mechanical device. For example, if A is a bank with custody of cash on deposit, B would be the company employees maintaining records of cash receipts and disbursements, and

===== Figure 5–1
Establishing accountability for assets

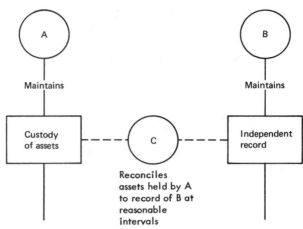

C might be a computer program that performs periodic bank reconciliations. Or, if A is a salesclerk with custody of cash receipts from sales, B
could be a cash register with a locked-in tape, and C could be the
departmental supervisor. Regardless of the nature of the parties involved, the principle remains the same: accounting records should be
maintained independently of custody of the related assets and should
be compared at reasonable intervals to asset quantities on hand.

Efficiency of operations. An effective organization plan should
enhance the efficiency of operations as well as contribute to internal
accounting control. When two or more departments participate in every
transaction, the work of one department is reviewed by another. Also,
each department has an incentive to demand efficient performance
from the others.

A typical purchase transaction illustrates how good organizational
structure enhances both internal control and the efficiency of operations. If the purchasing department fails to place a purchase order
promptly upon receipt of a purchase requisition from the material
stores department, the latter department may find itself without materials required by production departments. The material stores department, therefore, has an incentive to follow up purchase requisitions
and to demand prompt action by the purchasing agent. If the purchasing department orders an excessive or insufficient quantity, the responsibility for the error will be pinned down by reference to the purchase
requisition, the purchase order, and the receiving report, each of which
is prepared by an independent department.

Errors made by the receiving department in counting goods received
will normally be brought to light by the accounting department when it

compares the receiving report with the vendor's invoice and the purchase order. If defective materials are accepted by the receiving department, responsibility will be placed on the negligent department by personnel of the storeskeeping or production departments, which must utilize the materials in question.

On the other hand, if the various functional activities are not segregated by independent departments and all aspects of a purchase transaction are handled by employees reporting to the purchasing agent, then top management is less likely to learn of specific inefficiencies in purchasing activities.

Organizational independence of departments. Internal control is achieved largely through the organizational independence of accounting, operating, and custodial departments. This degree of independence is usually obtained by having designated department heads who are evaluated on the basis of the performance of their respective departments. The top executives of the major departments should be of equal rank and should report directly to the president or to an executive vice president. The partial organization chart in Figure 5–2 illustrates such an arrangement. If, for example, the controller were a line subordinate to the vice president of production, the organizational independence of the accounting department would be greatly impaired.

Illustrative case. During an examination of the Foster Company, the auditors' study of organizational lines of authority and their use of an internal control questionnaire disclosed that the receiving department personnel were under the direction of the purchasing agent. Accounts payable department employees had also been instructed to accept informal memoranda from the purchasing agent as evidence of receipt of merchandise and propriety of invoices.

Because of this deficiency in internal control, the auditors made a very thorough examination of purchase invoices and came across a number of large December invoices from one supplier bearing the notation: "Subject to adjustment at time of delivery of merchandise." Investigation of these transactions disclosed that the merchandise had not yet been delivered, but the invoices had been paid. The purchasing agent explained that he had requested the advance billing in an effort to reduce taxable income for the year under audit, during which profits had been higher than usual. Further investigation revealed that the purchasing agent held a substantial personal interest in the supplier making the advance billings, and that top management of the client company was not aware of this conflict of interests.

Responsibilities of finance and accounting departments. Finance and accounting are the two departments most directly involved in the financial affairs of a business enterprise. The division of responsibilities between these departments illustrates the separation of the accounting function from operations and also from the custody of assets. Under the direction of the *treasurer,* the finance department is responsible for financial operations and custody of liquid assets. Activities of this department include planning future cash requirements, establishing customer credit policies, and arranging to meet the short-

Figure 5–2
Partial organization chart

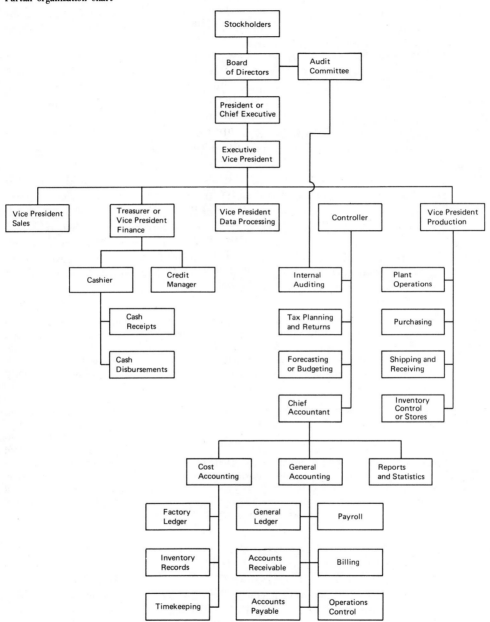

and long-term financing needs of the business. In addition, the finance department has custody of bank accounts and other liquid assets, invests idle cash, handles cash receipts, and makes cash disbursements. In short, it is the finance department that *conducts* financial activities.

The accounting department, under the authority of the *controller,* is responsible for all accounting functions and the design and implementation of internal control. With respect to financial activity, the accounting department *records* financial transactions, but does not handle financial assets. Accounting records establish *accountability* over assets, as well as providing the information necessary for financial reports, tax returns, and daily operating decisions. With respect to internal control, the accounting department maintains the independent records with which quantities of assets and operating results are compared. Often, this reconciliation function is performed by the *operations control group* or some other subdepartment within accounting.

Many of the subdepartments often found within accounting are illustrated in Figure 5–2. It is important for many of these subdepartments to be relatively independent of one another. For example, if the operations control group reconciles assets on hand to the accounting records, it is essential that the operations control personnel not maintain those records. Therefore, each subdepartment shown in the organization chart usually has its own employees and supervisor.

The accounting structure

To achieve internal control through separation of duties, the accounting system must be able to measure the performance and efficiency of the individual organizational units. An accounting system with this capability should include:

1. Adequate internal documentation to focus responsibility.
2. A chart of accounts classified in accordance with the responsibilities of individual supervisors and key employees.
3. A manual of accounting policies and procedures, and flowcharts depicting the established methods of processing transactions.
4. A financial forecast consisting of a detailed forecast of operations with provision for prompt reporting and analysis of variations between actual performance and budgetary standards.

Adequate documentation. A system of well-designed forms and documents is necessary to create a record of the activities of all departments. For example, how is the accounting department notified when a credit sale takes place? Usually notification is through a sales ticket prepared by the salesclerk when the sale occurs. Without such documentation, there would be virtually no record or control over the activities of the operating departments. Internally created documents are also used to create accountability for assets transferred from one department to another. Copies of these documents provide a trail of evidence that focuses responsibility for any chortages that may develop as the assets move from department to department.

The reliability of internally created documents is increased if two parties with *opposing interests* participate in preparation of the document. For example, when the stores department releases material to production, a *production order* is initialed by employees of each department. The stores department has an incentive to ascertain that quantities shown on the production order are not *understated*; otherwise, the stores department will be held responsible for goods no longer on hand. The production department, on the other hand, has an incentive to see that materials charged to its operations are not *overstated*.

Serial numbering of documents.   An internal control device of wide applicability is the use of serial numbers on documents. Serial numbers provide control over the number of documents issued. Checks, tickets, sales invoices, purchase orders, stock certificates, and many other business papers can be controlled in this manner. For some documents, such as checks, it may be desirable to account for every number of the series by a monthly or weekly inspection of the documents issued. For other situations, as in the case of serially numbered admission tickets, control may be achieved by noting the last serial number issued each day, and thereby computing the total value of tickets issued during the day. Adequate safekeeping and numerical control should be maintained at all times for unissued prenumbered documents.

Chart of accounts.   A chart of accounts is a classified listing of all accounts in use, accompanied by a detailed description of the purpose and content of each. How many accounts are needed? The number will depend upon the extent to which a company uses the accounts as a means of holding individuals responsible for custody of assets, for earning revenue, and for incurring expenses.

In too many cases the classification of accounts is looked upon as a mere listing of the items to be separately enumerated in the financial statements. A better approach is to view the chart of accounts as an internal control device consisting of separate accounts for recording the *responsibilities* of individual supervisors and employees. For example, a petty cash fund should be in the custody of a single employee; a separate account for such a fund is required if the accounts are to measure individual responsibility.

The principle of relating accounts and personal responsibility is by no means limited to the custody of assets; it is equally applicable to revenue and expense control. For every manager charged with obtaining revenue or incurring expense, separate revenue and expense accounts should be established to permit a clear measurement of the manager's performance. Just as machine operators may be held responsible for units of output, so should the department managers be held to account for the performance of the function entrusted to them.

Use of a chart of accounts that classifies operating results by responsible decision-makers is often termed *responsibility accounting.* A prerequisite to responsibility accounting is adequate internal documentation to focus responsibility for operating results. Responsibility accounting is hindered by any vagueness or inconsistency in the plan of organization and lines of responsibility. It is commonly found that for a given type of expense, such as repairs, several individuals have authority to make commitments; hence no one individual can be held responsible for excessive expenditures in this direction. Careful analysis of the chart of accounts and application of the test of clear segregation of individual responsibilities will often indicate a need of revision in lines of organizational responsibility. Even under the best of organization plans, certain expenses probably will not be clearly assignable to a single responsible individual. Obsolescence of plant and equipment, cost of performing work under product guarantees, and expenses associated with strikes or other industrial disputes are examples of such expenses. These expenses often result from policy decisions rather than from departmental operations and therefore should be segregated and clearly labeled.

Although classification of accounts along lines of individual responsibility is an essential step in achieving control of costs, it does not serve the purpose of providing management with cost figures for individual products. The techniques of cost accounting must be utilized for a reclassification, or distribution, of costs from the primary classification to a product basis.

Manual of accounting policies and procedures.   Every business organization, large or small, has a body of established methods of initiating, recording, and summarizing transactions. These procedures should be stated in writing, and in the form of flowcharts in a loose-leaf manual, and should be revised as the pattern of operating routines changes. If accounting procedures are clearly stated in writing, the policies set by management can be enforced efficiently and consistently. Uniform handling of like transactions is essential to the production of reliable accounting records and reports, and uniformity in the handling of transactions is possible only when definite patterns for processing routine transactions are made known to all employees.

Financial forecasts.   A financial forecast for an enterprise is an estimate of the most probable financial position, results of operations, and changes in financial position for one or more future periods.[1] It establishes definite goals and thus provides management with a yardstick for evaluating actual performance.

---

[1] *Guidelines for Systems for the Preparation of Financial Forecasts*, AICPA (New York, 1975), p. 3.

The simplest and most common application of forecasting is the cash forecast, in which the treasurer estimates, for perhaps a year in advance, the flow of cash receipts and disbursements classified by source of receipt and object of disbursement. The principal aim of the cash forecast is to ensure that sufficient funds are available at all times to meet maturing liabilities. In addition, the scheduling of anticipated receipts from all sources makes fraud involving the withholding of receipts more susceptible of detection. Similarly, the detailed planning of cash disbursements discourages the potential embezzler from any attempt to falsify the records of cash disbursements.

A more comprehensive forecasting program would include:

1. A sales forecast, consisting of estimated sales by product and by territory, based on analysis of past sales performance, current trends of prices and business volume, and appraisal of new products, territories, and distribution methods.
2. A production forecast, specifying the quantities necessary to meet the sales forecast, and detailing the quantity and cost of material, labor, and manufacturing overhead for given levels of output.
3. A distribution cost forecast, consisting of estimates of costs of selling, advertising, delivery, credit and collection, and other expenses appropriate to the estimated sales volume, classified by product or territory, and as variable, semivariable, and fixed.
4. A plant and equipment forecast, consisting of estimates of amounts required for the acquisition of new equipment and the maintenance of presently owned equipment.
5. A cash forecast, including an estimate of cash receipts and disbursements, short-term investments, and borrowing and repayments.
6. An estimated income statement, balance sheet, and statement of changes in financial position for the period encompassed by the forecast.

The completed forecast is summarized by preparing estimated financial statements for the coming year, supported by detailed analyses for segments of the business, such as territories, divisions, or branches. During the year monthly income statements should be prepared comparing actual operating results with forecast figures. These statements should be accompanied by explanations of all significant variations between forecast and actual results, with a definite fixing of responsibility for such variances.

In brief, a forecast is a control device, involving the establishment of definite standards of performance throughout the business. Failure to attain these standards is promptly called to the attention of appropriate levels of management through variance reports.

Internal auditing—its relationship to internal control

Another basic component of strong internal control is an internal auditing staff. The job of internal auditors is to investigate and appraise the system of internal control and the efficiency with which the various units of the business are performing their assigned functions, and to report their findings and make recommendations to top management. As representatives of top management, the internal auditors are interested in determining whether each branch or department has a clear understanding of its assignment, whether it is adequately staffed, maintains good records, protects cash and inventories and other assets properly, cooperates harmoniously with other departments, and in general carries out effectively the function provided for in the overall plan and organization of the business.

Internal auditors are *not* responsible for performing routine control procedures, such as reconciling bank statements, balancing subsidiary ledgers, or verifying the mathematical accuracy of invoices. These functions are usually performed by a separate unit within the accounting department, such as the operations control group shown in Figure 5–2. Internal auditors provide a higher level of internal control; they design and carry out audit procedures that test the efficiency of virtually all aspects of company operations.

Internal auditors contrasted with independent auditors. The independent auditors' objective is the expression of an opinion on the client's financial statements; the internal auditors' objective is not to verify financial statements, but to aid management in achieving the most efficient administration of the business. To this end, they appraise the effectiveness of internal controls in various departments, branches, or other organizational units of the company. Internal auditors' work is not limited to accounting controls; they also monitor administrative controls.

The similarities between independent audits and internal auditing pertain to mechanics and techniques, not to objectives and end results. Both internal auditors and independent auditors examine accounting records and procedures and prepare working papers, but the reasons motivating the two lines of work and the end results obtained are entirely different.

Audits by independent CPAs are termed *compliance audits* because the CPAs are primarily interested in determining whether the financial statements are in compliance with generally accepted accounting principles. Examinations by internal auditors are often called *operational audits* because the auditors are concerned with the *effect* of the existing policies and procedures upon the efficiency of operations. For example, in reviewing credit policies, independent CPAs are concerned primarily with determining the adequacy of the allowance for doubtful accounts. Internal auditors, on the other hand, are interested in whether employees are complying with existing policies and procedures and whether the existing policies and procedures might be changed to enhance the efficiency of operations. The end result of an operational audit is a report to management containing recommendations for improving operational performance. (Operational auditing is discussed further in Chapter 19.)

In companies that stress growth through acquisitions and mergers, the internal auditors may perform investigations of companies being considered for acquisition. In such an assignment, the role of the internal auditors is similar to that of an independent auditor. The investigation consists of gathering evidence to substantiate or disprove the other company's representations as to the collectibility of receivables, valuation of inventories, loss contingencies, volume of sales, trend of earnings, and related data in the financial statements.

Independence of internal auditors.   Since internal auditors are employees of the company they serve, they obviously cannot achieve the CPAs' independence in fact and in appearance. However, if internal auditors report directly to the audit committee of the board of directors, to the president, or other senior officer, they may achieve a greater degree of freedom, independence, and objectivity than if they report to an official of lesser rank in the organization.

Limitations of internal control

Internal control can do much to protect against fraud and assure the reliability of accounting data. Still, it is important to recognize the existence of inherent limitations in any system of internal control. Errors may be made in the performance of control procedures as a result of carelessness, misunderstanding of instructions, or other human factors. As dramatically illustrated in the Equity Funding management fraud, top management may circumvent internal control. Also, those control procedures dependent upon separation of duties may be circumvented by collusion among employees.

The extent of the internal controls adopted by a business is limited by cost considerations; to maintain a system of internal control so perfect as to make any fraud impossible would usually cost more than was warranted by the threat of loss from fraud. Particularly in a small business, it is often impracticable to separate completely the custody of assets from the function of record keeping. When a business has only a few employees, the opportunities for subdivision of duties are obviously somewhat limited. Despite these limitations, however, many actual defalcations could have been prevented or disclosed at an early stage if even the most simple and inexpensive of internal control practices had been followed.

Fidelity bonds

Strong internal control is not a guarantee against losses from dishonest employees. Neither is it possible to prevent fraud by emphasizing the selection of trustworthy employees. It is often the most trusted employees who engineer the biggest embezzlements. The fact that they are so highly trusted explains why they have access to cash, securities, and company records and are in a position that makes embezzlement possible.

Fidelity bonds are a form of insurance in which a bonding company agrees to reimburse an employer, within limits, for losses attributable to theft or embezzlement by bonded employees. Most employers require employees handling cash or other negotiable assets to be bonded. Individual fidelity bonds may be obtained by concerns with only a few employees; larger concerns may prefer to obtain a blanket fidelity bond covering many employees. Before issuing fidelity bonds, underwriters investigate thoroughly the past records of the employees to be bonded. This service offers added protection by preventing the employment of persons with dubious records in positions of trust. Bonding companies are much more likely to prosecute fraud cases vigorously than are employers; general awareness of this fact is another deterrent against dishonesty of the part of bonded employees.

Fidelity bonds are neither part of the system of internal control nor a substitute for internal control. If internal control is weak, losses may accumulate undiscovered until they exceed the fidelity coverage. Theft or defalcation must be discovered and the loss proved before recovery can be obtained from a bonding company. Moreover, inadequate internal control often causes other losses, as when management places reliance on inaccurate and misleading accounting data.

THE AUDITORS' REVIEW OF INTERNAL CONTROL

The generally accepted auditing standards set forth by the AICPA were presented in Chapter 1. The second standard of field work reads as follows:

> There is to be a proper study and evaluation of the existing internal control as a basis for reliance thereon and for the determination of the resultant extent of the tests to which auditing procedures are to be restricted.

In formulating this standard, the AICPA recognized that it is not possible for auditors to verify all, or even a major portion, of the great number of transactions comprising a year's operations in a large enterprise. In order that auditors make the most effective and searching investigation possible within reasonable time limits, they must determine whether the internal control in force is such as to ensure the integrity of the financial statements. The decisions based on an analysis of internal control will govern the extent of substantive testing and will designate those areas requiring most intensive examination.

Reliance by the auditors upon internal control

In expressing an opinion as to the fairness of financial statements, auditors rely upon (1) the effectiveness of internal control in preventing material errors in the accounting process, and (2) substantive tests to verify the amounts in the financial statements. Where internal accounting controls are strong, the auditors need rely less upon substantive testing. Conversely, where internal controls are weak, the auditors must place greater reliance upon their substantive tests. Thus, the auditors' study and evaluation of internal control is a major factor in determining the *nature, timing, and extent of the substantive testing* necessary to verify the financial statement items.

Since an adequate system of internal control is a major factor in the audit conducted by independent public accountants, the question arises as to what action they should take when internal control is found to be seriously deficient. Can the auditors complete a satisfactory audit and properly express an opinion on the fairness of financial statements of a company that has little or no internal control over its transactions? Although in theory the auditors might compensate for the lack of internal control by making a detailed verification of all entries in the accounts and of all transactions, this approach would generally be beyond the realm of practicability unless the business were quite small. In a large business the existence of adequate internal control over at least a considerable portion of the company's activities seems to be a prerequisite if the auditors are to establish that the company's financial statements reflect fairly its financial position and operating results.

Scope of the auditors' investigation of internal control

The auditors' investigation of internal control consists of two phases—the *study* and the *evaluation*. The study phase encompasses the first two steps of the audit process, as discussed in Chapter 4. First, the auditors review the client's internal control and prepare a description of the system in their working papers. Next, they conduct tests of compliance to determine how effectively the key internal control procedures are functioning. The critical evaluation of the weaknesses and strengths of internal control comprises the third step in the audit process. As part of their evaluation, the auditors expand their audit program to compensate for deficiencies in internal control. In areas of very strong internal control, the auditors will limit their substantive testing to the minimum necessary under the circumstances.

Review and description of internal control

As previously explained, the system of internal control is a comprehensive set of policies and procedures governing virtually every aspect of the client's business operations. In studying and evaluating this system, auditors generally find it useful to subdivide the overall system into its major transaction cycles.[2] The term *transaction cycle* refers to the policies and the sequence of procedures for processing a particular type of transaction. For example, the system of internal control in a manufacturing business might be subdivided into the following major transaction cycles:

1. *Sales and collection cycle*—involving procedures and policies for obtaining orders from customers, approving credit, shipping merchandise, preparing sales invoices, recording revenue and the account receivable, billing, and handling and recording cash receipts.

2. *Purchase or acquisition cycle*—including procedures for initiating purchases or inventory, other assets, or services; placing purchase orders; inspecting goods upon receipt and preparing receiving reports; recording liabilities to vendors; authorizing payment; and making and recording cash disbursements.

3. *Production cycle*—including procedures for storing materials, placing materials into production, assigning production costs to inventories, and accounting for the cost of goods sold.

4. *Payroll cycle*—including procedures for hiring, firing, and determining pay rates; timekeeping; computing gross payroll, payroll taxes, and amounts withheld from gross pay; maintaining payroll records and preparing and distributing paychecks.

5. *Financing cycle*—including procedures for authorizing, executing, and recording transactions involving bank loans, leases, bonds payable, and capital stock.

The transaction cycles within a particular company depend upon the nature of the company's business activities. A bank, for example, has no production cycle, but has both a lending cycle and a demand deposits cycle. Also, different auditors may elect to define a given company's transaction cycles in different ways. For example, the sales and collection cycle may alternatively be defined as two separate transaction cycles for (1) the processing and recording of credit sales, and (2) the handling and recording of cash receipts. The important point to recognize is that subdividing the overall system of internal control into transaction cycles enables the auditor to focus upon the internal control procedures that affect the reliability of specific elements of the financial statements.

---

[2] The transaction cycle approach to studying and evaluating internal control is the method recommended in the *Report of the Special Advisory Committee on Internal Accounting Control*, AICPA (New York, 1979).

Sources of information about internal control. How do auditors obtain the information about a client's system of internal control that enables them to describe the various transaction cycles in their working papers? One approach is to review the audit working papers from examinations made in prior years. When auditors are involved in repeat engagements, they will of course use all information about the client obtained in previous engagements. Their investigation will then stress the areas shown as having questionable controls in prior years. It is imperative, however, that auditors recognize that the pattern of operations is an ever-changing one, that internal controls that were adequate last year may now be obsolete, and that the established use of a given control procedure is no assurance that it is currently being applied in an effective and intelligent manner.

Auditors may ascertain the duties and responsibilities of client employees from organization charts, job descriptions, and interviews with client personnel. A review of the client's chart and text of accounts may provide information about employees' responsibilities as well as about accounting policies and procedures. Most clients have procedures manuals and flowcharts describing the approved practices to be followed in all phases of operations. Another excellent source of information is in the reports, working papers, and audit programs of the client's internal auditing staff. As the independent auditors obtain a working knowledge of the system of internal control, this information is recorded in the form of an internal control questionnaire, a written narrative, or flowcharts.

Internal control questionnaire. The traditional method of describing a system of internal control is the filling in of a standardized internal control questionnaire. Many public accounting firms have developed their own questionnaires for this purpose. The questionnaire usually contains a separate section for each major transaction cycle, enabling the work of completing the questionnaire to be divided conveniently among several audit staff members.

Most internal control questionnaires are so designed that a "no" answer to a question indicates a weakness in internal control. In addition, questionnaires usually provide for distinction between major and minor control weaknesses, indication of the sources of information used in answering questions, and explanatory comments regarding control deficiencies. An internal control questionnaire relating to cash receipts is illustrated in Figure 5–5.

Written narrative of internal control. An internal control questionnaire is intended as a means for the auditors to study a system of internal control. If completion of the questionnaire is regarded as an end in itself, there may be a tendency for the auditors to fill in the "yes" and "no" answers in a mechanical manner, without any real understanding or study of the problem. For this reason, some public accounting firms prefer to use written narratives or flowcharts in lieu of questionnaires. Written narratives usually follow the flow of each major transaction cycle, identifying the employees performing various tasks, documents prepared, records maintained, and the division of duties.

Flowcharts of internal control.   Many CPA firms now consider *systems flowcharts* to be more effective than questionnaires or narrative descriptions in developing an understanding of a client's data processing system and the related internal controls. A systems flowchart is a diagram—a symbolic representation of a system or a series of procedures with each procedure shown in sequence. To the experienced reader, a flowchart conveys a clear image of the system, showing the nature and sequence of procedures, division of responsibilities, sources and distribution of documents, and types and location of accounting records and files. The standard symbols used in systems flowcharting are illustrated in Figure 5–3; however, the symbols used and flowcharting technique varies somewhat among different public accounting firms.

Separate systems flowcharts are prepared for each major transaction cycle. In addition, each flowchart is subdivided into vertical columns representing the various departments (or employees) involved in processing the transactions. Departmental responsibility for procedures, documents, and records is shown by locating the related flowcharting symbol beneath the appropriate departmental heading. Flowcharts usually begin in the upper left-hand corner; directional flowlines then indicate the sequence of activity. The normal flow of activity is from top to bottom and from left to right. These basic concepts of systems flowcharting are illustrated in Figure 5–6.

We have previously indicated that questionnaires, narrative descriptions, and flowcharts are the three most common approaches to gaining an understanding of a system of internal control and describing that system in the auditors' working papers. What are the advantages and disadvantages of flowcharts in comparison to the two older techniques? The special advantage of a flowchart is that it provides a clearer, more specific portrayal of the client's system. There is less opportunity for misunderstanding, blank spots, or ambiguous statements when one uses lines and symbols rather than words to describe an internal control system. Furthermore, in each successive annual audit, the updating of a flowchart is a simple process requiring only that the auditor add or change a few lines and symbols.

A possible disadvantage of flowcharts is that internal control weaknesses are not identified as prominently as in questionnaires. A "no" answer in an internal control questionnaire is a conspicuous red flag calling attention to a dangerous situation. A flowchart may not provide so clear a signal that a particular internal control is absent or is not being properly enforced. Still, the trend is toward greater use of flowcharts by auditors.

Figure 5–3
Widely used flowcharting symbols

Basic symbols

Document any paper document, such as a check or sales invoice.

Manual process any manual operation, such as preparation of a sales invoice or reconciling a bank statement.

Process any operation, whether performed manually, mechanically, or by EDP. Often used interchangeably with the manual process symbol.

Offline storage a file or other storage facility for documents or EDP records.

Flowlines lines indicating the directional flow of documents. Normally downward or to right unless otherwise indicated by arrowheads.

Annotation used for explanatory comments, such as filing sequence (by date, alphabetical, etc.)

Connector exit to or entry from another part of the flowchart. Used to avoid excessive crossing of flowlines. Exit and entry connectors are keyed by letters or numbers.

Offpage connector indicates source or destination of items entering or exiting the flowchart.

Input/Output used in place of an offpage connector to indicate information entering or exiting the flowchart.

Decision indicates alternative courses of action resulting from a yes or no decision.

Special symbols for EDP systems

Punched card   Punched tape

Drum or disk

Magnetic tape

Illustration of written narrative, questionnaire, and flow-chart. The three methods of describing the system of internal control for cash receipts of a small company operating at only one location are illustrated at Figures 5–4 (written narrative), 5–5 (questionnaire), and 5–6 (flowchart).

Figure 5–4

Bennington Co., Inc.
Cash Receipts Procedures
December 31, 1984

All cash receipts are received by mail in the form of checks. Lorraine Martin, cashier, picks up the mail every morning at the post office and delivers it unopened to Helen Ellis, the head bookkeeper.

Ellis opens and distributes the mail. Customers' checks are given to Martin who records the remittances in the cash receipts journal, prepares duplicate deposit slips, and mails the day's receipts intact to First National Bank. The bank returns the validated duplicate deposit slip by mail and Ellis files them in chronological order. Ellis posts the accounts receivable subsidiary ledger from the cash receipts journal on a daily basis.

Any customers' checks charged back by the bank are given by Ellis to the manager, William Dale, who follows up and redeposits the checks. Ellis also forwards monthly bank statements unopened to Dale. Dale reconciles the monthly bank statement, compares the dates and amounts of deposits to the entries in the cash receipts journal, and reviews the propriety of sales discounts recorded in the cash receipts journal.

Martin, Ellis, and Dale are all bonded.

Conclusion:
Internal control over cash receipts is weak; there is no separation of cash handling and record keeping functions.

V. M. H.
11/6/84

A review of the three illustrations brings to light the advantages and disadvantages of each method for gathering evidence as to the nature of the client's internal control system. The written narrative is readily adaptable to unique internal control systems not covered by standardized questionnaires. However, written narratives generally are practical only for small companies. The questionnaire has the advantage of guid-

Figure 5–5

INTERNAL CONTROL QUESTIONNAIRE
CASH RECEIPTS – SALES CYCLE

Client *Bennington Co., Inc.*   Audit Date *December 31, 1984*

Names and Positions of Client Personnel Interviewed:
Lorraine Martin – Cashier; Helen Ellis – head bookkeeper; Wm. Dale – Manager

QUESTION	NOT APPL.	YES	NO	WEAKNESS MAJOR	WEAKNESS MINOR	REMARKS
1. Are all persons receiving or disbursing cash bonded?		✓				
2. Is all incoming mail opened by a responsible employee who does not have access to accounting records and is not connected with the cashier's office?			✓	✓		*H. Ellis is head bookkeeper*
3. Does the employee assigned to the opening of incoming mail prepare a list of all checks and money received?			✓		✓	*See mitigating control in #13*
4. a) Is a copy of the listing of mail receipts forwarded to the accounts receivable department for comparison with the credits to customers' accounts?	✓					
b) Is a copy of this list turned over to an employee other than the cashier for comparison with the cash receipts book?	✓					
5. Are receipts from cash sales and other over-the-counter collections recorded by sales registers, cash registers, and serially numbered receipts?	✓					
6. Are the daily totals of cash registers or other mechanical devices verified by an employee not having access to cash?	✓					
7. Are physical facilities and mechanical equipment for receiving and recording cash adequate and conducive to good control?		✓				
8. Is revenue from investments, rent, concessions, and similar sources scheduled in advance so that nonreceipt on due date would be promptly investigated?	✓					
9. Do procedures for sale of scrap materials provide for direct reporting to accounting department concurrently with transfer of receipts to cashier?	✓					
10. Are securities and other negotiable assets in the custody of someone other than the cashier?	✓					
11. Are collections by branch offices deposited daily in a bank account subject to withdrawal only by home-office executives?	✓					
12. Are each day's receipts deposited intact and without delay by an employee other than the accounts receivable bookkeeper?		✓				
13. Are duplicate deposit tickets signed by the bank teller and compared with the cash receipts record and mailroom list of receipts by an employee other than the cashier or accounts receivable bookkeeper?		✓				*W. Dale Manager*
14. Are the duplicate deposit tickets properly filed and available for inspection by auditors?		✓				*Chronological sequence*
15. Are N.S.F. checks or other items returned by the bank delivered directly to an employee other than the cashier and promptly investigated?		✓				*W. Dale Manager*
16. Is the physical arrangement of offices and accounting records designed to prevent employees who handle cash from having access to accounting records?			✓		✓	*Small Company doesn't permit this.*

Prepared By *V. M. Harris*   Date *11-6-84*   Manager Review _____   Date _____

Senior Review _____   Date _____   Partner Review _____   Date _____

ing the preparer through the investigation required for an adequate description of the internal control system. However, the fact that nearly one half of the questions are not applicable to a client as small as the illustrated Bennington Co., Inc. implies a major weakness of the questionnaire—its inflexibility. The flowchart, like the written narrative, can be readily tailored to a specific client system; but more exper-

Figure 5—6

BENNINGTON CO., INC.
CASH RECEIPTS SYSTEMS FLOWCHART
DECEMBER 31, 1984

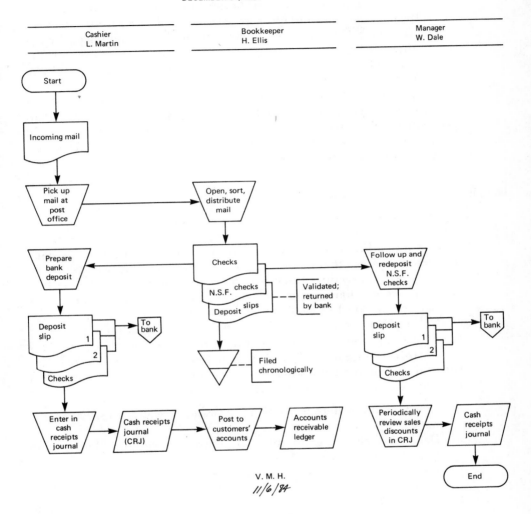

tise is required to prepare a flowchart than to write a narrative or to complete a questionnaire.

Walk-through test. After describing the system of internal control in their working papers, the auditors should verify this description by performing a walk-through of each transaction cycle. The term *walk-through* refers to tracing several transactions (perhaps only one or two) through each step in the cycle. To perform a walk-through of the sales and collection cycle, for example, the auditors might begin by selecting several sales orders and following the related transactions through the client's sequence of procedures. The auditors would determine whether such procedures as credit approval, shipment of merchandise, preparation of sales invoices, recording of the accounts receivable, and processing of the customers' remittances were performed by appropriate client personnel and in the sequence indicated in the audit working papers. If the auditors find that the system functions differently from the working paper description, they will amend the working papers to describe the actual system.

The purpose of the walk-through is to *test the completeness of the auditor's working papers,* not the reliability of the client's control procedures. To draw valid conclusions as to the reliability of specific accounting controls for the entire year under audit requires a far larger sample than one or two transactions.

Compliance tests of internal control procedures

The basic objective of compliance tests is to determine whether key internal control procedures have been operating effectively during the year under audit. Such tests are required before the auditors may place any reliance upon these control procedures. Compliance tests are an efficient audit procedure whenever the reduction in substantive testing resulting from reliance upon internal control exceeds the amount of audit work involved in performing compliance tests.

Preliminary evaluation of internal control. After completing their working paper description of internal control, auditors perform a *preliminary* evaluation of the system to determine which internal controls merit compliance testing. From a conceptual point of view, this preliminary evaluation involves the following steps:

1. Consider the different kinds of errors or irregularities that might occur.
2. Determine the types of internal control procedures that should prevent these errors or irregularities.
3. Determine whether such control procedures are present in the client's system.
4. Decide whether reliance upon these procedures would limit substantive testing sufficiently to justify performing tests of compliance.

This last consideration is highly subjective and requires both judgment and experience.

In some areas of the client's system, auditors often find that internal controls are so weak that they provide no basis for reliance, or that compliance tests would require more effort than the reduction in substantive testing that might result from reliance upon internal control. Under these circumstances, there is no purpose in conducting tests of compliance. In areas in which compliance tests are omitted, however, the auditors may place *no reliance* upon internal control in determining the nature, timing, and extent of the substantive testing procedures necessary to complete the audit.

In the audit of a small business, it may be possible to do sufficient substantive testing to express an opinion on the financial statements while placing little or no reliance upon internal control. In the audit of a large business, however, the auditors would normally disclaim an opinion if they were not able to place a reasonable degree of reliance upon the system of internal control.

Nature of compliance tests.   Compliance tests focus upon specific control procedures, rather than upon financial statement amounts or completed transactions. For example, assume that the client has a control procedure of requiring a second person to review the quantities, prices, extensions, and footing of each sales invoice. The purpose of this control procedure is to prevent material errors in the billing of customers and the recording of sales transactions. To test the effectiveness of this control procedure, the auditors might select a sample of, say, 60 sales invoices prepared throughout the year. They would compare the quantities shown on each invoice to the quantities listed on the related shipping documents, compare unit prices to the client's price lists, and verify the extensions and footings. The results of this test provide the auditors with evidence as to whether they may rely on the dollar amounts produced by the client's billing process. If numerous errors are found in the invoices, the auditors will expand their substantive procedures in the area of accounts receivable.

Evaluation of internal control

After the auditors have carried out their study of internal control (review and compliance testing), they must evaluate the system to determine the extent to which they may rely upon internal control. Based upon this evaluation, modifications are made in the audit program; audit procedures are expanded in areas of weak internal control and limited in areas of unusually strong controls. Only after an evaluation of internal control are the auditors in a position to draft a complete audit program suitably tailored to the engagement.

The study of internal control will have identified the areas of strength and weakness in the system. Significant weaknesses, as well as features of unusual strength, are summarized on a working paper that provides space for developing additional substantive tests to be performed in areas of weak controls and setting limitations on audit procedures in areas of strong controls. This working paper also contains a summary of recommendations to the client for strengthening weak points in the system. A working paper used to summarize the auditors' evaluation of internal control is illustrated in Figure 5-7. Notice that the extensions

Stever Manufacturing Company
Evaluation of Internal Control
December 31, 1984

Weaknesses in Internal Control

1. There is no established procedure for investigating and following up debit balances in accounts payable.

2. The accounts receivable bookkeeper prepares and issues all credit memoranda for sales returns and allowances.

Strengths in Internal Control

The depositary bank reconciles all of the client's bank accounts on the bank's data-processing equipment.

Extensions of Auditing Procedures

1. a. Obtain or prepare a listing of accounts payable debit balances at December 31, 1984.
   b. Mail confirmation requests to vendors having debit balances.
   c. Review credit standing of vendors having debit balances.
   d. Discuss with purchasing agent the prospects of additional purchases from debit balance vendors.
   e. Consider the need for an allowance for uncollectible debit balances.

2. a. Inspect copies of all credit memos issued during the period.
   b. Review with sales manager and controller all credit memoranda issued during the period.
   c. Confirm accounts of all customers to whom credit memoranda were issued during the period.

Limitations of Auditing Procedures

1. Perform no independent bank reconciliations at December 31, 1984. Obtain and review the bank's reconciliations.

Recommendations to Client

1. The accounts payable department should furnish a list of vendors with debit balances to the purchasing agent and the credit manager monthly. These individuals should follow up for procurement possibilities or collection of the debit balance.

2. The sales department should initiate all credit memoranda. Credit memos in excess of a stated minimum should be reviewed by the controller before being posted to the accounts receivable subsidiary ledger.

JHK JK
11/20/84

and limitations of audit procedures are described in detail to facilitate drafting a final version of the audit program.

Reliance on the work of internal auditors.   Many of the audit procedures performed by internal auditors are similar in nature to those employed by independent auditors. This raises the question of whether the independent auditors may rely on the work already performed by the internal auditors. The AICPA has addressed this issue in *SAS No. 9*, "The Effect of an Internal Audit Function on the Scope of the Independent Auditor's Examination."

The position taken in *SAS No. 9* is that the work of internal auditors cannot be substituted for the work of independent auditors. However, the independent auditors should consider the existence and quality of an internal audit function in their evaluation of the client's system of internal control. Through its contribution to internal control, the work of the internal auditors may reduce the amount of substantive testing performed by the independent auditors. In assessing the contribution of the internal audit function to internal control, the independent auditors should consider the *competence* and *objectivity* of the internal audit staff and *evaluate its work.*

On a test basis, the independent auditors should examine the work of the internal audit staff, considering such factors as the scope and quality of its audit procedures, the extent of the documentation in its working papers, and the appropriateness of its conclusions. In addition, the independent auditors should test specific transactions and compare their results with those obtained by the internal auditors. Upon completion of this investigation, the independent auditors have a sound basis for determining the extent to which they may limit their audit procedures in reliance upon the internal auditors' contribution to internal control.

To reduce the time and cost of an audit, the internal auditors may provide direct assistance to the CPAs in preparing working papers and performing certain audit procedures. The CPAs, however, should supervise and test any audit work done for them by the internal auditors. Also, the judgments regarding matters to be investigated, the effectiveness of internal control, and the fairness of the financial statements must be those of the independent auditors.

Preparation of a management letter

Deficiencies in internal control brought to light by the auditors' study and evaluation of the system should be communicated to the client along with the auditors' recommendations for corrective action. Discussions with management are the most effective way for auditors to communicate their findings to the client and explore possible courses of action. The content of these discussions is formally summarized and conveyed in writing to the client in a report called a *management letter.* This report serves as a valuable reference document for management and may also serve to minimize the auditors' legal liability in the event that a major defalcation or other loss results from a weakness in internal control. For these reasons, *SAS No. 20* **requires auditors to advise both senior management and the client's board of directors** of material weaknesses in internal accounting control.[3]

Many auditing firms place great emphasis upon providing clients with a thorough and well-planned management letter. These firms recognize that such a report can be a valuable and constructive contribution to the efficiency of the client's operations. The quality of the auditors' recommendations reflects their professional expertise and creative ability and the thoroughness of their investigation. No specific format exists for the preparation of management letters, since they are a communication sent only to the client. (Reports on internal control that are prepared for distribution to third parties are distinct from management letters and are discussed in Chapter 19.)

The management letter is usually prepared at the conclusion of the auditors' evaluation of internal control. It is desirable to submit this report well in advance of the balance sheet date. The amount of substantive testing necessary to complete the audit may be reduced if management is able to implement significant improvements in internal control before year-end.

Internal control in the small company

The preceding discussion of the system of internal control and its evaluation by the independent auditors has been presented in terms of large corporations. In the large concern, excellent internal control may be achieved by extensive subdivision of duties, so that no one person handles a transaction completely from beginning to end. In the very small concern, however, with only one or two office employees, there is little or no opportunity for division of duties and responsibilities. Consequently internal control tends to be weak, if not completely absent, unless the owner/manager recognizes the importance of internal control and participates in key activities.

Because of the absence of adequate internal control in small concerns, the independent auditors must make a much more detailed examination of accounts, journal entries, and supporting documents than is required in larger organizations. Although it is well to recognize that internal control can never be adequate in a small business, this limitation is no justification for ignoring available forms of control. Auditors can make a valuable contribution to small client companies by encouraging the installation of such control procedures are as practicable

---

[3] *Statement on Auditing Standards No. 20,* "Required Communication of Material Weaknesses in Internal Accounting Control," AICPA (New York, 1977), para. 1.

in the circumstances. The following specific practices are almost always capable of use in even the smallest business:

1. Record all cash receipts immediately.
   a. For over-the-counter collections, use cash registers easily visible to customers. Record register readings daily.
   b. Prepare a list of all mail remittances immediately upon opening of the mail and retain this list for subsequent comparison with bank deposit tickets and entries in the cash receipts journal.
2. Deposit all cash receipts intact daily.
3. Make all payments by serially numbered checks, with the exception of small disbursements from petty cash.
4. Reconcile bank accounts monthly and retain copies of the reconciliations in the files.
5. Use serially numbered sales invoices, purchase orders, and receiving reports.
6. Issue checks to vendors only in payment of approved invoices that have been matched with purchase orders and receiving reports.
7. Balance subsidiary ledgers with control accounts at regular intervals; prepare and mail customers' statements monthly.
8. Prepare comparative financial statements monthly in sufficient detail to disclose significant variations in any category of revenue or expense.

Adherence to these basic control practices significantly reduces the risk of material errors or major defalcation going undetected. If the size of the business permits a segregation of the duties of cash handling and record keeping, a fair degree of control can be achieved. If it is necessary that one employee serve as both accounting clerk and cashier, then active participation by the owner in certain key functions is necessary to guard against the concealment of fraud or errors. In a few minutes each day the owner, even though not trained in accounting, can create a significant amount of internal control by personally (1) reading daily cash register totals, (2) reconciling the bank account monthly, (3) signing all checks and canceling the supporting documents, (4) approving all general journal entries, and (5) critically reviewing comparative monthly statements of revenue and expense.

KEY TERMS INTRODUCED OR EMPHASIZED IN CHAPTER 5

Accounting controls   Internal controls of a nature that can directly affect the reliability of the accounting records and financial statements.

Administrative controls   Internal controls of a nature having no direct bearing upon the reliability of accounting data.

Compliance tests   Audit procedures designed to provide reasonable assurance that significant accounting controls within a client's system are in use and operating effectively.

Fidelity bonds A form of insurance in which a bonding company agrees to reimburse an employer for losses attributable to theft or embezzlement by bonded employees.

Foreign Corrupt Practices Act Federal legislation prohibiting payments to foreign officials for the purpose of securing business. The act also requires all companies under SEC jurisdiction to maintain a system of internal accounting control providing reasonable assurance that transactions are executed only with the knowledge and authorization of management.

Internal auditors Corporation employees who design and execute audit programs to test the efficiency of all aspects of internal control. The primary objective of internal auditors is to evaluate and improve the efficiency of the various operating units of an organization, rather than to express an opinion as to the fairness of financial statements.

Internal control questionnaire One of several alternative methods of describing a system of internal control in audit working papers. Questionnaires are usually designed so that "no" answers prominently identify weaknesses in internal control.

Operational audit A review of a department or other unit of a business to evaluate the efficiency of operations.

Operations control The routine reconciliation functions designed to achieve accountability for assets and to detect errors in accounting records. Examples include reconciliation of bank statements to accounting records and subsidiary ledgers to controlling accounts. Many operations control functions are performed in the accounting department, but some are performed by people whose principal duties do not involve accounting or control. For example, sales department supervisors often perform the operations control function of reconciling cash receipts to cash register tapes.

Organization plan The division of authority, responsibility, and duties among members of an organization.

Preliminary evaluation of internal control An evaluation of the client's system of internal accounting control made before the compliance testing phase of the audit. The purpose of this preliminary evaluation is to identify those accounting controls that merit compliance testing; controls upon which the auditors will place *no reliance* need not be tested. After the compliance testing phase of the audit, the auditors perform a more thorough evaluation of internal control to determine the extent to which they will rely upon the client's system and the nature, timing, and extent of their substantive test procedures.

Responsibility accounting An accounting system which separately accumulates the operating results attributable to specific decision-makers. Separate accounts for the assets, revenue, and expenses under the control of specific decision-makers and adequate internal documentation to focus responsibility are the basic elements of a responsibility accounting system.

Systems flowcharts A symbolic representation of a system or series of procedures with each procedure shown in sequence. Systems flowcharts are the most widely used method of describing a system of internal control in audit working papers.

Transaction cycle The sequence of procedures applied by the client in processing a particular type of recurring transaction. The auditors' working paper description of internal control is organized around the client's major transaction cycles.

Walk-through of the system A test of the accuracy and completeness of the auditors' working paper description of internal control. A walk-through is performed by tracing several transactions through each step of the related transaction cycle, noting whether the sequence of procedures actually performed corresponds to that described in the audit working papers.

Written narrative of internal control A written summary of a system of internal control for inclusion in audit working papers. Written narratives are more flexible than questionnaires, but are practical only for describing relatively small, simple systems.

GROUP I: REVIEW QUESTIONS

5–1. What is the basic purpose of a system of internal control? What measures comprise the system?

5–2. What is meant by internal accounting controls as contrasted with internal administrative controls? Give examples of each and explain which category is of more importance to the auditor.

5–3. Identify the basic features of a strong system of internal control.

5–4. How does separation of the record-keeping function from custody of assets contribute to internal control?

5–5. The owner of a medium-size corporation asks you to state two or three principles to be followed in dividing responsibilities among employees in a manner that will produce strong internal control.

5–6. One basic concept of internal control is that no one employee should handle all aspects of a transaction. Assuming that a general category of transactions has been authorized by top management, how many employees (or departments) should participate in each transaction, as a minimum, to achieve strong internal accounting control? Explain in general terms the function of each of these employees.

5–7. Explain the term *responsibility accounting.* Why is this concept an important factor in achieving internal control?

5–8. Compare the objectives of the internal auditor with those of the independent auditor.

5–9. How do the objectives of an operational audit differ from those of a financial compliance audit?

5–10. What reliance, if any, may independent auditors place upon the work of a client's internal audit staff?

5–11. What is the purpose of the study and evaluation of internal control required by generally accepted auditing standards?

5–12. A prospective client informs you that all officers and employees of the company are bonded, and he requests that under these circumstances you forego an evaluation of internal control in order to reduce the cost of an audit. Construct a logical reply to this request.

5–13. Suggest a number of sources from which auditors might obtain the information needed to prepare a description of internal control in the audit working papers.

5–14. Distinguish between a walk-through test of a transaction cycle and a compliance test of an accounting control procedure.

5–15. Compare the basic objective of the auditors' preliminary evaluation of internal control with those of the final evaluation of internal control that constitutes the third major step in the audit process.

5–16. Under what circumstances is compliance testing an *efficient* audit procedure?

5–17. Under what circumstances might auditors elect to forego tests of compliance for certain portions of a client's system of internal control?

5–18. After completing the study of internal control, how do auditors evaluate the system?

5–19. What is a management letter? At what stage of the audit should the management letter be prepared?

5–20. In view of the reliance the auditor places upon the system of internal control, how do you account for the fact that the auditors' standard report makes no reference to internal control in describing the scope of the examination?

5–21. Name the three factors you consider of greatest importance in protecting a business against losses through embezzlement.

5–22. You have discussed with the president of Vista Corporation several material weaknesses in internal control that have come to your attention during your audit. At the conclusion of this discussion, the president states that he will personally take steps to remedy these problems and that there is no reason for you to bring these matters to the attention of the board of directors. He explains that he believes the board should deal with major policy decisions and not be burdened with day-to-day management problems. How would you respond to this suggestion? Explain fully.

GROUP II: QUESTIONS REQUIRING ANALYSIS

5–23. Internal control comprises the plan of organization and all of the measures adopted to safeguard assets, enhance the reliability of the accounting records, promote compliance with managerial policies, and to encourage operational efficiency.

Required:
a. What is the purpose of the auditors' study and evaluation of the system of internal control?
b. What is the objective of a preliminary evaluation of internal control, performed before compliance testing?
c. How is the auditors' understanding of the client's system of internal control documented in the audit working papers?
d. What is the purpose of tests of compliance? (AICPA, adapted)

5–24. The audit process was described in Chapter 4 as a series of basic steps. Explain the relationship of each step of the audit process to the auditors' study and evaluation of internal control. For example—(*a*) *Review the system and prepare a description in the audit working papers* is the first step in the audit process and is the first part of the study phase of the auditors' investigation of internal control.

5–25. Henry Bailey, CPA, is planning the audit of The Neighborhood Store, a local grocery cooperative. Because The Neighborhood Store is a small business operated entirely by part-time volunteer personnel, internal controls are weak. Bailey has decided that he will not be able to rely on internal control to restrict audit procedures in any area. Under these circumstances, may Bailey omit study and evaluation of the system of internal control in this engagement?

5–26. Adherence to generally accepted auditing standards requires, among other things, a proper study and evaluation of the existing internal control. The most common approaches to reviewing the system of internal control include the use of a questionnaire, preparation of a written narrative, preparation of a flowchart, and combinations of these methods.

Required:
a. Discuss the advantages to CPAs of reviewing internal control by using:
(1) An internal control questionnaire.
(2) A written narrative.
(3) A flowchart.
b. If they are satisfied after completing their description of internal control that no material weaknesses exist in the system, is it necessary for the CPAs to conduct tests of compliance? Explain. (AICPA, adapted)

5–27. The process of gathering evidential matter to support an opinion on a client's financial statements involves several types of testing procedures. In the course of the examination, auditors perform detailed tests of samples of transactions from large-volume populations. Auditors may also audit various types of transactions by tracing a few transactions of each type through all stages of the accounting system.

Required:
What are the audit objectives associated with—
a. A sample of transactions from a large-volume population?
b. Tracing a few transactions of each type through all stages of the accounting system? (AICPA, adapted)

5–28. During your first examination of a manufacturing company with approximately 100 production employees, you find that all aspects of factory payroll are handled by one employee and that none of the usual internal controls over payroll is observed. What action will you take?

5–29. During your first examination of a medium-size manufacturing company, the owner explains that in order to establish clear-cut lines of responsibility for various aspects of the business, he has made one employee responsible of the purchasing, receiving, and storing of merchandise. A second employee has full responsibility for maintenance of accounts receivable records and collections from customers. A third employee is responsible for personnel records, timekeeping, preparation of payrolls, and distribution of payroll checks. The client asks your opinion concerning this plan of organization. Explain fully the reasons supporting your opinion.

5–30. Internal auditing is a staff function found in virtually every large corporation. The internal audit function is also performed in many smaller companies as a part-time activity of individuals who may or may not be called internal auditors. The differences between the audits by independent auditors and the work of internal auditors are more basic than is generally recognized.

Required:

a. Briefly discuss the auditing work performed by the independent public accountant and the internal auditor with regard to—
   (1) Auditing objectives.
   (2) General nature of auditing work.
b. In conducting their audit, the independent auditors must evaluate the work of the internal auditors. Discuss briefly the reason for this evaluation.
c. List the auditing procedures used by independent auditors in evaluating the work of the internal auditors. (AICPA, adapted)

5–31. The Carleton Company did not utilize the services of independent public accountants during the first several years of its existence. In the current year, at the suggestion of its banker, the company decided to retain McTavish and Company, a CPA firm, to conduct an audit of its financial statements in order to qualify for a larger bank loan. The auditors found the system of internal control to be "extremely weak or nonexistent." Under these circumstances what kind of audit report, if any, could McTavish and Company issue? Explain fully.

5–32. Select the best answer for each of the following questions. Explain the reason for your selection.

a. In connection with the study and evaluation of internal control during an audit of financial statements, independent auditors—
   (1) Give equal weight to internal accounting and administrative controls.
   (2) Emphasize internal administrative controls.
   (3) Emphasize those controls that are likely to detect management fraud.
   (4) Emphasize internal accounting controls.
b. In connection with the study of internal control, the auditor encounters the following flowcharting symbols:

The auditor should conclude that:
   (1) A master file is created by a manual operation.
   (2) A master file is created by a computer operation.
   (3) A document is generated by a manual operation.
   (4) A document is generated by a computer operation.

c. When an independent auditor decides that the work performed by internal auditors may have a bearing on the nature, timing, and extent of the independent auditor's procedures, the independent auditor should evaluate the competence and objectivity of the internal auditors. Relative to objectivity, the independent auditor should—
   (1) Consider the organizational level to which the internal auditors report the results of their work.
   (2) Test the internal auditors' work.
   (3) Consider the qualifications of the internal audit staff.
   (4) Review the training program in effect for the internal audit staff.

d. Effective internal control in a small company that has an insufficient number of employees to permit proper subdivision of responsibilities can best be enhanced by—
   (1) Employment of temporary personnel to aid in the separation of duties.
   (2) Direct participation by the owner in key record-keeping and control activities of the business.
   (3) Engaging a CPA to perform monthly write-up work.
   (4) Delegation to each employee full, clear-cut responsibility for a separate major transaction cycle. (AICPA, adapted)

GROUP III: PROBLEMS

5–33. At the Main Street Theatre the cashier, located in a box office at the entrance, receives cash from customers and operates a machine that ejects serially numbered tickets. To gain admission to the theater a customer hands the ticket to a door attendant stationed some 50 feet from the box office at the entrance to the theater lobby. The attendant tears the ticket in half, opens the door for the customer, and returns the stub to the customer. The other half of the ticket is dropped by the door attendant into a locked box.

Required:
   a. What internal controls are present in this phase of handling cash receipts?
   b. What steps should be taken regularly by the manager or other supervisor to give maximum effectiveness to these controls?
   c. Assume that the cashier and the door attendant decided to collaborate in an effort to abstract cash receipts. What action might they take?
   d. Continuing the assumption made in (c) of collusion between the cashier and the door attendant, what features of the control procedures would be likely to disclose the embezzlement?

5–34. Island Trading Co., a client of your CPA firm, has requested your advice on the following problem. It has three clerical employees who must perform the following functions:
   (1) Maintain general ledger.
   (2) Maintain accounts payable ledger.

(3) Maintain accounts receivable ledger.

(4) Maintain cash disbursements journal and prepare checks for signature.

(5) Issue credit memos on sales returns and allowances.

(6) Reconcile the bank account.

(7) Handle and deposit cash receipts.

Required:

Assuming that there is no problem as to the ability of any of the employees, the company requests your advice on assigning the above functions to the three employees in such a manner as to achieve the highest degree of internal control. It may be assumed that these employees will perform no other accounting functions that the ones listed and that any accounting functions not listed will be performed by persons other than these three employees.

a. List four possible unsatisfactory combinations of the above-listed functions.

b. State how you would recommend distributing the above functions among the three employees. Assume that, with the exception of the nominal jobs of the bank reconciliation and the issuance of credits on returns and allowances, all functions require an equal amount of time. (AICPA, adapted)

5–35. A description of some of the operating procedures of Old World Manufacturing Co. is given in succeeding paragraphs. For each of the activities described, you are to point out (*a*) the deficiencies, if any, in internal control, including an explanation of the errors or manipulations that might occur, and (*b*) recommendations for changes in procedures that would correct the existing weakness.

(1) When materials are ordered, a duplicate of the purchase order is sent to the receiving department. When the materials are received, one of four receiving clerks records the receipt by placing a check mark on the copy of the order, which is then sent to the accounting department to support the entry to Accounts Payable and to Purchases. The materials are then taken to the inventory storeroom where the quantity is entered on bin records.

(2) Time reports of employees are sent to a data processing department, which prepares punched cards for use in the preparation of payrolls, payroll checks, and labor cost distribution records. The payroll checks are compared with the payrolls and signed by the treasurer of the company, who returns them to the supervisor of the data processing department for distribution to employees.

(3) A sales branch of the company has an office force consisting of John Lane, the manager, and two assistants. The branch has a local bank account in which it deposits cash receipts. Checks drawn on this account require the manager's signature or the signature of the treasurer of the company. Bank statements and paid checks are returned by the bank to the manager, who retains them in his files after making the reconciliation. Reports of disbursements are prepared by the manager and submitted to the home office on scheduled dates. (AICPA, adapted)

5–36. You have been asked by the board of trustees of a local church to review its accounting procedures. As a part of this review you have prepared the following comments relating to the collections made at weekly services and record keeping for members' pledges and contributions:

(1) The church's board of trustees has delegated responsibility for financial management and internal audit of the financial records to the finance committee. This group prepares the annual forecast and approves major disbursements, but is not involved in collections or record keeping. No internal or independent audit has been considered necessary in recent years because the same trusted employee has kept church records and served as financial secretary for 15 years.

(2) The offering at the weekly service is taken by a team of ushers. The head usher counts the offering in the church office following each service. He then places the offering and a notation of the amount counted in the church safe. Next morning the financial secretary opens the safe and recounts the offering. He withholds about $100 to meet cash expenditures during the coming week and deposits the remainder of the offering intact. In order to facilitate the deposit, members who contribute by check are asked to draw their checks to cash.

(3) At their request a few members are furnished prenumbered, predated envelopes in which to insert their weekly contributions. The head usher removes the cash from the envelopes to be counted with the loose cash included in the offering and discards the envelopes. No record is maintained of issuance or return of the envelopes, and the envelope system is not encouraged.

(4) Each member is asked to prepare a contribution pledge card annually. The pledge is regarded as a moral commitment by the member to contribute a stated weekly amount. Based upon the amounts shown on the pledge cards, the financial secretary furnishes a letter to requesting members to support the tax deductibility of their contributions.

Required:
Describe the weaknesses and recommend improvements in procedures for—

a. Offerings given at weekly services.

b. Record keeping for members' pledges and contributions.

Organize your answer sheets as follows:

Weakness	*Recommended improvement*

(AICPA)

5–37. Prospect Corporation, your new audit client, processes its sales and cash receipts in the following manner:

(1) **Sales.** Salesclerks prepare sales invoices in triplicate. The original and second copy are presented to the cashier, the third copy is retained by the salesclerk in the sales book. When the sale is for cash, the customer pays the salesclerk, who presents the money to the cashier with the invoice copies.

A credit sale is approved by the cashier from an approved credit list. After receiving the cash or approving the invoice, the cashier validates the original copy of the sales invoice and gives it to the customer. At the end of each day the cashier recaps the sales and cash received, files the recap by date, and forwards the cash and the second copy of all sales invoices to the accounts receivable clerk.

The accounts receivable clerk balances the cash received with cash sales invoices and prepares a daily sales summary. Cash sales are posted by the accounts receivable clerk to the cash receipts journal, and the daily sales summary is filed by date. Cash from cash sales is included in the daily bank deposit (preparation of bank deposit is described with cash receipts in the following section). The accounts receivable clerk posts credit sales invoices to the accounts receivable ledger and then sends all invoices to the inventory control clerk in the sales department.

The inventory clerk posts to the inventory control cards and files the sales invoices numerically.

(2) **Cash receipts.** The mail is opened each morning by a mail clerk in the sales department. The mail clerk prepares a remittance advice (showing customer and amount paid) for each check and forwards the checks and remittance advices to the sales department supervisor. The supervisor reviews the remittance advices and forwards the checks and advices to the accounting department supervisor.

The accounting department supervisor, who also functions as credit manager in approving new credit and all credit limits, reviews all checks for payments on past-due accounts and then gives the checks and remittance advices to the accounts receivable clerk, who arranges the advices in alphabetical order. The remittance advices are posted directly to the accounts receivable ledger cards. The checks are endorsed by stamp and totaled. The total is posted to the cash receipts journal. The remittance advices are filed chronologically.

After receiving the cash from the previous day's cash sales from the cashier, the accounts receivable clerk prepares the daily deposit slip in triplicate. The original and second copy of the deposit slip accompany the bank deposit, and the third copy is filed by date. The bank deposit is sent directly to National Bank.

Required:
a. Prepare a systems flowchart of internal control over sales transactions as described in part 1 above.
b. Prepare a systems flowchart of internal control over cash receipts as described in part 2 above.

6

The audit of electronic data processing systems

The rapid growth of electronic data processing (EDP) for business use is having a greater impact upon public accounting than perhaps any other event in the history of this profession. Although the computer has created some challenging problems for professional accountants, it has also broadened their horizons and expanded the range and value of the services they offer. The computer is more than a tool for performing routine accounting tasks with unprecedented speed and accuracy. It makes possible the development of information that could not have been gathered in the past because of time and cost limitations. When a client maintains accounting records with a complex and sophisticated EDP system, auditors may find it helpful, and even necessary, to utilize the computer in performing many auditing procedures.

This chapter will call attention to some of the most significant ways in which auditing work is being affected by EDP, but cannot impart extensive knowledge of technical computer skills. Independent auditors will find additional familiarity with the computer, including technical skills such as programming, to be of ever-increasing value in the accounting profession.

Nature of an electronic data processing system

Before considering the impact of electronic data processing systems on the work of the independent certified public accountant, some understanding of the nature of a computer and its capabilities is needed. A business EDP system usually consists of a digital computer and peripheral equipment known as *hardware*; and equally essential *software,* consisting of various programs and routines for operating a computer.

Hardware. The principal hardware component of a digital computer is the *central processing unit* (CPU). The CPU consists of a *control unit,* which processes a program of instructions for manipulating data; a *storage unit,* consisting of many tiny magnetic rings or cores, for storing the program of instructions and the data to be manipulated; and an *arithmetic unit* capable of addition, subtraction, multiplication, division, and comparison of data at speeds measured in *microseconds* or *nanoseconds.*

Peripheral to the central processing unit are devices for recording input and devices for auxiliary storage, output, and communications. Peripheral devices in direct communication with the CPU are said to be *on-line,* in contrast to *off-line* equipment not in direct communication with the CPU.

A first step in the functioning of an electronic data processing system is to convert the data to machine-sensible form. This is the role of recording and input devices, such as card punches and readers, paper tape punches and readers, magnetic tape encoders, magnetic ink character readers, and optical scanners. Each of these devices either records data in some medium for later reading into the storage unit or communicates data direct to the CPU.

Auxiliary storage devices are utilized to augment the capacity of the storage unit of the CPU. Examples of auxiliary storage devices are magnetic tape, magnetic drums, and magnetic disk packs. Magnetic drums and disk packs have the advantage of *random access;* data on magnetic tapes must be stored sequentially.

Computers use special codes, *machine language,* to represent data being stored or processed within the computer. The purpose of a machine language is to permit all data to be expressed by combinations of only two symbols. Digital computer circuitry has two states in that any given circuit may be "on" or "off." By using an internal code capable of representing with two symbols any kind of data, the computer makes an on circuit represent one symbol and an off circuit represent the other. All data may then be expressed internally by the computer by a combination of on and off circuits. An example of a machine language is the *binary* number system.

Machines must also be used to translate the output of the computer back to a recognizable code or language. Output equipment includes card punches, printers, cathode ray tubes, and console display panels.

Software. Most important of the software components is the *program*—a series of instructions written in a language comprehensible to the computer. These instructions order the computer to process data.

Early-day programs were laboriously written in machine language, but today, programming languages such as COBOL (common business-oriented language) are much like English. Programming in COBOL and other *source languages* is made possible by another element of software, the *compiler,* which is a computer program utilized in translating a *source-language program* into machine language. The machine-language version of a program is called an *object program.*

Another important software component is the prewritten utility program for recurring tasks of data processing, such as sorting, sequencing, or merging data, language processing, and other routines closely related to the functioning of the computer. These prewritten utility programs are available from the computer manufacturer and do not generally pose any problem to the auditors because they are not likely to be the source of errors in computer output. Furthermore, they are technically so complex as to make examination by the auditors impracticable in most cases.

In concluding this brief discussion of the nature of an EDP system, two points deserve emphasis. First, computer *hardware* is extremely reliable, but this machine precision does not assure that the computer output will be reliable. Second, auditors have the same responsibility in auditing an EDP system as a manual system—which is to satisfy themselves that the financial statements produced reflect the interpretation and processing of transactions in conformity with generally accepted accounting principles.

Internal control in the electronic data processing system

The discussion of internal control in Chapter 5 stressed the need for a proper division of duties among employees operating a manual or punched-card accounting system. In such a system no one employee has the complete responsibility for a transaction, and the work of one person is verified by the work of another handling other aspects of the same transaction. This division of duties gives assurance of accuracy in records and reports and protects the company against loss from fraud or carelessness.

When a company converts to an EDP system, however, the work formerly divided among many people is performed by the computer. Consolidation of activities and integration of functions are to be expected, since the computer can conveniently handle many related aspects of a transaction. For example, when payroll is handled by a computer, it is possible to carry out a variety of related tasks with only a single use of the master records. These tasks could include the maintenance of personnel files with information on seniority, rate of pay, insurance, and the like; a portion of the timekeeping function; distribution of labor costs; and preparation of payroll checks and payroll records.

Despite the integration of several functions in an EDP system, the importance of internal control is not in the least diminished. The essential factors described in Chapter 5 for satisfactory internal control in a large-scale organization are still relevant. Separation of duties and clearly defined responsibilities are still key ingredients despite the change in departmental boundaries, as will be explained in later sections of this chapter. These traditional control concepts are augmented, however, by controls written into the computer programs and controls built into the computer hardware.

In recognition of the effect of EDP upon traditional control concepts, the AICPA issued *SAS No. 3*, "The Effects of EDP on the Auditor's Study and Evaluation of Internal Control." *SAS No. 3* classifies accounting controls in an EDP system into the categories of *general controls* and *application controls*. General controls relate to all EDP applications and include such considerations as: (*a*) the organization of the EDP department; (*b*) procedures for documenting, testing, and approving the original system and any subsequent changes; (*c*) controls built into the hardware (equipment controls); and (*d*) security for files and equipment. Application controls, on the other hand, relate to specific accounting tasks performed by EDP, such as the preparation of payrolls. Controls of this nature include measures designed to assure the reliability of input, controls over processing, and controls over output.

Organizational controls in an electronic data processing system

Because of the ability of the computer to process data efficiently, there is a tendency to combine many data processing functions in an EDP department. In a manual or mechanical system, certain combinations of functions are considered incompatible from a standpoint of achieving strong internal control. For example, the function of recording cash disbursements is incompatible with the responsibility for reconciling bank statements. Since one of these procedures serves as a check upon the other, assigning both functions to one employee would enable the employee to conceal his own errors. A properly programmed computer, however, has no tendency or motivation to conceal its errors. Therefore, what appears to be an incompatible combination of functions may be combined in an EDP department without weakening internal control.

When incompatible functions are combined in the EDP department, compensating controls are necessary to prevent improper human intervention with computer processing. A person with the opportunity to make unauthorized changes in computer programs or data files is in a position to exploit the concentration of data processing functions in the EDP department. For example, a computer program used to process accounts payable may be designed to approve a vendor's invoice for payment only when that invoice is supported by a purchase order and receiving report. An employee able to make unauthorized changes in that program could cause unsubstantiated payments to be made to specific vendors.

EDP programs and data files cannot be changed without the use of EDP equipment. With EDP equipment, however, they can be changed without leaving any visible evidence of the alteration. Thus, the organization plan of an EDP department should prevent EDP personnel from having unauthorized access to EDP equipment, programs, or data files. This is accomplished by providing definite lines of authority and responsibility, segregation of functions, and clear definition of duties for each employee in the department. The organizational structure of a

Figure 6–1
Organization of EDP department

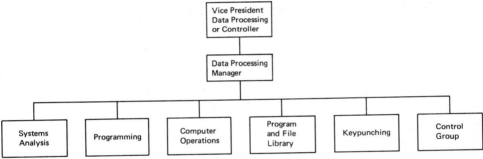

well-staffed EDP department, as illustrated in Figure 6–1, should include the following separation of responsibilities:

Data processing manager. A manager should be appointed to supervise the operation of the data processing department. This data processing manager may report to the controller, or perhaps to a vice president of data processing or information systems. It is desirable for the data processing department to have a substantial degree of autonomy from major user departments. When EDP is a section within the accounting department, the controller should not have direct contact with computer operations.

Systems analysis. Systems analysts are responsible for designing the EDP system. After considering the objectives of the business and its data processing needs, they determine the goals of the system and the means of achieving these goals. Utilizing system flowcharts and detail instructions, they outline the data processing system.

Programming. Guided by the specifications provided by the systems analysts, the programmers design program flowcharts for computer programs required by the system. They then code the required programs in computer language, generally making use of specialized programming languages, such as COBOL, and software elements, such as assemblers, compilers, and utility programs. They test the programs with *test decks* composed of genuine or dummy records and transactions and perform the necessary debugging. Finally, the programmers prepare necessary documentation, such as the computer operator instructions.

Computer operations. The computer operators manipulate the computer in accordance with the instructions developed by the programmers. On occasion the computer operators may have to intervene through the computer console during a run in order to correct an indicated error. All operator entries into the computer should be made through a console typewriter so that printed copies of the entries are available. The separation of computer operations from programming is an important one from the standpoint of achieving internal control. An employee performing both functions would have an opportunity to make unauthorized changes in computer programs.

Program and file library. The purpose of the file library is to protect computer programs, master files, transaction (detail) tapes, and other records from loss, damage, and unauthorized use or alteration. To assure adequate control, the librarian maintains a formal checkout system for making records available to authorized users.

In many systems, the library function is performed by the computer. The computer operators use special code numbers or passwords to gain access to programs and files stored within the system. The computer automatically maintains a log showing when these programs and files are used.

Keypunching. Keypunch operators transcribe data from source documents to punched cards, which are read into the computer by an input device. Keypunching is primarily associated with *batch processing* systems, in which a group (batch) of source documents is processed at one time. In an *on-line, real-time system*, data may be entered directly into the computer by user departments through remote *terminals* without being transcribed into punched cards. Even in the most sophisticated systems, however, many applications are handled by batch processing.

Control group. The control group of a data processing department reviews and tests all input procedures, monitors computer processing, handles the reprocessing of errors detected by the computer, and reviews and distributes all computer output. This group also reviews the console log of operator interventions with computer processing and the library log of program usage.

Besides segregation of functions, the data processing organization plan should provide for rotation of programmer assignments, rotation of operator assignments, mandatory vacations, and adequate fidelity bonds for employees. At least two of the qualified data processing personnel should be present whenever the computer facility is in use.

Careful screening procedures in the hiring of EDP personnel are also important in achieving strong internal control.

Organizational controls and computer-centered fraud

The history of computer-centered fraud shows that the persons responsible for frauds typically set up the system and control its use as programmer and operator.

Illustrative case. A programmer for a large bank wrote a program for identifying and listing all overdrawn accounts. Later, as operator of the bank's computer, he was able to insert a "patch" in the program to cause the computer to ignore overdrafts in his own account. The programmer-operator was then able to overdraw his bank account at will, without the overdraft coming to management's attention. The fraud was not discovered until the computer broke down and the listing of overdrawn accounts had to be prepared manually.

The number of personnel and the organizational structure will of course determine the extent to which segregation of duties is possible. As a minimum, the function of programming should be separated from the functions controlling input to the computer programs, and the function of the computer operator should be segregated from functions requiring detailed knowledge or custody of the computer programs. If one person is permitted to perform duties in several of these functions, internal control is weakened, and the opportunity exists for fraudulent data to be inserted in the system.

Access to assets by EDP personnel. Whenever the responsibilities for record keeping and custody of the related assets are combined, the opportunities for an employee to conceal the abstraction of assets are increased. Since EDP is basically a record-keeping function, it is highly desirable to limit the access of EDP personnel to company assets. However, EDP personnel have direct access to cash if EDP activity includes the preparation of signed checks. EDP personnel may also have indirect access to assets if, for example, EDP is used to generate shipping orders authorizing the release of inventory.

The combination of record keeping with access to assets seriously weakens internal control unless adequate *compensating controls* are present. One type of compensating control is the use of predetermined *batch totals,* such as document counts and totals of significant data fields, prepared in departments independent of EDP. For example, if EDP performs the function of printing checks, another department should be responsible for authorizing the preparation of the checks. The authorizing department should maintain a record of the total number and dollar amount of checks authorized. These independently prepared batch totals should then be compared with the computer output before the checks are released.

It is difficult for compensating controls to eliminate entirely the risk that results from EDP personnel having access to company assets. Auditors should therefore realize that the risk of computer-centered fraud is greatest in those areas in which EDP personnel have access to assets.

Management fraud. Organizational controls are reasonably effective in preventing an individual employee from perpetrating a fraud, but they do not prevent fraud involving collusion. If key employees or company officers conspire in an effort to commit fraud, internal controls that rely upon separation of duties can be rendered inoperative.

Illustrative case. Equity Funding Corporation of America went into bankruptcy after it was discovered that the company's financial statements had been grossly and fraudulently misleading for a period of years. A life insurance subsidiary of the company had been manufacturing bogus insurance policies of fictitious persons and then selling these policies to other insurance companies. When the fraud was discovered, Equity Funding's balance sheet included more than $120 million in fictitious assets, far exceeding the $75 million net income reported over the 13-year life of the company.

Perhaps the most startling revelation of the Equity Funding scandal was that numerous officers and employees of the company had worked together for years to perpetrate and conceal the fraud. The fictitious transactions had been carefully integrated into the company's computer-based accounting system. A wide variety of fraudulent supporting documents had been prepared for the sole purpose of deceiving auditors and governmental regulatory agencies. Upon disclosure of the activities, several members of top management were convicted of criminal charges.

The Equity Funding scandal is often described as a computer-based fraud. It was not because of the use of computers, however, that the company was able to deceive auditors and governmental investigators. Rather, the fraudulent activities were successfully concealed for a number of years because of the unprecedented willingness of a large number of company officers and employees to participate in the scheme. Collusion of the magnitude existing at Equity Funding would render any system of internal control ineffective.

Documentation

Internal control in an EDP department requires not only subdivision of duties, but also the maintenance of adequate documentation describing the system and procedures used in all data processing tasks. Although several *runs* through the computer may be necessary to perform all of the elements of a specific data processing task, the run is usually the basic unit of computer documentation. Documentation of each computer run is included in a *run manual*.

A run manual is prepared by either the systems analyst or the programmer and contains a complete description of the program used for the run. As a minimum, run documentation should include:

1. System flowcharts showing sources and nature of input, operations, and output.

2.   List and explanation of processing controls associated with the run.
3.   Record layouts showing the placement of data on punched cards, magnetic tape, and printouts.
4.   Program flowcharts showing the major steps and logic of each computer program.
5.   Program listings showing the detailed assembler and compiler printouts.
6.   Program approval and change sheets showing proper authorization for all initial programs and subsequent changes.
7.   Operator instructions for processing the programs.
8.   Test decks utilized in testing and debugging programs.

Complete run manuals may be utilized by systems analysts and programmers for making authorized changes in programs. Computer operators, on the other hand, should have access only to the instructions for processing the programs. If operators have access to the complete run manual, the opportunities for an operator to change or patch a program are increased.

Documentation is helpful to the auditors in reviewing the controls over program changes, evaluating controls written into programs, and determining the program logic. The auditors must also refer to format and layout information in the documentation in order to prepare test decks or special audit programs for testing the client's processing programs and computerized files. In other words, the auditors' study of internal control and their planning of an audit program to test the client's system require them to utilize the client's documentation.

Equipment controls

Modern electronic data processing equipment is highly accurate and reliable. Most errors in computer output result from erroneous input or an error in the program. Auditors, however, should be familiar with the equipment controls within a given system in order to appraise the reliability of the hardware, either for evaluating output or for searching for probable causes of erroneous output. Equipment controls are built into the computer by the computer manufacturer. Among the more common equipment or hardware controls are the following:

1.   Read after write. The computer reads back the data after they have been recorded in storage and verifies their accuracy.

2.   Dual read or *read after punch.* Data on magnetic tape or punched cards are read twice during the input phase, and the two readings are compared.

3.   Parity check. Data are processed by the computer in arrays of *bits* (binary digits of 1 or 0). In addition to bits necessary to represent the numeric or alphabetic character, a *parity* bit is added when necessary to make the sum of all the 1 bits always odd or even, depending upon the make of the computer. As data are transferred at rapid speeds between computer components, the parity check is applied by the computer to assure that bits are not lost during the transfer process.

4. *Echo check*. The echo check involves transmitting data received by an output device back to the source unit for comparison with the original data.

5. *Reverse multiplication*. In reverse multiplication, the roles of the original multiplicand and multiplier are reversed and the resultant product is compared to the original product.

A program of preventive maintenance is essential to assure the proper functioning of the equipment controls.

Security for files and equipment

All magnetic tape and punched card files should be properly identified by external labels and machine-readable internal *header* labels. The librarian should maintain a log recording all files checked out and returned to the library and the signature of the authorized person responsible for the file during the check-out period.

Generally, three generations of master files should be retained to enable reproduction of files lost or destroyed. Under this *grandfather-father-son* principle of file retention, the current updated master file is the *son;* the master file utilized in the updating run that produced the son is the *father;* and the previous father is the *grandfather*. Records of transactions for the current period and for the prior period also should be retained to facilitate updating the older master files in the event that the current master file is accidentally destroyed. The three generations should be stored in separate sections of the library, or in separate locations, to minimize the risk of losing all three generations at once.

When programs are stored in online storage devices, users should be required to enter a secret password in order to gain access to the programs. The computer should maintain a log of all program usage and should produce a warning if repeated attempts are made to gain access to programs by the use of incorrect passwords.

Safeguards are also necessary to protect the equipment against sabotage, fire, and water damage. The best way to prevent deliberate damage is to limit access to the facility to authorized personnel. Outsiders should be kept away from the facility, and EDP personnel should be carefully screened before employment. Management should always be alert to the possibility of damage by a disgruntled employee. Frequently, the location of the computer facility is kept relatively secret. The facility should have no windows and few doors; entrances should be controlled by guards or badge-activated locks. In addition, the computer room should be fire resistant, air-conditioned, and above possible flood levels.

Controls over input

Input controls are designed to provide assurance that data received for processing represent properly authorized transactions and are accurate and complete when read into the computer. Control over input begins with proper authorization for initiation of the transactions to be processed. EDP is primarily a record-keeping department and therefore should not be authorized to initiate transactions. When transaction data are originally recorded on hard-copy source documents, such as sales orders, authorization may be indicated by the appropriate person initialing the document. In on-line systems, transaction data may be entered directly into the computer from remote terminal devices located in the departments initiating the transactions. In these cases, access to the terminals must be limited to those persons authorized to initiate transactions. This may be accomplished by assigning to authorized terminal users an identification number that must be read into the terminal before the computer will accept the input data.

In most systems, transaction documents are collected into batches for processing in sequence as one lot. Input controls are necessary in batch processing to determine that no data are lost or added to the batch. The sequence of serial numbers of source documents comprising each batch should be accounted for. In addition, such batch totals as item counts and totals for significant data fields should be developed for each batch; these totals may be verified during each stage of the processing of the batch.

Provision should be made for verifying the accuracy of the conversion of source documents to machine-readable media. For keypunch operations, a verifier punch should test the accuracy of the mechanical key strokes, or, as an alternative, the punched cards may be interpreted and visually compared to the source documents. A *self-checking number* may also be utilized to promote the reliability of identification and account numbers included in the input data.

Control over processing

Processing controls are designed to assure the reliability and accuracy of data processing. A major method of achieving control over processing is the use of *program controls*, which are written into the computer programs. Common program controls include:

1. Item (or record) count. A count of number of items or transactions to be processed in a given batch.

2. Control total. The predetermined total of one field of information for all items in a batch. An example would be total sales for a batch of sales orders. This control protects against missing amounts, duplication, and transposition errors in input or processing.

3. Hash total. A total of one field of information for all items in a batch, used in the same manner as a control total. The difference between a hash total and a control total is that a hash total has no intrinsic meaning. An example of a hash total would be the sum of the employee social security numbers in a payroll application.

4. Validity (code validity) test. A comparison of employee, vendor, and other codes against a master file for authenticity.

5. Limit test. A test of the reasonableness of a field of data, given a predetermined upper and/or lower limit.

6. Self-checking number. A number containing redundant information, such as the sum of digits in another number, permitting a check for accuracy after the number has been transmitted from one device to another.

7. File labels. Labels used to ensure that the proper transaction file or master file is being used on a specific run. A *header label* is a machine-readable message at the beginning of a tape file, identifying the file and its release date. A *trailer label* is the last record in a file and contains such control devices as an item count and/or control totals.

In cases of exceptions or errors disclosed by program controls, the computer processing will halt, or the errors will be printed out. Error printouts should be transmitted directly to the control group for followup. The control group's responsibility includes ascertaining that corrections of errors are properly entered into the appropriate batches and that duplicate corrections are avoided.

The control group also monitors the operator's activities. A log maintained by the operator should be available to the control group. The log records the description of each run, the elapsed time for the run, operator console interventions, machine halts, master files utilized, and so on.

Controls over output

Output controls are designed to assure the reliability of computer output and to determine that output is distributed only to authorized personnel. Departments external to EDP can appraise the reliability of output by maintaining independent control totals of input and by reviewing the output returned by the data processing department. The EDP control group should have the responsibility for distributing the computer output to the appropriate recipients and for following up on exceptions and errors reported by the recipients.

Internal auditing and EDP

An internal audit function should exist separate and distinct from the work of the control group in the data processing department. The control group is primarily concerned with day-to-day maintenance of the internal accounting controls for data processing, whereas the internal auditors are interested in evaluating the overall efficiency of data processing operations and the related internal controls.

The internal auditors should participate in the design of the data processing system to ensure that the system provides a proper *audit trail* and includes adequate internal controls. Once the system becomes operative, internal auditors review all aspects of the system on a test basis to determine that prescribed internal controls are operating as planned. Among other things, the internal auditors will test to determine that no changes are made in the system without proper authorization, programming personnel are functionally separate from computer operating personnel, adequate documentation is maintained, input controls are functioning effectively, and the control group is performing its assigned functions.

Integrated test facility. One method used by internal auditors to test and monitor accounting controls in EDP applications is an *integrated test facility*. An integrated test facility is a subsystem of dummy records and files built into the regular data processing system. These dummy files permit test data to be processed simultaneously with regular (live) input without adversely affecting the live data files or output. The test data, which include all conceivable types of transactions and exceptions, affect only the dummy files and dummy output. For this reason, an integrated test facility is often called the "mini-company approach" to testing the system. Integrated test facilities may be used in either on-line, real-time, or batch processing systems.

The internal auditing staff monitors the processing of test data, studying the effects upon the dummy files, error reports and other output produced, and the followup of exceptions by the control group. An integrated test facility for payroll applications, for example, could be set up by including a fictitious department and records for fictitious employees in the payroll master file. Input data for the dummy department would be included with input data from actual departments. Internal auditors would monitor all output relating to the dummy department, including payroll records, error reports, and payroll checks. (In this situation, strict control would be necessary to prevent misuse of the dummy payroll checks.)

One problem with integrated test facilities is the risk that someone may manipulate the real data files by transferring data to or from the dummy files. Controls should exist to prevent unauthorized access to the dummy files, and the internal auditors should monitor all activity in these files.

Impact of EDP on the audit trail

In a manual or mechanical data processing system, an audit trail of hard copy documentation links individual transactions with the summary figures in the financial statements. Computers, on the other hand, are able to create, update, and erase data in computer-based records without any visible evidence of a change being made. During the early development of EDP systems, this capability led to some concern among accountants that electronic data processing would obscure or even eliminate the audit trail. Although it is technologically possible to design an EDP system that would leave no audit trail, such a system would be neither practical nor desirable. Valid business reasons exist for the inclusion of a hard copy audit trail in even the most sophisticated EDP systems.

An adequate audit trail is necessary to enable management to direct and control the operations of the business, to permit file reconstruction in the event of processing errors or computer failure, and to accommodate the needs of independent auditors and governmental agencies. The Internal Revenue Service, for example, sets forth the following requirements in Revenue Procedure 64–12:

> *Supporting Documents and Audit Trails.* The audit trail should be designed so that the details underlying the summary accounting data, such as invoices and vouchers, may be identified and made available to the Internal Revenue Service upon request.
>
> *Recorded or Reconstructible Data.* The records must provide the opportunity to trace any transaction back to the original source or forward to a final total. If printouts are not made of transactions at the time they are processed, then the system must have the ability to reconstruct these transactions.

Thus, fears that EDP would obscure the audit trail have not materialized. During the design of an EDP system, management will normally consult with both its internal auditors and independent auditors to assure that an adequate audit trail is built into the system. In an EDP system, of course, the audit trail may consist of computer printouts and data stored on punched cards and magnetic tapes, rather than the more traditional handwritten source documents, journals, and ledgers.

Implications of on-line, real-time systems

An on-line, real-time system is one in which users have direct (on-line) access to the computer, and the recording of transactions causes instantaneous updating of all relevant files. An example of an on-line, real-time (*OLRT*) system is frequently encountered in savings and loan associations. These systems allow a teller at any branch to update a customer's account immediately by recording deposits or withdrawals on a computer terminal.

When an OLRT system is in use, input need not be entered to the computer in batch runs. Elimination of the batch concept poses several problems for auditors. For example, original source documents may not be available to support input to the computer, and batch controls, such as control totals and item counts, may not be applicable. Also, the overall amount of hard copy included in the audit trail may be substantially reduced.

For the purpose of providing an audit trail in an OLRT system, account balances should be printed out periodically. In addition, daily printouts should be prepared listing the transactions entered through each terminal. If specified terminals are used for certain types of transactions, the transaction records will be grouped by type of transaction. Printouts of account balances and transactions should be stored in a separate location from the computer files so they can be used for file reconstruction if necessary.

In an OLRT system there is a greater degree of reliance upon the computer for internal control. Input and output errors are detected primarily through program controls. Control must be exercised to prevent manipulation of the system as a whole, since the amount of hard copy and the possibilities for output verification are substantially reduced. Security should be provided at each terminal to assure that transactions are initiated only by authorized personnel. A validity check of an identification number should be made before a terminal user can gain access to files. Passwords should be required to gain access to specific programs and files, and a self-checking digit should be used with account numbers to prevent input into the wrong accounts. Terminals should be operative only during regular processing hours.

A log of all input should be maintained at each input terminal. These logs should be reconciled with the daily record of transactions maintained and printed out by the computer.

A special problem in an OLRT system is the need to provide for continuing operations in the event of computer failure. Mechanical equipment should be kept available, whenever feasible, to permit the continuance of operations during computer downtime. For processing that can be handled only by computer, arrangements should be made for another computer facility to provide backup computer services on short notice.

The auditors' study and evaluation of internal control in an EDP system

Whether financial statements are produced by a manual, mechanical, or electronic data processing system, the auditors must conduct a proper study and evaluation of internal control. This investigation provides the auditors with a basis for assessing the extent to which the client's internal controls may be relied upon in determining the nature, timing, and extent of work necessary to complete the audit. In addition, their evaluation of internal control serves as the basis for the auditors' recommendations to the client for improving the system.

Regardless of the type of data processing system used by the client, the auditors' study and evaluation of internal control involves three distinct steps. The auditors must (1) review internal control and prepare a description of the system in their working papers, (2) conduct tests of compliance to determine that accounting controls are functioning as prescribed, and (3) evaluate the system to determine the extent to which internal controls may be relied upon.

Review of internal control

Auditors acquire an understanding of an EDP system by making inquiries, observing operations, inspecting records and documents, studying flowcharts, and reviewing run manuals. This understanding is then documented in the audit working papers by the use of either systems flowcharts or a specially designed internal control questionnaire.

Systems flowcharts. As explained in Chapter 5, systems flowcharts are the most commonly used technique for describing a system of internal control in audit working papers. An advantage of flowcharting, with respect to EDP systems, is that the EDP department should have systems flowcharts available for all computer applications as part of the standard documentation.

An illustration of a system flowchart for sales, accounts receivable, and cash receipts appears in Figure 6–2. The following description of the illustrated procedures and processing steps should be helpful in studying the illustrated flowchart.

1. Orders are received from sales representatives, and sales invoices are mechanically produced by a posting machine. A punched paper tape is a by-product of the writing of the sales invoice. Two copies of the invoice are mailed to the customer, one copy is sent to the shipping department, and one copy is filed offline. The punched paper tape of sales invoice transactions is converted to magnetic tape. The items on the magnetic tape are then sorted into the proper sequence on another magnetic tape.

2. Individual cash remittance advices from customers are received from the mail room and verified to a batch total, which is also received from the mail room. These remittances are keypunched on cards, and the cards are verified. The deck of punched cards is then converted to magnetic tape. The items on the magnetic tape are in turn sorted into proper sequence on another magnetic tape.

3. The accounts receivable master file is updated by processing both the sales transactions tape and the cash receipts transactions tape. A by-product of the updating of the accounts receivable master file is an *error report* for the run and a printout (on an on-line typewriter) of any job messages.

The client's documentation of EDP activities usually includes *program flowcharts* as well as systems flowcharts. Program flowcharts illustrate the detailed logic of specific computer programs. Auditors

Figure 6–2
System flowchart

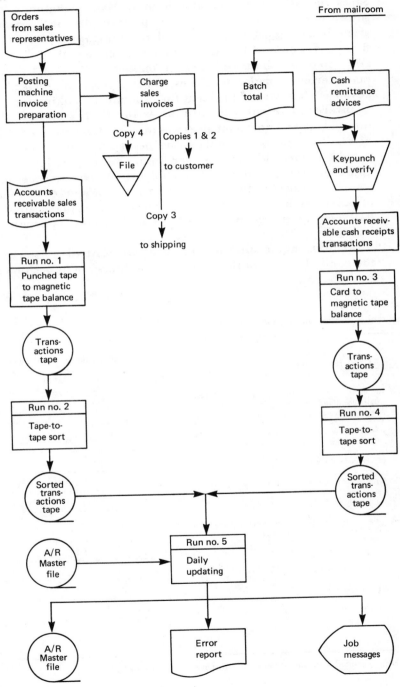

capable of interpreting program flowcharts may evaluate the program controls contained in specific computer applications and draw inferences regarding the computer output. Many computers will accept software routines that generate computer-made flowcharts of the programs in use. Auditors may use such routines to ensure that the program flowcharts contained in the documentation actually describe the programs in use. A shortcoming of this method is that even trained auditors may overlook a major deficiency within a program unless they know in advance what type of problem they should be looking for.

Internal control questionnaires for EDP systems. The use of internal control questionnaires was discussed in Chapter 5. In the audit of EDP systems, questionnaires are best suited for a study of organizational controls and controls over input and output. The questionnaire approach is not well suited to studying the effectiveness of program controls because neither the auditor nor the respondent is usually aware of situations in which program controls are inadequate. A portion of the EDP control questionnaire used by one national CPA firm is illustrated in Figure 6–3.

Preliminary evaluation of internal control. After completing their initial review of the system, the auditors are in position to make a

Figure 6–3
Internal control questionnaire for EDP systems—input controls

Section C -- Input Controls	Application (if additional columns are required, use additional pages)					
	#1			#2		
	Yes	No	N/A	Yes	No	N/A
C-1 Are initiating departments required to establish control over data submitted for processing (through the use of batch totals, document counts or other)?	___	___	___	___	___	___
C-2 Are there adequate controls over the creation of data and its conversion to machine-readable form?						
(a) Procedural controls	___	___	___	___	___	___
(b) Mechanical or visual verification	___	___	___	___	___	___
(c) Check digit	___	___	___	___	___	___
C-3 Is there adequate control over transmittal and input of data to detect loss or nonprocessing?	___	___	___	___	___	___
(a) Financial control totals	___	___	___	___	___	___
(b) Hash control totals	___	___	___	___	___	___
(c) Document counts	___	___	___	___	___	___
(d) Sequential numbering of input documents	___	___	___	___	___	___

Source: Reprinted with special permission of Laventhol & Horwath.

preliminary appraisal of the reliability of the client's accounting controls. If it appears that accounting controls may be sufficiently strong to provide a basis for reliance, the auditors must conduct tests of compliance before making their final evaluation of internal control. On the other hand, it may appear that accounting controls in some areas will not prove sufficiently reliable to justify the audit effort of compliance testing. In the interest of efficiency, the auditors may elect to place no reliance upon those accounting controls and omit the related compliance testing procedures.

Tests of compliance

Regardless of the nature of the client's data processing system, auditors must conduct tests of compliance if they are to place any reliance upon the client's internal controls. The purpose of these tests is to provide reasonable assurance that the internal controls described in the audit working papers are actually in use and operating as planned. The nature of the data processing system may, however, affect the specific procedures employed by the auditors in their compliance testing. In recognition of the effect of EDP upon these audit procedures, the AICPA issued an audit and accounting guide entitled *The Auditor's Study and Evaluation of Internal Control in EDP Systems*. This pronouncement describes the significant controls that should be present in EDP systems and provides guidelines for developing appropriate tests of compliance.

Auditors usually test general controls by observing the performance of duties by client personnel; reviewing authorizations, documentation, and approvals of programs and program changes; inspecting the equipment in use; and observing the security measures in force. The nature of general controls is such that their presence usually must be observed rather than determined by the examination of accounting data.

Procedures used to test applications controls vary significantly from one system or application to another. In a batch system, for example, input controls may be tested by accounting for the serial sequence of source documents in selected batches, verifying the computation of batch control totals, and comparing control totals to computer output. In an on-line real-time system, on the other hand, batch data are not available and the auditors must design entirely different compliance tests.

In testing processing controls, the auditors examine error reports printed by the computer, review the procedures performed by the EDP control group, and review the working papers of any testing done by the client's internal auditors. In addition, they must test the effectiveness of significant accounting controls written into the computer programs. Methods commonly used in compliance testing program controls include auditing "around the computer" and the use of test decks, controlled programs, and generalized audit software packages.

Auditing around the computer. One approach to testing processing controls in an EDP system is for the auditors to process input data manually on a test basis. The auditor's results are then compared to those obtained by the client's EDP department and any discrepancies are investigated. This technique is called auditing around the computer because the auditors bypass the computer rather than utilizing it in conducting their tests. As auditors have acquired greater expertise in auditing computer-based systems, testing procedures that make use of the computer (auditing *through the computer*) have tended to replace this older audit technique. However, auditing around the computer still can be very effective with respect to computer activities involving a risk of improper manipulation of EDP personnel.

Test decks. In the audit of a manual accounting system, the auditors trace sample transactions through the records from their inception to their final disposition. In the audit of an EDP system, a comparable approach is the use of a *test deck*. The test decks developed by the client's programmers may be utilized by the independent auditors once they have satisfied themselves by study of flowcharts and printouts that the tests are valid. Less desirably in terms of audit effort, the auditors may develop their own test decks.

Test decks should include all conceivable types of exceptions and errors in a process. Among these would be missing transactions, erroneous transactions, illogical transactions, out-of-balance batches, and out-of-sequence records. The auditors will carefully appraise the program controls and control group functions with respect to the test deck errors and exceptions. Dummy transactions and records used in test decks can be specially coded to avoid contamination of the client's genuine records and files. Test decks usually are used on a surprise basis so that the client's EDP personnel cannot modify the programs in anticipation of the auditors' tests.

Controlled programs. As an alternative or supplement to the test-deck approach, the auditors may monitor the processing of current data by using a duplicate program that is held under their control. They then compare their output to that developed by the client's copy of the program. They may also request the reprocessing of historical data with their controlled program for comparison with the original output. Reprocessing historical data may alert the auditors to undocumented changes in the client's programs.

Controlled programs are advantageous because the auditor may test the client's program with both genuine (live) and test data. A problem arises in testing historical data, however, since the client may not retain tape files beyond three generations.

Through controlled programs, auditors may test program controls without risk of contaminating the client's files. Also, the testing may be conducted at an independent computer facility without utilizing the client's computer or data processing personnel.

Generalized audit software.   Many large CPA firms have developed *generalized audit software* (computer programs), which may be used to test the reliability of the client's programs as well as to perform many specific auditing functions. This audit software is suited for use on a wide variety of computer systems.

One application of computer audit software is to verify the reliability of the client's programs through a process termed *parallel simulation.* The generalized audit software includes programs that can perform processing functions essentially equivalent to those of the client's programs. The generalized audit programs use the same files (transaction files and master files) as do the client's programs and should ideally produce the same results as were produced by the client. Thus, the

Figure 6–4
Flowchart of parallel simulation process

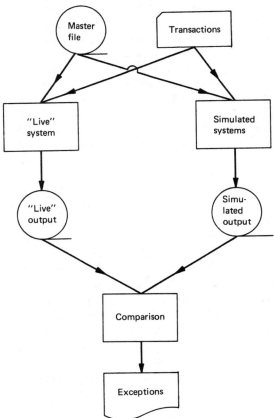

Source: Reprinted with special permission from *Tempo,* a quarterly journal published by Touche Ross & Co.

generalized audit programs simulate the client's processing of live data.

Although the generalized audit programs are likely to be less efficient than the client's programs, the output should be comparable in all material respects. The generalized audit software compares the simulated output to the client's records and prepares a listing of discrepancies. These discrepancies, of course, should be followed up and reconciled by the auditors. A flowchart of the parallel simulation process is illustrated in Figure 6–4.

The value of generalized audit software lies in the fact that the auditors are able to conduct independent processing of live data. Often, the verification of the client's output would be too large a task to be undertaken manually, but can be done efficiently through a parallel computer program. Even when manual verification would be possible, the use of a parallel program allows the auditors to expand greatly the size of the sample of transactions to be tested. An extensive examination of the client's files may become a feasible and economic undertaking. It is not necessary, however, to duplicate all of the client's data processing. Testing should be performed only to the extent necessary to determine the reliability of the client's financial reporting systems.

Generalized audit software and substantive testing. Audit software is available for a wide variety of audit applications. It is most widely used for retrieving data from the client's system for use by the auditors in substantiating account balances. In performing retrieval functions, the audit software *interfaces* with the client's master files and locates specific data requested by the auditors. The audit software may then be used to rearrange the data in a format more useful to the auditors, compare the data to other files, make computations, and select random samples. Applications of this nature include:

1. Examine the client's records for overall quality, completeness, and valid conditions. In auditing a manual system, the auditors become aware of the general quality, accuracy, and validity of the client's records through visual observation. Since the auditors do not have the same physical contact with computer-based records, the audit software may be used to scan the client's files for various improprieties. For example, the accounts receivable file may be scanned for account balances in excess of credit limits, and the depreciation expense may be recomputed for each item in the plant assets file. The great speed of the computer often makes it possible to perform such calculations for each item in the population, rather than having to rely upon a sample-based test.

2. Rearrange data and perform analyses. The audit software may be used to rearrange the data in the client's files into a format more useful to the auditors. For example, the accounts receivable file may be reorganized into the format of an aged trial balance. Data from the client's files may be printed out in the format of the auditors' working papers. In addition, the audit software can make analytical computations, such as computing turnover ratios to identify slow-moving inventory.

3.   Select audit samples.   Audit samples may be selected from the client's files on a random basis or using any other criteria specified by the auditors. Examples include selection of the inventory items to be test counted and the accounts receivable to be confirmed. An additional time savings may result if the audit software is used to print out the actual confirmation requests.

4.   Compare data on separate files.   When similar data is contained in two or more files, the audit software can compare the files and identify any discrepancies. For example, the changes in accounts receivable over a period of time may be compared to the details of the cash receipts and credit sales transactions files. Also, actual operating results may be compared to forecasts.

5.   Compare the results of audit procedures with the client's records.   Data obtained by the auditors may be converted to machine-readable form and compared to the data in computer-based files. For example, the results of the auditor's inventory test counts can be compared to the perpetual inventory file.

Using audit software: an illustration.   To illustrate some of the possible uses of generalized audit software, let us consider a specific example. Assume that an auditor is planning to observe a client's physical count of inventories at a specific date. All inventory is stored either in the client's distribution center or at a public warehouse. The client maintains computer-based perpetual inventory records, which are updated daily. This inventory file contains the following information:

Part number.	Cost per unit.
Description of item.	Date of last purchase.
Location.	Date of last sale.
Quantity on hand.	Quantity sold during the year.

The client has provided the auditor with a duplicate tape of the inventory file as of the date of the physical count.

The left-hand column in Figure 6–5 indicates typical inventory audit procedures the CPA might perform. The right-hand column indicates how the CPA's generalized audit software might be helpful in the performance of these procedures.

Auditors do not need extensive technical EDP knowledge in order to make use of generalized audit software. They will find it necessary to perform only a modest amount of programming. In fact, many CPA firms have found that they can train audit staff members to code specification sheets and operate a generalized audit program within a time span of a week or two. Because of the simplified procedures that have been developed, auditors can, after limited training, program and operate the generalized audit software independently—that is, without

===== Figure 6–5
Illustration of the uses of generalized audit software

Basic inventory audit procedure	How generalized audit software might be helpful
1. Observe the physical count, making appropriate test counts.	1. Determine which items are to be test counted by selecting from the inventory file a sample of items that provides the desired dollar coverage.
2. Test the mathematical accuracy of the inventory extensions and footings.	2. For each item in the inventory file, multiply the quantity on hand by the cost per unit, and add the extended amounts.
3. Compare the auditor's test counts to the inventory records.	3. Arrange the test counts in a tape format identical to the inventory file, and compare the two tapes.
4. Compare the client's physical count data to the inventory records	4. Compare the quantity of each item counted to the quantity on hand in the inventory file.
5. Perform a lower-of-cost-or-market test by obtaining a list of current costs per item from vendors.	5. Compare the current costs per unit to the cost per unit in the inventory file; print out extended value for each item, using lower of two unit costs, and add extended amounts.
6. Test purchases and sales cutoff.	6. List a sample of items on the inventory file for which the date of last purchase or last sale are on, or immediately before, the date of the physical count.
7. Confirm the existence of items located in public warehouses.	7. List items located in public warehouses.
8. Analyze inventory for evidence of obsolescence or slow-moving items.	8. List items from the inventory file for which the turnover ratio (quantity sold divided by quantity on hand) is low or for which the date of last sale indicates a lack of recent transactions.

Source: AICPA, adapted from Uniform CPA Examination.

assistance from the client's EDP personnel. On occasion, prepackaged software may not be available for a specific audit application. Most large CPA firms, however, have technical support groups that can design software routines to meet the specifications of the audit staff.

As previously mentioned, a number of the larger CPA firms have developed their own generalized audit software. Similar programs are available to other members of the profession through the AICPA.

Evaluation of internal control

Auditors evaluate internal control to determine the extent to which it may be relied upon to produce reliable accounting data. The extent of this reliance, in turn, determines the nature, timing, and extent of the substantive testing necessary for the auditors to express an opinion as to the fairness of the financial statements.

Conceptually, evaluating internal accounting controls over EDP activities is no different from evaluating other aspects of the system. Substantive testing procedures must be expanded in those areas where internal accounting controls are weak and may be restricted in areas where control is unusually strong. In evaluating accounting control over EDP activity, the auditors should consider the controls applied by user departments and internal auditing, as well as controls applied within the EDP department.

Computer service centers

Computer service centers provide data processing services to customers who do not do enough data processing to justify having their own computers. The customer delivers the input to the computer service center, and the service center processes the data and returns the output to the customer.

Computer service centers actually strengthen internal control because of increased subdivision of duties. Deliberate manipulation of a company's records is less likely because the persons doing the data processing do not have access to the company's assets. Also, since the service center processes input in small batches and provides hard-copy output to the customer, the independent auditors usually will have an adequate audit trail for evaluation of the processing conducted by the computer service center. Control totals, hash totals, and item counts may also be used effectively to ensure the reliability of the batch processing.

When their client uses a service center for data processing, the auditors ordinarily are able to evaluate internal control by auditing around the service center's computer, and possibly by using test decks. On occasion, the data processed by the service center may be material to the client's operations, and the client's controls over the data may not be adequate. In such situations, the auditors should consider visiting the service center to review, test, and evaluate the accounting controls in effect. To assist the auditors of clients using computer service centers, the AICPA has issued an audit guide entitled *Audits of Service-Center-Produced Records*.

Third-party reviews of service centers. Some service centers perform similar processing services for numerous clients. If the auditors of each client (called "user auditors") were to visit the service center for the purpose of reviewing accounting controls, they would probably all ask similar questions. To avoid such repetition, it may be advantageous for the service center to engage its own auditors to review and test the system of internal control at the service center and issue a report describing the system and their findings. The user auditors may then elect to rely upon this *third-party review* as an alternative to visiting the service center themselves. The cost of the third-party review may be borne by the service center, customers of the service center, or the user auditors.

Before relying upon a third-party review, the user auditors should take steps to satisfy themselves as to the independence and professional reputation of the third-party auditors. In addition, they should inquire of the service center management and the third-party auditors as to whether any significant changes have been made in accounting control at the service center subsequent to the third-party review.

Time-sharing systems

A time-sharing system consists of a large, fast, central computer that may be used simultaneously by a number of independent users at remote locations. Communication devices related to the computer permit translation of computer input into codes that are transmitted over telephone lines. Each user (subscriber) has on-line access to the central computer through a remote terminal. To use this terminal, either to enter input or receive output, the subscriber merely dials a telephone number and is automatically connected to the computer. The subscriber's files are maintained at the central computer facility. To prevent access to these files or other use of the computer by an unauthorized person, each subscriber is required to type an identification code into the terminal.

The subscribers to a commercial time-sharing system can, through their terminals, run programs, store these programs in the computer for subsequent use, use the programs developed by the time-sharing company, and store files of data in the computer for subsequent use. In brief, the user of a time-sharing system has available most of the services that would be available through ownership of a computer.

The central computer center should maintain controls to prevent unauthorized use of each customer's proprietary programs, loss or destruction of customers' data files, and alteration of customers' programs. Provision should also be made for file reconstruction. The internal controls most important to the auditors of a company having a time-sharing terminal are the client's control over input data and the program controls, such as item counts and control totals. Substantial hard-copy output is usually generated at the subscriber's access terminal; thus an adequate audit trail usually exists for verifying the reliability of data processing.

In most cases it is not feasible or necessary for the auditors to test or evaluate the internal control for the central computer; however, they may test the client's proprietary programs. Care must be taken so that test data do not permanently contaminate the client's files.

Large CPA firms have terminals in their offices across the country, all linked to national time-sharing networks. These terminals are used for such projects as forecasting financial statements with numerous input varibles, preparation of tax returns, selection of random samples for testing, staff training in computer skills, and also for administrative processes within the firm.

Auditing EDP systems—a look to the future

The computer was once viewed by some as a potential menace to auditors—a black box that threatened to make their task impossible by eliminating the audit trail. However, the public accounting profession has responded impressively to the challenges posed by the computer. Auditors have modified their procedures to fit electronic data processing systems and have harnessed the power of the computer to assist in the performance of many audit functions. Generalized computer audit programs have been developed that not only test the client's files and programs, but also perform simulations, capital budgeting applications, and other functions useful to both auditors and client. No longer are auditors dependent upon programmers in communicating with the computer. They have acquired the independent capacity to utilize the computer in achieving their goals.

As the routine clerical aspects of auditing are increasingly being delegated to the computer, auditors are able to broaden the scope of their activities and to emphasize the testing of management plans and policies. The use of computerized audit techniques may pave the way to the audit of quarterly financial statements as well as annual statements. Since interim financial statements are used as a basis for investment decisions, adding to their credibility through extension of the auditors' role is a logical consideration. (The auditors' responsibilities with respect to interim financial statements are discussed in Chapter 19.)

Computer audit programs for use with an on-line, real-time system are now being developed as an integral part of the client's EDP system. These programs select random samples of the processed data for subsequent review by both internal auditors and independent CPAs. Other audit functions might be made part of the system to ensure that all transactions processed meet stipulated criteria.

The painstaking work of developing input for a computer by use of punched cards or tape may be solved by improvements in optical scanning devices. A typewriter may be a sufficient input device if optical scanners capable of reading ordinary printed or typed material are available. In fact, auditors may type the evidence they gather on working papers, which will be read by optical scanners, automatically recorded on magnetic tape, and made available for processing by the computer.

The challenges of EDP are continuing to grow, and auditors will have to become increasingly familiar with EDP systems if they are to meet these challenges. Although staff auditors must have a good working knowledge of computer-based systems, they need not be computer specialists. In the audit of clients using sophisticated EDP systems, specialists in electronic data processing and specialists in statistical sampling may work with the audit team. The staff auditors, however, should have sufficient familiarity with EDP to design appropriate audit procedures for computer-based systems.

KEY TERMS INTRODUCED OR EMPHASIZED IN CHAPTER 6

Application controls Internal controls relating to a specific accounting task, such as preparation of a payroll.

Batch A group of transactions processed in sequence as one lot.

Boundary protection Protection against unauthorized entry (read or write) to a tape, disk, or other storage device.

Control total A total of one information field for all the records of a batch, such as the total sales dollars for a batch of sales invoices.

Disk A random access storage device consisting of a circular metal plate with magnetic material on both sides.

File An organized collection of related records, such as a customer file, which is usually arranged in sequence according to a key contained in each record.

File integrity The accuracy and reliability of data in a file.

General controls Internal accounting controls that relate to all EDP applications. The category includes organizational controls, documentation, equipment controls, and security controls.

Generalized audit software A group of computer programs used by auditors to locate and process data contained in a client's EDP-based records. The audit programs perform such functions as rearranging the data in a format more useful to the auditors, comparing records, selecting samples, and making computations. This software is compatible with a wide variety of different computer systems.

Hard copy Computer output in printed form, such as printed listings, reports, and summaries.

Hash total A meaningless control total such as the total of all invoice numbers in a batch of sales invoices, used to determine whether data are lost between operations.

Header label A machine-readable record at the beginning of a file that identifies the file.

Integrated test facility A set of dummy records and files included in an EDP system enabling test data to be processed simultaneously with live input.

Interface To run two or more files or programs simultaneously in a manner permitting data to be transferred from one to another.

Master file A file of relatively permanent data or information that is generally updated periodically.

Off-line Pertaining to peripheral devices or equipment not in direct communication with the central processing unit of the computer.

On-line Pertaining to peripheral devices or equipment in direct communication with the central processing unit of the computer.

Patch A new section of coding added in a rough or expedient way to modify a program.

Program flowchart A graphic representation of the major steps and logic of a computer program.

Random access Pertaining to a storage technique in which the time required to gain access to data is not significantly affected by the location of the data in storage. A disk is a random access device.

Record A group of related items or fields of data handled as a unit.

Record layout A diagram showing all the fields of data in a record and their arrangement in the record.

Self-checking number A number that contains a redundant suffixed digit (check digit) permitting the number to be verified for accuracy after it has been transferred from one device or medium to another.

Sequential access Pertaining to a storage technique in which the time required to gain access to data is related to the location of the data in storage. Magnetic tape is a sequential storage device.

Terminal An online input device. Many terminals are portable and may be connected to the computer through ordinary telephone lines. The method of entering data is usually a typewriter keyboard or an optical scanner.

Test deck A set of dummy records and transactions developed to test the adequacy of a computer program or system.

Third-party review (of a computer service center) An evaluation and report by an independent auditor on the internal accounting controls at a computer service center. Other auditors make use of this report in evaluating the internal control over data processing performed for their clients by the service center.

GROUP I: REVIEW QUESTIONS

6– 1.   Distinguish general controls from application controls, and give examples of the types of controls included in each of these broad categories.

6– 2.   Auxiliary storage devices used to augment the capacity of the storage unit of a computer include which of the following: (*a*) cathode-ray tubes, (*b*) magnetic drums, (*c*) card punches, (*d*) magnetic tape, (*e*) magnetic disk packs, (*f*) console display panels, (*g*) compilers, and (*h*) magnetic tape encoders?

6– 3.   An EDP department usually performs numerous data processing functions that would be separated in a manual system. Does this imply that separation of duties is not a practical means of achieving internal control in a computerized system? Explain.

6– 4.   What are the principal responsibilities of the control group in an electronic data processing department?

6– 5.   Explain briefly "on-line, real-time system."

6– 6.   Explain briefly the meaning of the terms *documentation* and *run manual* as used in an EDP department. How might a client's documentation be used by the auditors?

6– 7.   The number of personnel in an EDP department may limit the extent to which subdivision of duties is feasible. What is the minimum amount of segregation of duties that will permit satisfactory internal control?

6–8.   Compare the responsibilities and objectives of the EDP control group to those of the internal auditors with respect to EDP activities.

6–9.   What is an integrated test facility? How is it used?

6–10. Define and give the purpose of each of the following program or equipment controls:

   a.   Record counts.

   b.   Limit test.

   c.   Reverse multiplication.

   d.   Hash totals. (AICPA, adapted)

6–11. Most electronic data processing equipment manufacturers have built-in controls to ensure that information is correctly read, processed, transferred within the system, and recorded. One of these built-in controls is the parity bit.

   a.   What is the parity bit?

   b.   When would the parity bit control be used? (AICPA)

6–12. Distinguish equipment controls from program controls and give examples of each.

6–13. Differentiate between a systems flowchart and a program flowchart.

6–14. Auditors should be familiar with the terminology employed in electronic data processing. The following statements contain some of the terminology so employed. Indicate whether each statement is true or false.

   a.   A recent improvement in computer hardware is the ability to automatically produce error listings. Previously, this was possible only when provisions for such a report were included in the program.

   b.   The control of input and output to and from the EDP department should be performed by an independent control group.

   c.   An internal-audit computer program that continuously monitors computer processing is a feasible approach for improving internal control in OLRT systems.

   d.   An internal label is one of the controls built into the hardware by the manufacturer of a magnetic tape system.

   e.   A limit test in a computer program is comparable to a decision that an individual makes in a manual system to judge a transaction's reasonableness.

   f.   A principal advantage of using magnetic tape files is that data need not be recorded sequentially.

   g.   A major advantage of disk files is the ability to gain random access to data on the disk.

   h.   The term *grandfather-father-son* refers to a method of computer record security rather than to generations in the evolution of computer hardware.

   i.   A control total is an example of a self-checking number within a batch control.

   j.   When they are not in use, tapes, disks, and card files should be stored apart from the computer room under the control of a librarian.

6–15. Explain the fundamental differences between the use of a test deck and the use of generalized audit software.

6–16. Is it probable that the use of EDP will eventually eliminate the audit trail, making it impossible to trace individual transactions from their origin to the summary totals in the financial statements? Explain the reasons for your answer.

6–17. What is a computer service center? Does the use of a computer service center tend to strengthen or weaken a client's internal control? Explain.

6–18. Does a time-sharing system require the subscriber to deliver batches of data to a center for processing?

GROUP II: QUESTIONS REQUIRING ANALYSIS

6–19. What are the purposes of each of the following categories of application controls?
   a. Input controls.
   b. Processing controls.
   c. Output controls. (AICPA, adapted)

6–20. The first requirement of an effective system of internal control is a satisfactory plan of organization. Explain the characteristics of a satisfactory plan of organization for an EDP department, including the relationship between the department and the rest of the organization.

6–21. An effective system of internal control requires a sound system of records control, of operations and transactions (source data and their flow), and of classification of data within the accounts. For an EDP system, these controls include input controls, processing controls, and output controls. List the characteristics of a satisfactory system of input controls. Confine your comments to a batch-controlled system employing punched cards and to the steps that occur before the processing of the input cards in the computer. (AICPA, adapted)

6–22. Distinguish between batch processing and on-line, real-time (OLRT) processing. In which of these systems is strong internal accounting control over input most easily attained? Explain.

6–23. The use of test decks is one method of performing compliance tests of processing controls in an EDP system. Identify and discuss several other methods by which auditors may test internal processing controls over EDP activity.

6–24. Discuss how generalized audit software can be used to aid the auditor in examining accounts receivable in a fully computerized system. (AICPA, adapted)

6–25. Many companies have part or all of their data processing done by computer service centers.
   a. What controls should the company maintain to assure the accuracy of processing done by a service center?
   b. How do auditors test and evaluate internal control over applications processed for an audit client by a service center?
   c. What is a third-party review of a computer service center? Explain

the rationale behind third-party reviews and the procedures user auditors must employ before relying upon such reviews.

6–26. Select the best answers for each of the following questions. Explain the reasons for your selection.

a. Which of the following **best** describes a fundamental control weakness often associated with EDP systems?

(1) EDP equipment is more subject to mechanical error than manual processing is subject to human error.

(2) EDP equipment processes and records all similar transactions in a similar manner.

(3) EDP procedures for detection of invalid transactions are less effective than manual control procedures.

(4) Functions that normally would be separated in a manual system are combined in an EDP system.

b. A customer inadvertently ordered part number 12368 rather than part number 12638. In processing this order, the error would be detected by the vendor with which of the following controls?

(1) Batch total.

(2) Key punch verifying.

(3) Self-checking digit.

(4) Limit test.

c. Which of the following would **lessen** internal control in an EDP system?

(1) The computer librarian maintains custody of computer program instructions and detailed listings.

(2) Computer operators have access to operator instructions and detailed program listings.

(3) The control group is solely responsible for distribution of all computer output.

(4) Programmers write and debug programs that perform routines designed by the systems analysts.

d. Data Corporation has just completely computerized its billing and accounts receivable record keeping. You want to make maximum use of the new computer in your audit of Data Corporation. Which of the following audit procedures could not be performed through a computer program?

(1) Tracing audited cash receipts to accounts receivable credits.

(2) Selecting on a random number basis accounts to be confirmed.

(3) Examining sales invoices for completeness, consistency between different items, and reasonableness of amounts.

(4) Resolving differences reported by customers on confirmation requests.

GROUP III: PROBLEMS

6–27. The Central Valley Utility District is installing an electronic data processing system. The CPA who conducts the annual examination of the utility district's financial statements has been asked to recommend controls for the new system.

Required:

Discussed recommended controls over:

a.   Program documentation.

b.   EDP hardware.

c.   Tape files and programs. (AICPA, adapted)

6–28.   CPAs may audit around or through computers in the examination of the financial statements of clients who utilize computers to process accounting data.

Required:

a.   Describe the auditing approach referred to as auditing around the computer.

b.   Under what conditions do CPAs decide to audit through the computer instead of around the computer?

c.   In auditing through the computer, CPAs may use test decks.
    (1)   What is a test deck?
    (2)   Why do CPAs use test decks?

d.   How can the CPAs be satisfied that the computer programs presented to them for testing are actually those used by the client for processing accounting data? (AICPA, adapted)

6–29.   A CPA's client, The Outsider, Inc., is a medium-size manufacturer of products for the leisure time activities market (camping equipment, scuba gear, bows and arrows, and so on). During the past year, a computer system was installed, and inventory records of finished goods and parts were converted to computer processing. The inventory master file is maintained on a disk. Each record of the file contains the following information:

Item or part number.
Description.
Size.
Unit of measure code.
Quantity on hand.
Cost per unit.
Total value of inventory on hand at cost.
Date of last sale or usage.
Quantity sold or used this year.
Economic order quantity.
Code number of major vendor.
Code number of secondary vendor.

In preparation for year-end inventory, the client has two identical sets of preprinted inventory count cards. One set is for the client's inventory counts and the other is for the CPA's use to make audit test counts. The following information has been keypunched into the cards and interpreted on their face:

Item or part number.
Description.
Size.
Unit of measure code.

In taking the year-end inventory, the client's personnel will write the actual counted quantity on the face of each card. When all counts are complete, the counted quantity will be keypunched into the cards. The cards will be processed against the disk file, and quantity-on-hand figures will be adjusted to reflect the actual count. A computer listing will be prepared to show any missing inventory count cards and all quantity adjustments of more than $100 in value. These items will be investigated by client personnel, and all required adjustments will be made. When adjustments have been completed, the final year-end balances will be computed and posted to the general ledger.

The CPA has available generalized audit software that can process both cards and disk files.

Required:
a.   In general and without regard to the facts above, discuss the nature of generalized audit software and list the various types of uses of such software.
b.   List and describe at least five ways general purpose audit software can be used to assist in the audit of inventory of The Outsider, Inc. (For example, the software can be used to read the disk inventory master file and list items of high unit cost or total value. Such items can be included in the CPA's test counts to increase the dollar coverage of the audit verification.) (AICPA, adapted)

6–30.   You will be examining for the first time the financial statements of Central Savings and Loan Association for the year ending December 31. The CPA firm that examined the association's financial statements for the prior year issued an unqualified audit report.

At the beginning of the current year, the association installed an on-line, real-time computer system. Each teller in the association's main office and seven branch offices has an on-line input-output terminal. Customers' mortgage payments and savings account deposits and withdrawals are recorded in the accounts by the computer from data input by the teller at the time of the transaction. The teller keys the proper account by account number and enters the information in the terminal keyboard to record the transaction. The accounting department at the main office has both punched card and typewriter input-output devices. The computer is housed at the main office.

Required:
You would expect the association to have certain internal controls in effect because an on-line, real-time computer system is employed. List the internal controls that should be in effect solely because this system is employed, classifying them as:
a.   Those controls pertaining to input of information.
b.   All other types of computer controls. (AICPA, adapted)

6–31.   Lee Wong, CPA, is examining the financial statements of the Alexandria Corporation, which recently installed an off-line electronic computer. The following comments have been extracted from Wong's notes on computer operations and the processing and control of shipping notices and customer invoices:

To minimize inconvenience Alexandria converted without change its existing data processing system, which utilized tabulating equipment. The computer company supervised the conversion and has provided training to all computer department employees (except keypunch operators) in systems design, operations, and programming.

Each computer run is assigned to a specific employee, who is responsible for making program changes, running the program, and answering questions. This procedure has the advantage of eliminating the need for records of computer operations because each employee is responsible for his or her own computer runs.

At least one computer department employee remains in the computer room during office hours, and only computer department employees have keys to the computer room.

System documentation consists of those materials furnished by the computer company—a set of record formats and program listings. These and the tape library are kept in a corner of the computer department.

The corporation considered the desirability of program controls, but decided to retain the manual controls from its existing system.

Company products are shipped directly from public warehouses, which forward shipping notices to general accounting. There a billing clerk enters the price of the item and accounts for the numerical sequence of shipping notices from each warehouse. The billing clerk also prepares daily adding machine tapes (control tapes) of the units shipped and the unit prices.

Shipping notices and control tapes are forwarded to the computer department for keypunching and processing. Extensions are made on the computer. Output consists of invoices (in six copies) and a daily sales register. The daily sales register shows the aggregate totals of units shipped and unit prices, which the computer operator compares to the control tapes.

All copies of the invoice are returned to the billing clerk. The clerk mails three copies to the customer, forwards one copy to the warehouse, maintains one copy in a numerical file, and retains one copy in an open invoice file that serves as a detailed accounts receivable record.

Required:
Describe weaknesses in internal control over information and data flows and the procedures for processing shipping notices and customer invoices, and recommend improvements in these controls and processing procedures. Organize your answer sheets as follows:

Weakness	Recommended improvement

(AICPA, adapted)

Evidence—what kind and how much?

How important is the gathering of evidence to the independent auditor? All important—this is the very essence of auditing. A company's financial statements are the representations and assertions of the company's management. The role of the independent auditors is to perform an examination enabling them to express an opinion as to the fairness[1] of these representations. Thus, an audit may be regarded as the process of gathering and evaluating sufficient evidence to provide an adequate basis for expressing an opinion on financial statements.

Sufficient competent evidential matter

The third standard of field work states:

> *Sufficient competent evidential matter* is to be obtained through inspection, observation, inquiries, and confirmations to afford a reasonable basis for an opinion regarding the financial statements under examination. (Emphasis added.)

What constitutes "sufficient competent evidential matter"? This question arises repeatedly during the planning and performance of

---

[1] As discussed in Chapter 1 and in *SAS No. 5*, the concept of fairness embodies such specifics as conformity with generally accepted accounting principles and adequate disclosure.

every audit engagement. When an auditor is accused of negligence in the performance of an examination, the answer to this question may determine the CPA's innocence or guilt. To provide auditors with guidelines for answering this question, the Auditing Standards Board has issued *SAS No. 31*, "Evidential Matter," specifically addressing the nature, competence, and sufficiency of audit evidence.

Nature of evidential matter. Evidential matter is *any information that corroborates or refutes a premise*. The auditors' premise is that the financial statements present fairly the client's financial position and operating results. One major source of evidential matter is the client's accounting system, including journals, ledgers, and supporting documentary materials (such as checks, invoices, and minutes of meetings). The client's accounting system by itself, however, cannot be considered sufficient evidential matter to support the auditors' opinion on the financial statements. The auditors must also gather evidence through firsthand observation of assets and from a variety of sources outside of the client company.

The evidence gathered by auditors during the course of an examination may assume many forms. For example, observation of assets, confirmation of transactions by third parties, the auditors' judgmental evaluation of internal control, and information obtained in a telephone conversation may all be viewed as audit evidence.

Competence—a relative term. The competence of evidential matter refers to its *quality* or *reliability*. The relative competence of different types of evidential matter may vary greatly. Several factors contribute to the quality of evidential matter, including the following:

1. When auditors obtain evidence from independent sources *outside of the client company*, the reliability of the evidence is increased.

2. *Strong internal accounting control* contributes substantially to the quality of accounting records and other evidence created within the client organization.

3. The quality of evidence is enhanced when the auditors obtain the information *directly*—that is, by firsthand observation, correspondence, or computation, rather than by obtaining the information secondhand.

In addition, the competence of evidential matter is increased when the auditors are able to obtain additional information to support the original evidence. Thus, several pieces of related evidence may form a package of evidence that has greater competence than do any of the pieces viewed individually.

Sufficiency—a matter of judgment. The term *sufficient* relates to the *quantity* of evidence the auditors should obtain. The amount of evidential matter that is considered sufficient to support the auditors' opinion is a matter of professional judgment. However, the following considerations may be useful in evaluating the sufficiency of audit evidence:

1. The amount of evidence that is sufficient in a specific situation varies *inversely* with the competence of the evidence available. Thus, the less competent the evidential matter, the more of it that is needed to support the auditors' opinion.
2. The need for evidential matter is closely related to the concept of *materiality.* The more material an item, the greater the need for evidential matter as to its validity. Conversely, little or no evidence is needed to support items that are not material.
3. In every audit engagement, there is an element of risk that the auditors may overlook material error and issue an unqualified report when one is not warranted. This risk varies from one engagement to the next, depending upon such factors as the client's financial condition and line of business and the integrity of management. As the *relative risk* associated with a particular engagement increases, the auditors should require more evidence to support their opinion. (The concept of relative risk is discussed in more detail later in this chapter.)

Types of audit evidence

A fuller understanding of the competence of audit evidence may be gained by a brief consideration of the more important types of evidence gathered by the independent auditors as a basis for their opinion. The types of evidence to be discussed are as follows:

1. Internal control.
2. Physical evidence.
3. Documentary evidence.
    a. Documentary evidence created outside the client organization and transmitted directly to the auditors.
    b. Documentary evidence created outside the client organization and held by the client.
    c. Documentary evidence created and held within the client organization.
4. Accounting records.
5. Analytical review procedures (comparisons and ratios).
6. Computations.
7. Evidence provided by specialists.
8. Oral evidence.
9. Client letters of representations.

1.   Internal control as evidence

In verifying the financial statements by working back through the accounting records, it is not practicable for the auditors to examine every invoice, check, or other piece of documentary evidence. The solution lies in a study of the methods and procedures by which the company carries on its accounting processes. If these procedures are well designed and consistently followed, the end results in the form of financial statements will be valid. The auditors' approach is, therefore, to study and evaluate the system of internal control, including in this study a series of compliance tests to determine that the company's accounting procedures are actually working as intended.

An adequate system of internal control promotes accuracy and reliability in accounting data. Errors are quickly and automatically brought to light by the built-in proofs and cross-checks inherent in the system. Consequently, if the auditors find that the client company has a carefully devised system of internal control and that the prescribed practices are being consistently followed in day-to-day operations, they will regard the existence of this system of internal control as strong evidence of the validity of the amounts in the financial statements.

The auditors' opinion that financial statements are free from material error is a combination of their reliance upon (1) the effectiveness of the client's internal accounting controls in *preventing* the occurrence of such errors, and (2) the auditors' substantive tests to *detect* any material error that may have occurred. Thus, the adequacy of the client's internal accounting control is a major factor in determining how much evidence the auditors will need to gather from other sources. The stronger the internal control, the less evidence of other types that will be required as a basis for the auditors' opinion. When internal control is weak, the auditors must gather a correspondingly greater amount of other kinds of evidence.

2. Physical evidence

Actual observation or count of certain types of assets is the best evidence of their physical existence. The amount of cash on hand is verified by counting; inventories are also observed and counted. The existence of property and equipment, such as automobiles, buildings, office equipment, and factory machinery, may also be established by physical observation.

At first thought, it might seem that physical observation of an asset would be conclusive verification, but this is often not true. For example, if the cash on hand to be counted by the auditors includes checks received from customers, the making of a count provides no assurance that all of the checks will prove to be collectible when deposited. There is also the possibility that one or more worthless checks may have been created deliberately by a dishonest employee as a means of concealing from the auditors the existence of a cash shortage.

The physical observation of inventory may also leave some important questions unanswered. The quality and condition of merchandise or of goods in process are vital in determining salability. If the goods counted by the auditors contain hidden defects or are obsolete, a mere counting of units does not substantiate the dollar value shown on the balance sheet.

Illustrative case. During the observation of the physical inventory of a company manufacturing costly aircraft instruments, an auditor counted more than a hundred instruments of a given type, each of which had cost several hundred dollars to manufacture. After the inventory taking had been completed, the auditor was informed by the client that these instruments were defective and could not be sold. The defective instruments were identical in appearance with other satisfactory instruments.

Since auditors examine such widely differing businesses as breweries, mines, and jewelry stores, it is not possible for them to become expert in appraising the products of all their clients. However, CPAs should be alert to any clues that raise a doubt as to the quality or condition of inventories. CPAs often request clients to hire independent specialists to provide the auditors with information on quality or condition of inventories.

In the case of plant and equipment, the auditors' physical observation verifies the existence of the asset, but gives no proof of ownership. A fleet of automobiles used by salespeople and company executives, for example, might be leased rather than owned—or if owned might be subject to a mortgage. Further, physical observation does not substantiate the cost of the plant assets.

In summary, physical observation provides evidence as to the *existence* of certain assets, but generally needs to be supplemented by other types of evidence to determine the ownership, cost, and condition of these assets. For some types of assets, such as accounts receivable or intangible assets, even the existence of the asset cannot be verified through physical evidence.

3.   Documentary evidence

The most important type of evidence relied upon by auditors consists of documents. The worth of a document as evidence depends in part upon whether it was created within the company (for example, a sales invoice) or came from outside the company (as in the case of a vendor's invoice). Some documents created within the company (checks, for example) are sent outside the organization for endorsement and processing; because of this critical review by outsiders these documents are regarded as very reliable evidence.

In appraising the reliability of documentary evidence, the auditors should consider whether the document is of a type that could easily be forged or created in its entirety by a dishonest employee. A stock certificate evidencing an investment in marketable securities is usually elaborately engraved and would be most difficult to falsify. On the other hand, a note receivable may be created by anyone in a moment merely by filling in the blank spaces in one of the standard note forms available at any bank.

Documentary evidence created outside the client organization and transmitted directly to the auditors. The best quality of documentary evidence consists of documents created by independent parties outside the client's organization and transmitted directly to the auditors without passing through the client's hands. For example, in the verification of accounts receivable, the customer is requested by the client to write directly to the auditors to confirm the amount owed to the auditors' client. To assure that the customer's reply comes directly to the auditors and not to the client, the auditors will enclose with the confirmation request a return envelope addressed to the auditors' office. If the replies were addressed to the auditors at the client's place of business, an opportunity would exist for someone in the client's organization to intercept the customer's letter and alter the amount of indebtedness reported, or even destroy the letter.

Similar precautions are taken in the verification of cash in bank. The client will request the bank to advise the auditors directly in writing of the amounts the client has on deposit.

Other types of documents created outside the client's organization and transmitted directly to the auditors include letters from the client's attorneys describing any pending litigation and listings of insurance in force provided by the client's insurance broker. In each case, the client requests the outsider to furnish the information directly to the auditors in an envelope addressed to the auditors' office; and the auditors mail the request.

Documentary evidence created outside the client organization and held by the client. Many of the externally created documents referred to by the auditors will, however, be in the client's possession. Examples include bank statements, vendors' invoices and statements, property tax bills, notes receivable, contracts, customers' purchase orders, and stock and bond certificates. In deciding how much reliance to place upon this type of evidence, the auditors should consider whether the document is of a type that could be easily created or altered by someone in the client's employ. The auditors should be particularly cautious in accepting as evidence any documents that have been altered in any way. Of course, an alteration may have been made by the company originating the document to correct an accidental error. In general, however, business concerns do not send out documents marred by errors and corrections. The auditors cannot afford to overlook the possibility that an alteration on a document may have been made deliberately to misstate the facts and to mislead auditors or others who relied upon the document.

In pointing out the possibility that externally created documents in the client's possession *might* have been forged or altered, it is not intended to discredit this type of evidence. Externally created documents in the possession of the client are used extensively by auditors and are considered, in general, as a stronger type of evidence than documents created by the client.

Documentary evidence created and held within the client organization. No doubt the most dependable single piece of documentary evidence created within the client's organization is a paid check. The check bears the endorsement of the payee and a perforation or stamp indicating payment by the bank. Because of this review and processing of a check by outsiders, the auditors will usually look upon a paid check as a strong type of evidence. The paid check may be viewed as evidence that an asset was acquired at a given cost, or as a proof that a liability was paid, or an expense incurred. Of course the amount of the check might have been raised by an alteration subsequent to its payment, but protection against this possibility is afforded through the preparation of bank reconciliations, and also through comparison of paid checks with the entries on the bank statement and in the cash payment records.

Most companies place great emphasis on proper internal control of cash disbursements by such devices as the use of serial numbers on checks, signature (or two signatures) by responsible officials, and separation of the check-signing function from the accounting function. This emphasis on internal control over cash payments lends additional assurance that a paid check is a valid document.

Most documents created within the client organization represent a lower quality of evidence than a paid check because they circulate only within the company and do not receive critical review by an outsider. Examples of internally created documents that do not leave the client's possession are sales invoices, shipping notices, purchase orders, receiving reports, and credit memoranda. Of course, the original copy of a sales invoice or purchase order is sent to the customer or supplier, but the carbon copy available for the auditors' inspection has not left the client's possession.

The degree of reliance to be placed on documents created and used only within the organization depends on the adequacy of the system of internal control. If the accounting procedures are so designed that a document prepared by one person must be critically reviewed by another, and if all documents are serially numbered and all numbers in the series accounted for, these documents may represent reasonably good evidence. Adequate internal control will also provide for extensive subdivision of duties so that no one employee handles a transaction from beginning to end. An employee who maintains records or creates documents, such as credit memoranda, should not have access to cash. Under these conditions there is no incentive for an employee to falsify a document, since the employee creating documents does not have custody of assets.

On the other hand, if internal control is weak, the auditors cannot place much reliance on documentary evidence created within the organization and not reviewed by outsiders. There is the danger not only of fictitious documents created to cover theft by an employee, but also the possibility, however remote, that management is purposely presenting misleading financial statements and has prepared false supporting documents for the purpose of deceiving the auditors.

4. Accounting records as evidence

When auditors attempt to verify an amount in the financial statements by tracing it back through the accounting records, they will ordinarily carry this tracing process through the ledgers to the journals and on back to such basic documentary evidence as a paid check, invoice, or other original papers. To some extent, however, the ledger accounts and the journals constitute worthwhile evidence in themselves.

The dependability of ledgers and journals as evidence is indicated by the extent of internal control covering their preparation. Whenever possible, subsidiary ledgers for receivables, payables, and plant equipment should be maintained by persons not responsible for the general ledger. All general journal entries should be approved in writing by the controller or other official. If ledgers and journals are produced by an electronic data processing system, the safeguards described in Chapter 6 should be in effect. When controls of this type exist and the records appear to be well maintained, the auditors may regard the ledgers and journals as affording considerable support for the financial statements.

As a specific example, assume that the auditors wish to determine that the sale of certain old factory machinery during the year under audit was properly recorded. By reference to the subsidiary ledger for plant and equipment, they might ascertain that the depreciation accumulated during the years the machine was owned agreed with the amount cleared out of the Accumulated Depreciation account at the time of sale. They might also note that the original cost of the machine as shown in the plant ledger agreed with the credit to the Plant and Equipment control account when the machine was sold, and that the proceeds from sale were entered in the cash receipts journal. Assuming that the plant ledger, general ledger, and the cash receipts journal are independently maintained by three different employees, or are produced by an electronic data processing department with effective internal control, the agreement of these records offers considerable evidence that the sale of the machine was a legitimate transaction and properly recorded. Whether the auditors should go beyond this evidence and examine original documents, such as the bill of sale or a work order authorizing the sale, would depend upon the relative importance of the amount involved and upon other circumstances of the audit.

In addition to journals and ledgers, other accounting records providing evidential matter for independent auditors include sales summaries, trial balances, interim financial statements, and operating and financial reports prepared for management.

5.   Analytical review procedures as evidence

Analytical review procedures involve the study of trends, percentage changes, ratios, and other relationships among financial data. For example, current levels of revenue and expense may be compared to those of prior periods, to industry averages, to budgeted levels, and to relevant nonfinancial data, such as units produced or hours of direct labor. In addition, auditors study the percentage relationships of various items in the financial statements. Any unexpected fluctuations in these relationships should be explored until the auditors are satisfied that a valid reason exists for the abnormal relationship.

The fact that relationships among financial data appear normal is a relatively low quality of audit evidence. However, unusual fluctuations in these relationships may indicate serious problems in the financial statements. For this reason, *SAS No. 23* recommends that auditors apply analytical review procedures in every audit engagement.[2]

Illustrative Case.   In performing an analytical review for a marine supply store, the auditors noticed that uncollectible accounts expense, which normally had been running about 1 percent of net sales for several years, had increased in the current year to 6 percent of net sales. This significant variation caused the auditors to make a careful investigation of all accounts written off during the year and those presently past due. Most of the uncollectible accounts examined were found to be fictitious, and the cashier-bookkeeper then admitted that he had created those accounts to cover up his abstraction of cash receipts.

Analytical review procedures may be performed at various stages of the examination. For example, they may be useful in the early planning stage for directing the auditor's attention to areas requiring special investigation. Also, they may be applied during the audit to provide evidence as to the reasonableness of specific account balances. Finally, many CPA firms apply analytical review procedures at the end of the engagement as a final overview of the audited figures. This last application provides assurance that the auditors have not "failed to see the forest because of the trees." Since analytical review procedures provide evidence as to the reasonableness of specific account balances, they are regarded as substantive tests.

6.   Computations as evidence

Another form of audit evidence consists of computations made independently by the auditors to prove the arithmetical accuracy of the client's records. Computations differ from analytical review procedures. An analytical review involves the analysis of relationships among financial data, whereas computations simply verify mathematical processes. In its simplest form, an auditor's computation might consist of footing a column of figures in a sales journal or in a ledger account to prove the column total.

---

[2] *Statement on Auditing Standards No. 23*, "Analytical Review Procedures," AICPA (New York, 1978).

Independent computations may be used to prove the accuracy of such client calculations as earnings per share, depreciation expense, allowance for uncollectible accounts, revenue recognized on a percentage-of-completion basis, and provisions for federal and state income taxes. The computation of a client's pension liability normally involves actuarial assumptions and computations beyond an auditors area of expertese. Therefore, auditors usually enlist the services of an actuary to verify this liability.

7. Evidence provided by specialists

We have pointed out that CPAs may not be experts in such technical tasks as judging the quality of a client's inventory or making the actuarial computations to verify pension liabilities. Other phases of an audit in which CPAs lack the special qualifications necessary to determine the fairness of the client's representations include assessing the probable outcome of pending litigation and estimating the number of barrels of oil in an underground oil field.

In *SAS No. 11*, "Using the Work of a Specialist," the AICPA recognized the necessity for CPAs to consult with experts, when appropriate, as a means of gathering competent audit evidence. *SAS No. 11* defined a *specialist* as a person or firm possessing special skill or knowledge in a field other than accounting or auditing, giving as examples actuaries, appraisers, attorneys, engineers, and geologists. It is desirable that the specialist consulted by the auditors be unrelated to the client; however, in some instances it is acceptable for the specialist to have an existing relationship with the client. For example, the most logical specialist to consult regarding pending litigation would be the client's legal counsel. In any event, the auditors are responsible for ascertaining the professional qualifications and reputation of the specialist consulted.

Auditors cannot accept a specialist's findings blindly; they must obtain an understanding of the methods or assumptions used by the specialist and test accounting data furnished to the specialist by the client. The CPAs may accept the specialist's findings as competent audit evidence unless their tests cause them to believe the findings are unreasonable.

8. Oral evidence

Throughout their examination the auditors will ask a great many questions of the officers and employees of the client's organization. Novice auditors are sometimes afraid to ask questions for fear of seeming to be uninformed and inexperienced. Such an attitude is quite illogical; even the most experienced and competent auditors will ask a great many questions. These questions cover an endless range of topics—the location of records and documents, the reasons underlying an unusual accounting procedure, the probabilities of collecting a long past-due account receivable.

The answers auditors receive to these questions constitute another type of evidence. Generally, oral evidence is not sufficient in itself, but it may be useful in disclosing situations that require investigation or in corroborating other forms of evidence. For example, an auditor after making a careful analysis of all past-due accounts receivable will normally sit down with the credit manager and get that official's views on the prospects for collection of accounts considered doubtful. If the opinions of the credit manager are in accordance with the estimates of uncollectible accounts losses that have been made independently by the auditor, this oral evidence will constitute significant support of the conclusions reached. In repeat examinations of a business, the auditor will be in a better position to evaluate the opinions of the credit manager based on how well the manager's estimates in prior years have worked out.

9.   Representations letters as evidence

At the conclusion of the examination, auditors obtain from the client a written letter of representations summarizing the most important oral representations made during the engagement. Many specific items are included in this representations letter. For example, management usually represents that all liabilities known to exist are reflected in the financial statements. Most of the representations fall into the following broad categories:

1.   All accounting records, financial data, and minutes of directors' meetings have been made available to the auditors.
2.   The financial statements are complete and prepared in conformity with generally accepted accounting principles.
3.   All items requiring disclosure (such as loss contingencies, illegal acts, and related party transactions) have been properly disclosed.

SAS No. 19, "Client Representations," requires auditors to obtain a representations letter on every engagement and provides suggestions as to its form and content. These letters are dated as of the last day of field work (which also is the date of the audit report) and usually are signed by both the client's chief executive officer and chief financial officer.

A client representations letter is a low grade of audit evidence and *should never be used as a substitute for performing other audit procedures.* The financial statements already constitute written representations by the client; hence, a representations letter does little more than assert that the original representations were correct.

Illustrative case. The income statement of National Student Marketing Corporation (NSMC) included total gains of $370,000 from the sale of two subsidiary companies to employees of the subsidiaries. Consideration for the sales was notes receivable collateralized by 7,700 shares of NSMC stock. Because both subsidiaries had been operating at substantial losses, NSMC's independent auditors obtained written representations from three officers of NSMC that there were no indemnification or repurchase commitments given to the purchasers.

In *Accounting Series Release No. 173*, the SEC criticized the auditors for too great reliance on management representations regarding the sales. The SEC considered the sales to be sham transactions that would have been brought to light had the auditors sufficiently extended their auditing procedures. NSMC had executed various side agreements to assume all risks of ownership after the "sale" of one subsidiary, and had agreed to make cash contributions and guarantee a bank line of credit after "sale" of the other subsidiary. Further, the NSMC stock collateralizing the notes receivable had been given to the subsidiaries' "purchasers" by officers of NSMC.

Although representation letters are not a substitute for other necessary auditing procedures, they do serve several important audit purposes. One purpose is to *remind the client officers of their primary and personal responsibility for the financial statements.* Another purpose is to document in the audit working papers the client's responses to many questions asked by the auditors during the engagement. Also, a representation by management may be the only evidence available with respect to management's *future intentions.* For example, whether maturing debt is classified as a current or a long-term liability may depend upon whether management has both the ability and the *intention* of refinancing the debt.

Many CPA firms obtain a single letter of representations from client management covering numerous aspects of the financial position and operations of the client. Other auditors obtain separate representations for individual items. Subsequent chapters illustrate the latter type of letters of representations from clients.

The cost of obtaining evidence

CPAs can no more disregard the cost of alternative auditing procedures than a store manager can disregard a difference in the costs of competing brands of merchandise. Cost is not the primary factor influencing the auditors in deciding what evidence should be obtained, but cost is always an important consideration.

The cost factor may preclude the gathering of the ideal form of evidence and necessitate the substitution of other forms of evidence that are of lesser quality yet still satisfactory. For example, assume that the auditors find that the client has a large note receivable from a customer. What evidence should the auditors obtain to be satisfied that the note is authentic and will be paid at maturity? One alternative is for the auditors to correspond directly with the customer and obtain written confirmation of the amount, maturity date, and other terms of the note. This confirmation is evidence that the customer issued the note and regards it as a valid obligation. Second, the auditors might test the collectibility of the note by obtaining a credit report on the customer from Dun & Bradstreet, Inc., or from a local credit association. They might also obtain copies of the customer's most recent financial statements accompanied, if possible, by the opinion of an independent CPA. To carry our illustration to an extreme, the auditors might obtain permission to make an audit of the financial statements of the customer.

The cost of conducting this separate audit could amount to more than the note receivable the auditors wished to verify.

The point of this illustration is that auditors *do not* always insist upon obtaining the strongest possible evidence. They do insist upon obtaining evidence that is adequate under the circumstances. The more material the item to be verified, the stronger the evidence required by the auditors, and the greater the cost they may be willing to incur in obtaining it.

Relative risk

Is the risk of misstatement, or of fraud, or of violation of accounting principles about the same in all audits? Certainly not. In certain situations, which the auditors must learn to recognize, the risk of substantial error and misstatement in the accounts and in the financial statements is far greater than in other audits. When relative risk is above normal, the auditors should demand more and better evidence than they would normally require as a basis for their opinion. The following examples illustrate some relatively high-risk auditing situations:

1. *Weak internal control.* The system of internal control is itself one of the more important types of evidence utilized by the auditors. Internal control may be weak or absent in certain areas of the client's affairs or throughout the business. In this situation the auditors are on notice to exercise added caution and to gather other forms of detailed evidence to compensate for the weakness in internal control. This topic has already received attention in the chapter devoted to internal control.
2. *Unsound financial condition.* A company operating at a loss or hard pressed to pay its creditors is more likely to postpone writing off worthless receivables or obsolete inventories of merchandise, or perhaps to "forget" to record a liability, than is a strong, well-financed, profitable company.
3. *Revision of income tax rates or regulations.* When income tax rates are suddenly raised significantly, the reaction of some clients may be to look harder than ever for ways to minimize taxable income. The pressure of a heavy tax burden sometimes leads to the twisting of accounting principles and to interpretations of business transactions in a manner inconsistent with that of prior years. When any sharp change in tax rates or regulations is anticipated for the following year, an incentive exists for the client to shift income from one period to another.
4. *Unreliable management.* Despite careful investigation of the backgrounds of directors and management of a prospective client, a CPA firm may nevertheless be involved with clients having unscrupulous executives. Auditors should be wary of managers whose oral representations are found to be wholly or partially untrue.

5. *Complex business transactions.* Clients whose operations involve extremely complicated transactions represent a far greater risk to auditors than do clients with conventional operations. There is ever-present danger that the auditors, despite all of their evidence-gathering efforts, will not comprehend the *substance* of the complex activity.

6. *Clients who change auditors without clear justification.* A satisfactory client-auditor relationship should be a continuous one. When a company changes its independent CPA firm, the change may have resulted from dissatisfaction with the predecessor firm's services. All too often, however, companies change auditors because of disputes over financial statement presentation and disclosure. The new client who has changed auditors thus represents a high-risk situation for the successor auditors. (We have already pointed out in Chapter 2 the obligation of successor auditors to consult with the predecessor auditors to ascertain, among other matters, the predecessors' understanding of the reason for the client's change of auditors.)

7. *"High-flyer" speculative ventures.* The history of American business includes numerous examples of the rise and fall of companies that attempted to capitalize on fads, innovations, and other speculative ventures. Auditors of such operations are subject to far greater risk than are the auditors of long-time, successful, and more conventional companies.

The concept of relative risk may also be applied to the gathering of evidence on particular items in the financial statements. The very nature of some assets makes the risk of misstatement greater than for others. Assume that in a given business the asset of cash amounts to only half as much as the Buildings account. Does this relationship indicate that the auditors should spend only half as much time in the verification of cash as in the verification of the buildings? Cash is much more susceptible to error or theft than are plant and equipment, and the great number of cash transactions affords an opportunity for errors to be well hidden. The amount of audit time devoted to the verification of cash balances and of cash transactions during the year will generally be much greater in proportion to the dollar amounts involved than will be necessary for such assets as plant and equipment.

In some special audit engagements, the auditors are aware in advance that fraud is suspected and that the accounting records may include fictitious or altered entries. Perhaps the auditors have been engaged because of a dispute between partners or because of dissatisfaction on the part of stockholders with the existing management. The risks involved in such engagements will cause the auditors to assign different weights to various types of evidence than they otherwise would.

Illustrative case. Bruce Henry, a resident of New York, owned a 90 percent stock interest in a California automobile agency. The other 10 percent of the stock was owned by James

Barr, who also had a contract to act as general manager of the business. As compensation for his managerial services, Bar received a percentage of net income rather than a fixed salary. The reported net income in recent years had been large and increasing each year, with correspondingly larger payments to Barr as manager. However, during this period of reported rising income, the cash position of the business as shown by the balance sheet had been deteriorating rapidly. Working capital had been adequate when Barr took over as manager, but was now critically low.

Henry, the majority stockholder in New York, was quite concerned over these trends. He was further disturbed by reports that Barr was spending a great deal of time in Las Vegas and that he had placed several relatives on the payroll of the automobile agency. Henry decided to engage a CPA firm to make an audit of the business. He explained fully to the CPAs his doubts as to the fairness of the reported net income and his misgivings as to Barr's personal integrity. Henry added that he wished to buy Barr's stockholdings, but first needed some basis for valuing the stock.

An audit initiated under these circumstances obviously called for a greater amount of evidence and a greater degree of caution by the auditors than would normally be required. Oral evidence from Barr could not be given much weight. Documents created within the business might very possibly have been falsified. In brief, the degree of risk was great, and the auditors' approach was modified to fit the circumstances. More evidence and more conclusive evidence was called for than in a more routine audit of an automobile agency.

The outcome of the audit in question was a disclosure of a gross overstatement of inventories and the reporting of numerous fictitious sales. Commission payments were also found to have been made to persons not participating in the business.

Evidence provided by subsequent events

Evidence not available at the close of the period under audit often becomes available before the auditors finish their field work and write their audit report. The CPA's opinion on the fairness of the financial statements may be changed considerably by these *subsequent events.* The term *subsequent event* refers to an event or transaction that occurs after the date of the balance sheet but prior to the completion of the audit and issuance of the audit report. Subsequent events may be classified into two broad categories: (1) those providing additional evidence as to facts existing on or before the balance sheet date and (2) those involving facts coming into existence after the balance sheet date.

Type 1 subsequent events. The first type of subsequent event provides additional evidence as to *conditions that existed at the balance sheet date* and affects the estimates inherent in the process of preparing financial statements. This type of subsequent event requires that the financial statement amounts be *adjusted* to reflect the changes in estimates resulting from the additional evidence.

As an example, let us assume that a client's accounts receivable at December 31 included one large account and numerous small ones. The large amount due from the major customer was regarded as good and collectible at the year-end, but during the course of the audit engagement the customer entered bankruptcy. As a result of this information, the auditors might have found it necessary to insist on an increase in the December 31 allowance for uncollectible accounts. The bankruptcy of

sheet date, a major customer of the audit client declares bankruptcy, and a large receivable previously considered fully collectible now appears to be uncollectible. If the customer's bankruptcy resulted from a steady deterioration in financial position, the subsequent event provides evidence that the receivable actually was uncollectible at year-end, and the allowance for doubtful accounts should be increased. On the other hand, if the customer's bankruptcy stemmed from a casualty (such as a fire) occurring after year-end, the conditions making the receivable uncollectible came into existence after the balance sheet date. In this case, the subsequent event should be disclosed in a note to the financial statements.

Audit procedures relating to subsequent events

The period of time between the balance sheet date and the last day of field work is called the subsequent period. During this period, the auditors should determine that proper cutoffs of cash receipts and disbursements and sales and purchases have been made, and should examine data to aid in the evaluation of assets and liabilities as of the balance sheet date. In addition, the auditors should—

1. Review the latest available interim financial statements and minutes of directors', stockholders', and appropriate committees' meetings.
2. Inquire about matters dealt with at meetings for which minutes are not available.
3. Inquire of appropriate client officials as to loss contingencies, changes in capital stock, debt or working capital, changes in the current status of items estimated in the financial statements under audit, or any unusual adjustments made subsequent to the balance sheet date.
4. Obtain a letter from the client's attorney describing as of the last day of field work any pending litigation, unasserted claims, or other loss contingencies.
5. Obtain a letter of representations from the client concerning subsequent events. This letter also should be dated as of the last day of field work.

Generally, the auditors' responsibility for performing audit procedures to gather evidence as to subsequent events extends only through the last day of field work. However, even after completing normal audit procedures, the auditors have the responsibility to evaluate subsequent events *that come to their attention.* Suppose, for example, that the auditors completed their field work for a December 31 audit on February 3 and thereafter began writing their report. On February 12, before completing their report, the auditors were informed by the client that a lawsuit, which had been footnoted as a loss contingency in the December 31 financial statements, had been settled on February 11 by a substantial payment by the client. The auditors would have to insist that the loss contingency be changed to a real liability in the December 31 balance sheet and that the footnote be revised to show the settlement of the lawsuit subsequent to the balance sheet date. If the client agreed, the auditors would *dual-date* their report "February 3, except for Note __, as to which the date is February 12." Alternatively, the auditors might decide to return to the client's facilities for further review of subsequent events through February 12; in this case, the audit report would bear that date only.

Dual-dating extends the auditors' liability for disclosure through the later date *only with respect to the specified item.* Using the later date for the date of the report will extend the auditors' liability with respect to all areas of the financial statements.

Figure 7–1 summarizes the auditors' responsibilities for subsequent events with respect to the balance sheet date, the last day of field work, and the date upon which the audit report is actually issued.

Figure 7–1
Subsequent events

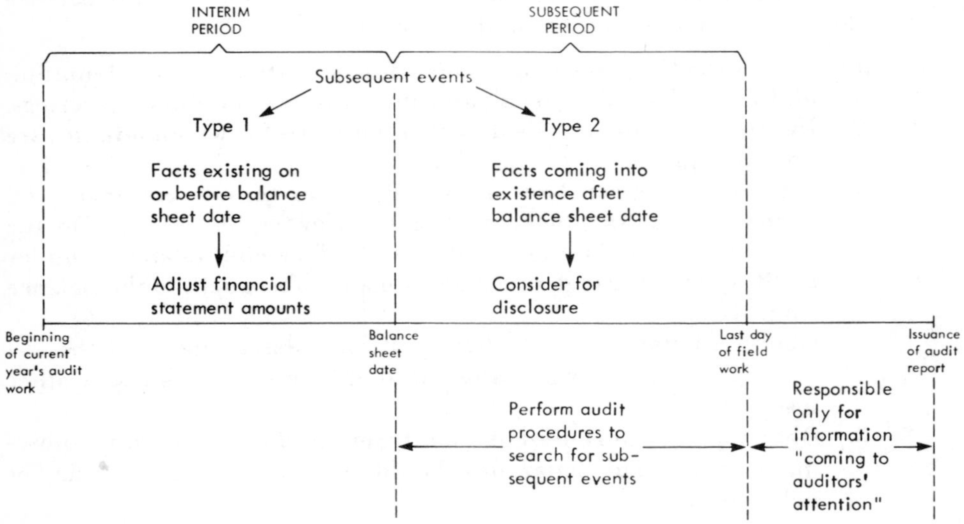

The auditors' S-1 review in an SEC registration.   The Securities Act of 1933 (Section 11[a]) extends the auditors' liability in connection with the registration of new securities with the SEC to the *effective date* of the registration statement—the date on which the securities may be sold to the public. In many cases, the effective date of the registration statement may be several days or even weeks later than the date the auditors completed their field work. Accordingly, on or as close as practicable to the effective date, the auditors return to the client's facilities to conduct an S-1 review, so-called because of the "Form S-1" title of the traditional SEC registration statement for new securities issues. In addition to completing the subsequent events review described in the preceding section, the auditors should read the entire prospectus and other pertinent portions of the registration statement. In addition, they should inquire of officers and other key executives of the client whether any events not reported in the registration statement have occurred that require amendment of the registration statement to prevent the audited financial statements therein from being misleading.

The auditors' subsequent discovery of facts existing at the date of their report

After the issuance of its audit report, a CPA firm may encounter evidence indicating that the client's financial statements contained material error or lacked required disclosures. The auditors must investigate immediately such subsequently discovered facts. If the auditors ascertain that the facts are significant and existed at the date of the audit report, they should advise the client to make appropriate disclosure of the facts to anyone actually or likely to be relying upon the audit report and the related financial statements. If the client refuses to make appropriate disclosure, the CPAs should inform each member of the client's board of directors of such refusal and then should notify regulatory agencies having jurisdiction over the client, and, if practicable, each person known to be relying upon the audited financial statements, that the CPAs' report can no longer be relied upon.

Evidence for related party transactions

How should auditors react if a corporation buys a parcel of real estate from one of its executive officers at an obviously excessive price? This situation illustrates the problems that may arise for auditors when the client company enters into *related party transactions.* The term *related parties* refers to the client entity and any other party with which the client may deal where one party has the ability to influence the other to the extent that one party to the transaction may not pursue its own separate interests. Examples of related parties include officers, directors, principal owners, and members of their immediate families; and affiliated companies, such as subsidiaries. A related party transaction is any transaction between related parties (except for normal compensation arrangements, expense allowances, and similar transactions arising in the ordinary course of business).

The primary concern of the auditors is that material related party transactions are *adequately disclosed* in the client's financial statements or footnotes. Disclosure of related party transactions should include: the nature of the relationship; a description of the transactions, including dollar amounts; and amounts due to and from related parties, together with terms and manner of settlement.

Since transactions with related parties are not conducted at arm's length, the auditors should be aware that the economic substance of these transactions may differ from their form. For example, a long-term, interest-free loan to an officer in substance includes an element of executive compensation equal to a realistic interest charge. If the auditors believe that related party transactions were executed at unrealistic prices or terms, and the dollar amounts are material, they must insist upon revision of the financial statements to properly describe the substance of the transactions.

SAS No. 6, "Related Party Transactions," suggests guidelines for identifying related parties and related party transactions. Common methods of identifying related parties include making inquiries of management and reviewing SAC filings, stockholders' listings, and conflict-of-interest statements obtained by the client from its executives. A list of all known related parties should be prepared at the beginning of the audit so that the audit staff may be alert for related party transactions throughout the engagement. This list is retained in the auditors' permanent file for reference and updating in successive engagements.

KEY TERMS INTRODUCED OR EMPHASIZED IN CHAPTER 7

Analytical review procedures   Substantive tests involving the study of trends, ratios, and other relationships among financial data and the subsequent investigation to determine the cause of any unusual relationships observed. Typical analytical review procedures involve comparisons of current financial data to that of prior periods, to industry averages, and to budgeted performance.

Competence   The competence of evidential matter relates to its quality.

Confirmation   A type of documentary evidence created outside the client organization and transmitted directly to the auditors.

Evidential matter   Any information that corroborates or refutes the auditors' premise that the financial statements present fairly the client's financial position and operating results.

Inspection   The auditors' evidence-gathering technique that provides documentary evidence.

Letter of representations   A single letter or separate letters prepared by officers of the client company at the auditors' request setting forth certain facts about the company's financial position or operations.

Material   Of substantial importance. Significant enough to affect evaluations or decisions by users of financial statements. Information that should be disclosed in order that financial statements constitute a fair presentation. Involves both qualitative and quantitative considerations.

Observation   The auditors' evidence-gathering technique that provides physical evidence.

Pro forma financial statements   Financial statements that give effect to subsequent events as though they had occurred as of the balance sheet date.

Related party transaction   A transaction in which one party has the ability to influence significantly the management or operating policies of the other party, to the extent that one of the transacting parties might be prevented from pursuing fully its own separate interests.

Relative risk   The danger in a specific audit engagement of substantial error and misstatement in the accounts and the financial statements.

S–1 review   Procedures carried out by auditors at the client company's facilities on or as close as practicable to the effective date of a registration statement filed under the Securities Act of 1933.

Specialist   A person or firm possessing special skill or knowledge in a field other than accounting or auditing, such as an actuary.

Subsequent event   An event occurring after the date of the balance sheet but prior to completion of the audit and issuance of the audit report.

Sufficient   Sufficient evidential matter is a measure of the quantity of the evidence.

GROUP I: REVIEW QUESTIONS

7–1.   In a conversation with you, Mark Rogers, CPA, claims that both the *sufficiency* and the *competence* of audit evidence are a matter of judgment in every audit. Do you agree? Explain.

7–2.   Identify and explain the considerations that guide the auditors in deciding how much evidence they must examine as a basis for expressing an opinion on a client's financial statements.

7–3.   "The best means of verification of cash, inventory, office equipment, and nearly all other assets is a physical count of the units; only a physical count gives the auditors complete assurance as to the accuracy of the amounts listed on the balance sheet." Evaluate this statement.

7–4.   As part of the verification of accounts receivable as of the balance sheet date, the auditors might inspect copies of sales invoices. Similarly, as part of the verification of accounts payable, the auditors might inspect purchase invoices. Which of these two types of invoices do you think represents the stronger type of evidence? Why?

7–5.   In verifying the asset accounts Notes Receivable and Marketable Securities, the auditors examined all notes receivable and all stock certificates. Which of these documents represents the stronger type of evidence? Why?

7–6.   Performing analytical review procedures involves two distinct steps. The first step is to compute relevant ratios, component percentages, and other predictable relationships among financial data. What is the second step?

7–7.   When in the course of an audit might the auditor find it useful to apply analytical review procedures?

7–8.   Give at least four examples of *specialists* whose findings might provide competent evidence for the independent auditors.

7–9.   What are the major purposes of obtaining letters of representations from audit clients?

7–10.   "In deciding upon the type of evidence to be gathered in support of a given item on the financial statements, the auditors should not be influenced by the differences in cost of obtaining alternative forms of evidence." Do you agree? Explain.

7–11.   The cost of an audit might be significantly reduced if the auditors relied upon a representations letter from the client instead of observing the physical counting of inventory. Would this use of a representation letter be an acceptable means of reducing the cost of an audit?

7–12.   What are subsequent events?

7–13.   Give three examples of subsequent events that might influence the auditors' opinion as to one or more items on the balance sheet.

7–14.   What are *related party transactions?*

7–15.   What disclosures should be made in the financial statements regarding material related party transactions?

7–16.   Evaluate the following statement: "Identifying related parties and obtaining a client letter of representations are two required audit procedures normally performed on the last day of field work."

GROUP II: QUESTIONS REQUIRING ANALYSIS

7–17.   One of the assets of Vista Corporation is 6,000 acres of land in a remote area of the Arizona desert. The land is held as a long-term investment and is carried in the accounting records at a cost of $200 per acre. A recent topographical map prepared by the U.S. Soil Conservation Service shows the land to be nearly flat with no standing bodies of water. The land is accessible only by aircraft or four-wheel-drive vehicles. Evaluate the merits of the auditors personally observing this land as a means of obtaining audit evidence.

7–18.   Analytical review procedures are substantive tests that are extremely useful in the initial audit planning stage.

Required:
a.   Explain why analytical review procedures are considered substantive tests.

b.   Explain how analytical review procedures may be useful in the initial audit planning stage.

c.   Might analytical review procedures be applied at any other stages of the audit process? Explain.

d.   List several types of comparisons a CPA might make in performing analytical review procedures. (AICPA, adapted)

7–19.   When analytical review procedures disclose unexpected changes in financial relationships relative to prior years, the auditors consider the possible reasons for the changes. Give several possible reasons for the following significant changes in relationships:

a.   The rate of inventory turnover (ratio of cost of goods sold to average inventory) has declined from the prior year's rate.

b.   The number of days' sales in accounts receivable has increased over the prior year. (AICPA, adapted)

7–20.   Rank each of the following examples of audit evidence in their order of *competence.* Arrange your answer in the form of a separate paragraph for each item. Explain fully the reasoning employed in judging the competence of each item.

a. Copies of client's sales invoices.

b. Auditors' independent computation of earnings per share.

c. Paid checks returned with bank statement.

d. Response from customer of client addressed to auditors' office confirming amount owed to client at balance sheet date.

e. Letter of representations by controller of client company stating that all liabilities of which she has knowledge are reflected in the company's accounts.

7–21. Marshall Land Company owns substantial amounts of farm and timber lands, and consequently property taxes represent one of the more important types of expense. What specific documents or other evidence should the auditors examine in verifying the Property Taxes Expense account?

7–22. Auditors are required on every engagement to obtain letters of representation from the client.

Required:

a. What are the objectives of the client's representations letters?

b. Who should prepare and sign the client's representations letters?

c. When should the client's representations letters be obtained?

7–23. The auditor's opinion on the fairness of financial statements may be affected by subsequent events.

Required:

a. Define what is commonly referred to in auditing as a subsequent event and describe the two general types of subsequent events.

b. Identify those auditing procedures that the auditor should apply at or near the completion of field work to disclose significant subsequent events. (AICPA, adapted)

7–24. On July 27, 1984, Arthur Ward, CPA, issued an unqualified audit report on the financial statements of Dexter Company for the year ended June 30, 1984. Two weeks later, Dexter Company mailed annual reports including the June 30, 1984, financial statements and Ward's audit report to 150 stockholders and to several creditors of Dexter Company. Dexter Company's stock is not actively traded on national exchanges or over the counter.

On September 5, 1984, the controller of Dexter Company informed Ward that an account payable for consulting services in the amount of $170,000 had inadvertently been omitted from Dexter's June 30, 1984, balance sheet. As a consequence, net income for the year ended June 30, 1984, was overstated $90,500, net of applicable federal and state income taxes. Both Ward and Dexter's controller agreed that the misstatements were material to Dexter's financial position at June 30, 1984, and operating results for the year then ended.

Required:

What should Arthur Ward's course of action be in this matter? Discuss.

7–25. In your examination of the financial statements of Wolfe Company for the year ended April 30, 1984, you find that a material account receivable is due from a company in reorganization under Chapter 10 of the Bankruptcy Act. You also learn that on May 28, 1984 several former members of the bankrupt company's management formed a new company and that the new company had issued a note to Wolfe Company that would pay off the bankrupt customer's account receivable over a four-year period. What presentation, if any, should be made of this situation in the financial statements of Wolfe Company for the year ended April 30, 1984? Explain.

7–26. John Reed is engaged in the audit of Brooke Corporation. While reviewing the company's notes payable, Reed encounters a three-year, 16 percent note in the amount of $1.5 million payable to Alan Davis, president of Brooke Corporation. The note was issued in conjunction with the purchase of a parcel of commercial real estate from Davis during the current year at a total price of $2.5 million. Discuss the audit significance of these findings and the actions, if any, that Reed should take.

7–27. Select the best answer for each of the following questions. Explain the reasons for your selection.

    a. As part of their examination, auditors must obtain a letter of representations from their client. Which of the following is *not* a valid purpose of such a letter?

        (1) To increase the efficiency of the audit by eliminating the need for such audit procedures as personal observation, inspection, and confirmation.

        (2) To remind the client's management of its primary and personal responsibility for the financial statements.

        (3) To document in the audit working papers the client's responses to certain verbal inquiries made by the auditors during the engagement.

        (4) To provide evidence in those areas dependent upon management's future intention.

    b. Which of the following statements best describes why auditors should investigate related party transactions?

        (1) Related party transactions are illegal acts.

        (2) The substance of related party transactions may differ from their form.

        (3) All related party transactions must be eliminated as a step in preparing consolidated financial statements.

        (4) Related party transactions are a form of management fraud.

    c. On August 15, the CPA completed field work on the audit of Cheyenne Corporation's financial statements for the year ended June 30. On September 1, before issuance of the auditor's report, an event occurred that the CPA and Cheyenne agree should be disclosed in a footnote to the June 30 financial statements. The CPA has not otherwise reviewed events subsequent to the completion of field work. The auditor's report should be dated:

        (1) September 1.

        (2) June 30, except for the footnote, which should be dated September 1.

(3) August 15, except for the footnote, which should be dated September 1.

(4) August 15.

d. Which event that occurred after the balance sheet date but prior to issuance of the auditor's report would not require disclosure in the financial statements?

(1) Sale of a bond or capital stock issue.

(2) A major drop in the quoted market price of the company's capital stock.

(3) Destruction of a factory as a result of a fire.

(4) Settlement of litigation when the event giving rise to the claim took place after the balance sheet date. (AICPA, adapted)

GROUP III: PROBLEMS

7–28. In the examination of financial statements, auditors must judge the validity of the audit evidence they obtain.

Required:

Assume that the auditors have evaluated internal control and found it satisfactory.

a. In the course of examination, the auditors ask many questions of client officers and employees.

(1) Describe the factors that the auditors should consider in evaluating oral evidence provided by client officers and employees.

(2) Discuss the validity and limitations of oral evidence.

b. Analytical review procedures include the computation of various balance sheet and operating ratios for comparison to prior years and industry averages. Discuss the validity and limitations of ratio analysis as evidential matter.

c. In connection with an examination of the financial statements of a manufacturing company, the auditors are observing the physical inventory of finished goods, which consists of expensive, highly complex electronic equipment. Discuss the validity and limitations of the audit evidence provided by this procedure. (AICPA, adapted)

7–29. In connection with her examination of the financial statements of Flowmeter, Inc., for the year ended December 31, 1983, Joan Hirsch, CPA, is aware that certain events and transactions that took place after December 31, 1983 but before she issues her report dated February 28, 1984 may affect the company's financial statements.

The following material events or transactions have come to her attention:

a. On January 3, 1984 Flowmeter, Inc., received a shipment of raw materials from Canada. The materials had been ordered in October 1983 and shipped FOB shipping point in November 1983.

b. On January 15, 1984 the company settled and paid a personal injury claim of a former employee as the result of an accident that had

occurred in March 1983. The company had not previously recorded
a liability for the claim.

  c.   On January 25, 1984 the company agreed to purchase for cash the
       outstanding stock of Porter Electrical Co. The business combina-
       tion is likely to double the sales volume of Flowmeter, Inc.
  d.   On February 1, 1984 a plant owned by Flowmeter, Inc., was dam-
       aged by a flood, resulting in an uninsured loss of inventory.
  e.   On February 5, 1984 Flowmeter, Inc., issued to an underwriting
       syndicate $2 million in convertible bonds.

Required:
For each of the above items, indicate how the event or transaction
should be reflected in Flowmeter's financial statements and explain the
reasons for selecting this method of disclosure. (AICPA, adapted)

7–30.   The financial statements of Wayne Company indicate that large
        amounts of notes payable to banks were retired during the period
        under audit. Evaluate the reliability of each of the following types of
        evidence supporting these transactions:
  a.   Debit entries in the Notes Payable account.
  b.   Entries in the check register.
  c.   Paid checks.
  d.   Notes payable bearing bank perforation stamp PAID and the date
        of payment.
  e.   Statement by client's treasurer that notes had been paid at maturity.
  f.   Letter received by auditors directly from bank stating that no in-
        debtedness on part of client existed as of the balance sheet date.

7–31.   During your examination of the accounts receivable of a new client, you
        notice that one account is much larger than the rest, and you therefore
        decide to examine the evidence supporting this customer's account.
        Comment on the relative reliability and adequacy of the following types
        of evidence:
  a.   Computor printout from accounts receivable subsidiary ledger.
  b.   Copies of sales invoices in amount of the receivable.
  c.   Purchase order received from customer.
  d.   Shipping document describing the articles sold.
  e.   Letter received by client from customer acknowledging the cor-
        rectness of the receivable in the amount shown on client's account-
        ing records.
  f.   Letter received by auditors directly from customer acknowledging
        the correctness of the amount shown as receivable on client's ac-
        counting records.

7–32.   In an examination of financial statements, CPAs are concerned with the
        accumulation of audit evidence.

Required:
  a.   What is the objective of the CPAs' accumulation of audit evidence
        during the course of their examination?
  b.   The source of documentary evidence is of primary importance in
        the CPAs' evaluation of its quality. Documentary evidence may be
        classified according to source. For example, one class originates

within the client's organization, passes through the hands of third
parties, and returns to the client, where it may be examined by the
auditors. List the classification of documentary evidence according
to source, briefly discussing the effect of the source on the reliability of the evidence. (AICPA, adapted)

7–33. What would you accept as satisfactory documentary evidence in support
of entries in the following?
a. Sales journal.
b. Sales returns register.
c. Voucher or invoice register.
d. Payroll register.
e. Check register. (AICPA, adapted)

7–34. Robertson Company had accounts receivable of $200,000 at December
31, 1983 and had provided an allowance for uncollectible accounts of
$6,000. After performing all normal auditing procedures relating to the
receivables and to the valuation allowance, the independent auditors
were satisfied that this asset was fairly stated and that the allowance for
uncollectible accounts was adequate. Just before completion of the
audit field work late in February, however, the auditors learned that
the entire plant of Thompson Corporation, a major customer, had been
destroyed by a flood early in February and that as a result Thompson
Corporation was hopelessly insolvent.

The account receivable from Thompson Corporation in the amount
of $44,000 originated on December 28; terms of payment were net 60
days. The receivable had been regarded as entirely collectible at December 31, and the auditors had so considered it in reaching their
conclusion as to the adequacy of the allowance for uncollectible accounts. In discussing the news concerning the flood, the controller of
Robertson Company emphasized to the auditors that the probable loss
of $44,000 should be regarded as a loss of the year 1984 and not of 1983,
the year under audit.

What action, if any, should the auditors recommend with respect to
the receivable from Thompson Corporation?

7–35. In connection with your examination of the financial statements of Hollis Mfg. Corporation for the year ended December 31, 1983, your review
of subsequent events disclosed the following items:
(1) January 7, 1984: The mineral content of a shipment of ore en route
to Hollis Mfg. Corporation on December 31, 1983 was determined
to be 72 percent. The shipment was recorded at year-end at an
estimated content of 50 percent by a debit to Raw Materials Inventory and a credit to Accounts Payable in the amount of $82,400.
The final liability to the vendor is based on the actual mineral
content of the shipment.
(2) January 15, 1984: Culminating a series of personal disagreements
between Ray Hollis, the president, and his brother-in-law, the
treasurer, the latter resigned, effective immediately, under an
agreement whereby the corporation would purchase his 10 percent
stock ownership at book value as of December 31, 1983. Payment is
to be made in two equal amounts in cash on April 1 and October 1,

1984. In December the treasurer had obtained a divorce from his wife, who is Ray Hollis's sister.

(3) January 31, 1984: As a result of reduced sales, production was curtailed in mid-January and some workers were laid off. On February 5, 1984 all the remaining workers went on strike. To date the strike is unsettled.

Required:

Assume that the above items came to your attention before completion of your audit field work on February 15, 1984. For each of the above items, discuss the disclosure that you would recommend for the item, listing all details that you would suggest should be disclosed. Indicate those items or details, if any, that should not be disclosed. Give your reasons for recommending or not recommending disclosure of the items or details. (AICPA, adapted)

8

Audit sampling

The preceding chapter discussed the need for sufficient, competent evidential matter as the basis for the auditors' report. Since the evolution of large business entities, auditors increasingly have had to rely upon sampling procedures as the only practical means of obtaining this evidence. This reliance upon sampling procedures is one of the basic reasons the auditors' report is regarded as an expression of opinion, rather than absolute certification of the fairness of financial statements.

Sampling, whether statistical or judgmental, is the process of selecting a sample from a larger group of items (called the **population** or **field**) and using the characteristics of the sample to draw inferences about the characteristics of the entire field of items. The underlying assumption is that the sample is **representative** of the population, meaning that the sample will possess essentially the same characteristics as the population. Inherent in the technique of sampling is the risk of **sampling error**—the possibility of selecting a sample that, purely by chance, **is not** representative of the population. Due to the ever-present risk of sampling error, there is always some degree of risk that sampling will lead to incorrect conclusions concerning the population. The risk that sampling error will cause auditors to reach a **different conclusion** than they would have reached by examining the entire population is called **sampling risk**.

As a general rule, sampling risk is reduced by increasing the size of the sample. When sample size is 100 percent of the population, the sample is by definition perfectly representative, and the risk of sampling error (material or otherwise) is eliminated entirely.[1] Large samples, however, are costly and time-consuming. A key element in efficient sampling is to balance the risk of material sampling error against the cost of using larger samples.

Comparison of statistical and nonstatistical sampling

A sample is said to be *nonstatistical* (or judgmental) when either sample size or composition of the sample is determined by the auditors' professional judgment rather than by the laws of probability. When sample size and composition are not determined by statistical methods, the sample results are not subject to statistical interpretation. Thus, judgmental sampling provides the auditors with no quantitative means of measuring the risk of material sampling error. The auditors may find themselves either taking larger and more costly samples than are necessary just to be safe, or unknowingly accepting a high degree of sampling risk.

An advantage of statistical sampling is that the *risk of material sampling error may be measured and controlled.* The auditors may specify in advance the reliability they require in their sample results and then compute a sample size that affords that degree of reliability. Since statistical sampling techniques are based upon the laws of probability, the auditors are able to control the extent of their risk in relying upon sample results. Thus, statistical sampling may assist auditors in (1) designing efficient samples, (2) measuring the sufficiency and competence of the evidence obtained, and (3) objectively evaluating sample results.

In the remainder of this chapter, we emphasize statistical sampling techniques. However, statistical sampling may involve additional costs in terms of auditor training, design of audit procedures, and selection of items for examination. For these reasons, nonstatistical samples are widely used by auditors, especially for tests of compliance and substantive tests of relatively small populations. Both statistical and nonstatistical sampling can provide auditors with sufficient competent evidential matter. *SAS No. 39,* "Audit Sampling," provides auditors with guidelines for planning, performing, and evaluating both statistical and nonstatistical samples.

---

[1] Auditors still may reach erroneous conclusions as a result of *nonsampling risk.* Nonsampling risk includes all possible sources of error not related to sampling. For example, the auditors may fail to apply appropriate audit procedures, or may fail to recognize errors in those documents or transactions they examine. Nonsampling risk can be reduced to negligible levels through such factors as proper planning, adequate supervision, and appropriate quality controls within the CPA firm. The topic of audit quality controls is discussed in Chapter 9.

Random selection

A common misinterpretation of statistical sampling is to equate this process with *random sampling.* Random sampling relates only to one step in the statistical sampling process; it is the method of *selecting* the items for inclusion in the sample. Random sampling, therefore, is only a part of the statistical sampling procedure and not the entire process. If auditors are to control the risk of sampling error, random sampling procedures must be used in conjunction with statistical measurement procedures for determining sample size and interpreting sample results. To emphasize this distinction, this text will use the term *random selection* rather than random "sampling" to refer to the procedure of selecting the items for inclusion in a sample.

The principle involved in unrestricted random selection is that every item in the population has an equal chance of being selected for inclusion in the sample. Since the items comprising a random sample are selected purely by chance, the person selecting the sample will not influence or bias the selection process. Although random selection results in an *unbiased sample,* that sample is not necessarily representative. The risk still exists that purely by chance a sample will be selected that does not possess essentially the same characteristics as the population. However, since the risk of a nonrepresentative random sample stems from the laws of probability, this risk may be measured by statistical formulas.

The concept of a random sample requires that the person selecting the sample will not influence or bias the selection either consciously or unconsciously. Thus, some type of impartial selection process is necessary to obtain a truly random sample. Techniques often used for selecting random samples include *random number tables, random number generators, and systematic selection.*

Random number tables

Perhaps the easiest method of selecting items at random is the use of a random number table. A portion of a random number table is illustrated in Figure 8–1.

The random numbers appearing in Figure 8–1 are arranged into columns of five digits. Except that the columnar arrangement permits the reader of the table to select numbers easily, the columns are purely arbitrary and otherwise meaningless. Each digit on the table is a random digit; the table does *not* represent a listing of random five-digit numbers. The columnar arrangement is for convenience only.

In using a random number table, the first step is to establish correspondence between the digits in the table and the items in the population. This is most easily done when the items in the population are

Figure 8–1
Table of random numbers

		Columns			
Row	(1)	(2)	(3)	(4)	(5)
1	04734	39426	91035	54839	76873
2	10417	19688	83404	42038	48226
3	07514	48374	35658	38971	53779
4	52305	86925	16223	25946	90222
5	96357	11486	30102	82679	57983
6	92870	05921	65698	27993	86406
7	00500	75924	38803	05386	10072
8	34862	93784	52709	15370	96727
9	25809	21860	36790	76883	20435
10	77487	38419	20631	48694	12638

consecutively numbered. On occasion, however, auditors may find it necessary to renumber the population to obtain correspondence. For example, if transactions are numbered A–001, B–001, and so on, the auditors may assign numbers to replace the alphabetic characters. Next, the auditors must select a starting point and a systematic route to be used in reading the random number table. Any route is permissible, as long as it is followed consistently.

To illustrate the use of a random number table, assume that a client's accounts receivable are numbered from 0001 to 5,000 and that the auditors want to select a random sample of 300 accounts for confirmation. Using the table in Figure 8–1, the auditors decide to start at the top of column 2 and to proceed from top to bottom. Reading only the first four digits of the numbers in column 2, the auditors would select 3942, 1968, and 4837 as three of the account numbers to be included in their sample. The next number 8692, would be ignored, since there is no account with that number. The next numbers to be included in the sample would be 1148, 592, 2186, and so on.

Duplicate numbers. In using a random number table, it is possible that the auditors will draw the same number more than once. If the auditors ignore a number that is drawn a second time and go on to the next number, they are *sampling without replacement.* This term means that an item once selected is not replaced into the population of eligible items, and consequently it cannot be drawn for inclusion in the sample a second time.

The alternative to sampling without replacement is *sampling with replacement.* This method requires that if a particular number is drawn two or more times, the number must be included two or more times in the sample. Sampling with replacement means that once an item has been selected, it is immediately replaced into the population of eligible items and may be selected a second time.

Statistical formulas can be used to compute sample size either with or without replacement. Sampling without replacement is the more efficient technique because it requires slightly smaller sample sizes.

Random number generators

Even when items are assigned consecutive numbers, the selection of a large sample from a random number table may be a very time-consuming process. Computer programs called *random number generators* may be used to provide any length list of random numbers applicable to a given population. Random number generators may be programmed to select random numbers with specific characteristics, so that the list of random numbers provide to the auditors includes only numbers present in the population. A random number generator is a standard program in all generalized audit software packages.

Systematic selection

An approach that is less time-consuming than selecting a random number for each item to be included in the sample is *systematic selection.* This technique involves selecting every nth item in the population following one or more *random starting points.*

To illustrate systematic selection, assume that auditors wish to examine 200 paid checks from a population of 10,000 checks. If only one random starting point is used, the auditors would select every 50th check (10,000 ÷ 200) in the population. As a starting point, the auditors would select at random one of the first 50 checks. If the random starting point is check No. 37, check Nos. 37, 87 (37 + 50), and 137 (87 + 50) would be included in the sample, as well as every 50th check number after 137. If the auditors had elected to use five random starting points, 40 checks (200 ÷ 5) would have to be selected from each random start. Thus, the auditors would select every 250th check number (10,000 ÷ 40) before and after each of the random starting points.

Selecting every nth item in the population results in a random sample only when positions in the population were assigned in random order. For example, if expensive inventory parts are always assigned an identification number ending in 9, systematic selection could result in a highly biased sample that would include only expensive items or only inexpensive items.

To prevent drawing a nonrandom or biased sample when systematic selection is used, the auditors should first determine that the population is arranged in random order. If the population is not in random order, each item to be included in the sample should be selected independently. Alternatively, the auditors might *stratify* the population into segments, each of which is arranged in random order, and apply systematic selection within each segment.

The systematic selection technique has the advantage of enabling the auditors to obtain a sample from a population of unnumbered documents or transactions. If the documents to be examined are unnumbered, there is no necessity under this method to number them either physically or mentally, as required under the random number table selection technique. Rather, the auditors merely count off the sampling interval to select the documents or use a ruler to measure the interval. Generalized audit software packages include routines for systematic selection of audit samples from computer-based files.

Stratification

Auditors often *stratify* a population before computing the required sample size and selecting the sample. Stratification is the technique of dividing a population into relatively homogeneous subgroups called strata. These strata then may be sampled separately; the sample results may be evaluated separately, or combined, to provide an estimate of the characteristics of the total population. Whenever items of extremely high or low values, or other unusual characteristics, are segregated into separate populations, each population becomes more homogeneous. It is easier to draw a representative sample from a relatively homogeneous population. Thus, it is frequently true that a smaller number of items must be examined to evaluate several strata separately than to evaluate the total population.

Besides increasing the efficiency of sampling procedures, stratification enables auditors to relate sample selection to the materiality, turnover, or other characteristics of items and to apply different audit procedures to each stratum. Frequently, auditors examine 100 percent of the stratum containing the most material items.[2] For example, in selecting accounts receivable for confirmation, auditors might stratify and test the population as follows:

Stratum	Composition of stratum	Method of selection used	Type of confirmation request*
1	All accounts of $10,000 and over	100% confirmation	Positive
2	Wholesale accounts receivable (under $10,000), all numbered with numbers ending in zero.	Random number table selection	Positive
3	All other accounts (under $10,000) in random order	Systematic selection	Negative

* A positive confirmation request asks the respondent to reply, indicating the amount owed; a negative request asks for a response only if the respondent does not agree with the amount indicated on the request. Confirmation of accounts receivable is discussed in more detail in Chapter 12.

---

[2] Any item sufficiently material that it may, by itself, constitute a material error in the financial statements should be substantiated separately, rather than by reliance upon sample results. Also, some populations (such as minutes of directors meetings) should be examined on a 100 percent basis, rather than on a sampling basis.

Block samples

A block sample consists of all items in a selected time period, numerical sequence, or alphabetical sequence. For example, in testing internal control over cash disbursements, the auditors might decide to vouch all disbursements made during the months of April and December. In this case, the sampling unit is months rather than individual transactions. Thus, the sample consists of two blocks selected from a population of 12. Block sampling cannot be relied upon to produce a representative sample unless the population is divided into a relatively large number of blocks.

Sampling plans

The statistical sampling procedures used to accomplish a specific audit objective are called a *sampling plan.* Sampling plans may be used to estimate many different characteristics of a population, but every estimate is either of (1) an occurrence rate or (2) a numerical quantity. The sampling terms corresponding to *occurrence rates* and *numerical quantities* are, respectively, *attributes* and *variables.*

Attributes sampling plans

Attributes sampling plans are used primarily in compliance tests of internal control. In tests of compliance, the auditors are interested in estimating the rate of compliance with (or deviation from) prescribed control procedures. Attributes sampling plans widely used by auditors include:

1. Estimation sampling for attributes (or attributes sampling). This plan enables auditors to estimate the occurrence rate of certain characteristics of a population. For example, the plan might be used to estimate the frequency of failures in a prescribed internal control procedure.

2. Discovery sampling. This form of attribute sampling is designed to locate at least one example of an item, providing that the item occurs within the population with at least a specified occurrence rate. Discovery sampling is used to search for *critical errors,* for which the existence of even a very low occurrence rate could have great significance.

Variables sampling plans

Variables sampling plans are widely used in substantive tests because they provide auditors with an estimate of a numerical quantity, such as an account balance. Major variables sampling plans include:

1. Mean-per-unit estimation. This plan enables auditors to estimate the average (mean) value of each item within the population. This estimate can then be converted into an estimate of the dollar value of the entire population.

2. Ratio or difference estimation. Although closely related, ratio estimation and difference estimation are two separate plans for estimating dollar amounts. These plans are more efficient than mean-per-unit estimation when differences between recorded amounts and appropriate dollar valuation are relatively common.

3. Dollar unit sampling. This plan also is used to estimate the dollar value of a population, but it is most efficient when differences between recorded and correct dollar amounts are relatively rare.

Dual-purpose sampling plans

Sometimes one sampling plan may be used for the dual purposes of (1) compliance testing an internal control procedure, and (2) substantiating the dollar amount of an account balance. Ratio estimation, difference estimation, and dollar unit sampling all lend themselves to dual-purpose testing. For example, difference estimation might be used to evaluate the effectiveness of the client's internal controls over recording the cost of sales and, based upon the same sample, to estimate the total overstatement or understatement in the cost of goods sold.

In order to understand any of these statistical sampling plans, the auditors must first be familiar with the meanings and interrelationships among certain statistical concepts, such as *occurrence rate, precision, confidence level* (or *reliability*), and *sample size. Occurrence rate* is the frequency with which a given characteristic occurs in the population being studied. Since the characteristic the auditors are interested in is frequently some type of error, an occurrence rate is often referred to as an *error rate.*

Precision

Whether the auditors' objective is estimating attributes or variables, the sample results may not be *exactly* representative of the population. Some degree of sampling error is usually present. In utilizing statistical sampling techniques, auditors are able to measure and control the risk of material sampling error by calculating precision and confidence level.

Precision is the range, set by + and − limits from the sample results, within which the true value of the population characteristic being measured is likely to lie. For example, assume a sample is taken to determine the occurrence rate of a certain type of error in the preparation of invoices. The sample indicates an error rate of 2.1 percent. We have little assurance that the error rate in the population is exactly 2.1 percent, but we know that the sample result probably approximates the population error rate. Therefore, we may set an *interval* around the sample result within which we expect the population error rate to be. A precision interval of ±1 percent would indicate that we expect the true population error rate to lie between 1.1 and 3.1 percent. The figures designating the upper and lower boundaries of the precision interval are the *precision limits.*

The less precision we require (meaning the wider the interval we allow), the more confident we may be that the true population characteristic lies within the precision interval. In the preceding example, a precision of ±2 percent would mean that we assume the population error rate to be between 0.1 percent and 4.1 percent. Obviously, it is more probable that the true population error rate will lie within this wider precision interval than within the narrower interval of ±1 percent. Remember, *less precision means a wider interval,* and *more precision means a narrower interval* because the true population characteristic is assumed to be closer to the sample results.

Precision may also be stated as a dollar value interval. For example, we may attempt to establish the total dollar value of receivables with a precision of ±$10,000. Precision may be viewed as the *maximum tolerable margin of sampling error.* The precision required by auditors usually is determined in light of the *materiality* of this tolerable margin of error.

Confidence level (reliability)

The true population characteristic may not always lie within our specified range of precision. Our confidence level is the *percentage of the time* we can expect the sample results to represent the true population characteristic within the specified precision interval. Confidence level measures the reliability of the sample, and the risk that the true population characteristic value lies outside the precision interval of the sample. The terms *confidence level* and *reliability* are used interchangeably.

Reliability of 95 percent means we can expect that 95 percent of the time the sample results will represent the true population characteristic value. Conversely, there is a 5 percent *risk* that the true population characteristic value *is not* within the precision interval of our sample result. This represents the risk that the amount of sampling error exceeds that allowed for by the precision interval.

Given a specific sample, the less precision we require the greater our level of confidence that the true population value lies within the precision interval. The greater the required precision, the lower will be our confidence level that the sample represents the population within the desired precision interval.

Sample size

The size of our sample has a direct effect upon both precision and reliability. With a very small sample, we cannot have high reliability unless we allow a very great range of precision. On the other hand, a sample of 100 percent of the population allows us 100 percent reliability with maximum precision (±0 percent).

In general, both confidence level and the degree of precision can be increased by increasing sample size. In other words, the greater the precision and/or confidence level desired by the auditors, the larger the sample that will be required.

Sample size is also affected by certain characteristics of the population being tested. As the population increases in size, the sample size necessary to represent the population with specified precision and reliability will increase, but not in proportion to the increase in population size. In estimation sampling for attributes, sample size also increases as the expected occurrence rate becomes larger. Finally, in sampling to estimate variables, greater variability among the item values in the population increases the required sample size. These relationships are summarized in Figure 8–2.

Figure 8–2
Factors affecting sample size

Factor	Change in factor*	Effect upon required sample size
Auditors' requirements:		
Precision	Increase (tighter)	Increase
Reliability	Increase	Increase
Population characteristics:		
Size	Increase	Small increase
Expected occurrence rate or Variability of item values	Increase	Increase

* As one factor changes, other factors are assumed to remain constant.

Estimation sampling for attributes

Estimation sampling for attributes enables auditors to determine, within prescribed limits of precision and confidence, the frequency of occurrence of specified characteristics in a population. This technique is widely used in compliance testing when auditors want to estimate the frequency of deviations from prescribed internal accounting control procedures. In compliance tests, deviations from prescribed procedures are commonly called *errors,* or *exceptions.*

Estimated exception rates are stated in percentages. If a sample indicates an exception rate of 3 percent with a precision interval of ±1 percent, the auditors could infer that between 2 and 4 percent of the items in the population contain the designated exception. Sampling for attributes does not provide dollar value information—that is, the sample results do not indicate the dollar magnitude of the exceptions or their effect upon the fairness of the financial statements. The sample results do provide the auditors with useful *qualitative* information as to whether the client's internal control procedures are operating effectively or in a haphazard manner. Comparison of current exception rates with those of prior years may also give the auditors an indication of whether internal accounting control is improving or deteriorating.

Defining an "exception."   When attribute sampling is used for compliance tests, the population usually consists of all transactions subject to a specific control procedure during the period under audit. Exceptions are defined as those *control failures* the auditors consider relevant to their evaluation of the effectiveness of the control procedure. The auditors' interpretation of the estimated exception rate will depend largely on how they have defined exceptions. If exceptions are defined to include every departure from prescribed procedures, no matter how trivial, a population could contain a relatively high error rate without lessening the reliability of the financial statements. On the other hand, if exceptions are defined only as fictitious transactions recorded in the accounting records, even a very low occurrence rate has serious implications.

If several types of compliance deviations are combined in the auditors' definition of exceptions, it is important that these errors are of similar audit significance. If serious and minor types of errors are combined in the definition, the significance of the occurrence rate is obscured.

Notice that compliance exceptions *do not necessarily indicate errors in the financial statements.* For example, the definition of a compliance deviation might include failure to secure approval for a specific transaction. However, if an unapproved transaction is properly recorded in the accounting records, this exception does not result in an error in the financial statements.

Determining precision and reliability.   How do auditors determine the appropriate precision interval and reliability for compliance tests? The answer depends upon many factors, including the importance of the control procedure, extent of the auditors' planned reliance upon the procedure, anticipated exception rate, type of transactions involved, and the existence or lack of compensating controls.

Compliance tests usually are designed to provide the auditors with assurance that error rates do not exceed acceptable levels. The *upper precision limit* is therefore of greater importance than the lower limit. Assume, for example, that auditors anticipate an error rate of 5 percent and stipulate a precision of ±3 percent. The relevant question is whether the auditors can accept an error rate range up to 8 percent, not whether they can accept an error rate of less than 2 percent. The lower precision limit is not pertinent to the objective of the test. For this reason, auditors generally use *one-sided precision* in estimation sampling for attributes—that is, they state precision only in terms of an upper precision limit. The upper precision limit may be regarded as the *maximum tolerable exception rate* that would permit the auditor to place reliance upon the internal control procedure.

Although precision and confidence level are not independent of one another, the auditors may view precision as the allowable margin of error, and the confidence level as establishing the risk of being wrong. Precision, then, should be determined by the potential effects of the exceptions on the financial statements. Confidence levels should be determined in light of the auditors' planned reliance upon the internal control procedure to restrict their substantive tests. Since the results of compliance tests play a major role in determining the nature, timing, and extent of other audit procedures, auditors usually demand a high level of reliability in these tests. In practice, the reliability level for compliance tests often is 90 or 95 percent, with an upper precision limit of 5 percent or less.

Tables for use in estimating error rates. To enable auditors to use estimation sampling for attributes without resorting to complex mathematical formulas, tables such as the one in Figure 8–3 have been developed. This illustration is one page of a set of tables in the AICPA's *An Auditor's Approach to Statistical Sampling*, vol. 6. The horizontal axis of the table is the anticipated exception rate in the population, and the vertical axis is the required sample size. The numbers in the body of the table are the upper precision limits (stated in percentages), which result from various sample sizes and occurrence rates.

To use this set of tables, the auditors must stipulate a desired reliability level, an anticipated exception rate, and a desired upper precision limit.[3] Sample size then may be determined by selecting the column designated by the anticipated occurrence rate, moving down the column to an acceptable upper precision limit, and reading the corresponding sample size from the extreme left column.

Figure 8–3 also may be used in the evaluation of sample results. When the table is used for this purpose, the horizontal axis is the exception rate actually observed in the sample. The intersection of the observed occurrence rate column with the row designating sample size indicates the upper precision limit of the sample results.

Illustration of estimation sampling for attributes

The following procedures for applying estimation sampling for attributes is predicated upon the use of the table in Figure 8–3; however, only slight modifications are necessary if other tables are used.

Determine the nature and objective of the tests to be made. Assume that the auditors wish to test the effectiveness of the client's internal control procedure of matching receiving reports with purchase invoices as a step in authorizing payment for purchases of materials. They are, therefore, interested in the clerical accuracy of the

---

[3] Some tables require the auditors to specify population size. Figure 8–3 assumes an infinite population. The effect on sample size when populations are finite but of significant size is not material.

— Figure 8–3

Table for use in estimation sampling for attributes:
Determination of sample size, one-sided upper precision limits (reliability level—95 percent)

Occurrence rate

Sample size	0.0	0.5	1.0	2.0	3.0	4.0	5.0	6.0	7.0	8.0	9.0	10.0	12.0	14.0	16.0	18.0	20.0	25.0	30.0	40.0	50.0
50	5.8			9.1		12.1		14.8		17.4		19.9	22.3	25.1	27.0	29.6	31.6		42.4	52.6	62.4
100	3.0		4.7	6.2	7.6	8.9	10.2	11.5	13.0	14.0	15.4	16.4	18.7	21.2	23.3	25.6	27.7	33.1	38.4	48.7	56.6
150	2.0			5.1		7.7		10.2		12.6		15.0	17.3	19.6	21.7	24.0	26.1		36.7	47.0	55.8
200	1.5	2.4	3.1	4.5	5.8	7.1	8.3	9.5	10.8	11.9	13.1	14.2	16.4	18.7	20.9	23.1	25.2	30.5	35.7	45.7	55.6
250	1.2			4.2		6.7		9.1		11.4		13.7	15.9	18.1	20.3	22.4	24.6		34.8	44.8	54.7
300	1.0		2.6	3.9	5.2	6.4	7.6	8.8	10.0	11.1	12.2	13.3	15.5	17.7	19.8	22.0	24.1	29.1	34.1	44.1	54.1
350	0.9			3.7		6.2		8.5		10.8		13.0	15.2	17.4	19.5	21.7	23.6		33.6	43.6	53.6
400	0.7	1.6	2.3	3.6	4.8	6.0	7.2	8.3	9.5	10.6	11.7	12.8	15.0	17.2	19.2	21.2	23.2	28.2	33.2	43.2	53.2
450	0.7			3.5		5.9		8.2		10.4		12.6	14.8	16.8	18.9	20.9	22.9		32.9	42.9	52.9
500	0.6		2.1	3.4	4.6	5.8	6.9	8.0	9.2	10.3	11.4	12.5	14.6	16.7	18.6	20.7	22.6	27.6	32.6	42.6	52.6
550	0.5			3.3		5.7		7.9		10.1		12.3	14.4	16.4	18.4	20.4	22.4		32.4	42.4	52.4
600	0.5	1.3	2.0	3.2	4.4	5.6	6.7	7.8	9.0	10.0	11.2	12.2	14.2	16.2	18.2	20.2	22.2	27.2	32.2	42.2	52.2
650	0.5			3.2		5.5		7.7		10.0		12.1	14.1	16.1	18.1	20.1	22.1		32.1	42.1	52.1
700	0.4		1.9	3.1	4.3	5.4	6.6	7.7	8.8	9.9	10.8	11.9	13.9	15.9	17.9	19.9	21.9	26.9	31.9	41.9	51.9
750	0.4			3.1		5.4		7.6		9.8		11.8	13.8	15.8	17.8	19.8	21.8		31.8	41.8	51.8
800	0.4	1.1	1.8	3.0	4.2	5.3	6.4	7.5	8.7	9.7	10.7	11.7	13.7	15.7	17.7	19.7	21.7	26.7	31.6	41.7	51.7
850	0.4			3.0		5.3		7.5		9.6		11.6	13.6	15.6	17.6	19.6	21.6		31.5	41.6	51.6
900	0.3		1.7	3.0	4.1	5.2	6.3	7.5	8.5	9.5	10.5	11.5	13.5	15.5	17.5	19.5	21.5	26.5	31.5	41.5	51.5
950	0.3			2.9		5.2		7.4		9.4		11.4	13.4	15.4	17.4	19.5	21.4		31.4	41.5	51.5
1,000	0.3	1.0	1.7	2.9	4.0	5.2	6.3	7.4	8.4	9.4	10.4	11.4	13.4	15.4	17.4	19.4	21.4	26.4	31.4	41.4	51.4
1,500	0.2		1.5	2.7	3.8	4.9	5.9	6.9	7.9	8.9	9.9	10.9	12.9	14.9	16.9	18.9	20.9	25.9	30.9	40.9	50.9
2,000	0.1	0.8	1.4	2.6	3.7	4.7	5.7	6.7	7.7	8.7	9.7	10.7	12.7	14.7	16.7	18.7	20.7	25.7	30.7	40.7	50.7
2,500	0.1		1.4	2.6	3.6	4.6	5.6	6.6	7.6	8.6	9.6	10.6	12.6	14.6	16.6	18.6	20.6	25.5	30.6	40.6	50.6
3,000	0.1	0.8	1.4	2.5	3.5	4.5	5.5	6.5	7.5	8.5	9.5	10.5	12.5	14.5	16.5	18.5	20.5	25.4	30.5	40.5	50.5
4,000	0.1	0.7	1.3	2.4	3.4	4.4	5.4	6.4	7.4	8.4	9.4	10.4	12.4	14.4	16.4	18.4	20.4	25.3	30.4	40.4	50.4
5,000	0.1	0.7	1.3	2.3	3.3	4.3	5.3	6.3	7.3	8.3	9.3	10.3	12.3	14.3	16.3	18.3	20.3	25.3	30.3	40.3	50.3

Source: AICPA, *An Auditor's Approach to Statistical Sampling*, vol. 6 (New York, 1974).

matching process and in determining whether the control procedure that requires the matching of purchase invoices and receiving reports is working. The auditors define an exception as any one or more of the following with respect to each invoice and the related receiver:

1. Any invoice not supported by a receiving document.
2. Any invoice supported by a receiving document that is applicable to another invoice.
3. Any differences between the invoice and the receiving document as to quantities shipped.
4. Any irregularities in the documents that were not subsequently corrected.
5. Any evidence of deliberate manipulation or circumvention of the internal control system.

For this type of test, the only testing procedure needed is inspection of the documents and matching of receivers with invoices.

Determine the field to be sampled. The client prepares a serially numbered voucher for every purchase of materials. The receiving report and purchase invoice are attached to each voucher. Since this compliance test is being performed during the interim period, the population to be tested consists of 7,600 vouchers for purchases of material during the first 10 months of the year under audit.

Determine the expected occurrence rate. In the audits of the previous three years, the auditors observed that exceptions of the type described above produced occurrence rates of 0.5 percent, 0.9 percent, and 0.7 percent in the respective years. No positive trend can be discerned from the figures for these three years; the auditors, therefore, select an expected occurrence rate of 1 percent, knowing that this rate is higher than any prior observed rates and that they can defend it on the basis of conservatism and reasonableness. The rate, however, is not so high as to result in an unreasonably large sample size.

Stipulate precision and confidence level. The auditors realize that errors in matching receiving reports with purchase orders can affect the financial statements through overpayments to vendors and misstatements of purchases and accounts payable. They also would like to rely upon this internal control procedure to limit their substantive testing of accounts payable, inventories, and the cost of goods sold. Based upon these considerations, the auditors decide upon a tolerable upper precision limit of 4.7 percent, with a confidence level of 95 percent.

Determine the required sample size from the table. Since the stipulated confidence level is 95 percent, the table in Figure 8–3 is applicable. Under the column for a 1 percent occurrence rate, the auditors find the stipulated upper precision limit of 4.7 percent; the corresponding sample size is 100 items.

Draw and inspect the sample. The auditors proceed to select 100 vouchers using an appropriate random selection technique. They then examine the vouchers and supporting documents for each of the types of exceptions previously defined.

Interpret the results of the examination. In interpreting the sample results, the auditors must consider not only the actual percentage of exceptions observed, but also the nature of the exceptions. There are three possibilities to be considered: (1) the actual occurrence rate is equal to, or less than, the expected rate; (2) the actual occurrence rate is more than the expected rate; and (3) one or more of the exceptions observed contain evidence of a deliberate manipulation or circumvention of the internal control system.

If the actual occurrence rate observed in the sample items examined is equal to or less than 1 percent and there is no evidence of a deliberate manipulation or circumvention of the internal control system, the auditors have completed their compliance test of this control procedure. They may conclude with 95 percent confidence that the error rate in the population does not exceed 4.7 percent.

Assume, however, that the error rate observed in the sample is 3 percent and none of the observed exceptions indicate deliberate manipulation or circumvention of internal control. Do the auditors still have 95 percent confidence that the population error rate does not exceed 4.7 percent? Referring to Figure 8–3, the auditors will find that a sample of 100 items with a 3 percent error rate provides 95 percent confidence only that the error rate does not exceed 7.6 percent. Thus, the sample results do not provide the auditors with assurance that the error rate does not exceed their stipulated upper precision limit.

In light of these results, the auditors should reduce their reliance upon the client's internal control in this area and increase their reliance upon their own substantive testing procedures.[4] This weakness in internal control may affect the auditors' substantive tests of inventories, accounts payable, and cash disbursements. As a preliminary step to any modification of their audit program, the auditors should investigate the cause of the unexpectedly high error rate. In addition, they may wish to expand their sample of vouchers to provide a more precise estimate of the population error rate.

There is no requirement that the auditors must continue to use statistical sampling techniques after their preliminary sample has indicated that the characteristics of the population do not meet their expectations. If the indicated error rate in the matching of purchase invoices with receivers is too high, the auditors may request that a thorough

---

[4] Alternatively, the auditors may increase their sample size in an attempt to achieve the stipulated upper precision limit of 4.7 percent. Now that the estimated occurrence rate is 3 percent, a sample of between 400 and 500 items would be required to achieve this precision. A compliance test involving such a large sample size would seldom be cost-effective.

examination be performed in this area by the client's employees under the auditors' supervision. Or, the auditors may be able to isolate the exceptions noted to a particular time period. Most of the exceptions may have been caused, for instance, by a replacement employee when a regular employee was on sick leave. If that is the case, the auditors may apply appropriate audit procedures to determine the dollar effect of errors occurring during that time period. The auditors should apply whatever audit procedures are appropriate to ensure that the excessive error rate has not led to material error in the financial statements.

Regardless of the occurrence rate observed, if one or more of the exceptions discovered by the auditors indicates fraud or circumvention of the internal control system, other auditing procedures become necessary. The auditors must evaluate the effect of the exception on the financial statements and adopt auditing procedures that are specifically designed to protect against the type of exception observed. The nature of the exception may be more important than its rate of occurrence.

The sample of 60

Auditors are always looking for ways to increase the efficiency of their audits. One approach to minimizing the time involved in compliance testing is to *assume a zero occurrence rate* for compliance deviations and to stipulate an upper precision limit of 5 percent and a reliability level of 95 percent. Although the figure is not shown in the table in Figure 8–3, these criteria indicate a sample size of 60 items. The auditors then select their sample and begin examining items.

If the auditors encounter no exceptions in their sample, they may conclude with 95 percent confidence that the exception rate does not exceed 5 percent, and they will place their planned degree of reliance upon the internal control procedure. On the other hand, if the auditors encounter *even one exception* in their sample, they will not be able to achieve the desired upper precision limit with a sample of only 60 items. Therefore, they must decide whether to increase the sample size or discontinue the compliance test and place no reliance upon the control procedure.

Let us consider the rationale for discontinuing a compliance test when a single exception is encountered. One exception in a sample of 60 items indicates an error rate of just under 2 percent. Figure 8–3 indicates that a sample of 150 items is needed to achieve an upper precision limit of 5 percent when the expected occurrence rate is 2 percent.[5] In

---

[5] Increasing the sample size to 150 offers no guarantee that the 5 percent upper precision limit can be achieved. If, for example, the auditors find 9 errors in 150 items (indicating an error rate of 3 percent), they would be faced with reducing their reliance upon internal control or increasing the sample size to the vicinity of 350 items. The fact that this problem may continue indefinitely is one argument for terminating the compliance test when the first error is encountered.

discontinuing the compliance test, the auditors are assuming that the reduction in substantive testing that might result from reliance upon the internal accounting control does not justify examining this large a sample. Whether or not this conclusion is valid depends upon the nature and time requirements of the related substantive tests.

Discovery sampling

Discovery sampling is actually a modified case of attribute sampling. The purpose of a discovery sample is to detect at least *one exception,* with a predetermined level of confidence, providing the exception exists with a specified occurrence rate in the population. One important use of discovery sampling is to locate examples of a suspected fraud.

Although discovery sampling is designed to locate relatively rare items, it cannot locate a needle in a haystack. If an exception exists within a population but has an insignificant occurrence rate (0.5 percent or less), no sampling plan can provide adequate assurance that an example of the exception will be encountered. Still, discovery sampling can (with a very high degree of confidence) ensure detection of exceptions occurring at a rate as low as 0.5 to 1 percent.

Discovery sampling is used primarily to search for *critical errors.* When an exception is critical, such as evidence of fraud, any occurrence rate may be intolerable. Consequently, if such an exception is discovered, the auditors may abandon their sampling procedures and undertake a thorough examination of the population. If no exceptions are found in discovery sampling, the auditors may conclude (with the specified reliability) that the critical error does not occur to the extent of the stipulated occurrence rate.

To use discovery sampling, the auditors must specify their desired level of confidence and stipulate the occurrence rate for the test. The required sample size then is computed as follows:

$$\text{Sample size} = \frac{\text{Reliability factor}}{\text{Stipulated occurrence rate}}$$

The *reliability factor* is *not* the same thing as the confidence or reliability level. For a given confidence level, the reliability factor for use in this formula is found from a table such as the one in Figure 8–4. The stipulated occurrence rate is stated as a decimal in the above formula— that is, a rate of 3 percent would be entered as 0.03.

To illustrate discovery sampling, assume that auditors have reason to suspect that someone has been preparing fraudulent purchase orders, receiving reports, and purchase invoices in order to generate cash disbursements for fictitious purchase transactions. In order to determine

Reliability factors for use in discovery sampling

Confidence level	Reliability factor
90%	2.3
95	3.0
96	3.2
97	3.4
98	3.7
99	4.3
99+	5.4

Source: AICPA, *An Auditor's Approach to Statistical Sampling*, vol. 6 (New York, 1974).

whether this has occurred, it is necessary to locate only one set of the fraudulent documents in the client's file of paid vouchers.

Assume the auditors wish to be 90 percent certain that their sample will bring to light a fraudulent voucher if the population contains 2 percent or more fraudulent items. Figure 8–4 indicates that the reliability factor corresponding to 90 percent confidence is 2.3. Dividing this reliability factor by the stipulated occurrence rate (.02), indicates that the auditors must examine a sample of 115 vouchers. If no fraudulent vouchers are found in this sample, the auditors will have 90 percent confidence that fraudulent vouchers are not present in the population to the extent of 2 percent. They have not, however, ruled out the possibility that one or more vouchers are fraudulent.

Discovery sampling and estimation sampling for attributes may be applied to the same sample. Auditors might examine a sample of vouchers once, simultaneously using discovery sampling to search for critical errors and estimation sampling to estimate the occurrence rates of various noncritical errors.

Sampling for variables

Although estimation sampling for attributes and discovery sampling are useful for testing internal control, these sampling plans do not provide results stated in dollars. Techniques that enable auditors to estimate dollar amounts are called *sampling for variables.* These techniques are very useful in such audit applications as estimating the dollar value of a client's inventories or accounts receivable or the aggregate dollar value of each age classification in an aging schedule of accounts receivable. Sampling for variables is used primarily in the auditors' substantive tests of account balances, whereas sampling for attributes is most widely used in compliance tests of internal accounting control procedures. Widely used variables sampling plans include *mean-per-unit estimation, ratio and difference estimation,* and *dollar-unit sampling.*

Mean-per-unit estimation

Mean-per-unit estimation (also called estimation sampling for variables) enables auditors to estimate the *average* dollar value of items in a population, with specified precision and reliability, by determining the *average* dollar value of items in a sample. If an estimate of the total dollar value of the population is desired, the estimated average value (the *sample mean*) may be multiplied by the number of items in the population.

Precision, in mean-per-unit estimation, is the maximum allowable difference between the auditors' estimate and the true population value. Since this sampling technique deals with averages, precision may be stated either with respect to the total population value or with respect to the average value per item. For example, assume that we wish to estimate the total value of a population containing 10,000 items with precision of ±$5,000. Assume also that the population has a total value of $180,000 and, therefore, a *true mean* of $18. If we select a sample with a mean of $17, we have missed estimating the true mean by only $1. However, our estimate of the total population value is $170,000 ($17 ×10,000 items), which is not within our stipulated precision of ±$5,000.

If our estimate of the total population is to be within ±$5,000, our estimate of the average item value must be within ±50 cents. This figure, ±50 cents, is our *sample precision.* Sample precision may be viewed as the required *precision per item*; it is found by dividing the stipulated precision for our estimate of the total population value by the number of items in the population.

Theory of mean-per-unit estimation

The assumption underlying mean-per-unit estimation is that the mean of a sample will, within a certain precision and confidence level, represent the true mean of the population. Sampling for variables is a more sophisticated statistical process than attribute or discovery sampling. Even if tables are used to determine the required sample size, the auditor needs some familiarity with statistical theory and terminology. Of particular importance are the concepts of *normal distribution, standard deviation, standard error of the sample means,* and *standard normal deviate.*

Normal distribution. Many populations, such as the heights of all men, may be described as normal distributions. A normal distribution is illustrated by the familiar bell-shaped curve, illustrated in Figure 8–5, in which the values of the individual items tend to congregate around the population *mean.* Notice that the distribution of individual

Figure 8–5
Normal distribution

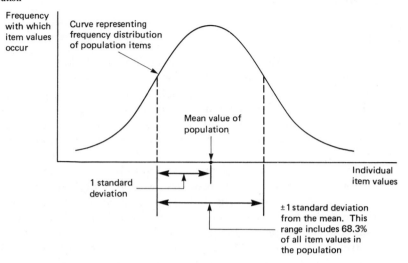

Frequency with which item values occur

Curve representing frequency distribution of population items

Mean value of population

1 standard deviation

Individual item values

±1 standard deviation from the mean. This range includes 68.3% of all item values in the population

item values is symmetrical on both sides of the mean. There is no tendency for deviations to be to one side rather than the other.

Even when the items within the population are **not** normally distributed, the concept of a normal distribution is relevant to sampling theory. If auditors were to draw from any population hundreds of samples of a given size, *the means of these samples would form a normal distribution* around the true population mean.

Standard deviation. The standard deviation of a population is a measure of the *variability* or *dispersion* of individual item values about the population mean.[6] The less variation among item values, the smaller the standard deviation; the greater the variation among item values, the larger the standard deviation. It is inherent in the definitions of normal distribution and standard deviation that 68.3 percent of the item values in a normal distribution fall within ±1 standard deviation of the population mean, that 95.4 percent fall within ±2 standard deviations, and that 99.7 percent fall within ±3 standard deviations. These percentage relationships hold true by definition; however, the dollar amount of the standard deviation will vary from one population to another.

[6] The standard deviation is the square root of the following quotient: the sum of the squares of the deviation of each item value from the population mean, divided by the number of items in the population. Symbolically, the formula for calculating the standard deviation is:

$$\sqrt{\frac{\Sigma(x - \overline{X})^2}{N}}$$

Auditors may obtain a reliable estimate of the dollar amount of the standard deviation by taking a *pilot sample* of approximately 50 items.[7] (The items examined in this pilot sample become part of the larger sample used for estimating the population mean.) Generalized audit software packages also include routines designed to estimate the standard deviation of a population either from a sample or from the population itself.

Standard error of the sample means.   If a series of samples of a given size as taken from a population, the means of these samples should form a normal distribution around the true population mean. The standard deviation of this normal distribution of sample means is called the *standard error of the sample means.* The words *standard error* are used in place of *standard deviation* to stress that deviation of sample means from the true mean is caused by *sampling error.*

The number of standard errors in the auditors' desired precision interval *determines the reliability of the sample results.* Since the standard error is the standard deviation of a distribution of all possible sample means, we know the percentage of sample means that will fall within a given number of standard errors of the true mean. For example, we know that 68.3 percent of all sample means fall within ±1 standard error of the true mean, that 95.4 percent fall within ±2 standard errors, and that 99.7 percent fall within ±3 standard errors. The numbers of standard errors in the precision intervals necessary to yield other levels of confidence may be determined from a table of *standard normal deviates.*

The larger the sample size, the more closely the sample means should represent the population mean. Thus, the standard error of a distribution of sample means may be reduced by increasing the sample size. The fact that a known percentage of sample means fall within a specified number of standard errors of the true mean enables auditors to control the reliability of their sample results. Selecting a sample size that limits the standard error to the desired amount enables them to control the precision of their estimate.

Standard normal deviate.   In estimation sampling for variables, reliability expresses the percentage of the time that the sample mean may be expected to fall within a specified interval of the population mean. The *standard normal deviate* is the *number of standard errors in this interval.* For example, we know by definition that 95.4 percent of all possible sample means fall within ±2 standard errors of

---

[7] An *estimate* of the standard deviation may be made from a sample by taking the square root of the following quotient: the sum of the squares of the deviation of each sample item value from the sample mean, divided by one less than the number of items in the sample. Symbolically, the formula for estimating the standard deviation is:

$$\sqrt{\frac{\Sigma(x - \bar{x})^2}{n - 1}}$$

the true mean. Thus, the reliability level of 95.4 percent has a standard normal deviate of 2, meaning that the sample mean may differ from the true mean by as much as two standard errors. The standard normal deviates corresponding to other levels of confidence are shown in Figure 8–6.

Figure 8–6
Table of standard normal deviates

Reliability*	Standard normal deviate (U)
68.3	±1.00
70	±1.04
75	±1.15
80	±1.28
85	±1.44
90	±1.64
95	±1.96
95.4	±2.00
99	±2.58
99.7	±3.00

* Percentage of the time that $\bar{x} - \overline{X}$ will be no more than U standard errors.

Determination of sample size

The factors affecting sample size in mean per unit estimation are (1) desired precision, (2) desired sample reliability, (3) variability among item values in the population, and (4) population size. The relationship of these factors to the required sample size are expressed by the following formula:[8]

$$\text{Sample size} = \left(\frac{\text{Standard normal deviate} \times \text{Estimated standard deviation}}{\text{Sample precision}}\right)^2$$

The procedures for mean-per-unit estimation now may be summarized as follows:

1. **Define the objectives of the test.** Estimation sampling for variables is generally used for substantive tests in which the auditors seek to gather evidence to support the value shown in the financial statements for a particular population.

---

[8] This formula is based upon an infinite population. The effect on sample size when the population is finite but of significant size is not material. Symbolically, this formula may be stated:

$$n = \left(\frac{US_{x_j}}{p}\right)^2$$

where n = Sample size, U = Standard normal deviate, S_{x_j} = Estimated standard deviation, and p = Precision stated in terms of the estimate of the mean value.

2. *Stipulate the desired precision and reliability.* The factors to be considered in stipulating precision and reliability are (*a*) the materiality of the maximum tolerable error and (*b*) the acceptable level of sampling risk. This topic is discussed in detail later in this chapter.

3. *Estimate the standard deviation of the population.* An estimate of the standard deviation may be made from a pilot sample or by using an appropriate computer program.

4. *Determine the required sample precision.* The precision with which the sample mean must approximate the true mean is determined by dividing the precision desired for the estimate of the population total by the number of items in the population.

5. *Determine the standard normal deviate corresponding to the desired reliability.* The standard normal deviate is determined from such tables as the one in Figure 8–6.

6. *Solve the formula for the required sample size.*

7. *Select the sample using random selection techniques.*

8. *Audit each item in the sample and compute the sample mean.* Since the sample mean is used to estimate the true value of the population, the auditors must apply appropriate audit procedures to determine the correct value of each item in the sample. These procedures might include independent computation of dollar amounts, confirmation by outside parties, and vouching transactions.

9. *Interpret the sample results.* The sample mean provides the auditors with an estimate of the true population mean, within prescribed precision and reliability.[9] If this estimate does not support the representations made in the client's financial statements, the auditors should investigate further to determine the cause and scope of the discrepancies. This may involve additional sampling to determine the true value of the population with greater precision and reliability. Ultimately, the auditors must require the client to correct any material misstatement of the population value if they are to render an unqualified report on the financial statements.

Illustration of mean-per-unit estimation

Assume that an audit client has an inventory of 10,000 head of beef cattle (steers) located in feed lots. The steers were purchased at various dates and at varying prices. The client's records show a value for the

---

[9] After determining the audited values of the sample items, the auditors should again estimate the standard deviation of the population. If the standard deviation exceeds that used in the computation of sample size, the auditors have underestimated the variability of the population, and their sample is too small to achieve the stipulated precision and reliability. In this case, the auditors must increase the sample size to that indicated by the new estimated standard deviation.

inventory equal to the purchase cost of the cattle plus the cumulative costs of feeding these cattle. The current price quotation for beef cattle of this grade is 90 cents per pound. As auditors, we wish to estimate the market value of the inventory to determine that the carrying value of the cattle in the accounting records does not exceed current market value.

In view of the dollar amounts involved and our assessment of sampling risk, we stipulate a precision of ±$200,000 for our estimate of the market value of the cattle. The client has no internal control procedure that would have caused a market value lower than cost to have been reflected in the accounting records. For this reason, we decide to require 95.4 percent reliability in our substantive test results.

By selecting a pilot sample of 50 steers and weighing each one to determine its market value, we estimate the standard deviation of the population at $90. Since estimation sampling for variables deals with average amounts, we must estimate the average market value per steer and multiply this estimate by the number of cattle in the inventory. If the estimate of total market value is to have a precision of ±$200,000 at the 95.4 percent confidence level, the estimate of average market value per steer must have a precision of ±$20 ($200,000 ÷ 10,000 steers). Referring to the table in Figure 8–6, we find the standard normal deviate corresponding to 95.4 percent reliability is ±2.00.

Using the sample size formula, we may now compute our required sample size:

$$\text{Sample size} = \left(\frac{\text{Standard normal deviate} \times \text{Estimated standard deviation}}{\text{Sample precision}} \right)^2$$

$$= \left(\frac{2.00 \times \$90}{\pm\$20} \right)^2 = \frac{32{,}400}{400} = 81 \text{ steers}$$

Since we have already sampled 50 steers, we need only to select on a random basis another 31 to complete our required sample of 81. Assuming our sample mean indicated an average market value of $610 per steer, we could be 95.4 percent confident that the current market value of the inventory is $6,100,000 ± $200,000. If our client's value for the cattle does not exceed our upper precision limit of $6,300,000, we would accept the client's figure as not being materially in excess of market value. If the client's book value exceeds $6,300,000 we would propose an adjusting entry to write down the carrying value of the cattle to market value.

Ratio and difference estimation

Mean-per-unit estimation estimates the average item value as the basis for estimating the total value of the population. Two alternatives to this approach are ratio and difference estimation. Although closely related, ratio estimation and difference estimation are two distinct sampling plans; each is appropriate under slightly different circumstances.

In ratio estimation, the auditors use a sample to estimate the *ratio* of the audited (correct) value of a population to its book value. This ratio is estimated by dividing the total audited value of a sample by the total book value of the sample items.[10] An estimate of the correct population value is obtained by multiplying this estimated ratio by the total book value of the population.

In applying difference estimation, the auditors use a sample to estimate the *average difference* between the audited value and book value of items in a population. The average difference is estimated by dividing the net difference between the audited value and book value of a sample by the number of items in the sample.[11] The total difference between the book value of the population and its estimated correct value is determined by multiplying the estimated average difference by the number of items in the population.

Use of ratio and difference estimation.   The use of ratio or difference estimation techniques requires that: (1) each population item has a book value, (2) the population book value corresponds to the sum of the item book values, (3) an audited value may be ascertained for each sample item, and (4) differences between audited and book values are relatively frequent. If the occurrence rate of differences is very low, a prohibitively large sample is required to disclose a representative number of errors.

Ratio estimation is most appropriate when the size of errors is nearly proportional to the book values of the items. In many cases, the size of transactions affecting an account may be nearly proportional to the account balance. Thus, mistakes in processing transactions affecting large accounts generally are larger than those affecting small accounts. When the size of errors is not nearly proportional to book value, difference estimation is the more appropriate technique.

Illustration of ratio and difference estimation

To illustrate the use of ratio and difference estimation techniques, assume that auditors wish to estimate the total value of a client's ac-

---

[10] Symbolically, this process is expressed:

$$\hat{R} = \frac{\Sigma a_j}{\Sigma b_j}$$

where $\hat{R}$ (pronounced R-caret) represents the estimated ratio of audited value to book value, a_j represents the audited value of each sample item, and b_j represents the book value of each sample item.

[11] Symbolically, the estimated difference is computed:

$$\hat{d} = \frac{1}{n} \sum_{j=l}^{n} (a_j - b_j)$$

where $\hat{d}$ represents the estimated average difference between audited value and book value; n represents the number of items in the sample; and a_j and b_j represent the audited and book values, respectively.

counts payable. The population consists of 4,000 accounts with an aggregate book value of $5 million. The auditors calculate the required sample size, randomly select the accounts to be sampled, and apply auditing procedures to establish the correct account balances. Assume that this sample consists of 200 accounts with a book value of $250,000, and that the audited value is determined to be $257,500.

Using ratio estimation, the auditors would estimate the ratio of audited value to book value to be 1.03 (computed $257,500 ÷ $250,000). Their estimate of the total population value, therefore, would be $5,150,000 (computed $5,000,000 × 1.03). If difference estimation is used, the auditors would estimate the average difference per item to be a $37.50 understatement ($7,500 net difference divided by 200 items). Multiplying $37.50 by the 4,000 accounts in the population indicates that the client's book value for accounts payable is understated by $150,000.

Each of these estimates would have a precision interval and reliability related to the auditors' sample size. The procedures for determining the required sample size in these sampling plans are more complex than in mean-per-unit estimation. To provide auditors with assistance in this area, the AICPA has issued *An Auditor's Approach to Statistical Sampling*, vol. 5, entitled "Ratio and Difference Estimation."

Dollar-unit sampling

Dollar-unit sampling is a technique that applies the theory of attributes sampling to estimating the total dollar amount of error in a population. This sampling plan may be used in dual-purpose tests, in which auditors evaluate the effectiveness of internal control and also estimate dollar effects of the errors upon the population.

Whereas most variables sampling plans define the population as a group of accounts or transactions, dollar-unit sampling defines the population as the *individual dollars* comprising the population's book value. Thus, a population of 5,000 accounts receivable with a total value of $2,875,000 is viewed as a population of 2,875,000 items (dollars), rather than 5,000 items (accounts). To illustrate the selection of the sample, assume that the first two customer accounts are each in the amount of $400, and that dollar 602 is selected at random for inclusion in the auditors' sample. Dollar 602 falls in the second customer account. Of course, to audit dollar 602, it is necessary to substantiate the balance of the second account. Verifying this account will also serve to substantiate dollars 401 through 800, in the event any of these dollars should also be included in the sample.

Dollar-unit sampling is efficient because the population is *automatically stratified by dollar amount*. A $2,000 account receivable, for example, has twice as much chance of being audited as does a $1,000 receivable, because the larger account has twice as many dollar units that might be selected for inclusion in the sample.

Illustration of dollar-unit sampling. To illustrate the application of attributes sampling theory to estimating dollar amounts, assume that we are auditing a population of accounts receivable with a total book value of $1 million. For purposes of our test, we will define an *exception* as a "fictitious dollar"—that is, one that does not belong in the population.[12] Now assume that we select a sample of 100 dollar units, audit the accounts containing those dollars, and find no exceptions. The attributes sampling table in Figure 8–3 (page 245) shows that we may have 95 percent confidence that the error rate (overstatement) in the population does not exceed 3 percent. Since the population value is $1 million, we have determined with 95 percent reliability that the population is not overstated by more than $30,000.

Evaluating sampling risk

In performing tests of compliance, the auditors are concerned with two aspects of sampling risk:

1. The risk of *underreliance* on internal control. As a result of sampling error, the sample results may cause the auditors not to rely upon an internal control procedure when, in fact, reliance is justified.
2. The risk of *overreliance* on internal control. This more important risk is the possibility that the sample results will cause the auditors to erroneously place more reliance upon an internal control procedure than is justified by the true effectiveness of that control.

Similarly, in performing substantive tests of account balances, there are two types of sampling risk:

1. The risk of *incorrect rejection* of a population. Also called *alpha risk*, this is the possibility that sample results will indicate that a population is materially misstated when, in fact, it is not.
2. The risk of *incorrect acceptance* of a population. Also called *beta risk*, this is the possibility that sampling error will cause the auditors to accept a population as free from material error when, in fact, material error does exist. This is the most hazardous type of sampling risk.

The risks of underreliance on internal control and of incorrect rejection of a population relate to the *efficiency* of the audit process. For example, if the auditors place too little reliance on internal control, they will perform more substantive testing than is necessary. This causes the audit to be inefficient, but it does not cause the auditors to overlook material errors in the financial statements. Similarly, if the auditors

---

[12] To simplify our illustration, we ignored the possibility that dollar units may be partially overstated without being totally fictitious. For example, if an account receivable with a $1,000 book value is determined to have a correct value of $750, a dollar unit within that account contains 25 percent overstatement and is a "partial" error.

incorrectly reject an account balance as containing material error, additional audit procedures will eventually lead to the correct conclusion. Thus, the risks of underreliance on internal control and of incorrect rejection reduce the efficiency, but not the effectiveness, of the audit.

The risk of overreliance on internal control and the risk of incorrect acceptance of a population relate to the *effectiveness* of the audit in detecting material errors. These risks are of primary concern to auditors; failure to detect material error may lead to accusations of negligence and to extensive legal liability.

Risk levels in compliance tests. The risk of overreliance on internal control may be described as the risk that the actual rate of compliance deviations exceeds the auditors' upper precision limit. This risk is equal to the complement of the specified confidence level—that is, 100 percent minus the confidence level. Since compliance tests generally are conducted at confidence levels of 95 or 90 percent, the risk of overreliance on a specific control procedure usually is limited to 5 or 10 percent.

The risk of underreliance on internal control is more difficult to quantify and often runs at very high levels, such as 50 percent or more. As previously stated, this risk will *not* cause the auditors to overlook material errors and is therefore not as serious as the risk of overreliance upon internal control. Furthermore, reducing the risk of underreliance to low levels requires such large sample sizes that the additional audit work usually cannot be justified.

Risk levels in substantive tests. Unfortunately, the complement of the reliability level used in a substantive test quantifies *only alpha risk*—that is, the risk of incorrectly rejecting a population when material error does not really exist. *Beta risk*—the risk of accepting a population containing material error—is both more difficult to measure and is of far greater importance to the auditors. Determining acceptable levels of beta risk and controlling sampling risk in substantive tests are topics discussed in the remaining sections of this chapter.

Acceptable levels of beta risk

How much beta risk is acceptable to an auditor? In large part, the answer depends upon how much reliance the auditor is able to place upon the client's system of internal control and upon other substantive tests, such as analytical review procedures. The *ultimate risk* that material errors exist in audited financial statements may be expressed as the joint product of three separate risks, as shown by the following equation:

$$UR = IC \times AR \times TD$$

where

UR = The ultimate risk of material error in the audited financial statements.

IC = The auditors' subjective evaluation of the risk that the client's system of internal control failed to prevent the occurrence of material error. (This risk embodies the results of the auditors' entire study and evaluation of internal control, not merely the results of compliance tests.)

AR = The risk that the auditors' analytical review procedures failed to bring the material error to the auditors' attention.

TD = The risk that the auditors' other substantive tests failed to detect the existence of the material error (beta risk). (TD stands for *Tests of Details,* a term used in *SAS No. 39,* "Audit Sampling.")

To illustrate the measurement of ultimate audit risk, assume that the auditors have assessed the risks of reliance upon internal control, analytical review procedures, and other substantive tests at 40 percent, 50 percent, and 20 percent, respectively. The ultimate risk of material error in the financial statements under these circumstances may be computed as follows:

$$UR = 0.4 \times 0.5 \times 0.2$$
$$UR = 0.04$$

Thus, the auditors still face a 4 percent ultimate risk that material error has evaded both the system of internal control and their substantive tests. Conversely, they have 96 percent confidence that the financial statements are free from material error.

In practice, auditors stipulate in advance the ultimate risk that they are willing to accept, rather than computing this statistic at the conclusion of the engagement. After determining the extent of their reliance upon the client's system of internal control and upon their analytical review procedures, the auditors may restate the ultimate risk formula as follows to solve for the *acceptable level of beta risk:*

$$TD = R \div (IC \times AR)$$

To illustrate, assume that the auditors are willing to accept 5 percent ultimate risk of material error in the client's accounts receivable. After studying and evaluating internal control over sales transactions, they decide to place 40 percent risk on the possibility of the system failing to detect a material error. In addition, they believe that there is a 50 percent risk of analytical review procedures failing to detect such an error. The allowable risk of failing to detect the error is substantive testing (beta risk) is computed as follows:

$$TD = .05 \div (.4 \times .5)$$
$$TD = .05 \div .2 = .25$$

Thus, the auditors must hold beta risk to 25 percent if they are to limit ultimate risk to 5 percent in this area of the financial statements.

Controlling beta risk

Beta risk and alpha risk may be controlled independently of one another. For example, we may design a sample that limits both beta risk and alpha risk to 10 percent, or we may hold beta risk to 5 percent while allowing alpha risk to rise to 50 percent or more. In establishing the acceptable level of beta risk, the auditors must consider the consequences of material error in the financial statements. In stipulating tolerable alpha risk, on the other hand, they should consider the *time* and *cost* involved in performing additional audit procedures if they cannot accept the population value based upon their sample results.

Control of alpha risk is simple; alpha risk is the compliment of the reliability level specified in the test. Thus, stipulating a reliability of, say, 80 percent automatically limits alpha risk to 20 percent. Beta risk, on the other hand, is *controlled by tightening or widening the precision interval,* rather than by changing the confidence level. The tighter the precision interval, the smaller the risk that auditors will incorrectly accept a population containing a material error. In mean-per-unit estimation, the precision interval required to obtain a desired level of beta risk may be determined from the following formula:

$$\text{Precision} = \frac{\text{Maximum tolerable error}}{1 + \dfrac{\text{Beta risk coefficient}}{\text{Alpha risk coefficient}}}$$

The maximum tolerable error is the maximum amount that the auditors would still consider immaterial. The *risk coefficients* are taken from a

Figure 8–7
Risk coefficients for alpha and beta risks

Acceptable level of risk (alpha or beta)	Alpha risk coefficient	Beta risk coefficient
1%	2.58	2.33
5	1.96	1.64
10	1.64	1.28
15	1.44	1.04
20	1.28	.84
25	1.15	.67
30	1.04	.52
40	.84	.25
50	.67	.0

table, such as the one in Figure 8– 7. Notice that the coefficients are different for alpha risk and for beta risk.

To illustrate, let us assume that auditors want to estimate the mean value of a client's accounts receivable. They have defined the maximum tolerable error in the account (material error) as ±$400,000 and have decided to limit alpha risk to 40 percent and beta risk to 25 percent. The stipulated confidence level for this test should be 60 percent (allowing 40 percent alpha risk), and the stipulated precision should be computed as follows:

$$\text{Precision} = \frac{\pm\$400,000}{1 + \frac{.67}{.84}} = \frac{\pm\$400,000}{1.7976} = \underline{\underline{\pm\$222,518}}$$

For practical purposes, the precision interval might be rounded to, perhaps, ±$220,000. Precision intervals should be rounded downward, not upward; rounding downward tightens the interval and, therefore, decreases beta risk.

KEY TERMS INTRODUCED OR EMPHASIZED IN CHAPTER 8

Alpha risk (risk of incorrect rejection)   The risk that sample results will support the rejection of a correct book value.

Beta risk (risk of incorrect acceptance)   The risk that sample results will support the acceptance of a book value which is, in fact, materially in error.

Compliance deviation   A defined departure from prescribed control procedures. This is the characteristic measured in tests of compliance. Also called exception, occurrence, or error.

Confidence level (reliability)   The percentage of time that the true population characteristic lies within the stated precision of the sample results.

Difference estimation   A sampling plan for estimating the average difference between the audited (correct) values of items in a population and their book values. Difference estimation is used in lieu of ratio estimation when the differences are not nearly proportional to book values.

Discovery sampling   A sampling plan for locating at least one exception, providing that the exception occurs in the population with a specified frequency. Discovery sampling is used to search for *critical errors*, such as evidence of fraud.

Dollar-unit sampling   A sampling plan that uses attributes sampling theory to estimate the dollar amount of error in a population. Used in both substantive and dual-purpose tests.

Dual-purpose test   A test designed to evaluation compliance with internal control and to substantiate the dollar amount of an account using the same sample.

Estimation sampling for attributes   A sampling plan enabling the auditors to estimate the occurrence rate of a specified characteristic in a population, with stipulated precision and reliability.

Exception   See *compliance deviation.*

Expected occurrence rate   An advance estimate of an occurrence rate. This estimate is necessary for determining the required sample size in an attribute sampling plan.

Mean   The average item value, computed by dividing total value by the number of items comprising total value.

Mean-per-unit estimation   A sampling plan enabling the auditors to estimate the average dollar value (or other variable) of items in a population by determining the average value of items in a sample. This plan also is called *estimation sampling for variables*.

Normal distribution   A frequency distribution in which item values tend to congregate around the mean with no tendency for deviation toward one side rather than the other. A normal distribution is represented graphically by a bell-shaped curve.

One-sided precision   A precision interval defined by only one precision limit. One-sided precision frequently is used in estimation sampling for attributes, because auditors are interested only in whether an error rate exceeds some upper limit, not whether it might be less than some lower limit.

Population   The entire field of items from which a sample might be drawn.

Precision   An interval around the sample results in which the true population characteristic is expected to lie. Precision may be considered the allowable margin of sampling error.

Precision limits   The points designating the upper and lower boundaries of the precision interval.

Random selection   Selecting items from a population in a manner in which every item has an equal chance of being included in the sample.

Ratio estimation   A sampling plan for estimating the ratio of the audited (correct) values of items to their book values. Extending the book value of the population by this ratio provides an estimate of audited total population value. Ratio estimation is a highly efficient technique when errors are nearly proportional to item book values.

Reliability   See *confidence level*

Representative sample   A sample possessing essentially the same characteristics as the population from which it was drawn.

Risk of incorrect acceptance   See *beta risk*.

Risk of incorrect rejection   See *alpha risk*.

Sample precision   Precision stated with respect to an estimate of the average (rather than total) value of a population. Sample precision may be viewed as *precision-per-item*; it is found by dividing the stipulated precision for the estimate of total value by the number of items in the population.

Sampling error   The difference between the characteristics of a sample and the characteristics of the population. Some sampling error is likely to exist in any sample. Auditors are able to control the risk of material sampling error through stipulating precision and reliability.

Sampling for attributes   Sampling plans designed to estimate the frequency of occurrence of a specified population characteristic.

Sampling for variables   Sampling plans designed to estimate a numerical measurement of a population, such as dollar value.

Sampling risk   The possibility of sampling error being sufficiently material to cause the auditors to reach an incorrect conclusion concerning the population.

Standard deviation   A measure of the variability or dispersion of item values within a population. In a normal distribution, 68.3 percent of all item values fall with ± 1 standard deviation of the mean, 95.4 percent fall within ± 2 standard deviations, and 99.7 percent fall within ±3 standard deviations.

Standard error of the sample means The standard deviation of a distribution of sample means. Since known percentages of all sample means fall within a given number of standard errors of the true mean, the number of standard errors in the auditors' precision interval determines the reliability of the sample results.

Standard normal deviate The number of standard errors in the stipulated precision interval. A table of standard normal deviates shows the standard normal deviates corresponding to stipulated confidence levels; this factor is then used in the computation of required sample size.

Stratification Dividing a population into two or more relatively homogeneous subgroups (strata). Stratification increases the efficiency of most sampling plans by reducing the variability of items in each stratum. The sample size necessary to evaluate the strata separately is often smaller than would be needed to evaluate the total population.

Systematic selection The technique of selecting a sample by drawing every nth item in the population, following a random starting point.

Ultimate risk The risk that audited financial statements contain material error.

GROUP I: REVIEW QUESTIONS

8–1. Define, and differentiate between, nonstatistical (judgmental) sampling and statistical sampling.

8–2. Define the terms *reliability* and *precision* as they are used in statistical sampling plans.

8–3. What statistical sampling plan appears to most useful in accomplishing the basic objectives of compliance tests? Explain.

8–4. Distinguish between sampling for attributes and sampling for variables.

8–5. Explain the meaning of *sampling without replacement* and *sampling with replacement*. Which method is more efficient?

8–6. In selecting items for examination an auditor considered three alternatives: (*a*) random number table selection, (*b*) systematic selection, and (*c*) random number generator selection. Which, if any, of these methods would lead to a random sample if properly applied?

8–7. Explain briefly the term *systematic selection* as used in auditing, and indicate the precautions to be taken if a random sample is to be obtained. Is systematic selection applicable to unnumbered documents? Explain.

8–8. Explain briefly how the auditors using statistical sampling techniques may measure the possibility that the sample drawn has characteristics not representative of the population.

8–9. What relationships exist between confidence level, precision, and sample size? (AICPA)

8–10. Assume population item values are randomly distributed between $0 and $10,000. Do these item values form a normal distribution?

8–11. Why is discovery sampling well suited to the detection of fraud?

8–12. What would be the difference in an estimation sampling for attributes plan and a variables sampling plan in a test of inventory extensions?

8– 13. What is meant by *standard error of the sample means?* Why is this measurement of significance to the auditor?

8– 14. What is meant by *one-sided precision?* Explain why this approach frequently is used in estimating exception rates.

8– 15. If a sample of 100 items indicates an error rate of 3 percent, should the auditors conclude that the entire population also has approximately a 3 percent error rate?

8– 16. What relationship exists between the expected occurrence rate and sample size?

8– 17. Explain what is meant by a precision of ±1 percent with reliability of 90 percent. (AICPA, adapted)

8– 18. Barker Company has an inventory with a book value of $4,583,231, which includes 116 product lines and a total of 326,432 units. How many items comprise this population for purposes of applying a dollar-unit sampling plan? Explain.

8– 19. The 12 following statements apply to unrestricted random sampling with replacement. Indicate whether each statement is true or false.

a. The auditors' prior knowledge of the materiality of the items to be tested may negate the need for random selection.

b. A rigid definition of the population of accounts receivable must specify that only active accounts with balances be included.

c. If a population consists mostly of accounts with large balances, it is acceptable to exclude accounts with small balances from the population to be sampled because the error in a small balance could not be material.

d. Excluding extremely large items from the definition of the population and evaluating them separately so that they have no chance of being included in the sample would violate the definition of unrestricted random sampling.

e. To be random a sample must be completely unbiased and its selection governed completely by chance.

f. The precision of an estimate of a population mean from a sample mean increases as the degree of confidence in the estimate increases.

g. It is likely that five different random samples from the same population would produce five different estimates of the true population mean.

h. A 100 percent sample would have to be taken to attain a precision range of ±$0 with 100 percent reliability.

i. The effect of the inclusion by chance of a very large or very small item in a random sample can be lessened by increasing the size of the sample.

j. The standard deviation is a measure of the variability of items in a population.

k. The larger the standard deviation of a population, the smaller the required sample size.

l. The standard error of the sample means will usually be less than the estimated standard deviation computed from a sample estimate. (AICPA, adapted)

8–20. In performing a substantive test of the book value of a population, auditors must be concerned with two aspects of sampling risk. What are these two aspects of sampling risk, and which aspect is of greater importance to auditors? Explain.

GROUP II: QUESTIONS REQUIRING ANALYSIS

8–21. Increasing attention is being given by CPAs to the application of statistical techniques to audit testing.

Required:

a. List and explain the advantages of applying statistical sampling techniques to audit testing.

b. List and discuss the decisions involving professional judgment that must be made by the CPAs in applying statistical sampling techniques to compliance testing.

c. You have applied estimation sampling for attributes techniques to the client's pricing of the inventory and discovered from your sampling that the occurrence rate exceeds your stipulated upper precision limit. Discuss the courses of action you can take. (AICPA, adapted)

8–22. The professional development department of a large CPA firm has prepared the following illustration to familiarize the audit staff with the relationships of sample size to population size and variability and the auditors' specifications as to precision and reliability.

	Characteristics of population 1 relative to population 2		Audit specifications as to a sample from population 1 relative to a sample from population 2	
	Size	*Variability*	*Specified precision*	*Specified confidence level*
Case 1	Equal	Equal	Equal	Higher
Case 2	Equal	Larger	Wider	Equal
Case 3	Larger	Equal	Tighter	Lower
Case 4	Smaller	Smaller	Equal	Lower
Case 5	Larger	Equal	Equal	Higher

Required:

For each of the five cases in the above illustration, indicate the relationship of the sample size to be selected from population 1 relative to the sample from population 2. Select your answer from the following numbered responses and state the reasoning behind your choice. The required sample size from population 1 is:

1. Larger than the required sample size from population 2.
2. Equal to the required sample size from population 2.
3. Smaller than the required sample size from population 2.
4. Indeterminate relative to the required sample size from population 2. (AICPA, adapted)

8–23. In performing a compliance test of sales order approvals, the CPAs stipulate an upper precision limit of 4.5 percent with desired reliability of 95 percent. They anticipate an error rate of 2 percent.

Required:
- *a.* What type of sampling plan should the auditors use for this test?
- *b.* Using the appropriate table or formula from this chapter, compute the required sample size for the test.
- *c.* Assume that the sample indicates an occurrence rate of 3 percent. May the CPAs conclude with 95 percent confidence that the population error rate does not exceed their upper precision limit of 4.5 percent?

8–24. An auditor has reason to suspect that fraud has occurred through forgery of the treasurer's signature on company checks. The population under consideration consists of 3,000 checks.

Required:
- *a.* Can discovery sampling rule out the possibility that any forged signatures exist among the 3,000 forged checks? Explain.
- *b.* If the population includes 15 forged signatures, how many checks would the auditor have to examine to have 90 percent confidence of encountering at least one forgery?

8–25. During an audit of Potter Company, an auditor needs to estimate the total value of the 5,000 invoices processed during June. The auditor estimates the standard deviation of the population to be $30. Determine the size sample the auditor should select to achieve a precision of ±$25,000 with 95.4 percent reliability. (AICPA, adapted)

8–26. Bock Company had two billing clerks during the year. Clerk A worked nine months, and clerk B worked three months. Assume the quantity of invoices per month is constant. If the same maximum tolerable occurrence rate and confidence level are specified for each population, should the ratio of the size of the sample drawn from clerk A's invoices to the size of the sample drawn from clerk B's invoices be 3 : 1? Discuss. (AICPA, adapted)

8–27. Ratio estimation and difference estimation are two widely used variables sampling plans.

Required:
- *a.* Under what conditions are ratio estimation or difference estimation appropriate sampling plans for estimating the total dollar value of a population?
- *b.* What relationship determines which of these two plans will be most efficient in a particular situation?

8–28. Chris York, CPA, is considering the use of dollar-unit sampling in examining the sales transactions and accounts receivable of Carter Wholesale Company.

Required:
- *a.* Is dollar-unit sampling used in compliance tests or substantive tests? Explain.
- *b.* How does the definition of the items in an accounts receivable

population vary between dollar-unit sampling and mean per unit estimation?

c. Should a population of accounts receivable be stratified by dollar value before applying dollar-unit sampling procedures? Discuss.

8–29. The auditors of Dunbar Electronics want to limit the ultimate risk of material error in the valuation of inventories to 2 percent. They believe that there exists only a 20 percent risk that material error could have bypassed the client's system of internal control and only a 50 percent risk that any existing material error would not have been brought to light by the auditors' analytical review procedures. What is the maximum **beta risk** (risk of incorrect acceptance) the auditors may allow in their substantive tests of inventories?

8–30. William Stafford, CPA, is considering the use of a mean per unit estimation sampling plan. Explain the factors that Stafford should consider in determining—

a. The acceptable level of alpha risk.

b. The maximum tolerable error in the population.

c. The acceptable level of beta risk.

8–31. Cathy Williams is auditing the financial statements to Morrison Industries. In the performance of a mean-per-unit estimation of credit sales, Williams has decided to limit alpha risk to 25 percent and beta risk to 10 percent. Williams considers the maximum tolerable error in this revenue account to be ±$500,000. Calculate (a) the confidence level and (b) the precision interval that Williams should use in the determination of sample size.

8–32. Select the best answer for each of the following questions. Explain the reasons for your selection.

a. What is the primary purpose of using stratification as a sampling method in auditing?

   (1) To increase the confidence level at which a decision will be reached from the results of the sample.

   (2) To determine the occurrence rate of a given characteristic in the population being studied.

   (3) To decrease the effect of variance in the total population.

   (4) To determine the precision range of the sample selected.

b. In estimating the total value of supplies on repair trucks, Baker Company draws random samples from two equal-size strata of trucks. The mean value of the inventory stored on the larger trucks (stratum 1) was computed at $1,500, with a standard deviation of $250. On the smaller trucks (stratum 2), the mean value of inventory was compted as $500, with a standard deviation of $45. If Baker had drawn an unrestricted sample from the entire population of trucks, the expected mean value of inventory per truck would be $1,000, and the expected standard deviation would be—

   (1) Exactly $147.50.

   (2) Greater than $250.

   (3) Less than $45.

   (4) Between $45 and $250, but not $147.50.

c. A CPA's test of the accuracy of inventory counts involves two storehouses. Storehouse A contains 10,000 inventory items, and storehouse B contains 5,000 items. The CPA plans to use sampling without replacement to test for an estimated 5 percent error rate. If the CPA's sampling plan calls for reliability of 95 percent and an upper precision limit of 7.5 percent for both storehouses, the ratio of the size of the CPA's sample from storehouse A to the size of the sample from storehouse B should be—

    (1)   More than 1:1 but less than 2:1.

    (2)   2:1.

    (3)   1:1.

    (4)   More than 0.5:1 but less than 1:1.

d.   Approximately 4 percent of the homogeneous items included in Barletta's finished-goods inventory are believed to be defective. The CPAs examining Barletta's financial statements decide to test this estimated 4 percent defective rate. They learn that a sample of 284 items from the inventory will permit specified reliability of 95 percent and specified precision of ±2.5 percent. If specified precision is changed to ±5 percent and specified reliability remains 95 percent, the required sample size becomes—

    (1)   72.

    (2)   335.

    (3)   436.

    (4)   1,543.   (AICPA, adapted)

GROUP III: PROBLEMS

8–33.   The use of statistical sampling techniques in an examination of financial statements does not eliminate judgmental decisions.

Required:

a.   Identify and explain four areas in which judgment may be exercised by CPAs in planning a statistical test.

b.   Assume that the auditors' sample shows an unacceptable error rate. Discuss the various actions that they may take based upon this finding.

c.   A nonstratified sample of 80 accounts payable vouchers is to be selected from a population of 3,200. The vouchers are numbered consecutively from 1 to 3,200 and are listed, 40 to a page, in the voucher register. Describe four different techniques for selecting a random sample of vouchers for review. (AICPA, adapted)

8–34.   To test the pricing and mathematical accuracy of sales invoices, the auditors selected a sample of 500 sales invoices from a total of 100,000 invoices that were issued during the years under examination. The 500 invoices represented total recorded sales of $22,500. Total sales for the year amounted to $5 million. The examination disclosed that of the 500 invoices audited, 15 were not properly priced or contained errors in extensions and footings. The 15 incorrect invoices represented $720 of the total recorded sales, and the errors found resulted in a net understatement of these invoices by $300.

Required:

Explain what conclusions the auditors may draw from the above information, assuming the sample was selected—

    a. On a judgment basis.

    b. As part of an estimation sampling for attributes plan using an expected occurrence rate of 3 percent, a stipulated upper precision limit of 5 percent, and reliability of 95 percent.

    c. As part of a difference estimation plan for estimating the total population value with precision of ±$50,000 and 80 percent reliability.

8–35. During your examination of the financial statements of Southwest Oil Company for the year ended June 30, you confirm accounts receivable from credit card customers. For purposes of the confirmation process, an error is defined as a misstatement of the June 30 balance of the accounts receivable control account and/or an individual customer's account balance, for other than in-transit items. As of June 30, there are approximately 30,000 accounts with balances ranging from $5 to $200 and averaging about $40. You select a sample of 500 accounts on a random basis; and after all accounts have been confirmed or otherwise examined through alternative procedures, your assistant shows you a working paper containing the following description of items considered by the assistant to be exceptions:

Number of sample item drawn	Nature of exception
002	Customer claims that payment was made on June 29. Our investigation discloses that the check was received from the customer on June 30, but it was not processed because of the large volume of cash receipts on that date. However, the check was deposited and recorded as a receipt on July 1.
086	The customer had purchased a set of tires that were found to be defective and returned them to one of the company's service stations in June. The service station issued a credit memo on July 2, which was received and recorded by the accounting office the following day.
121	The customer paid one of the company's branches for the entire account balance on July 1. Investigation discloses that the branch held its cash journal open to pick up all July 1 cash receipts as June 30 business.
157	Confirmation was returned by the customer's trustee in bankruptcy. The trustee states that the customer will be unable to pay; however, the credit manager feels that in the long run a partial collection is possible.
212	Customer claims that the account was paid in full before the middle of June. Investigation discloses that all open charges to this customer's account should have been charged to another account. There was a transposition in customer account numbers. Account 99026 was charged instead of Account 99062.
294	Customer claimed payment was mailed on June 29. Investigation shows that the payment was received and recorded on July 2.
302	Customer refuses to pay for delinquent charges on an installment plan purchase of automobile tires. For policy reasons, the client will not press for collection, and the amount will be charged off in July.
336	Customer claims that the account balance was paid on June 25. Investigation discloses that the payment was received on June 29 but was not accompanied by the payment slip. The company was unable to identify the payment and credited it to a suspense account pending identification.
426	Customer reported that the account balance should be $129.62 instead of $119.62 as shown by the statement. Investigation disclosed that the detail credit card slips were improperly footed.
487	Customer claims a bulk purchase container was returned for credit several months previously. Investigation discloses that a credit memo for the container inadvertently was not issued.

Required:

Prepare an analysis of each of the items in your assistant's working paper explaining whether or not the item should be considered an error for the purposes of your test. What error rate (in number of misstated customers' accounts) has your sample disclosed?

8–36. You desire to evaluate the reasonableness of the book value of the inventory of your client, Draper, Inc. You satisfied yourself earlier as to inventory quantities. During the examination of the pricing and extension of the inventory, the following data were gathered using appropriate unrestricted random sampling with replacement:

(1) Total items in the inventory (N) 12,700
(2) Total items in the sample (n) 400
(3) Total audited values of items in the sample $38,400
(4) Formula for estimated population standard deviation:

$$S_{X_j} = \sqrt{\frac{\sum\limits_{j=1}^{j=n} (x_j = x)^2}{n = 1}}$$

(5) $\sum\limits_{j=1}^{400} (x_j = \bar{x})^2$ 312,816

(6) Formula for estimated standard error of the sample means:

$$SE = \frac{S_{X_j}}{\sqrt{n}}$$

(7) Standard normal deviate coefficient corresponding to 95 percent reliability .... ±1.96

Required:

a. Based on the sample results, use estimation sampling for variables to estimate the total value of inventory. Show computations in good form where appropriate.

b. With what precision may the estimated population value in *part a*, above, represent the true population value at the 95 percent reliability level? (*Hint:* at the 95 percent reliability level, the precision interval is equivalent to a known number of standard errors of the mean.)

c. Independent of your answers to parts *a* and *b*, assume that the book value of Draper's inventory is $1,700,000, and based on the sample results the estimated total value of the inventory is $1,680,000. The auditors desire a confidence (reliability) level of 95 percent. Discuss the audit and statistical considerations the auditors must evaluate before deciding whether the sampling results support acceptance of the book value as a fair presentation of Draper's inventory. (AICPA, adapted)

8–37. In the audit of Potomac Mills, the auditors wish to test the costs assigned to manufactured goods. During the year, the company has produced 2,000 production lots with a total recorded cost of $5.9 million. The auditors select a sample of 200 production lots with an aggregate book value of $600,000 and vouch the assigned costs to the supporting documentation. Their examination discloses errors in the cost of 52 of the 200 production lots; after adjustment for these errors, the audited value of the sample is $582,000.

Required:
a. Show how the auditors would compute an estimate of the total cost of production lots manufactured during the year using each of the following sampling plans. (Do not compute the precision or reliability of these estimates.)
   (1) Mean-per-unit estimation.
   (2) Ratio estimation.
   (3) Difference estimation.
b. Explain why mean-per-unit estimation results in a higher estimate of the population value than does ratio estimation in this particular instance.

9

Audit working papers: Quality control for audits

Working papers are vitally important instruments of the auditing profession. The need for the auditors to acquire skill and judgment in the design and use of these basic tools is scarcely less than the need for a surgeon to master the use of operating instruments. Working papers are the connecting link between the client's records and the auditors' report. Working papers document all of the work done by the auditors and provide the justification for the auditors' conclusions as to the fairness of the financial statements.

Definition of working papers

The AICPA's Auditing Standards Board, in discussing standards of field work, has pointed out that "sufficient competent evidential matter is to be obtained through inspection, observation, inquiries, and confirmations to afford a reasonable basis for an opinion regarding the financial statements under examination." In building up this evidence, the auditors prepare working papers. Some of these may take the form of bank reconciliations or analyses of ledger accounts; others may consist of copies of correspondence, copies of minutes of directors' and stockholders' meetings, and lists of stockholders; still others might be organization charts or graphical presentations of plant layout. Working trial balances, audit programs, internal control questionnaires, a letter of representations obtained from the client, returned confirmation forms—all these various schedules, analyses, lists, notes, and documents form parts of the auditors' working papers.

The term *working papers* is thus comprehensive; it includes all the written records of the work performed by the auditors, the methods and procedures they followed, and the conclusions they developed. The *information contained in the working papers constitutes the principal evidence of the auditors' work and their resulting conclusions.*

Confidential nature of working papers

To conduct a satisfactory audit, the auditors must be given unrestricted access to all information about the client's business. Much of this information is confidential, such as the profit margins on individual products, tentative plans for business combinations with other companies, and the salaries of officers and key employees. Officers of the client company would not be willing to make available to the auditors information that is carefully guarded from competitors, employees, and others unless they could rely on the auditors maintaining a professional silence on these matters.

Much of the information gained in confidence by the auditors is recorded in their working papers; consequently, the working papers are confidential in nature. The *Code of Professional Ethics* developed by the AICPA includes the rule that: "A member shall not disclose any confidential information obtained in the course of a professional engagement except with the consent of the client." In interpreting this rule the AICPA Professional Ethics Executive Committee has expressed the opinion that one CPA firm selling its practice to another should not give the purchaser access to working papers without first obtaining permission from the clients involved.

Although the auditor is as careful as an attorney or physician to hold in confidence all information concerning a client, the communication between a client and a CPA is not privileged under the common law. In most states and under federal laws, a CPA firm may legally be required to produce its working papers in a court case and to disclose information regarding a client. In some states, however, statutes have granted a privileged status to communications between a client and the CPA.

Since audit working papers are highly confidential, they must be safeguarded at all times. Safeguarding working papers usually means keeping them locked in a briefcase during lunch and after working hours. If the client company wishes to keep some of its employees uninformed on executive salaries, business combinations, or other aspects of the business, the auditors obviously should not defeat this policy by exposing their working papers to unauthorized employees of the client. The policy of close control of audit working papers is also necessary because, if employees were seeking to conceal fraud or to mislead the auditors for any reason, they might make alterations in the papers. The working papers may identify particular accounts, branches, or time periods to be tested; to permit the client's employees to learn of these in advance would weaken the significance of the tests.

Ownership of working papers

Audit working papers are prepared on the client's premises, from the client's records, and at the client's expense, yet these papers are the exclusive property of the auditors. This ownership of working papers follows logically from the contractual relationship between the auditors and the client and has been supported in the courts.

Purposes of audit working papers

Audit working papers include all evidence gathered by the auditors and serve several major purposes: (1) to organize and coordinate all phases of the audit engagement; (2) to aid partners, managers, and senior accountants in reviewing the work performed by audit staff members; (3) to provide support for the auditors report; and (4) to provide evidence that the auditors complied with generally accepted auditing standards.

In addition, working papers provide information for preparation of income tax returns and for registration documents with the SEC and other governmental agencies, and also serve as a useful guide in subsequent engagements. Although clients may sometimes find it helpful to request information from the auditors' working papers of prior years, these working papers should not be regarded as a substitute for the client's own accounting records.[1]

To organize and coordinate audit work. Coordination of all phases of the audit work is achieved through the working papers. As each step of verification and analysis is performed, significant facts and relationships come to the attention of the auditors. Unless these matters are set down in writing when discovered, they are likely to be forgotten before they can be properly appraised in the light of information disclosed by other phases of the audit. By carefully planning the assignment of assistants to work on different papers, a senior auditor may efficiently coordinate and organize many phases of the examination work at one time. Thus the working papers show that the first standard of field work (adequate planning of the work and proper supervision of assistants) has been met.

The senior auditor may instruct each assistant to prepare a separate working paper on different items under examination and then proceed from one assistant to another, supervising the work done. Frequently the senior may prepare working paper headings and enter a few sample

---

[1] *Statement on Auditing Standards No. 1*, "Codification of Auditing Standards and Procedures," AICPA (New York, 1973), p. 70.

transactions, requesting assistants to complete the papers; in this manner, the auditor-in-charge initiates the examination of several items simultaneously and follows each project to completion. It is often not feasible for the auditor to carry out all verification work on a particular account at one time. For example, cash on hand may be counted on the first day of the investigation, but confirmation of bank balances not completed until several days later. As each phase is completed, the working papers are filed, to be expanded and added to as additional information is obtained. Thus the audit file on a given account may be begun early in the engagement, but may not be completed until after other phases of the audit have been fully carried out.

To aid supervisors in reviewing the work of audit staff members. When an audit covers several scattered branches of a company, working papers are of great assistance in organizing and coordinating the work. The records of each branch or subsidiary may be examined by different staff members, perhaps by individuals from different offices of the auditing firm. Working papers will then be prepared at each place of examination and sent to a central location to be assembled and reviewed before the writing of the report. Working papers of uniformly high quality are obviously of basic importance in audits of this type.

An audit does not end when the accountants leave the client's office. The report must be completed, or in some cases written in its entirety, tax returns prepared, and the entire engagement reviewed by a manager or partner. These last stages of the audit are made possible by the working papers. The managers or partners, with the working papers before them, have a view of the entire audit as an organized and coordinated whole; only then can they judge whether the audit meets professional auditing standards.

To support the report. Since audit reports are prepared from the working papers, it follows that audit working papers substantiate and explain the conclusions reached in the report. The auditors may on occasion be called upon to testify in court concerning the financial affairs of a client, or they may be required to defend in court the accuracy and reasonableness of their report. In all such cases, working papers are the principal means of substantiating the audit report. After completion of the study and evaluation of internal control, the auditors may draft a management letter on internal control to the client. In identifying existing weaknesses in internal control, and in developing recommendations to correct these weaknesses, the auditors will use the working papers as a principal source of information. Other essential contents of working papers in order to substantiate the report include the actions taken to resolve exceptions or other unusual matters discovered during the audit, and the auditors' conclusions on specific aspects of the engagement.

Compliance with auditing standards. The form and content of working papers should vary based on the requirements of the particular engagement. However, they should always be sufficient to illustrate that the financial statements or other information being reported on reconciles to the client's records, and that the CPAs have complied with the three standards of field work. The working papers should therefore demonstrate adequate planning of the audit and proper supervision of all staff members; a comprehensive study and evaluation of the client's system of internal control and the relation of the internal control evaluation to the audit program; and the accumulation of sufficient competent evidence to support the auditors' opinion on the client's financial statements.

Working papers and accountants' liability

The auditors' working papers are the principal record of the extent of the procedures applied and evidence gathered during the audit. If the auditors, after completing an engagement, are charged with negligence, their audit working papers will be a major factor in refuting or substantiating the charge. Working papers, if not properly prepared, are as likely to injure the auditors as to protect them. *To look over a set of working papers for supporting information is one thing; to look over these same papers for details that may be used to attack the auditors' conclusions is quite another.* This latter possibility suggests the need for public accounting firms to make a critical review of working papers at the end of each engagement and to give thought to the possibility that any contradictory statements, or evidence inconsistent with the conclusions finally reached, may be used to support charges of negligence at a later date.

Part of the difficulty in avoiding inconsistent and conflicting evidence in working papers is that the papers are prepared in large part by less experienced staff members. When the papers are reviewed by a supervisor or partner, the reviewer will give careful consideration to any questionable points. In studying these points the supervisors often give consideration to many other aspects of the audit, and of the client's records with which they are familiar; these other factors may lead the reviewer to the conclusion that an issue raised in the working papers does not warrant any corrective action. In some instances the reviewer may conclude that the assistant who prepared the paper has misinterpreted the situation. Years later, if a dispute arises and the working papers are being subjected to critical study by attorneys representing an injured client or third party, these questionable points in the papers may appear in a different light. The supervisor who cleared the issue based on personal knowledge of the client's business may not be available to explain the reasoning involved or the other special considerations present at the time of the audit. This long-range responsibility suggests that the supervisor should, at the time of deciding upon disposition of a troublesome point, insert an adequate explanation of the action in the working papers.

From time to time a public accounting firm should make a critical evaluation of its policies for preparation, review, and preservation of working papers. Recent experience in cases involving legal liability may lead some firms to considerable modification in the traditional handling of working papers.

Types of working papers

Since audit working papers document a variety of information gathered by the auditors, there are innumerable types of papers. However, there are certain general categories into which most working papers may be grouped; these are: (1) audit administrative working papers; (2) working trial balance and lead schedules; (3) adjusting journal entries and reclassification entries; (4) supporting schedules, analyses, reconciliations, and computational working papers; and (5) corroborating documents.

Audit administrative working papers. Auditing is a sophisticated activity requiring planning, supervision, control, and coordination. Certain working papers are specifically designed to aid the auditors in the planning and administration of engagements. These working papers include audit plans and programs, internal accounting control questionnaires and flowcharts, engagement letters, and time budgets. Memoranda of the planning process and significant discussions with client management are also considered administrative working papers.

Working trial balance. The working trial balance is a schedule listing the balances of accounts in the general ledger for the current and previous year, and also providing columns for the auditors' adjustments and reclassifications and for the final amounts that will appear in the financial statements. A working trial balance is the "backbone" of the entire set of audit working papers; it is the key schedule that controls and summarizes all supporting papers. This type of working paper will usually appear as shown below.

Process Company, Inc.
Working Trial Balance
December 31, 1984

TB-1

Working Paper Reference	Caption	Balance Final 12/31/83	per Ledger 12/31/84	Adjustments Dr. (Cr.)	Adjusted 12/31/84	Reclassifications Dr. (Cr.)	Final Balance 12/31/84
	Assets						
	Current Assets:						
A	Cash	481 443	742 186		742 186		742 186
B	Short-Term Investments	—	149 413		149 413		149 413
C	Accounts Receivable-Net	2 291 722	2 053 918	(91 096)	1 962 822		1 962 822
D	Inventories	2 701 814	2 942 117	(129 799)	2 812 318		2 812 318

Although most of these column headings are self-explanatory, a brief discussion of the third and fourth columns is appropriate. In the third column, the final adjusted balances from the previous year's audit are listed. Inclusion of the previous year's figures facilitates comparison with the corresponding amounts for the current year and focuses attention upon any unusual changes. Inclusion of the final figures from the prior year's audit also gives assurance that the correct starting figure is used if the auditors verify the year's transactions in a balance sheet account in order to determine the validity of the ending balance.

The fourth column provides for the account balances at the close of the year under audit; these balances usually are taken directly from the general ledger. The balances of the Revenue and Expense accounts should be included, even though these accounts have been closed into the Retained Earnings account prior to the auditors' arrival. Since the auditors ordinarily express an opinion on the income statement as well as the balance sheet, it is imperative that the audit working papers include full information on the revenue and expense accounts. The amount to be listed for the Retained Earnings account is the balance at the beginning of the year under audit. Dividends declared during the year are listed as a separate item, as is the computed net income for the year.

In many audits, the client furnishes the auditors with a working trial balance after all normal end-of-period journal entries have been posted. Before accepting the trial balance for their working papers, the auditors should trace the amounts to the general ledger for evidence that the trial balance is prepared accurately.

Lead schedules. Separate lead schedules (also called *grouping sheets* or *summary schedules*) are set up to combine similar general ledger accounts, the total of which appears on the working trial balance as a single amount. For example, a lead schedule for Cash might combine the following general ledger accounts: Petty Cash, $500; General Bank account, $348,216; Office Payroll Bank account, $1,500; Factory Payroll Bank account, $2,000; and Dividend Bank account, $500. Similar lead schedules would be set up for Accounts Receivable, Inventories, Stockholders' Equity, Net Sales, and for other balance sheet or income statement captions.

Adjusting journal entries and reclassification entries. During the course of an audit engagement, the auditors may discover various types of errors in the client's financial statements and accounting records. These errors may be large or small in amount; they may arise from the omission of transactions or from the use of incorrect amounts; or they may result from improper classification or cutoff, or from misinterpretation of transactions. Generally, these errors are accidental; however, the auditors may discover irregularities in the financial statements or accounting records.

To correct *material* errors or irregularities discovered in the financial statements and accounting records, the auditors draft *adjusting journal entries* (AJEs), which they recommend for entry in the client's accounting records. In addition, the auditors develop *reclassification entries* for items that, although correctly recorded in the accounting records, must be reclassified for fair presentation in the client's financial statements. For example, accounts receivable with *large credit balances* should be reclassified as a liability in the balance sheet.

Supporting schedules. Although all types of working papers may loosely be called schedules, auditors prefer to use this term to describe a listing of the elements or details comprising the balance in an asset or liability account at a specific date. Thus, a list of amounts owed to vendors making up the balance of the Trade Accounts Payable account is properly described as a *schedule.*

Analysis of a ledger account. An analysis of a ledger account is another common type of audit working paper. The purpose of an analysis is to show on one paper *all changes* in an asset, liability, equity, revenue, or expense account during the period covered by the audit. If a number of the changes are individually immaterial, they may be recorded as a single item in the analysis working paper.

To analyze a ledger account, the auditors first list the beginning balance and indicate the nature of the items comprising this balance. Next, the auditors list and investigate the nature of all debits and credits to the account during the period. These entries when combined with the beginning balance produce a figure representing the balance in the account as of the audit date. If any errors or omissions of importance are detected during this analysis of the account, the necessary adjusting journal entry approved by the client is entered on the working paper to produce the adjusted balance required for the financial statements.

Reconciliations. Frequently, auditors wish to prove the relationship between amounts obtained from different sources. When they do so, they prepare working papers known as reconciliations. These reconciliations provide evidence as to the accuracy of one or both of the amounts and are important to the audit of many accounts, including cash, accounts receivable, and inventories.

Computational working papers. Another type of supporting working paper is the computational working paper. The auditors' approach to verifying certain types of accounts and other figures is to make an independent computation and compare their results with the amounts shown by the client's records. Examples of amounts that might be verified by computation are the bonuses paid to executives, pension accruals, royalty expense, interest on notes, and accrued taxes. Bonuses, pensions, and royalties are ordinarily specified in contracts; by making computations based on the terms of the contracts, the auditors determine whether these items are stated in accordance with contractual requirements. Social security taxes are based on the amount of wages and salaries paid; the auditors' verification consists of applying the tax rates to the taxable wages and salaries for the period.

Corroborating documents.   Auditing is not limited to the examination of financial records, and working papers are not confined to schedules and analyses. During the course of an audit the auditors may gather much purely expository material to substantiate their report. One common example is copies of minutes of directors' and stockholders' meetings. Other examples include copies of articles of incorporation and bylaws; copies of important contracts, bond indentures, and mortgages; memoranda pertaining to examination of records; audit confirmations, letter of representations from the client, and lawyers' letters.

Organization of the working papers

The auditors usually maintain two files of working papers for each client: (1) current files for every completed examination and (2) a permanent file of relatively unchanging data. The current file (as for the 1984 audit) pertains solely to that year's examination; the permanent file contains such things as copies of the articles of incorporation, which are of continuing audit interest.

The current files.   The auditors' report for a particular year is supported by the working paper contained in the current files. Many CPA firms have found it useful to organize the current files around the arrangement of the accounts in the client's financial statements. The administrative working papers usually begin the current files, including a draft of the financial statements and the auditors' report. These working papers are followed by the working trial balance and the adjusting and reclassification entries. The remaining portion of the current files consists of working papers supporting the balances and other representations in the client's financial statements. It begins with working papers for each asset account and continues with papers for liabilities, owners' equity accounts, and revenue and expense accounts.

Each working paper in a file is assigned a reference number, and information is tied together through a system of cross-referencing. In this way a reviewer may trace amounts on the working trial balance back to the supporting working papers. Figure 9–1 illustrates a system of cross-referencing and a typical arrangement of the current files after the administrative working papers.

The permanent file.   The permanent file serves three purposes: (1) to refresh the auditors' memory on items applicable over a period of many years; (2) to provide for new staff members a quick summary of the policies and organization of the client; and (3) to preserve working papers on items that show relatively few or no changes, thus eliminating the necessity for their preparation year after year.

Much of the information contained in the permanent file is gathered during the course of the first audit of a client's records. A considerable portion of the time spent on a first audit is devoted to gathering and

===== Figure 9–1
Organization of the current files

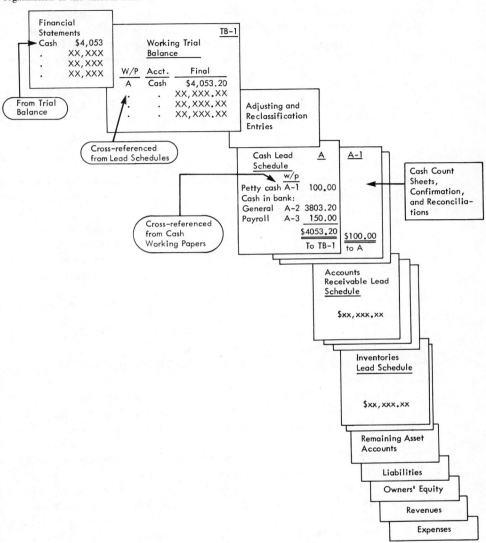

appraising background information, such as copies of articles of incorporation and bylaws, leases, patent agreements, pension plans, labor contracts, long-term construction contracts, charts of accounts, and prior years' tax returns.

Analyses of accounts that show few changes over a period of years are also included in the permanent file. These accounts may include land, buildings, accumulated depreciation, long-term investments, long-term liabilities, capital stock, and other owners' equity accounts. The initial investigation of these accounts must often include the transactions of many years. But once these historical analyses have been brought up to date, the work required in subsequent examinations will be limited to a review of the current year's transactions in these accounts. In this respect, the permanent file is a timesaving device because current changes in such accounts need only be added to the permanent papers without reappearing in the current working papers. Adequate cross-referencing in the working papers, of course, should be provided to show where in the permanent file such information is to be found.

Guidelines for preparation of working papers

We can now summarize in a few short paragraphs our basic guidelines for preparing working papers that will meet current professional standards.

A separate, properly identified working paper should be prepared for each topic. Proper identification of a working paper is accomplished by a heading that includes the name of the client company, a clear description of the information presented, and the applicable date or the period covered.

Complete and specific identification of documents examined, employees interviewed, and sites visited is essential for good working paper practice. The preparer of a working paper should date and sign or initial the working paper; the signatures or initials of the senior, manager, or partner who reviewed the working paper should also appear on the paper.

All working papers should be referenced and cross-referenced to the working trial balance or relevant lead schedule. Where reference is necessary between working papers, there must be adequate cross-referencing.

The nature of verification work performed by the auditors should be indicated on each working paper. A review of paid purchase invoices, for example, might be supplemented by inspection of the related purchase orders and receiving documents to substantiate the authenticity of the invoices examined; a description of this verification procedure should be included on the working paper. As audit working papers are prepared, the auditors will use several different symbols to identify specific steps in the work performed. These symbols, or *tick marks,* provide a very concise means of indicating the auditing procedures applied to particular amounts. Whenever tick marks are employed, they must be accompanied by a legend explaining their significance.

The working papers should include comments by the auditors indicating their conclusions on each aspect of the work. In other words, the auditors should take a stand on all findings. Figure 9–2 illustrates such

Figure 9–2
Preparation of a working paper

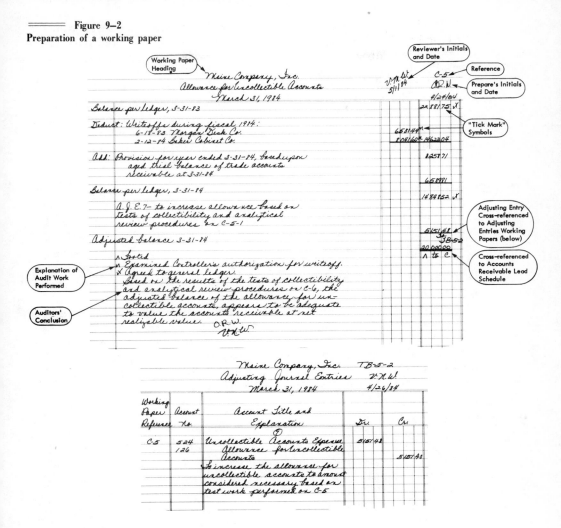

a conclusion related to the audit of the allowance for uncollectible account, along with other aspects of a properly prepared working paper.

The review of working papers

Working papers are reviewed at every supervisory level of a CPA firm. Senior auditors in charge of an engagement review the working papers of staff assistants; managers and supervisors scrutinize all working papers prepared by senior auditors and staff assistants; and partners make a final review of the entire set of working papers before signing the CPA firm's name to the audit report.

What do working paper reviewers look for? First, they seek indications that the audit was performed in accordance with generally accepted auditing standards—especially the standards of field work. Next, the reviewers judge whether the evidence accumulated during the audit supported the CPA firm's opinion on the client's financial statements.

QUALITY CONTROL FOR AUDITS

All enterprises must establish controls to ensure that their products and services adhere to a minimum level of quality. It is especially important for CPA firms to establish quality controls for the performance of audits. In Chapter 3 we discussed the serious consequences that can result from substandard performance on even a single engagement.

In recent years, the work of independent auditors has come under increasing criticism from Congress, the courts, the SEC, consumer activists, academicians, and CPAs themselves. Many critics have charged that the public accounting profession has done little to police its own ranks. The dismal performance of some CPA firms, brought to light in court cases and SEC actions, support these criticisms.

Quality control standards

The AICPA has taken steps to counteract the criticism described above. A new senior technical committee, the AICPA Quality Control Standards Committee, was formed to develop and issue quality control standards for CPA firms and to administer the AICPA's voluntary peer review program. Whereas an auditor, individually, is responsible for compliance with generally accepted auditing standards in an audit engagement, a firm of independent auditors should establish policies and procedures to control the quality of all their engagements. Elements of quality control are contained in the initial statement issued by the Quality Control Standards Committee.[2] That statement suggests that a firm consider establishing quality control policies and procedures in the following areas: independence, assigning personnel to engagements, consultation, supervision, hiring, professional development, advancement, acceptance and continuation of clients, and inspection. Most of the AICPA's quality control elements are obvious to professional CPAs; some elements have been considered at length in preceding pages of this

---

[2] Quality Control Standards Committee, *Statement on Quality Control Standards No. 1* (New York: American Institute of Certified Public Accountants, November 1979).

textbook. Only the elements of *consultation* and *inspection* will be discussed at this point.

Consultation. The AICPA recommends the establishment of policies and procedures to assure that independent auditors will consult with knowledgeable persons on critical questions in accounting and auditing. In large CPA firms, such consultation might be with partners or managers having expertise in specialized industries or SEC practice, or with the firm's technical research staff. Smaller CPA firms may refer questions to an appropriate group in the AICPA or in a state society of CPAs. The point to be stressed is that independent auditors should not attempt to solve complex accounting and auditing questions without the counsel of another expert.

Inspection. The inspection element deals with an internal audit type function. Most CPA firms have established programs in which review teams of partners and managers from various offices of the firm appraise the quality controls of other offices of the firm.

Division for CPA firms

Another response to the criticism of the profession, especially the legislative pressure of the 1970s, was the formation of the AICPA Division for CPA Firms. Previously, CPAs were subject only as individuals to ethical requirements and professional standards. No mechanism existed to discipline CPA firms for substandard performance. This legislative void was filled by the AICPA Division for CPA Firms.

The Division for CPA Firms actually includes two separate sections, the SEC Practice Section and the Private Companies Practice Section. CPA firms voluntarily join either, or both, sections based on the type of clients that they serve. Both sections require member firms to establish and maintain an adequate system of quality control and adhere to certain membership requirements. For example, the SEC Practice Section requires audit partners on SEC audit clients to be rotated at least every five years, and audit engagements for such clients must be subjected to review by a second partner. Members of the SEC Practice Section are also prohibited from performing certain executive recruiting services for SEC audit clients. Regular peer reviews and mandatory continuing education for firm personnel are part of the membership requirements of both firm sections.

The executive committees of the two sections have the power to sanction member firms for substandard performance. These sanctions may include additional personnel education requirements, fines, and expulsion from the division.

The Public Oversight Board

A vital part of the SEC Practice Section is the Public Oversight Board, which is made up of prominent individuals who are not members of the accounting profession. The Board oversees the activities of the SEC Practice Section and can intervene when the members of the Board think that the public's interest is not being served. Periodic reports inform the SEC and Congress about the activities of the Public Oversight Board.

Peer reviews

A major underpinning of the AICPA Division for Firms is the mandatory periodic peer reviews that are required of members of both sections. Member firms must subject their practice to an intensive review of their quality control policies and procedures by another CPA firm, or a review team authorized or appointed by one of the peer review committees of the two sections. Also, many firms that are not members of the AICPA Division for CPA Firms voluntarily submit their practice to periodic peer review.

Similar to evaluation of internal control, a peer review involves a study of the adequacy of the firm's established quality control policies and procedures and tests of compliance with the established controls. A major aspect of the tests of compliance consists of examination of working paper files and audit reports for selected engagements. These engagements are evaluated for compliance with established quality control policies and generally accepted auditing standards. The reviewers also examine many internal records of the CPA firm. They are especially interested in records concerning the promotion of employees, continuing education of firm personnel, staffing of audit engagements, client acceptance, and the employment of professional personnel. Based on the reviewers' study and tests of the quality controls, they issue a report that includes an opinion as to the adequacy of the reviewed firm's quality control system. Suggestions for improvement to the system are outlined in a letter issued by the reviewers to the reviewed firm.

KEY TERMS INTRODUCED OR EMPHASIZED IN CHAPTER 9

Adjusting journal entry A journal entry drafted by the auditors to correct a material error discovered in the financial statements and accounting records.

Administrative working papers Working papers specifically designed to help the auditors in planning and administration of the engagement, such as audit programs, internal control questionnaires and flowcharts, time budgets, and engagement memoranda.

Analysis A working paper showing all changes in an asset, liability, equity, revenue, or expense account during the period covered by the audit.

Corroborating documents Documents and memoranda included in the working papers that substantiate representations contained in the client's financial statements. These working papers include audit confirmations, lawyers' letters, copies of contracts, copies of minutes of directors' and stockholders' meetings, and letter of representations from the client's management.

Division for CPA Firms   A division of the AICPA providing a mechanism to regulate CPA firms. Firms may voluntarily join either or both sections; the SEC Practice Section and the Private Companies Practice Section.

Lead schedule   A working paper with columnar headings similar to those in a working trial balance, set up to combine similar ledger accounts, the total of which appears in the working trial balance as a single amount.

Peer review   The study and evaluation of a CPA firm's quality control policies and procedures by another CPA firm or a team of qualified CPAs.

Permanent file   A file of working papers containing relatively unchanging data, such as copies of articles of incorporation and bylaws, copies of minutes of directors', stockholders', and committees' meetings, and analyses of such ledger accounts as land and retained earnings.

Public Oversight Board   An independent group of prominent nonaccountants, who monitor the activities of the SEC Practice Section to provide assurance that the section is serving the public's interest.

Quality control standards   Standards for establishing quality control policies and procedures that provide reasonable assurance that all of a CPA firm's audits are conducted in accordance with professional standards.

Reclassification entry   A working paper entry drafted by the auditors to assure fair presentation in the client's financial statements, such as an entry to transfer accounts receivable credit balances to the current liabilities section of the client's balance sheet. Since reclassification entries do not correct errors in the client company's accounting records, they are not posted to the client's ledger accounts.

Tick mark   A symbol used in working papers by the auditor to indicate a specific step in the work performed. Whenever tick marks are used, they must be accompanied by a legend explaining their significance.

Working papers   Papers that document the evidence gathered by auditors to show the work they have done, the methods and procedures they have followed, and the conclusions they have developed in an examination of financial statements or another type of engagement.

Working trial balance   A working paper that lists the balances of accounts in the general ledger for the current and the previous year and also provides columns for the auditor's adjustments and reclassifications and for the final amounts that will appear in the financial statements.

GROUP I: REVIEW QUESTIONS

9– 1.   What has the AICPA done to help assure quality control by CPA firms?

9– 2.   What is the Public Oversight Board? What is its purpose?

9– 3.   What are the purposes of audit working papers?

9– 4.   Why are the final figures from the prior year's audit included in a working trial balance or lead schedules? Explain.

9– 5.   Should the working trial balance prepared by the auditors include revenue and expense accounts if the balances of these accounts for the audit year have been closed into retained earnings prior to the auditors' arrival? Explain.

9– 6.   Should the auditors prepare adjusting journal entries to correct all errors they discover in the accounting records for the year under audit? Explain.

9– 7.   In their review of audit working papers, what do managers and partners look for?

9– 8.   "Audit working papers are the property of the auditors, who may destroy the papers, sell them, or give them away." Criticize this quotation.

9– 9.   Describe a situation in which a set of audit working papers might be used by third parties to support a charge of gross negligence against the auditors.

9– 10. "I have finished my testing of footings of the cash journals," said the assistant auditor to the senior auditor. "Shall I state in the working papers the period for which I verified footings, or should I just list the totals of the receipts and disbursements I have proved to be correct?" Prepare an answer to the assistant's question, stressing the reasoning involved.

9– 11. Your CPA firm has been requested to perform a peer review of the firm of William & Stafford. What is involved in the performance of such an engagement? Discuss.

9– 12. Explain the meaning of the term *permanent file* as used in connection with audit working papers. What kinds of information are usually included in the permanent file?

9– 13. List several rules to be observed in the preparation of working papers that will reflect current professional practice.

9– 14. List the major types of audit working papers and give a brief explanation of each. For example, one type of audit working paper is an account analysis. This working paper shows the changes that occurred in a given account during the period under audit. By analyzing an account the auditors determine its nature and content.

GROUP II: QUESTIONS REQUIRING ANALYSIS

9– 15. Select the best answer for each of the following and give reasons for your choice.

a.   Which of the following is *not* a factor that affects the independent auditors' judgment as to the quantity, type, and content of working papers?

(1)   The timing and the number of personnel to be assigned to the engagement.

(2)   The nature of the financial statements, schedules, or other information upon which the auditor is reporting.

(3)   The need for supervision of the engagement.

(4)   The nature of the auditors' report.

b.   Audit working papers are used to record the results of the auditors' evidence-gathering procedures. When preparing working papers the auditors should remember that working papers should be—

    (1) Kept on the client's premises so that the client can have access to them for reference purposes.

    (2) The primary support for the financial statements being examined.

    (3) Considered as a part of the client's accounting records that is retained by the auditors.

    (4) Designed to meet the circumstances and the auditors' needs on each engagement.

  c. During the course of an audit engagement, auditors prepare and accumulate audit working papers. The primary purpose of the audit working papers is to—

    (1) Aid the auditors in adequately planning their work.

    (2) Provide a point of reference for future audit engagements.

    (3) Support the underlying concepts included in the preparation of the basic financial statements.

    (4) Support the auditors' opinion.

  d. Which of the following is *not* an element of quality control that should be considered by a firm of independent auditors?

    (1) Assigning personnel to engagements.

    (2) Consultation with appropriate persons.

    (3) Prohibition of overtime for staff assistants.

    (4) Supervision. (AICPA, adapted)

9–16. The partnership of Smith, Frank & Clark, a CPA firm, has been the auditor of Greenleaf, Inc., for many years. During the annual examination of the financial statements for the year ended December 31, 1984, a dispute developed over whether certain disclosures should be made in the financial statements. The dispute resulted in Smith, Frank & Clark's being dismissed and Greenleaf's engaging another CPA firm. Greenleaf demanded that Smith, Frank & Clark turn over all working papers applicable to the Greenleaf audits to it or face a lawsuit. Smith, Frank & Clark refused. Greenleaf has instituted a suit against Smith, Frank & Clark to obtain the working papers.

Required:

  a. Will Greenleaf succeed in its suit? Explain.

  b. Discuss the rationale underlying the rule of law applicable to the ownership of audit working papers. (AICPA, adapted)

9–17. "Working papers should contain facts and nothing but facts," said student A. "Not at all," replied student B. "The audit working papers may also include expressions of opinion. Facts are not always available to settle all issues." "In my opinion," said student C, "a mixture of facts and opinions in the audit working papers would be most confusing if the papers were produced as a means of supporting the auditors' position when their report has been challenged." Evaluate the issues underlying these arguments.

9–18. At twelve o'clock when the plant whistle sounded, George Green, an assistant auditor, had his desk completely covered with various types of working papers. Green stopped work immediately, but not wanting to leave the desk with such a disorderly appearance he took a few minutes to sort the papers into proper order, place them in a neat pile, and weight them down with a heavy ash tray. He then departed for lunch. The auditor-in-charge, who had been observing what was going on, was critical of the assistant's actions. What do you think was the basis for criticism by the auditor-in-charge?

9– 19. An important part of every examination of financial statements is the preparation of audit working papers.

Required:
   a. Discuss the relationship of audit working papers to each of the standards of field work.
   b. You are instructing an inexperienced staff assistant on her first auditing assignment. She is to examine an account. An analysis of the account has been prepared by the client for inclusion in the audit working papers. Prepare a list of the comments, commentaries, and notations that the staff assistant should make or have made on the account analysis to provide an adequate working paper as evidence of her examination. (Do not include a description of auditing procedures applicable to the account.) (AICPA, adapted)

9– 20. The preparation of working papers is an integral part of the auditors' examination of financial statements. On a recurring engagement the auditors review the working papers from their prior examination while planning the current examination to determine the papers' usefulness for the current engagement.

Required:
   a. (1)   What are the purposes or functions of audit working papers?
       (2)   What records of the auditors may be included in audit working papers?
   b. What factors affect the auditors' judgment of the type and content of the working papers for a particular engagement?
   c. To comply with generally accepted auditing standards, the auditors include certain evidence in their working papers, for example, "evidence that the engagement was planned and work of assistants was supervised and reviewed." What other evidence should the auditors include in audit working papers to comply with generally accepted auditing standards? (AICPA, adapted)

9– 21. You have been assigned by your CPA firm to complete the examination of the 1978 financial statements of Hamilton Manufacturing Corporation because the senior accountant and his inexperienced assistant, who began the engagement, were hospitalized as the result of an accident. The engagement is about one half completed. Your audit report must be delivered in three weeks, as agreed when your firm accepted the engagement. You estimate that by utilizing the client's staff to the greatest possible extent consonant with independence you can complete the engagement in five weeks. Your firm cannot assign an assistant to you.

   The working papers show the status of work on the examination as follows:
   (1) *Completed*—Cash, property and equipment, depreciation, mortgage note payable, and stockholders' equity.

(2) *Completed except as noted later*—Inventories, accounts payable, compliance tests of purchase transactions and payrolls.

(3) *Nothing done*—Trade accounts receivable, inventory price testing, accrued expenses payable, unrecorded liability test, compliance tests of sales transactions, payroll deductions compliance tests and observation of payroll check distribution, analysis of other expenses, analytical review procedures, vouching of December purchase transactions, audit report, internal control evaluation, internal control report, minutes, preparation of tax returns, subsequent events, and supervision and review.

Your review discloses that the assistant's working papers are incomplete and were not reviewed by the senior accountant. For example, the inventory working papers present incomplete notations, incomplete explanations, and no cross-referencing.

Required:

a. What field work standards have been violated by the senior accountant who preceded you on this assignment? Explain why you think the standards you list have been violated.

b. In planning your work to complete this engagement, you should scan working papers and schedule certain work as soon as possible and also identify work that may be postponed until after the audit report is rendered to the client.

   (1) List the areas on which you should plan to work first, say in your first week of work, and for each item explain why it deserves early attention.

   (2) State which work you believe could be postponed until after the audit report is rendered to the client, and give reasons why the work may be postponed. (AICPA, adapted)

GROUP III: PROBLEMS

9–22. Whitlow and Wyatt, CPAs, have been the independent auditors of Interstate Land Development Corporation for several years. During these years, Interstate prepared and filed its own annual income tax returns.

During 1984, Interstate requested Whitlow and Wyatt to examine to all the necessary financial statements of the corporation to be submitted to the Securities and Exchange Commission (SEC) in connection with a multistate public offering of 1 million shares of Interstate common stock. This public offering came under the provisions of the Securities Act of 1933. The examination was performed carefully and the financial statements were fairly presented for the respective periods. These financial statements were included in the registration statement filed with the SEC.

While the registration statement was being processed by the SEC, but before the effective date, the Internal Revenue Service (IRS) subpoenaed Whitlow and Wyatt to turn over all its working papers relating to Interstate for the years 1981–83. Whitlow and Wyatt initially refused to comply for two reasons. First, Whitlow and Wyatt did not prepare Interstate's tax returns. Second, Whitlow and Wyatt claimed that the working papers were confidential matters subject to the privileged communications rule. Subsequently, however, Whitlow and Wyatt did relinquish the subpoenaed working papers.

Upon receiving the subpoena, Whatt called Dunkirk, the chairman of Interstate's board of directors, and asked him about the IRS investigation. Dunkirk responded, "I'm sure the IRS people are on a fishing expedition and that they will not find any material deficiencies."

A few days later Dunkirk received written confirmation from the IRS that it was contending that Interstate had underpaid its taxes during the period under review. The confirmation revealed that Interstate was being assessed $800,000, including penalties and interest for the three years.

This $800,000 assessment was material relative to the financial statements as of December 31, 1984. The amount for each year individually exclusive of penalty and interest was not material relative to each respective year.

Required:

a.   Discuss the additional liability assumed by Whitlow and Wyatt in connection with the SEC registration engagement.

b.   Discuss the implications to Whitlow and Wyatt and its responsibilities with respect to the IRS assessment.

c.   Could Whitlow and Wyatt have validly refused to surrender the subpoenaed materials? Explain. (AICPA, adapted)

9–23.   Criticize the working paper (page 295) which you are reviewing as senior in charge of the November 30, 1984 audit of Pratt Company.

9–24.   One of the practical problems confronting the auditors is that of determining whether adjusting journal entries or other corrective actions are warranted by errors, omissions, and inconsistencies. The following items were noted by the auditors during their year-end examination of a small manufacturing partnership having net sales of approximately $1.6 million; net income of approximately $20,000; total assets of nearly $2 million; and total partners' capital of $300,000.

(1)   Proceeds of $250 from the sale of fully depreciated office equipment were credited to Miscellaneous Revenue rather than to Gain and Loss on Sale of Equipment, a ledger account that had not been used for several years.

(2)   The Trade Accounts Receivable control account showed a balance of $79,600. The individual accounts comprising this balance included three with credit balances of $320, $19, and $250, respectively.

(3)   Several debits and credits to general ledger accounts had been made directly without use of journal entries. The amounts involved did not exceed $500.

(4)   Credit memoranda were not serially numbered or signed, but a file of duplicates was maintained.

(5)   General journal entries did not include explanations for any but unusual transactions.

(6)   Posting references were occasionally omitted from entries in general ledger accounts.

Pratt Company
Cash   E-2

Per bank   specify date   44,874.50 ✓

Deposit in transit   837.50 ✓

Bank charges

                                                    2.80
                                             45,714.80

Outstanding checks:

    Check #'s   46.40

                10.00

                30.00

          1,013.60 ✓

          1,200.00 ✓

                10.00

              25.00 ✓

              15.00 ✓

              50.00 ✓

          1,002.00 ✓   3,402.00

Per ledger   specify date   42,312.80 ✓

✓ – Verified

R G H
12-2-84

Conclusion

(7) An expenditure of $200 for automobile repairs was recorded as a
     December expense, although shown by the invoice to be a No-
     vember charge.

(8) The auditors' count of petty cash disclosed a shortage of $20.

(9) Expenditures for advertising amounting to $8,000 were charged to
     the Advertising Expense account; other advertising expenses
     amounting to $3,000 had been charged to Miscellaneous Expense.

(10) On a bank loan of $300,000, negotiated September 5, for a period
     of four months at an annual interest rate of 6 percent, the entire
     amount of interest had been deducted in advance. The client's
     accountant had charged the full amount of interest to expense.
     He stated that he did not consider an entry to defer a part of the
     expense to the following year to be warranted by the amount
     involved.

Required:

You are to state clearly the position the auditors should take with respect to each of the above items during the course of an annual audit. If
adjusting journal entries are necessary, include them in your solution.

GROUP IV: CASE STUDIES IN AUDITING

9–25.   Bryan Instrument Manufacturing Company

During the examination of Bryan Instrument Manufacturing Company,
Dwight Bond, an assistant auditor, was assigned by the auditor-in-
charge to the verification of the trade accounts receivable. The receivables totaled more than $2 million and included accounts with gov-
ernmental agencies, national mail-order houses, manufacturers,
wholesalers, and retailers. Bond had recently read a study of credit
losses in this industry covering the past 10 years; and as a preliminary
step, he computed an allowance for uncollectible accounts by applying
to the total accounts receivable a percentage mentioned in the 10-year
study as the average rate of uncollectible account losses for the sales of
the entire industry. Application of this percentage to the Bryan Company's receivables indicated an uncollectible account loss of $90,000;
the allowance provided by the Company's management was $25,000.
The working paper showing the computation of the $90,000 estimate of
uncollectible account losses was placed in the file of working papers by
Bond.

After making this preliminary calculation, Bond undertook a careful study of the receivables; as a first step he obtained from the client a
classification of the accounts by type of customer and by age. He made a
careful analysis of individual accounts that appeared in any way doubtful, discussed all past-due accounts with the credit manager, and reviewed the company's prior history of uncollectible account losses. He
then reviewed his findings with the auditor-in-charge who, after further
investigation and discussion with the client management, took the position that the allowance for uncollectible accounts must be increased
from $25,000 to $40,000 or an unqualified opinion could not be given.

The client management was not convinced of the need for the increase but finally agreed to make the change.

While Bond was working on the accounts receivable, another staff assistant, Carla Roberts, was engaged in verification of inventory. Roberts overheard a stock clerk remark that the finished goods inventory was full of obsolete products that could never be sold. As a result of this chance remark, Roberts made tests of a number of items in the inventory, comparing the quantities on hand with the amount of recent sales. These tests indicated the quantities in inventory were reasonable and that the items were moving out to customers. Because of the technical nature of the instruments manufactured by the company, Roberts was not able to determine by observation whether the articles in stock were obsolete or unsalable for any other reason. She made a point of questioning officials of the company on the possibility of obsolescence in the inventory and was assured that no serious problem of obsolescence existed.

In preparing the working papers covering her investigation, Roberts included a separate memorandum quoting the remark she had overheard concerning the obsolescence of the inventory and added a suggestion of her own that this question of obsolescence be given special attention in succeeding examinations. She prepared a detailed description of certain portions of the inventory and suggested that in the succeeding examination the auditors determine whether these specific units were still on hand. During the review of the working papers, the auditor-in-charge questioned Roberts at length about the tests for obsolescence. He interviewed the employee who had made the remark about the impossibility of disposing of the finished goods inventory; the employee denied having made any such statement. The auditor-in-charge then discussed the issue with client officials and came to the conclusion that the inventory was properly valued and readily salable. In completing his review of the working papers, the auditor-in-charge added the following comment to the memorandum prepared by Roberts: "Question of obsolescence investigated and passed, but we should give consideration to this issue in succeeding examinations."

After all adjustments recommended by the auditors had been made, the financial statements of the company indicated a considerably weaker financial position than in prior years. The president complained that the adjustments insisted on by the auditors made the company's position look so bad that it would be difficult to obtain private long-term financing for which he had been negotiating. An unqualified audit report was issued.

Two months later, Bryan Instrument Manufacturing Company became insolvent. Principal causes of the failure, according to the president, were unexpectedly large credit losses and inability to dispose of inventories that had become obsolete because of newly designed products being offered by competitors in recent years. The president acknowledged that the company had made sales to customers of questionable credit standing because of the need for disposing of inventories threatened by obsolescence. Creditors of the company attempted to recover their losses from the auditors, charging the CPA firm with gross negligence and lack of independence in reviewing the valuation of the accounts receivable and inventory. Attention was directed to the working papers prepared by Bond and Roberts; it was charged that these papers showed the auditors had knowledge of the overvaluation of receivables and inventory but under pressure from the client had failed to disclose the facts.

Required:

a. Should the working paper showing the percentage calculation of a $90,000 allowance for uncollectible accounts have been prepared and retained? Explain. Comment on the industry rate of loss.

b. Should the working paper quoting the stock clerk's remark about obsolescence have been prepared and retained? Explain.

c. Did the auditor-in-charge handle his duties satisfactorily?

d. Do you think the working papers tended to support or injure the auditors' defense against the charges of the creditors? Explain.

e. Do you consider the creditors' charges to be well founded? Give reasons for your answer.

10

Examination of the general records; audit program design

In the early stages of an audit, the independent auditors must become familiar with many aspects of the client's business. For example, the auditors must obtain a knowledge of the client's organization plan, financial structure, physical facilities, products, accounting policies, and control procedures. However, information about the internal activities of the client is not in itself sufficient. If this information is to be interpreted and evaluated in a proper perspective, the auditors must also understand the business environment in which the client operates. State and federal laws and regulations, pending or threatened litigation, affiliations with other companies, and contracts with suppliers and customers are only a few of the factors in the business environment that may affect the client's internal activities. The auditors can gain considerable information about both the client's business environment and internal operations by examining the client's general records. The term *general records* is used to include the following categories.

1. Nonfinancial records.
    a. Articles of incorporation and bylaws.
    b. Partnership contract.
    c. Minutes of directors' and stockholders' meetings.
    d. Contracts with customers and suppliers.

    e. Contracts with officers and employees, including union agreements, stock option, profit-sharing, bonus, and pension plans.
    f. Governmental regulations directly affecting the enterprise.
    g. Correspondence files.
2. Financial records.
    a. Income tax returns of prior years.
    b. Financial statements and annual reports of prior years.
    c. Registration statements and periodic reports filed with the SEC.
3. Accounting records.
    a. General ledger.
    b. General journal.

Examining these records should provide the auditors with a concise picture of the client's policies and plans. As the engagement progresses, this understanding will enable the auditors to determine whether the transactions reflected in the accounts were properly authorized and executed in accordance with the directives of management. If audit staff members are thoroughly familiar with the history and problems of the business, the duties and responsibilities of key officials, and the nature and quality of the accounting records and procedures, then they are prepared to carry out each phase of the audit with confidence and understanding. If they do not acquire this background information before beginning the work of analyzing transactions and substantiating account balances, they are almost certain to proceed in a mechanical and routine manner, unaware of the real significance of much of the evidence examined.

Articles of incorporation and bylaws

In the first audit of a client's financial statements, a senior auditor will obtain copies of the articles of incorporation (or corporate charter) and bylaws. The ***articles of incorporation*** is the basic document filed with the state to evidence the legal existence of a corporation. It includes such information as the name of the company, date and state of incorporation, and number of authorized directors. In addition, the articles of incorporation describe the authorized capital structure, including classes of capital stock, number of shares authorized, par or stated values, liquidating preferences, voting rights, and dividend rates.

The ***bylaws*** help define the internal administrative structure of a corporation; they include the organizational structure, rules, and procedures adopted by the corporate stockholders. For example, the bylaws may stipulate the frequency of stockholders' meetings, the date and method for election of directors and selection of officers, and the powers and duties of directors and officers. Copies of both the articles of incorporation and the bylaws are retained in the auditors' permanent file for convenient reference during repeat engagements.

Partnership contract

In the audit of a business organized as a partnership, the partnership contract should be examined in much the same manner as the articles of incorporation and bylaws of corporate clients. The partnership contract represents an agreement among partners on the rules to be followed in the operation of the enterprise. The information available in a copy of the partnership contract usually includes the following:

1. The name and address of the firm.
2. The names and addresses of the individual partners.
3. The amount, date, and nature of the investment made by each partner.
4. The profit-sharing ratio, partners' salaries, interest on partners' capital, and restrictions on withdrawals.
5. The duties, responsibilities, and authority of each partner.
6. The provision for insurance on lives of partners.
7. The provisions concerning liquidation of the firm and distribution of assets.

In repeat examinations the auditors must ascertain whether any modification of the partnership contract has been made and obtain copies of the modifications for the permanent file. If no change has occurred since the preceding audit, a notation to that effect should be made.

Corporate minutes book

The corporate minutes book is an official record of the actions taken at meetings of directors and stockholders. Typical of the actions taken at meetings of stockholders is the extension of authority to management to acquire or dispose of subsidiaries and to adopt or modify pension or profit sharing plans for officers and employees. The stockholders also customarily approve the selection of a firm of independent auditors. Representatives of the auditing firm attend the stockholders' meeting for the purpose of answering questions that may arise concerning internal control and the financial operations of the business.

Minutes of the directors' meetings usually contain authorizations for important transactions and contractual arrangements, such as the establishment of bank accounts, setting of officers' salaries, declaration of dividends, and formation of long-term agreements with vendors, customers, and lessors. In addition, the minutes may document discussions by the board of pending litigation, investigations by regulatory agencies, or other loss contingencies.

Committees of the board. In large corporations, the board of directors often works through committees appointed to deal with special phases of operations. Common examples include an audit committee and an investment committee. As discussed in Chapters 4 and 5, the audit committee maintains close contact with both the independent CPAs and the company's internal auditors and may be involved in discussions of weaknesses in internal control, accounting policies, and possible illegal or fraudulent acts by management. The investment committee periodically reviews and approves the short-term investment activities of management. Minutes of the meetings of such committees are just as essential to the auditors' investigation as are the minutes covering the meetings of the entire board.

Procedure for review of minutes. In the first audit of a client, it may be necessary to review minutes recorded in prior years. Copies of these minutes will be preserved in the permanent file; as succeeding annual audits are made, the file will be appropriately expanded.

The auditor-in-charge will obtain from the secretary or other corporate officer copies of all minutes, including those of board committees, directors, and stockholders, for both regular and special meetings. These copies should be certified by a corporate officer and should be compared with the official minutes book to an extent sufficient to establish their completeness and authenticity.

In reviewing the minutes, the auditors will (1) note the date of the meeting and whether a quorum was present and (2) underscore or highlight such actions and decisions that, in their judgment, should influence the conduct of the audit. Nonessential material can be scanned rapidly, and highlighting can be limited to issues that warrant investigation during the course of the audit. For this phase of the audit work, there is no substitute for breadth of experience and maturity of judgment; for these factors make possible a sharp distinction between matters of real importance to the audit and those that may safely be passed by.

Major decisions in the minutes, such as declaration of dividends or authorization for borrowing, usually result in actions that need to be recorded in the accounting records. As the audit progresses, the auditors should trace authorized events from the minutes into the accounting records and cross-reference their copies of the minutes to the underlying account analyses. Similarly, events recorded in the accounting records that normally require authorization by directors should be traced and cross-referenced to the auditors' copies of the minutes.

Determining that all minutes are made available. How do the auditors know that copies of all minutes have been made available to them? First, they can review their permanent file to determine the identities of the boards' committees and the scheduled dates for regular meetings. Next, a typical practice at board and committee meetings is to approve the minutes of the preceding meeting. This practice enables the auditors to work backward from the most recent minutes to the oldest, noting the date of the previous minutes approved in the later meeting. Also, the auditors should obtain from management a letter representing that all minutes have been made available. The client's refusal to provide the auditors with copies of all minutes is a serious limitation of the scope of the auditors' examination. *SAS No. 2* advises auditors to issue a disclaimer of opinion on the financial statements when significant scope limitations are imposed by the client.[1]

Relationship of corporate minutes to audit objectives. The nature of the information to be highlighted in the minutes and the usefulness of this information to the auditors can be made clear by a few examples. Figure 10–1 shows several basic audit objectives and indicates for each objective certain relevant events that are likely to be documented in the minutes of the board and its committees.

Figure 10–1
Relationship of minutes to audit objectives

Audit objectives	Relevant information likely to be included in minutes of the board and its committees
1. Test cash transactions and substantiate cash balances in banks.	1a. The opening and closing of bank accounts require authorization by the board of directors. b. The authority to sign checks is delegated to specific officers by the board.
2. Substantiate investments in marketable securities and related investment income.	2a. The opening of brokerage accounts through which securities registered in the company name can be bought and sold require authorization by the board. b. Monthly summaries of all investment transactions are reviewed and approved by the investments committee of the board. c. Pledging of securities as collateral for a loan requires approval of the investments committee of the board.
3. Substantiate liabilities and disclosure of loss contingencies.	3a. The obtaining of bank loans requires advance approval by the board. b. Authority for the declaration of dividends payable rests with the board. c. Such issues as pending litigation, income tax disputes, accommodation endorsements, and other loss contingencies discussed by the board are documented in the minutes. d. The issuance of bonds payable or other long-term debt requires approval by the board. e. Unusual purchase commitments and sales commitments may be submitted to the board for approval. f. The selection of legal counsel, who in turn may have information regarding pending litigation or other loss contingencies, is approved by the board.

Contracts held or issued by client

Early in the audit engagement the auditors should obtain copies of the major contracts to which the client is a party. Information obtained

---

[1] *Statement on Auditing Standards No. 2,* "Reports on Audited Financial Statements," AICPA (New York, 1974), section 509, para. 12.

from an analysis of contracts may be helpful in interpreting such accounts as Advances from Suppliers, Progress Payments under Government Contracts, and Stock Options. In addition to production contracts with governmental agencies and other companies, the auditors may review contracts with suppliers for future delivery of materials, royalty agreements for use of patents, union labor contracts, leases, pension plans, stock options, and bonus contracts with officers.

The terms of existing contracts are often material factors in the measurement of debt-paying ability and in the estimating of future earnings. When examinations are being made in behalf of prospective investors, creditors, or purchasers of a business, the nature of contracts with customers may outweigh all other considerations in determining a market value for the business.

The procedure for examination of contracts will depend upon the length and nature of the contract in question. A contract from the federal government to an aircraft manufacturer may be a sizable volume with hundreds of pages of exhibits and specifications. Such contracts are generally accompanied by large numbers of change orders issued at frequent intervals throughout the life of the contract. When contracts are extremely long and technical, the auditors may find it necessary to rely upon summaries prepared by the client's staff or legal counsel. Data obtained in this manner should, of course, be verified by comparison with the basic contract to an extent considered reasonable in the circumstances.

The auditors may at times require the assistance of engineers, attorneys, and other specialists in the interpretation of important contracts. Most contracts include such accounting concepts as net income or working capital, but unfortunately those who draft the contracts may not in all cases understand the true meaning of the accounting terminology they employ. Skill in analyzing and interpreting the financial aspects of contracts appears to be a qualification of increasing importance to independent auditors.

Among the items auditors should usually note in reviewing contracts are the names and addresses of parties; effective date and duration of the contract; schedule for performance; provisions for price redetermination (such as cost-of-living adjustments); procedures for settlement of disputes; cancellation clauses; and provisions requiring audit of records to determine amounts owed.

Government regulations

Although independent auditors are not licensed to give legal advice or to interpret federal or state laws, they must be familiar with laws and regulations that affect the client's financial statements. Auditors should consult with the client's legal counsel—and their own attorneys if necessary—when they believe a legal problem affects performance of the audit or requires disclosure in the financial statements.

Among the laws and regulations with which auditors should be familiar are the following:

Foreign Corrupt Practices Act of 1977. This legislation contains two major parts. The first part makes it illegal to offer a bribe to a foreign official for the purpose of securing business. The second portion of the act requires companies to comply with certain accounting standards, including the maintenance of reasonably complete and accurate records and an adequate system of internal accounting control. The accounting standards portion of the act applies to all companies under SEC jurisdiction, regardless of whether or not they operate outside of the United States. The specific requirements regarding internal accounting control were discussed in Chapter 5.

State corporations codes. Laws governing the formation and operation of corporations vary among the states. The auditors should obtain a copy of the corporations code of each client's state of incorporation and become familiar with provisions of the code that affect such matters as legal or stated capital, par or no-par value stock, dividend declarations, and treasury stock.

Uniform Partnership Act. This act, in effect in most states, governs the operations of partnerships in areas not covered by the partnership contract.

State and federal corporate securities laws. Most states have blue-sky laws regulating the issuance of corporate debt and equity securities within their jurisdictions. In addition, the federal Securities Act of 1933 governs the interstate issuance of corporate securities, while the Securities Exchange Act of 1934 deals with the trading of securities on national exchanges and over the counter.

Uniform Commercial Code. This code has recently been adopted by most of the states; it regulates sales of goods, commercial paper (such as checks, bank collections, letters of credit, warehouse receipts, and bills of lading) investment securities, and secured transactions in personal property.

Antitrust laws. Federal antitrust laws are designed to promote competition; these laws provide civil and, in some cases, criminal liability for offenders. The Sherman Act of 1890 prohibits contracts (such as price-fixing) that result in unreasonable restraint of trade. The Clayton Act of 1914 strengthens the Sherman Act by outlawing specific practices that might "substantially lessen competition or tend to create a monopoly." The Robinson-Patman Act of 1936 amended the Clayton Act to prohibit price discrimination in interstate commerce unless justified by cost differences.

Labor laws. Federal laws regulating labor include the Fair Labor Standards Act of 1938 and 1939, and the Walsh-Healy Act of 1936. The Fair Labor Standards Act provides for a minimum wage, overtime premiums, and equal pay for men and women for equal work. The Walsh-Healy Act governs wages, hours, and working conditions of contractors having contracts with U.S. government agencies.

Social security. The Social Security Act of 1935 provides for payroll taxes on employers and employees to finance retirement and medical benefits for retired persons and certain surviving dependents. The employer has a liability for both the employer's share of the tax and the amounts withheld from employees.

Employee Retirement Income Security Act of 1974 (ERISA). This legislation, also known as the Pension Reform Act, affects virtually every private employee benefit play in the country. One consequence of the act is that CPAs have greater auditing responsibility for pension plans than in the past.

Cost accounting standards. The Cost Accounting Standards Board (CASB) is a government agency charged with developing cost accounting methods to be used by contractors with government contracts. The selling price in government contracts is often based upon the contractor's cost. The pronouncements of the CASB, *Cost Accounting Standards*, provide guidelines as to how *cost* is to be determined in government contracts.

Regulations for specific industries. Clients in regulated industries, such as insurance companies, banks, savings and loan associations, public utilities, airlines, truck lines, and railroads, are subject to additional specific controls often administered by federal and state regulatory commissions. Auditors with clients in these regulated areas will need to be familiar with the special laws and regulations that directly affect operation of these companies.

Temporary controls. In addition to the seemingly permanent statutes listed above, various temporary regulations are occasionally imposed by government that affect the transactions subject to review by the auditors. Examples include controls over wages, prices, and dividends. If violations are apparent, the auditors should inform both management and legal counsel of the client company and consider the possible existence of unrecorded liabilities in the form of fines or penalties.

Correspondence files

The general correspondence files of the client may contain much information of importance to the independent auditors, but it would be quite out of the question for them to plow through the great mass of general correspondence on file in search of pertinent letters. When the reading of corporate minutes, contract files, or other data indicates the existence of significant correspondence on matters of concern to the auditors, they should request the client to provide them with copies of such letters. In addition, the audit staff will usually review the client's correspondence with banks and other lending institutions, attorneys, and governmental agencies. Correspondence may generally be accepted as authentic; but if reason for doubt exists, the auditors may wish to confirm the contents of letters directly with the responsible persons.

Income tax returns of prior years

A review of federal, state, and foreign income tax returns of prior years will aid the auditors in planning any tax services required by the terms of the engagement. The possibility of assessment of additional income taxes exists with respect to the returns of recent years not yet cleared by tax authorities. By reviewing tax returns and revenue agents' reports, the auditors may become aware of any matters that pose a threat of additional assessments; they may also find a basis for filing a claim for a tax refund.

Other information the auditors can obtain from reviewing the prior-year tax returns of a new client includes the accounting principles used by the client for uncollectible accounts, inventory valuation, and depreciation, as well as the compensation and stock ownership of officers and the existence of affiliated organizations.

Financial statements and annual reports of prior years

Study of the financial statements and annual reports of prior years and of any available monthly or quarterly statements for the current year is a convenient way for the auditors to gain a general background knowledge of the financial history and problems of the business. If independent auditors have submitted audit reports in prior years, these documents may also be useful in drawing attention to matters requiring special consideration.

Reports to the SEC

Registration statements and periodic reports filed by the client with the SEC contain valuable information for the auditors—especially in a first audit. Included in this information will be the client's capital structure, a summary of earnings for the past five years, identity of affiliated companies, descriptions of the business and property of the client, pending legal proceedings, names of directors and executive officers of the client and their remuneration, stock option plans, and principal shareholders of the client.

Review and testing of the accounting records

Early in the examination, the auditors should review and test the journals and general ledger as part of the study of the client's internal control. A review of these records will inform the auditors as to the client's accounting procedures, the accounting records in use, and the control procedures in effect. The compliance testing verifies the mechanical accuracy of the records and provides assurance that the journals and ledger are actually achieving their respective purposes of recording and classifying transaction data.

The quality of accounting records may vary widely from one engagement to the next. Many clients maintain records that are carefully designed, well maintained, and easy to comprehend. The journals and ledgers of such clients are generally up-to-date, in balance, and virtually free from mechanical error. When the auditors ascertain that a client's accounting records are highly reliable, the audit work necessary to substantiate account balances may justifiably be minimized. At the other extreme, the accounting records of some clients may be typified by unrecorded transactions, unsupported entries, and numerous mechanical errors. In these cases, the auditors may have to perform extensive audit work to substantiate account balances. On occasion, the accounting records may be so inadequate that the auditors must disclaim an opinion on the financial statements.

Extent of testing.   If the client's accounting records and procedures are well designed and efficiently maintained, it is reasonable to devote less audit time to verifying the mechanical accuracy of the records than would be required in audits in which less satisfactory conditions prevail. The extent to which the auditors test the accounting records depends upon three factors: (1) the general appearance of the records; (2) the auditors' preliminary appraisal of the client's system of internal control, developed from the flow charts, written description, or questionnaire; and (3) the frequency and relative importance of any errors discovered during the actual testing. The first of these factors, the general appearance of the records, deserves some explanation. High-quality accounting records have basic characteristics which are readily apparent: journal entries include adequate written explanations, general journal entries are reviewed and approved by an officer before posting, and the records are legible, up-to-date, and properly cross-referenced. When records do not possess these characteristics, the existence of errors is a virtual certainty.

Testing of the accounting records may be done on a judgmental basis, or the auditors may use statistical sampling techniques. Sampling for attributes, discussed in Chapter 8, is a statistical sampling plan that may be used to estimate error occurrence rates within specified precision and levels of confidence.

The general ledger

The function of the general ledger is to accumulate and classify the transaction data posted from the journals. To ascertain that the ledger is being properly maintained, the auditors should conduct tests to determine that (1) account balances are mathematically correct, (2) all entries in the ledger were posted from journal entries, and (3) all journal entries were properly posted.

To test the mathematical accuracy of account balances, the auditors should verify the footings of some or all of the ledger accounts. The term *footings* is used among practicing accountants to designate column totals. "To foot," on the other hand, means to verify the total by adding the column.

For the second group of tests, the auditors must satisfy themselves that all entries in the general ledger were posted from authentic sources; that is, from entries in the journals. This procedure is important because the financial statements are drawn from the general ledger balances, and these balances conceivably could be falsified through the recording of unsupported debits or credits in the general ledger. The auditors can determine that entries in the ledger are properly supported by *tracing a sample of ledger entries back into the journals.* Ledger entries included in this sample are normally selected at random from entries made throughout the year. Of course, the auditors may test most or all of the entries in excess of some specified dollar amount.

Finally, to test the accuracy of the client's posting procedures, the auditors should *trace entries from the journals into the general and subsidiary ledgers.* The sample used for this test usually includes all entries made during several randomly selected periods of time. The auditors may also test journal entries that, for any reason, appear unusual.

Direction of testing.   In the two preceding paragraphs, two similar tests are described. In one test, ledger entries are traced back to the journals; in the other, journal entries are traced forward into the ledgers. The direction of the tracing is crucial to the effectiveness of the tests. The reasoning behind the direction of the tracing becomes apparent when we consider the nature of the errors for which the auditors are testing.

In the first test, the auditors are testing for unsupported entries in the ledger. Tracing ledger entries back to the journals may reveal the absence of supporting journal entries. On the other hand, the nonexistence of journal entries *cannot* be disclosed by tracing existing journal entries into the ledger.

In the second test, the auditors are testing for posting errors. If a journal entry was never posted, this omission can be detected only by tracing from the journal into the ledger. If certain items have been improperly omitted from ledger accounts, these missing amounts *cannot* be brought to light by tracing existing ledger entries back to their sources. Of course, some posting errors, such as transposition errors and posting to the wrong account, may be discovered by tracing in either direction.

Each of these two tests should be conducted in connection with testing the quality of the general ledger. However, each test is suited to disclosing different types of errors. In the design of audit procedures, careful consideration must be given to the nature of the errors that may exist. Otherwise, the audit procedures are likely to be ineffective and inconclusive.

Computer-based systems. A client utilizing electronic data processing may not maintain a traditional general ledger. Instead, an updated daily trial balance, showing beginning account balances, debit and credit transactions entries, and ending balances, is printed out by the computer. The auditors may test footings for selected daily trial balances; in addition, they should trace beginning account balances in the selected trial balances to the ending account balances of the previous day.

Errors disclosed by the test of the general ledger should be summarized on a separate working paper. Each error listed should be carefully investigated to determine its significance and probable cause. Although most errors are the result of clerical inaccuracy, the possibility of fraud as a motive must always be considered. In many cases the chief significance of an error lies in the directing of the auditors' attention to inadequate internal control.

The general journal

The general journal is an accounting record used to record all transactions for which special journals have not been provided. In its simplest form, the general journal has only a single pair of columns for the recording of debit and credit entries, but many variations from this basic design are encountered. A third column may be added to provide for entries to subsidiary ledgers, or various multicolumn forms may be used. The addition of a number of debit and credit columns is intended to facilitate the recording of transactions that occur so frequently as to make individual postings undesirable but are not sufficiently numerous to warrant the establishment of a special journal. Special journals are frequently used for recording routine business transactions. The review and testing of the special journals will be discussed in later chapters in conjunction with the audit of the related assets, liabilities, and underlying transactions.

Some companies maintain a system of journal vouchers. These are serially numbered documents, each containing a single, general journal entry, with full supporting details and bearing the signature of the controller or other officer authorized to approve the entry. A general journal in traditional form may be prepared from the journal vouchers, or that series of documents may be utilized in lieu of a general journal. Companies having electronic data processing equipment generally keypunch journal vouchers to serve as one of the transaction sources for the daily printout of the trial balance described in the preceding section.

The auditors should conduct tests of compliance to determine that entries in the general journal are based upon actual transactions and that these transactions have been properly recorded. Suggested procedures for testing the general journal follow:

1. Foot column totals of the journal.

The testing of footings in the general journal follows the pattern previously described for verification of ledger balances. A representative period for testing is selected, and all journal columns falling within that period are footed. Errors disclosed should be summarized on a working paper, investigated, and appropriate disposition made. With respect to the multicolumn form of general journal, it is necessary to cross-foot (add horizontally) the column totals and prove the equality of debits and credits. Discrepancies between the total of the debit columns and the total of the credit columns indicate either faulty addition or errors in individual entries.

2. Vouch selected entries to original documents.

To vouch a journal entry means to examine the original papers and documents supporting the entry. The term *voucher* is used to describe any type of supporting documentary evidence. For example, a journal entry recording the trade-in of a machine would be vouched by comparing it with a purchase order, supplier's invoice, sales contract, receiving report, and paid check—the vouchers for this entry. The auditors might not consider it necessary to examine all these documents if the evidence first examined appeared to provide adequate support for the entry. All general journal entries selected for compliance testing should be vouched.

Entries in the general journal should include clear, informative explanations; but, unfortunately, deviations from this principle are frequently encountered. The auditors should determine whether (1) the explanation is in agreement with the supporting documentation, and (2) the entry reflects the transaction properly in the light of generally accepted accounting principles.

The supporting evidence to be examined during the review of general journal entries may include purchase orders, invoices, receiving reports, sales contracts, correspondence, the minutes book, and partnership contract. Journal vouchers represent an internal control device; however, they should not be considered as original source documents supporting entries in the general journal. Verification of journal entries requires that the auditors refer to original invoices and other evidence previously described.

3. Scan the general journal for unusual entries.

The importance of certain types of transactions that are recorded in the general journal makes it desirable for auditors to scan this record for the entire period under audit, in addition to vouching all entries selected for testing. The following list is illustrative of the type of significant transactions for which the auditors should look in this scanning of the general journal:

1. The write-off of assets, particularly notes and accounts receivable: Collections from customers abstracted by employees and not recorded in the accounts may be permanently concealed if the accounts in question are written off as uncollectible. Any general journal entries involving loans receivable from officers require full investigation to provide assurance that such transactions are proper and have been authorized.

2. Assumption of liabilities: Transactions that create liabilities are normally recorded in special journals. Common examples of such transactions are the purchase of merchandise, materials, or equipment and the receipt of cash. General journal entries that bring liabilities into the record warrant close investigation to determine that they have received proper authorization and are adequately supported.

3. Any debits or credits to cash accounts, other than for bank charges and other bank reconciliation items: Most transactions affecting cash are recorded in special journals.

4. Creation of revenue: Transactions affecting operating revenue accounts are usually recorded in special journals. Operating revenue would be recorded in the general journal only if the underlying transaction were of an unusual nature or, for some reason, was being processed in a special manner. In either case, the auditors should verify the authenticity of the transaction and the propriety of the entry.

5. Unexplained or fragmentary transactions, the purpose and nature of which are not apparent from the journal entry: General journal entries with inadequate or unintelligible explanations suggest that the person making the entry did not understand the issues involved or was unwilling to state the facts clearly. Entries of this type, and entries that affect seemingly unrelated accounts, should be fully investigated.

6. Related party transactions: Transactions between the client and affiliated companies, directors, officers, and principal owners and their immediate families are not at arm's length and should be investigated to determine that the substance of the transactions has been fairly recorded. These transactions, as discussed in Chapter 7, should be reviewed by the auditors as to reasonableness of amounts, business purpose, and adequacy of disclosure.

Illustrative case. In a widely publicized management fraud, the financial statements of Equity Funding Corporation of America were inflated over a period of years by more than $120 million in fictitious assets and revenue. Although falsified journal entries were prepared to record fictitious transactions, there was frequently no documentation to support the journal entries. Large amounts of revenue were also recognized in journal entries that involved debits and credits to an illogical combination of accounts. Thorough investigation of unusual revenue-creating journal entries could have alerted the company's independent auditors to the fraud long before it reached mammoth proportions.

4. Determine that all general journal entries have received the approval of an officer.

An adequate system of internal control includes procedures for regular review and written approval of all general journal entries by the controller or other appropriate executive. The auditors should determine that such procedures have been consistently followed. In those cases in which a client official does not regularly review and approve journal entries, the auditors may deem it desirable to review the general journal with the controller and request an approval signature on each page. In such cases the internal control report to the client should include a suggestion that the client undertake regular review and approval of journal entries.

5. Trace selected transactions to general and subsidiary ledgers.

This procedure will usually be combined with the verification of postings to general ledger accounts. It is listed here for the purpose of emphasizing that a review of postings from the general journal should include the tracing of entries to subsidiary ledgers as well as to general ledger control accounts.

In tracing general journal entries to the ledgers, inspection of the posting reference is not sufficient; the entry should be traced directly into the account. The tracing of postings should be preceded by sufficient study of the client's chart of accounts to minimize the work required in locating accounts. In addition to tracing the posting of selected transactions, the auditors should ascertain that the column totals of a multicolumn general journal have been posted to the appropriate accounts.

Audit working papers for the examination of accounting records

Upon completing the review and testing of the accounting records, the auditors should prepare a working paper describing the records in use, the compliance tests and other audit procedure followed, the nature and significance of errors discovered, any suggestions for improving the accounting system, and the auditors' conclusion as to the overall quality of the accounting records. This working paper summarizes an important part of the auditors' study and evaluation of internal control and may serve as a reference for determining appropriate modifications in the audit program. At the beginning of the next annual audit, a review of this working paper will enable the auditors to concentrate upon the most significant aspects of the accounting records.

AUDIT PROGRAM DESIGN

An audit program is a detailed list of the audit procedures to be performed in the course of the examination. As discussed in Chapter 4, a tentative audit program is developed as part of the advance planning of an audit. This tentative program, however, requires frequent modification as the audit progresses. For example, the nature, timing, and extent of substantive test procedures are influenced by the auditor's study and evaluation of internal control. Thus, not until the study and evaluation of internal control has been completed can a final version of the audit program be drafted. Even this final version may require modification if the auditor's substantive tests disclose unexpected problems.

The audit program usually is divided into two major sections. The first section deals with the study and evaluation of the client's system of internal control, and the second section deals with the substantiation of specific financial statement amounts, as well as the adequacy of financial statement disclosures.

The systems portion of the program

The first part of the audit program is organized around the major *transaction cycles* in the client's system of internal control. For example, the systems portion of the audit program for a manufacturing company might be subdivided into separate programs for such areas as: (1) sales and collections cycle, (2) purchase cycle, (3) production cycle, (4) payroll cycle, and (5) financing cycle. (The activities comprising these specific transaction cycles are described in Chapter 5.) Audit procedures in the systems portion of the program typically include preparation of flowcharts for each transaction cycle, compliance tests of the significant internal accounting controls, and an evaluation of the strengths and weaknesses in internal control.

In conjunction with their evaluation of internal control, the auditors will make appropriate modifications in the substantive test portion of the audit program. For example, as a result of weaknesses in internal control in the sales cycle, the auditors may decide to perform more extensive substantive tests of accounts receivable and inventories.

The substantive test portion of the program

The portion of the audit program aimed at substantiating financial statement amounts usually is organized in terms of major balance sheet topics, such as cash, accounts receivable, inventories, and plant and equipment. Considering the importance of the income statement, why do audit programs emphasize the substantiation of balance sheet items? In part, this method of organizing the work may be a carry-over from the days when the auditor's objective was verification of the balance sheet alone. Even though present-day auditors are very much concerned with the reliability of the income statement, they still find the balance sheet approach to be an effective method of organizing their substantive audit procedures.

One advantage of the balance sheet approach is that highly competent evidence generally is available to substantiate assets and liabilities. Assets usually are subject to direct verification by such procedures as physical observation, inspection of externally created documentary evidence, and confirmation by outside parties. Liabilities usually can be verified by externally created documents, confirmation, and by inspecting paid checks after the liability has been paid.

In contrast, consider the nature of revenue and expense in double-entry accounting. The entry to record revenue or expense has two parts: first, the recognition of the revenue or expense, and second, the corresponding change in an asset or liability account. Revenue and expense have no tangible form; they exist only as entries in the client's accounting records, representing changes in owners' equity. Consequently, the best evidence supporting the existence of revenue or expense usually is the verifiable change in the related asset or liability account.

Indirect verification of income statement accounts. Figure 10–2 shows the relationship between income statement accounts and the related changes in cash or other balance sheet items. By substantiating the changes in the asset and liability accounts, the auditors indirectly verify revenue, cost of goods sold, and expenses. For example, most revenue transactions involve a debit to either Cash or Accounts Receivable. If the auditors are able to satisfy themselves that all cash receipts and all changes in accounts receivable during the year have been properly recorded, they have indirect evidence that revenue transactions have been accounted for properly.

Direct verification of income statement accounts. Not all of the audit evidence pertaining to income statement accounts is indirect. The verification of a major balance sheet item often involves several closely related income statement accounts that can be verified through computation or other direct evidence. For example, in substantiating the marketable securities owned by the client, it is a simple matter to compute the related interest revenue, dividends revenue, and gains or losses on sales of securities. In substantiating the balance sheet items of plant assets and accumulated depreciation, the auditors make computations that also substantiate depreciation expense. Uncollectible accounts expense is substantiated in conjunction with the balance sheet item Allowance for Doubtful Accounts. In addition to these computations, the auditor's *analytical review procedures* provide evidence as to the reasonableness of various revenue and expenses.

Comparison of the systems approach and the substantive approach. Auditing literature frequently refers to a CPA firm following a systems approach or a substantive approach to an audit. The *systems approach* involves heavy reliance upon the client's system of internal

= Figure 10-2

	Income statement items		Cash transactions		Balance sheet items	
Financial statement relationships						
	Revenue	=	Cash receipts from customers	−	Beginning balance of Accounts Receivable	+ Ending balance of Accounts Receivable
	Cost of Goods Sold	=	Cash payments for merchandise	−	Beginning balance of Accounts Payable	+ Ending balance of Accounts Payable
				+	Beginning balance of Inventory	− Ending balance of Inventory
	Expenses	=	Cash payments for expenses	−	Beginning balances of Accrued Expenses	+ Ending balances of Accrued Expenses
				+	Beginning balances of Prepaid Expenses	− Ending balances of Prepaid Expenses
Auditors' approach to substantiation	Verify indirectly by substantiating right-hand side of equation; also analytical review procedures and (if possible) direct computation.		Test transactions; reconcile to bank records.		Substantiate by reference to last year's audit working papers	Substantiate by substantive tests in current year.

control, whereas the substantive approach relies more heavily upon substantive testing as the basis for the auditor's opinion. Actually, every audit involves a blend of systems evaluation and substantive testing. Thus, *systems approach* and *substantive approach* are relative terms, indicating the emphasis that a particular CPA firm places in the systems or substantive portions of its audit program on a given engagement. Some CPA firms may lean toward one approach or the other as a matter of firm policy. However, in the audit of a client with weak internal control, the auditor has no choice but to emphasize the substantive approach.

Basic objectives of audit programs for asset accounts

In the next four chapters, we will consider the audit work to be done on the major asset categories, beginning with cash and concluding with plant assets and intangible assets. A sample audit program will be presented for each asset category to provide a framework for our discussion. It is important to remember that the audit programs presented in the text are merely illustrations of *typical* audit procedures. In actual practice, audit programs must be tailored to each client's business environment and system of internal control. The audit procedures comprising audit programs may vary substantially from one engagement to the next.

Each of the audit programs for an asset account will include perhaps 10 to 15 specific audit procedures. Although the procedures differ in each program, it is useful to realize that each audit program follows basically the same approach to verifying the balance sheet items and related income statement amounts. The audit program for every asset category includes procedures designed to accomplish the following *general objectives:*

Audit program for asset accounts
Stated in terms of general objectives

    I.   Study and evaluate internal control.
        A. Prepare a written description of the client's system of internal control.
        B. Conduct tests of compliance to determine the effectiveness of significant internal accounting control procedures.
        C. Evaluate the strength of internal control and modify the remaining audit procedures as necessary.
   II.   Substantiate account balances (substantive tests).
        A. Establish the *existence* and *ownership* of the assets.
        B. Determine the appropriate *valuation* of the assets.
        C. Establish a proper *cutoff* of transactions to be included in the period under audit.
        D. Verify the *related income statement amounts.*
        E. Determine the appropriate *financial statement presentation.*

In some cases, one of the above general objectives may be accomplished by a single audit procedure; in others, several procedures may be necessary to accomplish a single objective. However, these general objectives are *common to all audit programs for asset accounts.* Changes in these audit objectives, with respect to audit programs for liability and owners' equity accounts, will be discussed in later chapters.

Substantiation of account balances

The central purpose of the auditors' study and evaluation of internal control is to determine the nature and extent of the audit work necessary to substantiate account balances. In previous chapters considerable attention has been given to the study and evaluation of internal control; let us now discuss the objectives of the auditors' substantiation procedures.

Existence and ownership of assets

The first step in substantiating the balance of an asset account is to verify the existence and ownership of the asset. For assets such as cash on hand, marketable securities, and inventories, existence of the asset usually may be verified by physical inspection. When assets are in the custody of others, such as cash in banks and inventory on consignment, the appropriate audit procedure may be direct confirmation with the outside party. The existence of accounts receivable normally is verified by confirming with customers the amounts receivable. Verifying the existence of intangibles is more difficult; the auditors must gather evidence that costs have been incurred and that these costs represent future economic benefits.

On occasion, the same procedures that verify existence may also establish ownership of the assets. For example, confirming cash balances in bank accounts establishes the existence, ownership, and appropriate valuation of the cash. Similarly, inspecting marketable securities verifies both existence and ownership, because the registered owner's name usually appears on the face of the security certificate.

With other assets, such as plant and equipment, physical inspection establishes existence *but not ownership.* Plant and equipment may be rented or leased rather than owned. To verify the client's ownership of plant assets, the auditors must inspect documentary evidence such as property tax bills, purchase documents, and deeds.

Valuation of assets

Most assets are valued at cost. Therefore, a common audit procedure is to vouch the acquisition cost of assets to paid checks and other documentary evidence. If the acquisition cost is subject to depreciation or amortization, the auditors must evaluate the reasonableness of the cost allocation program and verify the computation of the remaining unallocated cost. Assets valued at lower-of-cost-or-market necessitate an investigation of current market prices as well as acquisition costs.

Establishing a proper cutoff

A problem inherent in the preparation of periodic financial statements is making a proper *cutoff* of transactions to be included in the period. The financial statements should reflect all transactions occurring through the end of the period and none that occur subsequently.[2] The term *cutoff* refers to the process of determining that transactions occurring near the balance sheet date are assigned to the proper accounting period.

Making a proper cutoff is complicated by the fact that invoices for many purchases and expenses of the current period may not arrive for several days or even weeks after the end of the period. For practical purposes, the preparation of financial statements cannot be delayed until all invoices have been received. Small items, such as utility bills, may be recorded in the period of payment rather than being accrued; as long as this method is followed consistently, no material error in the financial statements will result. Large items for which invoices have not been received should be recorded at estimated amounts. Two or three weeks are usually required for the accounting staff of a large company to complete the process of closing the accounts and preparing the financial statements.

The impact of cutoff errors upon the financial statements varies with the nature of the error. For example, a cutoff error in recording acquisitions of plant assets affects the balance sheet, but probably does not affect the income statement since depreciation usually is not recorded on assets acquired within a few days of year-end. On the other hand, a cutoff error in recording shipments of merchandise to customers affects both inventory and the cost of sales. In order to improve their financial picture, some clients may "hold their records open" to include in the current year cash receipts and revenue from the first part of the next period.

To verify the client's cutoff of transactions, the auditors should review transactions recorded shortly before and after the balance sheet date to ascertain that these transactions are assigned to the proper period. When such documents as checks, receiving reports, and shipping documents are serially numbered, noting the last serial number issued

---

[2] As discussed in Chapter 7, certain subsequent events may require adjustment to the financial statements. However, the fianancial statements are adjusted to reflect only those subsequent events that provide additional information regarding conditions existing on or before the balance sheet date.

during the period will assist the auditors in determining that a proper cutoff has been made in recording transactions.

Related income statement amounts

Income statement amounts often can be verified conveniently in conjunction with the substantiation of the related asset account. For example, after notes receivable have been verified, the related interest revenue can be substantiated by mathematically computing the interest applicable to the notes. In other cases, income statement amounts are determined by the same audit procedures used in determining the valuation of the related asset. Determining the undepreciated cost of plant assets, for example, necessitates computing (or testing) the depreciation expense for the period. Similarly, determining the net valuation of accounts receivable involves estimating the uncollectible accounts expense.

Some income statement items, such as sales revenue, do not lend themselves to verification by such direct audit procedures. However, when the auditors establish that accounts receivable are legitimate assets, and have been properly recorded, they have substantial *indirect* evidence that sales on account also have been properly measured.

Financial statement presentation

The concept of fair financial statement presentation embodies more than correct dollar amounts; the financial statements must also include adequate disclosure to enable users of the statements to interpret the information properly. Even after all dollar amounts have been substantiated, the auditors must perform procedures to assure that the financial statement presentation conforms to the requirements of authoritative accounting pronouncements and the general principle of adequate disclosure. Procedures falling into this category include the review of subsequent events; search for related party transactions; investigation of loss contingencies; review of disclosure of such items as leases, compensating balances, pledged assets, and inventory profits; and review of the statement of changes in financial position.

KEY TERMS INTRODUCED OR EMPHASIZED IN CHAPTER 10

Articles of incorporation   That part of the application to the state for a corporate charter that includes detailed information concerning the financial structure and other details of the business.

Bylaws   Rules adopted by the stockholders at the inception of a corporation to serve as general guidelines in the conduct of the business.

Cutoff   The process of determining that transactions occurring near the balance sheet date are assigned to the proper accounting period.

Journal voucher   A serially numbered document describing the details of a single journal entry and bearing the signature of the officer who approved the entry.

Minutes book   A formal record of the issues discussed and actions taken in meetings of stockholders and of the board of directors.

Substantive approach (to an audit)   An approach to auditing in which the auditor's opinion is based primarily upon the evidence obtained by substantiating the individual financial statement items. This approach places less emphasis upon the study and evaluation of internal control than does the systems approach and is particularly appropriate when internal control is weak.

Substantive tests   Tests of account balances and transactions designed to detect any material errors in the financial statements.

Systems approach (to an audit)   An approach to auditing in which the auditors place relatively high reliance upon their evaluation of the client's internal control and, therefore, perform a minimum of substantive testing. Whether an auditor follows a systems approach or a substantive approach is merely a matter of degree; every engagement involves both a system evaluation and substantive testing.

Trace   To follow data from one accounting record to another.

Transaction cycle   The sequence of procedures applied by the client in processing a particular type of recurring transaction. The term *cycle* reflects the idea that the same sequence of procedures is applied to each similar transaction. The auditors' study and evaluation of internal control often is organized around the client's major transactions cycles.

Vouch   To verify the accuracy and authenticity of entries in the accounting records by examining the original source documents supporting the entries.

GROUP 1: REVIEW QUESTIONS

10–1.   Since an audit is an examination of financial statements, why need auditors be concerned with records of a nonfinancial nature?

10–2.   During the first audit of a corporate client, the auditors will probably obtain a copy of the bylaws and review them carefully.

Required:
a.   What are bylaws of a corporation?
b.   What provisions of the bylaws are of interest to the independent auditors? Explain.

10–3.   State five significant provisions for which an auditor should particularly look in examining the articles of incorporation of a company and any amendments thereto. (AICPA)

10–4.   In connection with an annual audit of a corporation engaged in manufacturing operations, the auditors have regularly reviewed the minutes of the meetings of stockholders and of the board of directors. Name 10 important items that might be found in the minutes of the meetings held during the period under review that would be of interest and significance to the auditors. (AICPA)

10–5.   What should be the scope of an auditor's review of the corporate minutes book during the first audit of a client? During a repeat engagement?

10– 6.   Should the auditors make a complete review of all correspondence in the client's files? Explain.

10– 7.   What are the purposes of the audit procedures of (*a*) tracing a sample of journal entries forward into the ledgers, and (*b*) tracing a sample of ledger entries back into the journals?

10– 8.   Should the CPAs expect to find a traditional type of general ledger in the audit of a client utilizing electronic data processing equipment? Explain.

10– 9.   List three types of general journal entries for which the auditors would search in scanning the general journal for unusual entries, and explain why the journal entries you list are unusual.

10– 10. Charles Halstead, CPA, has a number of clients who desire audits at the end of the calendar year. In an effort to spread his work load more uniformly throughout the year, he is preparing a list of audit procedures that could be performed satisfactorily before the year-end balance sheet date. What work, if any, might be done on the general records in advance of the balance sheet date?

10– 11. What is the nature of the working papers used by the auditors to summarize the audit work performed on the accounting records?

10– 12. Why is audit work usually organized around balance sheet topics rather than income statement items?

10– 13. Identify the basic objectives of the auditors' substantiation procedures with respect to any major asset category.

10– 14. What is meant by making a proper year-end *cutoff*? Explain the effects of errors in the cutoff of sales transactions in both the income statement and the balance sheet.

GROUP II: QUESTIONS REQUIRING ANALYSIS

10– 15. Auditing literature frequently makes reference to the substantive approach and the systems approach to auditing.
a.   Distinguish between the substantive approach and the systems approach to an audit.
b.   Explain the circumstances under which each approach would be most appropriate.

10– 16. Listed below are several of the auditor's general objectives in performing substantive tests of an asset account:
(1)   Establish the existence and ownership of the asset.
(2)   Determine the appropriate balance sheet valuation of the asset.
(3)   Establish a proper cutoff of transaction.
(4)   Verify the related income statement amounts.
(5)   Determine the appropriate financial statement presentation.

Required:
Indicate the general objective (or objectives) of each of the following audit procedures:
a.   Count petty cash on hand.
b.   Locate on the client's premises a sample of the equipment items listed in the subsidiary plant and equipment ledger.

c. For all sales of investments in marketable securities, review brokers' advices to determine (*a*) the sales price, and (*b*) the date of sale.

d. Compare the unit cost of items in inventory to the current replacement cost being quoted by vendors.

e. Obtain a letter of representations from management stating that no inventory or accounts receivable have been pledged to secure specific liabilities.

f. Review the purchases journal for several days before and after the balance sheet date, noting the serial number of the receiving report for each recorded purchase.

10– 17. In a recent court case, the presiding judge criticized the work of a senior in charge of an audit in approximately the following language: "As to minutes, the senior read only what the secretary (of the company) gave him, which consisted only of the board of directors' minutes. He did not read such minutes as there were of the executive committee of the board. He did not know that there was an executive committee, hence he did not discover that the treasurer had notes of executive committee minutes which had not been written up."

Required:
How can the independent auditors be certain the client has provided them with minutes of all meetings of the board and committees thereof? Explain.

10– 18. Bonnie Cogan, CPA, is a senior auditor assigned to the first examination of the financial statements of Pioneer Mfg. Company, Inc., for the current year ended December 31. In scanning the client's general journal, Cogan noted the following entry dated June 30 of the current year:

Book To
Physical
Adjustment

Cost of Sales	186,453	
Raw Materials		84,916
Work in Process		24,518
Finished Goods		77,019

To adjust perpetual inventories to amounts of physical inventory taken this date.

The client-prepared income statement shows net sales and net income of approximately $5,500,000 and $600,000 respectively.

Required:
Do you think Cogan should investigate the above entry? Explain fully.

10– 19. Fred Murray, an assistant auditor, was instructed to use a discovery sampling plan to search for entries in the client's ledger that were not supported by entries in the journals. Murray defined the population as all journal entries made during the year. A statistical table for that size population indicated that a sample size of 300 was necessary to provide 95 percent confidence of finding at least one exception if the occurrence rate as 1 percent or greater. In conducting his test, Murray traced 300 randomly selected journal entries into the ledger and found no exceptions. Based upon this test, may Murray conclude with 95 percent confidence that at least 99 percent of the entries in the ledger are supported by journal entries? Explain fully.

10–20.   The partnership of Wheat Brothers operated successfully for many
years until the death of one of the brothers. The business was reorganized as a corporation at the beginning of the current year with John
Wheat, the surviving brother, elected to serve as president of the new
entity, Wheat Corporation. Mr. Wheat was also the largest stockholder.

To permit a cash settlement with the estate of the deceased partner,
the organization of the corporation involved obtaining outside capital.
This was readily accomplished by sale of capital stock to local resi-
dents who were familiar with the success and reputation of the business conducted by Wheat Brothers.

Near the close of the first year of operation as a corporation, John
Wheat, president of the company, retained you to perform a year-end
audit. Before the balance sheet date, you requested the secretary of
Wheat Corporation to provide you with the minutes books covering all
meetings of the stockholders, the board of directors, and any committees of the board. The secretary had held a responsible position in the
company throughout its years of operations as a partnership, during
which time the company had never been audited. He expressed some
reluctance to making available information that he regarded as highly
confidential, but finally he offered to provide you with a certified copy
of all resolutions relating to accounting matters that had been passed
by the stockholders, the board of directors, and committees of the
board. The secretary explained that some nonaccounting matters of a
highly confidential nature had been discussed in some of the board
meetings and that he considered it unwise for this confidential information to be made available to anyone other than directors of the
company.

The secretary also informed you that he had discussed your request
for the minutes books with Mr. Wheat, and that the president had
suggested that you might be elected to the board of directors at an
upcoming meeting. After such election, all records of the board and its
committees would automatically be available to you.

Required:
a.   What is the most likely explanation of the secretary's response to
your request?
b.   How would you respond to the statements by the secretary? Explain fully.

10–21.   Select the best answer for each of the following and give the reasons for
your choice.
a.   An auditor should examine the minutes of board of directors'
meetings:
(1)   Through the date of the financial statements.
(2)   Through the date of the audit report.
(3)   On a test basis.
(4)   Only at the beginning of the audit.
b.   Which of the following statements most appropriately summarizes
the auditor's responsibility for reviewing the client's correspondence files?
(1)   The auditor should review all correspondence for items relevant to the audit.

(2) The auditor should not review any correspondence; to do so would waste time more productively spent on gathering other evidence.

(3) The auditor should apply statistical selection techniques to draw a random sample of correspondence for review.

(4) The auditor should review correspondence with banks, other lending institutions, attorneys, and governmental agencies.

c. As one step in testing sales transactions, a CPA traces a random sample of sales journal entries to debits in the accounts receivable subsidiary ledger. This test provides evidence as to whether:

(1) Each recorded sale represents a bona fide transaction.

(2) All sales have been recorded in the sales journal.

(3) All debit entries in the accounts receivable subsidiary ledger are properly supported by sales journal entries.

(4) Recorded sales have been properly posted to customer accounts.

d. Which of the following is not a basic objective of the audit procedures applied to any major asset category?

(1) Verifying the appropriate valuation of the asset.

(2) Determining that transactions affecting the asset were recorded in the proper accounting period.

(3) Determining that the asset is fully insured against possible loss.

(4) Verifying related income statement amounts. (AICPA, adapted)

GROUP III: PROBLEMS

10–22. Precision Industries, Inc., is a manufacturer of electronic components. When a purchase order is received from a customer, a sales clerk prepares a serially numbered sales order and sends copies to the shipping and accounting departments. When the merchandise is shipped to the customer, the shipping department prepares a serially numbered shipping advice and sends a copy to the accounting department. Upon receipt of the appropriate documents, the accounting department records the sale in the accounting records. All shipments are *FOB shipping point.*

Required:

a. How can the auditors determine whether Precision Industries, Inc., has made a proper year-end cutoff of sales transactions?

b. Assume all shipments for the first five days of the following year were recorded as occurring in the current year. If not corrected, what effect will this cutoff error have upon the financial statements for the current year?

10–23. Kenneth J. Bryan, secretary of Jensen Corporation, has given you the minutes of the meetings of the board of directors. Summarize, in good form for the audit working papers, those contents of the following minutes that you consider to be of significance in the conduct of an annual audit.

Meeting of February 15, 1984

The meeting was called to order at 2:15 P.M. by H. R. Jensen, chairman of the board. The following directors were present:

John J. Savage	Ruth Andrews
Helen R. King	Dale H. Lindberg
Lee McCormick	Ralph Barker
H. R. Coleman	H. R. Jensen
George Anderson	Kenneth J. Bryan
Harold Bruce Smith	

Absent was Director J. B. Adams, who was in New York City on company business in connection with the opening of a sales office.

The minutes of the preceding meeting, December 15, 1983, were read by the secretary and duly approved as read.

Upon a motion by Ms. King, seconded by Mr. Savage, and unanimously carried, the secretary was instructed to notify the firm of Black, Bryson and MacDougal, Certified Public Accountants, of its selection to conduct an annual audit of the company's financial statements as of March 31, 1984.

President John J. Savage outlined the current status of negotiations leading toward the acquisition of a new factory site in San Diego, California, and recommended to the board the purchase of said property at a price not to exceed $600,000.

Ms. King offered the following resolution, which was seconded by Mr. Smith, and unanimously carried:

Resolved: That Mr. Savage hereby is authorized to acquire in behalf of the company the factory site located at Exmont and Donaldson Avenues, San Diego, California, at a price not in excess of $600,000, to be paid for in cash from the general funds of the corporation.

Upon a motion by Mr. Savage, seconded by Ms. King and carried unanimously, the secretary was instructed to arrange for the purchase from the estate of J. B. Williams, former director, 100 shares of the company's own stock at a price not in excess of $110 per share.

Mr. Savage, after discussing the progress of the company in recent months and its current financial condition, submitted the following resolution, which was seconded by Mr. Coleman and unanimously passed:

Resolved: That the following cash dividends are hereby declared, payable April 10, 1984, to stockholders of record on March 31, 1984.

   a.   The regular quarterly dividend of $1 per share of capital stock.

   b.   A special dividend of 50 cents per share of capital stock.

There being no further business brought before the meeting, the meeting was adjourned at 4 P.M.

Kenneth J. Bryan
Secretary

Meeting of March 15, 1984

The meeting was called to order at 2:15 P.M. by H. R. Jensen, chairman of the board. The following directors were present:

John J. Savage	Ruth Andrews
Helen R. King	Dale H. Lindberg
Lee McCormick	J. B. Adams
H. R. Coleman	H. R. Jensen
George Anderson	Kenneth J. Bryan
Harold Bruce Smith	

Absent was Director Ralph Barker.

The minutes of the preceding meeting, February 15, 1984, were read by the secretary and duly approved as read.

Chairman H. R. Jensen stated that nominations for the coming year were in order for the positions of president, vice president in charge of sales, vice president in charge of manufacturing, treasurer, controller, and secretary.

The following nominations were made by Ms. King, and there being no further nominations the nominations were declared closed:

President .... John J. Savage
Vice president—sales .... Otis Widener
Vice president—manufacturing .... Henry Pendleton
Treasurer .... Ruth Andrews
Controller .... Roger Dunn
Secretary .... Kenneth J. Bryan

The above nominees were duly elected.

Mr. McCormick then offered the following resolution, which was seconded by Mr. Coleman and unanimously carried:

Resolved: That the salaries of all officers be continued for the next year at the same rates currently in effect. These rates are as follows:

John J. Savage—president $150,000
Otis Widener—vice president—sales 70,000
Henry Pendleton—vice president—manufacturing 70,000
Ruth Andrews—treasurer 70,000
Roger Dunn—controller 70,000
Kenneth J. Bryan—secretary 50,000

Mr. Bryan offered the following resolution, which was seconded by Mrs. Andrews and unanimously carried:

Resolved: That the company establish a bank account at the United National Bank, San Diego, California, to be subject to check by either John J. Savage or Ruth Andrews.

There being no further business to come before the meeting, the meeting was adjourned at 4 P.M.

Kenneth J. Bryan
Secretary

10–24. Treefarm, Inc., is a closely held wholesale nursery that has never been audited. The business has been owned and operated by the same family for more than 20 years. All stockholders in the company are family members and also serve as directors and officers of the corporation. Treefarm's income statement shows a net income of $212,000 resulting from net sales of $925,000.

You are the senior auditor-in-charge of the first audit of Treefarm, Inc., for the year ended December 31, 1983. In your testing of the beginning account balances and review of the general journal, you encounter the following entries:

GENERAL JOURNAL

Date	Account	Debit	Credit
6/9/75	Accumulated Depreciation—Equipment	2,154.80	
	Accounts Payable—Ace Garage		2,154.80
	Ted, Vice President of Operations, had tractor rebuilt; repairs will extend useful life.		
5/19/79	Sales Returns & Allowances	6,422.00	
	Accounts Receivable—Valley Construction Co.		6,422.00
	Return of trees not used in Westridge housing development. See credit Memo. No. 732.		
1/10/80	Office Equipment	42,809.30	
	Notes Payable		42,809.30
	Agreed to pay ten-year annuity to Mary Jean in exchange for handcarved clock. Recorded at present value of annuity payments.		

12/31/80	Depreciation—Greenhouses	5,132.00	
	Accumulated Depreciation—Greenhouses		5,132.00
	Final year's depreciation on greenhouses scheduled for demolition in two months.		
12/31/82	Retained Earnings	38,528.37	
	Office Equipment		38,528.37
	Adjustment per journal Voucher No. 1795.		
8/24/83	Allowance for Uncollectible Accounts	32,710.00	
	Notes Receivable		32,710.00
	Notes receivable from Allan will not be collected in recognition of his promotion to treasurer.		

Required:

Which of the entries in the Treefarm, Inc., general journal would you investigate as being *unusual?* Explain fully.

10–25. A normal procedure in the audit of a corporate client consists of a careful reading of the minutes of meetings of the board of directors. One of the CPAs' objectives in reading the minutes is to determine whether the transactions recorded in the accounting records are in agreement with actions approved by the board of directors.

Required:

a. What is the reasoning underlying this objective of reconciling transactions in the corporate accounting records with actions approved by the board of directors? Describe fully how the CPAs achieve the stated objective after they have read the minutes of directors' meetings.

b. Discuss the effect each of the following situations would have on specific audit steps in the CPAs' examination and on the auditors' opinion:

   (1) The minutes book does not show approval for the sale of an important manufacturing division that was consummated during the year.

   (2) Some details of a contract negotiated during the year with the labor union are different from the outline of the contract included in the minutes of the board of directors.

   (3) The minutes of a meeting of directors held after the balance sheet date have not yet been written, but the corporation's secretary shows the CPAs notes from which the minutes are to be prepared when the secretary has time.

c. What corporate actions should be approved by stockholders and recorded in the minutes of the stockholders' meetings? (AICPA, adapted)

11

Cash and marketable securities

What are auditors looking for?

In audit work on cash (and other assets), auditors are on guard against *overstatement of asset values.* Assume, for example, that the client's balance sheet shows "Cash . . . . . $250,000." There is little chance that the client has more cash than shown; the real danger is that the actual cash is less than $250,000. If a cash shortage exists, it may have been concealed merely by the insertion of a fictitious check in the cash on hand at year-end, or by the omission of an outstanding check from the year-end bank reconciliation. In this case the amount of cash on hand and on deposit is actually less than the $250,000 amount shown in the balance sheet.

Auditors must also be alert for any *understatement of cash receipts* or *overstatement of cash disbursements.* Either of these misstatements can conceal a theft of cash by reducing the balance in the cash account to the amount remaining after the theft.

The auditors' objectives in examination of cash

In the examination of cash, the principal audit objectives are: (1) to study and evaluate the internal controls over cash transactions, and (2) to determine that cash is fairly presented in the client's financial statements.

After preparing a working-paper description of internal controls relating to cash, auditors conduct compliance tests to determine that cash transactions have been properly recorded throughout the year. The areas selected for testing and the size of the audit samples are determined according to the relative quality of internal control over cash receipts, cash disbursements, and cash forecasting. Compliance tests of cash transactions indicate the extent to which controls allegedly in use are actually being followed in practice. They indicate the general credibility of the accounting records.

The second objective—that of determining the fairness with which cash is presented as part of the client's overall financial position—is relatively simple, because cash, unlike other assets, poses virtually no problems of valuation. To substantiate the amount of cash shown on the balance sheet, auditors will conduct such substantive tests as confirming amounts on deposit by direct communication with banks and counting cash on hand.

How much audit time for cash?

The factor of materiality applies to audit work on cash as well as to other sections of the examination. The counting of a small petty cash fund, which is inconsequential in relation to the company's overall financial position, accomplishes little in achieving the auditors' objective of expressing an independent opinion on the financial statements. Nevertheless, auditors do devote a larger proportion of the total audit hours to cash than is indicated by the relative amount of cash shown on the balance sheet. This emphasis on cash transactions occurs despite the fact that scarcely any valuation problem exists for cash, whereas considerable audit time is expended on valuation problems in the work on inventories and accounts receivable.

Several reasons exist to explain the auditors' traditional emphasis on cash transactions. Liabilities, revenue, expenses, and most other assets flow through the cash account; that is, these items either stem from or result in cash transactions. Thus, the examination of cash transactions assists the auditors in the substantiation of many other items in the financial statements. If the auditors' study and evaluation of internal control over cash transactions discloses significant weaknesses, it is often necessary to extend the scope of audit work on cash and any other accounts that may be involved.

Another reason contributing to extensive auditing of cash is that cash is the most liquid of assets and offers the greatest temptation for theft, embezzlement, and misappropriation. Relative risk is high for liquid assets, and auditors tend to respond to high-risk situations with more intensive investigation. However, the detection of fraud is relevant to overall fairness of the client's financial statements only if such fraud is material in amount.

On occasion auditors may encounter evidence of small-scale employee fraud. After determining that such fraud could *not* have a material effect upon the financial statements, the auditors should discuss the situation with the client before investigating the matter further. This discussion will serve to alert the client to the situation, protect the auditors from charges of incompetence, and avoid wasting audit time on matters that are not material with respect to the financial statements and that may better be pursued by client personnel.

Internal control over cash transactions

Most of the functions relating to cash handling are the responsibility of the finance department, under the direction of the treasurer. These functions include handling and depositing cash receipts; signing checks; investing idle cash; and custody of cash, marketable securities, and other negotiable assets. In addition, the finance department must forecast cash requirements and make both short-term and long-term financing arrangements.

Ideally, the functions of the finance department and the accounting department should be integrated in a manner that provides assurance that—

1. All cash that should have been received *was* in fact received and recorded promptly and accurately.
2. Cash disbursements are made only for authorized purposes and are properly recorded.
3. Cash balances are maintained at adequate, but not excessive, levels by forecasting expected cash receipts and payments related to normal operations. The need for obtaining loans or for investing excess cash is thus made known on a timely basis.

A detailed study of the operating routines of the individual client is necessary in developing the most efficient control procedures, but there are some general guidelines to good cash-handling practices in all types of business. These universal rules for achieving internal control over cash may be summarized as follows:

1. Do not permit any one employee to handle a transaction from beginning to end.
2. Separate cash handling from record keeping.
3. Centralize receiving of cash as much as possible.
4. Record cash receipts immediately.
5. Encourage customers to obtain receipts and observe cash register totals.
6. Deposit each day's cash receipts intact.
7. Make all disbursements by check, with the exception of expenditures from petty cash.

8. Have bank reconciliations prepared by employees not responsible for the issuance of checks or custody of cash.

Several good reasons exist for the rule that each day's cash receipts should be deposited intact. Daily deposits mean that less cash will be on hand to invite "borrowing"; moreover, the deposit of each day's receipts as a unit tends to prevent the substituting of later cash receipts to cover a shortage. If company policy permits the paying of expenses out of cash receipts, fictitious disbursements and overstatement of actual payments are much more easily concealed than when liabilities are paid by check after proper verification. Any delay in depositing checks increases the risk that the checks will be uncollectible. Further, undeposited receipts represent idle cash, which is not a revenue-producing asset.

Internal control over cash receipts

Cash sales.   Control over cash sales is strongest when two or more employees (usually a salesclerk and a cashier) participate in each transaction with a customer. Restaurants and cafeterias often use a centrally located cashier who receives cash from the customer along with a sales ticket prepared by another employee. Theaters generally have a cashier selling prenumbered tickets, which are collected by a door attendant when the customer is admitted. If tickets or sales checks are serially numbered and all numbers accounted for, this separation of responsibility for the transaction is an effective means of preventing fraud.

Control features of cash registers.   In many retail establishments the nature of the business is such that one employee must make over-the-counter sales, deliver the merchandise, receive cash, and record the transaction. In this situation, dishonesty may be discouraged by proper use of cash registers and form-writing machines with locked-in copies. The protective features of cash registers include (1) visual display of the amount of the sale in full view of the customer, (2) a printed receipt, which the customer is urged to take with the merchandise, and (3) accumulation of a locked-in total of the day's sales. At the end of the day, the salesperson counts the cash in the drawer and turns in this amount without knowing the total sales recorded on the register. A supervisor inserts a key in the cash register, which permits a reading of the total sales for the day to be taken. Overages and shortages will inevitably occur from time to time, but a careful record of cash turned in and sales recorded by each salesperson will quickly disclose any unreasonable variations.

Electronic point-of-sale (POS) systems.   Many retail stores use various types of electronic cash registers, including on-line computer terminals. With some of these registers, a "wand" or an electronic scanner is used to read the sales price and other data from specially prepared price tags. The salesperson need only pass the wand over the price tags (or merchandise over the scanner) for the register to record automatically the sale at the appropriate price. Thus, the risk of a salesperson recording sales at erroneous prices is substantially reduced. Besides providing strong control over cash sales, electronic registers often may be programmed to perform numerous other control functions. For example, on-line registers may verify the credit status of charge account customers, update accounts receivable and perpetual inventory records, and provide special printouts accumulating sales data by product line, salesperson, department, and type of sale.

Control features of form-writing machines. Many businesses making sales over the counter find that internal control is strengthened by use of a machine containing triplicate sales tickets. As each sales check is written, two copies are ejected by the machine and a third copy is retained in a locked compartment. The retention of the third copy, which is not available to the salesclerk, tends to prevent a dishonest employee from reducing the store's copy of the sales check to an amount less than that shown on the customer's copy.

Collections from credit customers. In many manufacturing and wholesale companies, cash receipts consist principally of checks received through the mail. This situation poses little threat of defalcation unless one employee is permitted to receive and deposit these checks and also to record the credits to the customers' accounts. A typical system of internal control over cash received through the mail is described below.

Incoming mail usually is opened in the mailroom, where an employee prepares a *control listing* of the incoming cash receipts. This listing shows the amount received from each customer and identifies the customer by name or account number. Copies of the control listing are forwarded to the controller and to the employee responsible for the customers' accounts; cash receipts and customers' remittance advices are forwarded to the cashier.

Which controls tend to prevent the mailroom employee from abstracting the receipts from several customers, destroying the remittance advices, and omitting these receipts from the control listing? First, incoming cash receipts consist primarily of checks made payable to the company. Second, if customers' accounts are not credited for payments made, the customers will complain to the company. If these customers can produce paid checks supporting their claims of payment, and these checks do not appear on the mailroom control listings, responsibility for the abstraction is quickly focused upon the mailroom employee.

The cashier uses the checks and customers' remittance advices to record the cash received in the cash receipts journal. Then the cashier deposits the day's receipts intact in the bank. Control is exercised over the cashier by periodic reconciliation of the controller's copies of the

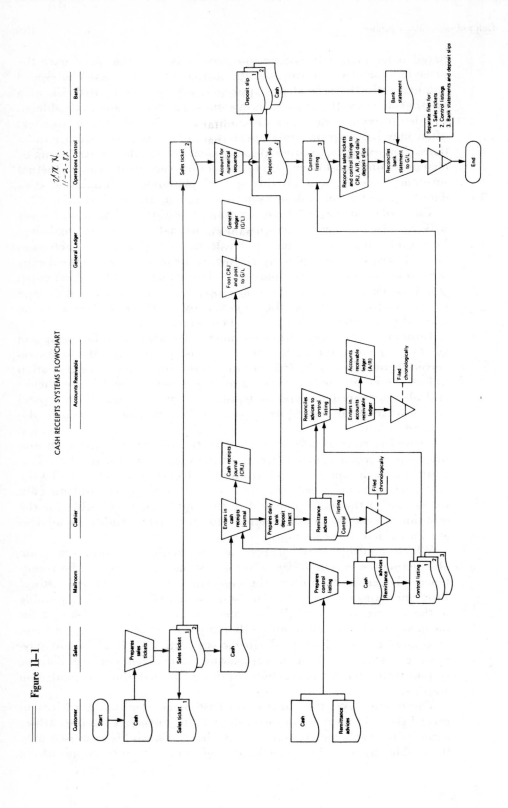

Figure 11–1

CASH RECEIPTS SYSTEMS FLOWCHART

mailroom control listings with the cash receipts journal and the detail of daily bank deposits.

After recording the cash receipts, the cashier forwards the remittance advices to the employee responsible for the customers' accounts ledger. This employee reconciles the remittance advices to his copy of the control listing and, when satisfied that all remittance advices are accounted for, posts credits to the customers' accounts. Strong internal control requires that the accounts receivable clerk have no access to the cash receipts, and that the customers' accounts be periodically reconciled with the general ledger. When the nature of operations permits, different employees should be assigned responsibility for (1) preparation of sales invoices, (2) maintenance of customers' accounts, (3) reconciling customers' ledgers with controlling accounts, (4) initial listing of cash receipts, (5) custody and depositing of cash receipts, and (6) collection activity on past-due accounts.

The division of responsibilities, sequence of procedures, and internal controls over cash sales and collections from customers are illustrated in the systems flowchart in Figure 11–1.

Lockbox control over cash receipts. Businesses receiving a large volume of cash through the mail often use a lockbox system to strengthen internal control and hasten the depositing of cash receipts. The lockbox is actually a post office box controlled by the company's bank. The bank picks up mail at the post office box several times a day, credits the company's checking account for cash received, and sends the remittance advices to the company. Internal control is strengthened by the fact that the bank has no access to the company's accounting records.

Internal control over cash disbursements

The dangers inherent in making disbursements out of cash receipts have already been discussed. To state the issue in positive terms, all disbursements should be made by check, except for payment of minor items from petty cash funds. Although the issuance of checks is somewhat more costly than making payments in cash, the advantages gained by use of checks usually justify the expense involved. A principal advantage is the obtaining of a receipt from the payee in the form of an endorsement on the check. Other advantages include (1) the centralization of disbursement authority in the hands of a few designated officials—the only persons authorized to sign checks, (2) a permanent record of disbursements, and (3) a reduction in the amount of cash kept on hand.

To secure in full the internal control benefits implicit in the use of checks, it is essential that all checks be prenumbered and all numbers in the series accounted for. Unissued prenumbered checks should be adequately safeguarded against theft or misuse. Voided checks should be defaced to eliminate any possibility of further use and filed in the regular sequence of paid checks. Dollar amounts should be printed on all checks by the computer or a check-protecting machine. This practice prevents anyone from altering a check by raising its amount.

Officials authorized to sign checks should review the documents supporting the payment and perforate these documents at the time of signing the check to prevent them from being submitted a second time. The official signing checks should maintain control of the checks until they are placed in the mail. Typically the check comes to the official complete except for signature. It is imperative that the signed checks not be returned to the custody of the employee who prepared them for signature.

Most companies issuing a large volume of checks use check-signing machines. These machines print the authorized signature, usually that of the treasurer, on each check by means of a facsimile signature plate. An item count of checks signed is provided by the machine, and a key is required to retrieve the signed checks. The facsimile signature plate should be removed from the machine and safeguarded when the machine is not in use.

Reconciliation of monthly bank statements is essential to adequate internal control over cash receipts and disbursements. Bank statements should be reconciled by an employee having no part in authorizing or accounting for cash transactions, or in handling cash. Statements from the bank should come unopened to this employee.

Illustrative case.   One large construction company ignored basic controls over cash disbursements. Unissued checks were stored in an unlocked supply closet, along with styrofoam coffee cups. The company check-signing machine deposited signed checks into a box that was equipped with a lock. Despite warnings from their independent auditors, company officials found it "too inconvenient" to keep the box locked or to pay attention to the check-counter built into the machine. The company maintained very large bank balances and did not bother to reconcile bank statements promptly.

A three-week-old bank statement and a group of paid checks were given to an employee with instructions to prepare a bank reconciliation. The employee noticed that the group of paid checks accompanying the bank statement was not complete. No paid checks could be found to support over $700,000 in charges on the bank statement. Further investigation revealed that more than $1 million in unauthorized and unrecorded checks had been paid from various company bank accounts. The checks had been issued out-of-sequence and had been signed by the company check-signing machine. The company was unable to determine who was responsible for the theft, and the money was never recovered.

Control features of a voucher system.   A voucher system is one method of achieving strong internal control over cash disbursements by providing assurance that all disbursements are properly authorized and reviewed before a check is issued. In a typical voucher system, the accounting department is responsible for assembling the appropriate documentation to support every cash disbursement. For example, before authorizing payment for merchandise purchased, the accounting department assembles copies of the purchase order, receiving report, and vendor's invoice, and determines that these documents are in agreement. After determining that the transaction is properly supported, an accounting employee prepares a voucher, which is filed in a tickler file according to the date upon which payment will be made.

A voucher, in this usage, is an authorization sheet that provides space for the initials of the employees performing various authorization functions. Authorization functions include such procedures as extending and footing the vendor's invoice; determining the agreement of the invoice, purchase order, and receiving report; and recording the transaction in the accounts. Transactions are recorded in a *voucher register* by an entry debiting the appropriate asset, liability, or expense accounts, and crediting Vouchers Payable.

On the payment date, the voucher and supporting documents are removed from the tickler file. A check is prepared *but not signed.* The voucher, supporting papers, and the check (complete except for signature) are forwarded to the finance department. The treasurer reviews the voucher before signing the check; the check is then mailed directly to the payee, and the voucher and all supporting documents are perforated to prevent reuse. The cancelled vouchers are returned to the accounting department, where an entry is made to record the cash disbursement (a debit to Vouchers Payable and a credit to Cash). Paid vouchers usually are filed by voucher number in a paid voucher file.

Strong internal control is inherent in this system because every disbursement is authorized and reviewed before a check is issued. Also, neither the accounting department nor the finance department is in a position to disburse cash without a review of the transaction by the other department. The operation of a voucher system is illustrated in the flowchart in Figure 11–2.

Internal control aspects of petty cash funds

Internal control over payments from an imprest petty cash fund is achieved at the time the fund is replenished to its fixed balance, rather than at the time of handing out small amounts of cash. When the custodian of a petty cash fund requests replenishment of the fund, the documents supporting each disbursement should be reviewed for completeness and authenticity and perforated to prevent reuse.

Petty cash funds are sometimes kept in the form of separate bank accounts. The bank should be instructed in writing not to accept for deposit in such an account any checks payable to the company. The deposits will be limited to checks to replenish the fund and drawn payable to the bank or to the custodian of the fund. The prohibition against deposit of checks payable to the company is designed to prevent the routing of cash receipts into petty cash, since this would violate the basic assumption of limited disbursements and review at time of replenishing the fund.

Figure 11–2
Flowchart of a voucher system

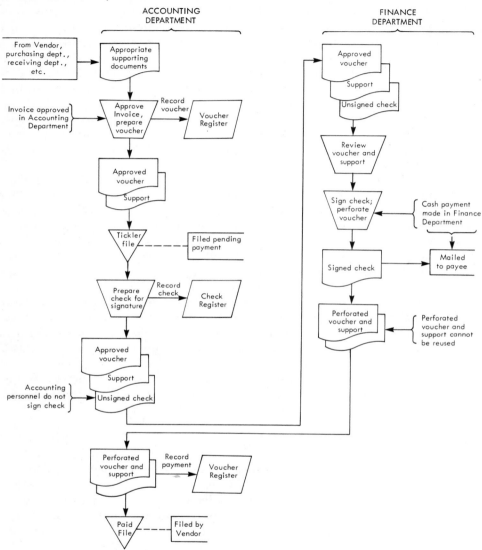

Internal control and the computer

Computer processing of cash transactions can contribute to strong internal control over cash. As previously discussed, control over cash sales may be strengthened by the use of on-line register terminals. Remittance advices or mailroom listings of customers' payments can be keypunched for processing by computer. Many companies use computers to issue checks and, subsequently, to prepare bank reconciliations. The daily computer processing of cash receipts and checks can provide management with a continually up-to-date cash receipts journal, check register, customers' accounts ledger, and cash balance. In addition to this, the computer can prepare reliable bank reconciliations even when thousands of checks are outstanding and can provide current information for cash planning and forecasting.

Audit working papers for cash

Auditors' working papers for cash should include a flowchart or a written description of internal controls. An internal control questionnaire is also often used, especially in larger companies. A related working paper will show the compliance tests of cash transactions and an evaluation of internal control over cash.

Additional cash working papers include a grouping sheet, cash counts, bank confirmations, bank reconciliations, outstanding check lists, lists of checks being investigated, recommendations to the client for improving internal control, and notes concerning proper presentation of cash in the client's balance sheet.

AUDIT PROGRAM FOR CASH

The following audit program indicates the general pattern of work performed by the auditors in the verification of cash. Selection of the most appropriate procedures for a particular audit will be guided, of course, by the nature of the internal controls in force and by other circumstances of the engagement.

A. Study and evaluation of internal control for cash

    1. Prepare a description of the internal control for cash and conduct a walk-through of the system.

    2. Prove footings of cash journals and trace postings to ledger accounts.

    3. Compare detail of cash receipts listings to cash receipts journal, accounts receivable postings, and authenticated deposit slips.

    4. Reconcile bank activity for one or more months with cash activity per the accounting records.

    5. Verify cash transactions in one or more selected expense accounts.

    6. Investigate any checks representing large or unusual payments to related parties.

    7. Evaluate internal control for cash.

B. Substantive tests of cash transactions and balances

    8. Send confirmation letters to banks to verify amounts on deposit.

    9. Count and list cash on hand.

10. Obtain or prepare reconciliations of bank accounts as of the balance sheet date.

11. Verify the client's cutoff of cash receipts and cash disbursements.

12. Obtain a cutoff bank statement containing transactions of at least seven business days subsequent to balance sheet date.

13. Trace all bank transfers for last week of audit year and first week of following year.

14. Determine proper balance sheet presentation of cash.

A. Study and evaluation

1. **Prepare a description of the internal control for cash and conduct a walk-through of the system.**

In the audit of a small business, auditors may prepare a written description of controls in force, based upon the questioning of owners and employees and upon firsthand observation. For larger companies, a flowchart or internal control questionnaire is usually employed to describe the system of internal control. An internal control questionnaire for cash receipts was illustrated in Chapter 5. Among the questions included in a questionnaire for cash disbursements are whether all disbursements (excepting those from petty cash) are made by prenumbered checks and whether voided checks are mutilated, preserved, and filed. The existence of these controls permits the auditors to determine that all disbursements have been recorded by accounting for the sequence of checks issued or voided during the period.

Also, the questionnaire should determine the presence of such controls as check-signing authority being restricted to executives not having access to accounting records, vouchers and supporting documents being presented with checks submitted for signature, and checks being mailed directly to the payee after being signed. Other sections of the internal control questionnaire, flowchart, or written description for cash cover cash disbursements for payroll and dividends and bank reconciliation procedures. All questions of the internal control questionnaire are designed to require affirmative answers when satisfactory controls exist.

After the auditors have prepared a flowchart (or other description) of internal control, they should conduct a walk-through of the system. The term "walk-through" means to trace a few transactions through each step of the system to determine that transactions actually are being processed in the manner indicated by the flowchart.

2. **Prove footings of cash journals and trace postings to ledger accounts.**

Compliance tests help to determine the effectiveness of the client's internal controls and the extent to which the auditors are justified in relying upon the client's accounting records. This procedure and the following ones relating to internal control are compliance tests.

The auditors prove the footings of the cash receipts and cash payments journals in order to verify the mechanical accuracy of the journals. Obviously, not much reliance could be placed on the accounting records if the journals were found to be full of errors and not in balance. The extent of the footings tests should be based upon the internal controls for cash described in the flowchart, questionnaire, or written description. For example, if one employee serves as both cashier and accountant, the auditors will generally test footings of most, if not all, of the journals. Cash embezzlements have been concealed by an understatement of the cash receipts journal Cash-Debit column or an overstatement of the Cash-Credit column of the cash disbursements journal. Generally, the Sales Discounts column total of the cash receipts journal will be overstated in the same amount as the cash column understatement, so that the journal will be in balance. In like manner, the Purchase Discounts column total of the cash disbursements journal may be understated to offset an overstatement of the Cash column total.

The auditors should trace the monthly postings of column totals from the cash receipts journal to the Cash account and to the controlling account for Accounts Receivable. Similar verification may be made for the totals posted from the cash payments journal to the Cash account and to the Accounts Payable account in the general ledger. If the testing of postings and footings discloses sloppy accounting work, with numerous errors and corrections, indistinct figures, and ambiguous totals, the scope of the auditors' work should be increased, for these are often the hallmarks of fraudulent manipulation of the records.

3. **Compare detail of cash receipts listings to cash receipts journal, accounts receivable postings, and authenticated deposit slips.**

Satisfactory internal control over cash receipts demands that each day's collections be deposited intact no later than the next banking day. This practice will minimize the opportunity for employees handling cash to "borrow" from the funds in their custody, and will facilitate comparison by the auditors of the cash receipts journal with the deposits per the bank.

To provide assurance that cash receipts have been deposited intact, the auditors should compare the detail of the original cash receipts listings (mailroom listings and register tapes) to the detail of the daily deposit tickets. The *detail* of cash receipts refers to a listing of the amount of each individual check and the total amount of currency comprising the day's receipts. In making a comparison of receipts and deposits, the auditors must emphasize the detail of cash receipts rather than relying upon daily or periodic totals. Agreement of total receipts and deposits for a period gives no assurance that worthless checks have not been substituted for currency or that shortages occurring early in the period have not been made up by subsequent deposits.

Comparison of the daily entries in the cash receipts journal with bank deposits may disclose a type of fraud known as *lapping.* Lapping means the concealment of a cash shortage by delaying the recording of cash receipts. If cash collected from customer A is withheld by the cashier, a subsequent collection from customer B may be entered as a credit to A's account. B's account will not be shown as paid until a collection from customer C is recorded as a credit to B. Unless the money abstracted by the cashier is replaced, the accounts receivable as a group remain overstated; but judicious shifting of the overstatement from one account receivable to another may avert protests from customers receiving monthly statements. The following schedule makes clear how a lapping activity may be carried on. In companies in which the cashier has access to the general accounting records, shortages created in this manner have sometimes been transferred to inventory accounts or elsewhere in the records for temporary concealment.

Date	Actually received from	Actual cash receipts	Recorded as received from	Receipts recorded and deposited	Receipts withheld
December 1	Abbott	$ 750			$ 750
	Crane	1,035	Crane	$1,035	
2	Barstow	750	Abbott	750	
	White	130	White	130	
3	Crawford	1,575	Barstow	750	825
	Miller	400	Miller	400	
		$4,640		$3,065	$1,575

If an employee who receives collections from customers is responsible for the posting of customers' accounts, lapping is most easily carried on. Familiarity with customers' accounts makes it relatively easy to lodge a shortage in an account that will not be currently questioned.

Duplicate deposit tickets in the possession of the client may be subject to alteration. If the auditors suspect that the duplicate slips have been altered, they should compare them with the originals on file at the bank. Most banks are willing to furnish auditors with copies of deposit tickets for comparison with the client's record of cash receipts.

4. **Reconcile bank activity for one or more months with cash activity per the accounting records.**

Reconciling the client's records of cash transactions with those of the bank is the most comprehensive compliance test of the client's controls over recording cash receipts and disbursements. This procedure, a *proof of cash,* involves the detailed study of the cash transactions

occurring within a specified test period. The starting point of this study
is preparation of a four-column bank reconciliation for one or more
months selected on a test basis. When internal control is weak, the
auditors may decide to reconcile bank activity with the accounting
records for the entire year under audit.

Satisfactory completion of the proof of cash will usually provide a
clear indication as to whether cash receipts and disbursements are
being properly handled and cash balances are accurately stated. In
addition, this work will enable the auditors to learn whether prescribed
internal controls are being effectively carried out in actual practice.

A proof of cash for the test period of September is illustrated in
Figure 11–3. Notice that this working paper is so organized that the first
and last columns reconcile the cash balance per bank and the balance
per accounting records at the beginning of the test period (column 1)
and at the end of this period (column 4). These outside columns are
equivalent to typical monthly bank reconciliations. The two middle
columns reconcile the bank's record of deposits with the client's record
of cash receipts (column 2) and the bank's record of paid checks with
the client's record of cash disbursements (column 3).

Next let us consider the source of the figures used in this reconciliation. The amounts in column 1 (Balance, August 31) are taken from the
client's bank reconciliation as of August 31. Similarly, the figures for
column 4 (Balance, September 30) are taken from the client's bank
reconciliation as of September 30. For column 2 (Deposits) the auditors
arrive at the $46,001 of deposits per the bank by adding the deposits
appearing on the September bank statement. The $45,338.50 of receipts
per the books is obtained from the debits to Cash in Bank account in
the general ledger. In column 3 the auditors compute the $40,362.90 of
checks paid by the bank by cross-footing the top line of the reconciliation and proving the figure by adding the paid checks. The bottom
figure in column 3 represents the disbursements per the accounting
records during September and is taken from the general ledger account.
The reconciling items listed in columns 2 and 3 are computed by the
auditors from analysis of the reconciling items at the beginning and end
of September.

After completing the four-column bank reconciliation form, the auditors should prove the footings of all four columns and make a detailed verification of the figures used in the reconciliation. The balances
taken from the client's bank reconciliations as of August 31 and September 30 should be traced to the bank statements and to the Cash in
Bank account in the general ledger.

**Verification of cash receipts and deposits during the test pe-
riod.**   To verify receipts and deposits for the month being tested, deposits listed on the bank statement should be compared with the client's
cash receipts record. This step will include not only a comparison of the
total receipts with the total deposits, but also a comparison of the date

Figure 11–3

The Fairview Corporation

Acct. No. 101   Proof of Cash for September 198X   8-4

December 31, 198X

	Balance 8/31/8X	Deposits	Checks	Balance 9/30/8X
Per bank statement	39,236.40 z	46,001.00 # ②	40,362.90	44,874.50 =
Deposits in transit:				
at 8/31/8X	600.00 z	(600.00)		
at 9/30/8X		837.50		837.50
Outstanding checks				
at 8/31/8X	(1,241.00) x		(1,241.00)	
at 9/30/8X			3,402.00	(3,402.00) ✓
Bank service charge:				
August	4.60		4.60	
September			(2.30)	2.30
Check of Customer A. G. Speeler charged back by bank 9/12/8X, redeposited 9/15/8X.		(900.00)	(900.00)	
Per books	38,600.00 #	45,338.50 #	41,625.70 #	42,312.80 #
			①	A-1

z = Traced to clients' 8/31/8X bank reconciliation and/or to September bank statement.

\# = Per adding machine tape at A-4-1.

x = Per adding machine tape at A-4-2.

✓ = Per adding machine tape at A-4-3.

= Traced to general ledger.

① = Vouched all September disbursements to paid vouchers and other supporting documents.

② = Obtained authenticated deposit slips for September from bank and compared with cash receipts journal. Compared detail of 10 deposit slips with original control listings and postings to customers' accounts.

Footed cash receipts journal and check register for September 198X. Accounted for numerical sequence of all checks issued September 198X — nos. 610-792. No exceptions to tests.

Conclusion: Client's records of cash receipts and disbursements appear reliable.

V. M. H. 10/16/8X

of each deposit with the date such funds were received by the company. Any failure to deposit each day's receipts intact should be investigated.

The misappropriation of cash receipts may sometimes be concealed by crediting the customers' accounts but debiting Sales Discounts rather than Cash. For this reason, auditors may verify all sales discounts recorded during the test period by computing the allowable discounts and noting the dates of invoices and customers' payments.

Verification of cash disbursements during the test period. Reconciling the client's record of cash disbursements to the bank's record of paid checks provides the auditors with assurance that all disbursements clearing the bank during the test period have been recorded in the accounting records. To determine that the nature of these disbursements is properly reflected in the accounts, the auditors will vouch disbursements for the test period to such supporting evidence as vouchers, approved vendors' invoices, and payroll records.

While vouching these disbursements, the auditors have an opportunity to test many of the controls over cash disbursements. For example, they will notice whether all paid vouchers and supporting documents have been perforated or cancelled. Also, they will determine whether agreement exists among the supporting documents and note the presence of all required authorization signatures.

One of the most important procedures in the verification of cash disbursements is to account for the sequence of check numbers issued during the period. All checks used should be paid, voided, or listed as outstanding on September 30. The auditors will examine any checks voided during the period and may also obtain the October bank statement to examine checks listed as outstanding on September 30.

Omitting an outstanding check from a bank reconciliation may conceal a cash shortage. Auditors should therefore determine that all check numbers not paid or voided during the test period are listed as outstanding on September 30. Another test of the client's bank reconciliation function is to determine that all checks listed as outstanding on August 31 were either paid in September or listed as outstanding in the September 30 bank reconciliation.

5. **Verify cash transactions in one or more selected expense accounts.**

Assume that an officer of an audit client has arranged for company checks to be sent to a department store in payment of personal expenditures. What account would probably be charged with this transaction? Experience shows that such accounts as Miscellaneous Expense, Entertainment Expense, and Sales Promotion Expense are among the accounts *most likely to be charged with improper disbursements.* Analysis of the cash transactions in one or more of these accounts is a desirable auditing procedure—one of which may focus considerable light on the adequacy of internal control over cash disbursements.

6. Investigate any checks representing large or unusual payments to related parties.

Any large or unusual checks payable to directors, officers, employees, affiliated companies, or to cash should be carefully reviewed by the auditors to determine whether the transactions (*a*) were properly authorized and recorded and (*b*) are adequately disclosed in the financial statements. If checks have been issued payable to cash, the auditors should determine who received these payments and why this form of check was used.

To provide assurance that cash disbursements to related parties were authorized transactions and were properly recorded, the auditors should determine that each such transaction has been charged to the proper account, is supported by adequate vouchers or other records, and was specifically approved before payment by an officer other than the one receiving the funds.

The need for financial statement disclosure of transactions with related parties was discussed in Chapter 7. To determine that such transactions are adequately disclosed, the auditors must obtain evidence concerning the relationship between the parties, the substance of each transaction (which may differ from its form), and the effect of each transaction upon the financial statements. Disclosure of related party transactions should include the nature of the relationships, a description of the transactions, and the dollar amounts involved.

7. Evaluate internal control for cash.

When the auditors have completed the procedures described in the preceding sections, they should evaluate the client's internal control for cash. As illustrated in Chapter 5, the internal control evaluation describes weaknesses and unusual strengths in internal control, related extensions or limitations of auditing procedures, and recommendations for inclusion in the internal control report to the client. The auditors then draft the portion of the audit program devoted to the substantive tests of cash transactions and balances.

B. Substantive tests

8. Send confirmation letters to banks to verify amounts on deposit.

One of the objectives of the auditors' work on cash is to substantiate the existence of the amount of cash shown on the balance sheet. A direct approach to this objective is to confirm amounts on deposit, count the cash on hand, and obtain or prepare reconciliations between bank statements and the accounting records.

Confirmation of amounts on deposit by direct communication with bank officials is necessary in all cases, even when unopened bank statements are made available to the auditors. The confirmation letters are prepared by the client, but they must be mailed personally by the auditors, with return envelopes enclosed that are addressed to the auditors' office. A standard form of bank confirmation request agreed upon by the AICPA and the Bank Administration Institute is widely used by the public accounting profession. This form is prepared in duplicate, the original to be retained by the bank and the duplicate to be returned to the auditors. An illustration of this form appears in Figure 11–4.

An important element of the confirmation letter is the request for disclosure of all indebtedness of the client to the bank. This request thus serves to bring to light any unrecorded liabilities to banks, as well as to confirm the existence of assets. Auditors should send confirmation letters to all banks in which the client has had deposits during the year, even though a deposit account may have been closed out during the period. It is entirely possible that a bank loan may continue after the closing of the deposit account. The same line of reasoning leads to the conclusion that confirmation letters are necessary even when the auditors obtain the bank statements and paid checks directly from the bank. Since every client maintains one or more bank accounts, the independent auditors will use bank confirmation requests on every audit engagement.

9. Count and list cash on hand.

Cash on hand ordinarily consists of undeposited cash receipts, petty cash funds, and change funds. The petty cash funds and change funds may be counted at any time before or after the balance sheet date; many auditors prefer to make a surprise count of these funds. If the client's internal audit staff regularly performs surprise counts of petty cash and change funds, the CPAs may review the internal auditors' working papers for these counts and conclude that it is unnecessary to include a count of petty cash and change funds among the procedures of the annual independent audit. If undeposited cash receipts constitute a material factor, a count at the balance sheet date is desirable; otherwise the auditors may verify the deposit in transit at year-end by referring to the date of deposit shown on the cutoff bank statement.

Whenever auditors make a cash count, they should insist that the *custodian of the funds be present throughout the count.* At the completion of the count, the auditors should obtain from the custodian a signed and dated acknowledgement that the funds were counted in the custodian's presence and were returned intact by the auditors. Such procedures avoid the possibility of an employee trying to explain a cash shortage by claiming that the funds were intact when turned over to the auditors. In some situations, the independent auditors may arrange for the client's internal auditing staff to assist under the CPAs' supervision in the count of large amounts of cash on hand.

A first step in the verification of cash on hand is to establish control over all negotiable assets, such as cash funds, securities and other investments, notes receivable, and warehouse receipts. Unless all nego-

Figure 11-4

STANDARD BANK CONFIRMATION INQUIRY
Approved 1966 by
AMERICAN INSTITUTE OF CERTIFIED PUBLIC ACCOUNTANTS
NABAC, THE ASSOCIATION FOR BANK AUDIT, CONTROL
AND OPERATION

E-1-1

DUPLICATE
To be mailed to accountant

January 16, 198X

Dear Sirs:

Your completion of the following report will be sincerely appreciated. **IF THE ANSWER TO ANY ITEM IS "NONE", PLEASE SO STATE.** Kindly mail it in the enclosed stamped, addressed envelope <u>direct</u> to the accountant named below.

Report from

Yours truly,

The Fairview Corporation
(ACCOUNT NAME PER BANK RECORDS)

(Bank)   Security National Bank

By   _Carl J. Forster_
          Authorized Signature

1000 Wilshire Boulevard

Los Angeles, California 90017

Bank customer should check here if confirmation of bank balances only (item 1) is desired. ☐

Name of Accountant
Douglas and Troon, CPAs
800 Hill Street
Los Angeles, California 90014

NOTE—If the space provided is inadequate, please enter totals hereon and attach a statement giving full details as called for by the columnar headings below.

Dear Sirs:

1. At the close of business on December 31, 198X our records showed the following balance(s) to the *credit* of the above named customer. In the event that we could readily ascertain whether there were any balances to the credit of the customer not designated in this request, the appropriate information is given below.

AMOUNT	ACCOUNT NAME	ACCOUNT NUMBER	SUBJECT TO WITHDRAWAL BY CHECK?	INTEREST BEARING? GIVE RATE
E-1 $44,874.50	General Account	123-5828	Yes	No
E-2 3,215.89	Payroll Account	123-6451	Yes	No

2. The customer was directly liable to us in respect of loans, acceptances, etc., at the close of business on that date in the total amount of $ 20,000.00 , as follows:

AMOUNT	DATE OF LOAN OR DISCOUNT	DUE DATE	INTEREST RATE	INTEREST PAID TO	DESCRIPTION OF LIABILITY, COLLATERAL, SECURITY INTERESTS, LIENS, ENDORSERS, ETC.
M-1 $20,000.00	10/1/8X	4/1/8X	15%	–	Unsecured

3. The customer was contingently liable as endorser of notes discounted and/or as guarantor at the close of business on that date in the total amount of $ None , as below:

AMOUNT	NAME OF MAKER	DATE OF NOTE	DUE DATE	REMARKS
$				

4. Other direct or contingent liabilities, open letters of credit, and relative collateral, were   None

5. Security agreements under the Uniform Commercial Code or any other agreements providing for restrictions, not noted above, were as follows (if officially recorded, indicate date and office in which filed):   None

Yours truly, (Bank) Security National Bank

Date January 12, 198X

By   _Jonathan Richards_
          Authorized Signature

Additional copies of this form are available from the American Institute of CPAs, 666 Fifth Avenue, New York, N. Y. 10019 tiable assets are verified at one time, an opportunity exists for a dishonest officer or employee to conceal a shortage by transferring it from one asset category to another.

Illustrative case. John Sidell, a key office employee in a small business, misappropriated $30,000 by withholding cash collections and postponing the required credits to accounts receivable from customers. The accounting records were in balance; but Sidell was aware that when the independent auditors confirmed the balances due from customers the shortage would be disclosed. He therefore "borrowed" negotiable securities from the office safe shortly before the annual audit and used them as collateral to obtain a short-term loan of $34,000. He intermingled the proceeds of this loan with the cash receipts on hand and credited the customers' accounts with all payments received to date. Mr. Sidell knew that unless the auditors insisted on verifying the securities owned by the business concurrently with their verification of cash, he would be able to abstract funds again after the cash had been counted, use these funds to pay off his loan, and return the "borrowed" securities to the safe before the auditors began their verification of investments. The defalcation was discovered when the auditors insisted on a simultaneous verification of all negotiable assets.

It is not uncommon to find included in cash on hand some personal checks cashed for the convenience of officers, employees, and customers. Such checks, of course, should not be entered in the cash receipts journal because they are merely substitutes for currency previously on hand. The auditors should determine that these checks are valid and collectible, thus qualifying for inclusion in the balance sheet figure for cash. This may be accomplished by the auditors taking control of the last bank deposit for the period and determining that it includes all checks received through year-end. The auditors will retain a validated deposit slip from this deposit for comparison to any checks subsequently charged back by the bank.

10. Obtain or prepare reconciliations of bank accounts as of the balance sheet date.

Determination of a company's cash position at the close of the period requires a reconciliation of the balance per the bank statement at that date with the balance per the company's accounting records. Even though the auditors may not be able to begin their field work for some time after the close of the year, they will prepare a bank reconciliation as of the balance sheet date or review the one prepared by the client.

If the year-end reconciliation has been made by the client before arrival of the auditors, there is no need for duplicating the work. However, the auditors should examine the reconciliation in detail to satisfy themselves that it has been properly prepared. Inspection of a reconciliation prepared by the client will include verifying the arithmetical accuracy, tracing balances to the bank statement and ledger account, and investigating the reconciling items. The total checks drawn during the month according to the cash disbursements journal should be equal to the total of the paid checks returned by the bank, plus the outstanding checks at the end of the period and minus the outstanding checks at the beginning of the period. The importance of a careful review of the client's reconciliation is indicated by the fact that a cash shortage may be concealed merely by omitting a check from the outstanding check list or by purposely making an error in addition on the reconciliation.

There are many satisfactory forms of bank reconciliations. The form most frequently used by auditors begins with balance per bank and ends with unadjusted balance per the accounting records. The format permits the auditors to post adjusting entries affecting cash directly to the bank reconciliation working paper, so that the final balance can be cross-referenced to the cash grouping sheet or to the working trial balance.

The mechanics of balancing the ledger account with the bank statement by no means complete the auditors' verification of cash on deposit. The authenticity of the individual items making up the reconciliation must be established by reference to their respective sources. The balance per the bank statement, for example, is not accepted at face value but is verified by direct confirmation with the bank, as described in the preceding pages. Other verification procedures associated with the reconciliation of the bank statement will now be discussed.

The auditors should investigate any checks outstanding for a month or more. If checks are permitted to remain outstanding for long periods, internal control over cash disbursements is weakened. Employees who become aware that certain checks have long been outstanding and may never be presented have an opportunity to conceal a cash shortage merely by omitting the old outstanding check from the bank reconciliation. Such omissions will serve to increase the apparent balance of cash on deposit and may thus induce an employee to abstract a corresponding amount of cash on hand.

The auditors' investigation of old outstanding checks will include examination of the voucher and other documents supporting the payment. Checks outstanding for long periods should be called to the attention of the client, who customarily will contact the payee to learn why the check has not been cashed or deposited. Payroll and dividend checks are the types most commonly misplaced or lost. It is good practice for the client to eliminate long-outstanding checks of this nature by an entry debiting the Cash account and crediting Unclaimed Wages or another special liability account. This will reduce the work required in bank reconciliations, as well as lessen the opportunity for irregularities.

11. **Verify the client's cutoff of cash receipts and cash disbursements.**

The balance sheet figure for cash should include all cash received on the final day of the year and none received subsequently. In other words, an accurate cutoff of cash receipts (and of cash disbursements) at year-end is essential to a proper statement of cash on the balance sheet. If the auditors can arrange to be present at the client's office at the close of business on the last day of the fiscal year, they will be able to verify the cutoff by counting the undeposited cash receipts. It will then be impossible for the client to include in the records any cash received after this cutoff point without the auditor being aware of such actions.

All customers' checks included in cash receipts should have been entered in the cash receipts journal before the auditors' cash count. The auditors should compare these checks, both as to name and amount, with the cash journal entries. If checks have been credited to accounts other than those of the drawers of the checks, a likelihood of lapping or other fraudulent activity is indicated.

Of course auditors cannot visit every client's place of business on the last day of the fiscal year, nor is their presence at this time essential to a satisfactory verification of cash. As an alternative to a count on the balance sheet date, auditors can verify the cutoff of cash receipts by determining that deposits in transit as shown on the year-end bank reconciliation appear as credits on the bank statement on the first business day of the new year. Failure to make *immediate* deposit of the closing day's cash receipts would suggest that cash received at a later time might have been included in the deposit, thus overstating the cash balance at the balance sheet date.

To ensure an accurate cutoff of cash disbursements, the auditors should determine the serial number of the last check written on each bank account on the balance sheet date and should inquire whether all checks up to this number have been placed in the mail. Some companies, in an effort to improve the current ratio, will prepare checks payable to creditors and enter these checks as cash disbursements on the last day of the fiscal year, although there is no intention of mailing the checks until several days or weeks later. When the auditors make a note of the number of the last check issued for the period, they are in a position to detect at once any additional checks that the client might later issue and seek to show as disbursements of the year under audit.

   12.   **Obtain a cutoff bank statement containing transactions of at least seven business days subsequent to balance sheet date.**

A *cutoff bank statement* is a statement covering a specified number of *business days* (usually 7 to 10) following the end of the client's fiscal year. The client will request the bank to prepare such a statement and deliver it to the auditors. Most auditors do not actually prepare a second bank reconciliation, but merely examine the cutoff statement closely to see that the year-end reconciling items such as deposits in transit and outstanding checks have cleared the bank in the interval since the balance sheet date.

With respect to checks that were shown as outstanding at year-end, the auditors should determine the dates on which these checks were paid by the bank. By noting the dates of payment of these checks, the auditors can determine whether the time intervals between the dates of the check and the time of payment by the bank were unreasonably long.

Unreasonable delay in the presentation of these checks for payment constitutes a strong implication that the checks were not mailed by the client until some time after the close of the year. The appropriate adjusting entry in such cases consists of a debit to Cash and a credit to a liability account.

In studying the cutoff bank statement, the auditors will also watch for any paid checks issued on or before the balance sheet date but not listed as outstanding on the client's year-end bank reconciliation. Thus, the cutoff bank statement provides assurance that the amount of cash shown on the balance sheet was not overstated by omission of one or more checks from the list of checks outstanding.

13.   **Trace all bank transfers for last week of audit year and first week of following year.**

The purpose of tracing bank transfers is to disclose overstatements of cash balances resulting from *kiting.* Many businesses maintain checking accounts with a number of banks and often find it necessary to transfer funds from one bank to another. When a check drawn on one bank is deposited in another, several days (called the float period) usually pass before the check clears the bank on which it is drawn. During this period, the amount of the check is included in the balance on deposit at both banks. Kiting refers to manipulations that utilize such temporarily overstated bank balances to conceal a cash shortage or meet short-term cash needs.

Auditors can detect manipulations of this type by preparing a schedule of bank transfers for a few days before and after the balance sheet date. This working paper lists all bank transfers and shows the dates that the receipt and disbursement of cash were recorded in the cash journals and on the bank statements. A partial illustration of a schedule of bank transfers is shown below.

	Bank accounts			Date of disbursement		Date of receipt	
Check No.	From	To	Amount	Books	Bank	Books	Bank
5897	General	Payroll	$30,620	12/28	1/3	12/28	12/28
6006	General	Branch 4	24,018	1/2	1/4	12/30	12/30
6029	Branch 2	General	10,000	1/3	1/5	1/3	12/31

Disclosure of kiting.   By comparing the dates in this working paper, auditors can determine whether any manipulation of the cash balance has taken place. The increase in one bank account and decrease in the other bank account should be recorded in the cash journals in the same accounting period. Notice that Check No. 6006 in the transfer schedule was recorded in the cash journals as a receipt on December 30 and a disbursement of January 2. As a result of recording the debit and credit parts of the transaction in different accounting periods, cash is overstated on December 31. For the cash receipts journal to remain in balance, some account must have been credited on December 30 to offset the debit to Cash. If a revenue account was credited, the results of operations were overstated along with cash.

Kiting may also be used to conceal a cash shortage. Assume, for example, that a financial executive misappropriates $10,000 from a company's general checking account. To conceal the shortage on December 31, the executive draws a check transferring $10,000 from the company's branch bank account to the general account. The executive deposits the transfer check in the general account on December 31, but records the transfer in the accounting records as occurring early in January. As of December 31, the shortage in the general account has been replaced, no reduction has yet been recorded in the branch account, and no shortage is apparent. Of course, the shortage will reappear in a few days when the transfer check is paid from the branch account.

A bank transfer schedule should disclose this type of kiting because the transfer deposit appears on the general account bank statement in December, while the transaction was not recorded in the cash journals until January. Check No. 6029 in the transfer schedule illustrates this discrepancy.

A third type of kiting uses the float period to meet short-term cash needs. For example, assume that a business does not have sufficient cash to meet the month-end payroll. The company might draw a check on its general account in one bank, deposit it in a payroll account in another bank, and rely upon subsequent deposits being made to the general account before the transfer check is presented for payment. If the transfer is properly recorded in the accounting records, this form of kiting will not cause a misstatement of the cash balance for financial reporting purposes (e.g., Check No. 5897). However, banks discourage this practice and may not allow the customer to draw against the deposit until the check has cleared the other account. In some deliberate schemes to defraud banks, this type of kiting has been used to create and conceal overdrafts of millions of dollars.

14. Determine proper balance sheet presentation of cash.

The balance sheet figure for cash should include only those amounts that are available for use in current operations. Most users of the balance sheet are not interested in the breakdown of cash by various bank accounts or in the distinction between cash on hand and on deposit. Consequently, all cash on hand and in banks that is available for general use is presented as a single amount on the balance sheet. Change funds and petty cash funds, although somewhat lacking in the general availability test, are usually not material in amount and are included in the balance sheet figure for cash.

A bank deposit that is restricted to use in paying long-term debt should not be included in cash. Certificates of deposit or time deposits are sometimes included in the balance sheet figure for cash, but if material in amount, they may be listed separately.

Window dressing. The term *window dressing* refers to actions taken shortly before the balance sheet date to improve the cash position or in other ways to create an improved financial picture of the company. For example, if the cash receipts journal is held open for a few days after the close of the year, the balance sheet figure for cash is improperly increased to include cash collections actually received after the balance sheet date. Another approach to window dressing is found when a corporate officer who has borrowed money from the corporation repays the loan just before the end of the year and then promptly obtains the loan again after the balance sheet has been prepared. This second example is not an outright misrepresentation of the cash position (as in the case of holding the cash receipts journal open), but nevertheless creates misleading financial statements that fail to portray the underlying economic position and operations of the company.

Not all forms of window dressing require action by the auditors. Many companies make strenuous efforts at year-end to achieve an improved financial picture by rushing shipments to customers, by pressing for collection of receivables, and sometimes by paying liabilities down to an unusually low level. Such efforts to improve the financial picture to be reported are not improper. Before giving approval to the balance sheet presentation of cash, the auditors must exercise their professional judgment to determine whether the client has engaged in window dressing of a nature that causes the financial statements to be misleading.

Interim audit work on cash

To avoid a concentration of audit work shortly after the year-end, CPA firms try to complete as many auditing procedures as possible on an interim basis during the year. The study and evaluation of internal control over cash, for example, can be performed in advance of the client's year-end. The audit work on cash at year-end can then be limited to such substantive tests as a review of the client's bank reconciliation, confirmation of year-end bank balances, investigation of the year-end cutoff, and a general review of cash transactions during the interval between the interim work on cash and the end of the period.

MARKETABLE SECURITIES

The most important group of investments, from the viewpoint of the auditor, consists of stocks and bonds, because they are found more frequently and usually are of greater dollar value than other kinds of investment holdings. Bank certificates of deposit, commercial paper issued by corporations, mortgages and trust deeds, and the cash surrender value of life insurance policies are other types of investments often encountered.

Investment of temporarily idle cash in selected types of marketable securities is an element of good financial management. Such holdings are regarded as a secondary cash reserve, capable of quick conversion to cash at any time, although producing a steady, but modest, rate of return. Management may also choose to maintain some investments in marketable securities on a semipermanent basis. The length of time such investments are held may be determined by the trend of the securities markets and by the company's income tax position, as well as by its cash requirements. Investments in securities may also exist for the purpose of maintaining control or influence over affiliated companies.

The auditors' objectives in examination of marketable securities

In the examination of investments in securities, the auditors attempt to determine that adequate internal control exists over the securities and the revenue from these investments. Other objectives include determining that the securities actually exist and are the property of the client, are fairly valued in accordance with generally accepted accounting principles, and are properly classified on the balance sheet. In addition to these objectives, the auditors' work is intended to determine that all revenue arising from the investments has been promptly collected and recorded. The verification of securities, therefore, may be considered as including the analysis of such related accounts as dividend revenue, interest earned, accrued interest, dividends receivable, and gain and loss on sale of securities. If the audit engagement includes the preparation of income tax returns, the procedures may be extended to obtain all necessary information, such as the dates of transactions and the tax basis of securities.

Internal control for marketable securities.

The major elements of an adequate system of internal control over marketable securities include the following:

1. Separation of duties between the executive authorizing purchase and sales of securities, the custodian of the securities, and the person maintaining the record of investments.
2. Complete detailed records of all securities owned, and the related revenue from interest and dividends.
3. Registration of securities in the name of the company.
4. Periodic physical inspection of securities by an internal auditor or an official having no responsibility for the authorization, custody, or record keeping of investments.

In many concerns, segregation of the functions of custody and record keeping is achieved by the use of an independent safekeeping agent, such as a stockbroker, bank, or trust company. Since the independent agent has no direct contact with the employee responsible for maintaining accounting records of the investments in securities, the possibilities of concealing fraud through falsification of the accounts are greatly reduced. The risks of physical loss or destruction are also minimized because the independent agent generally has fireproof vaults and other facilities especially designed to safeguard valuable documents. If securities are not placed in the custody of an independent agent, they should be kept in a bank safe-deposit box under the joint control of two or more of the company's officials. *Joint control* means that neither of the two custodians may have access to the securities except in the presence of the other. A list of securities in the box should be maintained there, and the deposit or withdrawal of securities should be recorded on this list along with the date and signatures of all persons present. The safe-deposit box rental should be in the name of the company, not in the name of an officer having custody of securities.

Complete detailed records of all securities owned, and of any securities held for others, are essential to a satisfactory system of internal control. These records frequently consist of a subsidiary record for each security, with such identifying data as the exact name, face amount or par value, certificate number, number of shares, date of acquisition, name of broker, cost, and any interest or dividends payments received. The purchase and sale of securities often is entrusted to a responsible financial executive, subject to frequent review by an investment committee of the board of directors.

The auditors may occasionally find that securities owned by the client are registered in the name of an officer or other individual rather than in the name of the company. Immediate registration in the company's name at date of purchase is the preferred practice, since this reduces the likelihood of fraudulent transfer or unauthorized use of the securities as collateral. Some bonds are payable to *bearer* and cannot be registered in the name of the owner. The registration of securities should not be considered as a substitute for the other control procedures described.

An internal auditor or other responsible employee should at frequent intervals inspect the securities on hand, compare the serial numbers and other identifying data of the securities examined with the accounting records, and reconcile the subsidiary record for securities with the control account. This procedure supplements the internal control inherent in the segregation of the functions of authorization, record keeping, and custodianship.

Internal control questionnaire

A questionnaire used by the auditors in studying and evaluating internal controls relating to securities will include such questions as the following. Are securities and similar instruments under the joint control of responsible officials? Are all persons having access to securities properly bonded? Is an independent safekeeping agent retained? Are all purchases and sales of securities authorized by a financial executive and reviewed by an investment committee of the board of directors?

Audit program for securities

Listed below are procedures typically performed by auditors to achieve the objectives described earlier.

A. Study and evaluation of internal control for securities

1. Prepare a description of the internal control for securities.
2. Trace transactions for purchases and sales of securities through the system.
3. Review reports by internal auditors on their periodic inspection of securities.
4. Review monthly reports by officer of client company on securities owned, purchased, and sold, and revenue earned.
5. Evaluate internal control for securities.

B. Substantive tests of securities transactions and year-end balances

6. Obtain or prepare analyses of securities investment accounts and related revenue accounts.
7. Inspect securities on hand and compare serial numbers with those shown on previous examination.
8. Obtain confirmation of securities in the custody of others.
9. Verify purchases and sales of securities during the year and for a short period subsequent to the balance sheet date.
10. Verify gain or loss on sales of marketable securities and obtain information for income tax returns.
11. Make an independent computation of revenue from securities by reference to dividend record books or other primary sources.
12. Investigate method of accounting for investments in subsidiary companies and investees other than subsidiaries.
13. Determine market value of securities at date of balance sheet.
14. Determine financial statement presentation for securities.

Audit procedures and working papers

The audit working papers describing the system of internal control may include a flowchart, questionnaire, or a written narrative. Next, selected transactions for purchase or sale of securities will be traced through the system to verify that the controls are being followed in actual practice. For example, a purchase of securities should be approved in minutes of the meetings of the investment committee, and documents from the stockbrokerage firm should show receipt of the order and its execution. Other evidence will be the broker's month-end statement, the stock certificate acquired, the entry in the subsidiary ledger for securities, and the monthly report of the treasurer showing all purchases, sales, current holdings, and revenue received from investments.

In large companies, the internal auditors may make surprise counts of all company-owned securities held in a bank safe-deposit box or other location. The independent auditors may reconcile the listing of securities at a given date as prepared by the internal auditors with the subsidiary ledger for securities and with the CPA firm's own working papers from the preceding year's audit.

A written monthly report of security transactions can be a valuable internal control device. In many companies the treasurer will submit to the investment committee of the board of directors a monthly report showing securities owned at the beginning of the month, all purchases, sales, gains, and losses during the month, the dividends and interest received, and the month-end holdings. Such reports are important evidence to the auditors in evaluating internal control.

An audit working paper may be prepared by analyzing changes in the securities investment account during the year. The beginning balances should agree with those in the working papers for the prior year's audit. If changes during the year are verified by reference to appropriate documents and controls, the ending balances should be valid. Gains and losses for the year as well as interest and dividends received may be listed on the same worksheet.

The auditors will count the securities owned by the client at year-end and compare the serial numbers on the certificates with those shown on previous examinations. This step *proves the existence and ownership of the securities.* The count ideally is made at the balance sheet date concurrently with the count of cash and other negotiable assets. If the securities are kept in a bank safe-deposit box, the client may instruct the bank in writing on the balance sheet date that no one is to have access to the box unless accompanied by the auditors. This arrangement makes it possible to count the securities at a more convenient time after the balance sheet date. The auditors should insist that a representative of the client be present throughout the count of the securities. To expedite the counting process, the auditors should have available a complete list of securities so that securities can quickly be checked off as counted.

Some client-owned securities may be in the hands of brokers or banks for transfer or safekeeping. In such cases a client-prepared confirmation request should be sent *by the auditors* directly to the holders and the reply mailed directly to the auditors' office in a self-addressed return envelope. A confirmation letter from a reliable financial institution independent of the client is an alternative to a firsthand inspection of securities.

In addition to vouching all changes in the investment account during the year to ***brokers' advices and statements*** and cash records, the auditors should review securities transactions for two or three weeks ***after*** the balance sheet date. The purpose is to assure that a correct cutoff of transactions was made. Sometimes sales occur shortly before the balance sheet date but go unrecorded until delivered to the broker early in the next period.

The auditors can make an independent computation of dividends that should have been received and recorded by referring to dividend record books published by investment advisory services. These books show dividend declarations, amounts, and payment dates for all listed stocks. Interest earned on bonds and notes also can be computed independently by the auditors and compared with recorded amounts in the client's records.

Current market quotations for all marketable securities owned by the client should be obtained by the auditors and included in the audit working papers. The presentation of marketable securities in financial statements is presently guided by *FASB Statement No. 12*, which requires use of the lower of the aggregate cost or market value determined at the balance sheet date.[1]

KEY TERMS INTRODUCED OR EMPHASIZED IN CHAPTER 11

Brokers' advice   A notification sent by a stockbrokerage firm to a customer reporting the terms of a purchase or sale of securities.

Certificate of deposit   A receipt issued by a bank for a deposit of funds for a specified time. Usually in denominations of $100,000 or more and bearing interest at a higher rate than for most bank savings accounts.

Check register   A journal used in a voucher system to record payment of vouchers. Since the cost distribution relating to voucher transactions is made in the voucher register, entries in the check register represent debits to Vouchers Payable and Credits to Cash.

Commercial paper   Unsecured short-term notes issued by most large corporations for periods of one year or less.

Confirmation letter (from bank)   Documentary evidence sent by the bank directly to the auditors confirming the client's bank account balances, outstanding loans, and other transactions involving the bank.

Confirmation request—securities   A letter prepared by the client and addressed to the broker, bank, or other holder of client-owned securities, requesting the holder to respond directly to the independent auditors giving full identification of the securities and the purpose for which held.

Control listing   A detailed listing of cash receipts that may be compared to entries in the accounting records and to bank deposits to assure that cash receipts remain intact as they pass through the system.

---

[1] *Statement of Financial Accounting Standards No. 12*, "Accounting for Certain Marketable Securities," Financial Accounting Standards Board (Stamford, Conn., 1975).

Cutoff bank statement A bank statement covering a specified number of business days (usually 7 to 10) after the client's balance sheet date. Auditors use this statement to determine that reconciling items shown on the year-bank reconciliation have cleared the bank within a reasonable time.

Dividend record book A reference book published monthly by investment advisory services reporting much detailed information concerning all listed and many unlisted securities. Includes dividend dates and amounts, current prices of securities, and other condensed financial data.

Kiting Manipulations causing an amount of cash to be included simultaneously in the balance of two or more bank accounts. Kiting schemes are based on the float period—the time necessary for a check deposited in one bank to clear the bank on which it was drawn.

Lockbox A post office box controlled by a company's bank at which cash remittances from customers are received. The bank picks up the remittances, immediately credits the cash to the company's bank account, and forwards the remittance advices to the company.

Proof of cash An audit procedure that reconciles the bank's record of cash activity with the client's accounting records for a test period. The working paper used for the proof of cash is a four-column bank reconciliation.

Remittance advice A document that accompanies cash remittances from customers identifying the customer and the amount of the remittance.

Voucher A document authorizing a cash disbursement. A voucher usually provides space for employees performing various approval functions to initial. (The term *voucher* may also be applied to the group of documents that support a cash disbursement.)

Voucher register A special journal used to record the liabilities for payment originating in a voucher system. The debit entries are the cost distribution of the transaction, and the credits are to Vouchers Payable. Every transaction recorded in a voucher register corresponds to a voucher authorizing future payment of cash.

Window dressing Action taken by the client shortly before the balance sheet date to improve the financial picture presented in the financial statements.

GROUP I: REVIEW QUESTIONS

11-1. The auditors' work on cash may include preparing a description of internal controls and the making of compliance tests. Which of these two steps should be performed first? What is the purpose of compliance tests?

11-2. Among the departments of J-R Company are a purchasing department, receiving department, accounting department, and finance department. If you were preparing a flowchart of a voucher system to be installed by the company, in which department would you show—

    a. The assemblying of the purchase order, receiving report, and vendor's invoice to determine that these documents are in agreement.

    b. The preparation of a check.

    c. The signing of a check.

    d. The mailing of a check to the payee.

    e. The perforation of the voucher and supporting documents.

11-3. What prevents the person who opens incoming mail from being able to abstract cash collections from customers?

11-4. Should an internal control questionnaire concerning cash receipts and disbursements be filled out for all audits? At what stage of an audit would you recommend use of the questionnaire?

11-5. An internal control questionnaire includes the following items. For each item, explain what is accomplished by the existence of the controls involved:

   a. Are each day's cash receipts deposited intact and without delay?

   b. If an imprest fund is represented by a bank account, has the bank been notified that no checks payable to the company should be accepted for deposit?

   c. Are payroll disbursements made from an imprest bank account restricted to that purpose?

   d. Are vouchers or other supporting documents stamped or perforated when checks are signed? (AICPA, adapted)

11-6. How can an auditor obtain assurance that cash receipts are being deposited intact?

11-7. Prepare a simple illustration of lapping of cash receipts, showing actual transactions and the cash receipts journal entries. (AICPA)

11-8. During the early months of the year, Joe Jones, the cashier in a small company was engaged in lapping operations, but he was able to restore the amount of cash borrowed by March 31 and refrained from any fraudulent acts after that date. Will the year-end audit probably disclose his lapping activities? Explain.

11-9. State one broad general objective of internal control over cash transactions for each of the following: cash receipts, cash disbursements, and cash balances.

11-10. In preparing a proof of cash, how does the auditor account for all checks issued during the test period?

11-11. An assistant auditor received the following instructions from her supervisor: "Here is a cutoff bank statement covering the first seven business days of January. Compare the paid checks returned with the statement and dated December 31 or earlier with the list of checks outstanding at December 31." What type of irregularity might this audit procedure bring to light? Explain.

11-12. During your audit of a small manufacturing firm, you find numerous checks of large amount drawn payable to the treasurer and charged to the Miscellaneous Expense account. Does this require any action by the auditor? Explain.

11-13. What information do CPAs request from a bank in the Standard Bank Confirmation Inquiry?

11-14. What action should be taken by the auditors when the count of cash on hand discloses a shortage?

11-15. "The auditors should send confirmation requests to all banks with which the client has had deposits during the year, even though some of these accounts have been closed prior to the balance sheet date." Do you agree? Explain.

11– 16. During your reconciliation of bank accounts in an audit, you find that a number of checks of small amount have been outstanding for more than a year. Does this situation call for any action by the auditor? Explain.

11– 17. Explain the objectives of each of the following audit procedures for cash:
  a. Obtain a cutoff bank statement subsequent to the balance sheet date.
  b. Compare paid checks returned with bank statement to list of outstanding checks in previous reconciliation.
  c. Trace all bank transfers during the last week of the audit year and the first week of the following year.
  d. Investigate any checks representing large or unusual payments to related parties.

11– 18. Explain two procedures by which auditors may verify the client's cutoff of cash receipts.

11– 19. What is the meaning of the term *window dressing* when used in connection with year-end financial statements? How might the term be related to the making of loans by a corporation to one or more of its executives?

11– 20. Under what conditions would CPAs accept a confirmation of the securities in the possession of a custodian in lieu of inspecting the securities themselves? (AICPA)

11– 21. What documents should be examined in verifying the purchases and sales of securities made during the year under audit?

11– 22. How can the auditors determine that all dividends applicable to marketable securities owned by the client have been received and recorded?

11– 23. What are the main objectives of the auditors in the examination of investments in securities?

11– 24. What information should be noted by the auditors during their inspection of securities on hand?

11– 25. Under what circumstances may securities owned by the client not be on hand at the balance sheet date?

11– 26. Are the auditors concerned with securities transactions subsequent to the balance sheet date? Explain.

11– 27. Assume that it is not possible for you to be present on the balance sheet date to inspect the securities owned by the client. What variation in audit procedures is appropriate if the inspection is not made until two weeks after the balance sheet date?

11– 28. One of your clients, which has never before invested in securities, recently acquired more than a million dollars in cash from the sale of real estate no longer used in operations. The president intends to invest this money in marketable securities until such time as the opportunity arises for advantageous acquisition of a new plant site. He asks you to enumerate the principal factors you would recommend to create a strong system of internal control over marketable securities.

GROUP II: QUESTIONS REQUIRING ANALYSIS

11–29. You are retained on October 1 by Wilson Manufacturing Company to perform an audit for the year ended December 31. Prior to the year-end you undertake a study of the new client's internal control over cash.

Virtually all of the cash receipts consist of checks received through the mail, but there is no prelisting of cash receipts before they are recorded in the accounts. You find that the incoming mail is opened either by the cashier or by the employee maintaining the accounts receivable subsidiary ledger, depending on which employee has time available. The controller stresses the necessity of flexibility in assignment of duties to the 20 employees comprising the office staff, in order to keep all employees busy and achieve maximum economy of operation.

Required:
a. Explain how prelisting of cash receipts strengthens internal control over cash.
b. List specific duties that should not be performed by an employee assigned to prelist the cash receipts in order to avoid any opportunity for that employee to conceal embezzlement of cash receipts. (AICPA, adapted)

11–30. Henry Mills is responsible for preparing checks, recording cash disbursements, and preparing bank reconciliations for Signet Corporation. While reconciling the October bank statement, Mills noticed that several checks totaling $937 had been outstanding for more than one year. Concluding that these checks would never be presented for payment, Mills prepared a check for $937 payable to himself, forged the treasurer's signature, and cashed the check. Mills made no entry in the accounts for this disbursement and attempted to conceal the theft by destroying the forged check and omitting the long-outstanding checks from subsequent bank reconciliations.

Required:
a. Identify the weaknesses in Signet Corporation's system of internal control.
b. Explain several audit procedures that might disclose the fraudulent disbursement.

11–31. Although the primary objective of an independent audit is not the discovery of fraud, the auditors in their work on cash take into consideration the high relative risk associated with this asset. One evidence of this attitude is evidenced by the CPA's alertness for signs of lapping.

Required:
a. Define *lapping.*
b. Explain the audit procedures that CPAs might utilize to uncover lapping.

11–32. During the examination of cash, the CPAs are alert for any indications of kiting.

Required:

a. Define *kiting.*

b. Explain the audit procedures that should enable the CPAs to uncover kiting.

11–33. Explain how each of the following items would appear in a four-column proof of cash for the month of November. Assume the format of the proof of cash begins with bank balances and ends with the unadjusted balances per the accounting records.

a. Outstanding checks at November 30.

b. Deposits-in-transit at October 31.

c. Check issued and paid in November, drawn payable to Cash.

d. The bank returned $1,800 in NSF checks deposited by the client in November; the client redeposited $1,450 of these checks in November and $350 in December, making no additional entries in the accounting records.

11–34. In the audit of a client with a fiscal year ending June 30, the CPAs obtain a July 10 bank statement directly from the bank. Explain how this cutoff bank statement will be used:

a. In the review of the June 30 bank reconciliation.

b. To obtain other audit information. (AICPA, adapted)

11–35. In the audit of Wheat, Inc., for the year ended December 31, you discover that the client had been drawing checks as creditors' invoices became due but had not been mailing the checks immediately. Because of a working capital shortage, some checks have been held for two or three weeks.

The client's controller informs you that unmailed checks totaling $48,500 were on hand at December 31 of the current year. He states that these December-dated checks had been entered in the cash disbursements journal and charged to the respective creditors' accounts in December because the checks were prenumbered. However, these checks were not actually mailed until early January. The controller wants to adjust the cash balance and accounts payable at December 31 by $48,500 because the Cash account had a credit balance. He objects to submitting to his bank your audit report showing an overdraft of cash.

Discuss the propriety of adjusting the cash balance and accounts payable by the indicated amount of outstanding checks.

11–36. Your are retained to audit the financial statements of John Brown, an individual with extensive investments in real estate and ranching. In reviewing the general ledger you notice an account entitled Davis Company, which has a debit balance of $150,000. Your investigation shows this to be the name of a local stockbrokerage firm with which your client had made a deposit for purchase of securities on margin. The only security transaction to date had been the purchase on December 10 of 3,000 shares of National Environmental Products at a price per share of $80. The brokerage fee on the transaction had been $1,566. No entry had been made for this purchase.

Give the adjusting entry or entries that you consider necessary for a proper presentation of these facts in the balance sheet at December 31.

11–37. Select the best answer for each of the following situations and give reasons for your choice.

    a. In the audit of a company with several bank accounts, which of the following audit techniques would be most effective in bringing to light any kiting activities by the client?

        (1) Review composition of authenticated deposit slips.

        (2) Review subsequent bank statements received directly from the banks.

        (3) Prepare a schedule of bank transfers.

        (4) Prepare year-end bank reconciliations.

    b. Which of the following is an internal control procedure that would prevent a paid voucher from being presented for payment a second time?

        (1) Vouchers should be prepared by individuals who are responsible for signing checks.

        (2) Vouchers should be approved by at least two responsible officials.

        (3) The date on a voucher should be within a few days of the date the voucher is presented for payment.

        (4) The official signing the check should compare the check with the voucher and should perforate or otherwise deface the voucher and supporting documents.

    c. In order to guard against the misappropriation of company-owned marketable securities, which of the following is the *best* course of action that can be taken by a company with a large portfolio of marketable securities?

        (1) Require that one trustworthy and bonded employee be responsible for access to the safekeeping area where securities are kept.

        (2) Require that employees who enter and leave the safekeeping area sign and record in a log the exact reason for their access.

        (3) Require that employees involved in the safekeeping function maintain a subsidiary control ledger for securities on a current basis.

        (4) Require that the safekeeping function for securities be assigned to a bank that will act as a custodial agent.

    d. Hall Company had large amounts of funds to invest on a temporary basis. The board of directors decided to purchase marketable securities and assigned the future purchase and sale decisions to a responsible financial executive. The best person(s) to make periodic reviews of the investment activity would be:

        (1) An investment committee of the board of directors.

        (2) The chief operating officer.

        (3) The corporate controller.

        (4) The treasurer.

GROUP III: PROBLEMS

11–38. The cashier of Mission Corporation intercepted customer A's check, payable to the company in the amount of $500 and deposited it in a bank account that was part of the company petty cash fund, of which he was custodian. He then drew a $500 check on the petty cash fund bank account payable to himself, signed it, and cashed it. At the end of the month, while processing the monthly statements to customers, he was able to change the statement to customer A to show that A had received credit for the $500 check that had been intercepted. Ten days later he made an entry in the cash receipts journal that purported to record receipt of a remittance of $500 from customer A, thus restoring A's account to its proper balance but overstating cash in bank. He covered the overstatement by omitting from the list of outstanding checks in the bank reconciliation two checks, the aggregate amount of which was $500.

Required:

Discuss briefly what you regard as the more important deficiencies in the system of internal control in the above situation and in addition include what you consider a proper remedy for each deficiency. (AICPA, adapted)

11–39. You are the senior in charge of the July 31, 198x audit of Reliable Auto Parts, Inc. Your newly hired staff assistant reports to you that she is unable to complete the four-column proof of cash for the month of April 198x, which you instructed her to do as part of the study of internal control for cash.

Your assistant shows you the following working paper that she has prepared:

RELIABLE AUTO PARTS, INC.
Proof of Cash for April 198x
July 31, 198x

	Balance 3/31/8x	Deposits	Checks	Balance 4/30/8x
Per bank statement	71,682.84	61,488.19	68,119.40	65,051.63
Deposits in transit				
At 3/31/8x	2,118.18			(2,118.18)
At 4/30/8x		4,918.16		4,918.16
Outstanding checks				
At 3/31/8x	(14,888.16)		14,888.16	
At 4/30/8x			(22,914.70)	22,914.70
Bank service charges				
March 198x	(22.18)		22.18	
April 198x			(19.14)	19.14
Note receivable collected by bank 4/30/8x		18,180.00		18,180.00
NSF check of customer L. G. Waite, charged back by bank 3/31/8x, redeposited and cleared 4/3/8x	(418.19)	418.19		
Balances as computed	58,472.49	85,004.54	60,095.90	108,965.45
Balances per books	59,353.23	45,689.98	76,148.98	28,894.23
Unlocated difference	(880.74)	39,314.56	(16,053.08)	80,071.22

Your review of your assistant's work reveals that the dollar amounts of all of the items in her working paper are correct. You learn that the accountant for Reliable Auto Parts, Inc., makes no journal entries for bank services charges or note collections until the month following the bank's recording of the item and that Reliable's accountant makes no journal entries whatsoever for NSF checks that are redeposited and cleared.

Required:

Prepare a corrected four-column proof of cash in good form for Reliable Auto Parts, Inc., for the month of April 198x.

11–40.   During the audit of Sunset Building Supply, you are given the following year-end bank reconciliation prepared by the client:

SUNSET BUILDING SUPPLY
Bank Reconciliation
December 31

Balance per 12/31 bank statement	$48,734
Add: Deposits in transit.......................................	4,467
	$53,201
Less: Checks outstanding	20,758
Balance per ledger, 12/31	$32,443

According to the client's accounting records, checks totaling $31,482 were issued between January 1 and January 14 of the following year. You have obtained a cutoff bank statement dated January 14 containing paid checks amounting to $50,440. Of the checks outstanding at December 31, $3,600 were not returned in the cutoff statement, and of those issued per the accounting records in January, $8,200 were not returned.

Required:

a.   Prepare a working paper comparing (1) the total of all checks returned by the bank or still outstanding with (1) the total per the client's records of checks outstanding at December 31 plus checks issued from January 1–14.

b.   Suggest four possible explanations for the situation disclosed in your working paper. State what action you would take in each case, including any adjusting entry you would propose.

11–41.   John Axton recently acquired the financial controlling interest of Pacific Imports, Inc., importers and distributors of cutlery. In his review of the duties of employees, Axton became aware of loose practices in the signing of checks and the operation of the petty cash fund.

You have been engaged as the company's CPA, and Axton's first request is that you suggest a system of sound practices for the signing of checks and the operation of the petty cash fund.

In addition to Axton, who is the company president, the company has 20 employees, including four corporate officers. About 200 checks are drawn each month. The petty cash fund has a working balance of about $200, and about $500 is expended by the fund each month.

Required:

Prepare a letter to Axton containing your recommendations for good internal control procedures for:

a. Signing checks. (Axton is unwilling to be drawn into routine check-signing duties.)

b. Operation of the petty cash fund. (Where the effect of the control procedure is not evident, give the reason for the procedure.) (AICPA)

11–42. In connection with the audit of Brookhurst Company for the year ended December 31, 198x you are given the following working paper prepared by an employee of the client:

BROOKHURST COMPANY
Bank Reconciliation
December 31, 198X

Balance per ledger, 12/31/8X		$51,524.58
Add:		
Deposit in transit, 12/31/8X		7,986.75
Debit memo for customer's check returned unpaid (check is on hand but no entry has been made on the books)		600.00
Bank service charge for December		6.50
		$60,417.83
Deduct:		
Outstanding checks, 12/31/8X (see detailed list below)	$6,803.25	
Credit memo for proceeds of a note receivable which had been left at the bank for collection but which has not been recorded as collected per books............................	1,190.00	
Check for an account payable entered on books as $722.70 but drawn by company and paid by bank as $1,257.00	534.30	8,527.55
Computed balance		$51,890.28
Unlocated difference		900.00
Balance per bank (agreed to confirmation).......		$50,990.28

adjust comp. record

should be added to book or deducted from bank balance

Outstanding checks, 12/31/8x

No.	Amount
573	$ 67.27
724	9.90
903	1,456.67
907	305.50
911	482.75
913	2,550.00
914	366.76
916	2,164.40
	$6,803.25

Required:

a. Prepare a corrected reconciliation for your working papers.

b. Prepare a journal entry for items that should be adjusted in the accounting records. (AICPA, adapted)

11–43. In connection with an examination of the financial statements of Morton, Inc., Jane Hill, CPA, is considering the necessity of inspecting marketable securities on the balance sheet date, May 31, or at some other date. The marketable securities held by Morton include negotiable bearer bonds, which are kept in a safe in the treasurer's office, and miscellaneous stocks and bonds kept in a safe deposit box at The

City Bank. Both the negotiable bearer bonds and the miscellaneous stocks and bonds are material to proper presentation of Morton's financial position.

Required:
   a. What are the factors that Hill should consider in determining the necessity for inspecting these securities on May 31, as opposed to other dates?
   b. Assume that Hill plans to send a member of her staff to Morton's offices and The City Bank on May 31 to make the security inspection. What instructions should she give to this staff member as to the conduct of the inspection and the evidence to be included in the audit working papers? (*Note:* Do not discuss the valuation of securities, the revenue from securities, or the examination of information contained in the accounting records of the company.)
   c. Assume that Hill finds it impracticable to send a member of her staff to Morton's offices and The City Bank on May 31. What alternative procedures may she employ to assure herself that the company had physical possession of its marketable securities on May 31, if the securities are inspected (1) May 28? (2) June 5? (AICPA, adapted)

11-44. A new client, Reyes Corporation, has retained you to audit its financial statements for the year ended June 30, 198x. On May 1, 198x, Reyes Corporation had borrowed $500,000 from Valley National Bank to finance plant expansion. The long-term note agreement provided for the annual payment of principal and interest over five years. The existing plant was pledged as security for the loan.

Because of unexpected difficulties in acquiring the building site, the plant expansion had not begun at June 30, 198x. To derive some revenue from the borrowed funds, management had decided to invest in stocks and bonds; and on May 16, 198x the $500,000 had been invested in marketable securities.

Required:
   a. How could you verify the securities owned by Reyes at June 30?
   b. In your audit of marketable securities, how would you—
      (1) Verify the dividend and interest revenue recorded?
      (2) Determine market value?
      (3) Establish the authority for securities purchases? (AICPA, adapted)

11-45. You are in charge of the audit of the financial statements of Hawk Corporation for the year ended December 31. The corporation has had the policy of investing its surplus cash in marketable securities. Its stock and bond certificates are kept in a safe-deposit box in a local bank. Only the president or the treasurer of the corporation has access to the box.

You were unable to obtain access to the safe-deposit box on December 31 because neither the president nor the treasurer was available. Arrangements were made for your staff assistant to accompany the treasurer to the bank on January 11 to examine the securities. Your assistant has never examined securities that were being kept in a safe-deposit box and requires instructions. To inspect all the securities on hand should not require more than one hour.

Required:

a. List the instructions that you would give to your assistant regarding the examination of the stock and bond certificates kept in the safe-deposit box. Include in your instructions the details of the securities to be examined and the reasons for examining these details.

b. Upon returning from the bank, your assistant reported that the treasurer had entered the box on January 4. The treasurer stated that the purpose of the January 4 visit to the safe-deposit box had been to remove an old photograph of the corporation's original building. The photograph was reportedly loaned to the local chamber of commerce for display purposes. List the additional audit procedures that are required because of the treasurer's action. (AICPA)

GROUP IV: CASE STUDIES IN AUDITING

11–46.   SUNCRAFT APPLIANCE CORPORATION

On October 21, Rand & Brink, a CPA firm, was retained by Suncraft Appliance Corporation to perform an audit for the year ended December 31. A month later James Minor, president of the corporation, invited the CPA firm's partners, George Rand and Alice Brink, to attend a meeting of all officers of the corporation. Mr. Minor opened the meeting with the following statement:

"All of you know that we are not in a very liquid position and our October 31 balance sheet shows it. We need to raise some outside capital in January, and our December 31 financial statements (both balance sheet and income statement) must look reasonably good if we're going to make a favorable impression upon lenders or investors. I want every officer of this company to do everything possible during the next month to ensure that, at December 31, our financial statements look as strong as possible, especially our current position, and our earnings."

"I have invited our auditors to attend this meeting so they will understand the reason for some year-end transactions that might be a little unusual. It is essential that our financial statements carry the auditors' approval, or we'll never be able to get the financing we need. Now what suggestions can you offer?"

The vice president for sales was first to offer suggestions: "I can talk some of our large customers into placing some orders in December that they wouldn't ordinarily place until the first part of next year. If we get those extra orders shipped, it will increase this year's earnings and also increase our current assets."

The vice president in charge of production commented: "We can ship every order we have now and every order we get during December before the close of business on December 31. We'll have to pay some overtime in our shipping department, but we'll try not to have a single unshipped order on hand at year-end. Also we could overship some orders, and the customers wouldn't make returns until January."

The controller spoke next: "If there are late December orders from customers that we can't actually ship, we can just label the merchandise as sold and bill the customers with December 31 sales invoices. Also, there are always some checks from customers dated December 31 that don't reach us until January—some as late as January 10. We can record all those customers' checks bearing dates of late December as part of our December 31 cash balance."

The treasurer offered the following suggestions: "I owe the company $50,000 on a call note I issued to buy some of our stock. I can borrow $50,000 from my mother-in-law about Christmas time and repay my note to the company. However, I'll have to borrow the money from the company again early in January, because my mother-in-law is buying an apartment building and will need the $50,000 back by January 15."

"Another thing we can do to improve our current ratio is to write checks on December 31 to pay most of our current liabilities. We might even wait to mail the checks for a few days or mail them to the wrong addresses. That will give time for the January cash receipts to cover the December 31 checks."

[handwritten margin note:] Can't take out of liability until you send them →

The vice president of production made two final suggestions: "Some of our inventory, which we had tentatively identified as obsolete, does not represent an open and shut case of being unsalable. We could defer any write-down until next year. Another item is some machinery we have ordered for delivery in December. We could instruct the manufacturer not to ship the machines and not to bill us before January."

After listening to these suggestions, the president, James Minor, spoke directly to Rand and Brink, the auditors. "You can see I'm doing my best to give you full information and cooperation. If any of these suggested actions would prevent you from giving a clean bill of health to our year-end statements, I want to know about it now so we can avoid doing anything that would keep you from issuing an unqualified audit report. I know you'll be doing a lot of preliminary work here before December 31, but I'd like for you not to bill us before January. Will you please give us your reactions to what has been said in this meeting?"

Required:

a. Put yourself in the role of Rand & Brink, CPAs, and evaluate *separately* each suggestion made in the meeting. What general term is applicable to most of the suggested actions?

b. Could you assure the client that an unqualified audit report would be issued if your recommendations were followed on all the matters discussed? Explain.

c. Would the discussion in this meeting cause you to withdraw from the engagement? Your answer on this point should be included as part of a statement to James Minor summarizing your firm's position as independent auditors.

12

Accounts and notes receivable; and sales transactions

The sales and collection cycle

Sales transactions and receivables from customers are so closely related that the two can best be considered jointly in a discussion of auditing objectives and procedures. In broad terms the sales and collection cycle embraces the receiving of orders from customers, the delivery and billing of merchandise to customers, and the recording and collection of accounts receivable. Receivables from customers include both accounts receivable and various types of notes receivable. One of the traditional objectives of the auditors in the verification of receivables has been to determine the genuineness of customers' accounts and notes. A good approach to this objective consists of a study and evaluation of the internal controls over the issuance of sales invoices, shipping documents, and other evidence of claims against customers. Before discussing internal control over sales and receivables, however, it is desirable first to consider the nature of the various claims that may be grouped under the classification of accounts and notes receivable and, second, to state the major objectives of the auditors in this phase of their examination.

Sources and nature of accounts receivable

Accounts receivable include not only claims against customers arising from the sale of goods or services, but also a variety of miscellaneous claims, such as advances to officers or employees, loans to subsidiaries, uncollected stock subscriptions, claims against railroads or other public carriers, claims for tax refunds, and advances to suppliers. Trade notes and accounts receivable should appear as a separate item in the current assets section of the balance sheet at their net realizable value. Other types of receivables may deserve separate listing if sufficiently material. If receivables have been pledged, disclosure of this fact is essential.

Some types of receivables do not qualify as current assets. Prominent among these are advances to officers, directors, and affiliated companies; such related party transactions are more commonly made for the convenience of the borrower rather than in the interest of the lending company, and presumably will be collected only at the convenience of the borrower. It is a basic tenet of statement presentation that transactions not characterized by arm's-length bargaining be fully publicized. Similar audit procedures are used in the verification of all types of receivables, although additional investigation may be required with respect to related party transactions—for example, loans to officers.

Sources and nature of notes receivable

Typically, notes and acceptances receivable are used for handling transactions of substantial amount; these negotiable documents are widely used by both industrial and commercial concerns. In banks and finance companies, notes receivable usually constitute the most important single asset.

An installment note or contract is a negotiable instrument that grants possession of the goods to the purchaser but permits the seller to retain title as collateral until the final installment under the note has been received. Installment notes are widely used in the sale of industrial machinery, farm equipment, tractors, and automobiles. Other transactions that may lead to the acquisition of notes receivable include the disposal of items of plant and equipment, the sale of divisions of a company, the issuance of capital stock, and the making of loans to officers, employees, and affiliated companies. Regardless of the type or source of the notes on hand, however, the auditors' objectives and procedures are sufficiently uniform that the following discussion is applicable to virtually all types of notes receivable.

The auditors' objectives in examination of receivables and sales

The principal objectives of the auditors in their examination of receivables and sales are to determine (1) the adequacy of internal control for sales transactions and receivables, (2) the validity or genuineness of the recorded receivables, (3) the approximate realizable value of this group of assets, and (4) the propriety of the amounts recorded as sales and as interest revenue.

Internal control of sales transactions and accounts receivable

Our discussion of internal control will be developed primarily in terms of the sales activities of manufacturing companies. When internal controls over sales on account are inadequate, large credit losses are almost inevitable. For example, merchandise may be shipped to customers whose credit standing has not been approved. Shipments may be made to customers without notice being given to the billing department—consequently no sales invoice is prepared. Sales invoices may contain errors in prices and quantities; and if sales invoices are not controlled by serial numbers, some may be lost and never recorded as accounts receivable. To avoid such difficulties, strong internal controls over credit sales are necessary. Usually internal control over credit sales is strengthened by a division of duties so that different departments or individuals are responsible for (1) preparation of the sales order, (2) credit approval, (3) issuance of merchandise from stock, (4) shipment, (5) billing, (6) invoice verification, (7) maintenance of control accounts, (8) maintenance of customers' ledgers, (9) approval of sales returns and allowances, and (10) authorization of write-offs of uncollectible accounts. When this degree of subdivision of duties is feasible, accidental errors are likely to be detected quickly through the comparison of documents and amounts emerging from independent units of the company, and the opportunity for fraud is reduced to a minimum.

Controlling customers' orders. The controlling and processing of orders received from customers require carefully designed operating procedures and numerous control devices if costly errors are to be avoided. Important initial steps include the registering of the customer's purchase order, a review of items and quantities to determine whether the order can be filled within a reasonable time, and the preparation of a sales order. The sales order is a translation of the terms of the customer's order into a set of specific instructions for the guidance of various divisions, including the credit, finished goods stores, shipping, billing and accounts receivable units. The action to be taken by the factory upon receipt of a sales order will depend upon whether the goods are standard products carried in stock or are to be produced to specifications set by the customer.

Credit approval. Before sales orders are processed, the credit department must determine whether goods may be shipped to the customer on open account. This department, supervised by a credit manager who reports to the treasurer or vice president of finance, monitors the financial condition of prospective and continuing customers by reference to the customers' periodic financial statements and published reports of credit agencies. For customers who do not meet standards for trade credit established by the finance committee of the board of directors, merchandise may be shipped on a cash-on-delivery (COD) basis.

Issuance of merchandise.   Companies that carry standard products in stock maintain a finished-goods storeroom supervised by a storeskeeper. The storeskeeper issues the goods covered by a sales order to the shipping department only after the sales order has been approved by the credit department. Perpetual inventory records of finished goods are maintained in the accounting department, not by the storeskeeper.

The shipping function.   When the goods are transmitted by the finished-goods storeroom to the shipping department, this group must arrange for space in railroad cars, aircraft, or motor freight carriers. Shipping documents, such as bills of lading, are created at the time of loading the goods into cars or trucks. The shipping documents are numerically controlled and are entered in a shipping register before being forwarded to the billing department. When shipments are made by truck, some type of gate control is also needed to ensure that all goods leaving the plant have been recorded as shipments. This may require the surrender to the gatekeeper of special copies of shipping documents.

The billing function.   Billing should be performed by a department not under the control of sales executives. The function is generally assigned to a separate section within the accounting, data processing, or finance departments. The billing section has the responsibility of (1) accounting for the serially numbered shipping documents, (2) comparing shipping documents with sales orders and customers' purchase orders and change notices, (3) entering pertinent data from these documents on the sales invoice, (4) applying prices and discounts from price lists to the invoice, (5) making the necessary extensions and footings, and (6) accumulating the total amounts billed. In the case of government contracts, the formal contract usually specifies prices, delivery procedures, inspection and acceptance routines, method of liquidating advances, and numerous other details, so that the contract is a most important source of information for preparation of the sales invoice.

Before invoices are mailed to customers, they should be reviewed to determine the propriety and accuracy of prices, credit terms, transportation charges, extensions, and footings. Daily totals of amounts invoiced should be transmitted directly to the general ledger accounting section for entry in control accounts. Copies of individual invoices should be transmitted to the accounts receivable section under control of transmittal letters, with a listing by serial number of all invoices being submitted.

In a company using an electronic data processing system, several of the billing and accounting processes described above are performed in a single processing run by the computer.

Collection of receivables.   As receivables are collected, the cashier will retain customers' remittance advices or prepare a comparable form, listing the credit to each customer's account. These remittance advices will then be forwarded to the accounts receivable section or the data processing department, which will record them in the appropriate accounts in the customers' ledger. The total reduction in accounts receivable will be posted periodically to the general ledger control account from the total of the accounts receivable column in the cash receipts journal. Credit memoranda will be handled in a parallel manner.

An *aged trial balance* of customers' accounts should be prepared at regular intervals for use by the credit department in carrying out its collection program. Under this system the general ledger and the subsidiary ledger for accounts receivable are developed from separate data by employees working independently of each other, thus assuring detection of nearly all accidental errors. Fraud becomes unlikely except in the event of collusion of two or more employees. The subsidiary ledger should be balanced periodically with the control account by an employee from the operations control group.

Write-off of receivables. Receivables judged by management to be uncollectible should be written off and transferred to a separate ledger and control account. This record may be of a memorandum nature rather than part of the regular accounting structure, but it is essential that the accounts that are written off be properly controlled. Otherwise any subsequent collections may be abstracted by employees without the necessity of any falsification of the records to conceal the theft.

Internal audit of receivables. In some large companies the internal auditors periodically take over the mailing of monthly statements to customers and investigate any discrepancies reported; or they may make extensive reviews of shipping reports, invoices, credit memoranda, and aged trial balances of receivables to determine whether authorized procedures are being carried out consistently.

The division of responsibility, sequence of procedures, and basic documentation of the handling of credit sales transactions are illustrated in the systems flowchart in Figure 12–1. Internal control over collections from customers is shown in the cash receipts systems flowchart in Figure 11–1 of Chapter 11.

Internal control of notes receivable

As previously stated, a basic element of internal control consists of the subdivision of duties. As applied to notes receivable, this principle requires that—

1. The custodian of notes receivable not have access to cash or to the general accounting records.
2. The acceptance and renewal of notes be authorized in writing by a responsible official who does not have custody of the notes.
3. The write-off of defaulted notes be approved in writing by respon-

sible officials, and effective procedures adopted for subsequent followup of such defaulted notes.

These rules are obviously corollaries of the general proposition that the authorization and recording functions should be entirely separate from the custodial function, especially for cash and receivables.

If the acceptance of a note from a customer requires written approval of a responsible official, the likelihood of fictitious notes being created to offset a theft of cash is materially reduced. The same review and approval should be required for renewal of a note; otherwise, an opportunity is created for the withholding of cash when a note is collected and the concealment of the shortage by unauthorized renewal of the paid note. The protection given by this procedure for executive approval of notes will be stronger if the internal auditing department periodically confirms notes directly with the makers.

The abstraction of cash receipts is sometimes concealed by failing to make any entry to record receipt of a partial payment on a note. Satisfactory control procedures for recording partial payments require that the date and amount of the payment and the new unpaid balance should be entered on the back of the instrument, with proper credit being given the debtor in the note register. Any notes written off as uncollectible should be kept under accounting control because occasionally debtors may attempt to reestablish their credit in later years by paying old dishonored notes. Any credit memoranda or journal vouchers for partial payments, write-offs, or adjustment of disputed notes should be authorized by proper officials and kept under numerical control.

Adequate internal controls over notes receivable secured by mortgages and trust deeds must include followup procedures that assure prompt action on delinquent property taxes and insurance premiums, as well as for nonpayment of interest and principal installments.

In many companies internal control is strengthened by the preparation of monthly reports summarizing note receivable transactions during the month and the details of notes owned at the end of the reporting period. These reports are often designed to focus executive attention immediately upon any delinquent notes and to require advance approval for renewals of maturing notes. In addition, a monthly report on notes receivable ordinarily will show the amounts collected during the month, the new notes accepted, notes discounted, and interest earned. The person responsible for reporting on note transactions should be someone other than the custodian of the notes.

Internal control and the computer

EDP systems permit sales and accounts receivable transactions to be processed by either a batch or an on-line, real-time system. Batch system

Figure 12–1

DIXIELINE INDUSTRIES LTD.
CREDIT SALES SYSTEMS FLOWCHART
DECEMBER 31, 198X

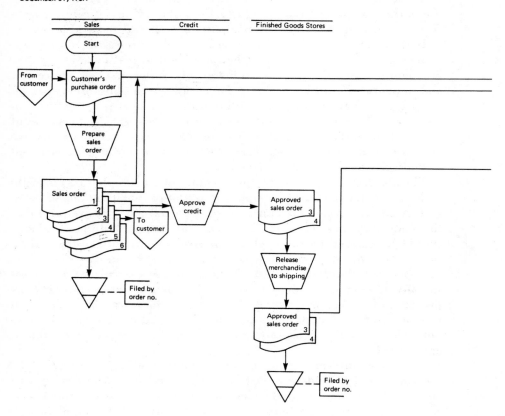

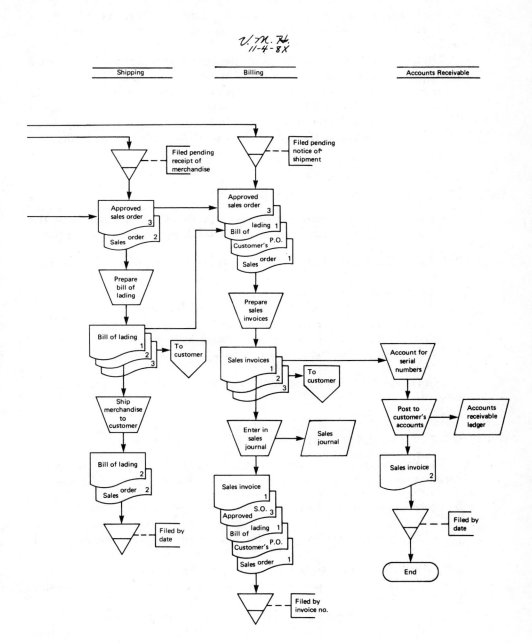

printouts usually include a daily sales journal (including sales returns and allowances) and a daily updated accounts receivable trial balance that reflects cash receipts and other accounts receivable transactions as well as sales.

The principal on-line, real-time printouts constitute a log of sales transactions in order of acceptance by the computer and a daily transactions journal for each computer terminal. In either situation, the traditional segregation of employee functions for sales and receivables is absent, and the auditors must study the internal control over EDP operations in appraising the internal control for sales transactions and receivables.

Audit working papers for receivables and sales

Besides preparing grouping sheets for receivables and net sales, the auditors obtain or prepare the following working papers, among others:

1. Aged trial balance of trade accounts receivable (often a computer printout).
2. Analyses of other accounts receivable.
3. Analysis of notes receivable and related interest.
4. Analysis of allowance for uncollectible accounts and notes.
5. Comparative analyses of sales transactions by month, by product or territory, or relating forecasted sales to actual sales.

Figure 12–2 illustrates an aged trial balance of trade accounts receivable.

AUDIT PROGRAM FOR RECEIVABLES AND SALES TRANSACTIONS

The following audit procedures are typical of the work done in the verification of notes and accounts receivable and sales transactions.

A. **Study and evaluation of internal control for receivables and sales**
    1. Obtain description of internal control for receivables and sales.
    2. Examine all aspects of a sample of sales invoices.
    3. Compare a sample of shipping documents to related sales invoices.
    4. Review the use and authorization of credit memoranda.
    5. Reconcile selected cash register tapes and sales tickets with sales journals.
    6. Review and confirm accounts and notes written off as uncollectible.
    7. Evaluate internal control for receivables and sales.

B.   Substantive tests of receivables and sales transactions

8.   Obtain or prepare an aged trial balance of trade accounts receivable and analyses of other accounts receivable.

9.   Obtain or prepare an analysis of notes receivable and related interest.

10.   Confirm accounts and notes receivable by direct communication with debtors.

11.   Inspect notes on hand and confirm those not on hand by direct communication with holders.

12.   Determine adequacy of allowance for uncollectible accounts and notes.

13.   Review the year-end cutoff of sales transactions.

14.   Verify interest earned on notes and accrued interest receivable.

15.   Ascertain whether any receivables have been pledged.

16.   Investigate fully any notes or accounts receivable from related parties.

17.   Obtain from client a letter of representations concerning notes and accounts receivable.

A.   Study and evaluation:

1.   Obtain description of internal control for receivables and sales.

The auditors' study and evaluation of internal controls over receivables and sales may begin with the preparation of a written description or flowchart or the filling in of an internal control questionnaire. Typical of the questions comprising an internal control questionnaire for receivables and sales are the following: Are orders from customers recorded and reviewed by a sales department? Are sales invoices prenumbered and all numbers accounted for? Are all sales approved by the credit department before shipment? The questionnaire should be viewed as an enumeration of matters to be investigated, rather than as questions to be disposed of with "yes" or "no" answers.

2.   Examine all aspects of a sample of sales invoices.

To determine that the internal controls portrayed in the flowchart are actually functioning in everyday operations, the auditors will select a sample of sales transactions for detailed compliance testing. The size of the sample and the transactions included therein may be determined by either statistical sampling or judgment sampling techniques. A generalized computer audit program is often used to select the invoices to be tested. To prove the extent of compliance with internal controls supposedly in force, the auditors should examine every aspect of the selected group of sales transactions.

In manufacturing companies the audit procedure for verification of a sales transaction that has been selected for compliance testing may begin with a comparison of the customer's purchase order, the client's sales order, and the duplicate copy of the sales invoice. The descriptions of items and the quantities are compared on these three documents and traced to the duplicate copy of the related shipping document. The credit manager's signature denoting approval of the customer's credit should appear on the sales order.

The extensions and footings on each invoice in the sample should be proved to be arithmetically correct. In addition, the date of each invoice should be compared with two other dates:

a. The date on the related shipping document, and
b. The date of entry in the accounts receivable subsidiary ledger.

Prices on the invoices can be verified by comparison with price lists, catalogs, or other sources used in preparing invoices. If a block sample of invoices covering transactions of a week or a month has been selected, the sequence of invoice serial numbers should also be reviewed for any missing numbers. Bills of lading and freight bills may also be compared with invoices as a further test of validity of the invoices.

After proving the accuracy of selected individual invoices, the auditors next trace the invoices to the sales journal. The footing of the sales journal is proven, and the total is traced to the general ledger account for sales.

In summary, this process of testing consists of tracing each selected transaction through the system from the receipt of the customer's order to the shipment of the goods and the subsequent collection of the account receivable. Testing in the opposite direction may also be used; for example, entries in the sales journal may be selected for vouching to supporting invoices, customer purchase orders, and shipping documents. By these tests, the auditors should obtain evidence that all sales are being accurately and promptly billed, that billings do not include any anticipated sales or extraneous transactions, and that the amounts billed are accurately and promptly recorded in customers' ledgers and in control accounts. If these conditions prevail, the auditors are entitled to rely upon the charges appearing in customers' accounts.

During their compliance tests of sales transactions, the auditors should be alert for indications of consignment shipments treated as sales. Many concerns that dispose of only a small portion of their total output by consignment shipments fail to make any distinction between consignment shipments and regular sales.

If the subsidiary records for receivables include some accounts with large debit entries and more numerous small credit entries, this should suggest to the auditors that goods have been shipped on consignment and that payments are being received only as the consignee makes sales. Notations such as "Consignment shipment" or "On approval" are sometimes found in subsidiary ledgers or on the duplicate copies of sales invoices. Numerous large returns of merchandise are also suggestive of consignment shipments.

A clearly defined company policy with respect to *cash discounts on sales* is a necessary element of good internal control over sales transactions. After discussing the policy with management, the auditors will scan the cash receipts journal to observe any deviations from established rates.

Another approach in reviewing the propriety of recorded cash discounts is to analyze by months the dollar amount of collections on receivables, the dollar amount of cash discounts allowed, and the percentage relationship of discounts to collections. Any significant variations should be fully investigated. Comparison, period by period, of the ratio of cash discounts to net credit sales is also a useful step in bringing to light variations of substantial amount.

The auditors should also investigate the controls for sales to related parties. Effective control over intercompany or interbranch transfers of merchandise often requires the same kind of formal procedures for billing, shipping, and collection functions as for sales to outsiders; hence these movements of merchandise are often invoiced and recorded as sales. When the operations of the several organizational units are combined or consolidated into one income statement, however, it is apparent that any transactions not representing sales to outsiders should be eliminated from consolidated sales. In the examination of a client that operates subsidiaries or branches, the auditors should investigate the procedures for recording movements of merchandise between the various units of the company.

3. Compare a sample of shipping documents to related sales invoices.

The preceding step in the audit program called for an examination of selected invoices and a comparison of such invoices with sales records and shipping documents. That procedure would not, however, disclose orders that had been shipped but not billed. To assure that all shipments are billed, it is necessary for the auditors to obtain a sample of shipping documents issued during the year and to compare these to sales invoices. In making this compliance test, particular emphasis should be placed upon accounting for all shipping documents by serial number. Any voided shipping documents should have been mutilated and retained in the files. The purposeful or accidental destruction of shipping documents before the creation of a sales invoice might go undetected if this type of test were not made. Correlation of serial numbers of sales orders, shipping advices, and sales invoices is highly desirable.

4. Review the use and authorization of credit memoranda.

All allowances to customers for returned or defective merchandise should be supported by serially numbered credit memoranda signed by an officer or responsible employee having no duties relating to cash handling or to the maintenance of customers' ledgers. Good internal control over credits for returned merchandise usually includes a requirement that the returned goods be received and examined before credit is given. The credit memoranda should then bear the date and serial number of the receiving report on the return shipment.

In addition to establishing that credit memoranda were properly authorized, the auditors should make tests of these documents similar to those suggested for sales invoices. Prices, extensions, and footings should be verified, and postings traced from the sales return journal or other accounting record to the customers' accounts in the subsidiary receivable ledgers.

5. **Reconcile selected cash register tapes and sales tickets with sales journals.**

In the audit of clients that make a substantial amount of sales for cash, the auditors may compare selected daily totals in the sales journal with cash register readings or tapes. The serial numbers of all sales tickets used during the selected periods should be accounted for and the individual tickets examined for accuracy of calculations and traced to the sale summary or journal.

6. **Review and confirm accounts and notes written off as uncollectible.**

If any accounts or notes receivable of significant amount were written off as uncollectible during the year, the auditors should determine that these write-offs were properly authorized. In the absence of proper authorization procedures, a dishonest employee could conceal permanently a theft of cash merely by a charge to accounts or notes receivable followed by a write-off of that asset.

A systematic review of the notes and accounts written off can conveniently be made by obtaining or preparing an analysis of the Allowance for Doubtful Accounts and Notes. Debits to the allowance may be traced to the authorizing documents and to the control record of accounts and notes written off; confirmation requests should be mailed to these debtors to determine that the account or note was genuine when it was first recorded in the accounts. Credit entries should be compared with the charges to Uncollectible Accounts and Notes Expense. Any write-off that appears unreasonable should be fully investigated. Charge-off of a note or account receivable from an officer, stockholder, or director is unreasonable on its face and warrants the most searching investigation by the auditors. The computation of percentages relating the year's write-offs to net credit sales, to the provision for uncollectible accounts and notes, and to the allowance for doubtful accounts and notes may be useful in bringing to light any abnormal write-offs.

7. **Evaluate internal control for receivables and sales.**

After completion of the description of internal control for receivables and sales, and the compliance tests of sales transactions, the auditors will have accumulated sufficient evidence to evaluate internal control for receivables and sales. In their evaluation, the auditors will identify those weaknesses that require extension of auditing procedures and those strengths that permit curtailment of procedures. The evaluation is thus closely integrated with the audit program for substantive tests of receivables and sales transactions.

B. Substantive tests:

8. Obtain or prepare an aged trial balance of trade accounts receivable and analyses of other accounts receivable.

An aged trial balance of trade accounts receivable at the audit date is commonly prepared for the auditors by employees of the client, often in the form of a computer printout. The client-prepared schedule illustrated in Figure 12–2 is a multipurpose form designed for the aging of

Figure 12–2

The Coast Company
Accounts Receivable—Trade
December 31, 198X

Acct. No. 121 G-1

Confirmation No.	Customer		Balance 12/31/8X	Billed In: December	November	October	Prior Months	Credit Balances	Collections Subsequent to 12/31/8X	Estimated Loss Acct. No. 125
1	Adams & Sons	cx	8255.60 y	7921.60 λ		334.00 λ			7921.60	334.00
2	Baker Company, Inc.	c	205.00 y		205.00 λ				205.00	
3	Cross Mfg. Co., Inc.	c	7310.20 y	1500.20 λ	1210.00 λ	500.00	4100.00 λ		4100.00	
	Douglas Supply Co.		22.00 y				22.00			22.00
4	Elastic Mfg. Co., Inc.	c	1250.00 y	1250.00 λ					1250.00	
	J. R. Farmer		3000.00 y	3000.00 λ						
64	Young Industries	cx	1825.00 y	1575.00 λ			250.00			912.50
	Zenith Co.		47.19 y	47.19 λ					47.19	
			78624.62	48801.67	21245.60	2875.20	6302.15	(600.00)		4100.00
	A.J.E. 12—Correct J.R. Farmer G-2		(3000.00)	(3000.00)						
			75624.62 √ u	45801.67 u	21245.60 u	2875.20 u	6302.15 u	(600.00)		4100.00 u
			G							G

A.J.E. 12		
Accounts Receivable—Officers	3000.00	
Accounts Receivable—Trade		3000.00
Correct classification of account receivable from J. R. Farmer, President.		

Prepared by client

u = Footed and cross-footed
√ – Agreed to general ledger } no differences noted.
y = Traced to accounts receivable subsidiary ledger
λ = Verified aging.
c = Confirmed; no exceptions.
cx = Confirmed with exceptions. See G-1-1.

See audit program (B-2) for extent of confirmation and other auditing procedures.

Conclusion:
The results of the confirmation and other tests described in the audit program (B-2) provide sufficient competent evidence of the genuineness of trade accounts receivable in the aggregate amount of $75,624.62.

V.N.H.
1/20/8–

customers' accounts, the estimating of probable credit losses, and the controlling of confirmation requests. The inclusion of so many phases of the examination of receivables in a single working paper is practicable only for small concerns with a limited number of customers.

The auditors also should obtain from the client analyses of any accounts receivable other than trade accounts. These analyses are needed because nontrade receivables may have arisen from transactions between *related parties,* rather than from transactions at arms'-length. Transactions between related parties require more than ordinary attention from the auditors. The nature of the transactions and the propriety of credits to the accounts should be studied.

When trial balances or analyses of accounts receivable are furnished to the auditors by the client's employees, some independent verification of the listing is essential. Determination of the proper extent of testing should be made in relation to the adequacy of the internal controls over receivables. The auditors should test footings, crossfootings and agings. In testing the aging, it is important to test some accounts classified as current, as well as those shown as past due. These selected individuals should be traced to the subsidiary ledgers. The totals of schedules prepared by client personnel should also be compared with related controlling accounts. In addition, the balances of the subsidiary ledger records should be verified by footing the debit and credit columns on a test basis. Generalized computer audit programs may be used to perform these tests when the client's accounts receivable are processed by an electronic data processing system.

9. Obtain or prepare an analysis of notes receivable and related interest.

An analysis of notes receivable supporting the general ledger control account may be prepared for the auditors by the client's staff. The information to be included in the analysis normally will include the name of the maker, date, maturity, amount, and interest rate. In addition to verifying the accuracy of the analysis prepared by the client, the auditors should trace selected items to the accounting records and to the notes themselves.

10. Confirm accounts and notes receivable by direct communication with debtors.

The term *confirmation* was defined in Chapter 7 as a type of documentary evidence secured from outside the client organization and transmitted directly to the auditors. Direct communication with debtors is the most essential and conclusive step in the verification of accounts and notes receivable. By confirming an account receivable, the auditors prove that the customer *exists.* Written acknowledgement of the debt by the debtor serves the dual purposes of (*a*) establishing the existence of the asset, and (*b*) providing some assurance that no lapping or other manipulations affecting receivables is being carried on at the balance sheet date. However, the confirmation of a receivable does not mean that it is collectible.

A better understanding of the emphasis placed on confirmation of receivables can be gained by a brief review of auditing history. Audit objectives and procedures were drastically revised in the late 1930s. Before that time the usual audit did not include procedures to assure that the receivables were genuine claims against existing companies or that inventories actually existed and had been accurately counted. For the auditors to confirm receivables (or to observe the taking of physical inventory) was considered too expensive and not particularly important. Auditors generally relied in that early era upon a written statement by management concerning the validity of receivables and the existence of inventories. This approach was drastically revised after some spectacular fraud cases involving millions of dollars in fictitious receivables and inventories showed the need for stronger audit evidence.

The following quotation from *SAS No. 1* summarizes the current status of the confirmation procedure.

> Confirmation of receivables . . . (is a) generally accepted auditing procedure. The independent auditor who issues an opinion when he has not employed . . . (confirmation) must bear in mind that he has the burden of justifying the opinion expressed.[1]

The circumstances of a particular audit engagement may make it impracticable or impossible for the auditors to confirm accounts receivable. If the auditors can satisfy themselves by using alternative procedures, the audit report need not mention the omission of the confirmation process.

An example of a situation in which it is impracticable or impossible to confirm receivables arises when sales are made to governmental agencies. The operating records and procedures of these agencies will not ordinarily enable them to confirm the amounts payable under government contracts and purchase orders. The auditors will, therefore, resort to alternative methods of verification—such as the examination of contracts, purchase orders, shipping documents, sales invoices, subsequent payments, and other similar evidence—to satisfy themselves that the receivable resulted from an actual order and shipment.

An important part of confirming notes and accounts receivable is determining the validity of the debtors' addresses. The auditors should investigate thoroughly if an excessive number of *individual* debtors have addresses that are post office boxes; the boxes may have been rented under fictitious debtors' names by employees of the client company engaged in accounts receivable fraud.

Illustrative case. In the Equity Funding Corporation of America fraud, fictitious receivables selected for confirmation by the auditors bore addresses of employees who were conspirators in the fraud. The fictitious confirmation requests were thus signed and returned to the auditors by the recipients.

---

[1] *Statement on Auditing Standards No. 1*, "Codification of Auditing Standards and Procedures," AICPA (New York, 1973), section 331, para. .01.

Figure 12–3
Positive form of accounts receivable confirmation request

Smith & Co.

1416 EIGHTEENTH STREET, LOS ANGELES, CALIFORNIA 90035

December 31, 198X

Martin, Inc.
6700 Holmes Street
Kansas City, Missouri 64735

Dear Sirs:

Please confirm directly to our auditors

ADAMS AND BARNES
Certified Public Accountants
1800 Avenue of the Stars
Los Angeles, California 90067

the correctness of the balance of your account payable to us as shown below and on the
enclosed statement at December 31, 198X. If the amount is not in agreement with your
records at that date, please provide any information which will aid our auditors in recording the
difference.

Your prompt return of this form in the enclosed stamped envelope is essential to the completion
of the auditors' examination of our financial statements and will be appreciatied.

Smith & Co.

By M. J. Crowley
(Controller)

THIS IS NOT A REQUEST FOR PAYMENT, BUT MERELY FOR
COMFIRMATION OF YOUR ACCOUNT.

— —

The statement of our account showing a balance of $24,689.00 due Smith & Co. at December 31,
198X is correct except as noted below.

Martin, Inc.

Date January 16, 198X   By Howard Martin

Exceptions: None

All requests for confirmation of notes and accounts receivable should be mailed in envelopes bearing the CPA firm's return address. A stamped or business reply envelope addressed to the office of the auditors should be enclosed with the request. The confirmation requests should be deposited personally by the auditors at the post office or in a government mailbox. These procedures are designed to prevent the client's employees from having any opportunity to alter or intercept a confirmation request or the customer's reply thereto. The entire process of confirming receivables will obviously contribute nothing toward the detection of overstated or fictitious accounts if the confirmation requests or replies from customers pass through the hands of the client. Requests returned as undeliverable by the post office may be of prime significance to the auditors and hence should be returned directly to their office.

Positive and negative confirmation requests. There are two methods of confirming receivables by direct communication with the debtor. In each type of communication, the *client* makes the formal request for confirmation although the auditors *control* the entire confirmation process.

The *positive method* consists of a request addressed to the debtor company asking it to confirm directly to the auditors the accuracy of the dollar amount shown on the confirmation request. The positive method calls for a reply in every case; the customer must state whether the balance shown is correct or incorrect. See Figure 12–3.

The *negative method* consists of a communication addressed to the debtor company asking it to advise the auditors *only* if the balance shown is incorrect. A negative confirmation request may be in the form of a letter or it may be made merely by applying a rubber stamp to the customer's regular monthly statement, or by attaching a gummed label bearing the words shown in Figure 12–4.

===== Figure 12–4
Negative form of accounts receivable confirmation request

Please examine this statement carefully. If it does not agree with your records, please report any differences to our auditors

    Adams and Barnes
    Certified Public Accountants
    1800 Avenue of the Stars
    Los Angeles, California 90064

A business reply envelope requiring no postage is enclosed for your convenience.

THIS IS NOT A REQUEST FOR PAYMENT

The greater reliability of the positive form of confirmation arises from the fact that the auditors are alerted to the need for further investigation if a reply is not received. When the negative form of confirmation is used, the lack of a reply from a given customer is interpreted as satisfactory evidence when in fact the customer may simply have ignored the confirmation request. The expense of sending negative confirmation requests is considerably less than for the positive form; thus, more customers can be contacted for the same cost.

The Auditing Standards Board of the AICPA has commented as follows on the positive and negative methods of confirming receivables:

> Because the use of the positive form results in either (a) the receipt of a response from the debtor constituting evidence regarding the debt or (b) the use of other procedures to provide evidence as to the validity and accuracy of significant nonresponding accounts, the use of the positive form is preferable when individual account balances are relatively large or when there is reason to believe that there may be a substantial number of accounts in dispute or with inaccuracies or irregularities. The negative form is useful particularly when internal control surrounding accounts receivable is considered to be effective, when a large number of small balances are involved, and when the auditor has no reason to believe the persons receiving the requests are unlikely to give them consideration. If the negative rather than the positive form of confirmation is used, the number of requests sent or the extent of the other auditing procedures applied to the receivable balance should normally be greater in order for the independent auditor to obtain the same degree of satisfaction with respect to the accounts receivable balance.
>
> In many situations a combination of the two forms may be appropriate, with the positive form used for large balances and the negative form for small balances.[2]

Size of sample. In the audit of companies with reasonably adequate systems of internal control, the confirmation process is limited to a sample of the accounts receivable. The sample should be sufficiently large to account for most of the dollar amount of the receivables, or it should be sufficiently representative to warrant the drawing of valid inferences about the entire population of receivables.

The size of the sample will vary with the materiality of accounts receivable in comparison with total assets. If accounts receivable are a relatively large asset, the size of the sample should be relatively large. The auditors' evaluation of the system of internal control is also a factor; weaknesses in internal control call for larger samples than when internal control is strong. The results of confirmation tests in prior years serve as another guide to the auditors in setting sample size; significant exceptions in prior years' confirmations signal the need for extensive

---

[2] *Statement on Auditing Standards No. 1* "Codification of Auditing Standards and Procedures," AICPA (New York, 1973), section 331, para. .05–.06.

confirmation of this year's receivables. Finally, the choice between the positive and negative forms of confirmation request influence the size of the sample. The number of confirmations is usually increased when the negative form is used.

In selecting the individual accounts to be confirmed, it is customary to include all customers with balances above a selected dollar amount and to select accounts on a random basis from the remaining receivables. Generalized computer audit programs are useful in stratifying computer-processed accounts receivable to facilitate the selection process described above.

Discrepancies in customers' replies. The auditors should resolve unusual or significant differences reported by customers; other exceptions may be turned over to employees of the client with the request that investigation be made and explanations furnished to the auditors. The majority of such reported discrepancies arise because of normal lags in the recording of cash receipts or sales transactions, or because of misunderstanding on the part of the customer company as to the date of the balance it is asked to confirm. Some replies may state that the balance listed is incorrect because it does not reflect recent cash payments; in such instances the auditors may wish to trace the reported payments to the cash records.

The percentage of replies to be expected for positive form confirmation requests will vary greatly according to the type of debtor. However, it is safe to say that replies to less than 50 or 60 percent of the dollar amount of confirmations requested would seldom, if ever, be considered satisfactory. Second and third requests, the latter usually by registered mail or telegram, are often found necessary to produce replies. When replies are not received on notes or accounts with substantial balances, the auditors should verify the existence, location, and credit standing of the debtor by reference to credit agencies or other sources independent of the client, as well as establish the authenticity of the underlying transactions by examination of supporting documents. Such documents include contracts, customer purchase orders, and copies of sales invoices and shipping advices.

Putting the confirmation process in perspective. When all expected replies to confirmation requests have been received, a summary should be prepared outlining the extent and nature of the confirmation program and the overall results obtained. Such a summary is a highly important part of the audit working papers.

After resolving all differences disclosed by confirming accounts receivable, the auditors are in a position to make a second more informed evaluation of the system of internal control. For example, if the number of significant errors exceeded what was anticipated from the auditors' original evaluation of internal control, the original evaluation was not valid. A new evaluation is necessary, and that may alter the remaining course of the audit.

The auditors face more than one type of risk in relying upon the confirmation process to form an opinion about the fairness of the accounts receivable as a whole. We have already recognized the risk that some accounts with erroneous balances may not be included in the sample confirmed, and also the risk that replies may not be received from some customers having erroneous balances. Finally, there is the risk that customers may routinely return confirmation requests without actually comparing the balance with their records. Such responses would give the auditors a false sense of security. Despite these risks, however, the confirming of accounts receivable provides valuable evidence and represents a most important part of the auditors' work.

It has sometimes been said that the best proof available to the auditors as to the validity of an account receivable is its collection during the course of their examination. But this statement requires qualification, as indicated by the following situation:

Illustrative case. During the first audit of a small manufacturing company the auditors sent confirmation requests to all customers whose accounts showed balances in excess of $1,000. Satisfactory replies were received from all but one account, which had a balance of approximately $10,000. A second confirmation request sent to this customer produced no response; but before the auditors could investigate further, they were informed by the cashier-accountant that the account had been paid in full. The auditors asked to examine the customer's check and the accompanying remittance advice, but were told that the check had been deposited and the remittance advice destroyed. Further questioning concerning transactions with this customer evoked such vague responses from the cashier-accountant that the auditors decided to discuss the account with the officers of the company. At this point the cashier-accountant confessed that the account in question was a fictitious one created to conceal a shortage and that to satisfy the auditors he had "collected" the account receivable by diverting current collections from other customers whose accounts had already been confirmed.

11.   Inspect notes on hand and confirm those not on hand by direct communication with holders.

The inspection of notes receivable on hand should be performed concurrently with the count of cash and securities to prevent the concealment of a shortage by substitution of cash for misappropriated negotiable instruments, or vice versa. Any securities held by the client as collateral for notes receivable should be inspected and listed at the same time. Complete control over all negotiable instruments should be maintained by the auditors until the count and inspection are completed.

Notes receivable owned by the client may be held by others at the time of the examination. Confirmation in writing from the *holder* of the note is considered as an acceptable alternative to inspection; it does not, however, eliminate the need for securing confirmation from the *maker* of the note. The confirmation letter sent to a bank, collection agency, secured creditor, or other holder should contain a request for verification of the name of the maker, the balance of the note, the interest rate, and the due date.

Confirmation of notes receivable discounted or pledged as collateral with banks is obtained in connection with the verification of cash on deposit, since the standard form of bank confirmation request includes specific inquiry on these matters.

Printed note forms are readily available at any bank; an unscrupulous officer or employee of the client company desiring to create a fictitious note could do so by obtaining a blank note form and filling in the amount, date, maturity, and signature. The relative ease of creating a forged or fictitious note suggests that physical inspection by the auditors represents a less significant and conclusive audit procedure in verification of notes receivable than for cash or securities.

12. Determine adequacy of allowance for doubtful accounts and notes.

If the balance sheet is to reflect fairly the financial position of the business, the receivables must be stated at net realizable value, that is, at face value less an adequate allowance for doubtful notes and accounts receivable. The measurement of income requires an impartial matching of revenue and related expenses. Since one of the expenses involved is the charge for uncollectible notes and accounts, the auditors' review of doubtful receivables should be looked upon as the verification of both income statement and balance sheet accounts.

As the audit approaches completion, considerable time will have elapsed since the balance sheet date. Consequently, many of the accounts receivable that were past due at the balance sheet date will have been collected; the others will be further past due. Thus the auditors have the advantage of hindsight in judging the collectibility of the receivables owned at the balance sheet date.

The auditors' best evidence of *collectibility* of accounts and notes receivable is payment in full by the debtors subsequent to the balance sheet date. The auditors should note in the working papers any such amounts received; in the illustrated trial balance of trade accounts receivable (Figure 12–2) a special column has been provided for this purpose. Since one of the auditors' objectives in the examination of notes and accounts receivable is the determination of their collectibility, it is highly important for the auditors to be aware of any collections on past-due accounts or matured notes during the period subsequent to the balance sheet date.

A note receivable, especially one obtained in settlement of a past-due account receivable, may involve as much credit risk as an account receivable. Provision for loss may reasonably be made for notes that have been repeatedly renewed, for installment notes on which payments have been late and irregular, for notes received in consequence of past-due accounts receivable, for defaulted notes, and for notes of companies known to be in financial difficulties. To appraise the collectibility of notes receivable, the auditors may investigate the credit standing of the makers of any large or doubtful notes. Reports from credit-rating agencies and financial statements from the makers of notes should be available in the client's credit department.

Evaluation of any collateral supplied by the makers of notes is another step in determining the collectibility of notes receivable. The auditors should determine current market value of securities held as collateral by the client by reference to market quotations or by inquiry from brokers. Attention of the client should be called to any cases in which the market value of the collateral is less than the note; the deficiency might have to be considered uncollectible.

To provide a basis for estimating the necessary size of the allowance for uncollectible accounts receivable, the auditors may take the following steps:

a. Examine the past-due accounts receivable listed in the aging schedule that have not been paid subsequent to the balance sheet date, noting such factors as the size and recency of payments, settlement of old balances, and whether recent sales are on a cash or a credit basis. The client's correspondence file may furnish much of this information.

b. Investigate the credit ratings for delinquent and unusually large accounts. An account with a single customer may represent a major portion of the total receivables.

c. Review confirmation exceptions for indication of amounts in dispute or other clues as to possible uncollectible accounts.

d. Summarize in a working paper those accounts considered to be doubtful of collection based on the preceding procedures. List customer names, doubtful amounts, and reasons considered doubtful.

e. Review with the credit manager the current status of each doubtful account, ascertaining the collection action taken and the opinion of the credit manager as to ultimate collectibility. Indicate on the doubtful accounts working paper the credit manager's opinion as to the collectible portion of each account listed, and provide for the estimated losses on accounts considered by the auditors to be uncollectible.

f. Compute ratios expressing the relationship of the valuation allowance to (1) accounts receivable, (2) net credit sales, and (3) accounts written off during the year, and compare to comparable ratios for prior years. Investigate any significant variations.

13. Review the year-end cutoff of sales transactions.

One of the more common methods of falsifying accounting records is to inflate the sales for the year by holding open the sales journal beyond the balance sheet date. Shipments made in the first part of January may be covered by sales invoices bearing a December date and included in December sales. The purpose of such misleading entries is to present a more favorable financial picture than actually exists. Since sales are frequently used as the base for computation of bonuses and commissions, an additional incentive for padding the Sales account is often present. A related abuse affecting accounts receivable is the practice of holding the cash journals open beyond the balance sheet date; auditing procedures designed to detect this practice were described in connection with the audit of cash transactions in Chapter 11.

To guard against errors in the cutoff of sales records (whether accidental or intentional), the auditors should compare the sales recorded several days before and after the balance sheet date with the duplicate sales invoices and shipping documents. The effectiveness of this step is largely dependent upon the degree of segregation of duties between the shipping, receiving, and billing functions. If warehousing, shipping, billing, and receiving are independently controlled, it is most unlikely that records in all these departments will be manipulated to disguise shipments of one period as sales of the preceding period. On the other hand, one individual who had control over both shipping records and billing documents could manipulate both sets of records if overstatement of the year's sales were attempted.

Fictitious sales, as well as predated shipments, are occasionally recorded at year-end as a means of "window dressing" the financial statements. The merchandise in question may even be shipped to customers without their prior knowledge, and subsequently returned. To guard against such manipulation, the auditors should review carefully all substantial sales returns following the balance sheet date that may apply to receivables originating in the year under audit. Consideration should be given to reflecting these returns in the current year's business by means of adjusting entries. Confirmation of accounts receivable, if made at the balance sheet date, should also serve to bring any large unauthorized shipments to the attention of the auditors.

14. Verify interest earned on notes and accrued interest receivable.

The most effective verification of the Interest Earned account consists of an **independent computation** by the auditors of the interest earned during the year on notes receivable. The working paper used to analyze notes receivable should show the interest rate and date of issuance of each note. The interest section of this working paper consists of four columns, which show for each note receivable owned during the year the following information:

a. Accrued interest receivable at the beginning of the year (taken from the preceding year's audit working papers).

b. Interest earned during the year (computed from the terms of the notes).

  c. Interest collected during the year (traced to cash receipts records).
  d. Accrued interest receivable at the end of the year (computed by the auditors).

These four columns comprise a self-balancing set. The beginning balance of accrued interest receivable (first column) plus the interest earned during the year (second column) and minus the interest collected (third column) should equal the accrued interest receivable at the end of the year (fourth column). The totals of the four columns should be crossfooted to ensure that they are in balance; in addition, the individual column totals should be traced to the balances in the general ledger.

If the interest earned for the year as computed by the auditors does not agree with interest earned as shown in the accounting records, the next step is an analysis of the ledger account. Any unaccounted-for credits in the Interest Earned account deserve particular attention because these credits may represent interest received on notes that have never been recorded.

Illustrative case.   In an examination of a company that held numerous notes receivable, the auditors made an independent computation of the interest earned during the year. The amount of interest earned shown by the accounting records was somewhat larger than the amount computed by the auditors. Careful analysis of entries in the Interest Earned account revealed one credit entry not related to any of the notes shown in the Notes Receivable account. Further investigation of this entry disclosed that a note had been obtained from a customer who was delinquent in paying his account receivable. The note receivable had not been recorded as an asset, but the account receivable that was replaced by the note had been written off as uncollectible.

Because of this situation the auditors made a thorough investigation of all accounts written off in recent years. Several of the former customers when contacted stated that they had been asked to sign demand notes for the balances owed and had been assured there would be no pressure for collection as long as interest was paid regularly. The existence of notes receivable totaling nearly a million dollars was brought to light; these notes were not recorded as assets and were not known to the officers of the client company. The note transactions had been arranged by a trusted employee who admitted having abstracted the interest payments received with the exception of one payment which, through oversight, he had permitted to be deposited and recorded as interest earned.

For financial institutions or other clients having numerous notes receivable, the auditors may verify interest computations on only a sample of the notes. In addition, they should test the reasonableness of total interest earned for the year by applying a weighted average rate of interest to the average balance of the Notes Receivable ledger account during the year.

  15. Ascertain whether any receivables have been pledged.

The auditors should inquire directly whether any notes or accounts receivable have been pledged or assigned. Evidence of the pledging of receivables may also be disclosed through the medium of bank confirmation requests, which specifically call for description of collateral securing bank loans. Analysis of the interest expense accounts may reflect charges from the pledging of receivables to finance companies.

Accounts receivable that have been pledged should be plainly labeled by stamping on the copy of the sales invoice a notice such as "Pledged to First National Bank under loan agreement of December 198x," and by inserting an identifying code in the accounts receivable records. Accounts labeled in this manner would be identified by the auditors in their initial review of receivables and confirmed by direct correspondence with the bank to which pledged. The auditors cannot, however, proceed on the assumption that all pledged receivables have been labeled to that effect, and they must be alert to detect any suggestions of an unrecorded pledging of accounts.

16. **Investigate fully any notes or accounts receivable from related parties.**

Loans by a corporation to its officers, directors, stockholders, or affiliates require particular attention from the auditors because these related party transactions are not the result of arm's-length bargaining by parties of opposing interests. Furthermore, such loans are often prohibited by state law or by the corporation's bylaws. It is somewhat difficult to reconcile substantial loans to insiders by a nonfinancial corporation with the avowed operating objectives of such an organization. The independent auditors have an obligation to stockholders, creditors, and others who rely upon audited statements to require disclosure of any self-dealing on the part of the management. It seems apparent that most loans to officers, directors, and stockholders are made for the convenience of the borrower rather than for the profit of the corporation. Because of the somewhat questionable character of such loans, they are sometimes paid off just before the balance sheet date and renewed shortly thereafter, in an effort to avoid disclosure in financial statements. Under these circumstances the renewed borrowing may be detected by the auditors through a scanning of notes and accounts receivable transactions subsequent to the balance sheet date.

17. **Obtain from client a letter of representations concerning notes and accounts receivable.**

The use of a letter of representations was described in Chapter 7. A single letter of representations may be obtained with sections for inventories, receivables, and so on; or separate ones may be obtained for different financial statement categories. The client's letter of representations is not a substitute for any auditing procedure and does not reduce the auditors' responsibility. However, it emphasizes to executives of the client company that primary responsibility for reliable financial statements rests with management rather than with the auditors. A letter of representations covering receivables follows:

With respect to your examination of the financial statements of _____ Company, I hereby make the following representations concerning accounts and notes receivable shown in the balance sheet at December 31, 19___, in the aggregate gross amount of $_____ .

1. All accounts and notes receivable represent valid claims against debtors for sales or other charges arising on or before December 31, 19___.

2. The accounts and notes receivable are unencumbered assets of the company.

3. Merchandise shipped on consignment has been identified as such in the records and is not included in accounts receivable.

4. All known uncollectible accounts and notes receivable have been written off.

5. The amount of $_____ provided for doubtful receivables is, in my judgment, sufficient to cover losses that may be sustained in realization of the notes and accounts receivable.

Signature of officer

Client company

Interim audit work on receivables and sales

Much of the audit work on receivables and sales can be performed one or two months before the balance sheet date. This interim work may consist of the study and evaluation of internal controls and, in some cases, the confirmation of accounts receivable as well. A decision to carry out the confirmation of receivables at an interim date rather than at year-end is justified only if internal controls for receivables are reasonably strong.

If interim audit work has been done on receivables and sales, the year-end audit work may be modified considerably. For example, if the confirmation of accounts receivable was performed at October 31, the year-end audit program would include preparation of a summary analysis of postings to the Accounts Receivable controlling account for the period from November 1 through December 31. This analysis would list the postings by month, showing the journal source of each. These postings would be traced to the respective journals, such as sales journal and cash receipts journal. The amounts of the postings would be compared with the amounts in preceding months and with the corresponding months in prior years. The purpose of this work is to bring to light any significant variations in receivables during the months between the interim audit work and the balance sheet date.

In addition to this analysis of the entries to the receivable accounts for the intervening period, the audit work at year-end would include obtaining the aging of the accounts receivable at December 31, confirmation of any large accounts in the year-end trial balance that are new or delinquent, and the usual investigation of the year-end cutoff of sales and cash receipts.

KEY TERMS INTRODUCED OR EMPHASIZED IN CHAPTER 12

Aged trial balance   A listing of individual customers' accounts classified by age. Serves as a preliminary step in estimating the collectibility of accounts receivable.

Confirmation   A type of documentary evidence that is created outside the client organization and transmitted directly to the auditors.

Consignment   A transfer of goods from the owner to another person who acts as the sales agent of the owner.

Interim audit work   Those audit procedures that can be performed before the balance sheet date. The purpose is to facilitate earlier issuance of the audit report.

Letter of representations   A written statement prepared by officers of the client company at the auditors' request making representations as to valuation and ownership of assets, disclosure of liabilities, and other aspects of the financial statements.

Negative confirmation   A confirmation request addressed to the debtor requesting a reply only if the balance shown on the monthly statement is incorrect.

Pledging of receivables   To assign to a bank, factor, finance company, or other lender an exclusive claim against accounts receivable as security for a debt. To hypothecate receivables without giving possession.

Positive confirmation   A confirmation request sent to the debtor asking it to confirm directly to the auditors the accuracy of the dollar amount shown on the request. Calls for a reply regardless of whether the amount is correct or incorrect.

GROUP I: REVIEW QUESTIONS

12–1.   Why should related party transactions, such as an advance by a corporation to its president, receive more than ordinary attention from independent auditors? Explain.

12–2.   Describe the role of the credit department in a manufacturing company.

12–3.   In selecting accounts receivable for confirmation, the auditors discover that the client company's records show the addresses of several individual customers to be post office boxes. What should be the auditors' reaction to this situation?

12–4.   Cite various procedures auditors employ that might lead to the detection of an inadequate allowance for doubtful accounts receivable. (AICPA, adapted)

12–5.   A CPA firm wishes to test the client's sales cutoff at June 30, 1984. Describe the steps that the auditors should include in this test. (AICPA, adapted)

12–6.   Several accounts receivable confirmations have been returned with the notation "verifications of vendors' statements are no longer possible because of our data processing system." What alternative auditing procedures could be used to verify these accounts receivable? (AICPA, adapted)

12–7. Explain the difference between a *customer's order* and a *sales order* as these terms might be used by a manufacturing company making sales on credit to customers in many cities.

12–8. The confirmation of accounts receivable is an important auditing procedure. Should the formal request for confirmation be made by the client or by the auditors? Should the return envelope be addressed to the client, to the auditors in care of the client, or to the auditors' office? Explain.

12–9. The controller of a new client operating a medium-size manufacturing business complains to you that he believes the company has sustained significant losses on several occasions because certain sales invoices were misplaced and never recorded as accounts receivable. What internal control procedure can you suggest to guard against such problems?

12–10. If you were preparing a credit sales system flowchart, what document would you show as—
   a. The source for posting debits to a customer's account in the accounts receivable ledger.
   b. Authorization to the finished goods stores to release merchandise to the shipping department.
   c. The source for preparing a sales order.

12–11. In the examination of credit memoranda covering allowances to customers for goods returned, how can the auditors ascertain whether the customer actually did return merchandise in each case in which accounts receivable were reduced?

12–12. Does the letter of representations obtained by the auditors from the client concerning accounts receivable usually include any representation as to collectibility? Explain.

12–13. What auditing procedures, if any, are necessary for notes receivable but are not required for accounts receivable?

12–14. During preliminary conversations with a new staff assistant you instruct her to send out confirmation requests for both accounts receivable and notes receivable. She asks whether the confirmation requests should go to the makers of the notes or to the holders of the notes in the case of notes that have been discounted. Give reasons for your answer.

12–15. In the examination of an automobile agency, you find that installment notes received from the purchasers of automobiles are promptly discounted with a bank. Would you consider it necessary to confirm these notes by a communication with the bank? With the makers? Explain.

12–16. Your review of notes receivable from officers, directors, stockholders, and affiliated companies discloses that several notes of small amount were written off to the allowance for uncollectible notes during the year. Have these transactions any special significance? Explain.

12–17. Worthington Corporation has requested you to conduct an audit so that it may support its application for a bank loan with audited financial statements. Worthington's president agrees that you shall have access to all records of the company and shall employ any audit procedures you deem necessary, except that you are not to communicate with customers. Under these circumstances will it be possible for you to issue an unqualified audit report? Explain.

12-18. Should short-term loans to officers and directors of a client company generally be shown on the balance sheet among the current assets? Explain.

12-19. Among specific procedures that contribute to good internal control over accounts receivable are (a) the approval of uncollectible account write-offs and credit memoranda by an executive and (b) the sending of monthly statements to all customers. State three other procedures conducive to strong internal control. (AICPA)

12-20. What additional auditing procedures should be undertaken in connection with the confirmation of accounts receivable where customers having substantial balances fail to reply after second request forms have been mailed directly to them? (AICPA, adapted)

12-21. In your first examination of Hydro Manufacturing Company, a manufacturer of outboard motors, you discover that an unusually large number of sales transactions were recorded just before the end of the fiscal year. What significance would you attach to this unusual volume?

12-22. In connection with a regular annual audit, what are the purposes of a review of sales returns and allowances subsequent to the balance sheet date? (AICPA, adapted)

12-23. An inexperienced clerk assigned to the preparation of sales invoices in a manufacturing company became confused as to the nature of certain articles being shipped, with the result that the prices used on the invoices were far less than called for in the company's price lists. What internal control procedures could be established to guard against such errors? Would errors of this type be disclosed in the normal audit by independent public accountants? Explain.

12-24. The accounts receivable section of the accounting department in Annandale Products Company maintains subsidiary ledgers that are posted from copies of the sales invoices transmitted daily from the billing department. How may the accounts receivable section be sure that it receives promptly a copy of each sales invoice prepared?

12-25. A company that ships goods to its customers must establish procedures to ensure that a sales invoice is prepared for every shipment. Describe procedures to meet this requirement.

GROUP II: QUESTIONS REQUIRING ANALYSIS

12-26. Tom Jones, CPA, is examining the financial statements of a manufacturing company with a significant amount of trade accounts receivable. Jones is satisfied that the accounts are properly summarized and classified, and are valued in accordance with generally accepted accounting principles. Jones plans to use accounts receivable confirmation requests to satisfy the third standard of field work as to trade accounts receivable.

Required:

    a. Identify and describe the two forms of accounts receivable confirmation requests and indicate what factors Jones should consider in determining when to use each.

    b. Assume Jones has received a satisfactory response to the confirmation requests. Describe how Jones could evaluate collectibility of the trade accounts receivable. (AICPA, adapted)

12–27.   In their work on accounts receivable and elsewhere in an audit, the independent auditors often make use of confirmations.

    a. What is an audit confirmation?

    b. What characteristics should an audit confirmation possess if a CPA firm is to consider it as valid evidence?

    c. Distinguish between a positive confirmation and a negative confirmation in the auditors' examination of accounts receivable.

    d. In confirming a client's accounts receivable, what characteristics should be present in the accounts if the CPA firm is to use negative confirmations? (AICPA, adapted)

12–28.   JoAnn Crane, the senior auditor-in-charge of examining the financial statements of Thorne Company, a small manufacturing company, was busy writing the audit report for another engagement. Accordingly, she sent Martin Joseph, a recently hired staff assistant of the CPA firm, to begin the audit of Thorne Company, with the suggestion that Joseph start with the accounts receivable. Using the preceding year's audit working papers for Thorne Company as a guide, Joseph prepared a trial balance of Thorne's trade accounts receivable, aged them, prepared and mailed positive confirmation requests, examined underlying documents plus other support for charges and credits to the Accounts Receivable ledger account, and performed such other work as he deemed necessary to assure the validity and collectibility of the accounts receivable. At the conclusion of Joseph's work, Crane traveled to Thorne Company to review Joseph's working papers. Crane found that Joseph had carefully followed the prior year audit working papers.

Required:

State how the three generally accepted auditing standards of field work were fulfilled, or were not fulfilled, in the audit of the accounts receivable of Thorne Company. (AICPA, adapted)

12–29.   Many CPAs consider determining the adequacy of the allowance for uncollectible accounts and notes to be the most difficult procedure of an audit. Do you agree? Explain.

12–30.   *a.* Why is confirmation of receivables a generally accepted auditing procedure where practicable and possible?

    b. What is the auditors' course of action when they discover that confirmation of a significant account receivable from an agency of the U.S. government is not practicable or possible?

12–31. *a.* What are the implications to the auditors if during their examination of accounts receivable some of a client's customers do not respond to the auditor's request for positive confirmation of their accounts receivable?

    b. What procedures should the auditors perform if there is no response to a second request for a positive confirmation? (AICPA, adapted)

12–32. You are conducting an annual audit of Granite Corporation, which has total assets of approximately $1 million and operates a wholesale merchandising business. The corporation is in good financial condition and maintains an adequate accounting system. Granite Corporation owns about 25 percent of the capital stock of Desert Sun, Inc., which operates a dude ranch. This investment is regarded as a permanent one and is accounted for by the equity method.

    During your examination of accounts and notes receivable, you develop the information shown below concerning three short-term notes receivable due in the near future. All three of these notes receivable were discounted by Granite Corporation with its bank shortly before the balance sheet date.

    (1) A 16 percent, 60-day note for $50,000 received from a customer of unquestioned financial standing.

    (2) A 15 percent, six-month note for $60,000 received from the affiliated company, Desert Sun, Inc. The affiliated company is operating profitably, but is presently in a weak cash position because of recent additions to buildings and equipment. The president of Granite Corporation intends to make an $80,000 advance with a five-year maturity to Desert Sun, Inc. The proposed advance will enable Desert Sun, Inc., to pay the existing 15 percent, $60,000 note at maturity and to meet certain other obligations.

    (3) A 14 percent, $20,000 note from a former key executive of Granite Corporation whose employment had been terminated because of chronic alcoholism and excessive gambling. The maker of the note is presently unemployed and without personal resources.

Required:

Describe the proper balance sheet presentation with respect to these discounted notes receivable. Use a separate paragraph for each of the three notes, and state any assumptions you consider necessary.

12–33. You are considering using the services of a reputable outside mailing service for the confirmation of accounts receivable balances. The service would prepare and mail the confirmation requests and remove the returned confirmations from the envelopes and give them directly to you.

    What reliance, if any, could you place on the services of the outside mailing service? Discuss and state the reasons in support of your answer. (AICPA)

12–34. An assistant auditor was instructed to "test the aging of accounts receivable as shown on the trial balance prepared by the client." In making this test, the assistant traced all past-due accounts shown on the trial balance to the ledger cards in the accounts receivable subsidiary ledger and recomputed the aging of these accounts. The assistant found no discrepancies and reported to the senior auditor that the aging work performed by the client was satisfactory.

Comment on the logic and adequacy of this test of the aging of accounts receivable.

12–35. During your annual examination of the financial statements of Wilshire Corporation, you undertook the confirmation of accounts receivable, using the positive form of confirmation request. Satisfactory replies were received from all but one of the large accounts. You sent a second and third request to this customer, but received no reply. At this point an employee of the client company informed you that a check had been received for the full amount of the receivable. Would you regard this as a satisfactory disposition of the matter? Explain.

12–36. Milton Chambers, CPA, was retained by Wall Corporation to perform an audit of its financial statements for the year ending December 31. In a preliminary meeting with company officials, Chambers learned that the corporation customarily accepted numerous notes receivable from its customers. At December 31 the client company's controller provided Chambers with a list of the individual notes receivable owned at that date. The list showed for each note the date of the note, amount, interest rate, maturity date, and name and address of the maker. After a careful study and evaluation of the internal control relating to notes receivable, Chambers turned his attention to the list of notes receivable provided to him by the controller.

Chambers proved the footing of the list and determined that the total agreed with the general ledger control account for notes receivable and also with the amount shown in the balance sheet. Next he selected 20 of the larger amounts on the list of notes receivable for detailed investigation. This investigation consisted of confirming the amount, date, maturity, interest rate, and collateral, if any, by direct communication with the makers of the notes. By selection of the larger amounts, Chambers was able to verify 75 percent of the dollar amount of notes receivable by confirming only 20 percent of the notes. However, he also selected a random sample of another 20 percent of the smaller notes on the list for confirmation with the makers. Satisfactory replies were received to all confirmation requests.

The president of Wall Corporation informed Chambers that the company never required any collateral in support of the notes receivable; the replies to confirmation requests indicated no collateral had been pledged.

No notes were past due at the balance sheet date, and the credit manager stated that no losses were anticipated. Chambers verified the credit status of the makers of all the notes he had confirmed by reference to audited financial statements of the makers and Dun & Bradstreet, Inc., credit ratings.

By independent computation of the interest accrued on the notes receivable at the balance sheet date, Chambers determined that the accrued interest receivable as shown on the balance sheet was correct.

Since Chambers found no deficiencies in any part of his examination, he issued an unqualified audit report. Some months later Wall Corporation became insolvent and the president fled the country. Chambers was sued by creditors of the company, who charged that his audit was inadequate and failed to meet minimum professional standards. You are to comment on the audit program followed by Chambers with respect to notes receivable *only.*

12–37.   Select the best answer for each of the questions below and explain fully the reason for your selection.

The following sales procedures were encountered during the regular annual audit of Marvel Wholesale Distributing Company.

Customer orders are received by the sales-order department. A clerk computes the dollar amount of the order and sends it to the credit department for approval. Credit approval is stamped on the order and returned to the sales-order department. An invoice is prepared in two copies, and the order is filed in the customer order file.

The customer copy of the invoice is sent to the billing department and held in the pending file awaiting notification that the order was shipped.

The shipping copy of the invoice is routed through the warehouse and the shipping department as authority for the respective departments to release and ship the merchandise. Shipping department personnel pack the order and prepare a three-copy bill of lading: the original copy is mailed to the customer, the second copy is sent with the shipment, and the other is filed in sequence in the bill of lading file. The invoice shipping copy is sent to the billing department.

The billing clerk matches the received shipping copy with the customer copy from the pending file. Both copies of the invoice are priced, extended, and footed. The customer copy is then mailed directly to the customer, and the shipping copy is sent to the accounts-receivable clerk.

The accounts-receivable clerk enters the invoice data in a sales-accounts-receivable journal, posts the customer's account in the subsidiary customer's accounts ledger, and files the shipping copy in the sales invoice file. The invoices are numbered and filed in sequence.

   a.   In order to gather audit evidence concerning the proper credit approval of sales, the auditors would select a sample of transaction documents from the population represented by the—

      (1)   Customer order file.
      (2)   Bill of lading file.
      (3)   Subsidiary customers' accounts ledger.
      (4)   Sales invoice file.

   b.   In order to determine whether the system of internal control operated effectively to minimize errors of failure to post invoices to customers' accounts ledger, the auditors would select a sample of transactions from the population represented by the—

      (1)   Customer order file.
      (2)   Bill of lading file.
      (3)   Subsidiary customers' accounts ledger.
      (4)   Sales invoice file.

    c. In order to determine whether the system of internal control operated effectively to minimize errors of failure to invoice a shipment, the auditors would select a sample of transactions from the population represented by the—

        (1) Customer order file.

        (2) Bill of lading file.

        (3) Subsidiary customers' accounts ledger.

        (4) Sales invoice file.

    d. In order to gather audit evidence that uncollected items in customers' accounts represented valid trade receivables, the auditors would select a sample of items from the population represented by the—

        (1) Customer order file.

        (2) Bill of lading file.

        (3) Subsidiary customers' accounts ledger.

        (4) Sales invoice file. (AICPA, adapted)

GROUP III: PROBLEMS

12–38. As part of his examination of the financial statements of Marlborough Corporation for the year ended March 31, 198x, Mark Wayne, CPA, is reviewing the balance sheet presentation of a $1,200,000 advance to Franklin Olds, Marlborough's president. The advance, which represents 50 percent of current assets and 10 percent of total assets, was made during the year ended March 31, 198x. It has been described in the balance sheet as "miscellaneous accounts receivable" and classified as a current asset.

    Olds informs the CPA that he has used the proceeds of the advance to purchase 35,000 shares of Marlborough's common stock, in order to forestall a take-over raid on the company. He is reluctant to have his association with the advance described in the financial statements because he does not have voting control and fears that this will "just give the raiders ammunition."

    Olds offers the following four-point program as an alternative to further disclosure:

    (1) Have the advance approved by the board of directors. (This can be done expeditiously because a majority of the board members are officers of the company.)

    (2) Prepare a demand note payable to the company with interest of 18 percent (the average bank rate paid by the company).

    (3) Furnish an endorsement of the stock to the company as collateral for the loan. (During the year under audit, despite the fact that earnings did not increase, the market price of Marlborough common rose from $20 to $40 per share. The stock has maintained its $40 per share market price subsequent to year end.)

    (4) Obtain a written opinion from the company attorney supporting the legality of the company's advance and the use of the proceeds.

Required:

    a. Discuss the proper balance sheet classification of the advance to Olds and other appropriate disclosures in the financial statements and footnotes. (Ignore SEC regulations and requirements, tax effects, creditors' restrictions on stock repurchase, and the presentation of common stock dividends and interest revenue.)

b. Discuss each point of Olds' four-point program as to whether or not it is desirable and as to whether or not it is an alternative to further disclosure.

c. If Olds refuses to permit further disclosure, what action should the CPA take? Discuss.

d. In his discussion with the CPA, Olds warns that the raiders, if successful, probably will appoint new auditors. What consideration should the CPA give to this factor? Explain. (AICPA, adapted)

12–39. Lawrence Company maintains its accounts on the basis of a fiscal year ending October 31. Assume that you were retained by the company in August to perform an audit for the fiscal year ending October 31, 198x. You decide to perform certain auditing procedures in advance of the balance sheet date. Among these interim procedures is the confirmation of accounts receivable, which you perform at September 30.

      The accounts receivable at September 30 consisted of approximately 200 accounts with balances totaling $956,750. Seventy-five of these accounts with balances totaling $650,725 were selected for confirmation. All but 20 of the confirmation requests have been returned; 30 were signed without comments, 14 had minor differences that have been cleared satisfactorily, and 11 confirmations had the following comments:

(1) We are sorry, but we cannot answer your request for confirmation of our account because Moss Company uses a computerized accounts payable voucher system.

(2) The balance of $1,050 was paid on September 23, 198x.

(3) The above balance of $7,750 was paid on October 5, 198x.

(4) The above balance has been paid.

(5) We do not owe you anything at September 30, 198x since the goods represented by your invoice dated September 30, 198x, Number 25,050, in the amount of $11,550, were received on October 5, 198x on FOB destination terms.

(6) An advance payment of $2,500 made by us in August 198x should cover the two invoices totaling $1,350 shown on the statement attached.

(7) We never received these goods.

(8) We are contesting the propriety of the $12,525 charge. We think the charge is excessive.

(9) Amount okay. As the goods have been shipped to us on consignment, we will remit payment upon selling the goods.

(10) The $10,000, representing a deposit under a lease, will be applied against the rent due to us during 1990, the last year of the lease.

(11) Your credit dated September 5, 198x in the amount of $440 cancels the above balance.

Required:

What steps would you take to clear satisfactorily each of the above 11 comments? (AICPA, adapted)

12–40. You are performing your first examination of the financial statements of Havers Company, Inc., a closely held corporation. The balance sheet at June 30, drafted by the controller of Havers, shows total assets of $9.5 million and stockholders' equity of $4 million.

  During the course of your examination of notes receivable, you discover that the corporation loaned $1.2 million on March 31 to the majority shareholder, on a 12 percent, unsecured note payable on demand. On June 30 Havers Company, Inc., sold this note without recourse to its depository bank. On the next day, July 1, Havers reacquired this note from the bank without recourse. The standard bank confirmation form returned to you by the bank shows no loss contingency at June 30 in connection with the $1.2 million note.

Required:

Discuss the implications of the above transactions as they affect the client's financial statements and your audit report.

12–41. The July 31, 198x general ledger trial balance of Aerospace Contractors, Inc., reflects the following accounts associated with receivables. Balances of the accounts are after all adjusting journal entries proposed by the auditors and accepted by the client.

Accounts receivable—commercial	$ 595,000
Accounts receivable—U.S. government	3,182,000
Allowance for uncollectible accounts and notes	75,000 cr.
Claims receivable—public carriers	7,000
Claims receivable—U.S. government terminated contracts	320,000
Due from Harwood Co., investee	480,000
Notes receivable—trade	15,000

  Remember that two or more ledger accounts are often combined into one amount in the financial statements in order to achieve a concise presentation. The need for brevity also often warrants the disclosure of some information parenthetically, as for example, the amount of the allowance for doubtful accounts.

Required:

a. Draft a partial balance sheet for Aerospace Contractors at July 31, 198x. In deciding upon which items deserve separate listing, consider materiality as well as the nature of the accounts.

b. Write an explanation of the reasoning employed in your balance sheet presentation of these accounts.

12–42. During your examination of the financial statements of Martin Mfg. Co., a new client, for the year ended March 31, 198x, you note the following entry in the general journal dated March 31, 198x:

Notes Receivable	550,000	
Land		500,000
Gain on Sale of Land		50,000

  To record sale of excess plant-site land to Ardmore Corp. for 8 percent note due 5 years from date. No interest payment required until maturity of note.

  Your review of the contract for sale between Martin and Ardmore, your inquiries of Martin executives, and your study of minutes of Martin's directors' meetings develop the following facts:

(1) The land has been carried in your client's accounting records at its cost of $500,000.

(2) Ardmore Corp. is a land developer and plans to subdivide and resell the land acquired from Martin Mfg. Co.

(3) Martin had originally negotiated with Ardmore on the basis of a 12 percent interest rate on the note. This interest rate was established by Martin after a careful analysis of Ardmore's credit standing and current money market conditions.

(4) Ardmore had rejected the 12 percent interest rate because the total outlay on a 12 percent note for $550,000 would amount to $880,000 at the end of five years; and Ardmore thought a total outlay of this amount would leave it with an inadequate return on the subdivision. Ardmore held out for a total cash outlay of $770,000, and Martin Mfg. Co. finally agreed to this position. During the discussions, it was pointed out that the present value of $1 due five years hence at an annual interest rate of 12 percent is approximately $.567.

Required:

Ignoring income tax considerations, is the journal entry recording Martin's sale of the land to Ardmore acceptable? Explain fully and draft an adjusting entry if you consider one to be necessary.

GROUP IV: CASE STUDIES IN AUDITING

12-43.   STAR FINANCE COMPANY

Star Finance Company, a small, new entity, is in the business of making small loans and investing in installment sales contracts purchased from dealers in automobiles, appliances, and other durable goods. Early in year 3, the company retained McGregor and Company, CPAs, to make an examination of the financial statements for the fiscal year ended February 28, year 3. James Smith, one of the partners in the CPA firm, went to the office of Star Finance to begin the audit. He took with him a senior auditor, Carol Brown, and spent some time explaining to Brown some of the differences between the handling of receivables in a finance company and in a merchandising concern. He stressed to Brown the importance in this business of obtaining bank loans and other capital, and of lending these funds to customers at higher interest rates. He added that *a finance company usually was not anxious to have a customer pay an account in full* because the company might then lose contact with him. On the contrary, Smith pointed out, the finance company would probably encourage its small-loan customers to obtain a new loan before the original one was paid off. If the customer could be developed into a more or less permanent borrower, the finance company would benefit from this relationship even though it never collected a loan in full. The important element, Smith commented, was to keep the customer in debt and paying interest charges.

One of the first steps taken by Smith and Brown was to obtain a trial balance of the general ledger. This trial balance showed installment loans receivable of $615,428. The allowance for doubtful loans was $6,473.

Early in the audit, Brown made tests to determine that the detail of the receivables was in agreement with the control account, and she sent out requests for confirmation of the balances due from the borrowers. In addition she made inquiries into the collectibility of the receivables. She found that the installment receivables consisted of 1,706 loans, of which 18 were classified by the company as delinquent; these 18 loans had aggregate uncollected balances of $5,167. However, in reviewing the receivables, Brown noticed quite a number of loans that were rather slow in collection; as a matter of fact, some of them showed no recent collections of principal.

After having developed this information, Brown made inquiries of the president of Star Finance Company as to the company's basis of considering an installment receivable as delinquent. She was informed that the company defined a delinquent loan as one upon which no collection had been received on either principal or interest within the last 60 days, or generally, therefore, 30 days from the due date; conversely, loans on which collections of principal or interest were being received currently (although not necessarily the full monthly payment) were considered as current. Furthermore, the president pointed out, all loans defined by the company as delinquent 90 days or more (which aggregated approximately $25,000) had been written off at February 28, year 3, by a charge against the allowance for loans.

The number of loans that seemed to be slow in collection continued to disturb Brown, and she made a further study of installment receivables and the recent payments thereon. This study covered 169 other loans classified by the company as current and indicated the following status:

	Number	Amount
Paying interest only	29	$ 12,557
All other (including some accounts on which all interest had been waived)	140	88,112
	169	$100,669

After comparing the results of this test with the amount of the allowance for doubtful loans, which amounted to only $6,473, Brown became further concerned as to the adequacy of the allowance. She decided to make some further inquiries into the status of these loans; thus she requested the controller of Star Finance Company to compile the following information as to the 169 loans (which she then tested):

	Total	Paying interest only	All others
Balance, February 28, year 2	$106,299	$12,313	$ 93,986
Add additional loans made	9,907	249	9,658
Total	116,206	12,562	103,644
Deduct collections received:			
Total collections	34,180	1,471	32,709
Less amount applied to interest	18,643	1,465	17,178
Remainder—applied to principal	15,537	6	15,531
Balance, February 28, year 3 (representing 169 accounts	$100,669	$12,556	$ 88,113

Brown conferred with Smith, and they agreed that the allowance was insufficient. Both Smith and Brown then discussed the matter with the president of Star Finance Company, and it was decided that further studies should be made by the company. At the conclusion of these studies, the company increased its allowance for doubtful loans from $6,473 to $34,182. This allowance, the company insisted, was sufficient to cover losses on collections of the receivables.

Brown was inclined to think that the allowance of $34,182 would be sufficient; after all it did represent better than 5 percent of the receivables and, furthermore, the company would be receiving interest in the future on all of its loans, out of which further provision could be made if necessary. Smith, however, did not agree. On the other hand, Smith was not sure that he could indicate in the audit report the amount of allowance that should be necessary because (1) he did not regard himself as being qualified as an appraiser to evaluate the loans and (2) the company had been in existence only a short time and hence did not have much background of credit experience.

The audit report, as finally issued by McGregor and Company, indicated that the client company was of the opinion its allowance for doubtful loans was sufficient. In a middle paragraph, the report broke down the installment loans receivable as follows:

Loans being collected in substantial accordance with
  contract terms, $509, 592 (less allowance for
  uncollectible loans $16,182) $493,410
Loans not being collected in substantial accordance
  with contract terms, $105,836 (less allowance for
  uncollectible loans $18,000) 87,836
     Total $581,246

The audit report also contained the following:

As to the allowances for losses carried by the company against its loans receivable, we are of the opinion, based largely on the company's collection experience and in the light of present conditions, that—
(1) The allowance of $16,182 carried against loans collected in substantial accordance with contract terms should be sufficient.
(2) The allowance of $18,000 carried against loans not being collected in substantial accordance with contract terms is insufficient, and losses substantially in excess of $18,000 may be expected thereon. However, inasmuch as the company has been in existence only a relatively short period of years and consequently does not have extensive experience as to losses and collections, and, further, since the ascertainment of adequate loss allowance in the absence of extensive loss experience is a technical matter for persons trained in small-loan operations and credits, we are unable to express an opinion as to the amount of loss allowance that should be required.

The opinion paragraph of the audit report stated: "In our opinion, except that the allowance for doubtful loans receivable not being collected in substantial accordance with contract terms is inadequate, the financial statements referred to above present fairly the financial position of the company at February 28, year 3 and the results of its operations and the changes in its financial position for the year then ended, in conformity with generally accepted accounting principles applied on a basis consistent with that of the preceding year."

On review of the audit report, the president of Star Finance Company claimed that McGregor and Company was putting him out of business and that the report would result in the bank (extending credit to the company) calling its line of credit; the president demanded that Smith change the report.

Required:

a. Do you agree with Smith's opinion that the allowance for doubtful loans was insufficient?

b. Do you think that Smith should have specified the amount of allowance he deemed to be sufficient?

c. Do you think that Smith should have been swayed by the statement of the president of Star Finance Company that the audit report would put him out of business, and if so, what else should Smith have done?

d. Was there anything else Smith could have done that he did not do?

13

Inventories and cost of goods sold

The interrelationship of inventories and cost of goods sold makes it logical for the two topics to be considered together. The internal controls that assure the fair valuation of inventories are found in the purchase (or acquisition) cycle. These controls include procedures for selection of vendors, ordering merchandise or materials, inspection of goods received, recording the liability to the vendor, and authorization and making of cash disbursements. In a manufacturing business, the valuation of inventories also is affected by the production cycle, in which various manufacturing costs are assigned to inventories, and the cost of inventories is then transferred to the cost of goods sold.

The selection of a valuation method and the need for consistency in its application also affect both inventories and cost of goods sold. During periods of inflation, the inadequacies of historical cost affect the validity of cost of goods sold as much as they affect inventories. Thus, it is not surprising that *FASB Statement No. 33*, "Financial Reporting and Changing Prices," calls for the disclosure of current replacement cost for both inventories and cost of goods sold.

The responsibilities of independent auditors with respect to inventories can best be understood by turning back to the time of the spectacular *McKesson & Robbins* fraud case. The hearings conducted by the SEC in 1939 disclosed that the audited financial statements of McKesson & Robbins, Inc., a drug company listed on the New York Stock Exchange, contained $19 million of fictitious assets, about one fourth of

413

the total assets shown on the balance sheet. The fictitious assets included $10 million of nonexistent inventories. How was it possible for the independent auditors to have conducted an audit and to have issued an unqualified report without discovering this gigantic fraud? The audit program followed for inventories in this case was in accordance with customary auditing practice of the 1930s. The significant point is that in that period it was customary to limit the audit work on inventories to an examination of records only; the standards of that era did not require any observation, physical count, or other actual contact with the inventories.

Up to the time of the *McKesson & Robbins* case, auditors had avoided taking responsibility for verifying the accuracy of inventory quantities and the physical existence of the goods. With questionable logic, many auditors had argued that they were experts in handling figures and analyzing accounting records but were not qualified to identify and measure the great variety of raw materials and manufactured goods found in the factories, warehouses, and store buildings of their clients.

The *McKesson & Robbins* case brought a quick end to such limited views of the auditors' responsibility. The public accounting profession was faced with the necessity of accepting responsibility for verifying the physical existence of inventories or of confessing that its audit function offered no real protection to investors or other users of financial statements. The profession met the challenge by adopting new standards requiring the auditors to observe the taking of the physical inventory and to confirm accounts receivable.

Subsequently, the AICPA issued *Statement on Auditing Standards Nos. 1* and *2*, which reaffirmed the importance of the auditors' observation of physical inventories but authorized the substitution of other auditing procedures under certain circumstances. *SAS No. 1* made a distinction between companies that determine inventory quantities solely by an annual physical count and companies with well-kept perpetual inventory records. The latter companies often have strong internal control over inventories and may employ statistical sampling techniques to verify the records by occasional test counts rather than by a complete annual count of the entire inventory. For these clients the auditors' observation of physical inventory may be limited to such counts as they consider appropriate, and may occur during or after the end of the period being audited.

The most difficult part of *SAS No. 1* to interpret is the provision that permits the auditors to substitute other audit procedures for the observation of inventories because it is *impracticable* or *impossible* for them to observe the physical inventory. The difficulty lies in defining the circumstances that make it *impracticable* or *impossible* to observe physical inventory. When observation of the physical inventory is determined to be impracticable or impossible, but the auditors are able to obtain competent evidence through the use of other auditing procedures, they may issue an unqualified opinion without making any disclosure of the omission of an observation of the physical inventory. However, the importance of physical contact with items of inventory, as well as inspection of records and documents, is stressed by *SAS No. 1* in stipulating that the use of alternative auditing procedures must always include observing or making some physical counts of inventories even though this occurs after the balance sheet date.

Critical importance of inventories to the auditors

Inventories have probably received more attention in auditing literature and in discussions among professional accountants than any other classification to be found in financial statements. The reasons for the special significance attached to the verification of inventories are readily apparent:

1. Inventories usually constitute the largest current asset of an enterprise and are more susceptible to major errors and manipulation than any other asset category.
2. Numerous alternative methods for valuation of inventories are sanctioned by the accounting profession, and different methods may be used for various classes of inventories.
3. The determination of inventory value directly affects the cost of goods sold and has a major impact upon net income for the year.
4. The verification of inventory quantity, condition, and value is inherently a more complex and difficult task than is the verification of most elements of financial position. Many items, such as precious gems, sophisticated electronic parts, and construction in progress, present significant problems of identification and valuation.

In this chapter the term *inventories* is used to include (1) goods on hand ready for sale, either the merchandise of a trading concern or the finished goods of a manufacturer; (2) goods in the process of production; and (3) goods to be consumed directly or indirectly in production, consisting of raw materials, purchased parts, and supplies.

The auditors' objectives in examination of inventories and cost of goods sold

The principal objectives of the auditors in the examination of inventories and cost of goods sold are to determine (1) the adequacy of internal controls; (2) the existence and ownership of the inventories; (3) that all inventories on hand are recorded; (4) the propriety of the valuation of inventories, including consideration of their quality and condition; (5) the fairness of the amount presented as cost of goods sold in the income statement; and (6) the adequacy of disclosures related to inventories and cost of goods sold.

The auditors' approach to the verification of inventories and cost of goods sold should be one of awareness to the possibility of intentional misstatement, as well as to the prevalence of accidental error in the determination of inventory quantities and amounts. Purposeful misstatement of inventories has often been employed to evade income taxes, to conceal shortages arising from various irregularities, and to mislead stockholders or other inactive owners as to profits and financial position.

Unaudited replacement cost information

In years of double-digit inflation, many investors question the usefulness of historical cost-based financial statements. They contend that such statements must be supplemented with measures of the effects of changing prices on the earnings and major assets of the company. In recognition of this problem, the SEC and FASB have both issued pronouncements requiring the supplementary disclosure of replacement costs and other changing price information. The SEC was first to issue disclosure requirements, which were announced in *Accounting Series Release No. 190*. However, these rules subsequently were withdrawn in light of the more comprehensive disclosures required by *FASB Statement No. 33*, "Financial Reporting and Changing Prices." The information must be disclosed by capital-intensive companies that meet certain size tests and may be presented in unaudited footnotes to the financial statements or in supplementary schedules. An integral part of the requirements is the disclosure of the current replacement cost of the company's inventories.

Note that this information is supplementary and not required for fair presentation of the basic financial statements. Consequently, *the auditors are not required to audit the information* in order to express an opinion on the fairness of the financial statements. Instead, the Auditing Standards Board established limited procedures to be applied to all FASB-required supplementary information.[1] These procedures require the following of auditors:

a. Inquire whether the information is presented in accordance with FASB requirements, whether the methods have changed from the prior period, and as to significant underlying assumptions.

b. Compare the information with management's responses, audited financial statements, and other information known to the auditors.

c. Consider obtaining written representations from management concerning the supplementary information.

d. Apply additional procedures as specified in Statements on Auditing Standards specifically related to the particular required supplementary information.

---

[1] *Statement on Auditing Standards No. 27*, "Supplementary Information Required by the Financial Accounting Standards Board," AICPA (New York, 1979).

e. Make additional inquiries if the preceding procedures indicate that the information may not be appropriately presented.

SAS No. 28, "Supplementary Information on the Effects of Changing Prices," provides specific guidance on the performance of these procedures with respect to the replacement cost information. These Statements on Auditing Standards require the auditors to expand their report to indicate an omission of the required current cost information, presentation that does not conform to FASB requirements, or narrative information that contains a misstatement of fact or is inconsistent with audited or other supplementary information.

Internal control of inventories and cost of goods sold

The importance of adequate internal control over inventories and cost of goods sold from the viewpoint of both management and the auditors can scarcely be overemphasized. In some companies, management stresses internal controls over cash and securities but ignores the problem of control over inventories. This attitude may be based on the outmoded notion that the primary purpose of internal control is to prevent and detect fraud. Since many types of inventories are composed of items not particularly susceptible to theft, management may consider internal controls to be unnecessary in this area. Such thinking ignores the fact that internal control performs other functions even more important than fraud prevention.

Good internal control is a means of providing accurate cost data for inventories and cost of goods sold as well as accuracy in reporting physical quantities. Inadequate internal controls may cause losses by permitting erroneous cost data to be used by management in setting prices and in making other decisions based on reported profit margins. If the accounts do not furnish a realistic picture of the cost of inventories on hand, the cost of goods manufactured, and the cost of goods sold, the financial statements may be grossly misleading both as to earnings and as to financial position.

Internal control procedures for inventories and cost of goods sold affect nearly all the functions involved in producing and disposing of the company's products. Purchasing, receiving, storing, issuing, processing, and shipping are the physical functions directly connected with inventories; the cost accounting system and the perpetual inventory records comprise the recording functions. Since the auditors are interested in the final products of the recording functions, it is necessary for them to understand and appraise the cost accounting system and the perpetual inventory records, as well as the various procedures and original documents underlying the preparation of financial data.

The purchasing function. Adequate internal control over purchases requires, first of all, an organizational structure which delegates to a separate department of the company exclusive authority to make all purchases of materials and services. The purchasing, receiving, and recording functions should be clearly separated and lodged in separate departments. In small companies, this type of departmentalized operation may not be possible; but even in very small enterprises, it is usually feasible to make one person responsible for all purchase transactions.

Serially numbered purchase orders should be prepared for all purchases, and copies forwarded to the accounting and receiving departments. The copy sent to receiving should have the quantities blacked out to assure that receiving personnel make independent counts of the merchandise received. Even though the buyer may actually place an order by telephone, the formal purchase order should be prepared and forwarded. In many large organizations, purchase orders are issued only after compliance with extensive procedures for (1) determining the need for the item, (2) obtaining of competitive bids, and (3) obtaining approval of the financial aspect of the commitment.

The receiving function. All goods received by the company—without exception—should be cleared through a receiving department that is independent of purchasing, storing, and shipping departments. The receiving department is responsible for (1) the determination of quantities of goods received, (2) the detection of damaged or defective merchandise, (3) the preparation of a receiving report, and (4) the prompt transmittal of goods received to the stores department.

The storing function. As goods are delivered to stores, they are counted, inspected, and receipted for. The stores department will then notify the accounting department of the amount received and placed in stock. In performing these functions, the stores department makes an important contribution to overall control of inventories. By signing for the goods, it fixes its own responsibility, and by notifying the accounting department of actual goods stored, it provides verification of the receiving department's work.

The issuing function. The stores department, being responsible for all goods under its control, has reason to insist that for all items passing out of its hands it be given a prenumbered requisition, which serves as a signed receipt from the department accepting the goods. Requisitions are usually prepared in triplicate. One copy is retained by the department making the request; another acts as the stores department's receipt; and the third is a notice to the accounting department for cost distribution. To prevent the indiscriminate writing of requisitions for questionable purposes, some organizations establish policies requiring that requisitions be drawn only upon the authority of a bill of materials, an engineering order, or a sales order. In mercantile concerns, shipping orders rather than factory requisitions serve to authorize withdrawals from stores.

The production function. Responsibility for the goods must be fixed, usually on factory supervisors or superintendents. Thus, from the time materials are delivered to the factory until they are completed and routed to a finished goods storeroom, a designated supervisor should be in control and be prepared to answer for their location and disposition.

The system of internal control over goods in process may include regular inspection procedures to reveal defective work. This aids in disclosing inefficiencies in the productive system and also tends to prevent inflation of the goods-in-process inventory by the accumulation of cost for goods that will eventually be scrapped.

Control procedures should also assure that goods scrapped during the process of production are promptly reported to the accounting department so that the decrease in value of goods-in-process inventories may be recorded. Scrapped materials may have substantial salvage value, and this calls for segregation and control of scrap inventories.

The shipping function. Shipments of goods should be made only after proper authorization has been received. This authorization will normally be an order from the sales department, although the shipping function also includes the returning of defective goods to suppliers. In this latter case the authorization may take the form of a shipping advice from a purchasing department executive.

One copy of the shipping authorization will go to the stores department; a second copy will be retained by the shipping department as evidence of shipment; and a third copy will be enclosed as a packing slip with the goods when they are shipped. These forms should be prenumbered and kept under accounting control. The control aspect of this procedure is strengthened by the fact that an outsider, the customer, will inspect the packing slip and notify the company of any discrepancy between this list, the goods ordered, and the goods actually received.

When the goods have been shipped, the shipping department will attach to a fourth copy of each shipping order the related evidence of shipment: bills of lading, trucking bills, carriers' receipts, freight bills, and so on. This facilitates subsequent audit by grouping together the documents showing that shipments were properly authorized and carried out. The shipping advice, with supporting documents attached, is then sent to the billing department, where it is used as the basis for invoicing the customer.

Established shipping routines should be followed for all types of shipments, including the sale of scrap, return of defective goods, and forwarding of materials and parts to subcontractors.

The cost accounting system. To account for the usage of raw materials and supplies, to determine the content and value of goods-in-process inventories, and to compute the finished-goods inventory, an adequate cost accounting system is necessary. This system comprises all the records, orders, requisitions, time tickets, and the like, needed in a proper accounting for the disposition of materials as they enter the flow of production and as they continue through the factory in the process of becoming finished goods. The cost accounting system also serves to accumulate labor costs and indirect costs that contribute to the goods-in-process and the finished-goods inventories. The cost accounting system thus forms an integral part of the internal control for inventories.

The figures produced by the cost system should be controlled by general ledger accounts. Two general types of systems are widely used. Under one, all transactions in a factory are passed through a factory ledger. The net balance of this ledger is represented by a factory ledger control in the general ledger. The other system records the cost of materials, labor, and factory overhead in individual goods-in-process accounts for each production order or process. These goods-in-process accounts are controlled by a single general ledger goods-in-process inventory account. In effect, a subsidiary goods-in-process ledger is produced by the cost system, which must at all times be represented in the general records.

Underlying this upper level of control between the factory records and the general ledger is found a system of production orders, material requisitions, job tickets or other labor distributions, and factory overhead distributions. Control is effected by having each production order properly authorized, recorded, and followed up. Payroll records are compiled only after all time tickets have been verified for accuracy. Indirect costs are distributed to the various job orders or processes through predetermined rates, which are adjusted to actual cost at the period's end. In addition, many cost systems have introduced methods of determining spoilage, idle labor, and idle machine time. These systems, known as standard costing, provide for the prompt pricing of inventories and for a control over operations through a study of variances between actual and standard figures. All these various types of cost accounting systems are alike in that all are designed to contribute to effective internal control by tracing the execution of managerial directives in the factory, by providing reliable and accurate inventory figures, and by safeguarding company assets.

The perpetual inventory system. Perpetual inventory records constitute a most important part of the system of internal control. These records, by showing at all times the quantity of goods on hand, provide information essential to intelligent purchasing, sales, and production-planning policies. With such a record it is possible to guide procurement by establishing points of minimum and maximum quantities for each standard item stocked.

The use of minimum/maximum stock quantities as a guide to reordering does not warrant placement of the ordering function in the hands of one employee and does not eliminate the need for review of decisions to order goods. Good internal control requires a regular review of prospective purchases before final authority is given for placing the order.

Illustrative case. A large aircraft manufacturer planned to adopt the practice of an annual Family Day, on which the families and friends of employees would be invited to visit the plant, go through the latest-model airplanes, and view movies concerning aircraft of the future. In anticipation of a crowd of more than 100,000 people, the plant protection department decided to erect numerous rope lanes to guide the crowds along a designated route. The plan required enormous quantities of rope, so a supervisor called the material stores department to see how much rope was in stock and whether additional amounts might be borrowed from neighboring plants. He was informed that through error the company had recently purchased 100,000 feet of rope when it had intended to buy only 10,000 feet. The plant protection department obtained the rope and used it in handling the Family Day crowds with the intention of returning it to the stores department in the next day or so. In the interim a stock clerk noticed that 100,000 feet of rope had been withdrawn from stores within the past week and that only a small quantity remained in stock. The stock clerk was accustomed to dealing in large quantities of various materials. Assuming that the withdrawal of 100,000 feet of rope during the past week was normal usage and that the company should have 10 weeks' supply on hand, the stock clerk prepared a "Rush" request for an order of 1 million feet of rope.

This colossal mistake was corrected through an internal control practice of requiring a supervisor to review and give written approval to all requests for orders of material before a purchase order was issued. The supervisor was puzzled as to why such quantities were needed and insisted upon a full investigation of the facts of the situation before he signed the request.

If perpetual inventory records are to produce the control implicit in their nature, it is desirable that the subsidiary records be maintained both in quantities and dollars for all stock, that the subsidiary records be controlled by the general ledger, that trial balances be prepared at reasonable intervals, and that both the detailed records and the general ledger control accounts be adjusted to agree with physical counts whenever taken.

Perpetual inventory records discourage inventory theft and waste, since storeskeepers and other employees are aware of the accountability over goods established by this continuous record of goods received, issued, and on hand. The records, however, must be periodically verified through the physical counting of goods.

Audit working papers for inventories and cost of goods sold

A great variety of working papers may be prepared by the auditors in their verification of inventories and cost of goods sold. These papers will range in form from written comments on the manner in which the physical inventory was taken to elaborate analyses of production costs of finished goods and goods in process. Selected working papers will be illustrated in connection with the audit procedures to be described in later sections of this chapter.

AUDIT PROGRAM FOR INVENTORIES AND COST OF GOODS SOLD

The following audit procedures for the verification of inventories and cost of goods sold will be discussed in detail in the succeeding pages.

The program is appropriate for a manufacturing company that takes a complete physical inventory to verify the perpetual inventories at the close of each fiscal year.

A. **Study and evaluation of internal control for inventories and cost of goods sold.**
    1. Obtain description of internal control for inventories and cost of goods sold and conduct a walk-through of the system.
    2. Make compliance tests of a sample of purchase transactions.
    3. Test the cost accounting system.
    4. Evaluate internal controls for inventories and cost of goods sold.

B. **Substantive tests of inventories and cost-of-goods-sold transactions.**
    5. Participate in advance planning of physical inventory.
    6. Observe the taking of physical inventory and make test counts.
    7. Obtain a copy of the completed physical inventory, determine its clerical accuracy, and trace test counts.
    8. Review inventory quality and condition.
    9. Review the bases and methods of inventory pricing.
    10. Test the pricing of inventories.
    11. Review the year-end cutoff of purchases and sales transactions.
    12. Perform analytical review procedures related to inventories and cost of goods sold.
    13. In the first audit of a client, investigate beginning inventories.
    14. Determine whether any inventories have been pledged, and review purchase and sales commitments.
    15. Determine proper financial statement presentation of inventories and cost of goods sold, including adequate disclosure.
    16. Obtain from client a letter of representations concerning inventories and cost of goods sold.

A. Study and evaluation:

    1. **Obtain description of internal control for inventories and cost of goods sold and conduct a walk-through of the system.**

    As previously indicated, the study of internal controls may involve the filling out of a questionnaire, the writing of descriptive memoranda, and the preparation of flowcharts depicting organizational structure and the flow of materials and documents. All these approaches utilize the same basic investigative techniques of interview and the conduct of a walk-through of the system to confirm that the system is accurately described.

During the review of internal controls over inventory, the auditors should become thoroughly conversant with the procedures for purchasing, receiving, storing, and issuing goods and for controlling production, as well as acquiring understanding of the cost accounting system and the perpetual inventory records.

The auditors should also give consideration to the physical protection for inventories. Any deficiencies in storage facilities, in guard service, or in physical handling that may lead to losses from weather, fire, flood, or theft may appropriately be called to the attention of management.

Should the auditors' study of internal control over inventories (or plant and equipment) include consideration of the client's insurance coverage? Management's policy as to the extent of insuring assets against fire, flood, earthquake, and other hazards will vary greatly from one company to another. The auditors' responsibility does not include a determination of what constitutes adequate insurance coverage. Consequently the auditors' report on financial statements need not contain any disclosure on the client's policies with respect to insurance coverage.

The matters to be investigated in the auditors' review of internal controls over inventory and cost of sales are fairly well indicated by the following questions: Are perpetual inventory records maintained for each class of inventory? Are the perpetual inventory records verified by physical inventories at least once each year? Do the procedures for physical inventories include the use of prenumbered tags, with all tag numbers accounted for? Are differences between physical inventory counts and perpetual inventory records investigated before the perpetual records are adjusted? Is a separate purchasing department responsible for purchasing all materials, supplies, and equipment? Are all incoming shipments, including returns by customers, processed by a separate receiving department? Are materials and supplies held in the custody of a stores department and issued only on properly approved requisitions?

2. Perform compliance tests of a sample of purchase transactions.

The proper recording of purchase transactions and of cash disbursements is essential to reliable accounting records. Therefore, the auditors must perform compliance tests of the key accounting control procedures in the client's purchasing transaction cycle. Compliance tests of this cycle may include the following steps:

1. Select a sample of purchase orders from purchasing department files.
2. Examine the purchase requisition or other authorization for each purchase order in the sample.

3. Examine the related vendor's invoice, receiving report, and paid check copy for each purchase order in the sample. Trace transactions to the voucher register and check register.
4. Review invoices for approval of prices, extensions, footings, freight and credit terms, and account distribution.
5. Compare quantities and prices in invoice, purchase order, and receiving report.
6. Trace postings from voucher register to general ledger and any applicable subsidiary ledgers.

3. Test the cost accounting system.

For a client in the manufacturing field, the auditors must become familiar with the cost accounting system in use, as a part of their study and evaluation of internal control. A wide variety of practices will be encountered for the costing of finished units. The cost accounting records may be controlled by general ledger accounts or operated independently of the general accounting system. In the latter case, the cost of completed units may be difficult or impossible to verify and may represent nothing more than a well-reasoned guess. Because cost accounting methods vary so widely, even among manufacturing concerns in the same industry, audit procedures for a cost accounting system must be designed to fit the specific circumstances encountered in each case.

In any cost accounting system, the three elements of manufacturing cost are direct materials costs, direct labor costs, and manufacturing overhead. Cost accounting systems may accumulate either actual costs or standard costs according to *processes* or *jobs.* The auditors' compliance tests of the client's cost accounting system must be designed to determine that costs allocated to specific jobs or processes are appropriately compiled.

To achieve this objective, the auditors must test the propriety of direct materials quantities and unit costs, direct labor-hours and hourly rates, and overhead rates and allocation bases. Quantities of direct materials charged to jobs or processes are vouched to materials requisitions, and unit materials costs are traced to the raw materials perpetual inventory records. The auditors should examine job tickets or time summaries supporting direct labor hours accumulations and should trace direct labor hourly rates to union contracts or individual employee personnel files.

The auditors must recognize that a variety of methods are generally accepted for the application of manufacturing overhead to inventories. A predetermined rate of factory overhead applied on the basis of machine-hours, direct labor dollars, direct labor hours, or some similar basis, is used by many manufacturing companies. The predetermined overhead rate is usually revised periodically, but nevertheless leads each year to some underabsorbed or overabsorbed overhead. The auditors will ordinarily insist that any significant amount of overabsorbed overhead be applied to a proportionate reduction in inventory and cost of sales. Underabsorbed overhead should generally be written off as a cost of the period; if material, it should be separately disclosed in the income statement.

A distinction between factory overhead, on the one hand, and overhead costs pertaining to selling or general administration of the business, on the other, must be made under generally accepted accounting principles, since selling expenses and general and administrative expenses usually are written off in the period incurred. The difference in the accounting treatment accorded to factory overhead and to non-manufacturing overhead implies a fundamental difference between these two types of cost. Nevertheless, as a practical matter it is often impossible to say with finality that a particular expenditure, such as the salary of a vice president in charge of production, should be classified as factory overhead, as general and administrative expense, or perhaps be divided between the two. Despite this difficulty, a vital procedure in the audit of cost of goods sold for a manufacturing concern is determining that factory overhead costs are reasonably allocated in the accounts. Failure to distribute factory costs to the correct accounts can cause significant distortions in the client's predetermined overhead rate and in over- or underapplied factory overhead. The auditors may find it necessary to obtain or prepare analyses of a number of the factory overhead subsidiary ledger accounts and to verify the propriety of the charges thereto. Then, the auditors must determine the propriety of the total machine-hours, direct labor hours, or other aggregate allocation base used by the client company to predetermine the factory overhead rate.

If standard costs are in use, it is desirable to compare standard costs with actual costs for representative items and to ascertain whether the standards reflect current materials and labor usage and unit costs. The composition of factory overhead, the basis for its distribution by department and product, and the effect of any change in basis during the year should be reviewed. The standard costs of selected products should be verified by testing computations, extensions, and footings and by tracing charges for labor, material, and overhead to original sources.

The auditors' study of a manufacturing company's cost accounting system should give special attention to any changes in cost methods made during the year and the effect of such changes on the cost of sales. Close attention should also be given to the methods of summarizing costs of completed products and to the procedures for recording the cost of partial shipments.

If the client company has supply contracts with U.S. government agencies, the auditors should determine whether standards issued by the Cost Accounting Standards Board were complied with. Cost accounting standards issued to date have dealt with such matters as consistency in estimating, accumulating, allocating, and reporting costs; and depreciation of plant assets.

4. Evaluate internal controls for inventories and cost of goods sold.

The description and compliance tests of the client's internal control for inventories and cost of goods sold provide the auditors with evidence as to weaknesses and strengths of the system. The auditors should appraise these weaknesses and strengths and design the remainder of their audit program for substantive tests of inventories and cost of sales accordingly.

B. Substantive tests:

5. Participate in advance planning of physical inventory.

Efficient and effective inventory taking requires careful planning in advance. Cooperation between the auditors and client personnel in formulating the procedures to be followed will prevent unnecessary confusion and will aid in securing a complete and well-controlled count. A first step in securing the desired elements of control and efficiency is the designation by the client management of an individual employee, often a representative of the controller, to assume responsibility for the physical inventory. This responsibility will begin with the drafting of procedures and will carry through to the final determination of the dollar value of all inventories.

In planning the physical inventory, the client should consider many factors, such as (1) selection of the best date or dates, (2) closing down certain departments of the plant, (3) segregating obsolete and defective goods, (4) establishing control over the counting process through the use of inventory tags, (5) achieving proper cutoff of sales and purchase transactions, and (6) arranging for services of engineers or other specialists to determine the quantity or quality of certain goods or materials.

Once the plan has been developed, it must be documented and communicated, in the form of written instructions to the personnel taking the physical inventory. These instructions normally will be drafted by the client and reviewed by the auditors, who will judge their adequacy. In evaluating the adequacy of the instructions, the auditors should consider the nature and materiality of the inventories, as well as the existing internal control. Normally, the auditors will insist that the inventory be taken at or near the balance sheet date. However, if the client has an effective system of internal control, including perpetual records, the auditors may be satisfied to observe inventory counts performed during the year. If the client plans to use a statistical sampling technique to estimate the quantities of inventories, the auditors will evaluate the statistical validity of the sampling method and the adequacy of the confidence level and precision. If the instructions for taking inventory are adequate, then the auditors' responsibility during the count is largely a matter of seeing that the instructions are followed conscientiously.

Some companies prepare two sets of instructions for the physical inventory: one set for the supervisors who will direct the count and a second set for the employees who will perform the detailed work of counting and listing merchandise. A set of instructions prepared by the controller of a large clothing store for use by supervisors is illustrated in Figure 13–1.

Advance planning by the senior auditor-in-charge is also necessary to assure efficient use of audit staff members during the inventory taking. The auditor-in-charge should determine the dates of the counts, number of auditors needed at each location, and the estimated time required. The senior should then assign auditors to specific locations and provide them with a written statement of their duties. The senior may also wish to arrange for the cooperation of the client's internal auditing staff during the count, and possibly for the assistance of the company's engineers or independent specialists.

When written instructions are prepared by the auditing firm for use of its staff in a particular engagement, these instructions are not made available to the client. Their purpose is to make sure that all auditors understand their assignments and can therefore work efficiently during the physical inventory. An example of inventory instructions prepared by a public accounting firm for the use of its own staff members is presented in Figure 13–2; these instructions relate to the same audit engagement described in the client's instructions to supervisors illustrated in Figure 13–1. In every case, the audit staff members will have copies of the client's inventory instructions in their possession during the inventory observation.

6. Observe the taking of physical inventory and make test counts.

It is not the auditors' function to *take* the inventory or to control or supervise the taking; this is the responsibility of management. The auditors *observe* the inventory taking in order to obtain sufficient competent evidence as to the *existence* and *ownership* of the client company's inventories. In brief, observation of inventory taking gives the auditors a basis for an opinion as to the credibility of representations by management as to inventory quantities.

To observe the inventory taking, however, implies a much more active role than that of a mere spectator. Observation by the auditors also includes determining that all usable inventory owned by the client is included in the count and that the client's employees comply with the written inventory instructions. As part of the process of observing the physical inventory, the auditors will be alert to detect any obsolete or damaged merchandise included in inventory. Such merchandise should be segregated by the client and written down to net realizable value. In

Figure 13–1

GLEN HAVEN DEPARTMENT STORES, INC.

Instructions for Physical Inventory,
August 5, 198X

TO ALL SUPERVISORS:

A complete physical inventory of all departments in each store will be taken Sunday, August 5, 198X beginning at 8:30 a.m. and continuing until completed. Employees are to report at 8:15 a.m. to receive their final briefing on their instructions, which are appended hereto.

Each count team should be formed and started by a supervisor, and should be periodically observed by that supervisor to assure that instructions are being complied with in the counting and listing processes.

A block of sequential prenumbered inventory sheets will be issued to each supervisor at 8:00 a.m. August 5, for later issuance to count teams. Each supervisor is to account for all sheets--used, unused, or voided. In addition, each supervisor will be furnished at that time with a listing of count teams under his supervision.

When a count team reports completion of a department, that team's supervisor should accompany a representative of the independent auditors, McDonald & Company, in performing test counts. A space is provided on each inventory sheet for the supervisor's signature as reviewer. When the independent auditors have "cleared" a department, the supervisor responsible should take possession of the count sheets. All completed count sheets are to be placed in numerical sequence and turned over to me when the entire inventory has been completed.

Before supervisors and employees leave the stores Saturday evening, August 4, they are to make certain that "housekeeping" is in order in each department, and that all merchandise bears a price ticket.

If you have any questions about these instructions or any other aspect of the physical inventory, please see me.

J. R. Adams

J. R. Adams
Controller
July 24, 198X

Figure 13–2

McDONALD and COMPANY

CERTIFIED PUBLIC ACCOUNTANTS

Glen Haven Department Stores, Inc.
Inventory Observation--Instructions for Audit Staff
August 5, 198X

We will observe physical inventory taking at the following stores of Glen Haven Department Stores, Inc., on August 5, 198X:

Store	Store Manager	Our Staff
Wilshire	J. M. Baker	John Rodgers, Faye Arnold
Crenshaw	Roberta Bryan	Weldon Simpkins
Valley	Hugh Remington	Roger Dawson

Report to assigned stores promptly at 8:00 a.m. Attached are copies of the Company's detailed instructions to employees who are to take the physical inventories and to supervisors who are to be in charge. These instructions appear to be complete and adequate; we should satisfy ourselves by observation that the instructions are being followed.

All merchandise counted will be listed on prenumbered inventory sheets. We should make occasional test counts to ascertain the accuracy of the physical counts. Test counts are to be recorded in working papers, with the following information included:
Department number
Inventory sheet number
Stock number
Description of item, including season letter and year
Quantity
Selling price per price tag

We should ascertain that adequate control is maintained over the prenumbered inventory sheets issued. Also, we should prepare a listing of the last numbers used for transfers, markdowns, and markups in the various departments and stores. Inventory sheets are not to be removed from the departments until we have "cleared" them; we should not delay this operation.

Each staff member's working papers should include an opinion on the adequacy of the inventory taking. The papers should also include a summary of time incurred in the observation.

No cash or other cutoff procedures are to be performed as an adjunct to the inventory observation.

short, during the inventory observation the auditors are alert for, and follow up on, any unusual problems not anticipated in the client's written inventory instructions or improperly dealt with by the client's inventory teams.

The auditors will also *make a record of the serial number of the final receiving and shipping documents issued before the taking of inventory* so that the accuracy of the cutoff can be determined at a later date. Shipments or receipts of goods taking place during the counting process should be closely observed and any necessary reconciliations made. Observation of the physical inventory by the auditors also stresses determining that the client is controlling properly the inventory tags or sheets. These should be prenumbered so that all tags can be accounted for.

During their inventory observation, the auditors will make test counts of selected inventory items. The extent of the test counts will vary widely, dependent upon the circumstances of the individual case, but in general should cover a representative cross section of the stock on hand. All test counts should be recorded in the audit working papers for subsequent comparison with the completed inventory listing.

Serially numbered inventory count tags are usually attached to each lot of goods during the taking of a physical inventory. The design of the tag and the procedures for using it are intended to guard against two common pitfalls: (*a*) accidental omission of goods from the count and (*b*) double counting of goods.

Many companies use two-employee teams to count the inventories. Each team is charged with a sequence of the serially numbered tags and is required to turn in to the physical inventory supervisor any tags voided or not used.

The actual counting, the filling in of inventory tags, and the pulling of these tags are done by the client's employees. While the inventory tags are still attached to the goods, the auditors may make such test counts as they deem appropriate in the circumstances. The auditors will list in their working papers the tag numbers for which test counts were made. The client employees will ordinarily not collect (pull) the inventory tags until the auditors indicate that they are satisfied with the accuracy of the count.

In comparing their test counts to the inventory tags, the auditors are alert for errors not only in quantities, but also in part numbers, descriptions, units of measure, and all other aspects of the inventory item. For test counts of goods-in-process inventory, the auditors must ascertain that the percentage or stage of completion indicated on the inventory tag is appropriate.

If the test counts made by the auditors indicate discrepancies, the goods are recounted at once by the client's employees and the error corrected. If an excessive number of errors is found, the inventory for the entire department or even for the entire company should be recounted.

The information listed on the inventory tags is transferred by the client to serially numbered inventory sheets. These sheets are used in pricing the inventory and in summarizing the dollar amounts involved. After the inventory tags have been collected, the client employee supervising the inventory will determine that all tags are accounted for by serial number. The auditors should ascertain that numerical control is maintained over both inventory tags and inventory sheets.

The test counts and tag numbers listed by the auditors in their working papers will be traced later to the client's inventory summary sheets. A discrepancy will be regarded not as an error in counting, but as a mistake in copying data from the tags, or as the result of a purposeful alteration of a tag, or creation of a fictitious tag.

Illustrative Case. The auditors of Crown Aluminum Corporation did not adequately review the control of physical inventory tags, even though their CPA firm's procedures required such a review. According to the SEC (*Accounting Series Release No. 157*), Crown personnel altered certain inventory tags and created other fictitious tags; the result was a $4.4 million overstatement of inventories with a carrying value of $9.2 million. In their review of Crown's physical inventory listing, the auditors did not discover that the fictitious and altered tags were listed in units of 50,000-pound aluminum coils; yet Crown did not manufacture or purchase aluminum coils in excess of 5,000 pounds. The CPA firm paid $875,000 to the parent company of Crown Aluminum Corporation in reimbursement of expenses incurred in the subsequent discovery and investigation of the fraud.

The preceding discussion has assumed that inventory tags and summaries are prepared manually. Clients using electronic data processing equipment may facilitate inventory counting and summarizing through the use of punched cards and machine-sensible pencils. Tag numbers, part numbers, descriptions, and unit prices may be prepunched into cards used as inventory tags. Count teams then record counts with pencils that are computer-sensible. The computer extends quantity times unit price for each punched card and prints out a complete inventory summary.

During the observation of physical inventories, the auditors should make inquiries to ascertain whether any of the materials or goods on hand are the property of others, such as goods held on consignment or customer-owned materials sent in for machine work or other processing.

Audit procedures applicable to goods held by the client on consignment may include a comparison of the physical inventory with the client's records of consigned goods on hand, review of contracts and correspondence with consignors, and direct written communication with the consignors to confirm the quantity and value of goods held at the balance sheet date and to disclose any client liability for unremitted sales proceeds or from inability to collect consignment accounts receivable.

Working papers will be prepared by each auditor participating in the observation of the inventory. These papers should indicate the extent of test counts, describe any deficiencies noted, and express an opinion as to whether the physical inventory appeared to have been properly taken in accordance with the client's instructions. The auditor-in-charge should prepare a concise summary memorandum indicating the overall extent of observation and the percentage of inventory value covered by quantity tests. The memorandum may also include comments on the consideration given to the factors of quality and condition of stock, the treatment of consigned goods on hand, and the control of shipments and receipts during the counting process. Figure 13–3 illustrates this type of memorandum.

Inventories in public warehouses and on consignment. The examination of warehouse receipts is not sufficient verification of goods stored in public warehouses. The AICPA has recommended direct confirmation in writing from outside custodians of inventories, and supplementary procedures when the amounts involved represent a significant proportion of the current assets or of the total assets of a concern. These supplementary procedures include review of the client's control procedures for investigating prospective warehouses and evaluating the performance of warehouses having custody of the client's goods. The procedures should also include establishing the existence, independence, and financial responsibility of warehouses or other concerns holding substantial quantities of goods belonging to the client. The auditors may refer to a business directory to verify the existence of a bonded public warehouse. If the amounts are quite material or any reason for doubt exists, they may decide to visit the warehouse, accompanied by a representative of the client, and observe a physical inventory of the client's merchandise stored at the warehouse.

The verification of goods in the hands of consignees may conveniently be begun by obtaining from the client a list of all consignees and copies of the consignment contracts. Contract provisions concerning the payment of freight and other handling charges, the extension of credit, computation of commissions, and frequency of reports and remittances require close attention. After review of the contracts and the client's records of consignment shipments and collections, the auditors should communicate directly with the consignees and obtain full written information on consigned inventory, receivables, unremitted proceeds, and accrued expenses and commissions as of the balance sheet date.

Often, the client may own raw materials that are processed by a subcontractor before being used in the client's production process. The auditors should request the subcontractor to confirm quantities and descriptions of client-owned materials in the subcontractor's possession.

Inventory verification when auditors are engaged after the end of the year. A company desiring an independent audit should engage the auditors well before the end of the year, so they can participate in advance planning of the physical inventory and be prepared to observe

=== **Figure 13–3**

THE WILSHIRE CORPORATION
Comments on Observation of Physical Inventory   D-9

December 31, 1984

1. Advance Planning of Physical Inventory.

A physical inventory was taken by the client on December 31, 1984. Two
weeks in advance of this date we reviewed the written inventory instructions
prepared by L. D. Frome, Controller. These instructions appeared entirely
adequate and reflected the experience gained during the counts of previous
years. The plan called for a complete closing down of the factory on December 31,
since the preceding year's count had been handicapped by movements of productive
material during the counting process. Training meetings were conducted by
Frome for all employees assigned to participate in the inventory; at these
meetings the written instructions were explained and discussed.

2. Observation of Physical Inventory.

We were present throughout the taking of the physical inventory on December 31,
1984. Prior to the count, all materials had been neatly arranged, labeled, and
separated by type. Two-employee inventory teams were used: one employee counting and
calling quantities and descriptions; the other employee filling in data on the serially
numbered inventory tags. As the goods were counted, the counting team tore off
the "first count" portion of the inventory tag. A second count was made later by
another team working independently of the first; this second team recorded the
quantity of its count on the "second count" portion of the tag.

We made test counts of the numerous items, covering approximately 30 percent
of the total inventory value. These counts were recorded on our working papers and
used as noted below. Our observation throughout the plant indicated that both the
first and second counts required by the inventory instructions were being performed
in a systematic and conscientious manner. The careful and alert attitude of employees
indicated that the training meetings preceding the count had been quite effective in
creating an understanding of the importance of an accurate count. Before the "second
count" portions of the tags were removed, we visited all departments in company with
Frome and satisfied ourselves that all goods had been tagged and counted.

No goods were shipped on December 31. We ascertained that receiving reports
were prepared on all goods taken into the receiving department on this day. We
recorded the serial numbers of the last receiving report and the last shipping advice
for the year 1984. (See D-9-1.) We compared the quantities per the count with
perpetual inventory records and found no significant discrepancies.

3. Quality and Condition of Materials.

Certain obsolete parts had been removed from stock prior to the count and reduced
to a scrap carrying value. On the basis of our personal observation and questions
addressed to supervisors, we have no reason to believe that any obsolete or defective
materials remained in inventory. During the course of inventory observation, we tested
the reasonableness of quantities of 10 items, representing 40 percent of the value
of the inventory, by comparing the quantity on hand with the quantity used in
recent months; in no case did we find that the quantity in inventory exceeded
three months' normal usage.

V. M. H.
1/3/85

the actual counting process. Occasionally, however, auditors are not engaged until after the end of the year and therefore find it impossible to observe the taking of inventory at the close of the year. For example, the illness or death of a company's individual practitioner CPA near the year-end might lead to the engagement of new auditors shortly after the balance sheet date.

Under these circumstances, the auditors may conclude that sufficient competent evidence cannot be obtained concerning inventories to permit them to express an opinion on the overall fairness of the financial statements. On the other hand, if circumstances are favorable, the auditors may be able to obtain satisfaction concerning the inventories by alternative auditing procedures. These favorable circumstances might include the existence of strong internal control, perpetual inventory records, availability of instructions and other records showing that the client had carried out a well-planned physical inventory at or near the year-end, and the making of test counts by the newly appointed auditors. If the auditors are to express an unqualified opinion, their investigation of inventories must include some physical contact with items of inventory and must be thorough enough to compensate for the fact that they were not present when the physical inventory was taken. Whether such alternative auditing procedures will be feasible and will enable the auditors to satisfy themselves depends upon the circumstances of the particular engagement.

7. Obtain a copy of the completed physical inventory, determine its clerical accuracy, and trace test counts.

The testing of inventory extensions and footings may disclose substantial misstatements of physical inventories. Often this test consists of "sight-footing" to the nearest hundred dollars or thousand dollars.

In testing extensions, the auditors should be alert for two sources of substantial errors—misplaced decimal points and incorrect extension of *count* units by *price* units. For example, an inventory listing that extends 1,000 units times $1.00C (per hundred) as $1,000 will be overstated $990. An inventory extension of 1,000 sheets of steel times $1 per pound will be substantially understated if each sheet of steel weighs more than one pound.

The auditors also should trace to the completed physical inventory their test counts made during the observation of physical inventory. During this tracing, the auditors should be alert for any indications that inventory tags have been altered or that fictitious inventory tags have been created. The auditors may compare inventory tag number sequences in the physical inventory listing to tag numbers noted in their audit working papers for the inventory observation.

Another test of the clerical accuracy of the completed physical inventory is the reconciliation of the physical counts to inventory records. Both the quantities and the values of the items should be compared to the company's perpetual records. The totals of various sections of inventory should also be compared with the corresponding control accounts. All substantial discrepancies should be investigated fully. The number, type, and cause of the discrepancies revealed by such comparisons are highly significant in appraising the adequacy of the system of internal control over inventories.

8. Review inventory quality and condition.

The auditors' responsibility for determining quality or condition of inventories is less rigorous than their responsibility for determining existence and ownership of inventories, for auditors do not claim to be experts in detecting deterioration or obsolescence of goods. However, an awareness of the problem and an alert attitude to recognize and act upon any evidence of unsatisfactory condition of goods is expected of the auditors.

To discharge their responsibility for inventory quality and condition, the auditors may have to rely upon the advice of a specialist. For example, the auditors of a retail jeweler might request the client to hire an independent expert in jewelry to assist the auditors in identifying the precious stones and metals included in the client's inventory. Similarly, the auditors of a chemical producer might rely upon the expert opinion of an independent chemist as to the identity of components of the client's inventories. Guidelines for using the work of a specialist are in Chapter 7.

The auditors should also be alert during the course of their inventory observation for any inventory of questionable quality or condition. Excessive dust or rust on raw materials inventory items may be indicative of obsolescence or infrequent use.

The auditors should also review perpetual inventory records for indications of slow-moving inventory items. Then, during the course of observing inventory taking, the auditors should examine these slow-moving items and determine that the client has identified the items as obsolete if appropriate.

9. Review the bases and methods of inventory pricing.

The auditors are responsible for determining that the bases and methods of pricing inventory are in accordance with generally accepted accounting principles. The investigation of inventory pricing often will emphasize the following three questions:

1. What method of pricing does the client use?
2. Is the method of pricing the same as that used in prior years?
3. Has the method officially selected by the client been applied consistently and accurately in practice?

For the first question—a method of pricing—a long list of alternatives is possible, including such methods as cost; cost or market, whichever is lower; the retail method; and quoted market price (as for metals and staple commodities traded on organized exchanges). The cost method, of course, includes many diverse systems, such as last-in, first-out; first-in, first-out; specific identification; weighted average; and standard cost.

The second question raised in this section concerned a change in method of pricing inventory from one year to the next. For example, let us say that the client has changed from the first-in, first-out method to the last-in, first-out method. The nature and justification of the change in method of valuing inventory and its effect on income should be disclosed in accordance with the provisions of *APB Opinion No. 20*, "Accounting Changes." In addition, the auditors must insert in the audit report a qualification concerning the lack of consistency in the two years.

The third question posed dealt with consistent accurate application in practice of the method of valuation officially adopted by the client. To answer this question the auditors must test the pricing of a representative number of inventory items.

10. Test the pricing of inventories.

The testing of prices applied to inventories of raw materials, purchased parts, and supplies by a manufacturing company is similar to the testing of prices of merchandise in a trading business. In both cases, cost of inventory items, whether last-in, first-out, first-in, first-out, weighted average, or specific identification, is readily verified by reference to purchase invoices. An illustration of a working paper prepared by an auditor in making price tests of an inventory of raw materials and purchased parts is presented in Figure 13–4.

Audit procedures for verification of the inventory values assigned to goods-in-process and finished goods are not so simple and conclusive as in the case of raw materials or merchandise for which purchase invoices are readily available. To determine whether the inventory valuation method used by the client has been properly applied, the auditors must make tests of the pricing of selected items of finished goods and goods-in-process. The items to be tested should be selected from the client's inventory summary sheets after the quantities established by the physical inventory have been priced and extended. Items of large total value may be selected for testing so that the tests will encompass a significant portion of the dollar amount of inventories. If statistical sampling is employed, the selection of items for testing will of course be on a random basis.

Lower-of-cost-or-market test. As a general rule, inventories should not be carried at an amount in excess of net realizable value. The lower-of-cost-or-market rule is a common means of measuring any loss of utility in the inventories. If the inventory includes any discontinued lines or obsolete or damaged goods, the client should reduce these items to net realizable value, which is often scrap value.

Illustrative case. During the first audit of an automobile agency, the auditors were observing the taking of the physical inventory of repair parts. They noticed a large number of new fenders of a design and shape not used on the current model cars. Closer inspection

Figure 13-4

The Wilshire Corporation
Test of Pricing-Raw Materials and Purchased Parts (Fifo)   D-5
December 31, 1984

Part No.	Description	Per Inventory Quantity	Price	Vendor	Per Vendor's Invoice Date	No.	Quantity	Price
8Z 182	Aluminum 48×144×.025	910 sheets	10.10	Hardy & Co.	12/18/84	5418	1,000	10.10 y
8Z 195	Aluminum 45×72×.032	84 sheets	9.01	Watson Mfg. Co.	11/28/84	2815	500	9.01 y
					12/22/84	3207	500	9.01 y
K 1125	Stainless steel .025×23	80,625 lbs.	.80	Ajax Steel Co.	12/3/84	K182	100,000	.80 y
K 1382	Stainless steel .031×17	65,212 lbs.	.82	Ajax Steel Co.	12/3/84	K182	75,000	.82 y
XL 3925	10 H.P. Electronic Motor	50 ea.	400.00	Cronyn Mfg. Co.	11/18/84	253	100	400.00 y
XJ 3821	¾ H.P. Electronic Motor	645 ea.	30.50	Long & Co.	12/29/84	E9821	650	30.50 y

Inventory value of raw materials and purchased parts selected for price testing — $301,825.56.

% of total raw materials and purchased parts selected for price testing — $\frac{\$301,825.56}{503,615.10} = 60\%$

See audit program B-4 for method of selecting raw materials and purchased parts for price testing.

y - agreed to prices on the vendor's invoice.

Conclusion:
Based on our tests, it appears that the pricing of raw materials and purchased parts is materially correct.

Prepared by: C.N.S.
1/4/85

Reviewed by: W.B.
1/7/85

revealed that the fenders (with a total inventory valuation of several thousand dollars) were for a model of automobile made seven years ago. The records showed that only one of this type of fender had been sold during the past two years. The automobile dealer explained that these fenders had been included in the parts inventory when he purchased the agency two years ago and that he had no idea as to why such a large stock had originally been acquired. He agreed that few, if any, of this model of fender would ever be sold. It had not occurred to him to write down the carrying value of these obsolete parts, but he readily agreed with the auditors' suggestion that the fenders, being virtually unsalable, should be reduced to scrap value.

11. Review the year-end cutoff of purchases and sales transactions.

An accurate cutoff of purchases is one of the most important factors in verifying the accuracy and completeness of the year-end inventory. Assume that a shipment of goods costing $10,000 is received from a supplier on December 31, but the purchase invoice does not arrive until January 2 and is entered as a January transaction. If the goods are included in the December 31 physical inventory but there is no December entry to record the purchase and the liability, the result will be an overstatement of both net income for the year and retained earnings and an understatement of accounts payable, each error being in the full amount of $10,000 (ignoring income taxes).

An opposite situation may arise if a purchase invoice is received and recorded on December 31, but the merchandise covered by the invoice is not received until several days later and is not included in the physical inventory taken at the year-end. The effect on the financial statements of recording a purchase without including the goods in the inventory will be to understate net income, retained earnings, and inventory.

How can the auditors determine that the liability to suppliers has been recorded for all goods included in inventory? Their approach is to *examine on a test basis the purchase invoices and receiving reports for several days before and after the inventory date.* Each purchase invoice in the files should have a receiving report attached; if an invoice recorded in late December is accompanied by a receiving report dated December 31 or earlier, the goods must have been on hand and included in the year-end physical inventory. However, if the receiving report carried a January date, the goods were not included in the physical count made on December 31.

A supplementary approach to the matching of purchase invoices and receiving reports is to examine the records of the receiving department. For each shipment received near the year-end, the auditors should determine that the related purchase invoice was recorded in the same period.

The effect on the financial statements of failing to include a year-end in-transit purchase as part of physical inventory is not a serious one, *provided* the related liability is not recorded until the following period. In other words, the primary point in effecting an accurate *cutoff of purchases is that both sides of a purchase transaction must be reflected in the same accounting period.* If a given shipment is included in the year-end physical inventory of the purchaser, the entry debiting Inventories and crediting Accounts Payable must be made. If the shipment is not included in the purchaser's year-end physical inventory, the purchase invoice must not be recorded until the following period.

Adjustments to achieve an accurate cutoff of purchases should of course be made by the client's staff; the function of the auditors should be to review the cutoff and determine that the necessary adjustments have been made.

Chapter 12 includes a discussion of the audit procedures for determining the accuracy of the sales cutoff. The sales cutoff is mentioned again at this point to emphasize its importance in determining the fairness of the client's inventory and cost of goods sold as well as accounts receivable and sales.

12. **Perform analytical review procedures related to inventories and cost of goods sold.**

Material errors in pricing, footings, and extensions of the physical inventory, as well as the recording of fictitious transactions, may be disclosed by analytical review procedures designed to establish the general reasonableness of the inventory figures.

A comparative summary of inventories classified by major types, such as raw materials, goods in process, finished goods, and supplies, should be obtained or prepared. Explanations should be obtained for all major increases or decreases from the prior year's amounts.

In certain lines of business, particularly retail and wholesale companies, gross profit margins may be quite uniform from year to year. Any major difference between the ending inventory estimated by the gross profit percentage method and the count of inventory at year-end should be investigated fully. The discrepancy may reflect theft of merchandise, or unrecorded or fictitious purchases or sales. On the other hand, it may be the result of changes in the basis of inventory valuation or of sharp changes in sales prices.

Another useful test is the computation of rates of inventory turnover, based on the relationship between the cost of goods sold for the year and the average inventory as shown on the monthly financial statements. These turnover rates should be compared with the rates prevailing in prior years. A decreasing rate of turnover suggests the possibility of obsolescence or of unnecessarily large inventories. Deliberate stockpiling in anticipation of higher prices or shortages of certain strategic materials will of course be reflected by a declining inventory turnover rate. Rates of turnover are most significant when computed for individual products or by departments; if compared on a company-wide basis,

substantial declines in turnover in certain sections of the client company's operations may be obscured by compensating increases in the
turnover rates for other units of the organization.

The auditors should also make certain that aggregate or unit inventories do not exceed the capacity of the client's production or storage
facilities. For example, in the audit of a manufacturer of chemicals, the
auditors should ascertain the total storage capacity of the client's containers, and determine that the aggregate quantity of chemicals in inventories does not exceed that capacity.

The auditors' review of purchase transactions will often include a
comparison of the volume of transactions from period to period. In this
study the purchase transactions may be classified by vendor and also by
type of product; comparisons made in this manner sometimes disclose
unusual variations of quantities purchased or unusual concentration of
purchases with particular vendors, indicating a possible conflict of
interest.

In addition to the analytical review of purchases and inventories, the
auditors should review all general ledger accounts relating to cost of
sales to make certain that they contain no apparent irregularities. Adjustments of substantial amount should be investigated to determine the
propriety of their inclusion in the cost of goods sold. If this review of
general ledger accounts were not made, the door would be left open for
all types of gross errors to remain undetected—such obvious errors, for
example, as closing miscellaneous revenue and expense into cost of
goods sold.

The auditors of a manufacturer client should obtain from the client
or prepare an analysis of cost of sales by month, broken down into raw
materials, direct labor, and factory overhead elements. The analysis
should also include a description of all unusual and nonrecurring
charges or credits to cost of goods sold. Figure 13–5 illustrates an analysis of cost of goods sold for a manufacturing concern.

13. **In the first audit of a client, investigate beginning inventories.**

The need for the auditors to be present to observe the taking of the
ending inventory has been strongly emphasized in auditing literature.
However, the figure for beginning inventory is equally significant in
determining the cost of goods sold and the net income for the year. In
the initial examination of a client, the auditors may not have been
present to observe the taking of inventory at the beginning of the year.
What procedures can they follow to obtain evidence that the beginning
inventories are fairly stated?

The first factor to consider is whether the client was audited by another firm of independent public accountants for the preceding year. If
a review of the predecessor firm's working papers indicates compliance
with generally accepted auditing standards, the new auditors can accept
the beginning inventories with a minimum of investigation. That mini-

Figure 13–5

The Constellation Company
Cost of Goods Sold
Year Ended December 31, 1984

Acct. No. 501   R-1

Month	Direct Materials	Direct Labor	Inventory Relief② Factory Overhead①	Scrap Sales Proceeds	Under-(Over) Absorbed Factory Overhead③	Total
Jan.	15 160.28	42 815.70 X	64 223.55 X	(819.72)	1 314.68	122 694.49 ∧
Feb.	18 142.55 X	47 922.18	71 883.27	(947.55) 4	(881.14) 4	136 119.31 ∧
Mar.	17 655.95	45 814.00	68 721.00 4	(742.88)	581.26	132 029.33 ∧
Apr.	20 944.16	50 822.16 X	75 333.24	(1 482.67)	(987.44) 4	144 029.45 ∧
May	19 446.82 X	48 144.76 X	72 217.14 X	(1 128.77) 4	(722.66)	137 957.29 ∧
June	22 814.70	52 581.22	78 877.83	(1 222.14)	381.14	153 416.75 ∧
July	21 214.14	51 158.16 X	77 373.24 X	(998.82)	(701.28)	148 469.44 ∧
Aug.	20 844.27 X	51 018.00	76 527.00 4	(1 008.44) 4	914.68 4	148 285.51 ∧
Sept.	19 842.10	49 827.14	74 740.71 X	(882.92)	(481.16)	143 045.87 ∧
Oct.	22 822.90	53 018.10 X	79 527.15 ∧	(1 871.28) 4	714.28 4	154 211.15 ∧
Nov.	20 476.20 X	48 218.70	72 328.05	(1 347.19)	(422.14)	139 253.57 ∧
Dec.	31 807.14	50 976.10 X	76 464.15 X	(1 548.02)	(781.16) 4	146 918.21 ∧
	341 171.21 ∧	592 140.22 ∧	888 010.33 ∧	(14 000.40) ∧	(1 170.99) ∧	1 706 350.37 ∧

Dec. 31, 1984   Adjustment of perpetual inventory to physical @ { D-1 / D-4 } inventory.   76 418.55

Prepared by client   Write-off of loss on fixed price contract No. AF-219-716   22 814.16

1 805 610.08
TO TB-3

∧ = Footed and cross-footed.
= Computation tested—no exceptions.
X = Traced to relief of perpetual inventory accounts—no exceptions.
4 = Vouched proceeds to remittance advice from scrap dealer and to certified weight tickets—no exceptions.

① 150% of direct labor dollars. See R-1-1 for our satisfactory test of this predetermined rate.

② Net overabsorbed factory overhead is less than 1% of total factory overhead applied, hence immaterial.

③ See referenced working paper for satisfactory tests of these write-offs.

④ See D-3 for our satisfactory study of internal control for cost accounting system for year ended December 31, 1984.

Conclusion: In our opinion, cost of goods sold for the year ended December 31, 1984 is fairly stated at the amount of $1,805,610.

mum might include the following steps: (*a*) study of the inventory valuation methods used; (*b*) review of the inventory records; (*c*) review of the inventory sheets used in taking the preceding year's physical inventory; and (*d*) comparison of the beginning and ending inventories, broken down by product classification.

If there had been no satisfactory audit for the preceding year, the investigation of the beginning inventories would include not only the procedures mentioned above, but also the following steps: (*a*) discussion with the person in the client's organization who supervised the physical inventory at the preceding balance sheet date; (*b*) study of the written instructions used in planning the inventory; (*c*) tracing of numerous items from the inventory tags or count sheets to the final summary sheets; (*d*) tests of the perpetual inventory records for the preceding period by reference to supporting documents for receipts and withdrawals; and (*e*) tests of the overall reasonableness of the beginning inventories in relation to sales, gross profit, and rate of inventory turnover. An investigation along these lines will sometimes give the auditors definite assurance that the beginning inventory was carefully compiled and reasonable in amount; in other cases, these procedures may raise serious doubts as to the validity of the beginning inventory figure. In these latter cases, the auditors will not be able to issue an unqualified opinion *as to the income statement.* They may be able, however, to give an unqualified opinion on the *balance sheet,* since this financial statement does not reflect the beginning inventories.

14. Determine whether any inventories have been pledged and review purchase and sales commitments.

The verification of inventories includes a determination by the auditors as to whether any goods have been pledged or subjected to a lien of any kind. Pledging of inventories to secure bank loans should be brought to light when bank balances and indebtedness are confirmed.

A record of outstanding purchase commitments is usually readily available, since this information is essential to management in maintaining day-to-day control of the company's inventory position and cash flow.

In some lines of business it is customary to enter into firm contracts for the purchase of merchandise or materials well in advance of the scheduled delivery dates. Comparison by the auditors of the prices quoted in such commitments with the vendors' prices prevailing at the balance sheet date may indicate substantial losses if firm purchase commitments are not protected by firm sales contracts. Such losses should be reflected in the financial statements.

The quantities of purchase commitments should be reviewed in the light of current and prospective demand, as indicated by past operations, the backlog of sales orders, and current conditions within the industry. If quantities on order appear excessive by these standards, the auditors should seek full information on this phase of operations. As a general rule, purchase commitments need not be mentioned in the financial statements unless significant losses are realized or the commitments are unusual in amount or nature.

Sales commitments are indicated by the client's *backlog* of unfilled sales orders. Losses inherent in firm sales commitments are generally recognized in the lower of cost or market valuation of inventories, with *market* being defined as the net realizable value of the goods-in-process or finished-goods inventories applicable to the sales commitments. In addition, the backlog may include sales orders for which no production has been started as of the balance sheet date. The auditors must review the client's cost estimates for these sales orders. If estimated total costs to produce the goods ordered exceed fixed sales prices, the indicated loss and a related liability should be recorded in the client's financial statements for the current period.

15. **Determine proper financial statement presentation of inventories and cost of goods sold, including adequate disclosure.**

One of the most important factors in proper presentation of inventories in the financial statements is disclosure of the inventory pricing method or methods in use. To say that inventories are stated at *cost* is not sufficient, because cost may be determined under several alternative assumptions, each of which leads to a substantially different valuation.

From the standpoint of analyzing the current earnings of the company, it is extremely important to know whether the reported profits have been inflated by prices changes, as has often been the case under first-in, first-out, or that the effect of price rises has been limited through the LIFO method of valuation. The users of the financial statements also need to know whether the carrying value of inventory approximates current cost (as with first-in, first-out) or whether inventories are stated at cost of an earlier period (as with the LIFO method).

Other important points in presenting inventories in the financial statements include the following:

1. Changes in methods of valuing inventory should be disclosed and the dollar effect and justification for the change reported, in accordance with *APB Opinion No. 20*. The auditors' report will contain a qualification in the opinion paragraph because of the lack of consistency between years.

2. Separate listing is desirable for the various classifications of inventory, such as finished goods, goods in process, and raw materials.

3. If any portion of the inventory has been pledged to secure liabilities, full disclosure of the arrangement should be made.

4. Replacement cost of inventories should be reported in accordance with *FASB Statement No. 33*, "Financial Reporting and Changing Prices."

Examples of disclosures of inventory pricing methods. In many large companies the cost of certain portions of the inventory is determined on one basis, and other portions of inventory on some other

═══════ **Figure 13—6**
Representations as to inventories and cost of goods sold

(Name of Accounting Firm)   Date _____
(Address)

Dear Sirs:

In connection with your examination of the financial statements of the X Company, for the period ended December 31, 19--, we make the following statements and representations concerning inventories and cost of goods sold:

1. Inventories consisting of the following classifications:

    Raw materials and purchased parts . . . . $ XXXX
    Goods in process . . . . $ XXXX
    Finished goods . . . . $ XXXX
    Supplies . . . . $ XXXX

        Total . . . . $ XXXX

    were on hand December 31, 19--, as determined by a physical inventory, taken under our supervision in accordance with written instructions.
2. All inventory quantities were determined by count, weight, or measurement.
3. All inventories owned, and only inventories owned, are included in the above summary, and no inventories have been pledged or hypothecated.
4. All liabilities for inventories have been recorded in the financial statements as of the above balance sheet date.
5. All raw materials, purchased parts, and supplies are stated at the lower of cost or market, with cost determined by the first-in, first-out method after deduction of all trade discounts, consistent with the basis employed in the preceding period.
6. Finished goods and goods in process are stated at manufacturing cost, except for items having a lower net realizable value after proper allowance for completion and disposal costs, consistent with the basis employed in the preceding period.
7. Proper provision has been made in cost of goods sold for obsolete, inactive, and damaged goods.
8. There are no purchase commitments in excess of current market price as of the above balance sheet date.
9. There are no sales commitments below inventory price and no purchase or sale commitments in excess of normal operations.

                                            Signed _____
                                            Title _____

basis. Typical of the disclosure of inventory pricing methods are the following examples taken from published financial statements:

ALPHA PORTLAND CEMENT COMPANY

Inventories—at cost or market, whichever is lower:

Finished cement at cost under LIFO method....................	$ 2,547,980
Raw materials, in process, packages, and operating supplies principally at average cost	1,907,376
Maintenance supplies and repair parts at or below cost	2,155,742

LEAR SIEGLER, INC.

Inventories—at the lower of cost (determined by the first-in, first-out method) or market:

Raw materials	$16,969,758
Work in process	8,110,027
Finished goods	17,068,834
	$42,148,619

Cost of goods sold is reported as a deduction from net sales to arrive at gross profit on sales for a multiple-step income statement. In a single-step income statement, cost of goods sold is included among the costs and expenses section of the income statement.

16. Obtain from client a letter of representations concerning inventories and cost of goods sold.

Public accounting firms generally obtain from clients a formal written statement concerning the overall accuracy of the inventories. The purpose of these representations is to emphasize to management that primary responsibility for the correctness of inventories and cost of sales and of the financial statements as a whole rests with the client rather than with the auditors. Officers or other executives asked to sign such representations are prone to attach greater significance to the process of taking, pricing, and summarizing the physical inventory than they otherwise would. The obtaining of the inventory representations does not in any way reduce the scope of the examination to be made by the auditors; nor does it lessen their responsibility.

The points usually covered in the inventory representations include quantities, titles, prices, commitments, and condition. An example of a form of inventories and cost of goods sold representations letter in common use is shown in Figure 13–6.

KEY TERMS INTRODUCED OR EMPHASIZED IN CHAPTER 13

Bill of lading A document issued by a common carrier acknowledging the receipt of goods and setting forth the provisions of the transportation agreement.

Confirmation A type of documentary evidence that is created outside the client organization and transmitted directly to the auditors.

Consignment A transfer of goods from the owner to another person who acts as the sales agent of the owner.

Cost Accounting Standards Board A five-member board established by Congress to narrow the options in cost accounting that are available under generally accepted accounting principles. Companies having significant supply contracts with certain U.S. government agencies are subject to the cost accounting standards established by the board.

Inventory profits   The amount of net income represented by the difference between the historical cost of an inventory item and its replacement cost at the time it is sold.

Observation   The auditors' evidence-gathering technique that provides physical evidence.

Periodic inventory system   A method of accounting in which inventories are determined solely by means of a physical inventory at the end of the accounting period.

Perpetual inventory system   A method of accounting for inventories in which control accounts and subsidiary ledgers are maintained to record receipts and issuances of goods, both in quantities and in dollar amounts. The accuracy of perpetual inventory records is tested periodically by physical inventories.

Purchase commitment   A contractual obligation to purchase goods at fixed prices, entered into well in advance of scheduled delivery dates.

Replacement cost information   Supplementary information required by *FASB Statement No. 33*. The information may be presented in "unaudited" notes to the financial statements or in supplementary schedules and must be disclosed by certain large corporations.

Sales commitment   A contractual obligation to sell goods at fixed prices, entered into well in advance of scheduled delivery dates.

Specialist   A person or firm possessing special skill or knowledge in a field other than accounting or auditing, such as an actuary.

GROUP I: REVIEW QUESTIONS

13–1.   A client company wishes to conduct its physical inventory on a sampling basis. Many items will not be counted. Under what general conditions will this method of taking inventory be acceptable to the auditors?

13–2.   Why is the information concerning the effects of changing prices required by *FASB Statement No. 33* not required to be audited?

13–3.   What lessons did the Crown Aluminum Corporation case provide for independent auditors?

13–4.   What types of procedures do the auditors perform concerning the replacement-cost information required by *FASB Statement No. 33?*

13–5.   How do the independent auditors use the client's backlog of unfilled sales orders in the examination of inventories?

13–6.   What are cost accounting standards?

13–7.   What are general objectives or purposes of the auditors' observation of the taking of the physical inventory? (Do not discuss the procedures or techniques involved in making the observation.) (AICPA)

13–8.   For what purposes do the auditors make and record test counts of inventory quantities during their observation of the taking of the physical inventory? Discuss. (AICPA)

13–9. What part, if any, do the independent auditors play in the planning for a client's physical inventory?

13–10. Once the auditors have completed their test counts of the physical inventory, will they have any reason to make later reference to the inventory tags used by the client's employees in the counting process? Explain.

13–11. The client's cost accounting system is often the focal point in the auditors' examination of the financial statements of a manufacturing company. For what purposes do the auditors review the cost accounting system? (AICPA)

13–12. What charges and credits may be disclosed in the auditors' analysis of the Cost of Goods Sold account of a manufacturing concern?

13–13. Explain the significance of the purchase order to adequate internal control over purchase transactions.

13–14. What segregation of duties would you recommend to attain maximum internal control over purchasing activities in a manufacturing concern?

13–15. Do you believe that the normal review of purchase transactions by the auditors should include examination of receiving reports? Explain.

13–16. Many auditors consider the substantiation of the figure for inventory to be a more difficult and challenging task than the verification of most other items on the balance sheet. List several specific factors that support this view.

13–17. "A well-prepared balance sheet usually includes a statement that the inventories are valued at cost." Evaluate this quotation.

13–18. Darnell Equipment Company uses the last-in, first-out method of valuation for part of its inventories and weighted-average cost for another portion. Would you be willing to issue an unqualified opinion under these circumstances? Explain.

13–19. "If the auditors can determine that all goods in the physical inventory have been accurately counted and properly priced, they will have discharged fully their responsibility with respect to inventory." Evaluate this statement.

13–20. When perpetual inventory records are maintained, is it necessary for a physical inventory to be taken at the balance sheet date? Explain.

13–21. The controller of a new client company informs you that most of the inventories are stored in bonded public warehouses. He presents warehouse receipts to account for the inventories. Will careful examination of these warehouse receipts constitute adequate verification of these inventories? Explain.

13–22. Hana Ranch Company, which has never been audited, is asked on October 1 by its bank to arrange for a year-end audit. The company retains you to make this audit and asks what measures, if any, it should take to ensure a satisfactory year-end physical inventory. Perpetual inventories are not maintained. How would you answer this inquiry?

13–23. Enumerate specific steps to be taken by the auditors to ascertain that a client's inventories have not been pledged or subjected to a lien of any kind.

GROUP II: QUESTIONS REQUIRING ANALYSIS

13–24.   Select the best answer for each of the following and explain fully the reason for your selection.

a.   Which of the following is the best audit procedure for the discovery of damaged merchandise in a client's ending inventory?

(1)   Compare the physical quantities of slow-moving items with corresponding quantities of the prior year.

(2)   Observe merchandise and raw materials during the client's physical inventory taking.

(3)   Review the management's inventory representation letter for accuracy.

(4)   Test overall fairness of inventory values by comparing the company's turnover ratio with the industry average.

b.   McPherson Corp. does not make an annual physical count of year-end inventories, but instead makes weekly test counts on the basis of a statistical plan. During the year Sara Mullins, CPA, observes such counts as she deems necessary and is able to satisfy herself as to the reliability of the client's procedures. In reporting on the results of her examination Mullins—

(1)   Can issue an unqualified opinion without disclosing that she did not observe year-end inventories.

(2)   Must comment in the scope paragraph as to her inability to observe year-end inventories, but can nevertheless issue an unqualified opinion.

(3)   Is required, if the inventories were material, to disclaim an opinion on the financial statements taken as a whole.

(4)   Must, if the inventories were material, qualify her opinion.

c.   The primary objective of a CPA's observation of a client's physical inventory count is to

(1)   Discover whether a client has counted a particular inventory item or group of items.

(2)   Obtain direct knowledge that the inventory exists and has been properly counted.

(3)   Provide an appraisal of the quality of the merchandise on hand on the day of the physical count.

(4)   Allow the auditor to supervise the conduct of the count so as to obtain assurance that inventory quantities are reasonably accurate.

d.   When the auditors test a client's cost accounting system, the auditors' tests are *primarily* designed to determine that

(1)   Quantities on hand have been computed based on acceptable cost accounting techniques that reasonably approximate actual quantities on hand.

(2)   Physical inventories are in substantial agreement with book inventories.

(3)   The system is in accordance with generally accepted accounting principles.

(4)   Costs have been properly assigned to finished goods, work-in-process and cost of goods sold. (AICPA, adapted)

13–25.   During the March 31 audit of a new client, Electronics Company, the auditors discovered that the client had acquired in a bulk purchase various raw materials used to produce parts for electronic data processing equipment. The bulk purchase had been completed more than a year previously, yet less than 10 percent of the raw materials had been used by Electronics Company since that time. The company's controller acknowledged that there might be some obsolete raw materials on hand from the bulk purchase; he claimed, however, that not enough time had elapsed to determine with assurance the complete degree of obsolescence. The controller therefore offered to write down to salvage value one third of the remaining raw materials from the bulk purchase. For the remainder, the controller offered to give the auditors a letter of representations stating that he believed the remaining materials to be not obsolete.

Will the controller's letter of representations provide sufficient, competent evidence for the auditors with respect to obsolescence of inventories? Discuss.

13–26.   You are engaged in the audit of Reed Company, a new client, at the end of its first fiscal year, June 30, 1985. During your work on inventories, you discover that all of the merchandise remaining in stock on June 30, 1985 had been acquired July 1, 1984 from Andrew Reed, the sole shareholder and president of Reed Company, for an original selling price of $10,000 cash and a note payable due July 1, 1987, with interest at 15 percent, in the amount of $90,000. The merchandise had been used by the president when he operated a similar business as a single proprietor.

How can you verify the pricing of the June 30, 1985 inventory of Reed Company? Explain.

13–27.   The observation of a client's physical inventory is a mandatory auditing procedure when practicable and possible for the auditors to carry out and when inventories are material.

Required:
   a.   Why is the observation of physical inventory a mandatory auditing procedure? Explain.
   b.   Under what circumstances is observation of physical inventory impracticable or impossible?
   c.   Why is the auditors' review of the client's control for inventory tags important during the observation of physical inventory? Explain.

13–28.   You have been asked to examine the financial statements of Wilson Corporation, a roadbuilding contractor that has never before been audited by CPAs. During your interim work, you learn that Wilson excludes a significant inventory item from its annual balance sheet. This inventory item, which Wilson management claims is approximately the same amount each year, is gravel that has been processed for use in road building and is placed at different road construction sites wherever it might be used. Wilson's controller states that any unused gravel at the completion of a construction contract is never moved to another job site; in fact, the gravel often disappears because of thefts during winter months when road construction is suspended.

Would you be able to issue an unqualified opinion on the financial statements of Wilson Corporation? Explain.

13–29. Grandview Manufacturing Company employs standards costs in its cost accounting system. List the audit procedures that you would apply to ascertain that Grandview's standard costs and related variance amounts are acceptable and have not distorted the financial statements. (Confine your audit procedures to those applicable to raw materials.) (AICPA, adapted)

13–30. At the beginning of your annual audit of Crestview Manufacturing Company's financial statements for the year ended December 31, 198x, the company president confides in you that Henry Ward, an employee, is living on a scale in excess of that which his salary would support.

The employee has been a buyer in the purchasing department for six years and has charge of purchasing all general materials and supplies. He is authorized to sign purchase orders for amounts up to $500. Purchase orders in excess of $500 require the countersignature of the general purchasing agent.

The president understands that the usual examination of financial statements is not designed, and cannot be relied upon, to disclose fraud or conflicts of interest, although their discovery may result. The president authorizes you, however, to expand your regular audit procedures and to apply additional audit procedures to determine whether there is any evidence that the buyer has been misappropriating company funds or has been engaged in activities that were conflicts of interest.

Required:

List the audit procedures you would apply to the company records and documents in an attempt to discover evidence within the purchasing department of defalcations being committed by the buyer. Give the purpose of each audit procedure. (AICPA, adapted)

13–31. A number of companies employ outside service companies that specialize in counting, pricing, extending, and footing inventories. These service companies usually furnish a certificate attesting to the value of the physical inventory.

Assuming that the service company took the client company's inventory on the balance sheet date:
a. How much reliance, if any, can the auditors place on the inventory certificate of outside specialists? Discuss.
b. What effect, if any, would the inventory certificate of outside specialists have upon the type of report the auditors would render? Discuss.
c. What reference, if any, would the auditors make to the certificate of outside specialists in their audit report? (AICPA)

13–32. Santa Rosa Corporation is a closely held furniture manufacturing company employing approximately one thousand employees. On December 15, the corporation retained the firm of Warren and Wood, Certified Public Accountants, to perform a December 31 year-end audit. The president of the corporation explained that perpetual inventory records were maintained and that every attention was given to maintaining a strong system of internal control. A complete count of inventories had been made at November 30 by the company's own employees; in addition, extensive test counts had been made in most departments at various intervals during the year. Although the company was not large, it employed an internal auditor and an assistant who had devoted their full time to analysis of internal control and appraisal of operations in the various organizational units of the company.

The certified public accountant who had audited Santa Rosa Corporation for several years had died during the current year, and the company had decided to forego an annual audit. The physical inventory had therefore been taken at November 30 without being observed by an independent public accountant. Shortly thereafter, a major stockholder in the company had demanded that new auditors be retained. The president explained to Warren and Wood that the company was too far behind on its delivery schedules to take time out for another physical inventory, but that all the papers used in the recent count were available for their review. The auditors reviewed these papers, made a thorough analysis of the internal controls over inventory, and made test counts at December 31 of large items representing 10 percent of the total value of inventory. The items tested were traced to the perpetual inventory records, and no significant discrepancies were found. Inventories at December 31 amounted to $4 million out of total assets of $9 million.

Required:
Assume that the auditors find no shortcomings in any aspect of the examination apart from the area of inventories. You are to prepare:
a. An argument setting forth the factors that indicate the issuance of an unqualified audit opinion.
b. An opposing argument setting for the factors that indicate the auditors should not issue an unqualified opinion.

13–33. One of the problems faced by the auditors in their verification of inventory is the possibility that slow-moving and obsolete items may be included in the goods on hand at the balance sheet date. In the event that such items are identified in the physical inventory, their carrying value should be written down to an estimated scrap value or other recoverable amount.

Prepare a list of the auditing procedures that the auditors should employ to determine whether slow-moving or obsolete items are included in the physical inventory.

13–34. During your observation of the November 30, 1984 physical inventory of Jay Company, you note the following unusual items:
a. Electric motors in finished goods storeroom not tagged. Upon inquiry, you are informed that the motors are on consignment to Jay Company.
b. A cutting machine (one of Jay's principal products) in the receiving department, with a large REWORK tag attached.
c. A crated cutting machine in the shipping department, addressed

to a nearby U.S. naval base, with a Department of Defense "Material Inspection and Receiving Report" attached, dated November 30, 1984 and signed by the Navy Source Inspector.

d. A small, isolated storeroom with five types of dusty raw materials stored therein. Inventory tags are attached to all of the materials, and your test counts agree with the tags.

Required:
What additional procedures, if any, would you carry out for each of the above? Explain.

13–35. Ace Corporation does not conduct a complete annual physical count of purchased parts and supplies in its principal warehouse, but uses statistical sampling instead to estimate the year-end inventory. Ace maintains a perpetual inventory record of parts and supplies and believes that statistical sampling is highly effective in determining inventory values and is sufficiently reliable to make a physical count of each item of inventory unnecessary.

Required:
a. Identify the audit procedures that should be used by the independent auditor that change or are in addition to normal required audit procedures when a client utilizes statistical sampling to determine inventory value and does not conduct a 100 percent annual physical count of inventory items.

b. List at least 10 normal audit procedures that should be performed *to verify physical quantities* whenever a client conducts a periodic physical count of all or part of its inventory. (AICPA, adapted)

13–36. Nolan Manufacturing Company retains you on April 1 to perform an audit for the fiscal year ending June 30. During the month of May, you made extensive studies of the system of internal control over inventories.

All goods purchased pass through a receiving department under the direction of the chief purchasing agent. The duties of the receiving department are to unpack, count, and inspect the goods. The quantity received is compared with the quantity shown on the receiving department's copy of the purchase order. If there is no discrepancy, the purchase order is stamped "OK—Receiving Dept." and forwarded to the accounts payable section of the accounting department. Any discrepancies in quantity or variations from specifications are called to the attention of the buyer by returning the purchase order to him with an explanation of the circumstances. No records are maintained in the receiving department, and no reports originate there.

As soon as goods have been inspected and counted in the receiving department, they are sent to the factory production area and stored alongside the machines in which they are to be processed. Finished goods are moved from the assembly line to a storeroom in the custody of a stock clerk, who maintains a perpetual inventory record in terms of physical units, but not in dollars.

What weaknesses, if any, do you see in the internal control over inventories?

GROUP III: PROBLEMS

13–37. David Anderson, CPA, is engaged in the examination of the financial
statements of Redondo Manufacturing Corporation for the year ended
June 30, 1985. Redondo's inventories at year-end include finished
merchandise on consignment with consignees and finished merchandise stored in public warehouses. The merchandise in public
warehouses is pledged as collateral for outstanding debt.

Required:
Normal inventory and notes-payable auditing procedures have been
satisfactorily completed. Describe the specific additional auditing
procedures that Anderson should undertake with respect to—
  a. Consignments out.
  b. Finished merchandise in public warehouses pledged as collateral
      for outstanding debt. (AICPA, adapted)

13–38. You have been engaged by the management of Alden, Inc., to review its
internal control over the purchase, receipt, storage, and issue of raw
materials. You have prepared the following comments, which describe
Alden's procedures.

  (1) Raw materials, which consist mainly of high-cost electronic com-
       ponents, are kept in a locked storeroom. Storeroom personnel
       include a supervisor and four clerks. All are well trained, compe-
       tent, and adequately bonded. Raw materials are removed from
       the storeroom only upon written or oral authorization of one of
       the production first-line supervisors.

  (2) There are no perpetual-inventory records; hence, the storeroom
       clerks do not keep records of goods received or issued. To com-
       pensate for the lack of perpetual records, a physical-inventory
       count is taken monthly by the storeroom clerks, who are well
       supervised. Appropriate procedures are followed in making the
       inventory count.

  (3) After the physical count, the storeroom supervisor matches quan-
       tities counted against a predetermined reorder level. If the count
       for a given part is below the reorder level, the supervisor enters
       the part number on a materials-requisition list and sends this list
       to the accounts payable clerk. The accounts-payable clerk pre-
       pares a purchase order for a predetermined reorder quantity for
       each part and mails the purchase order to the vendor from whom
       the part was last purchased.

  (4) When ordered materials arrive at Alden, they are received by the
       storeroom clerks. The clerks count the merchandise and agree
       the counts to the carrier's bill of lading. All bills of lading are
       initialed, dated, and filed in the storeroom to serve as receiving
       reports.

Required:
Describe the weaknesses in internal control and recommend improvements of Alden's procedures for the purchase, receipt, storage,
and issue of raw materials. Organize your answer sheet as follows:

Weaknesses	*Recommended improvements*

(AICPA, adapted)

13–39. You are an audit manager of the rapidly growing CPA firm of Raye and Coye. You have been placed in charge of three new audit clients, which have the following inventory features:

(1) Canyon Cattle Co., which maintains 15,000 head of cattle on a 1,000 square mile ranch, mostly unfenced, near the south rim of the Grand Canyon in Arizona.

(2) Rhoads Mfg. Co., which has raw materials inventories consisting principally of pig iron loaded on gondola freight cars on a siding at the company's plant.

(3) Strawser Company, which is in production around the clock on three shifts, and which cannot shut down production during the physical inventory.

Required:

What problems do you anticipate in the observation of physical inventories of the three new clients, and how would you deal with the problems?

13–40. Royal Meat Processing Company buys and processes livestock for sale to supermarkets. In connection with the examination of the company's financial statements, you have prepared the following notes based on your review of inventory procedures:

(1) Each livestock buyer submits a daily report of his or her purchases to the plant superintendent. This report shows the dates of purchase and expected delivery, the vendor and the number, weights and type of livestock purchased. As shipments are received, any available plant employee counts the number of each type received and places a check mark beside this quantity on the buyer's report. When all shipments listed on the report have been received, the report is returned to the buyer.

(2) Vendors' invoices, after a clerical review, are sent to the appropriate buyer for approval and returned to the accounting department. A disbursement voucher and a check for the approved amount are prepared in the accounting department. Checks are forwarded to the treasurer for signature. The treasurer's office sends signed checks directly to the buyer for delivery to the vendor.

(3) Livestock carcasses are processed by lots. Each lot is assigned a number. At the end of each day a tally sheet reporting the lots processed, the number and type of animals in each lot, and the carcass weight is sent to the accounting department, where a perpetual inventory record of processed carcasses and their weights is maintained.

(4) Processed carcasses are stored in a refrigerated cooler located in a small building adjacent to the employee parking lot. The cooler is

locked when the plant is not open, and a company guard is on duty when the employees report for work and leave at the end of their shifts. Supermarket truck drivers wishing to pick up their orders have been instructed to contact someone in the plant if no one is in the cooler.

(5) Substantial quantities of by-products are produced and stored, either in the cooler or elsewhere in the plant. By-products are initially accounted for as they are sold. At this time the sales manager prepares a two-part form: one copy serves as authorization to transfer the goods to the customer, and the other becomes the basis for billing the customer.

Required:

For each of the numbered notes (1) to (5) above, state the weaknesses, if any, in the present inventory procedures and your suggestions, if any, for improvement. (AICPA, adapted)

13–41. Payne Press Company is engaged in the manufacture of large-size presses under specific contracts and in accordance with customers' specifications. Customers are required to advance 25 percent of the contract price. The company records sales on a shipment basis and accumulates costs by job orders. The normal profit margin over the past few years has been approximately 5 percent of sales, after provision for selling and administrative expenses of about 10 percent of sales. Inventories are valued at the lower of cost or market.

Among the jobs you are reviewing in the course of your annual examination of the company's December 31 financial statements is Job No. 2357, calling for delivery of a three-color press at a firm contract price of $50,000. Costs accumulated for the job at the year-end aggregated $30,250. The company's engineers estimated that the job was approximately 55 percent complete at December 31. Your audit procedures have been as follows:

(1) Examined all contracts, noting pertinent provisions.
(2) Observed physical inventory of jobs in process and reconciled details to job order accounts.
(3) Compliance-tested input of labor, material, and overhead charges into the various jobs to determine that such charges were authentic and had been posted correctly.
(4) Confirmed customers' advances at year-end.
(5) Reconciled goods-in-process job ledger with control account.

Required:

With respect to Job No. 2357:

a. State what additional audit procedures, if any, you would follow and explain the purpose of the procedures.

b. Indicate the manner and the amount at which you would include Job No. 2357 in the balance sheet. (AICPA, adapted)

13–42. Late in December, your CPA firm accepted an audit engagement at Nash Jewelers, Inc., a corporation that deals largely in diamonds. The corporation has retail jewelry stores in several eastern cities and a diamond wholesale store in New York City. The wholesale store also sets the diamonds in rings and other quality jewelry.

The retail stores place orders for diamond jewelry with the wholesale store in New York City. A buyer employed by the wholesale store purchases diamonds in the New York diamond market; the wholesale store then fills orders from the retail stores and from independent customers and maintains a substantial inventory of diamonds. The corporation values its inventory by the specific identification cost method.

Required:

Assume that at the inventory date you are satisfied that Nash Jewelers, Inc., has no items left by customers for repair or sale on consignment and that no inventory owned by the corporation is in the possession of outsiders.

a. Discuss the problems the auditors should anticipate in planning for the observation of the physical inventory on this engagement because of the—

  (1) Different locations of inventories.

  (2) Nature of the inventory.

b. Assume that a shipment of diamond rings was in transit by corporation messenger from the wholesale store to a retail store on the inventory date. What additional audit steps would you take to satisfy yourself as to the gems that were in transit from the wholesale store on the inventory date? (AICPA, adapted)

GROUP IV: CASE STUDIES IN AUDITING

13–43.   WESTERN TRADING COMPANY

Western Trading Company is a sole proprietorship engaged in the grain brokerage business. At December 31, 1984, the entire grain inventory of the company was stored in outside bonded warehouses. The company's procedure of pricing inventories in these warehouses included comparing the actual cost of each commodity in inventory with the market price as reported for transactions on the commodity exchanges at December 31. A write-down was made on commodities in which cost was in excess of market. During the course of the 1984 examination, the auditors verified the company's computations. In addition to this, they compared the inventory prices with market prices at dates subsequent to the year-end. Before the end of the engagement, the market declined sharply for one commodity until its market price was below the average inventory price. The auditors suggested that the inventory be written down to give effect to this decline in market price subsequent to December 31, 1984. The company agreed, and a write-down of $7,000 was made.

The auditors also examined the trading position of the company and found that there was a short position in grain trading; that is, the sales negotiated for future delivery exceeded the total of year-end inventory and purchase contracts. The indicated loss on these contracts was reflected in the financial statements. After the above adjustments, the final net income for 1984 amounted to $30,000.

At December 31, 1985, the auditors made a similar examination of the financial statements of Western Trading Company. They found that the company had priced the inventory in the same manner as in 1984. The auditors followed procedures similar to those used in 1984 and at the end of their field work on February 2, 1986, noted that the inventories were priced at an amount that was not in excess of the market at that time. The trading position had been examined; the short position at the end of 1985 had an indicated gain of $4,000. No adjustment was proposed for this amount. Subsequent to the completion of the field work, but prior to the issuance of the audit report, there was a sharp decline in the market price of one commodity. The inventory was repriced by the auditors on the basis of the new market price, and the inventory value at December 31, 1985 was found to be in excess of market by approximately $21,000. The auditors proposed that the inventories be written down by $17,000 to this new market value, net of the gains on the subsequent sales. The management protested this suggestion, stating that in their opinion the market decline was only temporary and that prices would recover in the near future. They refused to allow the write-down to be made. Accordingly, the auditors took an exception in their audit report dated February 16, 1986, and the opinion paragraph of their report read as follows:

Except for the effect of the failure to record the market decline in grain inventories discussed in Note 2 to the financial statements, in our opinion, the financial statements referred to above present fairly the financial position of Western Trading Company at December 31, 1985 and the results of its operations and the changes in its financial position for the year then ended, in conformity with generally accepted accounting principles. Except for the matter discussed in Note 2 to the financial statements, these accounting principles were applied on a basis consistent with that of the preceding year.

Note 2 stated:

The company's grain inventories at December 31, 1984 were reduced by approximately $7,000 to reflect a decline in market value subsequent to that date. A similar market decline of approximately $21,000 subsequent to December 31, 1985 has not been recorded by the company. If this adjustment had been made as of December 31, 1985, the grain inventories shown on the accompanying balance sheet and the pretax accounting income for the year would have been reduced by $21,000.

At December 31, 1985, the net short market position of the company was 20,000 bushels of wheat; a gain of some $4,000 applicable thereto, based on the year-end market prices, has not been reflected in the accompanying financial statements.

Net income for the year 1985 amounted to $37,000 as shown by the company's income statement. Subsequent to the issuance of the auditors' report, the market reversed its downward trend and regained the level prevailing at February 2, 1986.

Required:

a. Does the lower-of-cost-or-market method include recognition of price declines subsequent to the balance sheet date? Explain.

b. To what extent should financial statements disclose by footnotes events subsequent to the balance sheet date?

c. If "adequate disclosure" of facts is achieved in the financial statements and accompanying notes, is the position taken by the auditors in their report thereby justified?

d. Were the auditors justified in issuing a qualified opinion in this case? Discuss fully, including alternative courses of action.

e. Would the entry proposed by the auditors have eliminated the necessity for a qualification if it had been made?

f. Was it necessary to comment on lack of consistency in valuation of inventories?

14

Property, plant, and equipment: Depreciation and depletion

The term *property, plant, and equipment* includes all tangible assets with a service life of more than one year that are used in the operation of the business and are not acquired for the purpose of resale. Three major groups of such assets are generally recognized:

1. *Land.* Land used in the operation of the business has the significant characteristic of not being subject to depreciation.
2. *Buildings, machinery, equipment,* and *land improvements,* such as fences and parking lots. Properties in this classification have limited service lives and are subject to depreciation.
3. *Natural resources* (wasting assets), such as oil wells, coal mines, and tracts of timber. These assets are subject to depletion and should be presented on the balance sheet as a separate subgroup.

Closely related to the property, plant, and equipment category are *intangible assets,* such as patents, franchises, and leaseholds. These assets are subject to amortization and should be shown as a separate subgroup on the balance sheet.

The auditors' objectives in examination of property, plant, and equipment

In the examination of property, plant, and equipment, the auditors try to determine the following: (*a*) the adequacy of internal control; (*b*) the existence and ownership of the plant assets; (*c*) the propriety of the

459

valuation methods used; (*d*) the reasonableness of the depreciation program; (*e*) the propriety of recorded revenue, gains and losses from plant assets; and (*f*) the fairness of the presentation of plant assets in the balance sheet and of depreciation in the income statement.

Contrast with audit of current assets

In many companies the investment in plant and equipment amounts to 50 percent or more of the total assets. However, the audit work required to verify these properties is usually a much smaller proportion of the total audit time spent on the engagement. The verification of plant and equipment is facilitated by several factors not applicable to audit work on current assets.

First, a typical unit of property or equipment has a high dollar value, and a relatively few transactions may lie behind a large balance sheet amount. Second, there is usually little change in the property accounts from year to year. The Land account often remains unchanged for a long span of years. The durable nature of buildings and equipment also tends to hold accounting activity to a minimum for these accounts. By way of contrast, such current assets as accounts receivable and inventory may have a complete turnover several times a year.

In the discussion of inventories in Chapter 13, considerable attention was given to the problem of an accurate *cutoff* at the year-end. The auditors must make extensive tests to prove that the year-end cutoff of purchases and sales of merchandise is accurate, because an error in cutoff may cause an error of corresponding amount in the year's pretax income. Errors in making a cutoff of the year's transactions do not pose a comparable problem in the case of plant and equipment acquisitions; a cutoff error in recording the purchase or retirement of equipment will ordinarily not significantly affect the determination of net income for the year. Of course such errors could cause slight inaccuracies in depreciation, or in the timing of gains and losses on retirements.

The auditors' examination of property, plant, and equipment does not include a determination of the adequacy of insurance coverage for several reasons. The amount of insurance is logically related to current value of plant and equipment, and the auditors are not appraisers of property values. Furthermore, the auditors' opinion on financial statements concerns the consistent application of generally accepted accounting principles rather than an evaluation of management's wisdom in deciding whether or not to carry insurance against some of the many risks inherent in property ownership.

Cost as the basis of valuation

Accounting authorities have long held that cost is the proper basis for valuing plant and equipment. The cost basis is a very satisfactory one during periods of stable price levels, for it gives a high degree of objectivity to the process of income measurement. During periods of severe inflation, however, the computation of depreciation expense in terms of the original cost of long-lived assets leads to the reporting of operating profits of questionable validity. The tremendous pressures generated by inflation and by tax rates create a demand that some type of current value be substituted for historical cost figures. The base for depreciation provisions would then be more in keeping with current replacement costs. Recognition of the inadequacies of conventional methods of computing depreciation has increased in recent years as the underlying assumption of stable price levels has become more and more unrealistic.

Under present standards, however, cost is the only accepted basis for valuing plant and equipment. Financial statements that presented property, equipment, and related depreciation on a basis other than cost would not be in conformity with generally accepted accounting principles and therefore could not receive unqualified approval from the auditors.

Unaudited replacement cost information

In an environment of continuing inflation, adequate financial reporting must take into consideration the effects of changing price levels on both earnings and assets. In other words, traditional cost-based financial statements must be supplemented by information on current replacement costs if the needs of investors and other users are to be met.

Both the SEC and the FASB have acted to require large corporations meeting certain size tests to disclose supplementary information of this nature. An important element of this information is the estimated current replacement cost of plant and equipment. Depreciation expense based on current replacement cost also must be disclosed. The SEC's action several years ago (Rule 3.17 of *Regulation S-X*) called upon large corporations to include replacement cost information in a separate supplement to financial statements. The SEC did not require that the replacement cost information be audited, but urged that standards be developed for the guidance of auditors. Later the Financial Accounting Standards Board in *FASB Statement No. 33* took broader action in requiring large corporations to disclose information on the effects of changing price levels.[1]

These disclosure requirements call for replacement cost information (including depreciation) to be shown in a footnote or in a supplementary section accompanying the financial statements. Notice that

---

[1] *FASB Statement No. 33*, "Financial Reporting and Changing Prices," FASB (Stamford, Conn., 1979).

replacement cost information is not to be substituted for historical cost in the financial statements.

Because replacement cost information is supplementary rather than part of the basic financial statements, the auditors' responsibility is much less with respect to this information than for data examined in accordance with generally accepted auditing standards. The replacement cost information *is not audited,* but is reviewed by the auditors. This review consists principally of reading the replacement cost information and making inquiries of management. Limited procedures for the review of replacement cost information as outlined in *SAS 27* were discussed in Chapter 13.

Most large corporations in making the supplementary disclosures required by *FASB Statement No. 33* present a three-column income statement. The three columns show (1) historical cost, (2) constant dollar amounts, and (3) current costs. The largest variation from historical cost is likely to be depreciation expense. In addition to the data in this multicolumn income statement, the supplementary information also shows the current cost of property, plant, and equipment.

In *SAS 28,* "Supplementary Information on the Effects of Changing Prices" (Section 554), the Auditing Standards Board recognizes that the FASB is encouraging experimentation within *FASB Statement No. 33* guidelines. Consequently, the auditors may encounter a variety of methods of measuring replacement cost and must evaluate numerous assumptions and judgmental decisions. If the auditors consider that the narrative explanations required to be included in annual reports to shareholders are in error or are inconsistent with the audited financial statements, the auditors' report should be expanded to describe the nature of the errors or inconsistencies.

Internal controls over plant and equipment

The principal purpose of internal controls relating to plant and equipment *is to obtain maximum efficiency from the dollars invested in plant assets.*

The amounts invested in plant and equipment represent a large portion of the total assets of many industrial concerns. The expenses of maintenance, rearrangement, and depreciation of these assets are a major factor in the income statement. The sheer size of the amounts involved makes carefully devised internal controls essential to the production of reliable financial statements. Errors in measurement of income will be material if assets are scrapped without their cost being removed from the accounts, or if the distinction between capital and revenue expenditures is not maintained consistently. The losses that inevitably arise from uncontrolled methods of acquiring, maintaining, and retiring plant and equipment are often greater than the risks of fraud in cash handling.

The plant and equipment budget

In large corporate enterprises the auditors may expect to find an annual plant budget that is used to forecast and control acquisitions and retirements of plant and equipment. Many small concerns also forecast expenditures for plant assets. Successful utilization of a plant budget presupposes the existence of reliable and detailed accounting records for plant and equipment. A detailed knowledge of the kinds, quantities, and condition of existing equipment is an essential basis for intelligent forecasting of the need for replacements and additions to the plant.

If the auditors can ascertain that acquisitions of plant and equipment, whether by purchase or construction, are made in accordance with prior budgetary authorizations and that any necessary expenditures not provided for in the budget are made only upon approval of a major executive, they will be able to minimize the routine testing of the year's acquisitions. Reference to the reports and working papers of the internal auditors is often a convenient method for the independent auditors to become familiar with the scope and dependability of the budgetary controls over plant and equipment.

Other major control devices

Other important internal controls applicable to plant and equipment are as follows:

1. A subsidiary ledger consisting of a separate record for each unit of property. An adequate plant and equipment ledger, usually on magnetic tape or punched cards in large concerns, facilitates the auditors' work in analyzing additions and retirements, in verifying the depreciation provision and maintenance expenses, and in comparing authorizations with actual expenditures.
2. A system of authorizations requiring advance executive approval of all plant and equipment acquisitions, whether by purchase, lease, or construction. Serially numbered capital work orders are a convenient means of recording authorizations.
3. A reporting procedure assuring prompt disclosure and analysis of variances between authorized expenditures and actual costs.
4. An authoritative written statement of company policy distinguishing between capital and revenue expenditures. A dollar minimum ordinarily will be established for capitalization; any expenditures of lesser amount automatically are classified as charges against current revenue.
5. A policy requiring all purchases of plant and equipment to be handled through the purchasing department and subjected to standard routines for receiving, inspection, and payment.
6. Periodic physical inventories, designed to verify the existence, loca-

tion, and condition of all property listed in the accounts and to disclose the existence of any unrecorded units.

7. A system of retirement procedures, including serially numbered retirement work orders, stating reasons for retirement and bearing appropriate approvals.

Audit working papers

Apart from a grouping sheet, the key working paper obtained or prepared by the auditors for property, plant, and equipment is a summary analysis such as that illustrated in Figure 14–1. A significant point to note in this working paper is the emphasis upon *changes during the current period*. The beginning balances of the plant and equipment accounts are usually readily determinable from the prior year's audit working papers. If the auditors are satisfied with the beginning balances and they verify fully the acquisitions and disposals of the current period, then the ending balances will have been firmly established. This audit approach clearly would not be suitable to current asset accounts that may turn over many times during the year, but it is appropriate for the property accounts with their relatively infrequent changes.

Among the other working papers commonly prepared in the audit of property, plant, and equipment are analyses of plant asset additions and retirements, analyses of repairs and maintenance expense accounts, and tests of depreciation provisions. The analyses of plant additions and retirements and the tests of depreciation are cross-indexed to the summary analysis, as illustrated in Figure 14–1.

Initial audits and repeat engagements

The auditing procedures listed in subsequent pages are applicable to repeat engagements and therefore concern only transactions of the current year. In the auditors' first examination of a new client that has changed auditors, the beginning balances of plant and equipment may be substantiated by reference to the predecessor firm's working papers. If, in previous years, audits were made by other reputable firms of public accountants, it is not customary to go beyond a general review of the past history of the plant and equipment as recorded in the accounts.

In a first audit of a company for which audits by independent public accountants have not been made previously, the ideal approach is a complete historical analysis of the property accounts. By thorough review of all major charges and credits to the property accounts since their inception, the auditors can determine whether the company has consistently followed good accounting practices in recording capital additions and retirements and in providing for periodic depreciation.

If the client has been in business for many years, the review of transactions in earlier years necessarily must be performed on a test basis in

Figure 14–1

The Mandeville Corporation

Summary of Property, Plant and Equipment and Accumulated Depreciation

December 31, 1974

K-1

Account No.	Description	Assets						Accumulated Depreciation			
		Balance 12/31/83	Additions	Retirements	Balance 12/31/84	Method	Rate	Balance 12/31/83	Provision	Retirements	Balance 12/31/84
151	Land	50,000 00	15,100 00		65,100 00						
152/3	Land Improvements	13,500 00	1,000 00		14,500 00 4	sl	5%	1,350 00	700 00		2,050 00 4
154/5	Buildings	450,000 00	49,500 00		499,500 00 4	sl	3%	29,200 00	14,242 00		43,442 00 4
156/7	Equipment	70,000 00	11,000 00	6,000 00	85,000 00 4	sl	10%	23,500 00	7,000 00	5,040 00	25,520 00 4
		583,500 00	76,600 00	6,000 00	664,100 00			54,050 00	23,002 00	5,040 00	71,012 00
			K-1-1		✗				K-1-2	K-1-1	✗

4 – Footed plant and equipment subsidiary ledger cards. No exceptions.

Conclusions:
As a result of our audit procedures for plant and equipment and related depreciation, it is our opinion that the 12/31/84 balances above are fairly stated.

2/14/74
1/9/85

order to stay within reasonable time limits. However, the importance of an analysis of transactions of prior years deserves emphasis. Only by this approach can the auditors be in a sound position to express an opinion as to the propriety of the current period's depreciation. If repair and maintenance expenses have been capitalized, or asset additions have been recorded as operating expenses, or retirements of property have gone unrecorded, the entire depreciation program is invalidated regardless of the care taken in the selection of depreciation rates. The auditors should make clear to the client that the initial examination of plant and equipment requires procedures that need not be duplicated in subsequent engagements.

AUDIT PROGRAM FOR PROPERTY, PLANT, AND EQUIPMENT

The following procedures are typical of the work required in many engagements for the verification of property, plant, and equipment. The procedures for accumulated depreciation are covered in a separate program on pages 475–76. Notice that the audit procedures do not include verification of current replacement cost or of depreciation based on replacement cost, which must be disclosed by large corporations. As indicated earlier in this chapter, replacement cost information is not *audited,* and the limited procedures for its review have already been discussed.

A. **Study and evaluation of internal control for property, plant, and equipment**
    1.   Obtain description of internal control for property, plant, and equipment.
    2.   Test property, plant, and equipment transactions.
    3.   Evaluate internal control for property, plant, and equipment.

B. **Substantive tests of property, plant, and equipment and related revenue and expenses**
    4.   Determine that the plant and equipment ledger is in agreement with the controlling accounts.
    5.   Verify legal ownership of property, plant, and equipment.
    6.   Verify additions to property during the year.
    7.   Make physical inspection of substantial additions and consider the need for a complete physical inventory of plant and equipment.
    8.   Obtain or prepare analyses of repair and maintenance expense accounts.
    9.   Verify retirements of property during the year.
    10. Investigate the status of property not in current use.
    11. Obtain or prepare a summary analysis showing changes during the year in property owned.

12. Review rental revenue from land, buildings, and equipment.
13. Verify property taxes expense by inspection of property tax bills and paid checks.
14. Determine proper balance sheet presentation.

A. Study and evaluation:

1. Obtain description of internal control for property, plant, and equipment.

In the study of internal control for plant and equipment, the auditors may utilize a written description, flowcharts, or an internal control questionnaire. The following are typical of the questions included in a questionnaire: Are plant ledgers regularly reconciled with general ledger control accounts? Are periodic physical inventories of plant assets compared with the plant ledgers? Are variances between plant budgets and actual expenditures for plant assets subject to review and approval of executives? Does the sale, transfer, or dismantling of equipment require written executive approval on a serially numbered retirement work order? Is there a written policy for distinguishing between capital expenditures and revenue expenditures?

2. Test property, plant, and equipment transactions.

The purpose of the compliance tests for property, plant, and equipment is to determine whether the internal controls established by the client are being followed consistently in practice. The auditors should be alert for any indications that the client's policy for distinguishing between capital expenditures and revenue expenditures has been violated.

3. Evaluate internal control for property, plant, and equipment.

The evaluation of internal control for plant assets includes an identification of weaknesses and unusual strengths in controls. The auditors then select the substantive tests necessary to provide sufficient competent evidence as to existence, ownership, and valuation of the client's property, plant, and equipment, given the quality of the internal control for plant assets.

B. Substantive tests:

4. Determine that the plant and equipment ledger is in agreement with the controlling accounts.

Before a detailed analysis of changes in property accounts during the year is made, it is necessary to determine that the individual plant asset records in the subsidiary ledger agree in total with the balances in the general ledger control accounts. This is also a desirable prerequisite to any tests of the ledger by observation of plant and equipment. Computer printouts or adding machine tapes prepared from the subsidiary property ledger should also be compared with the ending balances shown on the summary analysis obtained in procedure *11*.

5. Verify legal ownership of property, plant, and equipment.

To determine that plant assets are the property of the client, the auditors look for such evidence as a deed, title insurance policy, property tax bills, receipts for payments to mortgagee, and fire insurance policies. Additionally, the fact that rental payments are not being made is supporting evidence of ownership.

It is sometimes suggested that the auditors may verify ownership of real property and the absence of liens by examination of public records. This step is seldom taken, but a title search may in some circumstances be completed by a title insurance company for the auditors. Inspection of the documentary evidence listed above usually provides adequate proof of ownership. If some doubt exists as to whether the client has clear title to property, the auditors should obtain the opinion of the client's legal counsel.

In the first audit of a company, the auditors should obtain a copy of the deed for inclusion in the permanent file. The legal description in the deed should be compared with that in the title insurance policy or abstract of title. Possession of a deed is not proof of present ownership because in the sale of real property a new deed is usually prepared and the seller may retain the old one. This is true of title insurance policies as well. Better evidence of continuing ownership is found in tax bills made out in the name of the client and in fire insurance policies, rent receipts from lessees, and regular principal and interest payments to a mortgagee or trustee.

The disclosure of liens on property will usually be made during the examination of liabilities, but in the audit work on plant and equipment the auditors should be alert for evidence indicating the existence of liens. Purchase contracts examined in verifying the cost of property may reveal unpaid balances. Insurance policies may contain loss payable endorsements in favor of a secured party.

The ownership of automobiles and trucks can readily be ascertained by the auditors by reference to certificates of title and registration documents. The ease of transfer of title to automotive equipment, plus the fact that it is often used as collateral for loans, makes it important that the auditors verify title to such property.

6. Verify additions to property during the year.

The vouching of additions to the property accounts during the period under audit is one of the most important substantive tests of plant and equipment. The extent of the vouching is dependent upon the auditors' evaluation of internal control for plant and equipment expenditures. The vouching process utilizes a working paper analysis of the general ledger control accounts and will include the tracing of entries through the journals to the original documents, such as contracts, deeds, construction work orders, invoices, and authorization by directors.

The specific steps to be taken in investigating the year's property additions usually will include the following:

1. Examine authorizations for all major additions, including assets purchased and assets constructed.
2. Review changes during the year in construction in progress and examine supporting work orders, both incomplete and closed.
3. Trace transfers from the Construction in Progress account to the property accounts, observing propriety of classification. Determine that all completed items have been transferred.
4. On a test basis, vouch purchases of plant and equipment to invoices, deeds, contracts, or other supporting documents. Test extensions, footings, and treatment of discounts. Make certain revenue expenditures were not improperly capitalized.
5. Investigate all instances in which the actual cost of acquisitions substantially exceeded authorized amounts. Determine whether such excess expenditures were analyzed and approved by appropriate officials.
6. Investigate fully any debits to property accounts not arising from acquisition of physical assets.
7. Determine that the total cost of any plant and equipment assets purchased on the installment plan is reflected in the asset accounts and that the unpaid installments are set up as liabilities. Ascertain that all plant and equipment leases that in effect are installment purchases are accounted for as assets acquired. Interest charges should not be capitalized as a cost of the asset acquired.

The accounting for plant assets acquired in a trade-in or other exchange is specified by *APB Opinion No. 29*, "Accounting for Nonmonetary Transactions." No gain is recognized when a plant asset is exchanged for a similar plant asset. The asset acquired in the exchange is valued at the carrying amount of the asset given up plus any additional cash paid or amount owed.

Assets constructed by a company for its own use should be recorded at the cost of direct material, direct labor, and applicable overhead cost. However, auditors usually apply the additional test of comparing the total cost of self-constructed equipment with bids or estimated purchase prices for similar equipment from outside suppliers, and they take exception to the capitalization of costs substantially in excess of the amount for which the asset could have been purchased and installed.

Related party transactions. Assets acquired from affiliated corporations, from promoters or stockholders, or by any other type of related party transaction not involving arm's-length bargaining between buyer and seller, have often been recorded at inflated amounts. The auditors should inquire into the methods by which the sales price was determined, the cost of the property to the vendor, length of ownership by vendor, and any other available evidence that might indicate an arbitrarily determined valuation. When vendor and vendee are under common control, or for any reason arm's-length bargaining does not appear to have been present in the acquisition of plant and equipment, the notes to financial statements should contain full disclosure of the transaction.

7. **Make physical inspection of substantial additions and consider the need for a complete physical inventory of plant and equipment.**

It is customary for the auditors to make a physical inspection of any major items of plant and equipment *acquired* during the period under audit, but not to undertake the observation of a complete physical inventory of plant and equipment. At first thought, it may appear that verification of the existence of *all* plant and equipment listed in the financial statements and accounting records could best be accomplished through physical inspection by the auditors. Auditing procedures with respect to merchandise inventories and other current assets call for observation, inspection, or confirmation; and the Securities and Exchange Commission has in *Accounting Series Release No. 19* expressed the opinion that audit procedures should include physical inspection of plant and equipment to supplement the examination of entries in the accounting records. Current practice, however, does not include physical inspection as a standard procedure of verification, and casual inspection as part of a conducted plant tour can hardly be considered as verification. The omission of physical inspection from verification work in this area of the examination appears to be the result of several factors:

1. The risk of loss from theft or disappearance is slight, as compared with cash or other current assets.
2. Management, in general, has been reluctant to authorize frequent physical inventories of plant and equipment. This attitude is attributable to the cost and effort required for a physical inventory, and also may be based upon the outmoded notion that internal controls are applicable only to current assets.
3. The variety, quantity, and location of plant and equipment in large enterprises make a physical inventory difficult and time-consuming. It can be performed more satisfactorily by the internal auditing staff than by outside auditors.

In certain lines of business—as, for example, in construction work, where costly mobile equipment is often scrapped or sold upon authorization of a field supervisor—good audit practice would call for physical inspection as part of the verification procedures. In the audit of concerns owning substantial numbers of automobiles and trucks, physical inspection and verification of legal title are practicable and desirable measures.

8.   Obtain or prepare analyses of repair and maintenance expense accounts.

The auditors' principal objective in analyzing repair and maintenance expense accounts is to discover items that should have been
capitalized. Large concerns often have a written policy setting the minimum expenditure to be capitalized. For example, company policy may
prescribe that no expenditure for less than $500 shall be capitalized
regardless of the service life of the item purchased. In such cases the
auditors will analyze the repair and maintenance accounts with a view
toward determining the consistency of application of this policy as well
as compliance with generally accepted accounting principles. To
determine that the accounts contain only bona fide repair and maintenance charges, the auditors will trace the larger expenditures to written
authorizations for the transaction. Correctness of the amounts involved
may be verified by reference to vendors' invoices, to material requisitions, and to labor time records.

One particularly useful means of identifying any capital expenditures that are buried in the repair and maintenance accounts is to
obtain or prepare an analysis of the monthly amounts of expense with
corresponding amounts listed for the preceding year. Any significant
variations from month to month or between corresponding months of
the two years should be fully investigated. If maintenance expense is
classified by the departments serviced, the variations are especially
noticeable.

9.   Verify retirements of property during the year.

The principal purpose of this procedure is to determine whether any
property has been replaced, sold, dismantled, or abandoned without
having been reflected properly in the accounting records. Nearly every
thorough physical inventory of plant and equipment reveals missing
units of property: units disposed of without a corresponding reduction
of the accounts.

It is not unusual for a factory supervisor to order that a machine be
scrapped, without realizing that the accounting department has an
interest in such action. How is the accounting department expected to
know when a factory asset is retired? If a machine is sold for cash or
traded in on a new machine, the transaction will presumably involve
the use of documents, such as a cash receipts form or a purchase order;
the processing of these documents may bring the retirement to the attention of alert accounting personnel. Not all employees are alert,
however, and some are not sufficiently trained to recognize a clue to the
retirement of a plant asset. Moreover, many plant assets are scrapped
rather than being sold or traded in on new equipment; consequently,
there may be no paper work to evidence the disappearance of a machine.

One method of guarding against unrecorded retirements is enforce-
ment of a company-wide policy that no plant asset shall be retired from

use without prior approval on a special type of serially numbered work order. A copy of the retirement work order is routed to the accounting department. To supplement this policy, a physical inventory of plant and equipment should be taken on a test basis by the client at regular intervals. Together, these two measures provide reasonable assurance that retirements will be reflected in the accounting records.

What specific steps should the auditors take to discover any unrecorded retirements? The following measures often are effective:

1. If major additions of plant and equipment have been made during the year, ascertain whether old equipment was traded in or superseded by the new units.
2. Analyze the Miscellaneous Revenue account to locate any cash proceeds from sale of plant assets.
3. If any of the company's products have been discontinued during the year, investigate the disposition of plant facilities formerly used in manufacturing such products.
4. Inquire of executives and supervisors whether any plant assets have been retired during the year.
5. Examine retirement work orders or other source documents for authorization by the appropriate official or committee.
6. Investigate any reduction of insurance coverage to determine whether this was caused by retirement of plant assets.

10. Investigate the status of property not in current use.

Land, buildings, and equipment not in current use should be investigated thoroughly to determine the prospects for their future use in operations. Plant assets that are temporarily idle need not be reclassified, and depreciation may be continued at normal rates. On the other hand, idle equipment that has been dismantled, or for any reason appears unsuitable for future operating use, should be written down to an estimated realizable value and excluded from the plant and equipment classification. In the case of standby equipment and other property not needed at present or prospective levels of operation, the auditors should consider whether the carrying value is recoverable through future use in operations.

11. Obtain or prepare a summary analysis showing changes during the year in property owned.

At this point in the audit, the auditors have verified the beginning balances of plant and equipment assets by reference to the prior year's working papers or by carrying out procedures necessary in the audit of a new client. In addition to this, they have tested the additions and retirements of plant and equipment during the year. The auditors may now obtain or prepare the summary analysis illustrated in Figure 14–1, and cross-index it to the analyses of additions and disposals.

12. Review rental revenue from land, buildings, and equipment.

Many manufacturing companies retain the usual risks and rewards of ownership in connection with their leasing activities and thus qualify for the *operating method* of recording aggregate lease rentals received over the lives of the leases.

In verifying rental revenue from land and buildings, it is often desirable for the auditors to obtain or to sketch a map of the property and to make a physical inspection of each unit. This may disclose that premises reported as vacant are in fact occupied by lessees and are producing revenue not reflected in the accounting records. If the client's property includes an office or apartment building, the auditors should obtain a floor plan of the building as well as copies of all lease contracts. In this way they can account for all available rental space as revenue producing or vacant under terms of lease agreements and can verify reported vacancies by physical inspection at the balance sheet date. If interim audit work is being performed, vacancies should also be verified by inspection and discussion with management during each visit by the auditors during the year.

Examination of leases will indicate whether tenants are responsible for the cost of electricity, water, gas, and telephone service. These provisions should be reconciled with the handling of utility expense accounts. Rental revenue accounts should be analyzed in all cases, and the amounts compared with lease agreements and cash records.

13. Verify property taxes expense by inspection of property tax bills and paid checks.

The client's property taxes expense may be verified conveniently during the audit of the related plant assets. The auditors should obtain or prepare an analysis of prepaid taxes, taxes expense, and taxes payable and should vouch property tax payments to tax bills and paid checks.

14. Determine proper financial statement presentation.

The balance sheet or accompanying notes should disclose balances of major classes of depreciable assets. Accumulated depreciation may be shown by major class or in total, and the method or methods of computing depreciation should be stated. The total amount of depreciation should be disclosed in the income statement or supporting notes.

In addition, adequate financial statement presentation will ordinarily reflect the following principles:

1. Property, plant, and equipment can usually be summarized by the following major classes: Land and Land Improvements; Buildings and Leasehold Improvements; Machinery and Equipment; Furniture and Fixtures; and Construction in Progress.

2. Property not in current use should be segregated in the balance sheet.

3. Property pledged to secure loans should be clearly identified.
4. The basis of valuation should be explicitly stated. At present, cost is the generally accepted basis of valuation for plant and equipment; property not in use should be valued at estimated realizable value.
5. Companies subject to the requirements of *FASB Statement No. 33* should disclose current replacement cost and depreciation computed on the basis of replacement cost.

DEPRECIATION

The auditors' perspective toward depreciation

The auditors' approach to verification of depreciation expense is influenced by two factors not applicable to most other expenses. First, we must recognize that depreciation expense is an *estimate*. Determining the annual depreciation expense involves two rather arbitrary decisions by the client company: first, an estimate of the useful economic lives of various groups of assets, and second, a choice among several depreciation methods, each of which would lead to a different answer. The wide range of possible amounts for annual depreciation expense because of these arbitrary decisions by the client suggests that the auditors should maintain a perspective of looking for assurance of overall reasonableness rather than burying themselves in detailed calculations. Specifically, overall tests of the year's depreciation expense are of special importance.

A second unusual characteristic of depreciation expense is that, unlike other expenses, it has not been verified during the auditors' study and evaluation of internal control. The tests of transactions performed during the auditors' work on internal control include exchange transactions with outsiders, such as payments for advertising or rent, but do not include the internal allocations of cost that establish depreciation expense. Consequently, the auditors must place more emphasis upon the verification of year-end balances than would be needed if the reliability of the depreciation data had been established through tests of transactions.

Among the methods of computing depreciation expense most frequently encountered are the straight-line method and the declining-balance methods. Far less common, although quite acceptable, are methods based on units of output or hours of service. The most widely adopted types of accelerated depreciation methods are fixed-percentage-of-declining-balance, and sum-of-the-years'-digits. The essential characteristic of these and other similar methods is that depreciation is greatest in the first year and becomes smaller in succeeding years. The use of an accelerated method for income tax purposes does not mean that this method should necessarily be used for general accounting purposes. However, many accountants believe that accelerated methods constitute a logical and reasonable basis for allocating the cost of property to operating periods.

The auditors' objectives in auditing depreciation

The principal objectives of the auditors in examining depreciation methods and amounts are to determine (*a*) that the methods in use are acceptable ones, (*b*) that the methods are being followed consistently, and (*c*) that the calculations required by the chosen methods are accurately made. A more detailed picture of the auditors' objectives is conveyed by the audit program in the following section.

Audit program—depreciation expense and accumulated depreciation

The following outline of substantive tests to be performed by the auditors in reviewing depreciation is stated in sufficient detail to be largely self-explanatory. Consequently, no point-by-point discussion will be presented. Techniques for testing the client's provision of depreciation for the year and for analyzing the accumulated depreciation accounts are, however, discussed immediately following the audit program. Notice that the audit procedures do not include verification of the amount of depreciation based on replacement cost, which must be disclosed by large corporations. As indicated early in this chapter, replacement cost information is not *audited,* and the limited procedures for its review have already been discussed.

1. Review the depreciation policies set forth in company manuals or other management directives. Determine whether the methods in use are carefully designed and intended to allocate costs of plant and equipment assets equitably over their service lives.
   a. Inquire whether any extra working shifts or other conditions of accelerated production are present that might warrant adjustment of normal depreciation rates.
   b. Discuss with executives the possible need for recognition of obsolescence resulting from inventions or economic developments. For example, assume that a new, improved model of computer has recently become available and that it would fit the company's needs most effectively. Should the remaining estimated useful life of an older computer presently owned by the company be reevaluated in the light of this technological advance?
2. Obtain or prepare a summary analysis (see Figure 14–1) of accumulated depreciation for the major property classifications as shown by the general ledger control accounts, listing beginning balances, provisions for depreciation during the year, retirements, and ending balances.

    a. Compare beginning balances with the audited amounts in last year's working papers.

    b. Determine that the totals of accumulated depreciation recorded in the plant and equipment subsidiary records agree with the applicable general ledger control accounts.

3. Verify the provisions for depreciation.

    a. Compare rates used in current year with those employed in prior years, and investigate any variances.

    b. Test computations of depreciation provisions for a representative number of units and trace to individual records in property ledger. Be alert for excessive depreciation on fully depreciated assets.

    c. Compare credits to accumulated depreciation accounts for year's depreciation provisions with debit entries in related depreciation expense accounts.

4. Verify deductions from accumulated depreciation for assets retired.

    a. Trace deductions to the working paper analyzing retirements of assets during year.

    b. Test accuracy of accumulated depreciation to date of retirement.

5. Review the most recent audit report on depreciation made by the revenue agents from the Internal Revenue Service. Determine whether provisions and rates have been adjusted, when necessary, to agree with the findings of the Internal Revenue Service.

6. Compare the percentage relationships between accumulated depreciation and related property accounts with that prevailing in prior years, and discuss significant variations from the normal depreciation program with appropriate members of management.

Testing the client's provision for depreciation

We have emphasized the importance of determining the overall reasonableness of the amount of depreciation expense, which is usually a very material amount on the income statement. An *overall* test of the annual provision for depreciation requires the auditors to perform the following steps:

1. List the balances in the various asset accounts at the beginning of the year.

2. Deduct any fully depreciated assets, since these items should no longer be subject to depreciation.

3. Add one half of the asset additions for the year.

4. Deduct one half of the asset retirements for the year (exclusive of any fully depreciated assets).

These four steps produce average amounts subject to depreciation at the regular rates in each of the major asset categories. By applying the appropriate rates to these amounts, the auditors determine on an overall average basis the amount of the provision for depreciation. The computed amount is then compared with the client's figures. Precise agreement is not to be expected, but any material difference between the depreciation expense computed in this manner and the amount set up by the client should be investigated fully.

Verification of natural resources

In the examination of companies operating properties subject to depletion (mines, oil and gas deposits, timberlands, and other natural resources), the auditors follow a pattern similar to that used in evaluating the provision for depreciation expense and accumulated depreciation. They determine whether depletion has been recorded consistently and in accordance with generally accepted accounting principles, and they test the mathematical accuracy of the client's computations.

The depletion of timberlands is usually based on physical quantities established by cruising. The determination of physical quantities to use as a basis for depletion is more difficult in many mining ventures and for oil and gas deposits. The auditors often rely upon the opinions of such specialists as mining engineers and geologists about the reasonableness of the depletion rates being used for such resources. Under these circumstances, the auditors must comply with the provisions of *SAS No. 11*, "Using the Work of a Specialist" (discussed in Chapter 7).

If the number of tons of ore in a mining property could be accurately determined in advance, an exact depletion cost per ton could be computed by dividing the cost of the mine by the number of tons available for extraction. In reality the contents of the mine can only be estimated, and the estimates may require drastic revision as mining operations progress.

The auditors verify the ownership and the cost of mining properties by examining deeds, leases, tax bills, vouchers, paid checks, and other records in the same manner that they verify the plant and equipment of a manufacturing or trading concern. The costs of exploration and development work in a mine customarily are capitalized until such time as commercial production begins. After that date additional development work generally is treated as expense. The costs of drilling oil wells usually are capitalized. When an oil company leases land, it often makes an immediate payment followed by annual rental payments until production begins, after which time the landowner receives payment in the form of royalties. In the records of the oil company, the lease may be carried at the total of the payments made, including the cost of developmental work, with this total becoming the basis for depletion, or being written off if the property proves to be nonproductive. As an alternative some oil companies capitalize the bonus paid for a lease, but treat rental payments as an immediate charge to expense.

For some extractive companies the cost of the mine or oil deposit is negligible, and a "discovery" value or appraised value is substituted as the basis for computing depletion. The auditors' responsibility in this situation is the same as when they encounter appraised values in the accounting records of a manufacturing or mercantile business; the auditors must investigate the appraisal report, determine the basis of the appraisal values, trace the amounts from the report into the records, and insist upon appropriate disclosure in the financial statements.

Verification of intangible assets

The balance sheet caption *Intangible Assets* includes a variety of assets. All intangible assets are characterized by a lack of physical substance. Furthermore, they do not qualify as current assets, and they are nonmonetary—that is, they do not represent fixed claims to cash.

Among the more prominent intangible assets are goodwill, patents, trademarks, franchises, and leaseholds. Notice that investment in securities is *not* included in our list of intangibles. Since intangible assets are lacking in physical substance, their value lies in the rights or economic advantages afforded in their ownership. Because of their intangible nature, these assets may be more difficult to identify than units of plant and equipment. When a client treats an expenditure as creating an intangible asset, the auditors must look for objective evidence that a genuine asset has come into existence.

The auditors' substantiation of intangible assets may begin with an analysis of the ledger accounts for these assets. Debits to the accounts should be traced to evidence of payment having been made and to documentary evidence of the rights or benefits acquired. Credits to the accounts should be reconciled with the client's program of amortization or traced to appropriate authorization for the write-off of the asset.

One intangible asset that may still be large in amount yet of questionable future economic benefit is *goodwill.* Goodwill frequently arises in accounting for business combinations in which the price paid to acquire another company exceeds the fair value of the identifiable net assets acquired. When business combinations result in the recording of goodwill, the auditors should review the allocation of the lump-sum acquisition cost among tangible assets, identifiable intangible assets, and goodwill. Any allocation of total acquisition cost to goodwill should be considered for reasonableness and also traced to the authorization and subsequent approval in the minutes of the directors' meetings.

As part of an analysis of intangible asset accounts, the auditors should review the reasonableness of the client's amortization program. Amortization is ordinarily computed by the straight-line method over the years estimated to be benefited, but not in excess of forty years.

Examination of plant and equipment in advance of the balance sheet date

Most of the audit work on plant and equipment can be done in advance of the balance sheet date. For the initial audit of a new client, the time-consuming task of reviewing the records of prior years and establishing the beginning balances in the plant accounts for the current period should be completed before the year-end.

In repeat engagements, as well as in first examinations, the study and evaluation of internal control can be carried out at any convenient time during the year. Many auditing firms lighten their year-end work loads by performing interim work during October and November, including the analysis of the plant and equipment ledger accounts for the first 9 or 10 months of the year. After the balance sheet date, the work necessary on property accounts is then limited to the final two or three months' transactions. One of the major problems in managing an accounting practice is arranging a uniform work load for the staff throughout the year. A step toward the solution of this problem lies in performing most of the work on plant and equipment in advance of the balance sheet date.

KEY TERMS INTRODUCED OR EMPHASIZED IN CHAPTER 14

Capital expenditure An expenditure for property, plant, and equipment that is properly charged to an asset account.

Cruising The inspection of a tract of forestland for the purpose of estimating the total lumber yield.

Disclosure of replacement cost information Supplementary information to be shown in annual reports to shareholders by large corporations. Designed to reflect the effects of inflation by reporting the cost of replacing the plant and equipment at current prices and by computing the amount of depreciation based on replacement cost of depreciable assets in use.

Loss payable endorsement A clause in a fire or other casualty insurance policy providing for payments to lienholders of the insured property to the extent of their unpaid loans or the face amount of the insurance, whichever is less.

Operating method A method of accounting for lease revenue in which aggregate rentals are reported as revenue over the life of the lease, usually as rent becomes receivable under terms of the lease.

Revenue expenditure An expenditure for property, plant, and equipment that is properly charged to an expense account.

Work order A serially numbered accounting document authorizing the acquisition of plant assets. A separate series of retirement work orders may be used to authorize the retirement or disposal of plant assets, and a third variety consists of documents authorizing repair or maintenance of plant assets.

GROUP I: REVIEW QUESTIONS

14-1. Identify at least three elements of a strong system of internal control for property, plant, and equipment.

14– 2.   Summarize briefly the position of the FASB with respect to disclosure of replacement cost data for plant assets.

14– 3.   In the first audit of Newmark Company, Ralph James, CPA, discovered that several capital expenditures had been erroneously treated as revenue expenditures during the three-year history of the company. Describe the effects of these accounting errors on Newmark's financial statements for the current year, prior to correction of the errors.

14– 4.   Under what circumstances might the auditors use the work of a specialist during their audit of property, plant, and equipment? Explain.

14– 5.   Do the auditors question the service lives adopted by the client for plant assets, or do they accept the service lives without investigation? Explain.

14– 6.   How does the auditors' approach to replacement cost information prepared by an audit client differ from the auditors' approach to the historical cost of plant and equipment?

14– 7.   Should the independent auditors observe a physical inventory of property and equipment in every audit engagement? Discuss.

14– 8.   Hamlin Metals Company has sales representatives covering several states and provides automobiles for them and for its executives. Describe any substantive tests you would consider appropriate for the company's fleet of more than 100 automobiles, other than the verification procedures generally applicable to all property and equipment.

14– 9.   Explain the use of a system of authorizations for property and equipment additions.

14– 10. What is a principal objective of the auditors in analyzing a Maintenance and Repairs expense account?

14– 11. Gibson Manufacturing Company acquired new factory machinery this year and ceased using the old machinery. The old equipment was retained, however, and is capable of being used if the demand for the company's products warrants additional production. How should the old machinery be handled in the accounting records and on the financial statements?

14– 12. What objections do business executives have to the traditional practice of basing depreciation charges on original cost?

14– 13. Moultrie Company discovered recently that a number of its property and equipment assets had been retired from use several years ago without any entries being made in the accounting records. The company asks you to suggest procedures that will prevent unrecorded retirement of assets.

14– 14. Does a failure to record the retirement of machinery affect net income? Explain.

14– 15. What documentary evidence is usually available to the auditors in the client's office to substantiate the ownership of property, plant, and equipment?

14– 16. The auditors' verification of current assets such as cash, securities, and inventories emphasizes observation, inspection, and confirmation to determine the physical existence of these assets. Should the auditors take a similar approach to establish the existence of the recorded plant assets? Explain fully.

14–17. K–J Corporation has current assets of $5 million and approximately the same amount of plant and equipment. Should the two groups of assets require about the same amount of audit time? Give reasons.

14–18. You are making your first examination of Clarke Manufacturing Company. Plant and equipment represent a very substantial portion of the total assets. What verification, if any, will you make of the balances of the ledger accounts for Plant and Equipment as of the beginning of the period under audit?

14–19. Should the auditors examine public records to determine the legal title of property apparently owned by the client?

14–20. Cite various substantive tests the auditors could employ that might detect unrecorded retirements of property, plant, and equipment. (AICPA, adapted)

GROUP II: QUESTIONS REQUIRING ANALYSIS

14–21. Give the purposes of each of the following procedures that may be included in a system of internal control, and explain how each procedure contributes to strong internal control:

 a. Forecasting of expenditures for property, plant, and equipment.
 b. Maintaining a plant ledger for property, plant, and equipment. (AICPA, adapted)

14–22. During your audit of Pioneer Company, a new client in its first year of operations in Madison City, you find that the company has charged to the Rent Expense account all its payments for its land and building, which are leased from Madison City. The lease, which is for a 10-year term, provides for monthly rental payments sufficient to retire the principal and interest on an issue of 10 percent, 10-year serial general obligation bonds that Madison City issued to purchase the land and finance construction of the building. The lease provides that title to the real property will be transferred to Pioneer Company when the entire bond issue has been retired. The building has an estimated service life of 25 years.

Do you agree with Pioneer Company's accounting for lease rental payments? Explain.

14–23. Your new client, Ross Products, Inc., completed its first fiscal year March 31, year 10. During the course of your examination you discover the following entry in the general journal, dated April 1, year 9.

Building	2,400,000	
Mortgage Note Payable		1,400,000
Common Stock		1,000,000

To record (1) acquisition of building constructed by J. A. Ross Construction Co. (a sole proprietorship); (2) assumption of Ross Construction Co. mortgage loan for construction of the building; and (3) issuance of entire authorized common stock (10,000 shares, $100 par value) to J. A. Ross.

During your investigation, you learn that the entire authorized pre-ferred stock of Ross Products, Inc.—10,000 shares, $50 par value, had been issued to J. A. Ross for $500,000 cash. The cash was used to purchase the land for the building site from an unrelated party.

Required:
Explain how you would accomplish the following objective relating to the audit of this client's plant and equipment: "Determine the propri-ety of the valuation methods used."

14–24. Farmland, Inc., a business you have audited for several years, changed the estimated total service life of its machinery and equipment to 10 years from 8 years. The company included the cumulative effect of the accounting change, net of applicable income taxes, in its income statement for the year you are examining. Would you recommend a change in the company's accounting for the change in estimated ser-vice lives of machinery and equipment? Explain.

14–25. High Point Products, Inc., a closely held corporation, was incorpo-rated in 1975 but has never had an audit of its financial statements. The corporation is now in need of capital for expansion and plans to issue additional capital stock for sale to outsiders. To facilitate the stock issuance, High Point wishes to retain you to examine its 1984 transac-tions and render an opinion on its financial statements for the year ended December 31, 1984.

The company has expanded from one plant to three plants and has frequently acquired, modified, and disposed of all types of equip-ment. Plant assets have a net depreciated value of 70 percent of total assets and consist of land and buildings, diversified machinery, and equipment, and furniture and fixtures. Some property was acquired by donation from stockholders. Depreciation was recorded by several methods using various estimated service lives.

Required:
a. May you confine your examination solely to 1984 transactions as requested by this prospective client whose financial statements have not previously been examined? Explain.
b. Prepare an audit program for the January 1, 1984 balances of the Land, Building, and Equipment and Accumulated Depreciation accounts of High Point Products, Inc. You need not include substantive tests of 1984 transactions in your program (AICPA, adapted)

14–26. An executive of a manufacturing company informs you that no formal procedures have been followed to control the retirement of machinery and equipment. A physical inventory of plant assets has just been completed. It revealed that 25 percent of the assets carried in the ledger were not on hand and had presumably been scrapped. The accounting records have been adjusted to agree with the physical in-ventory. You are asked to outline internal control practices to govern future retirements.

14–27. List and state the purpose of all audit procedures that might rea-sonably be applied by the auditors to determine that all property and equipment retirements have been recorded in the accounting records. (AICPA)

14–28. Allen Fraser was president of three corporations: Missouri Metals Corporation, Kansas Metals Corporation, and Iowa Metals Corporation. Each of the three corporations owned land and buildings acquired for approximately $500,000. An appraiser retained by Fraser in 198x estimated the current value of the land and buildings in each corporation at approximately $3,000,000. The appraisals were recorded in the accounts. A new corporation, called Midwest Corporation, was then formed, and Fraser became its president. The new corporation purchased the assets of the three predecessor corporations, making payment in capital stock. The balance sheet of Midwest Corporation shows land and buildings "valued at cost" in the amount of $9,000,000, the carrying values to the vendor companies at the time of transfer to Midwest Corporation. Do you consider this treatment acceptable? Explain.

14–29. Shortly after you were retained to examine the financial statements of Case Corporation, you learned from a preliminary discussion with management that the corporation had recently acquired a competing business, the Mall Company. In your study of the terms of the acquisition, you find that the total purchase price was paid in cash and that the transaction was authorized by the board of directors and fully described in the minutes of the directors' meetings. The only aspect of the acquisition of the Mall Company that raises any doubts in your mind is the allocation of the total purchase price among the several kinds of assets acquired. This allocation, which had been specifically approved by the board of directors of Case Corporation, placed very high values on the tangible assets acquired and allowed nothing for goodwill.

You are inclined to believe that the allocation of the lump-sum price to the several types of assets was somewhat unreasonable, because the total price for the business was as much or more than the current replacement cost of the tangible assets acquired. However, as an auditor, you do not claim to be an expert in property values. Would you question the propriety of the directors' allocation of the lump-sum purchase price? Explain fully.

14–30. Select the best answer for each of the questions below and explain fully the reason for your selection.

  a. With respect to an internal control measure that will assure accountability for fixed asset retirements, management should implement a system that includes:

   (1) Continuous analysis of miscellaneous revenue to locate any cash proceeds from sale of plant assets.

   (2) Periodic inquiry of plant executives by internal auditors as to whether any plant assets have been retired.

   (3) Continuous utilization of serially numbered retirement work orders.

   (4) Periodic observation of plant assets by the internal auditors.

  b. The auditors may conclude that depreciation charges are insufficient by noting:

      (1)   Insured values greatly in excess of book values.

      (2)   Large amounts of fully depreciated assets.

      (3)   Continuous trade-ins of relatively new assets.

      (4)   Excessive recurring losses on assets retired.

  c. Which of the following is an internal accounting control weakness related to factory equipment?

      (1)   Checks issued in payment of purchases of equipment are not signed by the controller.

      (2)   All purchases of factory equipment are required to be made by the department in need of the equipment.

      (3)   Factory equipment replacements are generally made when estimated useful lives, as indicated in depreciation schedules, have expired.

      (4)   Proceeds from sales of fully depreciated equipment are credited to other income.

  d. Which of the following best describes the independent auditors' approach to obtaining satisfaction concerning depreciation expense in the income statement?

      (1)   Verify the mathematical accuracy of the amounts charged to income as a result of depreciation expense.

      (2)   Determine the method for computing depreciation expense and ascertain that it is in accordance with generally accepted accounting principles.

      (3)   Reconcile the amount of depreciation expense to those amounts credited to accumulated depreciation accounts.

      (4)   Establish the basis for depreciable assets and verify the depreciation expense.

GROUP III: PROBLEMS

14–31.   J. Barnes, CPA, has been retained to audit a manufacturing company with a balance sheet that includes the caption Property, Plant, and Equipment. Barnes has been asked by the company's management if audit adjustments or reclassifications are required for the following material items that have been included or excluded from Property, Plant, and Equipment.

    (1)   A tract of land was acquired during the year. The land is the future site of the client's new headquarters, which will be constructed in the following year. Commissions were paid to the real estate agent used to acquire the land, and expenditures were made to relocate the previous owner's equipment. These commissions and expenditures were expensed and are excluded from Property, Plant, and Equipment.

    (2)   Clearing costs were incurred to make the land ready for construction. These costs were included in Property, Plant and Equipment.

    (3)   During the land-clearing process, timber and gravel were recovered and sold. The proceeds from the sale were recorded as other income and are excluded from Property, Plant and Equipment.

    (4)   A group of machines was purchased under a royalty agreement,

which provides royalty payments based on units of production from the machines. The cost of the machines, freight costs, unloading charges, and royalty payments were capitalized and are included in Property Plant and Equipment.

Required:

a. Describe the general characteristics of assets, such as land, buildings, improvements, machinery, equipment, and fixtures that should normally be classified as Property, Plant, and Equipment, and identify audit objectives (i.e., how an auditor can obtain audit satisfaction) in connection with the examination of Property, Plant, and Equipment. *Do not discuss specific audit procedures.*

b. Indicate whether each of the above items numbered (1) to (4) requires one or more audit adjustments or reclassifications, and explain why such adjustments or reclassifications are required or not required. Organize your answer as follows:

Item number	Is audit adjustment or reclassification required? Yes or No	Reasons audit adjustment or reclassification is required or not required

(AICPA, Adapted)

14–32. As part of the annual audit of the financial statements of Mead Corporation, a manufacturer of office equipment, you have been assigned to examine the plant assets. The company maintains a detailed property ledger for all plant assets. You prepared an audit program for the property, plant, and equipment asset accounts but have yet to prepare one for accumulated depreciation and depreciation expense.

Required:

Prepare an audit program for the accumulated depreciation and depreciation expense accounts. (AICPA, adapted)

14–33. Nova Land Development Corporation is a closely held corporation engaged in purchasing large tracts of land, subdividing the tracts, and installing paved streets and utilities. The corporation does not construct buildings for the buyers of the land and does not have any affiliated construction companies. Undeveloped land usually is leased for farming until the corporation is ready to begin developing it.

The corporation finances its land acquisitions by mortgages; the mortgagees require audited financial statements. This is your first audit of the company, and you have now begun the examination of the financial statements for the year ended December 31.

Required:

The corporation has three tracts of land in various stages of development. List the audit procedures to be employed in the verification of the physical existence and title to the corporation's three landholdings. (AICPA, adapted)

14–34. You are engaged in the examination of the financial statements of Holman Corporation for the year ended December 31, 1984. The accompanying analyses of the Property, Plant, and Equipment, and related Accumulated Depreciation accounts have been prepared by the chief accountant of the client. You have traced the beginning balances to your prior year's audit working papers.

HOLMAN CORPORATION
Analysis of Property, Plant, and Equipment, and
Related Accumulated Depreciation Accounts
Year Ended December 31, 1984

	Assets			
Description	*Final* *12/31/83*	*Additions*	*Retirements*	*Per ledger* *12/31/84*
Land	$ 422,500	$ 5,000		$ 427,500
Buildings	420,000	17,500		437,500
Machinery and equipment.....	385,000	40,400	$26,000	399,400
	$1,227,500	$62,900	$26,000	$1,264,400

	Accumulated Depreciation			
Description	*Final* *12/31/83*	*Additions**	*Retirements*	*Per ledger* *12/31/84*
Buildings	$ 60,000	$ 5,150		$ 65,150
Machinery and equipment.....	173,250	39,220		212,470
	$233,250	$44,370		$277,620

* Depreciation expense for the year.

All plant assets are depreciated on the straight-line basis (no residual value taken into consideration) based on the following estimated service lives: building, 25 years; all other items, 10 years. The company's policy is to take one half-year's depreciation on all asset additions and disposals during the year.

Your examination revealed the following information:

(1) On April 1 the company entered into a 10-year lease contract for a die casting machine, with annual rentals of $5,000 payable in advance every April 1. The lease is cancelable by either party (60 days' written notice is required), and there is no option to renew the lease or buy the equipment at the end of the lease. The estimated service life of the machine is 10 years with no residual value. The company recorded the die casting machine in the Machinery and Equipment account at $40,400, the present value at the date of the lease, and $2,020 applicable to the machine has been included in depreciation expense for the year.

(2) The company completed the construction of a wing on the plant building on June 30. The service life of the building was not extended by this addition. The lowest construction bid received was $17,500, the amount recorded in the Buildings account. Company

personnel constructed the addition at a cost of $16,000 (materials, $7,500; labor, $5,500; and overhead, $3,000).

(3) On August 18, $5,000 was paid for paving and fencing a portion of land owned by the company and used as a parking lot for employees. The expenditure was charged to the Land account.

(4) The amount shown in the machinery and equipment asset retirement column represents cash received on September 5 upon disposal of a machine purchased in July 1980 for $48,000. The chief accountant recorded depreciation expense of $3,500 on this machine in 1984.

(5) Harbor City donated land and building appraised at $100,000 and $400,000, respectively, to Holman Corporation for a plant. On September 1, the company began operating the plant. Since no costs were involved, the chief accountant made no entry for the above transaction.

Required:

Prepare the adjusting journal entries that you would propose at December 31, 1984 to adjust the accounts for the above transactions. Disregard income tax implications. The accounts have not been closed. Computations should be rounded off to the nearest dollar. Use a separate adjusting journal entry for each of the above five paragraphs. (AICPA, adapted)

14–35. You are the senior accountant in the audit of Granger Grain Corporation, whose business primarily involves the purchase, storage, and sale of grain products. The corporation owns several elevators located along navigable water routes and transports its grain by barge and rail. Your staff assistant submitted the following working paper analysis for your review:

GRANGER GRAIN CORPORATION
Advances Paid on Barges under Construction—a/c 210
December 31, 1984

Advances made:

1/15/84—Ck. No. 3463—Jones Barge Construction Co.	$100,000[1]
4/13/84—Ck. No. 4129—Jones Barge Construction Co.	25,000[1]
6/19/84—Ck. No. 5396—Jones Barge Construction Co.	63,000[1]
Total payments	188,000
Deduct cash received 9/1/84 from City Life Insurance Co.	188,000[2]
Balance per general ledger—12/31/84	-0-

[1] Examined approved check request and paid check and traced to cash disbursements journal.

[2] Traced to cash receipts journal and to duplicate deposit ticket.

Required:

a. In what respects is this brief analysis incomplete for audit purposes? (Do not include any discussion of specific auditing procedures.)

b. What two different types of contractual arrangements may be inferred from your assistant's analysis?

c. What additional auditing procedures would you suggest that your staff assistant perform before you accept the working paper as being complete? (AICPA, adapted)

15

Accounts payable and other liabilities

Now that the several chapters dealing with the verification of assets have been completed and we are ready to consider the examination of liability accounts, it is appropriate to compare the auditors' work on assets with the work to be done on liabilities. We should bear in mind that management is almost always under some pressure to report increased earnings. An exaggeration of earnings is usually accompanied by an overstatement of assets or an understatement of liabilities. In the verification of every asset the auditors are constantly on guard against *overstated* asset values. Accounting records that overstate the amount of cash on hand or on deposit are suggestive of fraud, and the auditors' approach to this danger is a careful count of cash on hand and confirmation of amounts shown as on deposit with banks. Similarly, the threat of an overstated or fictitious account receivable necessitates direct communication with customers. The possibility of an overstated inventory requires that the auditors observe the physical count of goods. In carrying out these audit procedures, the auditors are on the alert for all types of errors, but they are particularly aware of the dangers of overstatement of asset accounts. Adjustments proposed by the auditors more often than not have the effect of reducing earnings and either reducing assets or increasing liabilities.

The auditors' concern with possible overstatement of asset values arises in part from the fact that creditors and investors may sustain serious losses if they extend credit or buy equity securities in reliance upon financial statements with inflated asset valuations. Nearly all law suits against CPA firms allege that the auditors failed to detect an over-statement of owners' equity. This overstatement of owners' equity may be caused by overstatement of assets or by understatement of liabilities. Either the overstatement of assets or the understatement of liabilities will cause earnings and owners' equity to be exaggerated. An old adage of public accounting is that a CPA is never sued because of the under-statement of owners' equity.

In our study of audit work on liabilities, the point to be emphasized is this: An *understatement of liabilities* will exaggerate financial strength of a company and conceal fraud just as effectively as *over-statement of assets*. Furthermore, the understatement of liabilities is usually accompanied by understatement of expenses and overstatement of net income. For example, dishonest management of a company could inflate net income for the year ended December 31 (and understate liabilities and overstate stockholders' equity at that date), merely by delaying the recording of bills for December operating expenses until they were paid in January. Audit procedures for liabilities should be designed to detect understatement, just as audit procedures for assets are designed to detect overstatement.

To overstate an asset account usually requires an improper entry in the accounting records, as by the recording of a fictitious transaction. Such improper entries can be detected by the auditors through verifica-tion of the individual items making up the balance of an asset account. Once a fictitious entry is detected, the individual responsible for the fraud has little alternative but to admit his acts. By way of contrast, it is possible to understate a liability account merely by *failing to make an entry* for a transaction creating a liability. The omission of an entry is less susceptible of detection than is a fictitious entry. If the omission is detected, there is at least a possibility of passing it off as an accidental error. Auditors have long recognized that the most difficult type of fraud to detect is fraud based on the *nonrecording* of transactions. Once transactions are entered in the records, there are many verifica-tion techniques available.

Another point of difference between the auditors' work on assets and liabilities is that liabilities generally do not present a problem of valua-tion. The amount of a liability is usually a matter of fact, whereas the proper valuation of an asset is a matter of opinion. (Income taxes pay-able and liabilities for pensions represent prominent exceptions to this generalization; the use of present values for long-term notes payable is another exception.) Much of the audit time devoted to assets is con-cerned with the propriety of the valuation methods used by the client. Consequently, the audit time required for verification of liability ac-counts may be considerably shorter than for verification of correspond-ing dollar amounts in asset accounts.

Meaning of accounts payable

The term *accounts payable* is used to describe short-term obligations arising from the purchase of goods and services in the ordinary
course of business. Typical transactions creating accounts payable
include the acquisition on credit of merchandise, raw materials, plant
assets, and office supplies. Other sources of accounts payable include
the receipt of services, such as legal and accounting services, advertising, repairs, and utilities. Interest-bearing obligations should not be
included in accounts payable, but shown separately as bonds, notes,
mortgages, or installment contracts.

Accounts payable arising from purchase of goods or services are usually evidenced by invoices and statements received from the suppliers.
In contrast, *accrued liabilities* (sometimes called accrued expenses)
generally accumulate on a time basis as a result of the company's obligation to pay salaries, pensions, interest, rent, taxes, and similar items.
Invoices or statements are not usually received for accrued liabilities.

The auditors' verification of these various types of short-term
liabilities is often divided into separate phases corresponding to balance sheet captions, such as accounts payable and accrued liabilities. In
terms of auditing procedures, liabilities arising from transactions with
outside suppliers differ significantly from payroll and other obligations
originating within the company. Moreover, purchases of merchandise
and materials make up the major portion of accounts payable transactions and require a corresponding amount of auditing activity. For these
reasons, it is convenient to center the discussion at present on accounts
payable and to deal separately with other current liabilities, such as
accrued expenses, taxes, and deferred credits to revenue.

The auditors' objectives in examination of accounts payable

The principal objectives of the auditors in the examination of accounts payable are to (1) determine the adequacy of internal controls
for the processing and payment of vendors' invoices; (2) prove that the
amount shown on the balance sheet is in agreement with the supporting
accounting records; and (3) determine that all liabilities existing at the
balance sheet date have been recorded.

Internal control over accounts payable

In thinking about internal control for accounts payable, it is important to recognize that the accounts payable of one company are the
accounts receivable of other companies. It follows that there is little
danger of a client permanently overlooking or misplacing a liability
because creditors will naturally maintain complete records of their
receivables and will speak up if payment is not received. Some com-

panies, therefore, may choose to minimize their record keeping of liabilities and to rely on creditors to call attention to any delay in making payment. This viewpoint is not an endorsement of inaccurate or incomplete records of accounts payable, but merely a recognition that the self-interest of creditors constitutes a protective feature of accounting for payables that is not present in the case of accounts receivable.

Discussions of internal control applicable to accounts payable are often extended to cover the functions of purchasing and receiving, as well as the activities of the accounts payable department. This is not surprising, for the end objective of controls in this area of operations is to provide assurance that the company receives value for all payments made; and this, in turn, requires proof that goods have been received in proper quantity and condition before vendors' invoices are approved. A first essential of adequate control is the segregation of duties so that a cash disbursement to a creditor will be made only upon approval of the purchasing, receiving, accounting, and finance departments. All purchase transactions should be evidenced by serially numbered purchase orders, copies of which are sent to the accounts payable department for comparison with vendors' invoices and receiving reports.

The receiving department should be independent of the purchasing department. Receiving reports should be prepared for all goods received. These documents should be serially numbered and prepared in a sufficient number of copies to permit prompt notification of receipts to the accounts payable department, purchasing department, and stores department. In smaller companies, vendors' packing slips often are utilized as receiving reports.

Within the accounts payable department, all forms should be stamped with the date and hour received. Vouchers and other documents originating within the department can be controlled through the use of serial numbers. Each step in the verification of an invoice should be evidenced by the entering of a date and signature on the voucher. The most effective means of assuring that routine procedures, such as the proof of extensions and footings and the review of the propriety of discounts taken, are carried out consistently is the requirement that a designated employee sign the voucher as each step in verification is completed. Comparison of the quantities listed on the invoice with those shown on the receiving report and purchase order, if carefully made, will prevent the payment of charges for goods in excess of those ordered and received. Comparison of the prices, discounts, and terms of shipment as shown on the purchase order and on the vendor's invoice provides a safeguard against the payment of excessive prices.

Separation of the function of invoice verification and approval from that of cash disbursement is another step that tends to prevent error or fraud. Before invoices are approved for payment, written evidence must be presented to show that all aspects of the transaction have been verified.

Another control procedure that the auditors may expect to find in a well-managed accounts payable department is regular monthly balancing of the detailed records of accounts payable to the general ledger control. These trial balances should be preserved as evidence of the performance of this procedure and as an aid in localizing any subsequent errors.

Monthly statements from vendors should be reconciled with the accounts payable ledger or list of open vouchers, and any discrepancies fully investigated. In some industries it is common practice to make advances to vendors, which are recovered by making percentage deductions from invoices. When such advances are in use, the auditors should ascertain what procedures are followed to assure that deductions from the invoices are made in accordance with the agreement.

Audit working papers for accounts payable

The principal working papers are a grouping sheet for accounts payable, trial balances of the various types of accounts payable at the balance sheet date, and confirmation requests for accounts payable. The trial balances are often in the form of computer printouts. In addition, the auditors usually prepare a listing of *unrecorded* accounts payable discovered during the course of the audit, as illustrated in Figure 15–1.

AUDIT PROGRAM

The examination of accounts payable usually requires audit work along the following lines. The first five procedures are performed as a part of the study and evaluation of internal control for accounts payable. The remainder of the audit program is performed on or subsequent to the balance sheet date.

A.   Study and evaluation of internal control for accounts payable
1. Prepare a description of the internal control for accounts payable.
2. Verify postings to the Accounts Payable controlling account for a test period.
3. Vouch to supporting documents all postings in selected accounts of the accounts payable subsidiary ledger.
4. Review cash discounts.
5. Evaluate internal control for accounts payable.

B.   Substantive tests of accounts payable transactions and balances
6. Obtain or prepare a trial balance of accounts payable as of the balance sheet date and reconcile with the general ledger.
7. Vouch balances payable to selected creditors by inspection of supporting documents.
8. Reconcile liabilities with monthly statements from creditors.

9. Confirm accounts payable by direct correspondence with vendors.
10. Compare cash payments subsequent to the balance sheet date with the accounts payable trial balance.
11. Search for unrecorded accounts payable.
12. Determine proper balance sheet presentation of accounts payable.
13. Obtain from client a letter of representations concerning liabilities.

A.   Study and evaluation:

1.   Prepare a description of the internal control for accounts payable.

One approach used by auditors in becoming familiar with a client's system of internal control for accounts payable is to prepare a flowchart or to use flowcharts prepared by the client. In some engagements the auditors may choose to prepare a narrative description covering such matters as the independence of the accounts payable department and the receiving department from the purchasing department. The auditors might also use a questionnaire to obtain a description of accounts payable controls. Typical of the questions are the following: Is an accounts payable trial balance prepared monthly and reconciled to the general ledger control account? Are monthly statements from vendors reconciled with accounts payable ledgers or unpaid vouchers? Are advance payments to vendors recorded as receivables and controlled in a manner that assures that they will be recovered by offset against vendors' invoices? Are debit memos issued to vendors for discrepancies in invoice prices, quantities, or computations? Are debit balances in vendors' accounts brought to the attention of the credit and purchasing departments?

2.   Verify postings to the Accounts Payable controlling account for a test period.

The validity of the amount in the general ledger controlling account for accounts payable is established by tracing postings for one or more months to the voucher register and cash payments journal. Any postings to the controlling account from the general journal during this test period should also be traced. This work is performed before the balance sheet date as part of a general compliance test of postings to all records. At the same time, the auditors should scrutinize all entries to the controlling account for the entire period under audit and should investigate any unusual entries.

3.   Vouch to supporting documents all postings in selected accounts of the accounts payable subsidiary ledger.

Testing the accuracy of the voucher register or the accounts payable ledgers by tracing specific items back through the cash payments journal, purchases journal, and other journals to original documents (such as purchase orders, receiving reports, invoices, and paid checks) is necessary to determine the adequacy of the system of internal control. If the functions of purchasing, receiving, invoice verification, and cash disbursement are delegated to separate departments and internal controls appear adequate, the tracing of individual items from the ledgers to the original records may be undertaken only to the extent necessary to determine that the system is operating properly.

The auditors may also make tests by following the audit trail in the opposite direction. By tracing a representative sample of entries from the journals to the accounts payable ledger, the auditors can verify that journal entries have been posted consistently to the subsidairy ledger.

4. Review cash discounts.

Some companies record purchase invoices in the voucher register at the net amount after deduction of any available cash discounts. It is also acceptable practice to record invoices at the gross amount before deduction of cash discounts. The net price method provides stronger internal control because it focuses attention on any discounts lost.

The auditors' concern with purchase discounts is based on the possibility of fraudulent manipulation by employees and also on the possibility of accidental loss through failure to take discounts. Numerous case histories of fraud relating to cash disbursements have involved the drawing of checks for the gross amount of an invoice paid within the discount period. The dishonest employee was then in a position to request a refund from the creditor, to substitute the refund check for currency, and to abstract cash in this amount without any further manipulation of the records.

The most convenient test of discounts when these are recorded separately is to compute the ratio of cash discounts earned to total purchases during the period and to compare this ratio from period to period. Any significant decrease in the ratio indicates a change in terms of purchases, failure to take discounts, or fraudulent manipulation.

5. Evaluate internal control for accounts payable.

Completion of the preceding audit procedures enables the auditors to evaluate internal control for accounts payable. The internal control evaluation provides the basis for selecting the necessary substantive tests for verification of accounts payable at the balance sheet date.

A rating of *strong* internal control over accounts payable often means that the auditors have found that serially numbered receiving reports are prepared promptly by the client for all goods received, that serially numbered vouchers are promptly prepared and recorded in the voucher register, and that payments are made promptly on the due dates and immediately recorded in the cash payments journal and accounts payable subsidiary ledger. Finally, at the end of each month, an employee who does not participate in processing accounts payable compares the individual accounts in the accounts payable subsidiary ledger with vendors' statements, and also compares the total of the subsidiary record with the general ledger controlling account. This favorable picture of internal control would enable the auditors to minimize substantive testing of accounts payable.

On the other hand, a rating of *weak* internal control over accounts payable often means that the auditors have found that the subsidiary record of accounts payable is not in agreement with the general ledger controlling account, that receiving reports and vouchers are not serially numbered and are used haphazardly, that purchase transactions often are not recorded until payment is made, and that many accounts payable are long past due. In this situation, the auditors must undertake extensive work if they are to determine that the balance sheet amount for accounts payable includes all liabilities in existence at the balance sheet date.

B.   Substantive tests:

    6.   Obtain or prepare a trial balance of accounts payable as of the balance sheet date and reconcile with the general ledger.

One purpose of this procedure is to prove that the liability figure appearing in the balance sheet is in agreement with the individual items comprising the detail records. A second purpose is to provide a starting point for substantive testing. The auditors will use the list of vouchers or accounts payable to select a representative group of items for careful examination.

Large companies with numerous accounts payable usually furnish the auditors with a computer-prepared trial balance. For a lesser volume of accounts, a manually completed listing may be used. In either case, the auditors should verify the footing and the accuracy of individual amounts in the trial balance.

If the schedule of individual items does not agree in total with the controlling account, the cause of the discrepancy must be investigated. In most situations the auditors will arrange for the client's staff to locate such errors and make the necessary adjustments. Agreement of the controlling account and the list of individual account balances is not absolute proof of the total indebtedness; invoices received near the close of the period may not be reflected in either the controlling account or the subsidiary records, and other similar errors may exist without causing the accounts to be out of balance.

    7.   Vouch amounts payable to selected creditors by inspection of supporting documents.

Another substantive test of the validity of the client-prepared trial balance of accounts payable is the vouching of selected creditors' balances to supporting vouchers, invoices, purchase orders, and receiving reports. This work is usually performed on a test basis and provides additional evidence on the internal control over accounts payable.

Many companies use a voucher system; and in this case, the verification of the individual vouchers is made most conveniently at the balance sheet date, when they will all be together in the unpaid voucher file. The content of the unpaid voucher file changes daily; as vouchers are paid, they are removed from the file and filed alphabetically by vendor. Consequently, it is difficult to determine at a later date what vouchers were outstanding at the year-end.

If the auditors cannot be present at the balance sheet date, they should ask the client to prepare a list of vouchers at that date with sufficient identifying data for each voucher to permit its being located some weeks later. This listing of vouchers payable at the end of the year should show the names of vendors, voucher numbers, dates, and amounts.

8. Reconcile liabilities with monthly statements from creditors

In some companies it is a regular practice each month to reconcile vendors' statements with the detailed records of payables. If the auditors find that this reconciliation is regularly performed by the client's staff, they may limit their review of vendors' statements to determining that the reconciliation work has been satisfactory.

If the client's staff has not reconciled vendors' statements and accounts payable, the auditors generally will do so. If internal control for accounts payable is weak, the auditors may control incoming mail to assure that all vendors' statements received by the client are made available to the auditors. Among the discrepancies often revealed by reconciliation of vendors' statements are charges by the vendor for shipments not yet received or recorded by the client. Normal accounting procedures do not provide for recording invoices as liabilities until the merchandise has been received. These in-transit shipments should be listed and a decision reached as to whether they are sufficiently material to warrant being recorded.

The purpose of this audit procedure is to assure that an accurate year-end cutoff of accounts payable has been made. The cutoff of accounts payable is closely connected with the cutoff of purchase invoices in determining the year-end inventory. When observing the taking of a physical inventory on December 31, the auditors will make a record of the serial numbers of the last receiving report issued. This number should be identified with the corresponding vendor's invoice on the list of accounts payable at December 31. Any invoices corresponding to earlier receiving reports represent liabilities at December 31; any invoices associated with later receiving reports should not be part of the year-end amount for accounts payable. In other words, the year-end cutoff must assure that a liability is recorded for any goods received on the last day of the year *and included in the physical inventory.* Otherwise, net income would be overstated by the full amount of the omitted invoice.

If a shipment of merchandise arrives on December 31 after the physical inventory has been completed, income will not be affected if the goods are omitted from inventory and the related vendor's invoice is omitted from purchases and accounts payable. Although the omission is a cutoff error, it is far less *material* than if the goods had been included in inventory but the liability had not been recorded.

In more general terms, we can say that the auditors in judging the materiality of unrecorded liabilities should consider the related unrecorded debits. If recording the transaction would mean adding an asset as well as a liability, the effect on the financial statements would be less significant than recording an invoice of like amount for which the debit belonged in an expense account. The auditors must be sure, however, that invoices have been recorded as liabilities for all goods received and included in the year-end physical inventory.

9. Confirm accounts payable by direct correspondence with vendors.

Confirmation requests should be mailed to vendors from whom substantial purchases have been made during the year, regardless of the balances of their accounts at the balance sheet date. An accounts payable confirmation request appears in Figure 15–1. Even accounts payable with zero balances at year-end should be confirmed if they represent major suppliers. These large suppliers can be identified by reference to the accounts payable subsidiary ledger, to computer printouts of purchase volume for individual suppliers, or by inquiry of purchasing department personnel. Other accounts to be confirmed by the auditors include those for which monthly statements are not available, accounts reflecting unusual transactions, accounts with parent or subsidiary corporations, and accounts secured by pledged assets.

Confirmation of accounts payable is not a mandatory procedure as is the confirmation of receivables. One reason is that the greatest hazard in the verification of liabilities is the existence of unrecorded liabilities. To confirm the *recorded accounts payable* does not prove whether any *unrecorded accounts payable* exist. However, sending confirmation requests to suppliers whose accounts show *zero balances* at year-end is designed to disclose unrecorded liabilities. Another factor to be noted in comparing the confirmation of accounts receivable and accounts payable is that the auditors will find in the client's possession externally created evidence such as vendors' invoices and statements that substantiate the accounts payable. No such external evidence is on hand to support accounts receivable. Finally, many of the recorded liabilities as of the balance sheet date will be paid before the auditors complete their examination. The act of payment serves further to substantiate the authenticity of recorded liabilities. For all these rea-

Packaging Systems, Inc.
9200 Channel Street
New Orleans, Louisiana 70128

January 2, 198X

Grayline Container, Inc.
4800 Madison Street
Dallas, Texas   75221

Dear Sirs:

Our independent auditors, Nelson & Gray, CPAs, are making an examination
of our financial statements. For this reason, please inform them in the space provided below the amount, if any, owed to you by this company at December 31, 198X.

Please attach an itemized statement supporting any balance owed, showing all
unpaid items. Your reply should be sent directly to Nelson & Gray, CPAs, 6500
Lane Avenue, New Orleans, Louisiana 70128. A stamped addressed envelope is enclosed for your reply. Thank you.

Sincerely,

Robert W. James

Robert W. James
Controller

- -

Nelson & Gray, CPAs

Our records show that the amount of $_____ was owed to us by
Packaging Systems, Inc., at December 31, 198X, as shown by the itemized statement
attached.

Date: *1 - 6 - 8X*   Signature   *Sharon Stale*

                                                        Title   *Controller*

sons the audit procedure of confirmation is of less importance for accounts payable than for accounts receivable.

**10.   Compare cash payments subsequent to the balance sheet
date with the accounts payable trial balance.**

The comparison of cash payments occurring after the balance sheet date with the accounts payable trial balance is an excellent means of disclosing any unrecorded accounts payable. All liabilities must eventually be paid, and will, therefore, be reflected in the accounts when paid if not when incurred. By close study of payments made subsequent to the balance sheet date, the auditors may find some items that should have appeared as liabilities on the balance sheet. Regular monthly expenses, such as rent and utilities, are often posted to the ledger accounts directly from the cash disbursements journal without any account payable or other liability having been set up. After having located such items, the auditors might decide against proposing any adjusting entry, but it is still essential that they have all the facts about omitted liabilities before they reach a decision as to the materiality of these items.

The auditors' comparison of cash payments occurring after the balance sheet date with the accounts payable trial balance also furnishes evidence of the validity of the recorded payables. Some clients retain copies of all checks issued; other clients maintain a cash disbursements journal only. In either case, the auditors should account for the numerical sequence of all checks issued between the balance sheet date, and the date of completion of field work.

11.   Search for unrecorded accounts payable.

Throughout the examination of accounts payable, the auditors are alert for any indication that liabilities may have been omitted from the records. The three preceding audit procedures are directly or indirectly concerned with bringing unrecorded accounts payable to light. The auditors should also consider such sources of potential unrecorded accounts payable as the following:

1.   Unmatched invoices and unbilled receivers. These documents are called work in process in a voucher system. The auditors should review such unprocessed documents at the balance sheet date to ascertain that the client has recorded an account payable where appropriate.

2.   Unpaid vouchers entered in the voucher register subsequent to the balance sheet date. Inspection of these records may uncover an item that should have been recorded as of the balance sheet date.

3.   Invoices received by the client after the balance sheet date. Not all vendors send invoices promptly when goods are shipped or services are rendered. Accordingly, the auditors' review of invoices received by the client in the subsequent period may disclose unrecorded accounts payable as of the balance sheet date.

4.   Other audit areas. A variety of unrecorded accounts payable may
     be discovered during the course of the entire audit. Examples are
     customers' deposits recorded as credits to accounts receivable; ob-
     ligations for securities purchased but not settled at the balance
     sheet date; unbilled contractor or architect fees for a building
     under construction at the audit date; and unpaid attorney or insur-
     ance broker fees. In all areas of the audit, the auditors should be
     alert for unrecorded payables.

A form of audit working paper used to summarize unrecorded accounts payable discovered by the auditors is illustrated in Figure 15–2.

When unrecorded liabilities are discovered by the auditors, the next
question is whether the omissions are sufficiently material to warrant
proposing an adjusting entry. Will the adjustment cause a sufficient
change in the financial statements to give a different impression of the
company's current position or of its earning power? As previously indicated in the discussion of the reconciliation of vendors' statements with
accounts payable, auditors seldom propose adjustments for the purpose
of adding shipments in transit to the year-end inventory unless the
shipments are unusually large.

As a further illustration of the factors to be considered in deciding
upon the *materiality* of an unrecorded transaction, let us use as an
example the December 31 annual audit of a small manufacturing company in good financial condition with total assets of $1 million and
preadjustment net income of $100,000. The auditors' procedures bring
to light the following unrecorded liabilities:

1.   An invoice for $1,400, dated December 30 and bearing terms of
     f.o.b. shipping point. The goods were shipped on December 30 but
     were not received until January 4. The invoice was also received
     and recorded on January 4.
         In considering the materiality of this omission, the first point is
     that net income is not affected. The adjusting entry, if made, would
     add equal amounts to current assets (inventories) and to current
     liabilities, hence would not change the amount of working capital.
     The omission does affect the current ratio very slightly. The auditor
     would probably consider this transaction as not sufficiently mate-
     rial to warrant adjustment.
2.   Another invoice for $4,000, dated December 30 and bearing terms
     of FOB shipping point. The goods arrived on December 31 and
     were included in the physical inventory taken that day. The invoice
     was not received until January 8 and was entered as a January trans-
     action.
         This error should be corrected because the inclusion of the goods
     in the physical inventory without recognition of the liability has
     caused an error of $4,000 in pretax income for the year. Since the
     current liabilities are understated, both the amount of working

Figure 15–2

The Palermo Company

Unrecorded Accounts Payable   N-1-1

December 31, 1984

Invoice Date	No.	Vendor and Description	Account Charged	Amount
12/31/84	2251	Hayes Mfg. Co. – invoice and shipment in transit	Inventories	10650 00
—	—	Fox & Williams – unpaid legal fees – see N-4	Legal Expenses	1000 00
12/28/84	428	Hart & Co. – machinery repairs (paid 1/18/85)	Repairs Exp.	12600 00
12/31/84	—	Allen Enterprises – Dec. 19 account sales for consigned goods	Sales	25680 00
—	—	Grant Co. – shipment received 12/31/84 per receiver no. 2907; invoice not yet received	Inventories	15820 00
—	—	Arthur & Baker – earned but unpaid architects' fee for building under construction – see K-3	Construction in Progress	23370 00
				89120 00
				M-1

A.J.E. 8

131	Inventories		26470 00	
156	Construction in Progress		23370 00	
401	Sales		25680 00	
518	Legal Expenses		1000 00	
527	Repairs Expense		12600 00	
203	Accounts Payable			89120 00

To record unrecorded accounts payable at 12/31/84

Above payables were developed principally in the audit of accounts payable. See audit program B-4 for procedures employed. In my opinion the $89,120 adjustment includes all material unrecorded accounts payable.

V.M.H.
1/28/85

capital and the current ratio are exaggerated. The owners' equity is also overstated. These facts point to the materiality of the omission and constitute strong arguments for an adjusting entry.

3.   An invoice for $1,500, dated December 31, for a new office safe. The safe was installed on December 31, but the invoice was not recorded until paid on January 15.

Since the transaction involved only asset and liability accounts, the omission of an entry did not affect net income. However, working capital and the current ratio are affected by the error since the debit affects a noncurrent asset and the credit affects a current liability. Most auditors would probably not propose an adjusting entry for this item.

4.   An invoice for $3,000 dated, December 31, for advertising services rendered during October, November, and December. The invoice was not recorded until paid on January 15.

The argument for treating this item as sufficiently material to warrant adjustment is based on the fact that net income is affected, as well as the amount of working capital and the current ratio. The adjusting entry should probably be recommended in these circumstances.

The preceding examples suggest that a decision as to the materiality of an unrecorded transaction hinges to an important extent on whether the transaction affects net income. Assuming that an omitted transaction does affect net income and there is doubt as to whether the dollar amount is large enough to warrant adjustment, the auditors should bear in mind that approximately half of the effect of the error on net income is eliminated by the present high level of corporate income taxes. In other words, an adjusting entry to record an omitted expense item of $10,000 will reduce aftertax income by approximately $5,000. If the adjusting entry is not made, the only ultimate effect is a shift of $5,000 between the net income of two successive years. As a general rule, the auditors should avoid proposing adjusting entries for errors in the year-end cutoff of transactions unless the effect on the statements is clearly significant. However, it should be borne in mind that a number of insignificant individual errors may be material in their *cumulative* effect on the financial statements.

12.   **Determine proper balance sheet presentation of accounts payable.**

Proper balance sheet presentation of accounts payable requires that any material amounts payable to related parties (directors, principal stockholders, officers, and employees) be listed separately from amounts payable to trade creditors.

Debit balances of substantial amount sometimes occur in accounts payable because of such events as duplicate payments made in error, return of merchandise to vendors after payment has been made, and advances to suppliers. If these debit balances are material, a reclassification entry should be made in the audit working papers so that the debit balances will appear as assets in the balance sheet rather than being offset against other accounts payable with credit balances.

If the client company acts as a consignee of merchandise, it is possible that sales of consigned goods shortly before the year-end may not have been set up as a liability to the consignor. An accurate determination of any amounts owing to consignors at the balance sheet date is one step in proper balance sheet presentation of liabilities.

Accounts payable secured by pledged assets should be disclosed in the balance sheet or a note thereto, and cross-referenced to the pledged assets.

   13.   **Obtain from client a letter of representations concerning liabilities.**

Most public accounting firms obtain written representations from clients concerning nearly all financial statement items. Although some accountants do not utilize representations by clients to this extent, it is standard practice to obtain a *liability representation* signed by responsible officers that all liabilities and contingent liabilities known to them are disclosed in the financial statements. Such a representation does not reduce the auditors' responsibility, but it often serves as an effective reminder to executives that management is primarily responsible for the fairness of financial statements.

OTHER LIABILITIES

Notes payable are discussed in the next chapter. In addition to the accounts payable previously considered, other items classified as current liabilities include—

1.   Amounts withheld from employees' pay.
2.   Sales taxes payable.
3.   Unclaimed wages.
4.   Customers' deposits.
5.   Accrued liabilities.

Amounts withheld from employees' pay

Payroll deductions are notoriously numerous; among the more important are social security taxes and individual income taxes. Although the federal and state governments do not specify the exact form of records to be maintained, they do require that records of amounts earned and withheld be adequate to permit a determination of compliance with tax laws.

Income taxes withheld from employees' pay and not remitted as of the balance sheet date constitute a liability to be verified by the auditors. Accrued employer payroll taxes may be audited at the same time. This verification usually consists of tracing the amounts withheld to the payroll summary sheets, testing computations of taxes withheld and accrued, determining that taxes have been deposited or paid in accordance with the federal and state laws and regulations, and reviewing quarterly tax returns.

Payroll deductions also are often made for union dues, charitable contributions, retirement plans, insurance, savings bonds, and other purposes. Besides verifying the liability for any such amounts withheld from employees and not remitted as of the balance sheet date, the auditors should review the adequacy of the withholding procedures and determine that payroll deductions have been properly authorized and accurately computed.

Sales taxes payable

In most sections of the country, business concerns are required to collect sales taxes imposed by state and local governments on retail sales. These taxes do not represent an expense to the business; the retailer merely acts as a collecting agent. Until the amounts collected from customers are remitted to the taxing authority, they constitute current liabilities of the business. The auditors' verification of this liability includes a review of the client's periodic tax returns. The reasonableness of the liability also is tested by a computation applying the tax rate to total taxable sales. In addition, the auditors should examine a number of sales invoices to ascertain that customers are being charged the correct amount of tax. Debits to the liability account for remittances to the taxing authority should be traced to copies of the tax returns and should be vouched to the paid checks.

Unclaimed wages

Unclaimed wages are, by their very nature, subject to misappropriation. The auditors, therefore, are particularly concerned with the adequacy of internal control over this item. A list of unpaid wages should be prepared after each payroll distribution. The payroll checks should not be left for more than a few days in the payroll department. Prompt deposit in a special bank account provides much improved control. The auditors will analyze the Unclaimed Wages account for the purpose of determining that (1) the credits represent all unclaimed wages after each payroll distribution, and (2) the debits represent only authorized payments to employees, remittances to the state under unclaimed property laws, or transfers back to general cash funds through approved procedures.

Customers' deposits

Many companies require that customers make deposits on returnable containers. Public utilities and common carriers also may require deposits to guarantee payment of bills or to cover equipment on loan to the customer. A review of the procedures followed in accepting and returning deposits should be made by the auditors with a view to disclosing any shortcomings in internal control. In some instances deposits shown by the records as refunded to customers may in fact have been abstracted by employees.

The verification should include obtaining a list of the individual deposits and a comparison of the total with the general ledger controlling account. If deposits are interest-bearing, the amount of accrued interest should also be verified. As a general rule, the auditors do not attempt to confirm deposits by direct communication with customers; but this procedure is desirable if the amounts involved are substantial or the internal control procedures are considered to be deficient.

Accrued liabilities

Most accrued liabilities represent obligations payable sometime during the succeeding period for services or privileges received before the balance sheet date. Examples include interest payable, accrued property taxes, accrued payrolls and payroll taxes, income taxes payable, and amounts accrued under service guarantees.

Unlike accounts payable, which result from executed contracts, accrued liabilities pertain to services of a continuing nature, with the related expense often measured on a time basis. The basic auditing steps for accrued liabilities are:

1. Examine any contracts or other documents on hand that provide the basis for the accrual.
2. Appraise the accuracy of the detailed accounting records maintained for this category of liability.
3. Test the computations made by the client in setting up the accrual.
4. Determine that accrued liabilities have been treated consistently at the beginning and end of the period.

If the accounting records are well maintained and internal control is reasonably satisfactory, there is no need for the auditors to make an independent computation of accrued liabilities. They should merely review the methods employed in setting up the accruals and test the arithmetical accuracy of the computations made by the employees of the company.

Accrued property taxes. Property tax payments are usually few in number and substantial in amount. It is, therefore, feasible for the audit working papers to include an analysis showing all of the year's property tax transactions. Tax payments should be verified by inspection of the property tax bills issued by local government units and by reference to the related paid checks. If the tax accruals at the balance sheet date differ significantly from those of prior years, an explanation of the variation should be obtained. The auditors should verify that property tax bills have been received on all taxable property or that an estimated tax has been accrued.

Accrued payrolls. The examination of payrolls from the standpoint of appraising the adequacy of internal controls and substantiating the expenditures for the period under audit is considered in Chapter 17. The present consideration of payrolls is limited to the procedures required for the verification of accrued payrolls at the balance sheet date.

Accrued gross salaries and wages appear on the balance sheets of virtually all concerns. The correctness of the amount accrued is significant in the determination of total liabilities and also in the proper matching of costs and revenue. The verification procedure consists principally of comparing the amounts accrued to the actual payroll of the subsequent period and reviewing the method of allocation at the balance sheet date. Payments made at the first payroll dates of the subsequent period are reviewed to determine that no *unrecorded* payroll liability existed as of the balance sheet date.

Pension plan accruals. Auditing procedures for the accrued liability for pension costs may begin with a review of the copy of the pension plan in the auditors' permanent file. Then consideration should be given to the provisions of the Employee Retirement Income Security Act (ERISA). Other steps include confirmation of the client's pension cost for the year by direct correspondence with the client's actuary and analysis of the related liability account, including confirmation of any payments to the trustee. In obtaining evidence from the client's actuary, the auditors should comply with the requirements of *SAS No. 11*, "Using the Work of a Specialist" (discussed in Chapter 7).

Accrued vacation pay. Closely related to accrued salaries and wages is the liability that may exist for accrued vacation pay. This type of liability arises from two situations: (1) an employee entitled by contract to a vacation during the past year may have been prevented from taking it by an emergency work schedule, and (2) an employee may be entitled to a future vacation of which part of the cost must be accrued to achieve a proper matching of costs and revenue.

The auditors' verification of accrued vacation pay may begin with a review of the permanent file copy of the employment contract or agreement stipulating vacation terms. The computation of the accrual should then be verified both as to arithmetical accuracy and for agreement with the terms of the company's vacation policy. The auditors should also ascertain whether the expense provision offsetting the vacation accrual qualifies as an income tax deduction. If not, income tax allocation will be required.

Service guarantees. The products of many companies are sold with a guarantee of free service or replacement during a rather extended warranty period. The costs of rendering such services should be recognized as expense in the year the product is sold rather than in a later year in which the replacement is made or repair service performed. If this policy is followed, the company will make an annual charge to expense and credit to a liability account based on the amount of the year's sales and the estimated future service or replacement. As repairs and replacements take place, the costs will be charged to the liability account.

The auditors should review the client's annual provision for estimated future expenditures and compute the percentage relationship between the amount in the liability account and the amount of the year's sales. If this relationship varies sharply from year to year, the client should be asked for an explanation. The auditors should also review the charges month by month to the liability account and be alert for the burial of other expenses in this account. Sudden variations in the monthly charges to the liability account require investigation. In general, the auditors should determine that the balance in the liability account for service guarantees moves in reasonable relationship with the trend of sales and is properly segregated into current and long-term portions in the balance sheet.

Current income tax laws prohibit the deduction of provisions for service guarantees; deductions are permitted only when actual expenditures are incurred. Accordingly, the auditors should ascertain that the client is properly allocating income taxes attributable to the nondeductible provisions.

Accrued commissions and bonuses. Accrued commissions to sales representatives and bonuses payable to managerial personnel also require verification. The essential step in this case is reference to the authority for the commission or bonus. The basic contracts should be examined and traced to minutes of directors' meetings. If the bonus or commission is based on the total volume of sales or some other objective measure, the auditors should verify the computation of the accrual by applying the prescribed rate to the amount used as a base.

Income taxes payable. Federal, state, and foreign income taxes on corporations represent a material factor in determining both net income and financial position. The auditors cannot express an opinion on either the balance sheet or income statement of a corporation without first obtaining evidence that the provision for income taxes has been properly computed. In the audit of small- and medium-size companies, it is customary for the audit engagement to include the preparation of the client's tax returns. If the income tax returns have been prepared by the client's staff or other persons, the auditors must nevertheless verify the reasonableness of the tax liability if they are to express an opinion on the fairness of the financial statements. In performing such a review of a tax return prepared by the client's staff or by others the auditors may sometimes discover an opportunity for a tax saving that has been overlooked; obviously such a discovery tends to enhance the client's appreciation of the services rendered by the auditors.

For businesses organized as single proprietorships or partnerships, no provision for income taxes appears on the income statement because taxes on the profits of these enterprises are payable by the individual owner or owners.

Taxable income often differs from pretax accounting income presented in the financial statements. If the difference between income as determined for tax purposes and income as determined by applying generally accepted accounting principles is substantial, allocation of income taxes is necessary to avoid a distortion of net income.

The auditors should analyze the Income Taxes Payable account and vouch all amounts to paid checks, income tax returns, or other supporting documents. The final balance in the Income Taxes Payable account will ordinarily equal the computed federal, state, and foreign taxes on the current year's income tax returns, less any payments thereon.

Besides reviewing the computation of the income tax liability for the current year, the auditors should determine the date to which income tax returns for prior years have been examined by IRS agents and the particulars of any disputes or additional assessments. Review of the reports of revenue agents is also an essential step. In the first audit of a new client, the auditors should review any prior years' income tax returns not yet examined by revenue agents to make sure that there has been no substantial underpayment of taxes that would warrant presentation as a liability.

Accrued professional fees. Fees of professional firms include charges for the services of attorneys, public accountants, consulting engineers, and other specialists who often render services of a continuing nature but present bills only at infrequent intervals. By inquiry of officers and by review of corporate minutes, the auditors may learn of professional services received for which no liability has yet been reflected in the accounts. Review of the expense account for legal fees is always essential because it may reveal damage suits, tax disputes, or other litigation warranting disclosure in the financial statements. Fees of public accountants for periodic audits are properly reflected in the accounts of the year subsequent to the period under audit. Accruals are desirable, however, for any other accounting services completed but unbilled as of the balance sheet date.

Balance sheet presentation

Accrued expenses—interest, taxes, rent, and wages—are included in the current liability section of the balance sheet and sometimes combined into one figure. Income taxes payable, however, may be sufficiently material to be listed as a separate item. Deferred federal income taxes resulting from tax allocations should be classified as current liabilities if they relate to current assets. Otherwise, deferred federal income taxes are classified as long-term.

Deferred credits to revenue for such items as rent or interest collected in advance that will be taken into earnings in the succeeding period are customarily included in current liabilities. Deposits on contracts and similar advances from customers also are accorded the status of current liabilities because the receipt of an advance increases the current assets total and because the goods to be used in liquidating the advance are generally included in current assets.

Time of examination

The nature and amount of trade accounts payable may change greatly within a few weeks' time; consequently, the auditors' verification of these rapidly changing liabilities is most effective when performed immediately after the balance sheet date. As stressed at the beginning of this chapter, failure to record a liability will cause an overstatement of financial position. Audit work on accounts payable performed before the balance sheet date is of little value if the client fails to record important liabilities coming into existence during the remaining weeks of the year under audit. For this reason many auditors believe that most of the audit work on accounts payable should be performed after the balance sheet date. Certainly, the auditors' search for unrecorded liabilities must be made after the balance sheet date because this search is concentrated on the transactions occurring during the first few weeks of the new year.

Some current liability accounts other than accounts payable are more suitable for preliminary audit work. The documents relating to accrued property taxes, for example, may be available in advance of the balance sheet date. Amounts withheld from employees' pay can be reviewed before the end of the year. The propriety of amounts withheld and of amounts remitted to the tax authorities during the year can be verified before the pressure of year-end work begins. The working papers relating to such liability accounts then may be completed very quickly after the end of the accounting period.

KEY TERMS INTRODUCED OR EMPHASIZED IN CHAPTER 15

Accrued liabilities (accrued expenses)   Short-term obligations for services of a continuing nature that accumulate on a time basis. Examples include interest, taxes, rent, salaries, and pensions. Generally not evidenced by invoices or statements.

Confirmation   Direct communication with vendors or suppliers to determine the amount of an account payable. Represents high quality evidence because it is a document created outside the client organization and transmitted directly to the auditors.

Consignment   A transfer of goods from the owner to another person who acts as the sales agent of the owner.

Subsequent period   The time extending from the balance sheet date to the date of the auditors' report.

Trade accounts payable   Current liabilities arising from the purchase of goods and services from trade creditors, generally evidenced by invoices or statements received from the creditors.

Vendor's statement   A monthly statement prepared by a vendor (supplier) showing the beginning balance, charges during the month for goods or services, amounts collected, and ending balance. This externally created document should correspond (except for timing differences) with an account in the client's accounts payable subsidiary ledger.

Voucher   A document authorizing a cash disbursement. A voucher usually provides space for employees performing various approval functions to initial. The term *voucher* may also be applied to the group of supporting documents used as a basis for recording liabilities or for making cash disbursements.

Voucher register   A special journal used in a voucher system to record liabilities requiring cash payment in the near future. Every liability recorded in a voucher register corresponds to a voucher authorizing future payment.

GROUP I: REVIEW QUESTIONS

15– 1.   Suggest two reasons the adjustments proposed by independent auditors more often than not call for reducing recorded earnings.

15– 2.   If a corporation overstates its earnings, are its liabilities more likely to be overstated or understated? Explain.

15– 3.   Law suits against CPA firms are most likely to allege that the auditors were negligent in not detecting which of the following? (*a*) overstatement of liabilities and earnings, (*b*) understatement of assets and earnings, (*c*) overstatement of owners' equity. Explain the reasoning underlying your choice.

15– 4.   Assume that a highly placed employee of a company has stolen company assets and is now planning to conceal the fraud by failing to make an accounting entry for a large transaction. Would the omission probably be for a transaction creating an asset or a liability? Explain.

15– 5.   Identify three audit procedures (other than "Search for unrecorded accounts payable") that are concerned directly or indirectly with disclosing unrecorded accounts payable.

15– 6.   What use should be made of monthly statements from vendors by personnel in the accounts payable department?

15– 7.   Is the confirmation of accounts payable by direct communication with vendors as useful and important an audit procedure as is the confirmation of accounts receivable? Explain fully. (AICPA)

15– 8.   During the verification of the individual invoices comprising the total of accounts payable at the balance sheet date, the auditors discovered some receiving reports indicating that the merchandise covered by several of these invoices was not received until after the balance sheet date. What action should the auditors take?

15– 9.   What do you consider to be the most important single procedure in the auditors' search for unrecorded accounts payable? Explain.

15–10. Whitehall Company records its liabilities in accounts payable subsidiary ledgers. The auditors have decided to select some of the accounts for confirmation by direct communication with vendors. The largest volume of purchases during the year had been made from Ranchero Company, but at the balance sheet date this account had a zero balance. Under these circumstances should the auditors send a confirmation request to Ranchero Company, or would they accomplish more by limiting their confirmation program to accounts with large year-end balances?

15–11. Compare the auditors' approach to the verification of liabilities with their approach to the verification of assets.

15–12. What is the purpose of the auditors in comparing cash payments subsequent to the balance sheet date with the trial balance of accounts payable at the year-end?

15–13. Most auditors are interested in performing as many phases of an examination as possible in advance of the balance sheet date. The verification of accounts payable, however, generally is regarded as something to be done after the balance sheet date. What specific factors can you suggest that make the verification of accounts payable less suitable than many other accounts for interim work?

15–14. The operating procedures of a well-managed accounts payable department will provide for the verification of several specific points before a vendor's invoice is recorded as an approved liability. What are the points requiring verification?

15–15. List the major responsibilities of an accounts payable department.

15–16. In achieving adequate internal control over operations of the accounts payable department, a company should establish procedures that will ensure that extensions and footings are proved on all invoices and that the propriety of prices is reviewed. What is the most effective means of assuring consistent performance of these duties?

15–17. Which do you consider the more significant step in establishing strong internal control over accounts payable transactions: the approval of an invoice for payment, or the issuance of a check in payment of an invoice? Explain.

15–18. Outline a method by which the auditors may test the propriety of cash discounts taken on accounts payable.

15–19. For what documents relating to the accounts payable operation would you recommend the use of serial numbers as an internal control procedure?

15–20. What internal control procedure would you recommend to call attention to failure to pay invoices within the discount period?

15–21. As part of the investigation of accounts payable, auditors sometimes vouch entries in selected creditors' accounts back through the journals to original documents, such as purchase orders, receiving reports, invoices, and paid checks. What is the principal purpose of this procedure?

15–22. Vendors's statements and accounts payable confirmations are both forms of documentary evidence created outside the client organization and useful in audit work on accounts payable. Which of these two represents higher quality evidence. Why?

15–23. What documentary evidence created outside the client's organization is particularly important to the auditors in verifying accrued property taxes?

15–24. What differences should auditors expect to find in supporting evidence for accrued liabilities as contrasted with accounts payable?

GROUP II: QUESTIONS REQUIRING ANALYSIS

15–25. The *subsequent period* in an audit is the time extending from the balance sheet date to the date of the auditors' report.

Required:
Discuss the importance of the subsequent period in the audit of trade accounts payable.

15–26. Compare the confirmation of accounts receivable with the confirmation of accounts payable under the following headings:
a. Generally accepted auditing procedures. (Justify the differences revealed by your comparison.)
b. Selection of accounts to be confirmed. (AICPA, adapted)

15–27. In connection with their examination of the financial statements of Davis Company, the auditors reviewed the Federal Income Taxes Payable account.

Required:
a. Discuss reasons why the auditors should review the federal income tax returns for prior years and the reports of internal revenue agents.
b. What information will these review provide? (Do not discuss specific tax return items.) (AICPA, adapted)

15–28. During the course of any audit, the auditors are always alert for unrecorded accounts payable or other unrecorded liabilities.

Required:
For each of the following audit areas (1) describe an unrecorded liability that might be discovered, and (2) state what auditing procedure(s) might bring it to light.
a. Construction in progress (property, plant, and equipment).
b. Prepaid insurance.
c. License authorizing the client to produce a product patented by another company.
d. Minutes of directors' meetings.

15–29. Describe the audit steps that generally would be followed in establishing the propriety of the recorded liability for federal income taxes of a corporation you are auditing for the first time. Consideration should be given the status of (a) the liability for prior years and (b) the liability arising from the current year's taxable income. (AICPA)

15–30. In the course of your initial examination of the financial statements of Sylvan Company, you ascertain that of the substantial amount of accounts payable outstanding at the close of the period, approximately 75 percent is owing to six creditors. You have requested that you be permitted to confirm the balances owing to these six creditors by communicating with the creditors, but the president of the company is unwilling to approve your request on the grounds that correspondence in regard to the balances—all of which contain some overdue items—might give rise to demands on the part of the creditors for immediate payment of the overdue items and thereby embarrass Sylvan Company.

In the circumstances, what alternative procedure would you adopt in an effort to satisfy yourself that the accounting records show the correct amounts payable to these creditors? (AICPA, adapted)

15–31. Select the best answer for each of the following and explain the reason for your selection.

  a. Which of the following audit procedures is *least* likely to be performed before the balance sheet date?

  (1) Observation of inventory.

  (2) Review of internal control over cash disbursements.

  (3) Search for unrecorded liabilities.

  (4) Confirmation of receivables.

  b. Which of the following is the *most* effecient audit procedure for the detection of unrecorded liabilities at the balance sheet date?

  (1) Confirm large accounts payable balances at the balance sheet date.

  (2) Compare cash disbursements in the subsequent period with the accounts payable trial balance at year-end.

  (3) Examine purchase orders issued for several days before the close of the year.

  (4) Obtain a letter as to existing liabilities from the client's attorney.

  c. Which of the following *best* explains why accounts payable confirmation procedures are *not* always used?

  (1) Inclusion of accounts payable balances on the liability certificate completed by the client allows the auditor to refrain from using confirmation procedures.

  (2) Accounts payable generally are insignificant and can be audited by utilizing analytic review procedures.

  (3) The auditor may be certain that the creditors will press for payment.

  (4) Reliable externally generated evidence supporting accounts payable balances is generally available for audit inspection on the client's premises.

  d. Under which of the following circumstances would it be advisable for the auditors to confirm accounts payable with creditors?

  (1) Internal accounting control over accounts payable is adequate, and there is sufficient evidence on hand to minimize the risk of a material misstatement.

(2)   Confirmation response is expected to be favorable, and accounts payable are of immaterial amounts.

ᴄ (3)   Creditors' statements are not available, and internal accounting control over accounts payable is unsatisfactory.

(4)   The majority of accounts payable balances are with associated companies.

GROUP III: PROBLEMS

15–32.   As part of your first examination of the financial statements of Marina del Rey, Inc., you have decided to confirm some of the accounts payable. You are now in the process of selecting the individual companies to whom you will send accounts payable confirmation requests. Among the accounts payable you are considering are the following.

Company	Amount payable at year-end	Total purchases from vendor during year
Dayco, Inc.	$ —	$1,980,000
Gearbox, Inc.	22,650	46,100
Landon Co.	65,000	75,000
Western Supply	190,000	2,123,000

Required:

a.   Which two of the above four accounts payable would you select as the most important to confirm? Explain your choice in terms of the audit objectives in sending accounts payable confirmation requests.

b.   Assume that you are selecting accounts receivable to be confirmed. Assume also that the four companies listed above are customers of your client rather than suppliers and that the dollar amounts are accounts receivable balances and total sales for the year. Which two companies would you select as the most important to confirm. Explain your choice.

15–33.   James Rowe, CPA, is the independent auditor of Raleigh Corporation. Rowe is considering the audit work to be performed in the accounts payable area for the current year's engagement.

The prior-year's working papers show that confirmation requests were mailed to 100 of Raleigh's 1,000 suppliers. The selected suppliers were based on Rowe's sample that was designed to select accounts with large dollar balances. A substantial number of hours was spent by Raleigh employees and by Rowe resolving relatively minor differences between the confirmation replies and Raleigh's accounting records. Alternate audit procedures were used for those suppliers that did not respond to the confirmation requests.

Required:

a.   Identify the accounts payable audit objectives that Rowe must consider in determining the audit procedures to be followed.

b. Identify situations in which Rowe should use accounts payable confirmations, and discuss whether Rowe is required to use them.

c. Discuss why the use of large dollar balances as the basis for selecting accounts payable for confirmation might not be the most efficient approach, and indicate what more efficient procedures could be followed when selecting accounts payable for confirmation. (AICPA, adapted) *should focus on customers w/ large # of transaction*

15–34. During the current year, your audit client, Video Corporation, was licensed to manufacture a patented type of television tube. The licensing agreement called for royalty payments of 50 cents for each tube manufactured by Video Corporation. What procedures would you follow in connection with your regular annual audit at December 31 to obtain evidence that the liability for royalties is correctly stated? (AICPA, adapted)

15–35. Nancy Howe, your staff assistant on the April 30, 1985 audit of Wilcox Company, was transferred to another audit engagement before she could complete the audit of unrecorded accounts payable. Her working paper, which you have reviewed and are satisfied is complete, appears on page 516.

Required:

Prepare a proposed adjusting journal entry for the unrecorded accounts payable of Wilcox Company at April 30, 1985. The amounts are material. (Do not deal with income taxes.)

15–36. You were in the final stages of your examination of the financial statements of Scott Corporation for the year ended December 31, 1984 when you were consulted by the corporation's president, who believes there is no point to your examining the 1985 voucher register and testing data in support of 1984 entries. He stated that (1) bills pertaining to 1984 that were received too late to be included in the December voucher register were recorded as of the year-end by the corporation by journal entry, (2) the internal auditors made tests after the year-end, and (3) he would furnish you with a letter representing that there were no unrecorded liabilities.

Required:

a. Should the independent auditors' test for unrecorded liabilities be affected by the fact that the client made a journal entry to record 1984 bills that were received late? Explain.

b. Should the independent auditors' test for unrecorded liabilities be affected by the fact that a letter is obtained in which a responsible management official represents that to the best of his knowledge all liabilities have been recorded? Explain.

c. Should the independent auditors' test for unrecorded liabilities be eliminated or reduced because of the internal audit tests? Explain.

d. Assume that the client company, which handled some government contracts, had no internal auditors but that auditors for a federal agency spent three weeks auditing the records and were just

Wilcox Company
Unrecorded Accounts Payable   M-1-1
April 30, 1985

Invoice Date	Vendor and Description	Amount
	Hill & Harper — unpaid legal fees at 4/30/85 (see attorney letter at M-4)	1000 √
4/1/85	Drew Insurance Agency — unpaid premium on fire insurance for period 4/1/85-3/31/88 (see insurance broker letter at J-1-1)	1800 √
4/30/85	Maup and Sage, Stockbrokers — advice for 100 shares of Madison Company Common Stock (settlement date 5/7/85)	2125 √
	Lane Company — shipment received 4/30/85 per receiver no. 3361 and included in 4/30/85 physical inventory; invoice not yet received (amount is per purchase order)	5863 √
		10 788 —

√ — Examined document described.

In my opinion, the $10,788 adjustment includes all material unrecorded accounts payable.

N.A.H.
5/29/85

completing their work at this time. How would the independent auditors' unrecorded liability test be affected by the work of the auditors for a federal agency?

e. What sources in addition to the 1985 voucher register should the independent auditors consider to locate possible unrecorded liabilities? (AICPA, adapted)

16

Debt and equity capital; loss contingencies

Business enterprises obtain substantial amounts of their financial resources by incurring interest-bearing debt and issuing capital stock. The acquisition and repayment of capital is sometimes referred to as the financing cycle. This transaction cycle includes the sequence of procedures for authorizing, executing, and recording those transactions that involve bank loans, mortgages, bonds payable, and capital stock. The payment of interest and dividends are an integral part of the financing cycle.

INTEREST-BEARING DEBT

Nearly every business borrows. A business with an excellent credit reputation may find it possible to borrow from a bank on a simple unsecured note. A business of lesser financial standing may find that obtaining bank credit requires the pledging of specific assets as collateral or that it must agree to certain restrictive covenants, such as the suspension of dividends.

Long-term debt usually is substantial in amount and often extends for periods of 30 years or more. Debentures, secured bonds, and notes payable (sometimes secured by mortgages or trust deeds) are the principal type of long-term debt. Debentures are backed only by the general credit of the issuing corporation and not by liens on specific assets. Since in most respects debentures have the characteristics of other corporate bonds, we shall use the term *bonds* to include both debentures and secured bonds payable.

The formal document creating bonded indebtedness is called the *indenture* or *trust indenture*. When creditors supply capital on a long-term basis, they often insist upon placing certain restrictions on the company. For example, the indenture often provides that a company may not declare dividends unless the amount of working capital is maintained above a specified amount. The acquisition of plant and equipment, or the increasing of managerial salaries, may be permitted only if the current ratio is maintained at a specified level and if net income reaches a designated amount. Another device for protecting the long-term credit is the requirement of a sinking fund or redemption fund to be held by a trustee. If these restrictions are violated, the indenture may provide that the entire debt is due on demand.

The auditors' objectives in examination of interest-bearing debt

The objectives of the auditors in their examination of interest-bearing debt are to determine that (1) internal controls are adequate; (2) all interest-bearing debt of the client has been recorded and represents bona fide obligations issued in accordance with federal and state laws; (3) interest payable and interest expense have been accurately computed, including the amortization of bond discount or premium; (4) the client company has met all requirements and restrictions imposed upon it by debt contracts; and (5) the interest-bearing debt and related expenses are properly presented in the financial statements and adequate informative disclosure is achieved.

Internal control over interest-bearing debt

Authorization by the board of directors. Effective internal control over interest-bearing debt begins with the authorization to incur the debt. The bylaws of a corporation usually require that borrowing be approved by the board of directors. The treasurer of the corporation will prepare a report on any proposed financing, explaining the need for funds, the estimated effect of borrowing upon future earnings, the estimated financial position of the company in comparison with others in the industry both before and after the borrowing, and alternative methods of raising the amount desired. Authorization by the board of directors will include review and approval of such matters as the choice of a bank, the type of security, the choice of a trustee, registration with the SEC, agreements with investment bankers, compliance with requirements of the state of incorporation, and listing of bonds on a securities exchange. After the issuance of long-term debt, the board of directors should receive a report stating the net amount received and its disposition, as for acquisition of plant assets, addition to working capital, or other purposes.

Use of an independent trustee. Bond issues are always for large amounts—usually many millions of dollars. Therefore, only large companies issue bonds; small companies obtain long-term capital through mortgage loans or other sources. Any company large enough to issue bonds and find a ready market for the securities will almost always utilize the services of a large bank as an independent trustee.

The trustee is charged with the protection of the creditors' interests and must continually review the issuing company's compliance with the provisions of the indenture. Besides, the trustee maintains detailed records of the names and addresses of the registered owners of the bonds, cancels old bond certificates and issues new ones when bonds change ownership, follows procedures to prevent over issuance of bond certificates, distributes interest payments, and distributes principal payments when the bonds mature. Use of an independent trustee largely solves the problem of internal control over bonds payable. Internal control is strengthened by the fact that the trustee does not have access to the issuing company's assets or accounting records and the fact that the trustee is a large financial institution with legal responsibility for its actions.

Interest payments on bonds and notes payable. The auditors appraisal of internal controls relating to bonds and notes payable must extend to the handling of interest payments. In the case of a note payable, there may be only one recipient of interest, and the disbursement may be controlled in the same manner as other cash payments.

Many corporations assign the entire task of paying interest to the trustee for either *bearer bonds* or *registered bonds*. Highly effective control is then achieved, since the company will issue a single check for the full amount of the semiannual interest payment on the entire bond issue. In the case of bearer bonds (coupon bonds), the trustee upon receipt of this check will make payment for coupons presented, cancel the coupons, and file them numerically. A second count of the coupons is made at a later date; the coupons then are destroyed and a cremation certificate delivered to the issuing company. The trustee does not attempt to maintain a list of the holders of coupon bonds, since these securities are transferable by the mere act of delivery. If certain coupons are not presented for payment, the trustee will hold the funds corresponding to such coupons for the length of time prescribed by statute. In the case of registered bonds, the trustee will maintain a current list of holders and will remit interest checks to them in the same manner as dividend checks are distributed to stockholders.

Audit working papers

A copy of the indenture relating to a bond issue should be placed in the permanent file. Analyses of ledger accounts for notes and bonds payable, and the related accounts for interest and discount or premium, should be obtained for the current working papers file or the permanent file. A grouping sheet is seldom required for short-term notes payable or for long-term debt.

AUDIT PROGRAM FOR INTEREST-BEARING DEBT

This audit program does not provide for the usual distinction between substantive testing and the study and evaluation of internal control. After the auditors have obtained a description of the client's system of internal control over interest-bearing debt, they usually do not conduct tests of compliance. Rather, since transactions are few in number but large in dollar amount, the auditors may follow the approach of substantiating the individual transactions. Thus, the audit program for interest-bearing debt consists primarily of substantive tests.

Audit procedures appropriate for the verification of interest-bearing debt include the following:

1. Obtain or prepare a description of internal control over interest-bearing debt.
2. Obtain or prepare analyses of interest-bearing debt accounts and related interest, premium, and discount accounts.
3. Examine copies of notes payable and supporting documents.
4. Obtain copy of indenture for bonds payable, and determine whether its provisions have been met.
5. Trace authority for issuance of interest-bearing debt to the corporate minutes.
6. Vouch borrowing and repayment transactions to supporting documents.
7. Confirm interest-bearing debt with payees or appropriate third parties.
8. Verify computation of interest expense, interest payable, and amortization of discount or premium.
9. Review notes payable paid or renewed after the balance sheet date.
10. Determine proper financial statement presentation of interest-bearing debt and related transactions.

1. Obtain or prepare a description of internal control over interest-bearing debt.

The study and evaluation of the client's internal control over interest-bearing debt often will involve the preparation of a written description and a flowchart, as well as the filling in of an internal control questionnaire. Some of the typical questions in this questionnaire are the following: Are interest-bearing liabilities incurred only under authorization of the board of directors? Is an independent trustee retained to account for all bond issuances, cancellations, and interest payments? Has the board of directors specified banks from which loans may be obtained? The questionnaire serves to remind the auditors of matters that should be investigated fully; the filling in of "yes" and "no" answers to the questions in itself is not a significant audit procedure.

2. Obtain or prepare analyses of interest-bearing debt accounts and related interest, premium, and discount accounts.

A notes payable analysis shows the beginning balance, if any, of each individual note, additional notes issued and payments on notes during the year, and the ending balance of each note. In addition, the beginning balances of interest payable or prepaid interest, interest expense, interest paid, and ending balances of interest payable or prepaid interest are presented in the analysis working paper.

An analysis of the Notes Payable account will serve a number of purposes: (*a*) the payment or other disposition of notes listed as outstanding in the previous year's audit can be verified; (*b*) the propriety of individual debits and credits can be established; and (*c*) the validity of the year-end balance of the account is proved through the step-by-step verification of all changes in the account during the year. Such a detailed analysis of notes payable is feasible and justified because normally there are not very many transactions and the dollar amounts are relatively large.

In the first audit of a client, the auditors will analyze the ledger accounts for Bonds Payable, Bond Issue Costs, and Bond Discount (or Bond Premium) for the years since the bonds were issued. The working paper is placed in the auditors' permanent file; in later audits any further entries in these accounts may be added to the analysis.

3. Examine copies of notes payable and supporting documents.

The auditors should examine the client's copies of notes payable and supporting documents such as mortgages and trust deeds. The original documents will be in the possession of the payees; but the auditors should make certain that the client has retained copies of the debt instruments and that their details correspond to the analyses described in the second procedure of this audit program.

4. Obtain copy of indenture for bonds payable and determine whether its provisions have been met.

In the first audit of a client or upon the issuance of a new bond issue, the auditors will obtain a copy of the bond indenture for the permanent file. The indenture should be carefully studied, with particular attention to such points as the amount of bonds authorized, interest rates and dates, maturity dates, descriptions of property pledged as collateral, provisions for retirement or conversion, duties and responsibilities of the trustee, and any restrictions imposed on the borrowing company.

The indenture provisions frequently require maintenance of a sinking fund, maintenance of stipulated minimum levels of working capital, and insurance of pledged property. The indenture also may restrict dividends to a specified proportion of earnings, limit management compensation, and prohibit additional long-term borrowing, except under stipulated conditions. Adequate comments should appear in the audit working papers as to the company's compliance with the provisions of the indenture. If the company has not complied fully with the requirements, the auditors should inform both the client and the client's legal counsel of the violation; explanation of the extent of noncompliance should also be included in the client's financial statements, and possibly in the audit report. In some cases of violation the entire bond issue may be due and payable on demand, and hence a current liability.

Illustrative case.   In the audit of a large construction company, the auditors found the client's working capital to be far below the minimum level stipulated in the indenture of long-term secured bonds payable. In addition to this, the client had allowed the required insurance coverage of pledged assets to lapse. These violations of the indenture were sufficient to cause the bond issue to become payable on demand.

Although the client agreed to reclassify the bond issue as a current liability, the auditors were unable to satisfy themselves that the client could meet the obligation if the bondholders demanded payment. Also, if the bondholders foreclosed on the pledged assets, the ability of the client to continue as a going concern would be questionable. Thus, even after the liability was reclassified as current, the auditors had to qualify their report as being subject to the client company's ability to meet its obligations and remain a going concern.

Auditors do not judge the legality of a bond issue; this is a problem for the client's attorneys. The auditors should be familiar, however, with the principal provisions of the federal Securities Act of 1933 and of the corporate blue-sky laws of the client's state of incorporation. They should ascertain that the client has obtained an attorney's opinion on the legality of the bond issuance. In doubtful cases they should consult the client's legal counsel.

   5.   **Trace authority for issuance of interest-bearing debt to the corporate minutes.**

The authority to issue interest-bearing debt generally lies in the board of directors. To determine that the bonds outstanding were properly authorized, the auditors should read the passages in the minutes of directors' (and stockholders') meetings concerning the issuance of debt. The minutes usually will cite the applicable sections of the corporate bylaws permitting the issuance of debt instruments, and may also contain reference to the opinion of the company's counsel concerning the legality of the issue. This information should be traced by the auditors to the original sources.

   6.   **Vouch borrowing and repayment transactions to supporting documents.**

The auditors must obtain evidence that transactions in interest-bearing debt accounts were valid. To accomplish this objective, the auditors trace the cash received from the issuance of notes, bonds, or mortgages to the validated copy of the bank deposit slip and to the bank statement. Any remittance advices supporting these cash receipts are also examined. The auditors can find further support for the net proceeds of a bond issue by refering to the underwriting contract and to the prospectus filed with the SEC.

Debits to a Notes Payable or a Mortgages Payable account generally represent payments in full or in installments. The auditors should examine paid checks for these payments; in so doing, they also will account for payments of accrued interest. The propriety of installment payments should be verified by reference to the repayment schedule set forth in the note or mortgage copy in the client's possession.

A comparison of canceled notes payable with the debit entries in the Notes Payable account provides further assurance that notes indicated as paid during the year have, in fact, been retired. The auditors' inspection of these notes should include a comparison of the maturity date of the note with the date of cash disbursement. Failure to pay notes promptly at maturity is suggestive of serious financial weakness. Payment prior to maturity, on the other hand, may be accompanied by a reduction in the amount of the liability on noninterest-bearing notes.

There is seldom any justification for a paid note to be missing from the files; a receipt for payment from the payee of the note is not a satisfactory substitute. If, for any reason, a paid note is not available for inspection, the auditors should review the request for a check or other vouchers supporting the disbursement and should discuss the transaction with an appropriate official.

In examining the canceled notes the auditors should also trace the disposition of any collateral used to secure these notes. A convenient opportunity for diversion of pledged securities or other assets to an unauthorized use may be created at the time these assets are regained from a secured creditor.

7. **Confirm interest-bearing debt with payees or appropriate third parties.**

Notes payable to banks are confirmed as part of the confirmation of bank balances. The standard bank confirmation form illustrated in the chapter on cash includes a request that the bank prepare a list of all borrowings by the depositor. The primary objective of this inquiry is to bring to light any unrecorded notes. As mentioned previously in the discussion of bank accounts, confirmation requests should be sent to all banks with which the client has done business during the year, since a note payable to a bank may be outstanding long after a deposit account has been closed.

Confirmation requests for notes payable to payees other than banks should be drafted on the client's letterhead stationery, signed by the controller or other appropriate executive, and mailed by the auditors. Payees should be requested to confirm dates of origin, due dates, unpaid balances of notes, interest rates and dates to which paid, and collateral for the notes.

The auditors may also substantiate the existence and amount of a mortgage liability outstanding by direct confirmation with the mortgagee. The information received should be compared with the client's records and the audit working papers. When no change in the liability account has occurred in the period under audit, the only major procedure necessary will be this confirmation with the creditor. At the same time that the mortgagee is asked to confirm the debt, it may be asked for an opinion as to the company's compliance with the mortgage or trust deed agreement.

Bond transactions usually can be confirmed directly with the trustee. The trustee's reply should include an exact description of the bonds, including maturity dates and interest rates; bonds retired, purchased for the treasury, or converted into stock during the year; bonds outstanding at the balance sheet date; and sinking fund transactions and balances.

8. Verify computation of interest expense, interest payable, and amortization of discount or premium.

Interest expense is of special significance to auditors because it indicates the amount of outstanding liabilities. In other words, close study of interest payments is a means of bringing to light any unrecorded interest-bearing liabilities.

Verification of interest expense and interest payable for notes or mortgages is usually a simple matter. The auditors test the accuracy of the client's interest expense and interest payable computations. In addition, the auditors should examine paid checks supporting interest payments and review the confirmations received from the payees to verify the dates to which interest on each note or mortgage has been paid.

The total bond interest expense for the period usually reflects not only the interest actually paid and accrued, but also amortization of bond premium or discount. The auditors will verify the amounts amortized by independent computations. The nominal interest on the bonds should be computed (interest rate times face value). Checks drawn in payment of interest are traced to the cash records. Any balance of interest expense that remains unpaid at the balance sheet date is traced to an accrued liability account. If the payment of interest to bondholders is handled through the independent trustee, a direct confirmation of the trustee's transactions should be obtained for the period under review.

9. Review notes payable paid or renewed after the balance sheet date.

If any of the notes payable outstanding at the balance sheet date are paid before completion of the audit engagement, the auditors will have available additional evidence on these liabilities. Renewal of notes maturing shortly after the balance sheet date may alter the auditors' thinking as to the proper classification of these liabilities.

In the discussion of notes receivable in Chapter 12, emphasis was placed on the necessity of close scrutiny of loans to officers, directors, and affiliates because of the absence of arm's-length bargaining in these related party transactions. Similar emphasis should be placed on the examination of notes payable to insiders or affiliates, although the opportunities for self-dealing are more limited than with receivables. The auditors should scan the notes payable records for the period between the balance sheet date and the completion of examination so that they may be aware of any unusual transactions, such as the reestablishment of an insider note that had been paid just prior to the balance sheet date.

10.   Determine proper financial statement presentation of interest-bearing debt and related transactions.

Because of the interest of creditors in the current liability section of the balance sheet and the inferences that may be drawn from various uses of notes payable, adequate informative disclosure is extremely important. Classification of notes by types of payees, as well as by current or long-term maturity, is desirable. Separate listing is needed for notes payable to banks, notes payable to trade creditors, and notes payable to officers, directors, stockholders, and affiliates.

Secured liabilities and pledged assets should be cross-referenced to one another with an explanation in the footnotes to the financial statements. In the event of financial difficulties and dissolution, creditors expect to share in the assets in proportion to their respective claims; and if choice assets, such as current receivables, have been pledged to one creditor, the risk to unsecured creditors is increased. Current liabilities should include not only those notes maturing within a period of 12 months (or a longer operating cycle), but also any installments currently payable on long-term obligations such as mortgages.

The essential point in balance sheet presentation of long-term liabilities is that they be adequately described. Each category of long-term debt should be stated under a separate title, which describes the type of debt, amounts authorized and issued, interest rate, maturity date, and any conversion or subordination features.

Long-term debt payable in the current period. Long-term liabilities include all debts that will not mature within the operating cycle and any debt that will mature but will not be liquidated from current assets. In other words, any bonds or notes falling due in the coming operating cycle that are to be paid from special funds or refinanced will be classified as long-term obligations regardless of maturity date. Before approving a long-term classification for maturing obligations, auditors must satisfy themselves that the client has both the *intent* and the *ability* to refinance the obligation on a long-term basis. Intent and ability to refinance are demonstrated by the client through either (1) refinancing the obligation on a long-term basis before the issuance of the audit report, or (2) entering into a financing agreement by that date, which clearly permits such refinancing. Any debt maturing currently and payable from current assets will be a current liability.

Restrictions imposed by long-term debt agreements. Most long-term debt agreements contain clauses limiting the borrowing company's right to pay dividends. Such a restriction is vitally significant to investors in common stocks. Consequently, the nature of the restriction should be clearly set forth in a footnote to the financial statement.

Unamortized bond premium or discount. Unamortized premium should be added to the face amount of the bonds or debentures in the liability section of the balance sheet. Similarly, unamortized discount should be deducted from the face amount of the debt.

Time of examination—interest-bearing debt

The review of internal control over interest-bearing debt may be carried out in advance of the balance sheet date. Analysis of the ledger accounts for interest-bearing debt and interest expense takes very little time in most audits because of the small number of entries. Consequently, most auditors prefer to wait until the end of the year before analyzing these accounts.

Audit procedures intended to bring to light any unrecorded liabilities cannot very well be performed in advance of the balance sheet date. Such steps as the confirmation of outstanding interest-bearing debt, the verification of accrued interest, and the investigation of notes paid or renewed shortly after the balance sheet date must necessarily await the close of the period being audited. We must conclude, therefore, that the opportunities for performing audit work in advance of the balance sheet date are much more limited in the case of interest-bearing debt than for most of the asset groups previously discussed.

EQUITY CAPITAL

Most of this section is concerned with the audit of stockholders' equity accounts of corporate clients; the audit of owners' equity in partnerships and sole proprietorships is discussed briefly near the end of the chapter.

In some respects, the audit of owners' equity is similar to that of long-term debt. Transactions are generally few in number, but material in amount. Consequently, each transaction requires careful attention. The auditors will find in many audit engagements that no change has occurred during the current year in the Capital Stock account, and perhaps only one or two entries have been made in the Retained Earnings account. Under these circumstances, the audit time required will be very small in relation to the dollar amounts in these accounts. The Capital Stock account often has a larger balance than the Cash account, but the audit work required for capital stock is usually far less.

The auditors' objectives in examination of owners' equity

The auditors' objectives in their examination of owners' equity are (1) to evaluate the internal control over stock certificates, stock transactions, and dividend payments; (2) to determine that all transactions during the year affecting owners' equity accounts were properly authorized and recorded; (3) to determine that legal requirements relating to corporate capital have been met; and (4) to determine that owners' equity is presented properly in the financial statements.

To accomplish these objectives, auditors need some familiarity with federal and state laws concerning securities and also with the rules and regulations of the Securities and Exchange Commission.

Internal control for owners' equity

There are three principal elements of strong internal control over capital stock and dividends. These three elements are (1) the proper authorization of transactions by the board of directors and corporate officers; (2) the segregation of duties in handling these transactions (especially the use of independent agents for stock registration and transfer and dividend payments); and (3) the maintenance of adequate records.

Control of capital stock transactions by board of directors

All changes in capital stock accounts should receive formal advance approval by the board of directors. The substantive tests for verifying an entry in a Capital Stock account, therefore, should include tracing the entry to an authorization in the minutes of directors' meetings.

Let us consider for a moment some of the specific steps relating to capital stock transactions that require authorization by directors. The board of directors must determine the number of shares to be issued and the price per share; if an installment plan of payment is to be used, the terms must be prescribed by the board. If plant and equipment, services, or any consideration other than cash are to be accepted in payment for shares, the board of directors must set the valuation on the noncash assets received. Transfers from retained earnings to the Capital Stock and Paid-In Capital accounts, as in the case of stock dividends, are initiated by action of the board. Stock splits and changes in par or stated value of shares also require formal authorization by the board.

Authority for all dividend actions rests with the directors. The declaration of a dividend must specify not only the amount per share, but also the date of record and the date of payment.

If a corporation handles its own capital stock transactions rather than utilizing the services of an independent registrar and stock transfer agent, the board of directors should pass a resolution designating those officers who are authorized to (1) sign stock certificates, (2) maintain records of stockholders, (3) have custody of unissued certificates, and (4) sign dividend checks. The signatures of two officers are generally required on stock certificates.

Independent registrar and stock transfer agent

In appraising the adequacy of internal control over capital stock, the first question that the auditors consider is whether the corporation employs the services of an independent stock register and a stock transfer agent or handles its own capital stock transactions. Internal control is far stronger when the services of an independent stock registrar and a stock transfer agent are utilized because the banks or trust companies acting in these capacities will have the experience, the specialized facilities, and the trained personnel to perform the work in an expert manner. Moreover, by placing the responsibility for handling capital stock certificates in separate and independent organizations, the corporation achieves to the fullest extent the internal control concept of separation of duties. The New York Stock Exchange and most other exchanges require that listed corporations utilize the services of an independent registrar.

The primary responsibility of the stock registrar is to avoid any overissuance of stock. The danger of overissuance is illustrated by the old story of a promoter who sold a 25 percent interest in a new corporation to each of 10 investors. To prevent such irregularities, the registrar must verify that stock certificates are issued in accordance with the articles of incorporation and the formal authorizations by the board of directors. The registrar obtains copies of the documents authorizing the total shares to be issued and maintains records of total shares issued and canceled. Each new certificate must be presented to the registrar for examination and registration before it is issued to a stockholder. The dangers of fraud and accidental error relating to improper issuance of stock certificates are greatly reduced when an independent registrar is employed.

Corporations with actively traded securities also employ independent *stock transfer agents.* Although the stock transfer agent maintains a record of the total shares outstanding, its primary responsibility is the maintaining of detail stockholder records (name and address of each stockholder) and carrying out transfers of stock ownership.

The stock certificate book

If the corporation does not utilize the services of an independent registrar and stock transfer agent, these functions usually are assigned by the board of directors to the secretary of the company. The stock certificates should be serially numbered by the printer; and from the time of delivery to the company until issuance, they should be in the exclusive custody of the designated officer.

The certificates often are prepared in bound books, with attached stubs similar to those in a checkbook. Each stub shows the certificate number and contains blank spaces for entering the number of shares represented by the certificate, the name of the stockholder, and the serial number of any previously issued certificate surrendered in exchange for the new one. Certificates should be issued in numerical sequence and not signed or countersigned until the time of issuance. When outstanding shares are transferred from one holder to another, the old certificate is surrendered to the company. The designated officer cancels the old certificate by perforating and attaching it to the corresponding stub in the certificate book.

The stockholders ledger

The stock certificate book is not in itself an adequate record of the capital stock outstanding. The certificates appear in the book in serial number order, and a single stockholder may own several certificates listed as various places in the certificate book.

A stockholders ledger provides a separate record for each stockholder, thus making it possible to determine at a glance the total number of shares owned by any one person. This record may be used in compiling the list of dividend checks or for any other communication with shareholders.

Internal control over dividends

The nature of internal control over the payment of dividends, as in the case of stock issuance, depends primarily upon whether the company performs the function of dividend payment itself or utilizes the services of an independent dividend-paying agent. If an independent dividend-disbursing agent is used, the corporation will provide the agent with a certified copy of the dividend declaration and with a check for the full amount of the dividend. The bank or trust company serving as stock transfer agent is usually appointed to distribute the dividend, since it maintains the detail records of stockholders. The agent issues dividend checks to the individual stockholders and sends the corporation a detailed list of the payments made. The use of an independent fiscal agent is to be recommended from the standpoint of internal control, for it materially reduces the possibility of fraud or error arising in connection with the distribution of dividends.

Audit working papers for owners' equity

In addition to the grouping sheet for owners' equity accounts, an analysis of each equity account is prepared by the auditors for the permanent file. A detailed analysis is essential for all aspects of a stock option plan: options authorized, issued, and outstanding. For a closely held corporation not served by a transfer agent, the auditors will often prepare for the permanent file a list of shareholders and the number of shares owned by each.

AUDIT PROGRAM—CAPITAL STOCK

The following procedures are typical of the work required in many engagements for the verification of capital stock:

1. Obtain or prepare a description of internal control over capital stock transactions.
2. Review articles of incorporation, bylaws, and minutes for provisions relating to capital stock.
3. Obtain or prepare analyses of the capital stock accounts.
4. Account for all proceeds from stock issues.
5. Confirm shares outstanding with the independent registrar and stock transfer agent.
6. For a corporation acting as its own stock registrar and transfer agent, reconcile the stockholder records with the general ledger.
7. Determine compliance with stock option plans and with other restrictions and preferences pertaining to capital stock.

Compliance tests usually are unnecessary in the audit of capital stock. Since transactions are so few in number, the auditors usually substantiate all transactions rather than rely upon the client's system of internal control. In addition to the preceding steps, the auditors must determine the appropriate financial statement presentation of capital stock. This topic will be discussed later in this chapter, along with the financial statement presentation of other elements of owners' equity.

1. Obtain or prepare a description of internal control over capital stock transactions.

Even though the examination of capital stock consists primarily of substantive tests, the auditors must acquire an understanding of the client's procedures for authorizing, executing, and recording capital stock transactions. This may be achieved by preparing a written description or flowchart of the system, or by filling in an internal control questionnaire. If the questionnaire approach is employed, typical questions to be answered might include the following: Does the company utilize the services of an independent registrar and stock transfer agent? Are stockholder ledgers and transfer journals maintained? Are entries in owners' equity accounts reviewed periodically by the controller? These questions should be regarded as identifying the areas to be investigated, rather than as items requiring simple yes or no answers.

2. Review articles of incorporation, bylaws, and minutes for provisions relating to capital stock.

In a first audit, copies of the articles of incorporation, bylaws, and minutes of the meetings of directors and stockholders obtained for the permanent file should be carefully read. The information required by the auditors for each issue of capital stock includes the number of shares authorized and issued, the par or stated value if any, dividend rates, call and conversion provisions, stock splits, and stock options. By gathering evidence on these points, the auditors will have some assurance that capital stock transactions and dividend payments have been in accordance with legal requirements and specific authorizations by stockholders and directors. Also, they will be able to judge whether the balance sheet contains all necessary information to describe adequately the various stock issues and other elements of corporate capital.

3.   Obtain or prepare analyses of the capital stock accounts.

In an initial audit engagement, capital stock accounts should be analyzed from the beginning of the corporation to provide the auditors with a complete historical picture of corporate capital. Analysis of capital stock includes an appraisal of the nature of all changes and the vouching of these changes to the supporting documents and records. All changes in capital stock should bear the authorization of the board of directors.

The analyses of capital stock accounts may be prepared in a manner that permits additions during later audit engagements. After the initial audit, if the analyses are kept in the auditors' permanent file, all that will be necessary is to record the current period's increases and decreases and to vouch these transactions. The auditors' then will have working papers showing all changes in capital stock from the inception of the corporation.

The auditors also should analyze the Treasury Stock account and prepare a list showing the number of shares of treasury stock on hand. All certificates on hand then may be inspected. If the certificates are not on hand, they should be confirmed directly with the custodian.

In their review of treasury stock transactions, the auditors should refer to permanent file copies of the minutes of directors' meetings to determine that (a) the acquisition or reissuance of treasury stock was authorized by directors, and (b) the price paid or received was in accordance with prices specified by the board.

4.   Account for all proceeds from stock issues.

Closely related to the analysis of Capital Stock accounts is the audit procedure of accounting for the receipt and proper disposition of all funds derived from the issuance of capital stock. The proceeds should be traced to the cash records and bank statements. SEC registration statements and contracts with underwriters may also be available as evidence of the amounts received from stock issues.

When assets other than cash are received as consideration for the issuance of capital stock, the entire transaction requires careful study. Generally the value of assets and services received in exchange for capital shares is established by action of the board of directors.

5. Confirm shares outstanding with the independent registrar and stock transfer agent.

The number of shares issued and outstanding on the balance sheet date may be confirmed by direct communication with the independent registrar and stock transfer agent. The confirmation request should be written by the client under the client's letterhead, but should be mailed by the auditors. Confirmation replies should be sent directly to the auditors, not to the client. All information contained in these replies should be traced to the corporate records. It is essential that the general ledger control accounts agree with the amount of stock issued as reported by the independent registrar and stock transfer agent. Because of the strong internal controls usually maintained over stock certificates, it is not customary to communicate with individual stockholders in establishing the number of shares outstanding.

6. For a corporation acting as its own stock registrar and transfer agent, reconcile the stockholder records with the general ledger.

When a corporation acts as its own transfer agent and registrar, the auditors must adopt alternative procedures as nearly as possible equivalent to direct confirmation with outside parties. These procedures include (a) accounting for stock certificate numbers, (b) examining canceled certificates, and (c) reconciling the stockholder ledger and stock certificate book with the general ledger.

The audit working papers should include a record of the last certificate number issued during the year. Reference to the working papers for the preceding audit, combined with the verification of certificate numbers issued during the current period, will enable the auditors to account for all certificates by serial number.

A working paper prepared during the auditors' examination of the stock certificate book of a small closely held corporation is designed to be utilized during several audits; it may be retained in the permanent file or forwarded to successive current files. Additionally, it is desirable for the auditors to inspect the unissued certificates to determine that all certificates purported to be unissued are actually on hand and blank.

An adequate system of internal control for corporations not utilizing the services of an independent registrar and stock transfer agent requires that all canceled stock certificates be perforated or marked in a manner precluding the possibility of further use. Canceled certificates should be attached to the corresponding stubs in the stock certificate book and permanently preserved. If reacquired certificates are not canceled properly, the danger exists that they may be reissued fraudulently by officers or employees. Auditors, therefore, will examine all canceled stock certificates on hand, noting in particular that these have been voided.

The general ledger account for capital stock shows the total par value or stated value of all shares outstanding, plus any treasury shares. The subsidiary records for capital stock contains an account for each stockholder. The stock certificate book contains all canceled certificates, and also open stubs for outstanding certificates. These three records must be reconciled by the auditors to establish the amount of outstanding stock and to rule out the possibility of an overissuance of shares. If this verification were not made, it would be possible for a dishonest official to issue unlimited amounts of stock and to withhold the proceeds from such sales.

A trial balance of the subsidiary stockholder records may be obtained from the client or prepared by the auditors and compared with the general ledger control account. In conjunction with this procedure, the total shares outstanding, as shown by the stock certificate book stubs, should also be reconciled with the controlling account and with the subsidiary trial balance. These procedures assure the auditors of the accuracy of the ledger account balances for capital stock.

> **7. Determine compliance with stock option plans and with other restrictions and preferences pertaining to capital stock.**

Many corporations grant stock options to officers and key employees as an incentive-type compensation plan. When stock options are granted, a portion of the authorized but unissued stock must be held in reserve by the corporation so that it will be in a position to fulfill the option agreements. Similarly, corporations with convertible debentures or convertible preferred stocks outstanding must hold in reserve a sufficient number of common shares to meet the demands of preferred stockholders and debenture holders who may elect to convert their securities into common stock.

The auditors must become thoroughly familiar with the terms of any stock options and stock purchase plans and with the conversion features in debenture bonds and preferred stock, so that they can determine whether the financial statements make adequate disclosure of these agreements. They must also verify the shares issued during the year through conversion or exercise of stock options, and must ascertain that the number of shares held in reserve at the balance sheet date does not exceed the corporation's authorized but unissued stock.

RETAINED EARNINGS AND DIVIDENDS

Audit work on retained earnings and dividends includes two major steps: (1) the analysis of retained earnings and any appropriations of retained earnings and (2) the review of dividend procedures for both cash and stock dividends.

The analysis of retained earnings and any appropriations of retained earnings should cover the entire history of these accounts. Such an analysis is prepared for the permanent file and is added to in each annual audit. Credits to the Retained Earnings account ordinarily represent amounts of net income transferred from the Income Summary account. Debits to the Retained Earnings account may include entries for net losses, cash and stock dividends, and for the creation or enlargement of appropriated reserves. Appropriations of retained earnings require specific authorization by the board of directors. The only verification necessary for these entries is to ascertain that the dates and amounts correspond to the actions of the board.

In the verification of cash dividends the auditors usually will perform the following steps:

1. Determine the dates and amounts of dividends authorized.
2. Verify the amounts paid.
3. Determine the amount of any preferred dividends in arrears.
4. Review the treatment of unclaimed dividend checks.

When reviewing minutes of the directors' meetings, the auditors should note the date and amount of each dividend declaration. This serves to establish the authority for dividend disbursements. The dividend payment may then be verified by multiplying the total number of shares as shown by the general ledger controlling account by the dividend per share.

The auditors' review of dividend declarations may reveal the existence of cash dividends declared but not paid. These declared but unpaid dividends must be shown as liabilities in the balance sheet. The auditors also may review the procedures for handling unclaimed dividends and ascertain that these items are recognized as liabilities. The amount of any accumulated dividends in arrears on preferred stock should be computed. If a closely held company has irregular dividend declarations or none at all, the auditors should consider whether the federal penalty surtax on unreasonably accumulated earnings might be assessed. In the verification of stock dividends, there is an additional responsibility of determining that the proper amounts have been transferred from retained earnings to capital stock and paid-in capital accounts for both large and small stock dividends.

Time of examination—stockholders' equity

The ledger accounts for capital stock, additional paid-in capital, and retained earnings ordinarily receive very few entries during the year. Consequently, most auditors agree that nothing can be gained by making a preliminary analysis of these accounts for a fraction of the year. It usually is more efficient to make the analysis in one step after the close of the period. Other audit procedures, such as the examination of the stock certificate book or the confirmation of outstanding shares with the independent registrar and stock transfer agent, also are performed at the year-end. In the first audit of a new client, some preliminary work can be done advantageously in obtaining and reviewing copies of the articles of incorporation and bylaws and in analyzing the capital accounts. For repeat engagements, however, there is usually little opportunity to perform audit work on owners' equity accounts before the end of the period.

Financial statement presentation of stockholders' equity

The presentation of capital stock in the balance sheet should include a complete description of each issue. Information to be disclosed includes the title of each issue; par or stated value; dividend rate if any; dividend preference; conversion and call provisions; number of shares authorized, issued, and in the treasury; dividends in arrears if any; and shares reserved for stock options or for conversions.

Treasury stock perferably is shown in the stockholders' equity section, at cost, as a deduction from the combined total of paid-in capital and retained earnings. In many states an amount of retained earnings equivalent to the cost of the treasury shares must be restricted. This restriction is disclosed by a footnote.

Changes in retained earnings during the year may be shown in a separate statement or combined with the income statement. The combined statement of income and retained earnings appears to be continuing in popularity. In this form of presentation the amount of retained earnings at the beginning of the year is added to the net income figure, dividends paid are subtracted from the subtotal, and the final figure represents the new balance of retained earnings.

One of the most significant points to consider in determining the presentation of retained earnings in the balance sheet is the existence of any restriction on the use of this retained income. Agreements with banks, bondholders, and other creditors very commonly impose limitations on the payment of dividends. These restrictions must be fully disclosed in the notes to financial statements.

AUDIT OF SOLE PROPRIETORSHIPS AND PARTNERSHIPS

Perhaps the most common reason for a small business to arrange for an independent audit is the need for audited financial statements in order to obtain a bank loan. Typically, a banker when approached by the owner of a small business applying for a loan will request audited financial statements as an aid to reaching a decision on the loan application.

It is natural for the owner of a business being audited for the first time to be concerned about the auditors' fee and to question whether all the procedures performed by the auditors are really necessary. The CPA retained to audit a small business, of course, will inquire as to the reason for the audit. If a bank loan is involved, the CPA may find it useful to arrange a joint meeting in which the owner, the banker, and the CPA discuss the objectives and scope of the examination. Such a meeting is helpful in making the small-business owner aware that the CPAs must have unlimited access to all information about the business. The owner then is more likely to cooperate fully with respect to such audit procedures as confirmation of receivables and observation of inventories.

Procedures for audit of partners' accounts. A most significant document underlying the partnership form of organization is the partnership contract. The auditors are particularly interested in determining that the distribution of net income has been carried out in accordance with the profit-sharing provisions of the partnership contract. Maintenance of partners' capital accounts at prescribed levels and restriction of drawings by partners to specified amounts are other points often covered in the contract; compliance with these clauses should be verified by the auditors in determining the propriety of the year's entries in the capital accounts. Partners' loan accounts also require reference to the partnership contract to determine the treatment intended by the partners.

Occasionally auditors may find that a partnership is operating without any written agreement of partnership. This situation raises a question of whether profits have been divided in accordance with the understanding existing between the partners. The auditors may appropriately suggest that the firm develop a written partnership contract; for their own protection the auditors may wish to obtain from each partner a written statement confirming the balance in his or her capital account and approval of the method used in dividing the year's earnings.

In general, the same principles described for the audit of corporate capital are applicable to the examination of the capital accounts and drawing accounts of a sole proprietorship or partnership. Analyses are made of all proprietorship accounts from the beginning of the business; the initial capital investment and any additions are traced to the cash and asset records; and the net income or loss for the period and any withdrawals are verified. In the case of a sole proprietorship, a common source of difficulty is the practice of intermingling business and personal transactions, making it necessary for the auditors to segregate personal net worth from business capital. Adjustments may also be required to transfer from expense accounts to the owner's drawing account any personal expenditures paid with company funds.

DISCLOSURE OF CONTINGENCIES

A *loss contingency* may be defined as a *possible* loss, stemming from past events, that will be resolved as to existence and amount by some future event. Central to the concept of a contingent loss is the idea of uncertainty—uncertainty both as to the amount of loss and whether, in fact, any loss has been incurred. This uncertainty is resolved when some future event occurs or fails to occur.

Most loss contingencies may also appropriately be called *contingent liabilities. Loss contingencies,* however, is a broader term, encompassing the possible impairment of assets as well as the possible existence of liabilities. The audit problem with respect to loss contingencies is twofold. First, the auditors must determine the existence of the loss contingencies. Because of the uncertainty factor, most loss contingencies do not appear in the accounting records, and a systematic search is required if the auditors are to have reasonable assurance that no important loss contingencies have been overlooked. Second, the auditors must appraise the probability that a loss has been incurred. This is made difficult both by the uncertainty factor and also by the tendency of the client management to maintain at least an outward appearance of optimism.

In *Statement No. 5,* the Financial Accounting Standards Board set forth the criteria for accounting for loss contingencies. Such losses should be reflected in the accounting records when both of the following conditions are met: (1) information available prior to the issuance of the financial statements indicates that it is *probable* that a loss had been sustained before the balance sheet date, *and* (2) the amount of the loss can be *reasonably estimated.* Recognition of the loss may involve either recognition of a liability or reduction of an asset. When a loss contingency has been accrued in the accounts, it is usually desirable to explain the nature of the contingency in a footnote to the financial statements and to disclose any exposure to loss in excess of the amount accrued.

Loss contingencies that do not meet both of the above criteria should still be disclosed when there is at least a *reasonable possibility* that a loss has been incurred. This disclosure should describe the nature of the contingency and, if possible, provide an estimate of the possible loss. If the amount of possible loss cannot be reasonably estimated, the disclosure should include either a range of loss or a statement that an estimate cannot be made.

Certain contingent liabilities traditionally have been disclosed in financial statements even though the possibility that a loss has occurred is remote. Such items include notes receivable discounted and guarantee endorsements. With the exception of those items for which disclosure is traditional, disclosure need not be made of loss contingencies when the possibility of loss is *remote.*

The procedures undertaken by auditors to ascertain the existence of loss contingencies and to assess the probability of loss vary with the nature of the contingent item. To illustrate these types of procedures, we will discuss several of the more frequent types of contingencies warranting financial statement disclosure.

1. Pending litigation.

Perhaps the most common loss contingency appearing in financial statements is that stemming from pending or threatened litigation. A *letter of inquiry* (or *lawyer's letter*) to the client's legal counsel is the auditors' primary means of obtaining evidence regarding pending and threatened litigation, as well as *unasserted claims* for which no potential claimant has yet demonstrated the intent to initiate legal action. In the past, many attorneys were reluctant to disclose information about such issues to auditors. They believed that such disclosure was a violation of their confidential relationship with their client and that it might adversely affect the outcome of the litigation. Auditors, on the other hand, thought that they could not issue an unqualified opinion on the financial statements of a client if they were not fully informed as to potential loss contingencies.

A joint effort by the AICPA and the American Bar Association was undertaken to resolve this conflict, and agreement was eventually reached between the professions. Subsequently, the AICPA issued *SAS No. 12,* "Inquiry of Client's Lawyer Concerning Litigation, Claims, and Assessments," to provide auditors with guidelines for this sensitive communication.

SAS No. 12 requires that auditors obtain from management a list describing and evaluating threatened or pending litigation. The auditors then should request the client's attorneys to comment on those areas where their views differ from those of management, or to provide an independent description of each item. The attorneys should also be requested to identify any pending or threatened litigation omitted from management's list.

Auditors must also inquire into the possibility of unasserted claims. Even though no potential claimant has exhibited an awareness of a claim, a loss contingency should be disclosed if it is (1) *probable* that a claim will be asserted and (2) *reasonably possible* that the outcome will be adverse. Thus, management and legal counsel should be asked to disclose any unasserted actions that meet these criteria.

Illustration of disclosure.   The following footnote to the financial statements of an aircraft manufacturer illustrates the disclosure of the contingent liability associated with pending litigation:

> A number of suits are pending against the Company as the result of accidents in prior years involving airplanes manufactured by the Company. It is believed that insurance carried by the Company is sufficient to protect it against loss by reason of suits involving the lives of passengers and damage to aircraft. Other litigation pending against the Company involves no substantial amount or is covered by insurance.

The balance sheet of another large corporation contained the following note concerning such contingent liabilities:

> The Company has suits pending against it, some of which are for large amounts. The Company is advised by counsel that, while it is impossible to ascertain the ultimate legal and financial responsibility in respect to such litigation as of December 31, 1983, it is their opinion that the ulti-

mate liability will not be materially important in relation to the total assets of the Company.

The refusal of a lawyer to furnish the information requested in the auditors' letter of inquiry would be a limitation of the scope of the auditors' examination and would necessitate qualification of the audit report. Even when all of the requested information is provided to the auditors and adequately disclosed in the financial statements, the uncertainty of the outcome of litigation may require the auditors to qualify their report. In such a situation, their report would be qualified as being subject to any adjustment necessary to reflect the resolution of the litigation. Various types of qualifications of audit reports are discussed further in Chapter 18.

2. Income tax disputes.

The necessity of estimating the income tax liability applicable to the year under audit was discussed in Chapter 15. In addition to the taxes relating to the current year's income, uncertainty often exists concerning the amount ultimately payable for prior years. A lag of two or three years often exists between the filing of income tax returns and the final settlement after review by the Internal Revenue Service. Disputes between the taxpayer and the IRS may create contingent liabilities not settled for several more years. The auditors should determine whether internal revenue agents have examined any returns of the client since the preceding audit, and if so, whether any additional taxes have been assessed.

3. Accommodation endorsements and other guarantees of indebtedness.

The endorsement of notes of other concerns or individuals is very seldom recorded in the accounts, but may be reflected in the minutes of directors' meetings. The practice is more common among small concerns—particularly when one person has a proprietary interest in several companies. Officers, partners, and sole proprietors of small organizations should be questioned as to the existence of any contingent liability from this source. Inquiry should also be made as to whether any collateral has been received to protect the company. The auditors may suggest the desirability of maintaining a record of any accommodation endorsements by inclusion of a pair of memorandum accounts in the general ledger.

4. Accounts receivable sold or assigned with recourse.

When accounts receivable are sold or assigned *with recourse,* a guarantee of collectibility is given. Authorization of such a transaction should be revealed during the auditors' reading of the minutes, and a clue also may be found during the examination of transactions and correspondence with financial institutions. Confirmation by direct communication with the purchaser or assignee is necessary for any receivables sold or assigned.

Commitments

Closely related to contingent liabilities are obligations termed *commitments.* The auditors may discover during their examination many of the following commitments: inventory purchase commitments, commitments to sell merchandise at specified prices, contracts for the construction of plant and equipment, pension or profit-sharing plans, long-term operating leases of plant and equipment, employee stock option plans, and employment contracts with key officers. A common characteristic of these commitments is the contractual obligation to enter into transactions *in the future.* All classes of material commitments may be described in a single note to financial statements; or they may be included in a "Contingencies and Commitments" footnote.

General risk contingencies

In addition to loss contingencies and commitments, all businesses face the risk of loss from numerous factors called *general risk contingencies.* A general risk contingency represents a loss that *might occur in the future,* as opposed to a loss contingency that *might have occurred in the past.* Examples of general risk contingencies are threat of a strike or consumer boycott, risk of price increases in essential raw materials, and risk of catastrophe.

General risk contingencies *should not be disclosed* in financial statements. Such disclosure would be confusing to investors, since the events that might produce a loss actually have not occurred, and since these risks are part of the general business environment. The lack of insurance coverage is a general risk contingency. Neither the adequacy nor the lack of insurance coverage need be presented in financial statements.

Audit procedures for loss contingencies

Although audit procedures vary with the individual type of loss contingency, the following steps are taken in most audits as a means of discovering these conditions:

1. Review the minutes of directors' meetings to the date of completion of field work. Important contracts, lawsuits, and dealings with subsidiaries are typical of matters discussed in board meetings that may involve loss contingencies.
2. Send a letter of inquiry to the client's legal counsel requesting:
    a. A description of the nature of pending and threatened litigation and of tax disputes.
    b. An evaluation of the likelihood of an unfavorable outcome in the matters described.
    c. An estimate of the probable loss or range of loss, or a statement that an estimate cannot be made.

 d. A description of any unasserted claims that, if asserted, have a reasonable possibility of an adverse outcome.

 e. A statement of the amount of any unbilled legal fees.

 3. Send a standard bank confirmation request to each bank with which the client has done business during the year. This standard form includes a request for information on any indirect or contingent liabilities of the client.

 4. Review correspondence with financial institutions for evidence of accommodation endorsements, guarantees of indebtedness, or sales or assignments of accounts receivable.

 5. Obtain a representations letter from the client indicating that all liabilities known to officers are recorded or disclosed.

Liability representations

Since contingent liabilities often are not entered in the accounting records, the officers of the company may be the only persons aware of the contingencies. It is therefore important that the auditors should ask the officers to disclose all liabilities and contingencies of which they have knowledge. To emphasize the importance of the request and to guard against any possible misunderstanding, the officers should be asked to sign a written liability representation, stating that all liabilities known to them are reflected in the accounts or otherwise disclosed in the financial statements.

Financial presentation of loss contingencies

Current practice utilizes supporting footnotes as a means of disclosure of loss contingencies. Presentation of information concerning loss contingencies should be limited to specific factual situations, such as accommodation endorsements, guarantees, and pending lawsuits. To fill the financial statements with vague generalities about the uncertainties of the future is more akin to fortune-telling than financial reporting.

KEY TERMS INTRODUCED OR EMPHASIZED IN CHAPTER 16

Additional paid-in capital   Capital contributed by stockholders in excess of the par or stated value of the shares issued.

Commitment   A contractual obligation to carry out a transaction at specified terms in the future. Material commitments should be disclosed in the financial statements.

Contingent liability   A possible liability, stemming from past events, that will be resolved as to existence and amount by some future event.

Debenture bond   An unsecured bond, dependent upon the general credit of the issuer.

General risk contingency   An element of the business environment that involves some risk of a future loss. Examples include the risk of accident, strike, price fluctuations, or natural catastrophe. General risk contingencies should not be disclosed in financial statements.

Indenture   The formal agreement between bondholders and the issuer as to the terms of the debt.

Lawyer's letter   A letter of inquiry sent by auditors to a client's legal counsel requesting a description and evaluation of pending or threatened litigation, unasserted claims, and other loss contingencies.

Liability representation   A written representation provided by key officers of the client that all liabilities and loss contingencies known to them are disclosed in the financial statements.

Loss contingency   A possible loss, stemming from past events, that will be resolved as to existence and amount by some future event. Loss contingencies should be disclosed in footnotes to the financial statements if there is a reasonable possibility that a loss has been incurred. In some instances, loss contingencies should be accrued in the accounts.

Sinking fund   Cash or other assets set aside for the retirement of a debt.

Stock certificate book   A book of serially numbered certificates with attached stubs. Each stub shows the corresponding certificate number and provides space for entering the number of shares represented by the certificate, name of the shareholder, and serial number of the certificate surrendered in exchange for the new one. Surrendered certificates are canceled and replaced in the certificate book.

Stockholders ledger   A record showing the number of shares owned by each stockholder. This is the basic record used for preparing dividend payments and other communications with shareholders.

Stock option plan   A formal plan granting the right to buy a specified number of shares at a stipulated price during a specified time. Stock option plans are frequently used as a form of executive compensation. The terms of such plans should be disclosed in financial statements.

Stock registrar   An institution charged with responsibility for avoiding overissuance of a corporation's stock. Every new certificate must be presented to the registrar for examination and registration before it is issued to a stockholder.

Stock transfer agent   An institution responsible for maintaining detailed records of shareholders and handling transfers of stock ownership.

Treasury stock   Shares of its own stock acquired by a corporation for the purpose of being reissued at a later date.

Unasserted claim   A possible legal claim of which no potential claimant has exhibited an awareness.

GROUP I: REVIEW QUESTIONS

16–1.   In addition to verifying the recorded liabilities of a company, the auditors must also give consideration to the possibility that other unrecorded liabilities exist. What specific steps may be taken by the auditors to determine that all of their client's interest-bearing liabilities are recorded?

16–2.   Two assistant auditors were assigned by the auditor-in-charge to the verification of long-term liabilities. Some time later, they reported to the auditor-in-charge that they had determined that all long-term liabilities were properly recorded and that all recorded long-term liabilities were genuine obligations. Does this determination constitute a sufficient examination of long-term liabilities? Explain.

16– 3. Explain the meaning of the term *liability representation.*

16– 4. Palmer Company has issued a number of notes payable during the year, and several of these notes are outstanding at the balance sheet date. What source of information should the auditors use in preparing a working-paper analysis of the notes payable?

16– 5. What is the principal reason for verifying the Interest Expense account in conjunction with the verification of notes payable?

16– 6. If the federal income tax returns for prior years have not as yet been reviewed by federal tax authorities, would you consider it necessary for the client to disclose this situation in footnotes to the financial statements? Explain.

16– 7. Audit programs for verification of accounts receivable and notes receivable often include investigation of selected transactions occurring after the balance sheet date as well as transactions during the year under audit. Are the auditors concerned with note payable transactions subsequent to the balance sheet date? Explain.

16– 8. Is the confirmation of notes payable usually correlated with any other specific phase of the audit? Explain.

16– 9. What is the meaning of the term *commitment* as used in accounting?

16– 10. Long-term creditors often insist upon placing certain restrictions upon the borrowing company for the term of the loan. Give three examples of such restrictions, and indicate how each restriction protects the long term creditor.

16– 11. Most corporations with bonds payable outstanding utilize the services of a trustee. What relation, if any, does this practice have to the maintenance of adequate internal control?

16– 12. "Auditors are not qualified to pass on the legality of a bond issue; this is a problem for the company's attorneys. It is therefore unnecessary for the auditors to inspect the bond indenture." Criticize this quotation.

16– 13. What information should be requested by the auditors from the trustee responsible for an issue of debentures payable?

16– 14. What are *general risk contingencies?* Do such items require disclosure in the financial statements?

16– 15. Compare the auditors' examination of owners' equity with their work on assets and current liabilities. Among other factors to be considered are the relative amounts of time involved and the character of the transactions to be reviewed.

16– 16. What do you consider to be the most important internal control device a corporation can adopt with respect to capital stock transactions?

16– 17. With respect to the examination of the Capital Stock account, how does the work in an initial audit differ from that required in a repeat engagement?

16–18. Comment on the desirability of audit work on the owners' equity accounts before the balance sheet date.

16–19. Name three situations that might place a restriction on retained earnings limiting or preventing dividend payments. Explain how the auditors might become aware of each such restricting factor.

16–20. Delta Company has issued stock options to four of its officers permitting them to purchase 5,000 shares each of common stock at a price of $25 per share at any time during the next five years. The president asks you what effect, if any, the granting of the options will have upon the balance sheet presentation of the stockholders' equity accounts.

16–21. Describe the significant features of a stock certificate book, its purpose, and the method of using it.

16–22. In the audit of a small corporation not using the services of an independent stock registrar and stock transfer agent, what use is made of the stock certificate book by the auditors?

16–23. What is the primary responsibility of an independent registrar with respect to capital stock?

16–24. How are changes in a corporation's contributed capital during the year disclosed in the financial statements?

16–25. What are *loss contingencies?* How are such items presented in the financial statements? Explain.

16–26. What is the usual procedure followed by the CPA in obtaining evidence regarding pending and threatened litigation against the client?

16–27. Explain how a loss contingency exists with respect to an *unasserted* claim. Should unasserted claims be disclosed in the financial statements?

16–28. What errors are commonly encountered by the auditors in their examination of the capital and drawing accounts of a sole proprietor?

16–29. Corporations sometimes issue their own capital stock in exchange for services and various assets other than cash. As an auditor, what evidence would you look for to determine the propriety of the values used in recording such transactions?

16–30. In your second annual examination of a corporate client, you find a new account in the general ledger, Treasury Stock, with a balance of $10,500. Describe the procedures you would follow to verify this item.

16–31. In examining the financial statements of Foster Company, you observe a debit entry for $20,000 labeled as Dividends in the Retained Earnings account. Explain in detail how you would verify this entry.

GROUP II: QUESTIONS REQUIRING ANALYSIS

16–32. Current pronouncements of the FASB require that under certain circumstances loss contingencies *be accrued* in the financial statements. Under other circumstances, loss contingencies may require *disclosure only in notes* to the financial statements, or may be *omitted entirely* from the financial statements and accompanying footnotes. You are to provide three separate examples of a loss contingency falling into each of these three categories.

16–33.   The only long-term liability of Range Corporation is a note payable for $1 million secured by a mortgage on the company's plant and equipment. You have audited the company annually for three preceding years, during which time the principal amount of the note has remained unchanged. The maturity date is 10 years from the current balance sheet date. You are informed by the president of the company that all interest payments have been made promptly in accordance with the terms of the note. Under these circumstances, what audit work, if any, is necessary with respect to this long-term liability during your present year-end audit?

16–34.   During your annual audit of Walker Distributing Co., your assistant, Jane Williams, reports to you that although a number of entries were made during the year in the general ledger account, Notes Payable to Officers, she decided that it was not necessary to audit the account because it had a zero balance at year-end.

Required:

Do you agree with your assistant's decision? Discuss. (AICPA)

16–35.   In an audit of a corporation that has a bond issue outstanding, the trust indenture is reviewed and confirmation as to the issue is obtained from the trustee. List eight matters of importance to the auditors that might be found either in the indenture or in the confirmation obtained from the trustee. Explain briefly the reason for the auditors' interest in each of the items. (AICPA)

16–36.   You are retained by Columbia Corporation to make an examination of its financial statements for the fiscal year ended June 30, and you begin work on July 15. Your survey of internal control indicates a fairly satisfactory condition, although there are not enough employees to permit extensive subdivision of duties. The company is one of the smaller units in the industry, but has realized net income of about $300,000 in each of the last three years.

Near the end of your field work you overhear a telephone call received by the president of the company while you are discussing the audit with him. The telephone conversation indicates that on May 15 of the current year the Columbia Corporation made an accommodation endorsement of a 60-day, $130,000 note issued by a major customer, Brill Corporation, to its bank. The purpose of the telephone call from Brill was to inform your client that the note had been paid at the maturity date. You had not been aware of the existence of the note before overhearing the telephone call.

Required:

a.   Do you think the auditors would be justified from an ethical standpoint in acting on information acquired in this manner?

b.   Should the balance sheet as of June 30 disclose the contingent liability? Give reasons for your answer.

c.   Prepare a list of auditing procedures that might have brought the contingency to light. Explain fully the likelihood of detection of the accommodation endorsement by each procedure listed.

16–37.   You are the audit manager in the examination of the financial statements of Midwest Grain Storage, Inc., a new client. The company's records show that as of the balance sheet date, approximately 15 million bushels of various grains are in storage for the Commodity Credit Corporation, an agency of the U.S. government.

In your review of the audit senior's working papers, you ascertain the following facts:

(1) All grain is stored under a Uniform Grain Storage Agreement, which holds Midwest responsible for the quantity and quality of the grain.

(2) Losses due to shrinkage, spoilage, and so forth are inherent in the storage of grain. Midwest's losses, however, have been negligible due to the excellence of its storage facilities.

(3) Midwest carries a warehouseman's bond covering approximately 20 percent of the value of the stored grain.

In the loss contingencies section of the working papers, the senior auditor has made the following notation: "I propose recommending to Midwest's controller that the contingent liability for grain spoilage and shrinkage be disclosed in a note to the financial statements."

Required:
Do you concur with the senior's proposal? Explain.

16–38. You are engaged in the examination of the financial statements of Armada Corporation, a publicly owned company, for the year ended August 31, 1984. The balance sheet, reflecting all of your audit adjustments accepted by the client to date, shows total current assets, $5,000,000; total current liabilities, $3,500,000; and stockholders' equity, $1,500,000. Included in current liabilities are two unsecured notes payable—one payable to United National Bank in the amount of $400,000 due October 31, 1984, the other payable to First State Bank in the amount of $300,000 due September 30, 1984. On September 30, the last scheduled date for your audit field work, you learn that Armada Corporation is unable to pay the $312,000 maturity value of the First State Bank note; that Armada executives are negotiating with First State Bank for an extension of the due date of the note; and that nothing definite has been decided as to the extension.

Required:
a. Should this situation be disclosed in footnotes to Armada Corporation's August 31 financial statements?
b. After the question of financial statement disclosure has been resolved to the auditor's satisfaction, might this situation have any effect upon the audit report?

16–39. Linda Reeves, CPA, receives a telephone call from her client, Lane Company. The company's controller states that the board of directors of Lane has entered into two contractual arrangements with Ted Forbes, the company's former president, who has recently retired. Under one agreement, Lane Company will pay the ex-president $7,000 per month for five years if he does not compete with the company during that time in a rival business. Under the other agreement, the company will pay the ex-president $5,000 per month for five years for such advisory services as the company may request from the ex-president.

Lane's controller asks Reeves whether the balance sheet as of the date the two agreements were signed should show $144,000 in current liabilities and $576,000 in long-term liabilities, or whether the two agreements should be disclosed in a contingencies note to the financial statements.

Required:

How should Linda Reeves reply to the controller's questions? Explain.

16–40. During an audit engagement, Robert Wong, CPA, has satisfactorily completed an examination of accounts payable and other liabilities and now plans to determine whether there are any loss contingencies arising from litigation, claims, or assessments.

Required:

What are the audit procedures Wong should follow with respect to the existence of loss contingencies arising from litigation, claims, or assessments? Do not discuss reporting requirements.

16–41. Valley Corporation has a stock option plan designed to provide extra incentive to its officers and key employees. A footnote to the financial statements includes a description of the plan and lists the number of options for shares that have been authorized, the number granted, the number exercised, and the number expired. The option price and the market price per share on the grant dates and the exercise dates are also shown.

Required:

a. In view of the fact that the information concerning the stock option plan appears in a footnote, rather than in the body of the financial statements, what responsibility, if any, do the independent auditors have for this information?

b. List the audit procedures, if any, that you believe should be applied to the stock option plan information.

16–42. Select the best answer choice for each of the following, and justify your selection in a brief statement.

a. When no independent stock transfer agent is employed and the corporation issues its own stocks and maintains capital stock records, canceled stock certificates should—

(1) Be perforated to prevent reissuance and attached to the corresponding stubs.

(2) Not be perforated, but segregated from other stock certificates and retained in a canceled certificates file.

(3) Be destroyed to prevent fraudulent reissuance.

(4) Be perforated and sent to the secretary of state.

b. Which of the following is the most important consideration of an auditor when examining the stockholders' equity section of a client's balance sheet?

(1) Changes in the capital stock account are verified by an independent stock transfer agent.

       (2)   Stock dividends and/or stock splits during the year under audit were approved by the stockholders.

       (3)   Stock dividends are capitalized at par or stated value on the dividend declaration date.

       (4)   Entries in the capital stock account can be traced to a resolution in the minutes of the board of directors' meetings.

   c.   An audit program for the examination of the retained earnings account should include a step that requires verification of the—

       (1)   Gain or loss resulting from the disposition of treasury shares.

       (2)   Market value used to charge retained earnings to account for a two-for-one stock split.

       (3)   Authorization for both cash and stock dividends.

       (4)   Approval of the adjustment to the beginning balance as a result of a write-down of an account receivable.

   d.   If a company employs a capital stock registrar and/or transfer agent, the registrar or agent, or both, should be requested to confirm directly to the auditors the number of shares of each class of stock—

       (1)   Surrendered and canceled each year.

       (2)   Authorized at the balance sheet date.

       (3)   Issued and outstanding at the balance sheet date.

       (4)   Authorized, issued, and outstanding during the year.

GROUP III: PROBLEMS

16–43.   You were engaged to examine the financial statements of King Corporation for the year ended June 30.

       On May 1, of the current year, the corporation borrowed $500,000 from Second National Bank to finance plant expansion. The long-term note agreement provided for the annual payment of principal and interest over five years. The existing plant was pledged as security for the loan.

Required:

   a.   What are the audit objectives in the examination of long-term debt?

   b.   Prepare an audit program for the examination of the long-term note agreement between King and Second National Bank. (AICPA, adapted)

16–44.   In your first audit of Hydrafoil Company, a manufacturer of specially designed boats capable of transporting passengers over water at very high speeds, you find that sales are made to commercial transportation companies. The sales price per unit is $200,000, and with each unit sold, the client gives the purchasing company a certificate reading as follows:

Hydrafoil Company promises to pay to _____ the sum of $12,000 when the boat designated as Serial No. _____ is permanently retired from service and evidence of such retirement is submitted.

The president of Hydrafoil Company explains to you that the purpose of issuing the certificates is to ensure contact with customers when they are in the market for new equipment. You also learn that the company makes no journal entry to record a certificate when it is issued. Instead, the company charges an expense account and credits a liability account $100 per month for each outstanding certificate, based on the company's experience that its hydrafoil boats will be rendered obsolete by new, more efficient models in approximately 10 years from the date of sale.

Required:

Do you concur with Hydrafoil Company's accounting for the certificates? You may assume that the 10-year service life of the product (and therefore of the certificates) is an accurate determination. Explain your position clearly.

16–45. The following covenants are extracted from the indenture of a bond issue of Case Company. The indenture provides that failure to comply with its terms in any respect automatically advances the due date of the loan to the date of noncompliance (the regular due date is 20 years hence). Give any audit procedures or reporting requirements you think should be taken or recognized in connection with each one of the following:

(1) "The debtor company shall endeavor to maintain a working capital ratio of 2 to 1 at all times; and in any fiscal year following a failure to maintain said ratio, the company shall restrict compensation of officers to a total of $500,000. Officers for this purpose shall include chairman of the board of directors, president, all vice presidents, secretary, controller, and treasurer."

(2) "The debtor company shall keep all property that is security for this debt insured against loss by fire to the extent of 100 percent of its actual value. Policies of insurance comprising this protection shall be filed with the trustee."

(3) "The debtor company shall pay all taxes legally assessed against property that is security for this debt within the time provided by law for payment without penalty, and shall deposit receipted tax bills or equally acceptable evidence of payment of same with the trustee."

(4) "A sinking fund shall be deposited with the trustee by semiannual payments of $300,000, from which the trustee shall, in its discretion, purchase bonds of this issue." (AICPA, adapted)

16–46. You are engaged in the first audit of a corporation. The corporation has both a stock transfer agent and an independent registrar for its capital stock. The transfer agent maintains the record of stockholders, and the registrar determines that there is no overissue of stock. Signatures of both are required to validate stock certificates.

It has been proposed that confirmations be obtained from both the transfer agent and the registrar as to the stock outstanding at balance sheet date. If such confirmations agree with the accounting records, no additional work is to be performed as to capital stock.

If you agree that obtaining the confirmations as suggested would be sufficient in this case, give the justification for your position. If you do not agree, state specifically all additional steps you would take and explain your reasons for taking them. (AICPA, adapted)

16–47.   You are engaged in the audit of Phoenix Corp., a new client, at the close of its first fiscal year, April 30, 1984. The accounts had been closed before the time you began your year-end field work.

You review the following stockholders' equity accounts in the general ledger:

Capital Stock

		5/1/83 CR1	500,000
		4/28/84 J12–5	50,000

Paid-In Capital in Excess of Stated Value

		5/1/83 CR1	250,000
		2/2/84 CR10	2,500

Retained Earnings

4/28/84 J12–5	50,000	4/30/84 J12–14	800,000

Treasury Stock

9/14/83 DC5	80,000	2/2/84 CR10	40,000

Income Summary

4/30/84 J12–13	5,200,000	4/30/84 J12–12	6,000,000
4/30/84 J12–14	800,000		

Other information in your working papers includes the following:

(1)   Phoenix's articles of incorporation filed April 17, 1983 authorize 100,000 shares of no-par-value capital stock.

(2)   Directors' minutes include the following resolutions:

4/18/83   Established $50 per share stated value for capital stock.

4/30/83   Authorized issue of 10,000 shares to an underwriting syndicate for $75 per share.

9/13/83   Authorized acquisition of 1,000 shares from a dissident holder at $80 per share.

2/1/84   Authorized reissue of 500 treasury shares at $85 per share.

4/28/84   Declared 10 percent stock dividend, payable May 18, 1984, to stockholders of record May 4, 1984.

(3)   The following costs of the May 1, 1983 and February 2, 1984 stock issuances were charged to the named expense accounts: Printing Expense, $2,500; Legal Fees, $17,350; Accounting Fees, $12,000; SEC Fees, $150.

(4)   Market values for Phoenix Corp. capital stock on various dates were:

9/13/83	$78.50
9/14/83	79.00
2/2/84	85.00
4/28/84	90.00

(5)   Phoenix Corp.'s combined federal and state income tax rates total 55 percent.

Required:

a.   Adjusting journal entries at April 30, 1984.

b.   Stockholders' equity section of Phoenix Corp.'s April 30, 1984 balance sheet.

16–48.   Robert Hopkins was the senior office employee in Griffin Equipment Company and enjoyed the complete confidence of the owner, William Barton, who devoted most of his attention to sales, engineering, and production problems. All financial and accounting matters were entrusted to Hopkins, whose title was office manager. Hopkins had two assistants, but their only experience in accounting and financial work had been gained under Hopkins's supervision. Barton had informed Hopkins that it was his responsibility to keep him (Barton) informed on financial position and operating results of the company but not to bother him with details.

The company was short of working capital and would occasionally issue notes payable in settlement of past-due open accounts to suppliers. The situations warranting issuance of notes were decided upon by Hopkins, and the notes were drawn by him for signature by Barton. Hopkins was aware of the weakness in internal control and finally devised a scheme for defrauding the company through understating the amount of notes payable outstanding. He prepared a note in the amount of $24,000 payable to a supplier to whom several invoices were past due. After securing Barton's signature on the note and mailing it to the creditor, Hopkins entered the note in the Notes Payable account of the general ledger as $4,000, with an offsetting debit of $4,000 to the creditor's account payable.

Several months later when the note matured, a check for $24,000 plus interest was issued and properly recorded, including a debit of $24,000 to the Notes Payable account. Hopkins then altered the original credit in the account by changing the figure from $4,000 to $24,000. He also changed the original debit to Accounts Payable from $4,000 to $24,000. This alteration caused the Notes Payable account to have a balance in agreement with the total of other notes outstanding. To complete the fraud, Hopkins called the supplier to whom the check had been sent and explained that the check should have been for only $4,000 plus interest.

Hopkins explained to the supplier that the note of $24,000 originally had been issued in settlement of a number of past-due invoices, but that while the note was outstanding, checks had been sent in payment of all the invoices. "In other words," said Hopkins over the telephone, "we made the mistake of giving you a note for those invoices and then going ahead and sending you checks for them as soon as our cash position had improved. Then we paid the note at maturity. So please excuse our mistakes and return the overpayment." After reviewing the record of invoices and checks received, the supplier agreed he had been overpaid by $20,000 plus interest and promptly sent a refund, which Hopkins abstracted without making any entry in the accounts.

Required:

a. Assuming that an audit by independent CPAs was made while the note was outstanding, do you think that the $20,000 understatement of the Notes Payable account would have been detected? Explain fully the reasoning underlying your answer.

b. If the irregularity was not discovered while the note was outstanding, do you think that an audit subsequent to the payment of the note would have disclosed the fraud? Explain.

c. What internal control procedures would you recommend for Griffin Equipment Company to avoid fraud of this type?

GROUP IV: CASE STUDIES IN AUDITING

16–49.   CONTRACTOR'S INSPECTION &
                                    DISBURSEMENT SERVICE, INC.

Contractor's Inspection & Disbursement Service, Inc., furnishes a control service for building contractors. Contractors of limited financial standing are required by certain lending institutions to engage such a service to make regular progress inspections of their projects and to control the disbursement of funds advanced to the contractor by the lenders. The funds are advanced by the bank and deposited in a separate bank account for each contractor; the service controls these accounts. Disbursements are made on the basis of approved invoices supported by release and lien waivers where necessary.

One of the larger financial institutions has become apprehensive over the financial condition of Contractor's Inspection & Disbursements Service, Inc., and has threatened to discontinue referrals of its borrowers to this service unless the stockholders' equity of the corporation can be increased to at least $150,000. The financial position of the service at present is as follows:

Assets

Cash	$ 25,000
Accounts receivable	200,000
Other assets	25,000
Total	$250,000

Liabilities and Stockholders' Equity

Accounts payable	$ 50,000
Deferred revenue	125,000
Stockholders' equity	75,000
Total	$250,000

Note: This statement does not include any funds held for account of contractors.

The present billing procedure of the service is to bill the contractor as soon as construction begins and the first funds are received from the bank. In most cases the fee is payable out of the first advance from the bank, so that accounts receivable generally are collected promptly; in some agreements the fee is not payable until the construction is completed. At the time the fee is billed, deferred revenue is credited, and this deferred revenue subsequently is taken into income pro rata over the period of construction. Therefore, there is always a substantial balance of deferred revenue representing the advance charges for control services that have not been rendered.

The stockholders of the company either do not have the necessary additional capital required by the lending institution or they are reluctant to transfer such capital from other investments. Therefore, the controller has proposed the following:

A new corporation, Contractor's Inspection & Disbursement Company, will be formed. To it will be transferred all collectible accounts receivable, as well as cash and other assets, and all liabilities except the deferred revenue. After this transfer the balance sheet of the new company will appear as follows:

Assets

Cash.....................................	$ 25,000
Accounts receivable	150,000
Other assets	25,000
Total	$200,000

Liabilities and Stockholders' Equity

Accounts payable	$ 50,000
Capital stock	150,000
Total	$200,000

The balance sheet of Contractor's Inspection & Disbursement Service, Inc. (the old company), will appear as follows:

Assets

Cash	-0-
Accounts receivable	$ 50,000
Other assets	-0-
Investment in Contractor's Inspection & Disbursement Company	150,000
Total	$200,000

Liabilities and Stockholder's Equity

Deferred revenue	$125,000
Stockholders' equity	75,000
Total	$200,000

To compensate for the failure to transfer the deferred revenue to the new company, the old company will sign an agreement guaranteeing to complete any control contracts the new company may be financially unable to carry out and to take over certain problem jobs when they arise. (In the past the old company frequently has had to take over a contractor's work and finish the job when the contractor became hopelessly delinquent.) Through this agreement, the old company intends to indemnify the new company for any such occurrences. The old company will adjust the balance of deferred revenue in its accounting records at the end of each year to show the correct amount of deferred revenue.

In establishing accounting policies for the new company, the controller proposes to take all fees into income as they are billed, without any deferral. He says he is justified in doing this because many companies operate on a cash basis, and he thinks such a procedure is in order if it helps accomplish the objective of increasing the stockholders' equity of the organization to the level of $150,000, as required by the bank. He also points out that income tax regulations require the inclusion of deferred revenue in taxable income when it is received. Thus the method of accounting adopted for the new company would be in accordance with income tax reporting requirements.

The controller has outlined this procedure to the bank official handling the case, and this official has agreed that the proposed reorganization will be satisfactory to the bank. However, you were not present during the conference, and there is nothing in writing to assure you that the bank official fully understood just what was being done. It is understood that the bank will be given financial statements of only the new company and that it no longer will be interested in the old company.

You were asked to perform an examination and submit an opinion as to the balance sheet of the new company in a report to the bank. Your engagement also contemplates making annual audits of the new company.

Required:

a. What kind of an opinion would you give on the beginning balance sheet?

b. In your report at the end of the first year, can you give an opinion that the income statement presents fairly the results of operations for the year? Explain fully.

17

Further verification of revenue and expenses

Today, with greater and greater emphasis being placed upon corporate earnings as an indicator of the health and well-being of our industrialized economy, the income statement is of fundamental importance to management, stockholders, creditors, employees, and government. The relative level of corporate earnings is now a key factor in the determination of such issues as wage negotiations, income tax rates, price controls, subsidies, and government fiscal policy. It must be remembered that the function of the independent public accountants is to give integrity to financial statements—to give assurance to all who use these statements that the net earnings reported each year have been determined in accordance with generally accepted accounting principles, in an unbiased manner, and on a basis consistent with that of the preceding year. Acceptance of this responsibility is the best evidence that public accounting has reached the status of a profession. The development of the profession is most apparent when we recall that not long ago auditors were largely concerned with protecting creditors against overstatement of asset values, rather than serving the needs of all the varied groups that play a part in our economy.

Conservatism in the measurement of income

Conservatism in the valuation of assets means that when two (or more) reasonable alternative values are indicated, the accountant will

555

choose the lower of the two. Of course, the principles used in valuing assets, such as inventories and accounts receivable, also have an effect upon the measurement of income. The traditional policy of choosing the lower of two possible valuations for an asset has the supplementary effects of minimizing net income for the current period and of minimizing owners' equity. The doctrine of conservatism is a powerful force influencing distinctions between capital and revenue expenditures; this force always is exerted in favor of treating borderline cases as expenses of the period.

Another aspect of conservatism in the measurement of income is the policy of not recording revenue until the point of delivery of goods or services; at this point, the revenue is realized through the receipt of cash or the acquisition of a receivable or the equivalent. The other side of income measurement is the recognition of expenses; in this area, conservatism requires that all expenses associated with the revenue of the period be recognized, even though some of these expenses (as for pension plans or for the warranty of products sold) are not subject to precise measurement until a later date.

Most auditors have a considerable respect for the doctrine of conservatism. In part, this attitude springs from the concept of legal liability to third parties. Bankers, creditors, and investors who have sustained losses as a result of the failure of auditors to detect overstated assets and exaggerated earnings have time and again collected heavy damages from public accounting firms and have damaged many a professional reputation. Financial statements that *understate* financial position and operating results almost never lead to legal action against the auditors who approve these statements. Nevertheless, leaders of the public accounting profession must recognize that overemphasis on conservatism in financial reporting is a narrow and shortsighted approach to meeting the needs of our society. To be of greatest value, financial statements should present fairly, rather than understate, financial position and operating results.

The auditors' approach to verification of income

Accountants generally agree that the measurement of income is the most important single function of accounting. A fair and informative income statement is then surely as important as, if not more important than, the balance sheet. Nevertheless, audits continue to be organized in terms of balance sheet topics. The reasons for organizing audit work in this manner were discussed in Chapter 10.

As the significance of the income statement increased, auditors began to verify income statement accounts concurrently with related balance sheet accounts. Depreciation expense, for example, is most conveniently verified along with the plant and equipment accounts. Once the existence and cost of depreciable assets are established, the verification of depreciation expense is merely an additional step. On the other hand, to verify depreciation expense without first establishing the nature and amount of assets owned and subject to depreciation would obviously be a cart-before-the-horse approach. The same line of reasoning tells us that the auditors' work on inventories, especially in determining that inventory transactions were accurately cut off at the end of the period, is a major step toward the verification of the income statement figures for sales and cost of goods sold. Much of the material in the preceding six chapters of this book has related to income statement accounts, although the sequence of topics has followed a balance sheet arrangement.

When the balance sheets at the beginning and end of an accounting period have been fully verified, the net income for the year is fairly well established, although considerable additional work remains to be done before the auditors can express a professional opinion that the income statement presents fairly the results of operations.

Let us emphasize the fact that the auditors' examination of revenue and expense transactions should be much more than an incidental by-product of the examination of assets and liabilities. Critical examination of revenue and expense accounts may bring to light errors, omissions, and inconsistencies not disclosed in the examination of balance sheet accounts. An example of such deficiencies in accounting for revenue and expense transactions is failure to distinguish properly between capital and revenue expenditures.

Audit by analytical review

Analytical review procedures, as defined by *SAS No. 23*, are substantive tests of financial information carried out by study and comparison of related amounts.[1] For example, the client's gross profit percentage for the current year is compared with the percentage for the preceding year. If the gross profit percentage has risen or fallen significantly, the auditors should *investigate this fluctuation.* We can assume that the relationship existing between financial elements (such as this percentage of gross profit to sales) will remain relatively unchanged unless we know of underlying conditions that have changed during the year. The tendency for relationships between certain accounts or elements of financial statements to remain fairly constant makes available to the auditors a wealth of evidence as to the overall reasonableness of the client's recorded revenue and expenses.

The use of analytical review procedures gives the auditors a better perspective and understanding of current trends in the client's business. This approach also draws attention to possible errors in the financial statements, and indicates the need to expand or reduce the extent

---

[1] *Statement on Auditing Standards No. 23,* "Analytical Review Procedures," AICPA (New York, 1978).

of other substantive tests. Analytical review procedures are sometimes referred to as auditing by comparison. The monthly totals of individual revenue and expense accounts can be compared with the corresponding monthly figures of the preceding year. For example, repairs expense for June of the current year is compared with repairs expense incurred in June of the prior year. This comparison may disclose variations caused by unusual items that warrant investigation.

Comparison of *actual* revenue and expenses with *budgeted amounts* also may draw the auditors' attention to areas requiring detailed analysis. Significant variations should be explored fully. Comparison of revenue and expense accounts with nonfinancial data is another means of bringing to light circumstances that require investigation. For example, the CPAs should investigate unusual relationships between production records stated in gallons or pounds with the related dollar amounts of sales. Financial statement ratios for the current year should be compared with ratios for prior years and with similar information for other companies in the same industry. For this purpose, industry statistics are available from numerous financial and industry publications. Figure 17–1 illustrates a working paper that compares major income statement categories for the year under audit with the prior year amounts and industry averages.

Significant variations disclosed by analytical review can be used not only to increase the efficiency of the audit, but also with a view toward the development of suggestions to management of means of reducing expenses and expanding revenue. The relative profitability or unprofitability of particular products or territories, as well as the development of significant trends in certain types of revenue and expense, may be disclosed by this process of analytical review. The value of auditing services is certain to be increased in the eyes of management if the auditors will expand this approach to include a thorough appraisal of the methods of controlling both revenue and expenses.

REVENUE

Audit objectives

In the examination of revenue, the principal objectives of the auditors are: (1) to study and evaluate internal control, with particular emphasis upon the use of accrual accounting to record revenue; (2) to verify that all earned revenue has been recorded and all recorded revenue has been earned; and (3) to identify and interpret significant trends and variations in the dollar amounts of various categories of revenue.

Relationship of revenue to balance sheet accounts

The auditors' review of sales activities was considered in connection with accounts receivable in Chapter 12. As pointed out previously, most

===== Figure 17–1

Cheviot Corporation
Corporation Income Statement
Year Ended December 31, 1984

R-1-4

| | 1983 | | 1984 | | Industry Statistics |
	$	%	$	%	%
Sales	548784 –√	100	610740 –∩▽	100	100
Cost of Goods Sold	374658 –√	68	403070 –∩∅	66	65
Gross Profit	174126 –	32	207670 –∅	34	35
Selling Expenses	55484 –√	10	85654 –∩∆	14	15
General and Administrative Expenses	79634 –√	15	87557 –∩∅	14	12
Income before Taxes	39008 –	7	34459 – ∅	6	8
Taxes	12873 –√	2	6869 –∩✗	1	3
Net Income	26135 –	5	27590 – ∅	5	5

∧ Footed

∩ Agreed to the general ledger.

√ Agreed to the prior year working papers.

∅ Amount appears reasonable in relation to prior year results and industry statistics.

▽ See audit procedures performed on Sales, R-1-2.

∆ Large increase in Selling Expenses is due to the addition of a salesman to the sales staff. Based on a review of the payroll records the increase in the account appears reasonable.

✗ Decrease in tax rate is due to the realization of several thousand dollars in investment tax credit related to purchases of equipment. See tax accrual working paper, O-3.

Conclusion:
The comparative analysis revealed no unusual fluctuations that could not be adequately explained.

revenue accounts are verified by the auditors in conjunction with the audit of a related asset or liability. The following list summarizes the revenue verified in this manner:

Balance sheet item	Revenue
Accounts receivable	Sales
Notes receivable	Interest
Securities and other investments	Interest, dividends, gains on sales, share of investee's income
Property, plant, and equipment	Rent, gains on sale
Intangible assets	Royalties

A common characteristic of the revenue items listed above is that most, if not all, are accounted for on the accrual basis. Accrual basis accounting for revenue results in stronger internal control, because it requires the recording of a receivable when the revenue is earned. Once the receivable is recorded, some followup is inevitable. Additional assurance is provided that attention will be drawn to any delay in the receipt of cash, or any failure to record a cash receipt. For example, if dividends earned are recorded as receivables by an accrual entry at the date of record, any failure to receive or to record dividend checks will be readily apparent.

Miscellaneous revenue

One category of revenue not included in the above listing, but of interest to the auditors, is miscellaneous revenue. Miscellaneous revenue, by its very nature, is a mixture of minor items, some nonrecurring and others likely to be received at irregular intervals. Consequently, many companies do not accrue such revenue, but merely debit Cash and credit Miscellaneous Revenue when cash is received. The weakness inherent in this procedure is not of particular significance if the amounts involved are minor and infrequent. However, the weakness can become serious if revenue of substantial amount is misclassified as Miscellaneous Revenue, a practice sometimes followed because of its convenience.

Illustrative case.　An old story in public accounting circles concerns the auditors who inquired of a new client how extensive was the classification by the company of revenue and expenses. "Just two of each," was the reply, "general and miscellaneous."

For the reasons indicated above, the auditors should obtain an analysis of the Miscellaneous Revenue account. Among the items the auditors might find improperly included as miscellaneous revenue are the following:

1. Collections on previously written-off accounts or notes receivable. These collections should be credited to the allowance for doubtful accounts and notes receivable.
2. Write-offs of old outstanding checks or unclaimed wages. In many states unclaimed properties revert to the state after statutory periods; in such circumstances these write-offs should be credited to a liability account rather than to miscellaneous revenue.
3. Proceeds from sales of scrap. Scrap sales proceeds should generally be applied to reduce cost of goods sold, under by-product cost accounting principles.
4. Rebates or refunds of insurance premiums. These refunds should be offset against the related expense or unexpired insurance.
5. Proceeds from sales of plant assets. These proceeds should be accounted for in the determination of the gain or loss on the assets sold.

The auditors should propose adjusting journal entries to classify correctly any material items of the types described above that have been included in miscellaneous revenue by the client. Before concluding the work on revenue, the auditors should perform the analytical review procedures described earlier in this chapter and investigate unusual fluctuations. Material amounts of unrecorded revenue may be discovered by these procedures, as well as significant misclassifications affecting revenue accounts.

EXPENSES

The auditors' work relating to purchases and cost of goods sold was covered, along with inventories, in Chapter 13. We are now concerned with audit objectives and procedures for other types of expenses.

Audit objectives

In the examination of payrolls, selling expenses, and general and administrative expenses, the auditors study and evaluate the internal controls in force and try to determine whether expenses have been recognized in the proper accounting period. In other words, the auditors want evidence that expenses have been properly matched with revenue. They also consider whether expenses have been properly classified and are reasonable in amount, as compared with budgeted amounts, with expenses of prior years, and with the sales of the current year.

The work required to attain these objectives has in large part already been performed in connection with the verification of balance sheet accounts. Let us consider for a moment the number of expense accounts for which we have already outlined verification procedures in the chapters dealing with balance sheet topics:

Relationship of expenses to balance sheet accounts

Balance sheet item	*Expenses (and costs)*
Accounts and notes receivable	Uncollectible accounts and notes expense
Inventories	Purchases and cost of goods sold
Property, plant, and equipment	Depreciation, repairs and maintenance, and depletion
Prepaid expenses and deferred charges	Various related expenses, such as rent, property taxes, advertising, postage, and others
Intagible assets	Amortization
Accrued liabilities	Commissions, fees, bonuses, product warranty expenses, and others
Interest-bearing debt	Interest

In the following sections, we shall complete our review of expenses by considering additional audit objectives and procedures for payrolls, and for selling, and general and administrative expenses, other than those listed above. The audit of payroll is presented as a unit without regard to the division of salaries and wages between manufacturing operations and other operations. Manufacturing salaries and wages are, of course, charged to inventories, either directly or by means of the allocation of factory overhead.

The budget—a vital element in controlling costs and expenses

In approaching the examination of costs and expenses, perhaps the most important single question to raise is the following: "Does the client have a good budgeting program?" The existence of a good budgeting program means that department heads, first-line supervisors, and other supervisors who authorize expenditures have prepared a year in advance a statement of the expenses that must be incurred for a given volume of operations. These estimates of expenses to be incurred have been assembled and summarized by the accounting department and reviewed and approved by top management. A definite plan of operations exists; standards of performance have been set; and, month by month, the costs and expenses actually incurred are compared with the amounts shown by the budget. Any significant discrepancy between budgeted expenses and actual expenses immediately receives the attention of management, and the supervisor responsible for the expenses in question is called upon for an explanation. When a budgeting program of this type is in operation, the integrity of the accounts is greatly increased: the opportunities for misclassification of expenses, for omission of transactions, and for fraud are reduced to a minimum.

Much of the audit work on costs and expenses, therefore, may be devoted to a study of the client's budgeting program. If the auditors find that the client does not prepare a budget, or merely makes a pretense of using budgeting techniques, the conduct of the audit must be modified accordingly. One of the most effective substitutes for comparison of actual expenses with budgeted expenses is to compare the expenses of each month with the expenses of the corresponding month for the preceding year. Other procedures to be stressed in the absence of budgeting controls include close review of variations in gross profit margins and extensive analysis of ledger accounts for expenses.

Payrolls

The payroll in many companies is by far the largest operating cost, and, therefore, deserves the close attention of the auditors. In the past, payroll frauds were common and often substantial. Today, however, payroll frauds are more difficult to conceal for several reasons: (1) extensive subdivision of duties relating to payroll, (2) use of computers for preparation of payrolls, and (3) necessity of frequent reports to government, listing employees' earnings and tax withholdings.

The principal objectives of the auditors in the examination of payrolls are:

1. To determine that the authorized records and procedures are so designed and operated as to provide adequate internal control.
2. To determine that the client has complied with government regulations concerning social security taxes, unemployment insurance, worker's compensation insurance, wages and hours, income tax withholding, and other federal, state, and local requirements concerning employment.
3. To determine that the company is complying with terms of union agreements as to wage rates, vacation pay, and similar items.
4. To suggest methods of simplifying and improving payroll procedures.

Internal control

The establishment of strong internal control over payrolls is particularly important for several reasons. Although payroll frauds are infrequent today, compared to the past, the possibility of large-scale payroll fraud still exists. Such frauds may involve listing fictitious persons on the payroll, overpaying employees, and continuing employees on the payroll after their separation from the company. A second reason for emphasizing internal control over payrolls is that a great mass of detailed information concerning hours worked and rates of pay must be processed quickly and accurately if workers are to be paid promptly and without error. Good employee relations demand that paychecks be ready on time and be free from error. As pointed out in previous chapters, internal control is a means of securing accuracy and dependability in accounting data as well as a means of preventing fraud.

Still another reason for emphasizing the importance of internal control over payrolls is the existence of various payroll tax laws and income tax laws, which require that certain payroll records be maintained and that payroll data be reported to the employee and to governmental agencies. Complete and accurate records of time worked are also necessary if a company is to protect itself against lawsuits under the Fair Labor Standards Act.

Methods of achieving internal control.

Budgetary control of labor costs.   To control payroll costs means to avoid waste and to obtain the maximum production from the dollars expended for services of employees. As a means of establishing control over payroll costs, many companies delegate to department heads and other supervisors responsibility for the control of costs in their respective units of the business. The supervisor may be requested at the beginning of each year to submit for the budget an estimate of departmental labor costs for the coming period. As the year progresses and actual labor costs are compiled, the controller submits monthly reports to top management comparing the budgeted labor costs and the actual labor costs for each department. The effectiveness of this control device will depend largely upon the extent to which top management utilizes these reports and takes action upon variances from the budget.

Reports to governmental agencies.   Another important internal control over payroll lies in the necessity of preparing reports to government agencies showing the earnings and tax deductions for all employees. This type of control is not concerned with holding labor costs to a minimum, but is an effective means of preventing and detecting payroll fraud. Now that every employee must have a social security number and the employer must report earnings and deductions for each employee, the opportunities for payroll fraud are greatly reduced. In a few cases, falsified reports to government agencies have been prepared as part of a payroll fraud, but this involves such extensive scheming and falsification of records as to make fraud of this type rather unlikely.

Subdivision of duties.   Most important of all internal controls over payroll is the division of payroll work among several departments of the company. Payroll activities include the functions of employment, timekeeping, payroll preparation and record keeping, and the distribution of pay to employees. For strong internal control, each of these functions should be handled by a separate department of the company. Combination of these functions in a single department or under the authority of one person opens the door to payroll fraud. These several phases of payroll activities will now be considered individually.

The employment function

The first significant step in building a strong system of internal control over payrolls is taken by the personnel department when a new employee is hired. At this point, the authorized rate of pay should be entered on a pay-rate record. The employee also should sign a payroll deduction authorization specifying any amounts to be withheld, and a withholding tax exemption certificate. These records should be kept in the personnel department; but a notice of the hiring of the new employee, the rate of pay, and the payroll deductions should be sent to the payroll department. Notice of employment and of the authorized pay rate also is sent to the head of the department in which the employee is to work.

Under no circumstances is the payroll department justified in adding a name to the payroll without having received the formal authorization notice from the personnel department. When an employee's rate of pay is changed, the new rate will be entered on the pay-rate record that is maintained in the personnel department. An authorization for the new rate must be sent to the payroll department before the change can be made effective on the payroll. Upon the termination of an employee, notice of termination is sent from the personnel department to the payroll department. The work of the payroll department and the propriety of names and pay rates used in preparing the payroll, therefore, rest upon formal documents originating outside the payroll department.

An adequate system of internal control demands that the addition and removal of names from the company payroll, as well as rate changes and reclassification of employees, be evidenced by written approval of an executive in the personnel department and by the head of the operating department concerned. To permit the payroll department to initiate changes in pay rates, or to add names to the payroll without formal authorization from the personnel department, is to invite payroll fraud.

Timekeeping

The function of timekeeping consists of determining the number of hours (or units of production) for which each employee is to be paid. The use of electronic time-recording equipment is of considerable aid in establishing adequate internal control over the timekeeping function. Reports prepared by timekeepers who travel through the plant and contact an employee only once or twice during the day may be less dependable than time reports prepared by supervisors, whose duties keep them in continuous contact with a small group of employees.

Internal control can be improved by the practice of regular comparison of the time reports prepared by timekeepers or supervisors with time clock records showing arrival and departure times of employees. If pay is based on piecework, a comparison may be made between the reports of units produced and the quantities that are added to the perpetual inventory records.

Salaried employees receiving a fixed monthly or weekly salary may not be required to use time clocks. Some companies require salaried employees to fill out a weekly or semimonthly report indicating the time devoted to various activities. If a salaried employee is absent, the department head usually has authority to decide whether a pay reduction should be made.

Undesirable practices related to the timekeeping function include permitting employees to maintain their own records of time worked or units completed and basing payment on these records without any independent verification. Combination of the timekeeping function with that of payroll preparation is also extremely dangerous from an internal control standpoint. If time clock records are to contribute significantly to internal control, it is imperative that all employees punch their own time cards and no others. Any overtime worked by employees paid on an hourly basis should be approved in writing by the appropriate supervisor.

Payroll records and payroll preparation

The payroll department has the responsibility of computing the amounts to be paid to employees and of preparing all payroll records. It is imperative that the payroll department should **not** perform the related functions of timekeeping, employment, or distribution of pay to employees. The output of the payroll department may be thought of as: (1) the payroll checks (or pay envelopes, if wages are paid in cash); (2) individual employee statements of earnings and deductions; (3) a payroll journal; (4) an employees' ledger, summarizing earnings and deductions for each employee; (5) a payroll distribution schedule, showing the allocation of payroll costs to direct labor, overhead, and various departmental expense accounts; and (6) quarterly and annual reports to the government showing employees' earnings and taxes withheld. If the client utilizes an electronic data processing installation, many of these functions may be delegated to the data processing department.

The computation of the payroll is made from the work hours reported by the timekeeping department, and from authorized pay rates and payroll deductions reported by the personnel department.

The auditors may find payroll records and procedures varying in complexity from a manual "write it once" system to the most sophisticated computerized techniques. However, they should expect the client's system to include such basic records as time cards, payroll journals, labor distributions, and employee earnings records.

Distributing paychecks or cash to employees

The distribution of paychecks or pay envelopes to employees is the task of the paymaster. If employees are paid in cash, a copy of the payroll register is forwarded from the payroll department, and the paymaster uses this record as a guide to filling the payroll envelopes. These envelopes preferably should be prepared by the payroll department. If employees are paid by check, the checks may be made ready for signature in the payroll department and forwarded to the paymaster for signature.

Under no circumstances should the signed payroll checks or pay envelopes containing cash be returned to the payroll department. Neither is it acceptable to turn paychecks or pay envelopes over to supervisors in the operating departments for distribution to employees. The function of distributing paychecks should be lodged exclusively with an employee who should perform no other payroll activity. When delivering a check to an employee, the paymaster will require proof of identity by presentation of a badge or by signing of a receipt. A check or pay envelope for an absent employee should be retained and never turned over to another employee for delivery. When the absentees later pick up their pay, they should be required to sign a receipt.

Most companies that pay employees by check use a special payroll bank account. A voucher for the entire amount of the weekly payroll may be prepared in the general accounting department based on the payroll summary prepared in the payroll department. This voucher is sent to the treasurer, who issues a check on the general bank account for the amount of the payroll. The check is deposited in the special payroll bank account, and checks to individual employees are drawn on this bank account. It also is the practice of some companies to have printed on the check a statement that this type of check is not valid if issued for an amount in excess of a specified dollar amount.

If wages are paid in cash, any unclaimed wages should be deposited in the bank and credited to a special liability account. Subsequent disbursement of these funds to employees then will be controlled by the necessity of drawing a check and preparing supporting documents. The auditors should investigate thoroughly all debits to the Unclaimed Wages account. The dangers inherent in permitting unclaimed pay envelopes to be retained by the paymaster, returned to the payroll clerk, or intermingled with petty cash are apparent.

Description of internal control for payroll

Typical of the questions to be answered by the auditors for the completion of an internal control questionnaire, a systems flowchart, or other record of payroll internal controls are the following: Are employees paid by check? Is a payroll bank account maintained on an imprest basis? Are the activities of timekeeping, payroll compilation, payroll check signing, and paycheck distribution performed by separate departments or employees? Are all operations involved in the preparation of payrolls subjected to independent verification before the paychecks are distributed? Are employee time reports approved by supervisors? Is the payroll bank account reconciled monthly by an employee having no other payroll duties?

AUDIT PROGRAM FOR PAYROLLS

The following audit procedures are representative of the work generally completed to establish the propriety of payments for salaries, wages, bonuses, and commissions:

1. Obtain description of internal control for payrolls.
2. Make compliance tests of payroll transactions for one or more pay periods, including the following specific procedures:
    a. Trace names and wage or salary rates to records maintained by personnel department.
    b. Trace time shown on payroll to time cards and time reports approved by supervisors.
    c. If payroll is based on piecework rates rather than hourly rates, reconcile earnings with production records.
    d. Determine basis of deductions from payroll and compare with records of deductions authorized by employees.
    e. Test extensions and footings of payroll.
    f. Compare total of payroll with total of payroll checks issued.
    g. Compare total of payroll with total of labor cost summary prepared by cost accounting department.
    h. If wages are paid in cash, compare receipts obtained from employees with payroll.
    i. If wages are paid by check, compare paid checks with payroll and compare endorsements to signatures on withholding tax exemption certificates.
    j. Review subsequent payment of unclaimed wages, comparing receipts with payroll records, wage rates, and time reports.
3. Observe the use of time clocks by employees reporting for work, and investigate time cards not used.
4. Plan a surprise observation of one of the paycheck distributions, including control of payroll records and an accounting for all employees listed.
5. Determine that payrolls for the year do not exceed the number of weekly or monthly pay periods and that all payrolls have been properly approved.
6. Obtain or prepare a summary of compensation of officers for the

year and trace to contracts, minutes of directors' meetings, or other authorization.

7. Investigate any extraordinary fluctuations in salaries, wages, and commissions.

8. Test computations of compensation earned under profit-sharing plans.

9. Test commission earnings by examination of contracts and detailed supporting records.

10. Test pension payments by reference to authorized pension plans and to supporting records.

The fourth procedure in the above list, calling for the auditors to plan a surprise observation of a regular distribution of paychecks to employees, deserves special consideration. The auditors' objective in observing the distribution of checks or cash to employees on a regular payday is to determine that every name on the company payroll is that of a bona fide employee presently on the job. This audit procedure is particularly desirable if the various phases of payroll work are not sufficiently segregated by departments to afford good internal control. The history of payroll frauds shows that permitting one person to have custody of employment records, time cards, paychecks, and employees' earnings records has often led to the entering of fictitious names on the payroll, and to other irregularities, such as use of excessive pay rates and continuance of pay after the termination of an employee.

The auditors' observation of a paycheck distribution should be on a surprise basis, and may conveniently be done at some time other than the peak of the audit work season. Efficient planning of the payroll observation requires that the auditors know in advance the general procedure and timing of payroll preparation and distribution. Without any prior announcement, the auditors should appear on a regular payday and take control of the paychecks or pay envelopes. Before the distribution to employees is begun, the auditors will compare the name and amount on each check or envelope with the corresponding entry in the payroll register. The auditors must make sure that they have a check or envelope for every employee on the payroll register. The footings of the payroll register should also be verified so that there is no doubt that the auditors are accounting for the distribution of every dollar of the payroll. In a company so large that the auditors cannot conveniently observe the distribution of the entire payroll, the test may be limited to one or more selected departments.

The auditors first will determine that they have possession of all the checks or envelopes comprising the payroll. They will then accompany representatives of the client around the plant as all the checks or envelopes are distributed to employees. The whole procedure will be meaningless unless the auditors establish the identity of each employee receiving payment.

AUDIT PROGRAM FOR SELLING, GENERAL, AND ADMINISTRATIVE EXPENSES

For other expenses not verified in the audit of balance sheet accounts, the following substantive tests are appropriate. The extent to which the analytical review procedures are applied is dependent upon the auditors' evaluation of internal control for expenses.

1. Perform analytical review procedures related to the accounts.
   a. Compare actual expenses and budgeted expenses.
   b. Compare monthly operating expenses with those of prior years, both in dollar amounts and expressed as a percentage of net sales.
   c. Investigate all significant fluctuations and unusual relationships disclosed by comparison of expenses with the budget and with amounts of prior years.
   d. Obtain or prepare analyses of expense accounts selected as a result of the analytical review procedures.
2. Obtain or prepare an analysis of professional fees expense.
3. Obtain or prepare analyses of critical expenses in income tax returns.

1. Perform analytical review procedures related to the accounts.

Analytical review procedures should be performed as a part of the audit of all significant selling, general, and administration expenses. Typical analytical review procedures applied to expense accounts include comparisons with budgeted amounts and amounts incurred in prior years.

a. Compare actual expenses and budgeted expenses.

The effectiveness of a good budgeting program in controlling expenses was discussed earlier in this chapter. In the examination of companies that prepare budgets, the auditors should compare actual and budgeted expenses and analyze variances from the budget. Often management will have investigated thoroughly the variances from the budget and will be able to provide logical explanations. The existence of a good budgeting program may reduce considerably the audit time that otherwise would be devoted to analysis of expense accounts.

b. Compare monthly operating expenses with those of the prior year, both in dollar amounts and expressed as a percentage of net sales.

Even though a budget is not prepared by the client, the auditors may still apply analytical review procedures by obtaining or preparing analyses that compare the various operating expenses month by month with the figures for corresponding months of the preceding year. One of the previously mentioned audit objectives was determining whether expenses had been correctly classified. The issue of classification is most important as between factory overhead costs, on the one hand, and selling, general, and administrative expenses, on the other. Factory overhead costs may properly be carried forward as part of inventory cost, whereas the expenses of selling, general, and administrative functions usually are deducted from revenue in the period incurred. Consequently, an error in classification may cause an error in the net income of the period. The auditors' review of the propriety of classification of expenses can be linked conveniently with the comparison of monthly amounts of the various expenses. Comparison of yearly totals is accomplished by inclusion of amounts for the preceding year on the auditors' grouping sheets or working trial balance, but this procedure should be supplemented by comparison of expenses on a month-by-month basis.

> **c. Investigate all significant variations disclosed by comparison of expenses with the budget and with amounts of prior years.**

The principal methods of investigating significant variations in expenses are inquiry of management and analyses of ledger accounts. Analyses of expense accounts involve tracing entries in the accounts back to the voucher register, or to the cash disbursements journal if the company records expenses only at time of making payment. From these accounting records, reference may be made to invoices, receiving reports, purchase orders, or other supporting evidence.

> **d. Obtain or prepare analyses of expense accounts selected as a result of the analytical review procedures.**

As a result of the above procedures, the auditors will have chosen certain expense accounts for further verification. The client should be requested to furnish analyses of the accounts selected, together with related vouchers and other supporting documents, for the auditors' review. An illustration of an expense account analysis is presented in Figure 17–2.

Which expense accounts are most likely to contain errors and are most important for the auditors to analyze? Generally, auditors have found that the accounts for traveling expense, entertainment, contributions, professional fees, officers' compensation, repairs and maintenance, and miscellaneous expense should be analyzed.

> **2. Obtain or prepare an analysis of professional fees expense.**

As indicated in the preceding paragraph, the auditors should analyze professional fees expense. This analysis often will disclose legal and audit fees properly chargeable to costs of issuing stock or debt instruments, or to costs of business combinations. A study of professional fees expense for a new client will inform the auditors of fees charged by the predecessor CPAs. Also, the analysis of professional fees expense furnishes the names of attorneys to whom letters should be sent requesting information as to pending litigation and other loss contingencies. Figure 17–2 illustrates an analysis of professional fees expense.

Figure 17–2

Cheviot Corporation

Acct. No. 547   Professional Fees Expense   R-3-7

Year Ended December 31, 1984

Date	Reference	Payee	Description	Amount	
Various	Various	Hale and Hale	Monthly retainer for legal services - 12 × $500	6000 —	
3/5/84	CD411	Jay & Wall, CPAs	Fee for 1983 audit	7500 —	4
5/2/84	CD602	Hale and Hale	Fee for legal services relating to acquisition of real property adjoining San Diego plant	3000 —	4
9/18/84	CD1018	Hale and Hale	Fee for legal services relating to modification of installment sales contract forms	400 —	4
12/31/84			Balance per ledger	16900 —	
12/31/84	A.J.E. 41		To capitalize 5/2/84 disbursement as part of cost of land	K-1 (3000 —)	
12/31/84			Adjusted balance	13900	
				R-3	

A.J.E. 41

Land   3000 —
     Professional Fees   3000 —
To capitalize legal
fees reobtaining land.

Prepared by clients

n – Footed and agreed to general ledger balance.
4 – Examined billing and copy of client's check in payment thereof.

Conclusion:
     Professional fees expense is fairly presented in the adjusted amount of $13,900.

V. M. H.
1/9/85

J. Agee
C. M.
1/12/85

C. M.
1/12/85

3. Obtain or prepare analyses of critical expenses in income tax returns.

Income tax returns in use at present generally require schedules for officers' salaries, taxes, contributions, and casualty losses. In addition to these, officers' expense account allowances are presented in the analysis of officers' salaries. Accordingly, the auditors should obtain or prepare analyses of any of these expenses that were not analyzed in connection with the audit of payrolls or with procedure *d* of this audit program. The auditors should bear in mind that details of these expenses will probably be closely scrutinized when the state or federal revenue agents examine the client's tax returns.

INCOME STATEMENT PRESENTATION

How much detail in the income statement?

One of the more interesting problems of statement presentation of revenue and expenses is the question of how much detailed operating information may be disclosed without causing the income statement to become unreasonably long and complex. As a minimum, the income statement should show the net sales revenue, cost of goods sold, selling expenses, general and administrative expenses, income taxes, and net income. Such special events as discontinued operations, extraordinary items, and the effects of accounting changes should be presented in the income statement in accordance with the requirements of the FASB.

Reporting earnings per share

FASB pronouncements require that companies with shares owned by the public present earnings per share on the face of the income statement. For these companies, per share figures should be reported for income from continuing operations, income before extraordinary items, cumulative effects of accounting changes, and net income. The computations should be based upon the weighted average number of actual and *equivalent* common shares outstanding during the year. In addition to these *primary* earnings per share, companies with a complex capital structure may be required to report *fully diluted* earnings per share.

Reporting by diversified companies

The business combination movement in recent years has created many large conglomerate corporations by bringing together companies in quite unrelated industries. Although the word *conglomerate* is usually applied to a large family of corporations created by business combinations, other companies have achieved the same degree of diversification among unrelated industries through internal development and expansion. The term *diversified company* is therefore more appropriate for our use in considering the special financial reporting problems created by the emergence of this new type of business entity.

For the diversified company carrying on operations in several unrelated industries, we may well question whether the traditional form of income statement constitutes a fair presentation. Would the income statement be more useful to financial analysts and others if it showed separately the revenue and operating results of the various industry segments comprising the diversified company? In the past, an investor or financial analyst easily could associate a given corporation with a specific industry. Since this is hardly possible for many of the new, large, diversified companies, a worthwhile analysis of the income statement may require disclosure of profitability of the several industry segments.

The Financial Accounting Standards Board requires companies with shares owned by the public to include certain business segment information in their annual financial statements. This disclosure includes information concerning the company's operations in different industries, its foreign operations, and its sales to major customers. Since the information is required for fair presentation of the financial statements in conformity with generally accepted accounting principles, it must be audited to provide a basis for an unqualified opinion on the financial statements. Accordingly, *SAS No. 21*, "Segment Information," states that the auditors should perform the following procedures related to the business segment information:

1. Evaluate the reasonableness of management's methods of compiling the information.
2. Consider whether the information is presented in sufficient detail; apply analytical review procedures to test its reasonableness.
3. Evaluate the reasonableness of methods used in allocating operating expenses among segments.

Examination of the statement of changes in financial position

Ordinarily, the auditors' examination of the client's statement of changes in financial position does not include the performance of substantive tests. The statement is prepared from selected account balances from other financial statements and from analyses of increases and decreases in these balances. Therefore, the amounts included in the statement of changes in financial position are audited in conjunction with the audit of balance sheet and income statement accounts. Additional procedures to examine the statement consist solely of review procedures to evaluate the presentation and clerical accuracy of the statement.

The statement of changes in financial position should disclose all aspects of the company's financing and investing activities and all significant sources and uses of funds. Its format should include presentation of funds provided or used by operations and by extraordinary items. The concept of funds used in preparation of the statement should be appropriate for the company's business. For example, the working capital concept of funds is not appropriate for a financial institution with a balance sheet that is not classified as to current and noncurrent assets and liabilities. The auditors should trace the amounts included in the statement to other financial statement balances and amounts included in audit working papers. They should ascertain that a statement of changes in financial position is presented for each year in which an income statement is presented, and that the statement is presented on a basis consistent with that of prior years.

KEY TERMS INTRODUCED OR EMPHASIZED IN CHAPTER 17

Analytical review procedures Ratio, trend, and comparative analysis designed to detect unusual fluctuations in financial statement balances or other questionable items that require investigation.

Conservatism An accounting doctrine for asset valuation in which the lower of two alternative acceptable asset valuations is chosen.

Extraordinary item An event or transaction that is distinguished by its unusual nature and by the infrequency of its occurrence.

Fully diluted earnings per share A pro forma presentation that reflects the dilution of earnings per share that would have occurred if all contingent issuances of common stock that individually would reduce earnings per share had taken place at the beginning of the period.

Primary earnings per share A presentation of earnings per share based on outstanding common shares and those securities that are in substance equivalent to common shares and have a dilutive effect.

Public company A company whose securities are traded on an organized exchange or that is required to file financial statements with the SEC.

Segment A component of an entity whose activities represent a separate major line of business or class of customer.

GROUP I: REVIEW QUESTIONS

17–1. How should the independent auditors advise the client to present discontinued operations in the income statement?

17–2. Why does the auditors' examination of the statement of changes in financial position usually not involve a substantiation of the statement amounts?

17–3. Describe how the auditors use analytical review procedures in the examination of selling, general, and administrative expenses.

17–4. When you are first retained to examine the financial statements of Wabash Company, you inquire whether a budget is used to control costs and expenses. The controller, James Lowe, replies that he personally prepares such a budget each year, but that he regards it as a highly confidential document. He states that you may refer to it if necessary, but he wants you to make sure that no employee of the firm sees any of the budget data. Comment on this use of a budget.

17–5. What influence does the existence of a good budgeting program in the client's business have on the conduct of an audit?

17–6. During an initial audit, you observe that the client is not complying with federal regulations concerning wages and hours. Would you (a) report the violation to regulatory authorities, (b) discuss the matter with the client, (c) ignore the matter completely, (d) withdraw from the engagement, or (e) follow some other course of action? Explain.

17–7. What standards did the FASB enact for disclosures of operating details on the income statements of diversified companies?

17–8. What division of duties among independent departments is desirable to achieve maximum internal control over payrolls?

17–9. What specific procedures are suggested by the phrase "compliance test of payroll transactions?"

17–10. Identify three revenue accounts that are verified during the audit of balance sheet accounts; also, identify the related balance sheet accounts.

17–11. Identify three items often misclassified as miscellaneous revenue and state how the misclassified items should be accounted for.

17–12. How are analytical review procedures used in the verification of revenue?

17–13. Identify three expense accounts that are verified during the audit of balance sheet accounts; also, identify the related balance sheet accounts.

17–14. For which expense accounts should the auditors obtain or prepare analyses to be used in preparation of the client's income tax returns?

17–15. What safeguards should be employed when the inaccessibility of banking facilities makes it desirable to pay employees in cash?

17–16. You are asked by a client to outline the procedures you would recommend for disposing of unclaimed wages. What procedures do you recommend?

17–17. What auditing procedure can you suggest for determining the reasonableness of selling, general, and administrative expenses?

17–18. During the examination of the financial statements of Harvest Company, the auditors compared the monthly amounts of individual revenue and expense accounts with the corresponding data for the prior year. They also compared various ratios for the current and prior years. What auditing term is used to describe these procedures? What is the purpose of these comparisons?

GROUP II: QUESTIONS REQUIRING ANALYSIS

17–19. The Wickerson Corporation is a public company with diversified operations, including several foreign subsidiaries. The management of the company has prepared Wickerson's financial statements including disclosure of the business segment information required by *FASB Statement No. 14.*

Required:

List the procedures that the auditors should perform to audit the business segment information.

17–20. In a properly planned examination of financial statements, the auditors coordinate their reviews of specific balance sheet and income statement accounts.

Required:

Why should the auditors coordinate their examinations of balance sheet accounts and income statement accounts? Discuss and illustrate by examples. (AICPA, adapted)

17–21. In your first examination of the financial statements of Willman Company, you discover that the company has included in the Miscellaneous Revenue account a $10,000 commission from Bradley Realtors, Inc. Your investigation discloses that Bradley negotiated Willman's purchase for $500,000 of a tract of land from Payne Company, and that Payne had paid Bradley's commission of $50,000 on the sale.

Required:

Would you take exception to Willman Company's accounting for the commission received from Bradley Realtors, Inc.? Explain.

17–22. During your regular audit of Payton Company, you discover that the company signed a 10-year lease on a building at the beginning of the company's fiscal year. The lease, which is an operating lease, requires monthly rental payments of $1,000 per month for the last nine years of the lease only. Nancy James, controller of Payton Company, explains that the lessor waived the first year's rent because the building had remained vacant for a long period. James states that, in her view, Payton Company had incurred no rent expense for the fiscal year your audit covers. Do you agree? Explain.

17–23. Your new audit client, Coin-O-Mat Company, leases coin-operated laundry equipment to military bases. Usage of the equipment requires the insertion of coins into metered receptacles, which record expired time of equipment operation. How can you determine whether all revenue earned by Coin-O-Mat Company has been recorded in the accounting records?

17–24. Bowden Company owed property taxes of $5,972. Through error Morton Bryant, who served the company as office manager, cashier, and accountant, paid the tax bill twice. Realizing his error after having mailed the second check, he wrote to the county officials requesting a refund.

When the refund was received some weeks later, Bryant substituted the check from the city for cash receipts and abstracted $5,972 in currency.

Would this error and theft probably be discovered in an audit by independent public accountants? Indicate what auditing procedure, if any, would disclose the facts.

17–25. Barton Company is a highly diversified public company with segments that manufacture and sell antibiotics, dairy products, hospital supplies, toiletries, and chemicals. In what form should the income statement of Barton Company be prepared?

17–26. Select the best answer for each of the following, and explain fully the reason for your selection.

    a. Which of the following analytical review procedures should be applied to the income statement?

        (1) Select sales and expense items and trace amounts to related supporting documents.

        (2) Ascertain that the net income amount in the statement of changes in financial position agrees with the net income amount in the income statement.

        (3) Obtain from the proper client representatives the beginning and ending inventory amounts that were used to determine costs of sales.

        (4) Compare the actual revenues and expenses with the corresponding figures of the previous year and investigate significant differences.

    b. Which of the following is the *best* way for the auditors to determine that every name on a company's payroll is that of a bona fide employee presently on the job?

        (1) Examine personnel records for accuracy and completeness.

        (2) Examine employees' names listed on payroll tax returns for agreement with payroll accounting records.

        (3) Make a surprise observation of the company's regular distribution of paychecks.

        (4) Visit the working areas and confirm with employees their badge or identification numbers.

    c. Which of the following *best* describes the independent auditors' approach to obtaining satisfaction concerning depreciation expense in the income statement?

        (1) Verify the mathematical accuracy of the amounts charged to income as a result of depreciation expense.

        (2) Determine the method for computing depreciation expense, and ascertain that it is in accordance with generally accepted accounting principles.

        (3) Reconcile the amount of depreciation expense to those amounts credited to accumulated depreciation accounts.

        (4) Establish the basis for depreciable assets, and verify the depreciation expense.

    d. Proper internal control over the cash payroll function would mandate which of the following?

        (1) The payroll clerk should fill the envelopes with cash and a computation of the net wages.

        (2) Unclaimed pay envelopes should be retained by the paymaster.

        (3) Each employee should be asked to sign a receipt.

        (4) A separate checking account for payroll should be maintained. (AICPA, adapted)

GROUP III: PROBLEMS

17–27. Susan Antonio, CPA, is conducting the 1984 audit of the financial statements of Johnson Company and has been given the following statement of changes in financial position:

JOHNSON COMPANY
Statement of Changes In Financial Position
For the Year Ended December 31, 1984
(Amounts in $000)

Funds provided	
Operations:	
Net income from operations	$46,000
Add or (deduct) items not requiring outlay of working capital in the current period:	
Depreciation	5,500
Deferred income taxes	1,500
Investment in unconsolidated subsidiary (net of cash dividends paid)	(1,700)*
From operations prior to extraordinary loss	$51,300
Extraordinary loss	(13,000)
From operations after extraordinary loss	$38,300
Proceeds from exercise of stock options	2,700*
Total	$41,000
Funds used	
Cash dividends paid on common and preferred stock	$15,000*
Increase in long-term investments (net of allowance)	3,000 ⎫
Allowance for unrealized losses on noncurrent marketable equity securities	5,000 ⎭ *
Increase in working capital	18,000
Total	$41,000
Changes in working capital-increase (decrease)	
Cash and short-term investments	$(9,000)
Accounts receivable	17,000
Inventories	18,000
Accounts payable and accrued liabilities	(7,000)
Other current assets and liabilities	(1,000)
Increase in working capital	$18,000

Antonio has completed necessary auditing procedures on the balance sheet, income statement, and statement of stockholders' equity and is satisfied that these statements are fairly presented with adequate disclosures in the statements and in the footnotes. Antonio has not yet examined the statement of changes in financial position.

Required:

a. What *general* steps should be followed by Antonio to examine the statement of changes in financial position of the Johnson Company? *Do not discuss the presentation or verification of any specific item on the statement.*

b. What additional specific steps should be followed by Antonio to verify each of the four items marked with an asterisk (*) on the statement of changes in financial position of the Johnson Company? (AICPA, adapted)

17–28. In connection with an examination of the financial statements of Olympia Company, the auditors are reviewing procedures for accumulating direct labor hours. They learn that all production is by job order and that all employees are paid hourly wages, with time-and-one-half for overtime hours.

Olympia's direct labor hour input process for payroll and job-cost determination is summarized in the following flowchart:

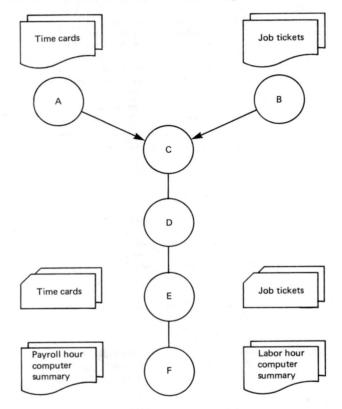

Steps A and C are performed in timekeeping, step B in the factory operating departments, step D in payroll audit and control, step E in data preparation (keypunch), and step F in computer operations.

Required:
For each input processing step A through F—
a.   List the possible errors or discrepancies that may occur.
b.   Cite the corresponding control procedure that should be in effect for each error or discrepancy.
Note: Your discussion of Olympia's procedures should be limited to the input for direct labor hours, as shown in steps A through F in the flowchart. Do not discuss personnel procedures for hiring, promotion,

termination, and pay rate authorization. In step F do not discuss equipment, computer program, and general computer operational controls. Organize your answer for each input-processing step as follows:

Step	Possible errors or discrepancies	Control procedures
A		

(AICPA, adapted)

17–29. Rita King, your staff assistant on the April 30, 1985 audit of Maxwell Company, was transferred to another assignment before she could prepare a proposed adjusting journal entry for Maxwell's Miscellaneous Revenue account, which she had analyzed per the working paper below. You have reviewed the working paper and are satisfied with King's procedures. You are convinced that all the Miscellaneous Revenue items should be transferred to other accounts. Maxwell Company's state of incorporation has an Unclaimed Properties Law.

Maxwell Company

Acct. No. 430   Miscellaneous Revenue   Q-2

Year Ended April 30, 1985

C.M. 5/19/85

Date	Description	Reference	Amount
5/8/84 through 4/7/85	Proceeds of sale of scrap from manufacturing process (total of 12 monthly sales)	Various CR	5843 ✓
7/18/84	Writeoff of old outstanding checks: nos. 118—$500; 214—$400; 407—$200	GJ 7-4	1100 ✓
9/22/84	Recovery of previously written-off account receivable from Wilson Company	CR 9-1	4381 ✓
2/6/85	Cash proceeds from sale of machine. Cost of $10,000 and accumulated depreciation of $8,000 as of 2/6/85 not removed from accounts.	CR 2-1	3500 ✓
4/28/85	Refund of premium overcharge on fire insurance policy no. 1856, for period 4/1/85 - 3/31/86	CR 4-1	600 ✓
4/30/85	Balance per ledger		15424

✓ – Traced to cash receipts journal or general journal; vouched to appropriate supporting documents.

R.A.K. 5/18/85

Required:

Draft a proposed adjusting journal entry at April 30, 1985 for Maxwell Company's Miscellaneous Revenue account.

17–30. Rowe Manufacturing Company has about 50 production employees and uses the following payroll procedures.

The factory supervisor interviews applicants and on the basis of the interview either hires or rejects the applicants. After being employed, the applicant prepares a W–4 form (Employee's Withholding Exemption Certificate) and gives it to the supervisor. The supervisor writes the hourly rate of pay for the new employee in the corner of the W–4 form and then gives the form to a payroll clerk as notice that the applicant has been employed. The supervisor verbally advises the payroll department of pay rate adjustments.

A supply of blank time cards is kept in a box near the entrance to the factory. Each employee takes a time card on Monday morning, signs it, and notes in pencil on the time card the daily arrival and departure times. At the end of the week the employees drop the time cards in a box near the door to the factory.

The completed time cards are taken from the box on Monday morning by a payroll clerk. Two payroll clerks divide the cards alphabetically between them, one taking the A to L section of the payroll, and the other taking the M to Z section. Each clerk is fully responsible for one section of the payroll. The payroll clerks compute the gross pay, deductions, and net pay; post the details to the employees' earnings records; and prepare and number the payroll checks. Employees are automatically removed from the payroll when they fail to turn in a time card.

The payroll checks are manually signed by the chief accountant and given to the supervisor, who distributes the checks to the employees in the factory and arranges for the delivery of the checks to the employees who are absent. The payroll bank account is reconciled by the chief accountant, who also prepares the various quarterly and annual payroll tax reports.

Required:

List your suggestions for improving Rowe Manufacturing Company's system of internal control for factory hiring practices **and** payroll procedures. (AICPA, adapted)

17–31. Your client is a shopping center with 30 store tenants. All leases with the store tenants provide for a fixed rent plus a percentage of sales, net of sales taxes, in excess of a fixed dollar amount computed on an annual basis. Each lease also provides that the lessor may engage CPAs to audit all records of the tenant for assurance that sales are being properly reported to the lessor.

You have been requested by your client to audit the records of Traders Restaurant to determine that the sales totalling $390,000 for the year ended December 31, 1984 have been properly reported to the lessor. The restaurant and the shopping center entered into a five-year lease on January 1, 1984. Traders Restaurant offers only table service; no liquor is served. During meal times there are four or five waitresses in attendance who prepare handwritten prenumbered restaurant checks for the customers. Payment is made at a cash register, operated by the proprietor, as the customer leaves. All sales are for cash. The proprietor also is the accountant. Complete files are kept of restaurant checks and cash register tapes. A daily sales journal and general ledger are also maintained.

Required:

List the auditing procedures that you would employ to verify the total annual sales of Traders Restaurant. (AICPA, adapted)

17–32. City Loan Company has 100 branch loan offices. Each office has a manager and four or five employees who are hired by the manager. Branch managers prepare the weekly payroll, including their own salaries, and pay employees from cash on hand. The employees sign the payroll sheet signifying receipt of their salary. Hours worked by hourly personnel are inserted in the payroll sheet from time reports prepared by the employees and approved by the manager.

The weekly payroll sheets are sent to the home office, along with other accounting statements and reports. The home office compiles employee earnings records and prepares all federal and state payroll tax returns from the weekly payroll sheets.

Salaries are established by home office job-evaluation schedules. Salary adjustments, promotions, and transfers of full-time employees are approved by a home office salary committee based upon the recommendations of branch managers and area supervisors. Branch managers advise the salary committee of new full-time employees and terminations. Part-time and temporary employees are hired without referral to the salary committee.

Required:

a. How might funds for payroll be diverted in the above system?
b. Prepare a payroll internal audit program to be used in the home office to audit the branch office payrolls of City Loan Company. (AICPA, adapted)

GROUP IV: CASE STUDIES IN AUDITING

17–33. **TIMBER PRODUCTS CORPORATION**

During the first audit of Timber Products Corporation, the auditor, James Wills, CPA, found the payroll activities to be concentrated in the hands of an experienced and trusted employee, Richard Cardiff. Cardiff prepares a payroll register from time reports. The register is presented for approval of the treasurer, who then issues a check for the total amount of the payroll. Cardiff cashes this check, fills pay envelopes for all of the company's 400 hourly employees, and distributes the pay envelopes to the employees.

In verifying the hourly payroll, the auditor selected two test periods, the first week in July and the second week in December. For these test periods, he proved the accuracy of the footings and the extensions on the payroll register. The totals shown by the payroll register corresponded with the checks issued for the total payrolls. Employee names and rates of pay were traced to a file of employment records maintained by Cardiff. These records indicated the date of employment, the job classification, and the hourly rate of pay. When an employee was reclassified to a higher pay classification, the date and nature of the reclassification were noted on these records. When employees terminated, their records were transferred to another file.

In support of the hours worked during the test period, the auditor found time reports on file for all employees, showing time of arrival and departure each day. Cardiff stated that he personally observed the punching in and out of employees and had custody of the time reports.

Cardiff produced for inspection by the auditor an envelope containing $97 in cash, which he stated to be the pay due a former employee who had left in the middle of November without claiming the fraction of a week's pay due him.

The auditor's examination of the payroll register, employment records, and checks for the total payroll during the two periods selected for testing revealed no discrepancies. A comparison of the payroll during the year under audit with the payroll for the two preceding years on a month-to-month basis indicated no significant variation. The auditor also compared the number of employees in each job classification with the number employed in such jobs in the two preceding years and compared the rates of pay for various jobs during the three-year period. He noted that the output of the company during these three years had been fairly stable. Inquiries made of officers substantiated this lack of trend and evoked the observation that profits were down slightly.

Officers and supervisory employees of the company were paid by check on a monthly basis. The auditor traced these payments to salary authorizations in the minutes of directors' meetings and found no exceptions. Although his tests had served to substantiate the accuracy of the payroll records, the auditor felt somewhat concerned over the lack of internal control caused by the delegation of so much responsibility to Cardiff. Consequently, the auditor decided to observe employees punching in and out of the plant on the time clock, and observe (on a surprise basis) the distribution of pay envelopes by Cardiff to the employees.

The auditor's observation of employees arriving at and leaving the plant disclosed no improper use of time reports. When the auditor appeared without warning on payday and informed Cardiff that he wished to observe the distribution of pay envelopes, Cardiff expressed some impatience with this procedure. Cardiff explained that he had a very busy day in prospect and proposed to distribute pay envelopes at intervals during the day as his other duties took him to various parts of the plant. The auditor insisted on carrying out this observation of the payoff and accompanied Cardiff until the last pay envelope had been delivered, although this process was interrupted a good many times while Cardiff attended to other matters. Cardiff knew all of the 400 employees personally and did not require any identification from them. The auditor inquired if the employees were required to carry identification badges, but was informed that this practice had been abandoned because the plant was so small that Cardiff knew each employee. Furthermore, when badges had been required in prior years, employees frequently came to work without them. When an employee reported for work without a badge, he was refused admission to the plant, but this practice led to so much lost time and employee resentment that the company had discontinued the use of badges. Cardiff added that since the use of badges had been discontinued, each employee was required to sign a receipt for his pay.

Since his surprise observation of the payoff and his other verification procedures had revealed no irregularities, the auditor concluded that the payroll records were dependable, despite the concentration of duties in the hands of Cardiff. Other phases of the audit were completed satisfactorily, and an unqualified audit report was issued by the auditor.

Several months later, a sudden illness of Richard Cardiff caused an officer of the company to take over the payroll work temporarily. The officer discovered that 10 fictitious employees were on the payroll and had been on the payroll continuously for three years, with consequent loss to the company of approximately $600,000. The company sought to recover a part of its losses from the auditor on the grounds that he must have been guilty of gross negligence not to have discovered that approximately 2½ percent of the payroll was fictitious. The auditor attempted to defend himself against the charges by emphasizing his surprise observation of the payoff, which he stated was evidence of his having gone beyond normal auditing procedures in recognition of the weakness in internal control. The auditor contended that a padded payroll could not have avoided detection by this test, but Cardiff explained that during the payday in question, when accompanied by the auditor, he had delivered five extra pay envelopes to one employee and five more to another, both employees being good friends of his and willing to "help him out of a tight spot."

The pay envelopes delivered to these employees had been presented to them at various hours during the day at various locations in the plant, and the auditor had apparently not remembered having seen the employees previously.

Required:

a. Did the audit conform to generally accepted auditing standards? Explain.

b. Discuss the purpose and effectiveness of the auditor's observation of the distribution of pay to employees.

c. Do you believe Timber Products Corporation had a valid claim against the auditor? Explain.

d. Would this payroll fraud have been prevented if the company had paid its employees by check rather than in cash? Explain.

18

Audit reports

The expressing of an independent and expert opinion on the fairness of financial statements is the most important and valuable service rendered by the public accounting profession. This opinion provides users of financial statements with *reasonable assurance* that the information is in conformity with generally accepted accounting principles. The opinion is expressed through the auditors' standard report, consisting of a concise description of the scope of the examination and a statement of the auditors' opinion on the financial statements. If there is a deficiency within the financial statements, the auditors must modify their standard report. An explanation of the reason for the modification is generally provided in a middle paragraph.

In this chapter we emphasize the auditors' standard report and situations that require modification of this report. In addition, we shall consider special reports, in which the auditors attest to elements of financial statements or to financial statements prepared on the cash basis or any comprehensive basis of reporting other than generally accepted accounting principles.

Financial statements

The reporting phase of an auditing engagement begins when the independent auditors have completed their field work and their proposed adjustments have been accepted and recorded by the client. Before writing their report, the auditors must review the client-prepared financial statements for form and content, or draft the financial statements on behalf of the client.

The financial statements on which the independent auditors customarily report are the balance sheet, the income statement, the statement of retained earnings, and the statement of changes in financial position. Often, the statement of retained earnings is combined with the income statement. In some cases, the retained earnings statement may be expanded to a statement of stockholders' equity. Financial statements generally are presented in comparative form for the current year and the preceding year and are accompanied by explanatory footnotes. The financial statements for a parent corporation usually are consolidated with those of the subsidiaries.

Financial statement disclosures

The purpose of notes to financial statements is to achieve adequate disclosure when information in the financial statements proper is insufficient to attain this objective. Although the notes, like the financial statements themselves, are representations of the client, the independent auditors generally assist in drafting the notes. The writing of notes to financial statements is a challenging task because complex issues must be summarized in a clear and concise manner. Adequate disclosure in the footnotes to the financial statements is necessary for the auditors to issue an unqualified opinion on the financial statements.

In addition to footnote disclosures, many companies are required by the FASB or the SEC to present *supplementary information.* Such information is not a required part of the basic financial statements, but is presented in *unaudited supplementary schedules* accompanying the financial statements.

Recent pronouncements by the Financial Accounting Standards Board and the Securities and Exchange Commission have required extensive additions to disclosures in financial statements. Listed below are a few of the many items for which supplementary disclosures are now mandatory. For each of the sample items listed, reference is made to the FASB *Statement of Financial Accounting Standards (SFAS)*, or to the AICPA *Accounting Principles Board Opinion (APBO)*, or to the SEC *Accounting Series Release (ASR)*, which mandates the disclosure.

1. Footnote disclosure of significant accounting policies, such as principles of consolidation, and the basis of valuation and amortization of assets (*APBO 22*).
2. Footnote disclosure of accounting changes (*APBO 20*).
3. Footnote disclosure of the significant aspects of business combinations (*APBO 16*).
4. Supplementary disclosure of selected interim financial data (*ASR 177*).

5. Supplementary disclosure of the effects of changing prices on in-
    come from continuing operations, inventory, and property, plant
    and equipment (*SFAS 33*).

In drafting financial reporting disclosures, the auditors should keep
in mind that disclosures are meant to supplement the information in
the financial statements and not to *correct* improper financial statement presentation. Thus, a footnote or supplementary schedule, no
matter how skillfully drafted, does not compensate for the erroneous
presentation of an item in the financial statements.

The auditors' standard report

For convenient reference the auditors' standard report, which was
introduced and discussed in Chapter 1, is presented again:

> We have examined the balance sheet of X Company as of December 31,
> 198x and the related statements of income, retained earnings and changes
> in financial position for the year then ended. Our examination was made
> in accordance with generally accepted auditing standards and, accord-
> ingly, included such tests of the accounting records and such other audit-
> ing procedures as we considered necessary in the circumstances.
>
> In our opinion, the financial statements referred to above present
> fairly the financial position of X Company as of December 31, 198x and
> the results of its operations and the changes in its financial position for the
> year then ended, in conformity with generally accepted accounting prin-
> ciples applied on a basis consistent with that of the preceding year.

The standard audit report illustrated above is appropriate for a *firm*
of certified public accountants. A CPA performing an audit as an individual practitioner should use *I* instead of *we* in the auditors' standard
report.

Restatement of basic points concerning the standard report

Among the major points made in Chapter 1 concerning the standard
report were the following:

1. The financial statements (including footnotes and supplementary
    information) are the statements of the client, not of the auditors.
    The auditors' product is their report, in which they express their
    opinion about the client's financial statements.
2. The statement in the audit report that an examination has been
    made in accordance with "generally accepted auditing standards"
    refers to an official statement of standards adopted by the member-
    ship of the American Institute of Certified Public Accountants.
    This official set of standards includes general standards (such as
    independence), standards of field work (such as the gathering of
    sufficient evidence), and standards of reporting. In this chapter we

are particularly concerned with standards of reporting. Four standards of reporting have been enunciated by the AICPA and deserve careful attention. These four standards require the following:

a. A clear statement as to whether the financial statements are prepared in accordance with generally accepted accounting principles.

b. A statement as to the consistency with which accounting principles have been applied in the current and preceding periods.

c. Adequate disclosure in the financial statements (or notes thereto).

d. Clear indication of the character of the examination and the degree of responsibility assumed by the auditors. This fourth standard of reporting has not always been easy to enforce; it will be discussed at more length later in this chapter.

3. The auditors' opinion indicates whether the financial statements "present fairly. . . ." In *SAS No. 5* the AICPA emphasized that the auditors' judgment as to fairness of financial statement presentation should be applied within the framework of generally accepted accounting principles. In essence, the quality of *presenting fairly* may be equated with *not being misleading*.

4. The auditors' opinion that the financial statements were prepared in conformity with "generally accepted accounting principles applied on a basis consistent with that of the preceding year" gives assurance to bankers, stockholders, and other interested persons that these statements may reasonably be compared with the company's statements in prior years, and with statements of other companies in the industry. The banker or stockholder is thereby enabled to weigh the merits of one company against another.

A compendium of generally accepted accounting principles may be found in the AICPA's loose-leaf service entitled *Professional Standards*. All currently effective *FASB Statements*, *APB Opinions*, and *Accounting Research Bulletins* are integrated in volumes 3 and 4 of *Professional Standards*.

EXPRESSION OF AN OPINION BY THE AUDITORS

The principal alternatives in reporting on financial statements may be summed up as follows:

1. An unqualified opinion.
2. A qualified opinion.
3. An adverse opinion.
4. A disclaimer of opinion.

These alternatives are based on the fourth standard of reporting adopted by the membership of the AICPA, which reads as follows:

The report shall either contain an expression of opinion regarding the financial statements, taken as a whole, or an assertion to the effect that an opinion cannot be expressed. When an overall opinion cannot be expressed, the reasons therefore should be stated. In all cases where an auditor's name is associated with financial statements, the report should contain a clear-cut indication of the character of the auditor's examination, if any, and the degree of responsibility he is taking.

This standard does not prevent the auditors from expressing separate opinions on the balance sheet and the income statement. For example, they may express an unqualified opinion on the balance sheet and disclaim an opinion or express a qualified or adverse opinion on the income statement.

Unqualified opinions

The unqualified opinion (illustrated on page 588) is, of course, the most desirable opinion from the client's point of view. The auditors express an unqualified opinion on the client's financial statements when there has been no unresolvable restriction on the scope of the examination and the auditors have no significant exceptions as to the fairness and applicability of the accounting principles reflected in the financial statements, the consistency of their application, and the adequacy of informative disclosures in the financial statements.

The unqualified opinion usually contains the precise wording illustrated in the auditors' standard report. However, such circumstances as reliance upon other auditors or emphasis on a special matter may justify a deviation from the standard wording.

Reliance upon other auditors.   On occasion it may be necessary for the principal auditors of a company to rely upon another CPA firm to perform a portion of the audit work. The most common situation in which CPAs rely upon the work of other auditors is in the audit of consolidated entities. If certain subsidiaries have been audited by other CPA firms, the auditors of the parent company may decide to rely upon the work of these other CPAs rather than conduct another examination of the subsidiaries. In other situations, the auditors of a multibranch client may retain another CPA firm to perform audit procedures at a specific branch location. When more than one CPA firm participates in an engagement, some modification of the conventional unqualified opinion may be necessary. The principal auditors must decide how much responsibility they will assume for the engagement and, thus, whether to make reference to the other CPA firm in their audit report. The two courses of action open to the principal auditors in this situation are described as follows in *SAS No. 1:*

If the principal auditor decides to assume responsibility for the work of the other auditor insofar as that work relates to the principal auditor's expression of an opinion on the financial statements taken as a whole, no reference should be made to the other auditor's examination. On the other hand, if the principal auditor decides not to assume that responsibility, his report should make reference to the examination of the other auditor and should indicate clearly the division of responsibility between himself and the other auditor in expressing his opinion on the financial statements.

In all cases the principal auditors should satisfy themselves as to the professional reputation and independence of the other auditors participating in the engagement. This may be done by making inquiries of professional organizations and others having knowledge of the other auditors' reputation. It may also be desirable to obtain written representations from the other auditors. If the principal auditors engage the services of another CPA firm of good professional reputation and independent status, the principal auditors usually determine the scope of the second firm's engagement and assume full responsibility for the work done. In this case, it is unnecessary for the principal auditors to mention in the audit report that they used the services of an agent. In other cases, however, the client may act directly to retain a second firm of auditors to examine the financial statements of a distant subsidiary company; in these circumstances, the auditors examining the parent company might not accept responsibility for the work of the other auditors and consequently may disclose in the scope paragraph the use of other public accountants for the examination of the subsidiary company. An unqualified opinion may be issued if neither CPA firm had any significant exceptions; however, the report should be worded to show the joint responsibility for the opinion, as in the following illustration:

We have examined the consolidated balance sheet of X Company and subsidiaries as of December 31, 198x and the related consolidated statements of income, retained earnings, and changes in financial position for the year then ended. Our examination was made in accordance with generally accepted auditing standards and, accordingly, included such tests of the accounting records and such other auditing procedures as we considered necessary in the circumstances. We did not examine the financial statements of B Company, a consolidated subsidiary, which statements reflect total assets and revenue constituting 20 percent and 22 percent, respectively, of the related consolidated totals. These statements were examined by other auditors whose report thereon has been furnished to us, and our opinion expressed herein, insofar as it relates to the amounts included for B Company, is based solely upon the report of the other auditors.

In our opinion, based on our examination and the report of other auditors, the consolidated financial statements referred to above present fairly the financial position of X Company and subsidiaries at December 31, 198x and the results of their operations and the changes in their financial position for the year then ended, in conformity with generally accepted accounting principles applied on a basis consistent with that of the preceding year.

Departures from officially recognized accounting principles. Rule 203 of the AICPA *Code of Professional Ethics* provides that auditors usually should express a qualified or adverse opinion when financial statements contain a material departure from authoritative FASB pronouncements or *APB Opinions*. However, unusual circumstances may be encountered in which application of an officially recognized principle would result in misleading financial statements. An unqualified opinion may be issued in these circumstances, but the auditors must disclose the departure in a middle paragraph of their report.

Emphasis of a matter. Another modification of the standard audit report occurs when the auditors choose to emphasize a matter regarding the client's financial statements. For example, the auditors may add a paragraph to their unqualified audit report calling attention to a significant subsequent event described in a note to the financial statements. If the conventional wording is used in the opinion paragraph, such an audit report is unqualified.

Conditions preventing issuance of an unqualified opinion. The auditors are not always able to give the "clean bill of health" indicated by the model report on page 588. Among the reasons that may prevent the issuance of an unqualified opinion are the following:

1. The examination may not have been made in accordance with generally accepted auditing standards.
    a. Internal control may be so seriously inadequate that a satisfactory examination cannot be performed within reasonable time limits.
    b. The client may place restrictions on the scope of the auditors' examination, as, for example, not permitting the confirmation of accounts receivable, not taking a physical inventory, which the auditors must observe, or not permitting the auditors to examine a subsidiary company or to visit a distant branch location where an important portion of the company's assets are located.

        Under the circumstances described above, the auditors will generally *disclaim* an opinion on the financial statements. In some situations where the exceptions as to the scope of the examination are less serious, the auditors may *qualify* their opinion, using the words *except for* in their qualification.

2. For reasons beyond the control of the client or the auditors, it may not have been possible to perform certain necessary auditing procedures.
    a. In a first audit if inventory records are very poor, there may be no way to verify the beginning inventories; consequently, the

       cost of goods sold and net income for the year cannot be verified. If beginning inventories were substantial, the auditors must *disclaim* an opinion on the income statement and statements of retained earnings and changes in financial position. If the auditors have no other exceptions, they may express an *unqualified opinion* on the balance sheet.

    b.   Substantial uncertainties may prevent the auditors from determining or estimating the resolution of a significant contingency, such as a pending lawsuit. In this situation the auditors typically will issue a *qualified opinion* with the words *"subject to"* emphasizing the uncertainty. If the uncertainty is sufficiently important, the auditors may *disclaim* an opinion on the financial statements.

3.   The financial statements may not present fairly the client's financial position and operating results.

    a.   The financial statements may not have been prepared in accordance with generally accepted accounting principles. When the auditors find that assets have been improperly valued, that liabilities have been omitted or that other violations of generally accepted accounting principles exist, their first reaction will be to attempt to persuade management of the client company to revise the statements. In most cases, management will agree, and the deficiencies will be remedied. Occasionally, however, management will not agree to the changes considered necessary by the auditors, and consequently an unqualified opinion cannot be issued. If the violations of generally accepted accounting principles are extremely serious, the auditors will issue an *adverse opinion* on the financial statements. Less serious problems concerning accounting principles warrant a *qualified* opinion with the words *"except for"*.

    b.   Accounting principles may not have been applied consistently as compared with the preceding year. An unqualified audit report cannot be issued if the client company has changed its method of inventory valuation, if it has adopted a new method of computing depreciation, or if it has made other material changes in accounting principle as compared with the preceding year. The auditors issue an *"except for" qualified opinion* to call attention to the change in accounting principle, its justification, and its effects on the financial statements.

    c.   Fairness in financial statements often hinges on the issue of what constitutes adequate informative disclosure. Assume, for example, that pending legislation indicates that a certain type of business, such as the operation of a race track, may soon be outlawed. Disclosure of this threat to continued existence of the business is essential to a fair presentation. A similar contingency requiring disclosure is the existence of lawsuits in the process of litigation. The client company's failure to disclose such significant matters in notes to the financial statements customarily necessitates the issuance of an *"except for" qualified opinion* by the auditors. Only in extreme cases of inadequate disclosure would the auditors have to issue an *adverse opinion.*

The types of audit reports appropriate under the preceding conditions are summarized in Figure 18–1.

Figure 18–1

Departures from an unqualified audit report

	Nature of auditors' exception			
		Inability to perform necessary auditing procedures		
	*Examination not in accordance with GAAS**	*Beginning inventories in first audit*	*Major uncertainty*	*Financial statements not presented fairly*
Usual type of report	Disclaimer of opinion	Disclaimer on operations statements; unqualified opinion on balance sheet	"Subject to" qualified opinion	"Except for" qualified opinion
	or	*or*	*or*	*or*
Less frequent type of report	"Except for" qualified opinion (when departure from GAAS not extremely serious)	"Except for" qualified opinion on operations statements (when beginning inventories not extremely material)	Disclaimer of opinion (when uncertainty is extremely critical)	Adverse opinion (when departures from GAAP† are extreme)

* GAAS—generally accepted auditing standards
† GAAP—generally accepted accounting principles

Qualified opinions

A qualified opinion is a modification of the unqualified opinion stating that *except for* the *effects* of some limitation on the scope of the examination, a change in accounting principle, or some unsatisfactory financial statement presentation, the financial statements are fairly presented. If the client's financial statements were affected by an inability to resolve some significant uncertainty, the words *"subject to"* are included in the opinion paragraph.

The materiality of the exception governs the use of the qualified opinion. The exception must be sufficiently significant to warrant mentioning in the auditors' report, but it must not be so significant as to necessitate a disclaimer of opinion or an adverse opinion. Consequently, the propriety of a qualified opinion in the event of a significant exception is a matter for careful professional judgment by the auditors.

The audit reports for all qualified opinions, except those dealing with changes in accounting principle, should have a *separate explanatory paragraph* disclosing the reasons for the qualification. The opinion paragraph of a qualified report includes the appropriate qualifying language and a reference to the explanatory paragraph.

Limitations on scope of examination. We have pointed out that limitations on the scope of the auditors' examination may result from failure to comply with generally accepted auditing standards (weak internal control or client-imposed restrictions), or from inability of the auditors to perform necessary auditing procedures (inability to verify beginning inventories of a new client or major uncertainties). If the scope limitations are not so material as to require a disclaimer of opinion, the auditors would issue a qualified opinion such as the following:

> We have examined the balance sheet of Y Company as of December 31, 19x5 and the related statements of income, retained earnings and changes in financial position for the year then ended. Except as explained in the following paragraph, our examination was made in accordance with generally accepted auditing standards and, accordingly, included such tests of the accounting records and such other auditing procedures as we considered necessary in the circumstances.
>
> We did not observe the taking of the physical inventory at December 31, 19x4, since that date was before the time we were engaged initially as auditors for the Company. Due to the nature of the Company's records, we were unable to obtain evidence as to the inventory quantities by means of other auditing procedures.
>
> In our opinion, *except for the effects of such adjustments, if any, as might have been determined to be necessary had we been able to observe the physical inventory at December 31, 19x4,* the accompanying statements of income, retained earnings and changes in financial position present fairly the results of Y Company's operations and the changes in its financial position for the year ended December 31, 19x5 in conformity with generally accepted accounting principles applied on a basis consistent with that of the preceding year. Also in our opinion, the accompanying balance sheet presents fairly the financial position of Y Company as of December 31, 19x5, in conformity with generally accepted accounting principles applied on a basis consistent with that of the preceding year.

Major uncertainty affecting a client's business. If substantial uncertainty exists as to the outcome of an important matter affecting the client's financial statements, the auditors are not able to accumulate sufficient competent evidential matter and hence must usually issue an opinion *"subject to"* the outcome of the pending uncertainties. The term *uncertainty* does not include matters whose outcome is merely *difficult* to estimate. As emphasized by the AICPA in *SAS No. 2:*

Matters are not to be regarded as uncertainties . . . unless their outcome is not susceptible of reasonable estimation, . . .

Following is an example of an audit report qualified as to uncertainty. Since the wording of the standard scope paragraph is not affected, that paragraph is omitted from the illustration, and only the middle paragraph and opinion paragraph are shown.

(Standard scope paragraph)

As discussed in Note 8 to the financial statements, the Company is defendant in a lawsuit alleging infringement of certain patent rights and claiming royalties and punitive damages. The Company has filed a counter action, and preliminary hearings and discovery proceedings on both actions are in progress. Company officers and counsel believe the Company has a good chance of prevailing, but the ultimate outcome of the lawsuits cannot be determined at this time, and no provision for any liability that may result has been made in the financial statements.

In our opinion, *subject to the effects, if any, on the financial statements of the ultimate resolution of the matter discussed in the preceding paragraph,* the financial statements referred to above present fairly the financial position of X Company as of December 31, 198x and the results of its operations and the changes in its financial position for the year then ended, in conformity with generally accepted accounting principles applied on a basis consistent with that of the preceding year.

Question about a company's continued existence. A special type of significant uncertainty concerns the ability of a client company to continue to operate as a going concern. Under generally accepted accounting principles, both assets and liabilities are recorded and classified on the assumption that the company will continue to operate. Assets, for example, may be presented at amounts that are significantly greater than their liquidation values.

During the course of an audit, the auditors may become aware of events that seriously threaten the client's continued existence. Questions of continued existence usually hinge on a company's ability to meet its financial obligations, without restructuring its debt or changing its operations. However, other factors, such as the loss of key employees or major customers, also may render doubtful the continued existence of a client company as a going concern. *SAS No. 34* indicates that the auditors should assume that the client is a going concern unless contrary evidence comes to their attention.[1] Conditions that may challenge the applicability of the going-concern assumption include negative cash flows from operations, defaults on loan agreements, adverse financial ratios, loss of key employees, and loss of primary assets. When such conditions come to the auditors' attention, they should consider

---

[1] *Statement on Auditing Standards No. 34,* "The Auditor's Considerations When a Question Arises about an Entity's Continued Existence," AICPA (New York, 1981).

whether the conditions are mitigated by other factors. For example, management may have other available sources of financing, creditors may be willing to restructure the client's debt, or unprofitable segments of the business may be offered for sale.

After considering evidence contrary to the assumption of a going concern, and also considering any mitigating factors and management's plans, the auditors may conclude that a substantial doubt remains about the client's ability to continue in operation. If the implications of the loss of going-concern status are significant to the financial statements, a qualified audit report is appropriate. The auditors should qualify their opinion subject to the recoverability of the assets and the appropriate classification of assets and liabilities. The middle paragraph of the report should refer to the disclosures containing information on the client's ability to continue as a going concern.

Qualifications as to accounting principles or disclosure. The auditors sometimes must qualify their opinion because they do not agree with the accounting principles used in preparing the statements or because they believe disclosures in the statements are inadequate. Usually when the auditors' objections are carefully explained, the client will agree to change the statements in an acceptable manner. If the client does not agree to make the suggested changes, the auditors will be forced to qualify their opinion (or if the exception is sufficiently material, to issue an adverse opinion). An example of an audit report with the opinion paragraph qualified as to the accounting principles follows:

(Standard scope paragraph)

As more fully described in Note 4 to the financial statements, the Company has excluded certain lease obligations from property and debt in the accompanying balance sheet. In our opinion, generally accepted accounting principles require that such obligations be included in the balance sheet.

In our opinion, *except for the effects of not capitalizing lease obligations, as discussed in the preceding paragraph,* the financial statements referred to above present fairly the financial position of X Company as of December 31, 19xx and the results of its operations and the changes in its financial position for the year then ended, in conformity with generally accepted accounting principles applied on a basis consistent with that of the preceding year.

It is important to remember that the third standard of reporting states that

Informative disclosures in the financial statements are to be regarded as reasonably adequate unless otherwise stated in the report.

Therefore, the auditors should issue a qualified or adverse report if they consider the disclosure in the client's financial statements to be inadequate. *SAS No. 32,* "Adequacy of Disclosure in Financial Statements," requires omitted information to be disclosed in the auditors' report, if it is practicable to do so. The word *practicable* in this context means that the information can reasonably be obtained and that its inclusion in the report would not cast the auditors in the role of the preparer of the information. For example, the omission by the client of a statement of changes in financial position would not cause the auditors to include such a statement in their report.

To illustrate the wording of a report qualified for lack of adequate disclosure, assume that a client failed to disclose a significant restriction on the payment of dividends. The last two paragraphs of the auditors' report might appear as follows after a standard scope paragraph:

> On January 15, 19x5, the company issued debentures in the amount of $30,000,000 for the purpose of financing plant expansion. The debenture agreement restricts the payment of future cash dividends to earnings after December 31, 19x4.
>
> In our opinion, except for the omission of the information in the preceding paragraph, the aforementioned financial statements present fairly the financial position of X Company as of December 31, 19x5, and the results of its operations and the change in its financial position for the year then ended, in conformity with generally accepted accounting principles applied on a basis consistent with that of the preceding year.

Consistency qualifications. If a client company makes a change in accounting principle (including a change in the reporting entity), the nature of, justification for, and effect of the change is reported in a note to the financial statements for the period in which the change was made. Any such change having a material effect upon the financial statements will also require qualification of the auditors' report, even though they are in full agreement with the change. The auditors' qualification as to consistency appears in the *opinion paragraph* of their report, rather than in a *separate paragraph.*

Conditions surrounding a consistency qualification may be varied. For example, the accounting change may be one that requires retroactive restatement of preceding years' financial statements, instead of inclusion of the cumulative effect of the change in the current year's income statement. Further, the auditors may be reporting on comparative financial statements for more than one year, rather than on the current year's statements only. The auditors' consistency qualifications must be tailored to fit these varied conditions.

An example of an audit report on financial statements for a single year, but which statements include the cumulative effects of an accounting change, would read as follows, following the standard scope paragraph.

(Standard scope paragraph)

> In our opinion, the financial statements referred to above present fairly the financial position of X Company as of December 31, 198x and the results of its operations and the changes in its financial position for the

year then ended, in conformity with generally accepted accounting principles, which, *except for the change, with which we concur, in the
method of computing depreciation as described in Note 1 to the
financial statements,* have been applied on a basis consistent with that
of the preceding year.

In the preceding example, Note 1 would describe fully the nature of
and justification for the change in method of computing depreciation
and the related effect upon net income. If the auditors did not concur
with any aspects of the change or its disclosure, they would qualify their
opinion or issue an adverse opinion, as appropriate.

A change in accounting estimate, such as the estimated service life of
a patent, and a changed condition unrelated to accounting, such as the
sale of a plant, do not require a consistency qualification by the auditors
if they are properly disclosed in notes to the financial statements.

If the auditors are reporting on the financial statements for the first
accounting period of a newly organized company, no previous accounting period exists. Accordingly, the auditors should not refer to consistency, unless there had been a change in accounting principle during
the first accounting period that had not been retroactively applied for
the entire period.

"Explained opinions."   Some audit reports have been issued containing a qualification worded in such a cautious manner that it could
be interpreted as no qualification at all. Typically, the opinion paragraph following an ambiguous qualification might contain the expression "with the foregoing explanation as to inventories, the accompanying financial statements present fairly. . . ." Such indecisive or contradictory audit reports are not satisfactory. The acceptable alternatives
in such cases are to issue an unqualified opinion, or a qualified opinion
that incorporates the words *except for* or *subject to.*

Adverse opinions

An adverse opinion is the opposite of an unqualified opinion; it is an
opinion that the financial statements *do not* present fairly the financial
position, results of operations, and changes in financial position of the
client, in conformity with generally accepted accounting principles.
When the auditors express an adverse opinion, they must have accumulated sufficient evidence to support their unfavorable opinion.

The auditors should express an adverse opinion if the statements are
so lacking in fairness that a qualified opinion would not be warning
enough. If the auditors know the statements to be an unfair presentation, they cannot disclaim an opinion. Whenever the auditors issue an
adverse opinion, they should disclose in a separate paragraph of their
report the reasons for the adverse opinion and the principal effects of
the adverse opinion on the client company's financial position and
operating results.

Thus, an audit report that included an adverse opinion might include a standard scope paragraph, a middle paragraph describing the reasons for the adverse opinion and the principal effects of the subject matter of the adverse opinion, and an opinion paragraph, such as the one following:

> In our opinion, because of the effects of the matters discussed in the preceding paragraph, the financial statements referred to above *do not present fairly*, in conformity with generally accepted accounting principles, the financial position of X Company as of December 31, 198x or the results of its operations and changes in its financial position for the year then ended.

Unless the auditors have specific exceptions as to consistency, they should make no reference to consistency in an audit report containing an adverse opinion. An expression of opinion on consistency would imply the application of generally accepted accounting principles, and thus soften the impact of the adverse opinion.

Adverse opinions are rare because most clients follow the recommendations of the independent auditors with respect to fair presentation in financial statements. One possible source of adverse opinions is the actions of regulatory agencies that prescribe accounting practices not in accordance with generally accepted accounting principles.

Disclaimer of opinion

A disclaimer of opinion is no opinion. In an audit engagement, a disclaimer is required when substantial restrictions upon the scope of the auditors' examination or other conditions preclude their compliance with generally accepted auditing standards.

Restrictions imposed by client. In some engagements, the client will impose restrictions limiting the auditors' compliance with generally accepted auditing standards. Examples are the prohibition of inventory observation and receivables confirmation. Since inventories and receivables are usually important factors in determining both financial position and operating results, the auditors (if prohibited by the client from observing the physical inventory or confirming receivables) must qualify the scope paragraph of their report. Generally, failure to observe the physical inventory or to confirm receivables will represent such a material shortcoming in the scope of the examination that the auditors will not be able to express an opinion on the fairness of the financial statements taken as a whole.

Another example of a client-imposed restriction on the scope of the audit is the client's denial of permission for the auditors to examine the financial statements of a significant subsidiary company or branch, or to apply required auditing procedures to the financial statements of a significant investee company.

When the client imposes restrictions that limit significantly the scope of the audit, the CPA firm *generally must disclaim an opinion* on the client's financial statements. In a separate paragraph of the audit report, the auditors should describe all substantive reasons for the disclaimer of opinion, and should disclose any reservations they have regarding fairness of the financial statements. In a disclaimer of opinion, the auditors should not describe the auditing procedures actually performed; to do so might dilute the impact of the disclaimer.

An example of a disclaimer of opinion follows:

> The Company did not take a physical inventory of merchandise, stated at $863,198, in the accompanying financial statements as of December 31, 198x. The Company's records do not permit the application of adequate alternative procedures regarding the inventories.
>
> Since the Company did not take a physical inventory and we were unable to apply adequate alternative procedures regarding inventories, as noted in the preceding paragraph, the scope of our work was not sufficient for us to express, and *we do not express, an opinion on the financial statements referred to above.*

Disclaimer because of uncertainty. In *SAS No. 2*, the AICPA took the position that a *qualified opinion* is generally appropriate for a material uncertainty that is described adequately in notes to the client's financial statements. However, the institute did not rule out the issuance of a *disclaimer of opinion* because of major uncertainty. If a disclaimer because of uncertainty is issued by the auditors, it should be in the same format as the disclaimer of opinion illustrated above.

Other disclaimers issued by CPAs. In this section, we have discussed only disclaimers of opinion issued in *audit* engagements. CPA firms issue disclaimers of opinion in many other types of engagements; these disclaimers are dealt with in Chapter 19.

An audit report in which the CPA firm disclaims an opinion on the fairness of the financial statements is not likely to be of much use to the client. Consequently, the auditors should consider at the beginning of the engagement what obstacles may exist to their expression of an opinion and should reach an understanding with the client as to any special problem that may prevent the endorsement of the statements.

Negative assurance clause in audit report

Statements of *negative assurance* have sometimes been included in audit reports to comfort or reassure a client when the auditors cannot express an unqualified opinion. For example:

> Our examination did not include confirmation of accounts receivable or observation of physical inventory. Consequently, we do not express an opinion on the fairness of the financial statements referred to above. However, nothing came to our attention that would lead us to question the fairness of the amounts shown for receivables and inventories.

The purpose of such a statement is to soften the disclaimer of opinion, and to avoid giving the impression of a blunt denial of responsibility by the auditors. Such statements of negative assurance are likely to be misleading; they encourage the reader to believe that the amounts shown for receivables and inventory are dependable. Furthermore, they are a violation of the AICPA reporting standards, which include a requirement that "in all cases where the auditor's name is associated with financial statements, the report should contain a clear-cut indication of the character of the auditor's examination, if any, and the degree of responsibility [the auditor] is taking."

For the auditors to report that "nothing came to their attention" that would cause them to doubt the amounts shown for receivables or inventories creates confusion as to what responsibility, if any, the auditors are assuming. If the auditors made no investigation of these items, then there was little opportunity for anything unfavorable to come to their attention. The use of negative assurance in letters for underwriters, reviews of financial statements, and compliance reports are issues taken up later in this chapter and in Chapter 19.

Comparative financial statements in audit reports

The AICPA has long supported the presentation of comparative financial statements for a series of accounting periods in annual or interim reports to shareholders. Comparative statements show changes and trends in the financial position and operating results of a company over an extended period, and thus are more useful to investors and creditors than are financial statements for a single period.

When comparative financial statements are presented by the client company, the auditors should report upon the statements of prior periods if the CPA firm has examined them. The scope paragraph should specify the periods for which the statements were examined, and the opinion paragraph of an unqualified report should be worded as follows:

> In our opinion, the financial statements referred to above present fairly the financial position of X Company as of December 31, 19x4 and December 31, 19x5 and the results of its operations and the changes in its financial position for the years then ended, in conformity with generally accepted accounting principles applied on a consistent basis.

New information or changed conditions may cause the auditors to alter their opinion on prior year financial statements. A significant uncertainty that existed in the prior year, for example, may have been resolved. The auditors may express a different type of opinion than was expressed previously providing that the reason for the change in opinion is set out in a separate paragraph in the current report.

If the client has changed auditors, the reports of both auditors are generally included in the client's annual report. The report of the predecessor auditors should bear its original date and be reissued only after the predecessor auditors have obtained a letter of representations from the current auditors regarding events or conditions that might cause the predecessor auditors to change their original opinion. The predecessor auditors should also read the current year's financial statements and the comparative financial statements for any matters that might affect the continued appropriateness of their opinion.

If the financial statements of prior comparative periods were unaudited or were examined by another CPA firm whose report is not presented, these facts should be disclosed in the applicable financial statements or in the current auditors' report. Any significant exceptions to the prior year's statements should be disclosed by the auditors in their current report.

Dating the audit report; dual dating

The audit report usually is dated as of the day the audit field work was completed, regardless of the date the report is actually issued. The completion of audit field work in most cases also signifies the completion of all important audit procedures. However, if an event subsequent to the date of field work completion, but before issuance of the audit report, requires disclosure in a note to the audited financial statements, the auditors have two options for dating their report. They may use *dual dating,* such as "February 10, 19xx, except for Note 7 as to which the date is February 22, 19xx"; or they may date the report as of the later date. If the auditors choose the second option, they should return to the client's premises and apply additional auditing procedures to disclose other subsequent events through the later date.

Reports to the SEC

Many audit clients are subject to the financial reporting requirements of the federal laws administered by the SEC. Two principal laws, the Securities Act of 1933 and the Securities Exchange Act of 1934, provide for a multitude of reports requiring audited financial statements. The most important of these reports, or *forms,* are the following:

1. Forms S-1, S-7, or S-16. These forms are the "registration statements" for clients planning to issue securities to the public.
2. Form 10. This is the principal device for registering securities for trading on a national securities exchange.
3. Form 10-K. This report is filed annually with the SEC by companies subject to the periodic reporting provisions of the Securities Acts.

The report includes audited financial statements and other detailed financial information.

4. Proxy Statement. Companies planning to solicit proxies for the election of directors at shareholders' meetings often are required to submit audited financial statements in the proxy statements mailed to shareholders.

5. Form 8-K. This is a "current report" filed for any month in which significant events occur for a company subject to the Securities Acts. If the significant event is a business combination, audited financial statements of the acquired company often are required in the current report.

The preceding points represent only a brief summary of the complex reporting requirements of the SEC. The auditors dealing with these reports should be well versed in the requirements of each form, as well as in the provisions of the SEC's *Regulation S-X*, which governs the form and content of financial statements and supporting schedules required to be filed with the various forms.

The auditors' responsibility for information accompanying audited financial statements

Audited financial statements are often included in three types of reports: (1) annual reports to shareholders, (2) reports to the SEC, and (3) auditor-submitted financial reports. Included in these documents is a considerable amount of information in addition to the audited financial statements. The auditors' responsibility for this other information depends on the type of report and the nature of the information.

FASB required supplementary information. Certain companies are required by the FASB to present *supplementary information* in their annual reports. An example of this type of information is the disclosure of the effects of changing prices required by *FASB Statement No. 33.* This supplementary information is not required for fair presentation of the financial statements in conformity with generally accepted accounting principles and may be presented in "unaudited" notes to the financial statements or in other supplementary schedules in annual reports. Therefore, the auditors need not audit the information to express an opinion on the financial statements. The auditors' responsibility for supplementary information required by the FASB is described in *SAS No. 27,* which establishes limited procedures to be applied to the information.[2] These procedures include inquiries of management regarding the appropriate presentation of the supplementary information, and comparisons of the information with audited and other data known to the auditors. The AICPA has also issued statements that

---

[2] *Statement on Auditing Standards No. 27,* "Supplementary Information Required by the Financial Accounting Standards Board," AICPA (New York, 1979).

specify specific inquiries and comparisons to be performed regarding particular supplementary information. For example, *SAS No. 28* establishes procedures to be applied to the information on the effects of changing prices required by *FASB Statement No. 33*.[3]

If required supplementary information is omitted or not appropriately presented, or the auditors are not able to complete their limited procedures, these facts should be described in an additional paragraph in the auditors' report. Since the information is not required for fair presentation of the financial statements, the inclusion of the additional paragraph does not constitute a qualification of the auditors' opinion.

Other information in client-prepared documents. Audit reports on the financial statements of large companies usually are included in an annual report to shareholders and in reports to the SEC. These annual reports contain information other than audited financial statements and required supplementary information, as, for example, discussion of the company's plans and prospects for the future. In *SAS No. 8*, "Other Information in Documents Containing Audited Financial Statements," the AICPA set forth guidelines for the independent auditors with respect to such information. The auditors should read the other information and consider whether it, or its manner of presentation, is materially inconsistent with information appearing in the audited financial statements or footnotes. If the other information is inconsistent and the auditors conclude that neither the audited financial statements nor the audit report requires revision, they should request the client to revise the other information. If the client refuses to do so, the auditors should consider such alternatives as (1) revising the audit report to describe the inconsistency, (2) withholding use of their audit report by the client, or (3) withdrawing from the engagement. The auditors should also be alert for, and discuss with the client, any other types of material misstatements included in the other information.

Information accompanying financial statements in auditor-submitted documents. The auditors often type and reproduce financial reports for their clients, particularly for small companies with few shareholders. These documents may contain information in addition to the audited financial statements and the auditors' report. The *accompanying information* generally supplements or analyzes the basic financial statements, but is not necessary for the presentation of the statements in accordance with generally accepted accounting principles. When the auditors submit a document that contains audited financial statements and accompanying information to their clients or others, they should report on all the information. If the auditors have audited the information, they should express an opinion that it is fairly stated in all material respects in relation to the financial statements

---

[3] *Statement on Auditing Standards No. 28*, "Supplementary Information on the Effects of Changing Price," AICPA (New York, 1980).

taken as a whole. Otherwise, the auditors should provide a disclaimer of opinion on the information.

Reporting on audits of personal financial statements

Financial statements for individuals have been audited and made public by a number of political candidates in recent years. Personal financial statements are also often required for credit applications and for income tax and estate tax planning. To provide guidelines for such statements, the AICPA has issued an Industry Audit Guide entitled *Audits of Personal Financial Statements.* The Guide states that the basic financial statements for individuals or families—the statement of assets and liabilities and the statement of changes in net assets—should utilize dual money columns, one for *cost* and the other for *estimated value.* The statements should reflect the accrual basis of accounting, including income tax allocation for differences between cost and tax bases, and provide, in the *estimated value* column, for accured income taxes on unrealized appreciation of assets.

An unqualified audit report for personal financial statements includes the two paragraphs of the report, expressing an opinion only on the *cost* column amounts in the financial statements. In a third paragraph, the auditors assert that they have determined that the amounts in the *estimated value* column are presented on the bases described in the statements or footnotes. The auditors do not express an opinion on the amounts shown as estimated values.

Presently under discussion by the AICPA are proposed standards that would require the presentation of estimated values only in personal financial statements. If these standards are adopted, new standards for the audit of personal financial statements must be developed.

Special reports

Although the term *special report* might be applied to all the reports we have considered other than the auditors' standard report, the AICPA, in *SAS No. 14,* "Special Reports," has applied the term only to reports on the following:

1. Financial statements prepared on a basis other than generally accepted accounting principles, such as the cash basis or a basis prescribed by regulatory authorities.
2. Specific elements of financial statements, such as rentals, royalties, profit-sharing, or income taxes.
3. Compliance with such contractual arrangements as bond indentures, or with requirements of governmental regulatory agencies.
4. Financial information presented in prescribed forms or schedules that require a prescribed form of auditors' report.

In all special reports, the independent CPAs must describe the scope of their engagement and report clearly on their findings. We shall limit our discussion to the first three types of special reports.

Basis other than generally accepted accounting principles (GAAP)

Auditors are sometimes requested to audit financial statements that are prepared on a comprehensive basis other than generally accepted accounting principles. The auditors' report should describe the basis of accounting or refer to a footnote that provides such a description. Also, the individual financial statements should be carefully labeled to avoid the implication that they present financial position and results of operations in accordance with GAAP. A common type of financial statements prepared on a basis other than GAAP is cash basis financial statements.

Reports on cash basis statements. Is an independent CPA firm justified in issuing the standard report for a small company that uses the cash basis of accounting? This question is a practical one, for many such organizations do retain CPAs and request that all work necessary be done to permit issuance of an unqualified audit report.

It is sometimes argued that if a company does not have significant amounts of inventory, plant and equipment, or accrued revenue and expenses, financial statements prepared on the basis of cash receipts and disbursements will be approximately the same as if prepared on the accrual basis. Even if we grant that cash basis statements for *some* organizations in *some* years will not differ significantly from statements based on the accrual basis, this line of argument still appears to ignore the real issue. That issue may be stated as follows: are cash basis statements prepared in accordance with *generally accepted accounting principles* as that phrase is used in the standard audit report? The answer is *no.* However, this fact does not condemn the cash basis of accounting nor prevent the auditors from expressing an opinion on cash basis statements. It is important that cash basis financial statements disclose that the reporting is being done on the cash basis.

Financial statements prepared on the cash basis of accounting do not present fairly either financial position or changes therein or operating results for the period; such statements merely summarize the cash transactions for the period. The auditors' opinion attached to cash basis statements may serve a very useful purpose, but the opinion should omit any reference to conformity with generally accepted accounting principles and should recognize the statements for what they are.

The following wording is suggested for a report on cash basis financial statements:

> We have examined the statement of assets and liabilities arising from cash transactions of X Company as of December 31, 198x and the related statement of revenue collected and expenses paid for the year then ended. Our examination was made in accordance with generally accepted audit-

ing standards and, accordingly, included such tests of the accounting records and such other auditing procedures as we considered necessary in the circumstances.

As more fully described in Note 1, the Company's policy is to prepare its financial statements on the basis of cash receipts and disbursements; consequently, the financial statements do not include certain assets, liabilities, revenue, and expenses. Accordingly, the financial statements are not intended to present financial position and results of operations in conformity with generally accepted accounting principles.

In our opinion, the financial statements referred to above present fairly the assets and liabilities arising from cash transactions of X Company as of December 31, 198x and the revenue collected and expenses paid during the year then ended, on the basis indicated in the preceding paragraph, which basis is consistent with that used in the preceding year.

The essence of the audit report is the expression of an opinion as to whether the statements fairly present what they purport to present. The wording of the footnote mentioned in the report will vary from case to case in order to give an accurate indication of the content of statements, because the cash basis or modified cash basis sometimes includes accounting records of various assets other than cash.

Specified elements, accounts, or items

Auditors may be engaged to express an opinion on specified elements, accounts, or items of a financial statement. For example, auditors are often requested by lessees to provide reports solely on their revenues. Such reports are required by the provisions of their lease agreements and are used to compute lease payments that are contingent on the lessee's revenue. In such cases, the auditors modify the standard report to indicate the information examined, the basis of accounting used, and whether the information is presented fairly on that basis. It should be noted that materiality for such engagements is determined in relation to the information presented; it is generally less than would be used in the audit of the financial statements.

SAS No. 35 provides guidance when the auditors are engaged to report on *the application of agreed-upon procedures* to specified elements, accounts, or items of a financial statement.[4] These engagements differ from those discussed above because the agreed-upon procedures are not adequate for the auditors to form an opinion on the fairness of the information. Therefore, it is very important that the *report is restricted* to informed individuals who have a clear understanding of the procedures performed. A discussion between the auditors and the individuals or their representatives concerning the

---

[4] *Statement on Auditing Standards No. 35*, "Special Reports—Applying Agreed-Upon Procedures to Specified Elements, Accounts, or Items of a Financial Statement," AICPA (New York, 1981).

extent of the procedures will generally accomplish this objective. The CPAs' report on the results of applying agreed-upon procedures should (1) indicate the information to which the procedures were applied, (2) indicate the intended distribution of the report, (3) enumerate the procedures performed, (4) state the CPAs' findings, (5) disclaim an opinion on the information, and (6) state that the report does not extend to the financial statements taken as a whole.

Compliance reports

Regulatory requirements and debt agreements often require companies to provide compliance reports prepared by their independent auditors. A common example of such reports are those prepared for bond trustees as evidence of the company's compliance with restrictions contained in the bond indenture. The maintenance of certain financial ratios and restrictions on the payment of dividends are provisions that are commonly contained in such documents. If the auditors have audited the applicable financial statements of the company, they can issue a report that provides negative assurance as to the client's compliance with the requirements.

KEY TERMS INTRODUCED OR EMPHASIZED IN CHAPTER 18

Accompanying information   Information included with the financial statements in a document submitted by the CPAs to their client or others.

Accounting change   A change in an accounting principle, in an accounting estimate, or in the reporting entity. Changes in accounting principle and in the reporting entity result in *consistency qualifications* in the auditors' standard report.

Adverse opinion   An opinion that the financial statements *do not* present fairly financial position, reuults of operations, and changes in financial position, in conformity with generally accepted accounting principles.

Disclaimer of opinion   A form of report in which the auditors state that they do not express an opinion on the financial statements.

Dual dating   Dating of audit reports with two dates: the date of completion of field work, and the date of a significant subsequent event described in a note to the financial statements. The latter date is later than the former.

Negative assurance   An improper statement sometimes included with a disclaimer of opinion, stating that nothing came to the attention of the auditors that would indicate any lack of fairness in various elements of the financial statements.

Principal auditors   Auditors who use the work and reports of other independent CPAs who have examined the financial statements of one or more subsidiaries, branches, or other segments of the principal auditors' client.

Professional Standards   A four-volume publication of the AICPA, of which volumes 3 and 4 represent a compendium of generally accepted accounting principles.

Qualified opinion   A modification of the auditor's standard report, employing an *except for* or *subject to* clause to limit the auditor's endorsement of the financial statements. A qualified opinion indicates that except for some limitation on the scope of the examination, some departure from generally accepted accounting principles, some inconsistency in the use of accounting principles, or subject to some unresolved uncertainty, the financial statements are fairly presented. An explanatory paragraph is included in the report to make clear the nature of the modification. If the qualification pertains solely to an inconsistency in application of accounting principles, this explanatory paragraph is not used.

Special report A report by independent CPAs that includes different wording from the standard audit report on financial statements. The different wording is necessary to identify the basis on which the subject financial information is prepared, or to describe the character of the engagement.

Supplementary information Information required in the financial reports of certain companies by the FASB. The information is not required for fair presentation of the financial statements in accordance with generally accepted accounting principles, but auditors must apply limited procedures to the information.

Unqualified opinion An opinion that the financial statements present fairly financial position, results of operations, and changes in financial position, in conformity with generally accepted accounting principles.

GROUP I: REVIEW QUESTIONS

18– 1. What must predecessor auditors do in order to reissue their report on comparative financial statements?

18– 2. What standard for *fairness* was established by *SAS No. 5*?

18– 3. The auditors plan to add a separate paragraph to their standard audit report to call attention to a significant subsequent event described in a note to the financial statements. Will the auditors' action result in a *qualified opinion?* Explain.

18– 4. Why are comparative financial statements preferable in financial reports?

18– 5. What is the independent auditors' obligation with respect to information in client-prepared annual reports to shareholders other than the audited financial statements?

18– 6. When auditors submit documents to their clients that contain audited financial statements, what are their responsibilities concerning information that accompanies the financial statements?

18– 7. Compare the audit report issued on cash basis financial statements with the auditors' standard report.

18– 8. What is the function of notes to financial statements?

18– 9. Your client refuses to include a statement of changes in financial position among the financial statements for the current year. Would this prevent you from issuing an unqualified audit report?

18– 10. Describe the reports containing audited financial statements customarily filed by a company subject to the reporting requirements of the SEC.

18– 11. How do *special reports* differ from the auditors' standard report?

18– 12. Wade Company has been your audit client for the last several years. At the beginning of 1985 the company changed its method of inventory valuation from average cost to LIFO. The change, which had been under consideration for some time, was in your opinion a logical and proper step for the company to take. What effect, if any, would this change have upon your standard audit report for the year ended December 31, 1985?

18–13. List several factors that would prevent the issuance of an unqualified audit report.

18–14. In the annual examination of Powell Company the auditors did not confirm accounts receivable from customers, at the client's request. During the course of the examination, virtually all the accounts receivable outstanding at the balance sheet date were collected and the auditors examined the checks and remittance advices received from customers. Under these circumstances, can the auditors issue an unqualified audit report? Explain.

18–15. What procedures do auditors apply to supplementary information required by the FASB?

18–16. What are compliance reports?

GROUP II: QUESTIONS REQUIRING ANALYSIS

18–17. Select the best answer for each of the following and explain fully the reason for your selection.

a. The fourth reporting standard requires the auditors' report to either contain an expression of opinion regarding the financial statements, taken as a whole, or an assertion to the effect that an opinion cannot be expressed. The objective of the fourth standard is to prevent

(1) The CPAs from reporting on one basic financial statement and not the others.

(2) The CPAs from expressing different opinions on each of the basic financial statements.

(3) Misinterpretations regarding the degree of responsibility the auditors are assuming.

(4) Management from reducing its final responsibility for the basic financial statements.

b. After performing all necessary procedures the predecessor auditors reissue a prior-period report on financial statements at the request of the client without revising the original wording. The predecessor auditors should

(1) Delete the date of the report.

(2) Dual-date the report.

(3) Use the reissue date.

(4) Use the date of the previous report.

c. For which of the following accounting changes would an auditors' report normally *not* contain a consistency qualification?

(1) A change in principle that does not result in noncomparable statements because the previous year's statements are not presented.

(2) A change to a principle required by a new FASB pronouncement.

(3) A change in principle properly reported by restating the financial statements of prior years.

(4) A change in an accounting estimate.

d. If the auditors wish to issue a qualified opinion because the financial statements include a departure from generally accepted accounting principles, the auditors' report should have an explanatory paragraph referring to a footnote that discloses the principal effects of the subject matter of the qualification. The qualification should be referred to in the opinion paragraph by using language such as

(1) "With the exception of."

(2) "When read in conjunction with the footnotes."

(3) "With the foregoing explanation."

(4) "Subject to the departure explained in the footnotes." (AICPA, adapted)

18–18. While performing your audit of Williams Paper Company, you discover evidence that indicates that Williams may not have the ability to continue as a going concern.

Required:

a. Discuss the types of information that may indicate a going concern problem.

b. Discuss the factors that might mitigate evidence that is contrary to the assumption of continued existence.

c. Explain the auditors reporting obligation in such situations.

18–19. What type of audit report (unqualified opinion, qualified opinion, adverse opinion, disclaimer of opinion) should the auditors *generally* issue in each of the following situations? Explain.

a. Client-imposed restrictions limit significantly the scope of the auditors' procedures.

b. The auditors decide to make reference to the report of another CPA firm as a basis, in part, for the auditors' opinion.

c. The auditors believe that the financial statements have been stated in conformity with generally accepted accounting principles in all respects other than those contingent on the outcome of a material uncertainty.

18–20. The following statement is representative of attitudes and opinions sometimes encountered by CPAs in their professional practices: "It is important to read the footnotes to financial statements, even though they often are presented in technical language and are incomprehensible. The auditors may reduce their exposure to third-party liability by stating something in the footnotes that contradicts completely what they have presented in the balance sheet or income statement."

Required:

Evaluate the above statement and indicate—

a. Areas of agreement with the statement, if any.

b. Areas of misconception, incompleteness or fallacious reasoning included in the statement, if any. (AICPA, adapted)

18–21. Criticize the following audit report:

June 2, 1985

Mr. Richard Thomas
Thomas Enterprises

We have examined the accounts and records of Thomas Enterprises (a sole proprietorship) at April 30, 1985, and present herewith a statement of financial position as at April 30, 1985, and the related statement of income for the year then ended.

Our examination included such tests as we considered necessary to generally satisfy ourselves as to the reasonableness of the aforementioned statements. However, we did not perform all tests required by statute so that we might issue an independent accountants' opinion.

Farley, Jackson & Co., CPAs

18–22. During your examination of the financial statements of Raymond Company for the current year, you discover that the company has included in its income statement the material cumulative effect, net of applicable income taxes, of a change in depreciation expense for prior years resulting from an increase during the current year in the estimated service lives of plant assets. Will you be able to express an unqualified opinion on Raymond Company's financial statements for the current year? Explain.

18–23. Comment upon the following: "The auditors' standard report was adopted substantially in its present form over 40 years ago. Considerable accounting literature has been devoted to the wording used in it, and its intended meaning is fairly well understood by the accounting profession and by the more sophisticated users of auditors' reports. However, despite continuous efforts on the part of the profession to educate the vast mass of less sophisticated users—those who consciously, but somewhat innocently, rely on the reports—the auditors' role still seems to be misunderstood. Most users think of the financial statements themselves, and probably even more so the notes, as comprising part of the auditors' report rather than being the representations of management. The report itself does little to dispel this notion or to make clear that the auditors are only expressing their opinion on management's report."

18–24. Upon completion of the examination of the client's financial statements the CPA firm, in its report, must either express an opinion or disclaim an opinion on the financial statements. The opinion may be unqualified, qualified, or adverse.

Required:
a. Under what general conditions may a CPA firm express an unqualified opinion on the client's financial statements?
b. Define and distinguish among (1) a qualified opinion, (2) an adverse opinion, and (3) a disclaimer of opinion on the statements. (AICPA, adapted)

18–25. Many CPA firms are engaged to report on specified elements, accounts, and items of financial statements.

Required:

a. Discuss the two types of reports that may be provided for specified elements, accounts, and items of financial statements.

b. Why should reports on the application of agreed-upon procedures to information be restricted as to its distribution?

18–26. What type of audit report would be issued in each of the following cases? Justify your choice.

a. Bowles Company is engaged in a hazardous trade and cannot obtain insurance coverage from any source. A material portion of the company's assets could be destroyed by a serious accident. The company has an excellent safety record and has never suffered a catastrophe.

b. Draves Company owns substantial properties, which have appreciated significantly in value since the date of purchase. The properties were appraised and are reported in the balance sheet at the appraised values with full disclosure. The CPA firm believes that the values reported in the balance sheet are reasonable.

c. The CPA firm is examining the financial statements that are to be included in the annual report to the stockholders of Eagle Company, a regulated company. Eagle's financial statements are prepared as prescribed by a regulatory agency of the U.S. government, and some items are not presented in accordance with generally accepted accounting principles. The amounts involved are somewhat material and are adequately disclosed in footnotes to the financial statements.

d. London Company has material investments in stocks of subsidiary companies. Stocks of the subsidiary companies are not actively traded in the market, and the CPA firm's engagement does not extend to any subsidiary company. The CPA firm is able to determine that all investments are carried at original cost, and the auditors have no reason to suspect that the amounts are not stated fairly.

e. Slade Company has material investments in stocks of subsidiary companies. Stocks of the subsidiary companies are actively traded in the market, but the CPA firm's engagement does not extend to any subsidiary company. Management insists that all investments shall be carried at original costs, and the CPA firm is satisfied that the original costs are fairly stated. The CPA firm believes that the client will never ultimately realize a substantial portion of the investments, and the client has fully disclosed the facts in footnotes to the financial statements. (AICPA, adapted)

18–27. Rose & Co., CPAs, has satisfactorily completed the examination of the financial statements of Bale & Booster, a partnership, for the year ended December 31, 1985. The financial statements that were prepared on the entity's income tax (cash) basis include footnotes indicating that the partnership was involved in continuing litigation of material amounts relating to alleged infringement of a competitor's patent. The amount of damages, if any, resulting from this litigation could not be determined at the time of completion of the engagement. The prior years' financial statements were not presented.

Required:

Based upon the information presented, prepare an auditor's report that includes appropriate explanatory disclosure of significant facts. (AICPA, adapted)

18–28.   Lando Corporation is a domestic company with two wholly owned domestic subsidiaries. Michaels, CPA, has been engaged to examine the financial statements of the parent company and one of the subsidiaries and to act as the principal auditor. Thomas, CPA, has examined the financial statements of the other subsidiary whose operations are material in relation to the consolidated financial statements.

The work performed by Michaels is sufficient for Michaels to serve as the principal auditor and to report as such on the financial statements. Michaels has not yet decided whether to make reference to the examination made by Thomas.

Required:

a.   There are certain required audit procedures that Michaels should perform with respect to the examination made by Thomas, whether or not Michaels decides to make reference to Thomas in Michaels' auditor's report. What are these audit procedures?

b.   What are the reporting requirements with which Michaels must comply if Michaels decides to name Thomas and make reference to the examination of Thomas? (AICPA, adapted)

GROUP III: PROBLEMS

18–29.   Roscoe, CPA, has completed the examination of the financial statements of Excelsior Corporation as of and for the year ended December 31, 1985. Roscoe also examined and reported on the Excelsior financial statements for the prior year. Roscoe drafted the following report for 1985.

March 15, 1986

We have examined the balance sheet and statements of income and retained earnings of Excelsior Corporation as of December 31, 1985. Our examination was made in accordance with generally accepted accounting standards and accordingly included such tests of the accounting records as we considered necessary in the circumstances.

In our opinion, the above mentioned financial statements are accurately prepared and fairly presented in accordance with generally accepted accounting principles in effect at December 31, 1985.

Roscoe, CPA
(Signed)

Other information:

(1)   Excelsior is presenting comparative financial statements.

(2)   Excelsior does not wish to present a statement of changes in financial position for either year.

(3)   During 1985 Excelsior changed its method of accounting for long-term construction contracts and properly reflected the effect of the change in the current year's financial statements and restated the prior year's statements. Roscoe is satisfied with Excelsior's

justification for making the change. The change is discussed in footnote 12.

(4) Roscoe was unable to perform normal accounts receivable confirmation procedures, but alternate procedures were used to satisfy Roscoe as to the validity of the receivables.

(5) Excelsior Corporation is the defendant in litigation, the outcome of which is highly uncertain. If the case is settled in favor of the plaintiff, Excelsior will be required to pay a substantial amount of cash that might require the sale of certain fixed assets. The litigation and the possible effects have been properly disclosed in footnote 11.

(6) Excelsior issued debentures on January 31, 1984, in the amount of $10 million. The funds obtained from the issuance were used to finance the expansion of plant facilities. The debenture agreement restricts the payment of future cash dividends to earnings after December 31, 1990. Excelsior declined to disclose this essential data in the footnotes to the financial statements.

Required:

Consider all facts given, and rewrite the auditors' report in acceptable and complete format, incorporating any necessary departures from the standard report.

Do not discuss the draft of Roscoe's report, but identify and explain any items included in *"Other information"* that need not be part of the auditors' report. (AICPA, adapted)

18–30. Upon completion of all field work on September 23, 1985, the following standard report was rendered by Timothy Ross to the directors of Rancho Corporation.

To the Directors of
Rancho Corporation:

We have examined the balance sheet and the related statement of income and retained earnings of Rancho Corporation as of July 31, 1985. In accordance with your instructions, a complete audit was conducted.

In many respects, this was an unusual year for Rancho Corporation. The weakening of the economy in the early part of the year and the strike of plant employees in the summer of 1985 led to a decline in sales and net income. After making several tests of sales records, nothing came to our attention that would indicate that sales have not been properly recorded.

In our opinion, with the explanation given above and with the exception of some minor errors that are considered immaterial, the financial statements referred to above present fairly the financial position of Rancho Corporation at July 31, 1985 and the results of its operations for the year then ended, in conformity with pronouncements of the Accounting Principles Board and the Financial Accounting Standards Board applied consistently throughout the period.

Timothy Ross, CPA
September 23, 1985

Required:

List and explain deficiencies and omissions in the auditors' report. The type of opinion (unqualified, qualified, adverse, or disclaimer) is of no consequence and need not be discussed.

Organize your answer sheet by paragraph (scope, explanatory, and opinion) of the auditor's report. (AICPA, adapted)

18–31. Your client, Quaid Company, requests your assistance in rewriting the footnote presented below, to make it clearer and more concise.

> *Note 6.* The indenture relating to the long-term debt contains certain provisions regarding the maintenance of working capital, the payment of dividends, and the purchase of the company's capital stock. The most restrictive of these provisions requires that: (*a*) working capital will be maintained at not less than \$4,500,000; (*b*) the company cannot pay cash dividends or purchase its capital stock, if after it has done so, working capital is less than \$5,000,000; and (*c*) cash dividends paid since January 1, 1981, plus the excess of capital stock purchased over the proceeds of stock sold during the same period, cannot exceed 70 percent of net earnings (since January 1, 1981) plus \$250,000. At December 31, 1985, \$2,441,291 of retained earnings was available for the payment of dividends under this last provision, as follows:

Net earnings since January 1, 1981	\$5,478,127
70 percent of above	\$3,834,688
Additional amount available under indenture	250,000
	4,084,688
Cash dividends paid since January 1, 1981	1,643,397
Retained earnings available	\$2,441,291

Required:
Rewrite the footnote in accordance with your client's instructions.

18–32. Jiffy Clerical Services is a corporation that furnishes temporary office help to its customers. Billings are rendered monthly based on predetermined hourly rates. You have examined the company's financial statements for several years. Following is an abbreviated statement of assets and liabilities on the modified cash basis as of December 31, 19—.

Assets:

Cash	\$20,000
Advances to employees	1,000
Equipment and autos, less accumulated depreciation	25,000
Total assets	\$46,000

Liabilities:

Employees' payroll taxes withheld	\$ 8,000
Bank loan payable	10,000
Estimated income taxes on cash basis profits....................	10,000
Total liabilities	\$28,000
Net assets	\$18,000

Represented by:

Common stock	\$ 3,000
Cash profits retained in the business	15,000
	\$18,000

Required:

a. Prepare the report you would issue covering the statement of assets and liabilities as of December 31, 19—, as summarized above, and the related statement of cash revenue and expenses for the year ended that date.

b. Briefly discuss and justify your modifications of the conventional short-form audit report on accrual basis statements.

18–33. Global Company, an audit client of your CPA firm, has several wholly owned subsidiaries in foreign countries that are audited by other independent auditors in those countries. The financial statements of all subsidiaries were consolidated with the financial statements of the parent company, and the foreign auditors' reports were furnished to your CPA firm.

You are now preparing your firm's opinion on the consolidated balance sheet and statements of income, retained earnings, and changes in financial position for the year ended June 30, 19—. These statements were prepared on a comparative basis with those of last year.

Required:

a. How would you evaluate and accept the independence and professional reputations of the foreign auditors?

b. Under what circumstances may the principal auditors assume responsibility for the work of another CPA firm to the same extent as if they had performed the work themselves?

c. Assume that both last year and this year you were willing to utilize the reports of the other independent auditors in expressing your opinion on the consolidated financial statements, but were unwilling to take full responsibility for performance of the work underlying their opinions. Assuming your examination of the parent company's financial statements would allow you to render an unqualified opinion, prepare (1) the necessary disclosure to be contained in the scope paragraph and (2) the complete opinion paragraph of your firm's audit report.

d. What modification(s), if any, would be necessary in your firm's report if the financial statements for the prior year were unaudited? (AICPA, adapted)

18–34. Various types of accounting changes can affect the second reporting standard of the generally accepted auditing standards. This standard reads, "The report shall state whether such principles have been consistently observed in the current period in relation to the preceding period."

Assume that the following list describes changes that have a material effect on a client's financial statements for the current year.

(1) A change from the completed-contract method to the percentage-of-completion method of accounting for long-term construction-type contracts.

(2) A change in the estimated service lives of previously recorded plant assets based on newly acquired information.

(3) Correction of a mathematical error in inventory pricing made in a prior period.

(4) A change from prime costing to full absorption costing for inventory valuation.

(5) A change from presentation of financial statements of individual companies to presentation of consolidated financial statements.

(6) A change from deferring and amortizing preproduction costs to recording such costs as an expense when incurred because future benefits of the costs have become doubtful. The new accounting method was adopted in recognition of the change in estimated future benefits.

(7) A change to including the employer share of FICA taxes as "Retirement benefits" on the income statement from including it with "Other taxes."

(8) A change from the FIFO method of inventory pricing to the LIFO method of inventory pricing.

Required:

Identify the type of change that is described in each item above; state whether any modification is required in the auditors' report as it relates to the second standard of reporting; and state whether the prior years' financial statements should be restated when presented in comparative form with the current year's statements. Organize your answer sheet as shown below.

For example, a change from the Lifo method of inventory pricing to Fifo method of inventory pricing would appear as shown.

Item no.	Type of change	Should auditors' report be modified?	Should prior year's statements be restated?
Example	An accounting change from one generally accepted accounting principle to another generally accepted accounting principle.	Yes	Yes

(AICPA, adapted)

18–35. Nancy Miller, CPA, has completed field work for her examination of the financial statements of Nickles Company for the year ended March 31, 1985 and now is preparing her audit report. Presented below are four independent and unrelated assumptions concerning this examination:

Assumption 1

The CPA was engaged on April 15, 1985 to examine the financial statements for the year ended March 31, 1985 and was not present to observe the taking of the physical inventory of March 31, 1985. Her alternative procedures included examination of shipping and receiving documents with regard to transactions during the year under review, as well as transactions since the year end; extensive review of the inventory-count sheets; and discussion of the physical inventory procedures with responsible company personnel. She has also satisfied herself as to inventory valuation and consistency in valuation method. Inventory quantities are determined solely by means of physical count. (*Note:* Assume that the CPA properly is relying upon the examination of another auditor with respect to the beginning inventory.)

Assumption 2

During the year ended March 31, 1985, Nickles's new Pollution Control System Division incurred developmental costs that are material to the company's financial statements and are presented in the balance sheet as deferred research and development costs. The pollution-control equipment developed thus far has performed well in controlled laboratory simulations, but it has not been tested in a practical setting. Nickles cannot afford to proceed further with this project, but in management's opinion sufficient governmental funds can be obtained to fully develop functioning equipment that can be sold at a price that will permit recovery of these costs. There is support for management's optimism, but no commitment of governmental funds has been received to date. Nickles' board of directors refuses to write off development costs applicable to the Pollution Control Systems division.

Assumption 3

As of April 1, 1985, Nickles has an unused balance of $1,378,000 of federal income tax net operating loss carryover that will expire at the end of the company's fiscal years as follows: $432,000 in 1986, $870,000 in 1987, and $76,000 in 1988. Nickles's management expects that the company will have enough taxable income to use the loss carryover before it expires.

Assumption 4

On February 28, 1985, Nickles paid cash for all of the outstanding stock of Ashworth, Inc., a small manufacturer. The business combination was consummated as of that date and has been accounted for as a purchase.

Required:

For each assumption described above discuss:

a.   In detail, the appropriate disclosures, if any, in the financial statements and accompanying footnotes.
b.   The effect, if any, on the audit report. For this requirement assume that Nickles makes the appropriate disclosures, if any, recommended in "*a*."

Note: Complete your discussion of each assumption (both "*a*" and "*b*") before beginning discussion of the next assumption. In considering each independent assumption, assume that the other three situations did not occur. Organize your answer sheet as follows:

Assumption number	(a) Financial statements and footnotes	(b) Audit report

(AICPA, adapted)

18–36. Presented below are three independent, unrelated audit or other reports. The corporation being reported on, in each case, is profit oriented and publishes general-purpose financial statements for distribution to owners, creditors, potential investors, and the general public. Each of the following reports contains deficiencies.

Report I

We have examined the consolidated balance sheet of Belasco Corporation and subsidiaries as of December 31, 1985 and the related consolidated statements of income, retained earnings and changes in financial position for the year then ended. Our examination was made in accordance with generally accepted auditing standards and, accordingly, included such tests of the accounting records and such other auditing procedures as we considered necessary in the circumstances. We did not examine the financial statements of Seidel Company, a major consolidated subsidiary. These statements were examined by other auditors whose report thereon has been furnished to us, and our opinion expressed herein, insofar as it relates to Seidel Company, is based solely upon the report of the other auditors.

In our opinion, except for the report of the other auditors, the financial statements referred to above present fairly the financial position of Belasco Corporation and subsidiaries at December 31, 1985 and the results of its operations and the changes in its financial position for the year then ended, in conformity with generally accepted accounting principles applied on a basis consistent with that of the preceding year.

Report II

The accompanying balance sheet of Jones Corporation as of December 31, 1985 and the related statements of income, retained earnings and changes in financial position for the year then ended were not audited by us; however, we confirmed cash in the bank and performed a general review of the statements.

During our engagement, nothing came to our attention to indicate that the financial statements referred to above do not present fairly the financial position of Jones Corporation at December 31, 1985 and the results of its operations and the changes in its financial position for the year then ended, in conformity with generally accepted accounting principles applied on a basis consistent with that of the preceding year; however, we do not express an opinion on them.

Report III

I made my examination in accordance with generally accepted auditing standards. However, I am not independent with respect to Mavis Corporation because my wife owns 5 percent of the outstanding common stock of the company. The accompanying balance sheet as of December 31, 1985 and the related statements of income, retained earnings, and changes in financial position for the year then ended were not audited by me; accordingly, I do not express an opinion on them.

Required:

For each report describe the reporting deficiencies, explain the reasons therefor, and briefly discuss how the report should be corrected. Each report should be considered separately. When discussing one report, ignore the other two. **Do not discuss the addressee, signatures, and date. Also do not rewrite any of the reports.** Organize your answer sheet as follows:

Report no.	Deficiency	Reason	Correction

(AICPA, adapted)

19

Other reports by CPAs

Reports issued by CPAs are not limited to audit opinions; CPAs also issue reports relating to a variety of accounting services. When these accounting services involve the compilation or review of financial statements, the term *unaudited financial statements* is used. The word *unaudited* emphasizes the fact that a CPA's name may be associated with financial statements in some manner even though no audit has been performed. For publicly owned companies, a common example is a report on the auditors' review of quarterly or other interim financial statements. For smaller companies with stock not publicly owned, CPAs often compile or review the financial statements and therefore issue reports that identify these statements as *unaudited financial statements*.

Compilation and review services involve much less work than an audit. In fact, compiling financial statements involves little more than the preparation of financial statements from the books and records of the company. No procedures are performed by the CPAs to substantiate the fairness of the financial statement balances.

CPAs also render services and issue reports that do not involve financial statements. *Letters for underwriters* report the results of work done by CPA firms to aid securities underwriters in their investigations of registration statements required under the Securities Act of 1933. Accountants also may be called upon to review and report on a *financial forecast*. These reports communicate the results of an extensive

623

investigation of the assumptions underlying the forecast. When CPAs are requested to report on *internal accounting control*, the report may take various forms depending on the scope and specific objectives of the engagement.

An operational audit, as indicated in Chapter 1, is an examination of a department or other unit of a business or governmental organization to measure the efficiency of operations. Independent accountants occasionally are engaged to perform operational audits and report the results to management. However, such audits more commonly are performed by governmental and internal auditors.

Unaudited financial statements

The standards applicable to engagements involving unaudited financial statements vary depending on whether the client is a public or a nonpublic company. The Auditing Standards Board issues standards that apply to engagements involving the unaudited financial statements of *companies with stock traded on an organized exchange* or *companies in the process of registering their securities for sale* (public companies). Standards for the compilation and review of the financial statements of *nonpublic companies* are issued by the Accounting and Review Services Committee.

Disclaimers on unaudited financial statements of public companies

Certified public accountants may draft or otherwise be associated with the financial statements of public companies, without performing an examination in accordance with generally accepted auditing standards. CPAs are considered to be *associated* with financial statements when they consent to the use of their name in a document containing the statements, or when they prepare or assist in preparing the statements.

SAS No. 26, "Association with Financial Statements," provides the following guidelines for CPAs associated with the unaudited financial statements of public companies:

1. CPAs have no responsibility for applying any auditing procedures to unaudited financial statements, except to read the statements for obvious material errors.

2. When CPAs are associated with unaudited financial statements, a disclaimer of opinion should accompany the statements, and each page of the financial statements should be clearly marked as "unaudited." Suggested wording for the disclaimer is as follows:

> The accompanying balance sheet of XYZ Corporation as of December 31, 19x1 and the related statements of income, retained earnings, and

changes in financial position for the year then ended were not audited by us and, accordingly, we do not express an opinion on them.

3. If the CPAs know that unaudited financial statements are not in accordance with generally accepted accounting principles, or do not contain adequate informative disclosures, they should insist upon appropriate revision or should state their reservations in the disclaimer of opinion. If necessary, the CPAs should withdraw from the engagement and refuse to be associated with the financial statements.

CPA firm not independent.   Although a CPA firm that is not independent of its client cannot perform an audit, it may be associated with *unaudited* financial statements of that client. In such cases, the CPAs must issue a special disclaimer of opinion, which discloses the lack of independence. The AICPA has suggested the following language for the independence disclaimer.

> We are not independent with respect to XYZ Company, and the accompanying balance sheet as of December 31, 19x1, and the related statements of income, retained earnings, and changes in financial position for the year then ended were not audited by us and, accordingly, we do not express an opinion on them.

Notice that the accountant's report does not explain why the CPA firm is not independent of the client. The Auditing Standards Board believes it would be confusing to users of the report if these reasons were spelled out.

Reports on unaudited interim financial data

In *Accounting Series Release No. 177*, the SEC required disclosure of selected interim (quarterly) financial data in a note to the annual financial statements of public companies.[1] The commission permits the required note to be labeled unaudited, even though it is a part of the notes to audited financial statements. Also, in *ASR No. 177*, the SEC urged companies it supervises to have independent CPAs review the unaudited interim financial data reported in Form 10-Q, which is filed with the Commission within 45 days following the end of each of a company's first three fiscal quarters.

Guidance for CPAs engaged to review unaudited financial data is contained in *SAS No. 36*, "Review of Interim Financial Information." The principal procedures for a review of interim financial data include inquiries of client-company officers and other executives regarding the accounting and internal control system; analytical review of the interim financial data by reference to prior interim information, budgets, and

---

[1] Currently, this information also may be presented as supplementary information anywhere within the financial report.

other data; reading of minutes of meetings of stockholders, board of directors, and committees of the board; and obtaining written representations from management regarding the presentation and completeness of the interim financial data. *SAS No. 36* provides the following format for reporting the results of the review:

> We have made a review of the balance sheet and related statements of income, retained earnings, and changes in financial position of ABC Company and consolidated subsidiaries as of September 30, 19x1 and for the three-month and nine-month periods then ended, in accordance with standards established by the American Institute of Certified Public Accountants.
>
> A review of interim financial information consists principally of obtaining an understanding of the system for the preparation of interim financial information, applying analytical review procedures to financial data, and making inquiries of persons responsible for financial and accounting matters. It is substantially less in scope than an examination in accordance with generally accepted auditing standards, the objective of which is the expression of an opinion regarding the financial statements taken as a whole. Accordingly, we do not express such an opinion.
>
> Based on our review, we are not aware of any material modifications that should be made to the accompanying financial statements for them to be in conformity with generally accepted accounting principles.

Each page of the interim financial data should be clearly marked as "unaudited" and the report date should be the date of completion of the review. Interim review reports should be modified to describe a departure from generally accepted accounting principles.

Compilation and review for nonpublic companies

Corporations that do not offer their securities for sale to the public (nonpublic companies) are not required to have independent audits of their financial statements. No SEC requirement exists to mandate an annual audit for them. Bankers and other creditors may be willing to provide capital on the basis of unaudited financial statements, especially if a CPA is involved to some extent in the compilation or review of the financial statements. The argument against a full-scale audit is one of cost versus benefits. However, even companies for which an audit would not be cost-efficient may want to utilize the services of a CPA. To be more responsive to the needs of these prospective clients, the AICPA established the Accounting and Review Services Committee, a senior technical committee that issues *Statements on Standards for Accounting and Review Services (SSARS)*.

Accounting and review services are not auditing services; they do not involve the performance of observation, confirmation, or other procedures to corroborate the financial statements. The need to establish a clear understanding with the client concerning the nature of such services was illustrated by the outcome of the *1136 Tenants Corporation* case (discussed in Chapter 3). CPAs must avoid the implication that they are performing audits when they are engaged to perform accounting or review services. Accordingly, it is very important that the CPAs prepare an *engagement letter* clearly specifying the nature of the services to be provided and the degree of responsibility the CPAs are assuming. The letter should include a discussion of the limitations of the services and a description of the report to be issued.

Compilation services for nonpublic companies. A *compilation* involves the preparation of financial statements from the accounting records and other representations of management. The CPAs are not obligated to make inquiries or to perform other procedures to corroborate or review the information. Consequently, *no assurance is expressed* by the CPAs regarding the fairness of the financial statements. A compilation report includes a disclaimer of opinion. However, CPAs do not accept patently unreasonable information. They evaluate the financial information in light of their knowledge of the company's transactions and accounting system, and the accounting principles and practices of the company's industry—knowledge that must be acquired to perform a compilation. They reject any information that appears to be incorrect, incomplete, or otherwise unsatisfactory. Also, compiled financial statements are read by the CPAs for appropriate form and obvious material errors.

Financial statements compiled by a CPA firm should be accompanied by the following standard report:

> The accompanying balance sheet of XYZ Company as of December 31, 19xx and the related statements of income, retained earnings, and changes in financial position for the year then ended have been compiled by us.
>
> A compilation is limited to presenting in the form of financial statements information that is the representation of management (owners). We have not audited or reviewed the accompanying financial statements and, accordingly, do not express an opinion or any other form of assurance on them.

The date of the accountant's report is the date the compilation is completed, and each page of the financial statements should be marked "See Accountants' Compilation Report."

A nonpublic company may request CPAs to compile financial statements that omit substantially all of the disclosures required by generally accepted accounting principles. Such statements are generally prepared for internal use only—that is, for the sole use of the management of the company. CPAs may compile such financial statements provided the omission is clearly indicated in the CPAs' report. In such situations, the accountants should add the following last paragraph to their compilation report:

> Management has elected to omit substantially all of the disclosures (and the statement of changes in financial position) required by generally

accepted accounting principles. If the omitted disclosures were included in the financial statements, they might influence the user's conclusions about the company's financial position, results of operations, and changes in financial position. Accordingly, these financial statements are not designed for those who are not informed about such matters.

Compilations when the CPAs are not independent.   Since compilation reports are not intended to provide any assurance as to the fairness of the financial statements, CPAs may perform the services even when they are not independent of the client. The accountants should indicate their lack of independence by adding the following last paragraph to their compilation report:

We are not independent with respect to XYZ Company.

Review services for nonpublic companies.   A review of financial statements involves the performance of inquiry and analytical review procedures. This work provides the accountants with a reasonable basis for expressing *limited assurance* that the statements require no material modification to be in accordance with generally accepted accounting principles. The objective of a review of financial statements differs significantly from the objective of an audit. When performing a review, the CPAs *do not* evaluate internal accounting control or obtain other corroborative evidence necessary to express an opinion on the financial statements. Therefore, the level of assurance that the financial statements conform to generally accepted accounting principles is limited; the extent of the assurance provided falls between the little or no assurance provided by a compilation and the reasonably high degree of assurance provided by an audit.

To evaluate the responses to their inquiries and the results of other review procedures, the independent accountants should develop a knowledge of the accounting principles and practices in the client's industry and a thorough understanding of the client's business. The CPAs' understanding of the client's business should include a general understanding of the company's organization, its methods of operations, and the nature of its financial statement accounts.

The procedures for a review of the financial statements of nonpublic companies are similar to those performed in a review of the *interim* financial statements of a public company. These procedures include inquiries of officers and other executives; analytical review of the financial data by reference to prior financial statements, budgets, and other operating data; and inquiries concerning the actions taken in meetings of stockholders, board of directors, and committees of the board. The CPAs' inquiries should focus on whether the financial statements are in accordance with generally accepted accounting principles consistently applied, and also on changes in business activities and significant subsequent events. Additional procedures should be performed if the accountants become aware that information may be incorrect, incomplete, or otherwise unsatisfactory. The CPAs should perform these procedures to the extent considered necessary to provide limited assurance that there are no material modifications that should be made to the statements.

The accountants' standard report on a review of a company's financial statements reads as follows:

> We have reviewed the accompanying balance sheet of XYZ Company as of December 31, 19xx, and the related statements of income, retained earnings, and changes in financial position for the year then ended, in accordance with standards established by the American Institute of Certified Public Accountants. All information included in these financial statements is the representation of the management of XYZ Company.
>
> A review consists principally of inquiries of company personnel and analytical procedures applied to financial data. It is substantially less in scope than an examination in accordance with generally accepted auditing standards, the objective of which is the expression of an opinion regarding the financial statements taken as a whole. Accordingly, we do not express such an opinion.
>
> Based on our review, we are not aware of any material modifications that should be made to the accompanying financial statements in order for them to be in conformity with generally accepted accounting principles.

The date of completion of the review procedures should be used as the date of the report, and each page of the financial statements should be labeled "See Accountants' Review Report."

Departures from generally accepted accounting principles. Compilation and review reports are not altered in cases involving a lack of consistent application of generally accepted accounting principles or the existence of major uncertainties. However, a modification of the report is required when the accountants are aware of a material departure from generally accepted accounting principles. The departure and its effects on the financial statements, if known, is described in a separate paragraph of the compilation or review report. The following is an example of a report paragraph that discusses a departure from generally accepted accounting principles:

> As disclosed in note 5 to the financial statements, generally accepted accounting principles require that land be stated at cost. Management has informed us that the company has stated its land at appraised value and that, if generally accepted accounting principles had been followed, the land account and stockholders' equity would have been decreased by $500,000.

Reports on comparative financial statements. As with audited financial statements, accountants who have compiled or reviewed comparative financial statements are obligated to report on these statements. In many cases, the accountants write one report covering the current year's financial statement and the financial statements presented for comparative purposes. However, if the accountants are compiling the current year's financial statements, they should not update a review report on prior financial statements. To do so would imply that the CPAs have applied review procedures up to the date of the current report. Such situations call for the accountants to reissue their prior report carrying its original date with an indication that review procedures were not extended beyond that date, or include the following reference to the prior report in the current report:

> The accompanying 19x1 financial statements of XYZ Company were previously reviewed by us and our report dated March 1, 19x2 stated that we were not aware of any material modifications that should be made to those statements in order for them to be in conformity with generally accepted accounting principles. We have not performed any procedures in connection with that review engagement after the date of our report on the 19x1 financial statements.

A reference similar to the one above should also be included in the current report when another CPA firm, whose report is not presented, compiled or reviewed the comparative financial statements.

Letters for underwriters

Investment banking firms that underwrite a securities issue often request independent auditors who examined the financial statements and schedules in the registration statement to issue a letter for the underwriters. This letter, commonly called a *comfort letter,* usually covers the following:

1. A statement as to the auditors' independence.
2. An opinion as to whether the audited financial statements and schedules in the registration statement comply in all material respects with the applicable requirements of the Securities Act of 1933 and related rules of the SEC.
3. Negative assurances as to whether any *unaudited* financial statements or condensed financial statements included in the registration statement comply with the 1933 Act and SEC pronouncements, and are fairly presented on a basis consistent with the *audited* financial statements.
4. Negative assurances as to whether during a specified period following the date of the latest financial statements in the registration statement there has been any change in long-term debt or capital stock, or any decrease in other specified financial statement items.

Comfort letters help the underwriters in fulfilling their obligation to perform a reasonable investigation of the securities registration statement. No definitive criteria exist for the underwriters' "reasonable investigation." Therefore, the underwriters should approve the adequacy of the CPAs' procedures serving as a basis for the comfort letter. The independent auditors engaged in writing these letters should consult *SAS No. 38, "Letters for Underwriters,"* which contains guidelines and illustrations of typical letters.

Reviews of financial forecasts

Securities analysts are giving increasing attention to financial forecasts by corporations. A related trend is the inclusion of forecasts in annual reports and prospectuses describing new issues of securities. Users of these forward-looking data are requesting assurances that the forecasts are not overly optimistic statements of expected future results. Consequently, the AICPA has issued a *Guide for a Review of a Financial Forecast*, which indicates the CPA's responsibility in such engagements.

A financial forecast is defined as the most probable future financial position, results of operations, and changes in financial position for an entity. The objective of a review of such information is to provide the CPAs with a belief that (1) the forecast is presented in accordance with AICPA guidelines for presentation of a financial forecast and (2) that the assumptions provide a reasonable basis for the forecast.

Before issuing a review report, the CPAs perform an extensive examination of the underlying assumptions to satisfy themselves that management has identified all key assumptions and that the assumptions are suitably supported. The reasonableness of all significant assumptions must be questioned by inspecting supporting data, making inquiries of management, and performing analytical review procedures.

Accountants can make an objective verification of past earnings and vouch for their accuracy; they cannot read the future and, therefore, their report must not indicate that they vouch for the accuracy of a forecast of future results. Rule 201 of the AICPA *Code of Professional Ethics* specifically prohibits such indications. Instead, a report on a review of a financial forecast should include the following:

1. An identification and description of the forecast information.
2. An indication that a review in accordance with AICPA standards was performed.
3. A statement that the report will not be updated for future events.
4. A conclusion as to the presentation of the forecast in accordance with AICPA guidelines, and whether the assumptions provide a reasonable basis for the forecast.
5. An indication that the attained result will deviate from the forecast and that the deviation may be material.

Reports on internal accounting control

We have pointed out in earlier chapters that the auditors, following their study and evaluation of internal control, usually issue a management letter to the client describing weaknesses in the existing internal control and making recommendations for improvement. A management letter should not be confused with a report to regulatory agencies or other outside groups on a company's internal control. The management letter is an informal report intended only for management. Since it is an informal communication, no standard format has been developed. The management letter is written for internal use by persons having a detailed knowledge of the company's operations and interested in making improvements in internal control. Such a letter need not carry the extensive warnings and precautions needed in a report to outsiders.

In recent years, groups outside the client company have become interested in obtaining internal control reports prepared by CPA firms. Regulatory agencies may want such reports because of the reports' relevance to regulatory purposes or to the agencies' examination functions. However, if a report on internal control similar to the management letter were sent to regulatory agencies or other outside groups, they might misinterpret it and reach unwarranted conclusions. In summary, a report on internal accounting control to be sent to regulatory agencies or other outsiders should employ the most careful and cautious wording. The report should make clear that it relates to accounting controls only, that the extent of internal control is limited by cost factors, that errors and irregularities may occur despite the existence of controls, and that controls functioning at the time of the review may no longer be in force. *SAS No. 30,* "Reporting on Internal Accounting Control," provides CPAs with guidelines for the form and content of such a report.

Opinions on internal accounting control. The objectives of internal accounting control are to provide management with reasonable assurance that assets are safeguarded and financial records are reliable for the preparation of financial statements. The CPA's opinion on internal accounting control expresses the CPA's assurance as to whether the client's existing controls are sufficient to meet these objectives. If the CPA's study and evaluation disclose material weaknesses in the system, those weaknesses should be described in the report.

When reviewing a system of internal accounting control for the purpose of expressing an opinion, the CPA's should (1) plan the scope of the engagement, (2) review the system design, (3) test compliance with prescribed procedures, and (4) evaluate the test results. These steps are similar to those used in a study and evaluation of internal accounting control for audit purposes, but the scope of the study differs. Tests of the system for audit purposes are not comprehensive. Consequently, the study and evaluation of internal accounting control for audit purposes generally is not adequate to express an opinion on the system taken as a whole.

An unqualified opinion on a company's system of internal accounting control should be expressed as follows:

We have made a study and evaluation of the system of internal accounting control of XYZ Company and subsidiaries in effect at April 1, 19xx. Our study and evaluation was conducted in accordance with standards established by the American Institute of Certified Public Accountants.

The management of XYZ Company is responsible for establishing and maintaining a system of internal accounting control. In fulfilling this responsibility, estimates and judgments by management are required to assess the expected benefits and related costs of control procedures. The objectives of a system are to provide management with reasonable, but not absolute, assurance that assets are safeguarded against loss from unauthorized use or disposition and that transactions are executed in accordance with management's authorization and recorded properly to permit the preparation of financial statements in accordance with generally accepted accounting principles.

Because of inherent limitations in any system of internal accounting control, errors or irregularities may occur and not be detected. Also, projection of any evaluation of the system to future periods is subject to the risk that procedures may become inadequate because of changes in conditions or that the degree of compliance with the procedures may deteriorate.

In our opinion, the system of internal accounting control of XYZ Company and subsidiaries in effect at April 1, 19xx, taken as a whole, was sufficient to meet the objectives stated above insofar as those objectives pertain to the prevention or detection of errors or irregularities in amounts that would be material in relation to the consolidated financial statements.

The opinion should be modified if material weaknesses are disclosed by the study and evaluation, or if the scope of the study is restricted.

The CPA's opinion should not extend to an indication that the company is in compliance with the accounting provisions of the Foreign Corrupt Practices Act. This is a legal determination rather than one made by accountants.

Restricted use reports on internal accounting control. CPAs may prepare reports covering only limited areas of the client's system of internal accounting control. Such limited reports may be prepared for the exclusive use of management or some specified third party, such as a regulatory agency. These reports should describe the limited purpose of the study and evaluation and indicate that distribution of the report is limited. The CPAs should indicate clearly that they are not expressing an opinion on the system taken as a whole and that weaknesses may exist that did not come to their attention.

Operational audits

The term *operational audit* refers to a comprehensive examination of an operating unit of an organization to evaluate its performance measured by the objectives set by management. A *financial audit* focuses on the measurement of financial position and results of operations, but an operational audit focuses on the efficiency and effectiveness of specific operating units within an organization. The operational auditor appraises the administrative controls over such varied activities as purchasing, receiving, shipping, office services, advertising, and engineering.

The major users of an operational audit report are managers at various levels. Top management needs assurance that every component of the organization is working to attain the organization's goals. For example, management needs the following:

1. Assurance that its plans (as set forth in statements of objectives, programs, budgets, and directives) are comprehensive, consistent, and understood at the operating levels.
2. Objective information on how well its plans and policies are being carried out in all areas of operations.
3. Reassurance that all operating reports can be relied on as a basis for action.
4. Information on weaknesses in administrative controls, particularly as to possible sources of waste.
5. Aid in measuring the efficiency of operations by feedback of information on the quality and cost of the work and adherence to schedule.

In attempting to meet these managerial needs, operational auditors sample the work performed to see whether it is in accordance with approved procedures. They verify the accuracy and consistency of the information contained in operating reports, and they study the format of these reports to determine whether the information is presented in a meaningful form.

Above all, the operational auditors are alert for indications of, and opportunities for, improvement. The auditors' traditional protective responsibility for seeing that the company's assets are safeguarded against fraud is expanded to a responsibility to provide protection against all kinds of waste. A company may have such a strong system of internal control over its cash, inventories, and other personal property that it will never suffer a serious loss from fraud or theft, yet will lose substantial amounts of its assets through hidden waste.

Waste comes in many guises—for example, the waste of materials by poor planning of purchases or inadequate storage protection; waste of personnel by overstaffing or poor scheduling; waste of equipment by improper planning of requirements; waste of capital by failure to bill and collect receivables properly or maintenance of excessive inventories; improper investments or failure to use idle funds productively; and countless others. Not the least of the sources of potential waste for which the operational auditors must be alert is the temptation to recommend the imposition of too costly administrative control measures that cannot be justified by the safeguards or results achieved.

The operational audit report is issued to top management of the organization and summarizes the auditors' findings. The report generally includes suggested improvements in the internal administrative controls of the organization and a list of situations in which compliance with administrative controls is less than adequate.

Currently, economic pressures are forcing companies and government at all levels to economize, resulting in an increased demand for the information provided by operational audits. The demand has been so pronounced that operational auditing has become an extension of the internal audit function of most large companies. Also, governmental auditors engage extensively in evaluating the economy and effectiveness of various government programs. The not-for-profit nature of governmental units makes them especially suited to operational audits. To a lesser extent, the management advisory services departments of many CPA firms perform operational audits for both profit and not-for-profit enterprises.

KEY TERMS INTRODUCED OR EMPHASIZED IN CHAPTER 19

Compilation of financial statements The preparation of financial statements by CPAs based on representations of management, with the expression of no assurance concerning the statements' compliance with generally accepted accounting principles.

Comfort letter A letter issued by the independent auditors to the underwriters of securities registered with the SEC under the Securities Act of 1933. Comfort letters deal with such matters as the auditors' independence and the compliance of unaudited data with requirements of the SEC.

Financial forecast Estimates of a company's most probable financial position, results of operations, and changes in financial position for one or more future periods.

Management letter A letter issued only to the audit committee of the client company's board of directors following the auditors' study and evaluation of the client's existing internal accounting control. In the letter, the auditors describe weaknesses in the existing internal control and make recommendations for improvement.

Nonpublic company A company other than one whose securities are traded on a public market or that makes a filing with a regulatory agency in preparation for sale of securities on a public market.

Operational audit A study of the efficiency and effectiveness of an organization or an activity within an organization. Operational auditing is performed by the internal audit departments of many companies and by government and independent accountants.

Opinion on internal accounting control A report by the CPAs as to whether the company's system of internal accounting control is adequate to provide reasonable assurance that assets are safeguarded and financial information is reliable. The opinion is issued upon completion of a comprehensive study and evaluation of the system.

Public company A company whose stock is traded on a public market or a company in the process of registering its stock for public sale.

Review of a financial forecast   An extensive evaluation of the basis for and presentation of a financial forecast. The report on a review of a financial forecast expresses an opinion on the reasonableness of the forecast's underlying assumptions.

Review of financial statements   The performance of inquiry and analytical review procedures that are not equivalent to an audit made in accordance with generally accepted auditing standards. The procedures provide the CPAs with a basis to provide limited assurance that the financial statements are in accordance with generally accepted accounting principles.

GROUP 1: REVIEW QUESTIONS

19– 1.   What are the types of procedures that are performed in the *review* of financial statements?

19– 2.   Evaluate this statement: "All companies should be audited."

19– 3.   Under what circumstances should a compilation or review report be modified?

19– 4.   How does a review of financial statements differ from an audit?

19– 5.   What types of services may be performed by CPAs involving the financial statements of a nonpublic company? Explain.

19– 6.   If the CPAs are not independent with respect to a public client, but are associated with the client's financial statements, what type of report is appropriate? Discuss.

19– 7.   Can the CPAs report on a nonpublic client's financial statements that omit substantially all disclosures required by generally accepted accounting principles? Explain.

19– 8.   What should the accountants do if they discover that the financial statements they are compiling contain a material departure from generally accepted accounting principles?

19– 9.   What is the purpose of a comfort letter? Discuss.

19– 10.   What is the objective of a review of a financial forecast?

19– 11.   Can a CPA firm vouch for the achievability of a financial forecast? Discuss.

19– 12.   Should a management letter be issued to the general public? Explain.

19– 13.   List the steps involved in expressing an opinion on a system of internal accounting control.

19– 14.   What is an operational audit?

19– 15.   Who is the major user of operational audit reports? Discuss.

GROUP II: QUESTIONS REQUIRING ANALYSIS

19– 16.   Select the best answer for each of the following and explain fully the reason for your selection.

    a.   Which of the following would not be included in a CPAs' report based upon a review of the financial statements of a nonpublic entity?

    (1) A statement that the review was in accordance with generally accepted auditing standards.

    (2) A statement that all information included in the financial statements are the representations of management.

    (3) A statement describing the principal procedures performed.

    (4) A statement describing the CPAs' conclusions based upon the results of the review.

b. Which of the following best describes the operational audit?

    (1) It requires the constant review by internal auditors of the administrative controls as they relate to the operations of the company.

    (2) It concentrates on implementing financial and accounting control in a newly organized company.

    (3) It attempts and is designed to verify the fair presentation of a company's results of operations.

    (4) It concentrates on seeking out aspects of operations in which waste would be reduced by the introduction of controls.

c. The CPAs should not normally refer to which one of the following subjects in a comfort letter to underwriters?

    (1) The independence of the CPAs.

    (2) Changes in financial-statement items during a period subsequent to the date and period of the latest financial statements in the registration statement.

    (3) Unaudited financial statements and schedules in the registration statement.

    (4) Management's determination of line-of-business classifications.

d. Which of the following procedures is not included in a review engagement of a nonpublic entity?

    (1) Inquiries of management.

    (2) Inquiries regarding events subsequent to the balance sheet date.

    (3) Any procedures designed to identify relationships among data that appear to be unusual.

    (4) A study and evaluation of internal control (AICPA, adapted).

19–17. An accountants' report was appended to the financial statements of Worthmore, Inc., a public company. The statements consisted of a balance sheet as of November 30 and statements of income and retained earnings for the year then ended. The first two paragraphs of the report contained the wording of the standard unqualified report, and a third paragraph read as follows:

    The wives of two partners of our firm owned a material investment in the outstanding common stock of Worthmore, Inc. during the fiscal year ending November 30. The aforementioned individuals disposed of their holdings of Worthmore, Inc., on December 3 in a transaction that did not result in a profit or a loss. This information is included in our report in order to comply with certain disclosure requirements of the *Code of Professional Ethics* of the American Institute of Certified Public Accountants.

               Bell & Davis
               Certified Public Accountants

Required:

    a. Was the CPA firm of Bell & Davis independent with respect to the examination of Worthmore, Inc.'s financial statements? Explain.

    b. Do you find Bell & Davis' report satisfactory? Explain. (AICPA, adapted)

19–18. Sarah Mann, CPA, has been engaged to compile the 1985 annual financial statements of Southwest, Inc., a small nonpublic company. The 1984 financial statements of the company are presented in Southwest's annual report for comparative purposes. Since she had previously reviewed the financial statements of the prior year, Sarah was aware that she should report on both years. She has prepared a report in the following form:

Board of Directors
Southwest, Inc.

    (The standard compilation report for the 1985 financial statements)
    (The standard review report for the 1984 financial statements)

March 31, 1986   Sarah Mann, CPA

Required:

    a. Explain the deficiency in this form of reporting.

    b. Explain two ways in which Sarah Mann might properly report on the financial statements.

19–19. You are a CPA retained by the manager of a cooperative retirement village to do write-up work. You are expected to compile unaudited financial statements accompanied by a standard compilation report. In performing the work you discover that there are no invoices to support $25,000 of the manager's claimed disbursements. The manager informs you that all the disbursements are proper.

Required:

Explain the steps that you should take in this situation. (AICPA, adapted)

19–20. You have been asked by Ambassador Hardware Co., a small nonpublic company, to submit a proposal for the audit of the company. After performing an investigation of the company, including its management and accounting system, you advise the president of Ambassador that the audit fee will be approximately $10,000. Ambassador's president was somewhat surprised at the fee, and after discussions with members of the board of directors, he concluded that the company could not afford an audit at this time.

Required:

    a. Discuss management's alternatives to having their financial statements audited in accordance with generally accepted auditing standards.

    b. What should Ambassador's management consider when selecting the type of service that you should provide? Explain.

19–21. Andrew Wilson, CPA, has assembled the financial statements of Texas Mirror Co., a small public company. He has not performed an audit of the financial statements in accordance with generally accepted auditing standards. Wilson is confused about the standards applicable to this type of engagement.

Required:

a. Explain where Wilson should look for guidance concerning this engagement.
b. Discuss the concept of association with financial statements.
c. Explain Wilson's responsibilities with respect to a preparation of unaudited financial statements.

19–22. You have been engaged by the management of Pippin, Inc., a nonpublic company, to review the company's financial statements for the year ended December 31, 1984. To prepare for the engagement you consult the *Statements on Standards for Accounting and Review Services.*

Required:

a. Discuss the procedures required for the performance of a review of financial statements.
b. Explain the content of the report on a review of financial statements.
c. Discuss your responsibilities if you find that the financial statements contain a material departure from generally accepted accounting principles.

19–23. In connection with a public offering of first mortgage bonds by Guizzetti Corporation, the bond underwriter has asked Guizzetti's CPAs to furnish them with a comfort letter giving as much assurance as possible on Guizzetti's unaudited financial statements for the three months ended March 31. The CPAs had expressed an unqualified opinion on Guizzetti's financial statements for the year ended December 31, the preceding year; they have also performed a review of Guizzetti's financial statements for the three months ended March 31. Nothing has come to their attention that would indicate that the March 31 statements are not properly presented.

Required:

a. Explain what can be stated about the unaudited financial statements in the letter.
b. Discuss other matters that are typically included in comfort letters.

19–24. The management of Williams Co. is considering issuing corporate debentures. To enhance the marketability of the bond issue, management has decided to include a financial forecast in the prospectus. Williams management has requested that your CPA firm review the financial forecast to add credibility to the prospective information.

Required:

a. Explain what is involved in the review of a financial forecast.
b. Discuss the content of the report on a review of a financial forecast. (Do not write a report.)

19–25. You have been performing a financial audit for Wallace Shoe Co. for several years. The president of Wallace Shoe Co. has recently read an article on the benefits of operational auditing and has come to you with several questions about such audits.

Required:

a. Explain the difference between a financial audit and an operational audit.
b. Discuss the major users of operational audit reports.
c. Discuss the types of auditors that perform operational audits.

GROUP III: PROBLEMS

19–26. Norman Lewis, an inexperienced member of your staff, has compiled the financial statements of Williams Grocery. He has submitted the following report for your review:

> The accompanying financial statements have been compiled by us. A compilation is an accounting service, but we also applied certain analytical review procedures to the financial data.
>
> As explained in note 3, the company changed accounting principles in accounting for its inventories. We have not audited or reviewed the accompanying financial statements, but nothing came to our attention to indicate that they are in error.

Required:
Describe the deficiencies in the report, give reasons why they are deficiencies, and briefly discuss how the report should be corrected. Do not discuss the addressee, signature, and date. Organize your answer sheet as follows:

Deficiency	Reason	Correction

19–27. Upon completion of a study and evaluation of the internal accounting control of Weaver Corporation, the following opinion on internal control was issued by Milburn and Jones, CPAs.

To the Board of Directors of Weaver Corporation:

> We have made a study and evaluation of the system of internal control of Weaver Corporation. Our study and evaluation was conducted as a part of our audit of Weaver Corporation.
>
> Our management advisory division established Weaver Corporation's system of internal control, and we take responsibility for maintaining the system.
>
> In our opinion, the system of internal control of Weaver Corporation is sufficient to prevent or detect all errors and irregularities. We also believe that the system is adequate to assure that Weaver Corporation is not in violation of the internal accounting control provisions of the Foreign Corrupt Practices Act.

April 23, 1984   Milburn and Jones, CPAs

Required:
List and explain the deficiencies and omissions in the opinion and explain how it might be corrected. Organize your answer as follows:

Deficiency or omission	Correction

19–28. The financial statements of Tiber Company have never been audited by independent CPAs. Recently Tiber's management asked Anthony Burns, CPA, to provide an opinion on Tiber's internal accounting control; this management advisory services engagement will not include an examination of Tiber's financial statements. Following completion of his study and evaluation, Burns plans to prepare a report that is consistent with the requirements of *SAS No. 30* dealing with reports on internal accounting control.

Required:

a. Describe the inherent limitations that should be recognized in considering the potential effectiveness of any system of internal accounting control.

b. Explain and contrast the review of internal accounting control that Burns might make as part of an examination of financial statements with his study and evaluation to express an opinion on the system, covering each of the following:

(1) Objectives of review or study.
(2) Scope of review or study.
(3) Nature and content of reports.

Organize your answer for part *b* as follows:

Examination of financial statements	Opinion on internal accounting control
1. Objective	1. Objective
2. Scope	2. Scope
3. Report	3. Report

(AICPA, adapted)

19–29. Brown, CPA, received a telephone call from Calhoun, the sole owner and manager of a small corporation. Calhoun asked Brown to compile the financial statements for the corporation and emphasized that the statements were needed in two weeks for external financing purposes. Calhoun was vague when Brown inquired about the intended use of the statements. Brown was convinced that Calhoun thought Brown's work would constitute an audit. To avoid confusion Brown decided not to explain to Calhoun that the engagement would only be to compile the financial statements. Brown, with the understanding that a substantial fee would be paid if the work was completed in two weeks, accepted the engagement and started the work at once.

During the course of the work, Brown discovered an accrued expense account labeled Professional Fees and learned that the balance in the account represented an accrual for the cost of Brown's services. Brown suggested to Calhoun's bookkeeper that the account name be changed to Fees for Limited Audit Engagement. Brown also reviewed several invoices to determine whether accounts were being properly classified. Some of the invoices were missing. Brown listed the missing invoice numbers in the working papers with a note indicating that there should be a followup on the next engagement. Brown also discovered that the available records included the fixed asset values at estimated current replacement costs. Based on the records available, Brown compiled a balance sheet, income statement, and statement of stockholder's equity. In addition, Brown drafted the footnotes, but decided that any mention of the replacement costs would only mislead the readers. Brown suggested to Calhoun that readers of the financial statements would be better informed if they received a separate letter from Calhoun explaining the meaning and effect of the estimated replacement costs of the fixed assets. Brown mailed the financial statements and footnotes to Calhoun with the following note included on each page:

The accompanying financial statements are submitted to you without complete audit verification.

Required:
Identify the inappropriate actions of Brown, and indicate what Brown should have done to avoid each inappropriate action.

Organize your answer sheet as follows:

Inappropriate action	*What Brown should have done to avoid inappropriate action*

(AICPA, adapted)

19–30. The limitations on the CPA's professional responsibilities when they are associated with unaudited financial statements are often misunderstood. These misunderstandings can be substantially reduced if the CPAs follow professional pronouncements in the course of their work, and take other appropriate measures.

Required:
The following list describes seven situations CPAs may encounter, or contentions they may have to deal with in their association with and preparation of *unaudited* financial statements. Briefly discuss the extent of the CPAs responsibilities and, if appropriate, the actions they should take to minimize any misunderstandings. Number your answers to correspond with the numbering in the following list.

1. The CPAs were engaged by telephone to perform write-up work including the compilation of financial statements. The client believes that the CPAs have been engaged to audit the financial statements and examine the records accordingly.

2. A group of investors who own a farm that is managed by an independent agent engage CPAs to compile quarterly unaudited financial statements for them. The CPAs prepare the financial statements from information given to them by the independent agent. Subsequently, the investors find the statements were inaccurate because their independent agent was embezzling funds. They refuse to pay the CPAs' fee and blame them for allowing the situa-

tion to go undetected, contending that they should not have relied on representations from the independent agent.

3.   In comparing the trial balance with the general ledger the CPAs find an account labeled Audit Fees in which the client has accumulated the CPAs' quarterly billings for accounting services including the compilation of quarterly unaudited financial statements.

4.   Unaudited financial statements for a public company were accompanied by the following letter of transmittal from the CPAs.

> We are enclosing your company's balance sheet as of June 30, 1974 and the related statements of income and retained earnings and changes in financial position for the six months then ended to which we have performed certain auditing procedures.

5.   To determine appropriate account classification, the CPAs examined a number of the client's invoices. They noted in their working papers that some invoices were missing, but did nothing further because it was felt that the invoices did not affect the unaudited financial statements they were compiling. When the client subsequently discovered that invoices were missing, he contended that the CPAs should not have ignored the missing invoices when compiling the financial statements and had a responsibility to at least inform him that they were missing.

6.   The CPAs compiled a draft of unaudited financial statements from the client's records. While reviewing this draft with their client, the CPAs learned that the land and building were recorded at appraisal value.

7.   The CPAs are engaged to compile the financial statements of a nonpublic company. During the engagement, the CPAs learn of several items that by generally accepted accounting principles would require adjustments of the statements and footnote disclosure. The controller agrees to make the recommended adjustments to the statements, but says that she is not going to add the footnotes because the statements are unaudited. (AICPA, adapted)

Index

T

U

V

W

*This book has been set VIP, in 10 and 9 point
Bodoni, leaded 2 points. Chapter numbers are 36
point American Typewriter Medium; chapter titles are 24 point American Typewriter Medium.
The size of the type page is 30 by 48 picas.*